# MORNINGSTAR®
# ETFs100™

Annual Sourcebook
2006 Edition

Introduction by
Dan Culloton,
Editor

# Table of Contents

There has been a lot of hype about exchange-traded funds recently, and, for once, there is something to all of it.

Cheap, flexible, tax efficient, and transparent, ETFs have been hailed as one of greatest investing innovations in years. Their numbers have multiplied and assets have ballooned since the first ETF made its debut in 1993; the industry's growth shows no sign of abating as the variety of ETFs increases and more professional and individual investors try them out. This dizzying pace of expansion can be disorienting. There are about 200 ETFs on the market as of this writing, and there are more on the way. Their investment objectives range from the broad and commonplace to the narrow and quixotic. StreetTracks Total Market ETF TMW, for example, aims for nothing more than the return of the broad domestic-equity market, while PowerShares Lux Nanotech Portfolio PXN purports to track the nascent nanotechnology industry. It can be hard to figure out which of the many available ETFs are legitimate investment tools that can help you attain your financial goals, and which are distracting novelties.

That is where this, the inaugural edition of Morningstar's ETFS 100, comes in. We've taken the rapidly expanding ETF universe and singled out 100 for close attention. There was no magic formula to selecting our candidates; we simply focused on the largest, most actively traded ETFs first and then filled out the ranks with funds that offered low-cost, diversified alternatives in categories in which there is a paucity of affordable conventional mutual funds with experienced managers and credible records. The result is a large menu of investment choices, ranging from inflation-protected bond ETFs to sector and international funds.

For each member of the ETFS 100, we provide a one-page report that includes all the data you need to do your due diligence on a given fund, including 10 years worth of performance history, a snapshot of the ETF's risk profile, details about its advisor and the construction methodology of its benchmark, and an indication if the fund is trading below or above the fair value of its underlying holdings. Tying all of the data on the report page together is Morningstar's Take: our analyst's critical evaluation of whether a particular ETF is worth buying or not.

Because ETFs are still new to many people, we've included more than 20 articles on everything from ETF basics to how to use them in fund and stock portfolios. And, of course, the book is full of data tables and rankings of both the ETFS 100 and the broad ETF universe. The ETFS 100 has the data and analysis to help you safely and profitably incorporate ETFS into your portfolio, whether you are new to ETFS or looking for new ideas. Happy hunting.

Dan Culloton
Editor
*Morningstar* ETFS *100*

# The Year in Review

ETFs experienced in 2005 another year
of impressive growth.

**by Dan Culloton, Editor,
Morningstar ETFs 100**

By many measures 2005 was another strong year for exchange-traded funds. A record number of new ETFs began trading; asset growth and inflows stayed healthy; and awareness of and interest in ETFs spread. There were also signs that ETFs finally had injected some much needed price competition into the fund industry, as Fidelity Investments cut the expense ratios of its traditional index funds and Vanguard lowered the fees for some of its funds' exchange-traded share classes. Lower costs are always better for shareholders, but ETFs also continued to make good on their promise to deliver tax-efficient equity exposure to shareholders. Most of the funds avoided capital gains distributions in 2005. The following is a look at the year that was and the year that will be for ETFs.

### Leaders and Laggards

ETFs, which are all still index funds, acted like their counterparts in the conventional mutual fund universe. Most broad equity ETF categories ended the year in positive territory. Broad market ETFs, such as **Vanguard Total Stock Market** VTI and **StreetTracks Total Market ETF** TMW, were up more than 6% for the year to date through Dec. 30, 2005.

International and energy-focused ETFs turned in the strongest performances. Latin America, emerging-markets, and natural-resources funds, buoyed by soaring energy and commodity stocks (such as oil company Petroleo Brasileiro), led the way. **iShares MSCI Brazil** EWZ and **iShares MSCI South Korea** EWY each gained more than 50% through Dec. 30. The **Energy Select Sector SPDR** XLE and **Vanguard Energy VIPERs** VDE still posted robust gains of about 40%, despite stumbling as oil prices moderated in the fourth quarter.

Communication, technology, and large-growth ETFs turned in the worst performances, though only the average communications fund lost money. The **iShares S&P Global Telecommunications Index** IXP shed 6.7% through the end of December as large holdings such as phone service providers **Vodafone** VOD and **Verizon Communications** VZ got

hammered over concerns about risky acquisitions and fierce competition.

### When You're Hot, You're Hot

More new ETFs hit the market in 2005 than ever before. In terms of sheer numbers of new funds launched, 2005 was the year of PowerShares. Of the record-breaking 51 new ETFs to hit the market in 2005, PowerShares Capital Management launched 32, or more than 60% of them. The Wheaton, IL-based firm has quickly established itself and pushed the boundaries of ETFs with its quasi-actively managed funds, but most of its offerings track little known or dangerously narrow benchmarks.

There were no blockbuster new offerings. The biggest new ETF in terms of assets, **Vanguard Emerging Markets Stock Viper** VWO, which launched in March 2005, had $450 million by the end of November, beating **iShares Comex Gold** IAU, which rolled out in January 2005 and had more than $300 million. That's a far cry from 2004's biggest launch, **StreetTracks Gold Shares** GLD, which gathered more than $1 billion in a few weeks. The Vanguard Emerging Markets VIPER deserves some attention because it has a lower expense ratio than its closest rival, **iShares MSCI Emerging Markets** EEM. Each of these funds, however, is in a hot category (emerging markets and precious metals), and it's usually a bad idea to chase performance.

ETFs kept growing in 2005. In the first 11 months of the year total ETF assets grew to $289 billion, or 28% from the end of 2004, according to the Investment Company Institute. Net new issuance of ETF shares was running a little ahead of 2004's pace, according to the ICI. Through Nov. 30 ETFs issued $48 billion in net new shares, versus $46 billion for the same period last year.

Barclays Global Investors' iShares family remains the biggest of the ETF groups. Indeed, though the end of November Barclays was one of fastest growing fund families, exchange-traded or otherwise, of 2005; iShares garnered $39.3 billion in net new money and had more than $116 billion in total assets, according to Financial Research Corp. The most popular iShares included the broad-based international fund, **iShares MSCI EAFE** EFA, which was one of the 10 best-selling funds of all kinds with $6.5 billion in net inflows through the first 11 months of the year, according to FRC. **iShares MSCI Emerging Markets** EEM and **iShares MSCI Japan** EWJ also were hot sellers, taking in nearly $4 billion in net inflows each. There's a good case to be made for investing overseas, but single-country and emerging-markets funds are notoriously volatile, and buying them solely for their recent strong absolute performance is a bad idea.

### A Faster Track?

Much sooner than expected, the Securities and Exchange Commission approved the first ETF based on currency. The **Rydex Euro Currency Shares** FXE, which tracks the price of the European Union's currency versus the dollar, began trading in December. We're not that excited about the fund as an investment; currency movements are too fickle for most investors to mess with. The offering's relatively quick approval (less than a year) could be a sign that the SEC is getting more comfortable with exotic ETF proposals. Previously, alternative asset class ETFs, such as those tracking the price of gold, had taken nearly two years to secure approval.

### Barra Gets the Boot

Standard & Poor's, which publishes the style-based equity benchmarks used by iShares and dozens of other funds, decided to drop a style index construction methodology (developed by risk-management firm Barra) that relied only on price/book value to determine if a stock should be classified as growth or value. There is a lot of academic work supporting the use of price/book value as a gauge of growth or value; in reality, however, relying on one factor has undesirable ramifications for index funds. The Barra S&P style indexes proved to be unrealistic measures of the growth and value universes and forced index fund managers to turn their portfolios over more often as stocks migrated based on their price/book values.

Those were among the reasons Standard & Poor's adopted new style bogies derived from a multifactor model created by **Citigroup** C. The Citigroup indexes will still draw their constituents from the same S&P large-, mid-, and small-cap indexes, but it will look at seven valuation and growth factors instead of one to figure out where a stock belongs. Unlike the Barra indexes, they will also allow stocks that have both value and growth characteristics to reside in both value and growth indexes, which should control turnover. Barclays' iShares funds began tracking the new indexes in December 2005.

### Index Fund Price War

Fidelity Investments put some pressure on ETFs as it tussled with Vanguard. Fidelity first cut the retail share class expense ratios of its conventional equity index funds to a competitive 0.10%.

Later it rolled out a new Advantage share class for its index funds that charged an even lower 0.07% for investors with at least $100,000. The move was aimed at rival Vanguard, which has long offered cheaper Admiral share classes for big investors. But the battle also throws a gauntlet at the feet of ETFs. The expense ratio for Fidelity's Advantage class matches the cheapest ETFs', and unlike ETFs, Fidelity's funds can be bought without a commission. The Fidelity offerings, regardless of share class, are therefore likely better choice for investors putting money into their funds on a regular basis.

### What's Next?

Investors can expect more alternative asset class ETFs in 2006. The SEC has approved the Deutsche Bank Commodity Index, which will use futures to track a production-weighted benchmark of aluminum, gold, wheat, corn, heating oil, and sweet light crude. Barclays has a similar offering in the works: iShares GSCI Commodity-Indexed Trust. There's also an iShares Silver ETF and several funds that plan to track the price of oil, though they all may not secure regulatory approval.

There will be more action on actively managed ETFs. A handful of firms have filed applications with the SEC or proposed active ETF formats, including the American Stock Exchange and a firm founded by a former Amex executive. It remains to be seen, however, if the wait will be worth it.

Someone may introduce more fixed-income ETFs; there are still only six. Investors are also sure to see more ETFs tracking indexes purporting to offer an alternative to traditional market-cap weighted indexes. Rydex Investments, for example, hopes to launch six ETFs based on the "pure" versions of the S&P/Citigroup style benchmarks that weight their constituents by their style scores.

Judging from the frenetic pace of ETF launches we saw in 2005, its safe to say investors will see a fair amount of trend hopping. For example, there were five new dividend focused ETFs launched in 2005 and Barclays, State Street Global Advisors, and PowerShares all rolled out or planned to roll out more thinly sliced ETFs tracking hot areas, such as homebuilding or the oil and gas industries. Just remember if they build it, you don't have to come-- until you're sure it fits your goals and risk profile. Ⅲ

# How to Use This Book

Tips for getting the most out of your
*Morningstar ETFs 100*

**by Christine Benz,
Associate Director
of Fund Analysis, and
Dan Culloton, Editor,
Morningstar ETFs 100**

When it comes to selecting conventional funds, Morningstar has long advocated focusing on fundamental analysis and eschewing past performance trends. Though exchange-traded funds are different from their traditional counterparts, the same rule applies. Successful ETF investing begins not by checking last year's leaders' lists, but by researching expenses, index methodology, and the competence of the advisor. True, looking at the best-performing ETFs for any given time period can provide important clues about market trends, and that's why this book includes plenty of rankings. (See Pages 165-189.) But to truly understand an ETF and the role it might play in a portfolio, investors have to examine its holdings, understand how its index is built and how its manager tracks it, and evaluate the ETF's risk level.

Toward that end, this inaugural edition of *Morningstar ETFs 100* is chock-full of all the data and analysis you need to make informed decisions. Read on as we walk through some of the best tools for doing just that. (The Glossary that begins on Page 193 provides you with specific definitions of all of the data points in the book.)

### Morningstar's Take
The text box in the lower left-hand quadrant of each individual ETF page is the analysis, or "Morningstar's Take." Reading the analysis is an essential first step as you attempt to determine whether an ETF is appropriate for your goals and risk tolerance. In it, a Morningstar analyst sums up all of an ETF's salient points by assessing its historical risk/reward profile relative to its peer group and competing conventional mutual funds, discussing how the ETF's benchmark is constructed, and noting and evaluating any recent changes to that methodology. And because Morningstar analysts speak regularly with ETF sponsors and advisors and have Morningstar's extensive database at their fingertips, the analysis can provide glimpses into individual ETFs that you won't find anywhere else.

### Morningstar Price to Fair Value Measure
This gives investors a way to use Morningstar stock research to evaluate ETF portfolios. In addition to its staff of more than two dozen mutual fund analysts, Morningstar has 85 in-house equity analysts researching and estimating fair values for more than 1,700 stocks. The price/fair value ratio basically taps that research to offer a bottom-up assessment of whether an ETF portfolio is cheap or expensive by gauging if its holdings, on average, are trading above or below their Morningstar fair value estimates.

First we calculate the market value of all the holdings in the ETF for which we have fair value estimates. Then we use the fair value estimates of those stocks to calculate what we believe is the fair value of the same portfolio. Lastly, we compare the two numbers and calculate a ratio of the market value compared with the fair value. A reading higher than 1 means the ETF is overvalued; lower than 1 indicates it's undervalued.

Because Morningstar does not estimate a fair value for every stock an ETF might own, the relevance of the results of the price/fair value depends on how many stocks in a given portfolio have received fair value estimates and the percentage of that portfolio's assets these stocks represent. You can see how pertinent the measure is by looking at the "Hit Rate," which shows the percentage of the ETF's market capitalization covered by Morningstar equity analysts. Our stock coverage is pretty comprehensive for the vast majority of domestic large-cap ETFs.

### Style Boxes/Morningstar Categories
The Morningstar style box, the nine-square grid that appears toward the bottom right-hand corner of each individual fund page, is designed to give you a visual snapshot of the type of securities an ETF owns. For stock funds, the style box shows you the size of companies in which an ETF invests, as well as whether it focuses on growth- or value-oriented securities. For bond ETFs, the style box depicts an ETF's sensitivity to interest rates as well as the average credit quality of the bonds in the portfolio. Armed with three years' worth of style boxes, we determine an ETF's Morningstar Category placement, which reflects how the ETF has invested its assets over the past three years. (The Morningstar Category appears in the top right-hand corner of each ETF page).

As a general rule of thumb, large-blend or large-value ETFs make the best core stock holdings, because they invest in the well-established companies that tend to dominate the market, and because they're not as volatile as their large-growth counterparts. For those seeking a core bond ETF holding, the intermediate-term bond category will generally be the best hunting ground. Such ETFs are typically well diversified across government and corporate bonds and have some (although not extreme) sensitivity to interest-rate changes. There aren't many fixed-income ETFs to choose from currently, but that could change in the future.

Just as Morningstar's style boxes and categories can help you make smart ETF selections, they can also help you determine how to put the ETFs together into a well-diversified package. While you need not buy an ETF in every single Morningstar Category, building a portfolio of ETFs with varying investment styles is a sensible diversification strategy.

### Sector Weightings
Sector weightings, which appear in the bottom right-hand corner of each stock ETF page, pick up where an ETF's investment style box leaves off. Examining an ETF's sector weightings is an essential step on the road to understanding how an ETF will behave and how you might use it to build a diversified portfolio. After all, ETFs may land in different Morningstar Categories, but if their sector compositions are similar, it's possible that their performances will be, too.

### Strategy
In this area Morningstar's analyst sums up the ETF's investment process; for index ETFs this means how their benchmarks are constructed and how the ETFs' advisors go about tracking the bogies. How does the fund's index define the asset class it is trying to measure? How does it weight its constituents? How often does it rebalance? What method does the manager use to mimic the index's returns—exact replication or representative sampling? The strategy section tries to address all of these questions and could help you differentiate between ETFs that purport to track the same areas of the market.

### Tables and Charts
For those of you who love lists, pages 165-189 include an impressive array of ETF data and rankings. In general, selecting ETFs from a list of short-term leaders is a poor investment strategy. But checking out the lists of top-performing ETFs over longer time frames—over the past five and 10 years, for example—can provide you with great ideas for further research. The lists of leaders and laggards over various time frames can also be a good way to get up to speed on recent market trends. Small-value ETFs dominate the three- and five-year diversified, domestic-equity ETFs' leader list on page 176, for example, whereas large-cap-dominated ETFs bring up the rear over these time frames. ▮

# The Morningstar Stock-ETF Page

In this six-page walk-through, we briefly describe how each section of the page is relevant to your fund research and offer some tips on using these features to better analyze funds. More-detailed discussions of the elements presented in this section appear in the Glossary.

**A** Investment Value Graph

**B** Management

**C** Strategy

**D** Performance

**E** Tax Analysis

**F** Morningstar's Take

**G** Operations

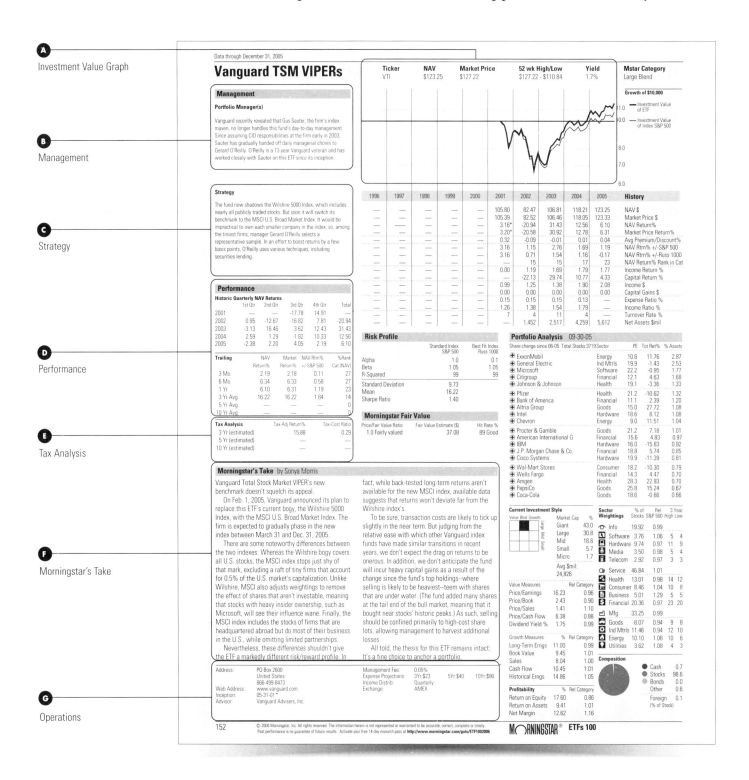

### A. Investment Value Graph

The Investment Value graph line shows an ETF's performance trend, derived from the ETF's historical growth of $10,000. It provides a visual depiction of how an ETF has amassed its returns, including the performance swings its shareholders have endured along the way. The growth of $10,000 begins at the date of the ETF's inception. (If the ETF has been in existence for more than 10 years, then growth of $10,000 begins at the first year listed on the graph.) Also, featured in the graph is the performance of an index (S&P 500 or MSCI EAFE, for example), which allows investors to compare the performance of the ETF with the performance of the benchmark index.

### B. Management

The portfolio manager(s) is the individual or individuals responsible for the overall investment operations of the ETF, including the buying and selling required for index ETFs to track their benchmarks. In many cases managers are also involved in selecting benchmarks for new ETFs. To help investors know who is running an ETF, we detail an ETF's management with a brief biography. We note the manager's background, experience, analytical support, other ETFs managed, and whether the manager invests in his or her own ETF.

### C. Strategy

While the Morningstar Category gives investors an idea of the kind of investments an ETF makes, it does not fully capture the nuances of the ETF's methodology for capturing the returns of the market segment it claims to represent. In this section, Morningstar's analysts explain how an ETF's benchmark selects securities for inclusion, how often it rebalances, when it decides to kick issues out, how it controls turnover, and how risky a given index may be. On the equity side, the strategy description often focuses on what size and type of company on which an ETF's index focuses. For style-based ETFs this includes a discussion of how the index defines growth and value stocks. With bond ETFs, the strategy section explains how the ETF goes about matching the duration, credit quality, and maturity of its benchmark index.

### D. Performance

The quarterly returns show the performance investors have seen over each calendar quarter in the past five years. This section is a good spot to quickly test your risk tolerance. Find the largest quarterly loss; if it makes you uneasy, you should probably look for less-volatile ETFs. The trailing returns section illustrates performance over short and long periods. We compare returns against appropriate benchmarks and peers, with 1 as the best percentile and 100 as the worst.

### E. Tax Analysis

This section lists an ETFs tax-adjusted returns and the percentage-point reduction in annualized returns that results from taxes, called the tax-cost ratio. For context, each figure is then given a percentile rank in the ETF's category (1 is the best percentile; 100 is the worst). Examine the two returns figures together because high tax-adjusted returns do not necessarily mean the ETF is tax-efficient. Also, an ETF could be very tax-efficient, but if returns are poor to begin with, an investor will still pocket a low sum. ETFs rarely make capital gains distributions, but dividend payouts can affect their tax efficiency.

### F. Moningstar's Take

Our analysts interpret the data on the page and interview the ETF's manager to explain the methodologies guiding investment decisions. They then succinctly detail how and why an ETF has succeeded or failed, and what role—if any—it should play in your portfolio.

### G. Operations

Here we list where to write or call to obtain investment information about the ETF. We also list the ETF's management fee, income distribution frequency, inception date, and exchange on which it trades.

# The Morningstar Stock-ETF Page (continued)

**H** Morningstar Category

**I** History

**J** Portfolio Analysis

**K** Risk Profile

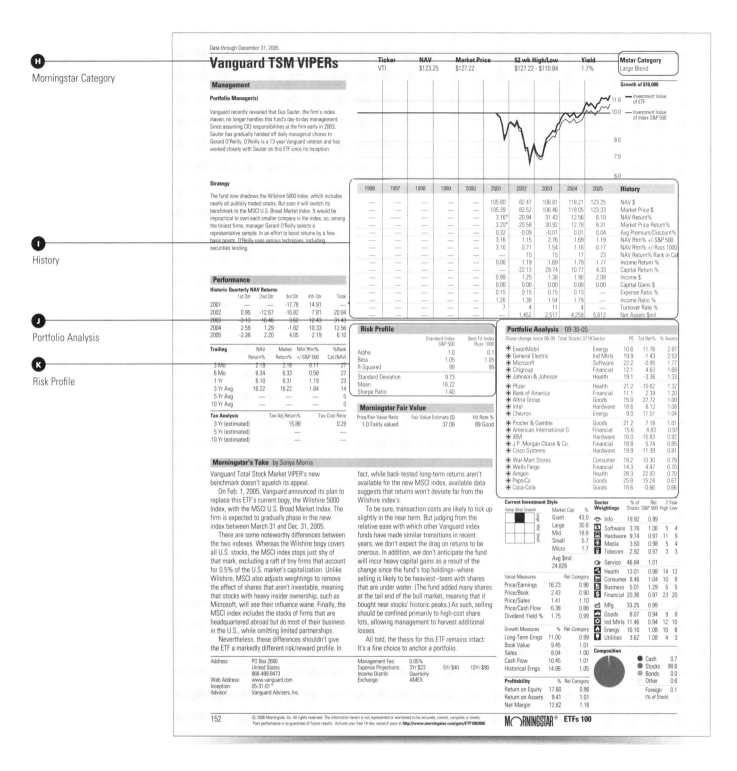

Data through December 31, 2005

## Vanguard TSM VIPERs

| | Ticker | NAV | Market Price | 52 wk High/Low | Yield | Mstar Category |
|---|---|---|---|---|---|---|
| | VTI | $123.25 | $127.22 | $127.22 - $110.84 | 1.7% | Large Blend |

### Management

**Portfolio Manager(s)**

Vanguard recently revealed that Gus Sauter, the firm's index maven, no longer handles this fund's day-to-day management. Since assuming CIO responsibilities at the firm early in 2003, Sauter has gradually handed off daily managerial chores to Gerard O'Reilly. O'Reilly is a 13-year Vanguard veteran and has worked closely with Sauter on this ETF since its inception.

**Strategy**

The fund now shadows the Wilshire 5000 Index, which includes nearly all publicly traded stocks. But soon it will switch its benchmark to the MSCI U.S. Broad Market Index. It would be impractical to own each smaller company in the index, so, among the tiniest firms, manager Gerard O'Reilly selects a representative sample. In an effort to boost returns by a few basis points, O'Reilly uses various techniques, including securities lending.

### Performance

**Historic Quarterly NAV Returns**

| | 1st Qtr | 2nd Qtr | 3rd Qtr | 4th Qtr | Total |
|---|---|---|---|---|---|
| 2001 | — | — | -17.78 | 14.91 | — |
| 2002 | 0.95 | -12.67 | -16.82 | 7.81 | -20.94 |
| 2003 | -3.13 | 16.46 | 3.62 | 12.43 | 31.43 |
| 2004 | 2.59 | 1.29 | -1.82 | 10.33 | 12.56 |
| 2005 | -2.38 | 2.20 | 4.05 | 2.19 | 6.10 |

| Trailing | NAV Return% | Market Return% | NAV Rtrn% +/-S&P 500 | %Rank Cat.(NAV) |
|---|---|---|---|---|
| 3 Mo | 2.19 | 2.18 | 0.11 | 27 |
| 6 Mo | 6.34 | 6.33 | 0.58 | 27 |
| 1 Yr | 6.10 | 6.31 | 1.19 | 23 |
| 3 Yr Avg | 16.22 | 16.22 | 1.84 | 14 |
| 5 Yr Avg | — | — | — | 0 |
| 10 Yr Avg | — | — | — | 0 |

| Tax Analysis | Tax-Adj Return% | Tax-Cost Ratio |
|---|---|---|
| 3 Yr (estimated) | 15.88 | 0.29 |
| 5 Yr (estimated) | — | — |
| 10 Yr (estimated) | — | — |

### History

| | 1996 | 1997 | 1998 | 1999 | 2000 | 2001 | 2002 | 2003 | 2004 | 2005 | History |
|---|---|---|---|---|---|---|---|---|---|---|---|
| | — | — | — | — | — | 105.80 | 82.47 | 106.81 | 118.21 | 123.25 | NAV $ |
| | — | — | — | — | — | 105.39 | 82.52 | 106.46 | 118.05 | 123.33 | Market Price $ |
| | — | — | — | — | — | 3.16* | -20.94 | 31.43 | 12.56 | 6.10 | NAV Return% |
| | — | — | — | — | — | 3.20* | -20.58 | 30.92 | 12.78 | 6.31 | Market Price Return% |
| | — | — | — | — | — | 0.32 | -0.09 | -0.01 | 0.01 | 0.04 | Avg Premium/Discount% |
| | — | — | — | — | — | 3.16 | 1.15 | 2.76 | 1.69 | 1.19 | NAV Rtrn% +/-S&P 500 |
| | — | — | — | — | — | 3.16 | 0.71 | 1.54 | 1.16 | -0.17 | NAV Rtrn% +/-Russ 1000 |
| | — | — | — | — | — | — | 15 | 15 | 17 | 23 | NAV Return% Rank in Cat |
| | — | — | — | — | — | 0.00 | 1.19 | 1.69 | 1.79 | 1.77 | Income Return % |
| | — | — | — | — | — | — | -22.13 | 29.74 | 10.77 | 4.33 | Capital Return % |
| | — | — | — | — | — | 0.99 | 1.25 | 1.38 | 1.90 | 2.08 | Income $ |
| | — | — | — | — | — | 0.00 | 0.00 | 0.00 | 0.00 | 0.00 | Capital Gains $ |
| | — | — | — | — | — | 0.15 | 0.15 | 0.15 | 0.13 | — | Expense Ratio % |
| | — | — | — | — | — | 1.26 | 1.38 | 1.54 | 1.79 | — | Income Ratio % |
| | — | — | — | — | — | 7 | 4 | 11 | 4 | — | Turnover Rate % |
| | — | — | — | — | — | — | 1,452 | 2,517 | 4,259 | 5,612 | Net Assets $mil |

### Risk Profile

| | Standard Index S&P 500 | Best Fit Index Russ 1000 |
|---|---|---|
| Alpha | 1.0 | 0.1 |
| Beta | 1.05 | 1.05 |
| R-Squared | 99 | 99 |
| Standard Deviation | 9.73 | |
| Mean | 16.22 | |
| Sharpe Ratio | 1.40 | |

### Morningstar Fair Value

| Price/Fair Value Ratio | Fair Value Estimate ($) | Hit Rate % |
|---|---|---|
| 1.0 Fairly valued | 37.08 | 89 Good |

### Portfolio Analysis 09-30-05

Share change since 06-05  Total Stocks:3719

| Sector | PE | Tot Ret% | % Assets |
|---|---|---|---|
| ⊕ ExxonMobil | Energy | 10.6 | 11.76 | 2.87 |
| ⊕ General Electric | Ind Mtrls | 19.9 | -1.43 | 2.53 |
| ⊕ Microsoft | Software | 22.2 | -0.95 | 1.77 |
| ⊕ Citigroup | Financial | 12.1 | 4.63 | 1.68 |
| ⊕ Johnson & Johnson | Health | 19.1 | -3.36 | 1.33 |
| ⊕ Pfizer | Health | 21.2 | -10.62 | 1.32 |
| ⊕ Bank of America | Financial | 11.1 | 2.39 | 1.20 |
| ⊕ Altria Group | Goods | 15.0 | 27.72 | 1.08 |
| ⊕ Intel | Hardware | 18.6 | 8.12 | 1.08 |
| ⊕ Chevron | Energy | 9.0 | 11.51 | 1.04 |
| ⊕ Procter & Gamble | Goods | 21.2 | 7.18 | 1.01 |
| ⊕ American International G | Financial | 15.6 | 4.83 | 0.97 |
| ⊕ IBM | Hardware | 16.0 | -15.83 | 0.92 |
| ⊕ J.P. Morgan Chase & Co. | Financial | 18.8 | 5.74 | 0.85 |
| ⊕ Cisco Systems | Hardware | 19.9 | -11.39 | 0.81 |
| ⊕ Wal-Mart Stores | Consumer | 18.2 | -10.30 | 0.79 |
| ⊕ Wells Fargo | Financial | 14.3 | 4.47 | 0.70 |
| ⊕ Amgen | Health | 28.3 | 22.93 | 0.70 |
| ⊕ PepsiCo | Goods | 25.8 | 15.24 | 0.67 |
| ⊕ Coca-Cola | Goods | 18.6 | -0.66 | 0.66 |

**Current Investment Style**

| Market Cap | % |
|---|---|
| Giant | 43.0 |
| Large | 30.8 |
| Mid | 18.8 |
| Small | 5.7 |
| Micro | 1.7 |

Avg $mil: 24,826

| Value Measures | | Rel Category |
|---|---|---|
| Price/Earnings | 16.23 | 0.96 |
| Price/Book | 2.43 | 0.90 |
| Price/Sales | 1.41 | 1.10 |
| Price/Cash Flow | 6.38 | 0.88 |
| Dividend Yield % | 1.75 | 0.99 |

| Growth Measures | % | Rel Category |
|---|---|---|
| Long-Term Erngs | 11.00 | 0.99 |
| Book Value | 9.45 | 1.01 |
| Sales | 8.04 | 1.00 |
| Cash Flow | 10.45 | 1.01 |
| Historical Erngs | 14.86 | 1.05 |

| Profitability | % | Rel Category |
|---|---|---|
| Return on Equity | 17.60 | 0.86 |
| Return on Assets | 9.41 | 1.01 |
| Net Margin | 12.62 | 1.16 |

**Sector Weightings**

| | % of Stocks | Rel S&P 500 | 3 Year High Low |
|---|---|---|---|
| ↻ Info | 19.92 | 0.99 | |
| Software | 3.76 | 1.06 | 5  4 |
| Hardware | 9.74 | 0.97 | 11  9 |
| Media | 3.50 | 0.98 | 5  4 |
| Telecom | 2.92 | 0.97 | 3  3 |
| ↻ Service | 46.84 | 1.01 | |
| Health | 13.01 | 0.98 | 14  12 |
| Consumer | 8.46 | 1.04 | 10  8 |
| Business | 5.01 | 1.29 | 5  5 |
| Financial | 20.36 | 0.97 | 23  20 |
| Mfg | 33.25 | 0.99 | |
| Goods | 8.07 | 0.94 | 9  8 |
| Ind Mtrls | 11.46 | 0.94 | 12  10 |
| Energy | 10.10 | 1.08 | 10  6 |
| Utilities | 3.62 | 1.08 | 4  3 |

**Composition**

| | |
|---|---|
| Cash | 0.7 |
| Stocks | 98.6 |
| Bonds | 0.0 |
| Other | 0.6 |
| Foreign | 0.1 |

(% of Stock)

### Morningstar's Take by Sonya Morris

Vanguard Total Stock Market VIPER's new benchmark doesn't squelch its appeal.

On Feb. 1, 2005, Vanguard announced its plan to replace this ETF's current bogy, the Wilshire 5000 Index, with the MSCI U.S. Broad Market Index. The firm is expected to gradually phase in the new index between March 31 and Dec. 31, 2005.

There are some noteworthy differences between the two indexes. Whereas the Wilshire bogy covers all U.S. stocks, the MSCI index stops just shy of that mark, excluding a raft of tiny firms that account for 0.5% of the U.S. market's capitalization. Unlike Wilshire, MSCI also adjusts weightings to remove the effect of shares that aren't investable, meaning that stocks with heavy insider ownership, such as Microsoft, will see their influence wane. Finally, the MSCI index includes the stocks of firms that are headquartered abroad but do most of their business in the U.S., while omitting limited partnerships.

Nevertheless, these differences shouldn't give the ETF a markedly different risk/reward profile. In fact, while back-tested long-term returns aren't available for the new MSCI index, available data suggests that returns won't deviate far from the Wilshire index's.

To be sure, transaction costs are likely to tick up slightly in the near term. But judging from the relative ease with which other Vanguard index funds have made similar transitions in recent years, we don't expect the drag on returns to be onerous. In addition, we don't anticipate the fund will incur heavy capital gains as a result of the change since the fund's top holdings--where selling is likely to be heaviest--teem with shares that are under water. (The fund added many shares at the tail end of the bull market, meaning that it bought near stocks' historic peaks.) As such, selling should be confined primarily to high-cost share lots, allowing management to harvest additional losses.

All told, the thesis for this ETF remains intact: It's a fine choice to anchor a portfolio.

| | | | | |
|---|---|---|---|---|
| Address: | PO Box 2600 United States 866-499-8473 | Management Fee: | 0.05% | |
| | | Expense Projections: | 3Yr:$23  5Yr:$40  10Yr:$90 | |
| Web Address: | www.vanguard.com | Income Distrib: | Quarterly | |
| Inception: | 05-31-01 * | Exchange: | AMEX | |
| Advisor: | Vanguard Advisers, Inc. | | | |

**Growth of $10,000**
— Investment Value of ETF
— Investment Value of Index S&P 500

3 1833 04647 443 0

152

MORNINGSTAR® ETFs 100

## Ⓗ Morningstar Category

The Morningstar Category is the first stage of digging into the ETF's portfolio. We sort ETFs into peer groups based on the types of securities the ETFs hold. Each category is assigned using a fundamental analysis of an ETF's portfolio over a three-year period. It is important to analyze the types of securities an ETF holds. Portfolio analysis, and an ETF's category, can tell you a lot about an ETF's performance and future volatility. For example, investors can expect bumpier rides with ETFs in the small-cap growth category-those that focus on small, rapidly growing companies-than with large-cap value ETFs, which focus on well-established companies that are trading cheaply. In addition to portfolio analysis, the Morningstar categories also can help you diversify and evaluate the role an ETF might play in your portfolio. For example, you might head to the more-volatile categories (the small-cap groups or emerging markets) if you decided to spice up your large-cap-laden portfolio. Or you might want to tone down a growth-oriented portfolio with a value ETF or two.

## Ⓘ History

Use this table to spot trends over the past 10 years. Pay particular attention to the following statistics.

### Expense Ratio

This percentage tells you how much it costs to own the ETF each year. Generally ETFs are much cheaper than traditional mutual funds with expense ratios that are a fraction of that of the average conventional mutual fund. The average expense ratio is 0.36% for domestic stock ETFs, 0.68% for international ETFs, and 0.17% for fixed-income ETFs.

### Turnover Rate

Virtually all ETFs are index funds and should have low turnover relative to conventional mutual funds. However, turnover still matters. Depending on how they are constructed, the benchmarks of smaller-cap and style-base indexes can have higher turnover as stocks that get larger or smaller, or cheaper or more expensive, migrate in and out of the benchmarks. To keep up with the changes, ETFs may have to sell securities. Higher turnover drives up an ETF's costs because more brokerage commissions are being paid. Higher-turnover ETFs also could be less tax-efficient, although the unique structure of ETFs allows them to avoid many gains. Still if an ETF has a high turnover rate, check its tax efficiency. And watch for significant year-to-year changes in the turnover rate: It could indicate a change in the ETF's benchmark.

## Ⓙ Portfolio Analysis

Analyzing an ETF's portfolio will give you an understanding of the ETF's performance and potential volatility. First, note the ETF's total holdings: The ETF with fewer stocks will get more kick from its best performers, but if just a few holdings falter, the ETF will lag. All things being equal, an ETF with 50 or fewer stocks will be more volatile than an ETF holding twice as many issues. Next, check the percentage of assets devoted to each security. An ETF following a concentrated index will have large hunks of the ETF's assets (more than 5% per stock) invested in its top holdings. Now identify each stock's sector to gain insight into where an ETF's top holdings are concentrated and where its vulnerabilities lie. Then check the stocks' P/E ratios; a high P/E is another indication of possible future volatility. Each stock's year-to-date returns tell you which securities in which sectors are driving the performance of the ETF up or down.

## Ⓚ Risk Profile

These numbers provide views of risk. Alpha, beta, and R-squared are three Modern Portfolio Theory statistics that measure how much you can expect an ETF to follow a market index and whether the ETF has added or subtracted value versus that benchmark. We compare all domestic- and international-equity ETFs with the S&P 500 and a Best Fit Index (the index with which the ETF has the highest correlation).

### Alpha

Alpha measures excess returns per unit of risk. The higher the alpha the better. A positive alpha indicates the ETF performed better in the past than its beta would predict. A negative alpha indicates the ETF performed worse. Below these statistics, standard deviation measures risk as volatility by showing the range within which an ETF's monthly returns have landed. The larger the number, the wider the range and more volatile the ETF has been. To set an ETF's standard deviation in context, compare it with others in the ETF's category. The mean represents the annualized total return for an ETF over the trailing three years.

### Beta

Beta measures an ETF's volatility relative to its benchmark. A beta of more than 1.0 means the ETF is more volatile than the index and should outperform it when the index is rising and underperform it when the index is falling. A beta of less than 1.0 works the opposite way. The iShares Dow Jones Real Estate Index's beta of 0.98 versus the Dow Jones Wilshire REIT Index means it's just as volatile as that bogy. The ETF's beta of 0.43 versus the S&P 500 means its less volatile than the broad market.

# The Morningstar Stock-ETF Page (continued)

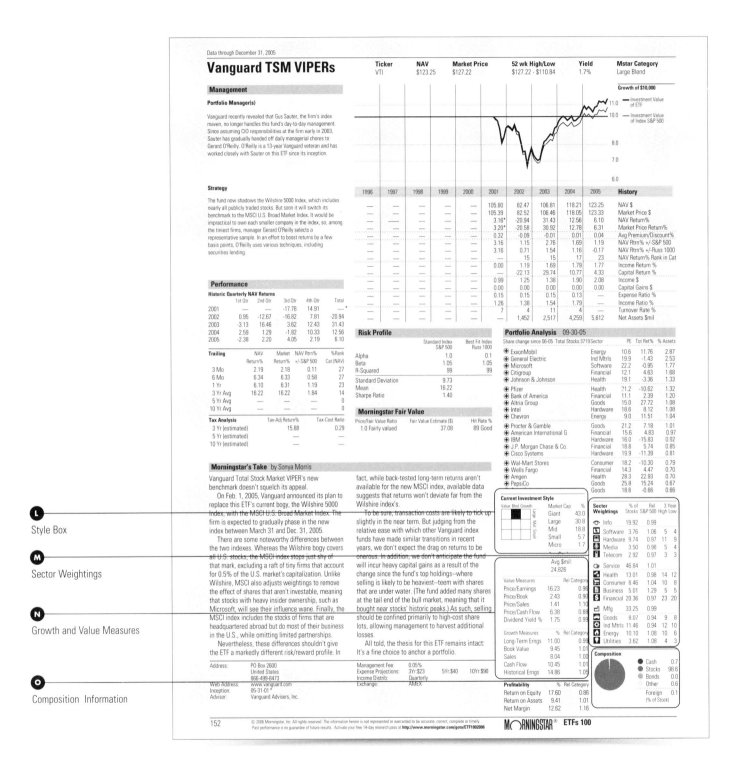

Data through December 31, 2005

## Vanguard TSM VIPERs

| | Ticker VTI | NAV $123.25 | Market Price $127.22 | 52 wk High/Low $127.22 - $110.84 | Yield 1.7% | Mstar Category Large Blend |
|---|---|---|---|---|---|---|

### Management

**Portfolio Manager(s)**

Vanguard recently revealed that Gus Sauter, the firm's index maven, no longer handles this fund's day-to-day management. Since assuming CIO responsibilities at the firm early in 2003, Sauter has gradually handed off daily managerial chores to Gerard O'Reilly. O'Reilly is a 13-year Vanguard veteran and has worked closely with Sauter on this ETF since its inception.

**Strategy**

The fund now shadows the Wilshire 5000 Index, which includes nearly all publicly traded stocks. But soon it will switch its benchmark to the MSCI U.S. Broad Market Index. It would be impractical to own each smaller company in the index, so, among the tiniest firms, manager Gerard O'Reilly selects a representative sample. In an effort to boost returns by a few basis points, O'Reilly uses various techniques, including securities lending.

### Performance

**Historic Quarterly NAV Returns**

| | 1st Qtr | 2nd Qtr | 3rd Qtr | 4th Qtr | Total |
|---|---|---|---|---|---|
| 2001 | — | — | -17.78 | 14.91 | — * |
| 2002 | 0.95 | -12.67 | -16.82 | 7.81 | -20.94 |
| 2003 | -3.13 | 16.46 | 3.62 | 12.43 | 31.43 |
| 2004 | 2.59 | 1.29 | -1.82 | 10.33 | 12.56 |
| 2005 | -2.38 | 2.20 | 4.05 | 2.19 | 6.10 |

| Trailing | NAV Return% | Market Return% | NAV Rtrn% +/-S&P 500 | %Rank Cat.(NAV) |
|---|---|---|---|---|
| 3 Mo | 2.19 | 2.18 | 0.11 | 27 |
| 6 Mo | 6.34 | 6.33 | 0.58 | 27 |
| 1 Yr | 6.10 | 6.31 | 1.19 | 23 |
| 3 Yr Avg | 16.22 | 16.22 | 1.84 | 14 |
| 5 Yr Avg | — | — | — | 0 |
| 10 Yr Avg | — | — | — | 0 |

| Tax Analysis | Tax-Adj Return% | Tax-Cost Ratio |
|---|---|---|
| 3 Yr (estimated) | 15.88 | 0.29 |
| 5 Yr (estimated) | — | — |
| 10 Yr (estimated) | — | — |

### Morningstar's Take by Sonya Morris

Vanguard Total Stock Market VIPER's new benchmark doesn't squelch its appeal.

On Feb. 1, 2005, Vanguard announced its plan to replace this ETF's current bogy, the Wilshire 5000 Index, with the MSCI U.S. Broad Market Index. The firm is expected to gradually phase in the new index between March 31 and Dec. 31, 2005.

There are some noteworthy differences between the two indexes. Whereas the Wilshire bogy covers all U.S. stocks, the MSCI index stops just shy of that mark, excluding a raft of tiny firms that account for 0.5% of the U.S. market's capitalization. Unlike Wilshire, MSCI also adjusts weightings to remove the effect of shares that aren't investable, meaning that stocks with heavy insider ownership, such as Microsoft, will see their influence wane. Finally, the MSCI index includes the stocks of firms that are headquartered abroad but do most of their business in the U.S., while omitting limited partnerships.

Nevertheless, these differences shouldn't give the ETF a markedly different risk/reward profile. In fact, while back-tested long-term returns aren't available for the new MSCI index, available data suggests that returns won't deviate far from the Wilshire index's.

To be sure, transaction costs are likely to tick up slightly in the near term. But judging from the relative ease with which other Vanguard index funds have made similar transitions in recent years, we don't expect the drag on returns to be onerous. In addition, we don't anticipate the fund will incur heavy capital gains as a result of the change since the fund's top holdings--where selling is likely to be heaviest--teem with shares that are under water. (The fund added many shares at the tail end of the bull market, meaning that it bought near stocks' historic peaks.) As such, selling should be confined primarily to high-cost share lots, allowing management to harvest additional losses.

All told, the thesis for this ETF remains intact: It's a fine choice to anchor a portfolio.

| Address: | PO Box 2600 United States 866-499-8473 | Management Fee: | 0.05% |
|---|---|---|---|
| | | Expense Projections: | 3Yr:$23  5Yr:$40  10Yr:$90 |
| | | Income Distrib: | Quarterly |
| Web Address: | www.vanguard.com | Exchange: | AMEX |
| Inception: | 05-31-01 * | | |
| Advisor: | Vanguard Advisers, Inc. | | |

152

© 2006 Morningstar, Inc. All rights reserved. The information herein is not represented or warranted to be accurate, correct, complete or timely. Past performance is no guarantee of future results. Activate your free 14-day research pass at http://www.morningstar.com/goto/ETF1002006

MORNINGSTAR® ETFs 100

**L** — Style Box

**M** — Sector Weightings

**N** — Growth and Value Measures

**O** — Composition Information

**Growth of $10,000**

| | 1996 | 1997 | 1998 | 1999 | 2000 | 2001 | 2002 | 2003 | 2004 | 2005 | History |
|---|---|---|---|---|---|---|---|---|---|---|---|
| | — | — | — | — | — | 105.80 | 82.47 | 106.81 | 118.21 | 123.25 | NAV $ |
| | — | — | — | — | — | 105.39 | 82.52 | 106.46 | 118.05 | 123.33 | Market Price $ |
| | — | — | — | — | — | 3.16* | -20.94 | 31.43 | 12.56 | 6.10 | NAV Return% |
| | — | — | — | — | — | 3.20* | -20.58 | 30.92 | 12.78 | 6.31 | Market Price Return% |
| | — | — | — | — | — | 0.32 | -0.09 | -0.01 | 0.01 | 0.04 | Avg Premium/Discount% |
| | — | — | — | — | — | 3.16 | 1.15 | 2.76 | 1.69 | 1.19 | NAV Rtrn% +/-S&P 500 |
| | — | — | — | — | — | 3.16 | 0.71 | 1.54 | 1.16 | -0.17 | NAV Rtrn% +/-Russ 1000 |
| | — | — | — | — | — | — | 15 | 15 | 17 | 23 | NAV Return% Rank in Cat |
| | — | — | — | — | — | 0.00 | 1.19 | 1.69 | 1.79 | 1.77 | Income Return % |
| | — | — | — | — | — | — | -22.13 | 29.74 | 10.77 | 4.33 | Capital Return % |
| | — | — | — | — | — | 0.99 | 1.25 | 1.38 | 1.90 | 2.08 | Income $ |
| | — | — | — | — | — | 0.00 | 0.00 | 0.00 | 0.00 | 0.00 | Capital Gains $ |
| | — | — | — | — | — | 0.15 | 0.15 | 0.15 | 0.13 | — | Expense Ratio % |
| | — | — | — | — | — | 1.26 | 1.38 | 1.54 | 1.79 | — | Income Ratio % |
| | — | — | — | — | — | 7 | 4 | 11 | 4 | — | Turnover Rate % |
| | — | — | — | — | — | — | 1,452 | 2,517 | 4,259 | 5,612 | Net Assets $mil |

### Risk Profile

| | Standard Index S&P 500 | Best Fit Index Russ 1000 |
|---|---|---|
| Alpha | 1.0 | 0.1 |
| Beta | 1.05 | 1.05 |
| R-Squared | 99 | 99 |
| Standard Deviation | 9.73 | |
| Mean | 16.22 | |
| Sharpe Ratio | 1.40 | |

### Morningstar Fair Value

| Price/Fair Value Ratio | Fair Value Estimate ($) | Hit Rate % |
|---|---|---|
| 1.0 Fairly valued | 37.08 | 89 Good |

### Portfolio Analysis 09-30-05

Share change since 06-05 Total Stocks:3719

| Sector | | PE | Tot Ret% | % Assets |
|---|---|---|---|---|
| ⊕ ExxonMobil | Energy | 10.6 | 11.76 | 2.87 |
| ⊕ General Electric | Ind Mtrls | 19.9 | -1.43 | 2.53 |
| ⊕ Microsoft | Software | 22.2 | -0.95 | 1.77 |
| ⊕ Citigroup | Financial | 12.1 | 4.63 | 1.68 |
| ⊕ Johnson & Johnson | Health | 19.1 | -3.36 | 1.33 |
| ⊕ Pfizer | Health | 21.2 | -10.62 | 1.32 |
| ⊕ Bank of America | Financial | 11.1 | 2.39 | 1.20 |
| ⊕ Altria Group | Goods | 15.0 | 27.72 | 1.08 |
| ⊕ Intel | Hardware | 18.6 | 8.12 | 1.08 |
| ⊕ Chevron | Energy | 9.0 | 11.51 | 1.04 |
| ⊕ Procter & Gamble | Goods | 21.2 | 7.18 | 1.01 |
| ⊕ American International G | Financial | 15.6 | 4.83 | 0.97 |
| ⊕ IBM | Hardware | 16.0 | -15.83 | 0.92 |
| ⊕ J.P. Morgan Chase & Co. | Financial | 18.8 | 5.74 | 0.85 |
| ⊕ Cisco Systems | Hardware | 19.9 | -11.39 | 0.81 |
| ⊕ Wal-Mart Stores | Consumer | 18.2 | -10.30 | 0.79 |
| ⊕ Wells Fargo | Financial | 14.3 | 4.47 | 0.70 |
| ⊕ Amgen | Health | 28.3 | 22.93 | 0.70 |
| ⊕ PepsiCo | Goods | 25.8 | 15.24 | 0.67 |
| | Goods | 18.6 | -0.66 | 0.66 |

**Current Investment Style**

| Value Blend Growth | Market Cap | % |
|---|---|---|
| | Giant | 43.0 |
| | Large | 30.8 |
| | Mid | 18.8 |
| | Small | 5.7 |
| | Micro | 1.7 |
| | Avg $mil: | 24,826 |

| Value Measures | | Rel Category |
|---|---|---|
| Price/Earnings | 16.23 | 0.96 |
| Price/Book | 2.43 | 0.90 |
| Price/Sales | 1.41 | 1.10 |
| Price/Cash Flow | 6.38 | 0.88 |
| Dividend Yield % | 1.75 | 0.99 |

| Growth Measures | % | Rel Category |
|---|---|---|
| Long-Term Erngs | 11.00 | 0.99 |
| Book Value | 9.45 | 1.01 |
| Sales | 8.04 | 1.00 |
| Cash Flow | 10.45 | 1.01 |
| Historical Erngs | 14.86 | 1.05 |

| Profitability | % | Rel Category |
|---|---|---|
| Return on Equity | 17.60 | 0.86 |
| Return on Assets | 9.41 | 1.01 |
| Net Margin | 12.62 | 1.16 |

**Sector Weightings**

| | % of Stocks | Rel S&P 500 | 3 Year High Low |
|---|---|---|---|
| ⌖ Info | 19.92 | 0.99 | |
| Software | 3.76 | 1.06 | 5  4 |
| Hardware | 9.74 | 0.97 | 11  9 |
| Media | 3.50 | 0.98 | 5  4 |
| Telecom | 2.92 | 0.97 | 3  3 |
| Service | 46.84 | 1.01 | |
| Health | 13.01 | 0.98 | 14 12 |
| Consumer | 8.46 | 1.04 | 10  8 |
| Business | 5.01 | 1.29 | 5  5 |
| Financial | 20.36 | 0.97 | 23 20 |
| Mfg | 33.25 | 0.99 | |
| Goods | 8.07 | 0.94 | 9  8 |
| Ind Mtrls | 11.46 | 0.94 | 12 10 |
| Energy | 10.10 | 1.08 | 10  6 |
| Utilities | 3.62 | 1.08 | 4  3 |

**Composition**

| | % |
|---|---|
| ● Cash | 0.7 |
| ● Stocks | 98.6 |
| ● Bonds | 0.0 |
| ● Other | 0.6 |
| Foreign | 0.1 |
| (% of Stock) | |

## R-squared

For beta and alpha to be reliable measures of risk and reward, an ETF must have a high correlation with its index, as measured by R-squared. R-squared indicates how marketlike an ETF is. A high R-squared (between 85 and 100) indicates the ETF's performance patterns have been in line with the index's. An ETF with a low R-squared (70 or less) doesn't act much like the index. Index ETFs' should have R-squared of 100 when compared against their own or similar indexes, but the measure can vary when they are compared against a different bogy. The iShares Dow Jones Real Estate Index, for example, has an R-squared of 99 versus the Dow Jones Wilshire REIT Index, but an R-squared of 9 versus the S&P 500. That means the ETF is more like the REIT index.

## Sharpe Ratio

The Sharpe ratio is a risk-adjusted measure. The higher the Sharpe ratio (1.0 is pretty good), the better the ETF's risk-adjusted performance has been.

## L Style Box

For stock ETFs, Morningstar assigns style-box classifications based on portfolios' scores for growth measures, value measures, and average weighted market cap. For example, ETFs that invest predominantly in large-cap, fast-growing firms with high valuations typically land in large growth. By contrast, ETFs that specialize in smaller, slower-growing firms with modest valuations are assigned to the small-value style box.

## M Sector Weightings

Learn which sectors of the economy the ETF invests in to gauge how diversified the ETF is. An ETF that has more than 25% of assets concentrated in one sector is almost certain to carry more risk than a more-diversified offering. Knowing the ETF's weightings can help you maintain a well-diversified portfolio. Weightings are displayed relative to the S&P 500 for domestic-stock ETFs and to the category for international-stock ETFs. (We show relative subsector breakdowns for ETFs in our specialty categories.) The last two columns of the section give an ETF's historical range of the percentage of assets held in each sector.

## N Growth and Value Measures

This section lists an ETF portfolio's current averages for various portfolio statistics, including price/earnings, price/cash flow, and historical earnings growth. To provide perspective, we compare these measures with the ETFs' category average.

## O Composition Information

This section shows the percentage of assets devoted to cash, stocks, bonds, and other, along with what percentage of stock assets are invested in foreign securities. All ETFs should be nearly fully invested, though they typically will carry a trace of cash for settlement purposes.

# The Morningstar Bond-ETF Page

In this two-page walk-through, we spotlight sections that are unique to the bond-fund page and offer some advice on using the page to select a bond fund. More-detailed discussions of the elements presented in this section appear in the Glossary.

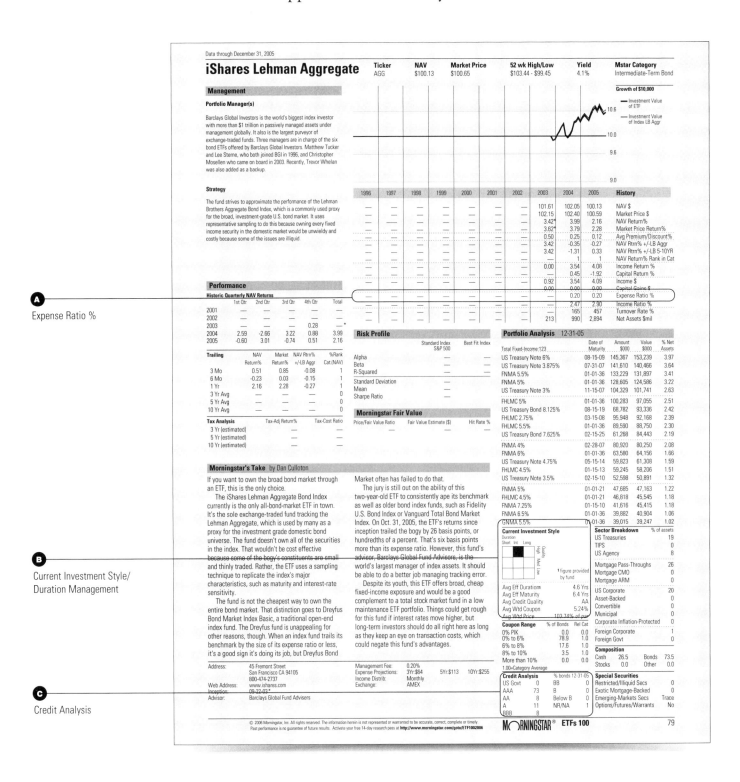

**A** — Expense Ratio %

**B** — Current Investment Style/Duration Management

**C** — Credit Analysis

### Ⓐ Expense Ratio %

It's critical to look for bond ETFs with low expenses. Expenses can eat into total returns and income payments.

### Ⓑ Current Investment Style / Duration

The bond style box is based on an ETF's credit quality and its duration. Check the ETF's average credit quality and average effective duration in the column next to the style box. Credit quality is an important aspect of any bond ETF, as it measures the creditworthiness of the ETF's holdings. An ETF with an average credit quality of AAA, for example, is less likely to get stung by defaults than an ETF with an average credit quality of BBB. Duration is equally important, as it measures an ETF's overall interestrate risk. The longer an ETF's duration, the more sensitive the ETF is to shifts in interest-rates. When rates fall, ETFs with longer durations benefit; when interest-rates climb, shorter-duration ETFs are beneficial. First-time bond-ETF buyers, especially those looking to cushion their stock-heavy portfolios, probably should stick with ETFs in the intermediate-term range (3.5 to six years). Intermediate-term bond funds have offered yields and returns similar to long-term bond funds but with less volatility.

### Ⓒ Credit Analysis

Average credit quality provides a snapshot of a portfolio's overall credit quality, while the Credit Analysis section shows the percentage of fixed-income securities that fall within each credit-quality rating, as assigned by Standard & Poor's or Moody's. The lower a bond's rating, the greater its default risk and the higher its yield. Bonds rated BBB and above are considered investment-grade issues; those rated BB and below are high-yield, commonly called junk bonds. Pay particularly close attention to an ETF's weightings in below B and nonrated bonds. Often these issues are riskier bonds that are in danger of defaulting or that have already defaulted. They are also typically less liquid than higher-quality bonds. That's why it's a good idea to diversify with a good mix of high- and low-quality bonds (lean more toward the high-quality side).

# ETFs 101

## What are exchange-traded funds, and how do they work?

by Dan Culloton, Editor, Morningstar ETFs 100

They have been hailed as innovative tools for a new generation of savvy investors and derided as "beautiful shotguns"—elegantly designed products that can be dangerous in the hands of the inexperienced or intemperate. Although they've been around for a dozen years, they recently have become increasingly pervasive alternatives to mutual funds. They're still a tiny niche of the $8.5 trillion traditional fund industry, but they're growing rapidly. We're talking, of course, about exchange-traded funds, or ETFs.

### Understanding ETFs

ETFs are index mutual funds that can be bought and sold throughout the trading day on an exchange like a stock. Like regular mutual funds, they can offer one-stop diversified equity exposure to investors who don't have the time or the inclination to pick their own stocks. Unlike their forebears, though, ETFs' share prices are set throughout the day by the laws of supply and demand, not once per day at 4 P.M. EST. You also can do just about anything with an ETF that you can do with a stock, including set market, limit, and stop-loss orders, buy them on margin (or with borrowed money), and sell them short. ETFs often have lower expense ratios than even the cheapest traditional index funds, but you must pay brokerage commissions to trade them. Those transaction costs can add up quickly for frequent traders or those who like to make regular investments.

The flexibility of exchange-traded funds is the source of both their popularity and potential peril. Understanding them can help put those attractions and hazards in perspective. This article will focus on ETFs' origins, inner workings, and main purveyors.

### A Brief History

The antecedents of ETFs stretch back to the advent of program trading in the 1970s and 1980s, which allowed large institutional investors to buy and sell whole portfolios of stocks in one fell swoop. In the late 1980s and early 1990s, stock exchanges in America and Canada experimented with versions of ETFs, but the **SPDR** SPY (short for Standard and Poor's Depositary Receipts) was the most successful early form. The American Stock Exchange and State Street Global Advisors launched the fund, which tracks the S&P 500 Index, in January 1993, and it attracted more than $400 million in assets that year.

Growth was slow at first. The American Stock Exchange added **MidCap SPDRs** MDY, which followed the S&P MidCap 400 Index, in 1995, and Morgan Stanley's country-specific international ETFs, known as WEBS, or World Equity Benchmark Shares, followed in 1996. Funds tracking the Dow Jones Industrial Average and the NASDAQ 100 indexes hit the market in 1998 and 1999, respectively. By the end of the decade the Investment Company Institute estimated there were about 30 ETFs with nearly $34 billion in assets under management.

The late 1990s' bull market and the growing popularity of do-it-yourself, online trading helped set the stage for ETFs' most dramatic growth spurt. In 2000 Barclay's Global Investors began launching dozens of ETFs tracking everything from broadly diversified indexes, such as the S&P 500, to impossibly narrow ones, such as the South African stock market. Expansion continued apace thereafter. From 2000 to the end of 2005 the number of ETFs more than doubled to nearly 200 and total assets under management more than tripled to nearly $300 billion. The offerings have gotten increasingly exotic, too. Firms have launched new ETFs tracking the price of gold and micro-cap stocks and have floated proposals for funds offering exposure to silver, currencies, oil, and other commodities.

### Nuts and Bolts

Like mutual funds, ETFs are baskets of securities (typically stocks) that continuously create and redeem shares. However, most individual investors can't buy ETF shares from or sell them to investment companies the way they can with traditional fund shares. That's because ETF shares can only be bought and sold directly from the fund in 50,000 share lots known as creation units. Even then the transactions are done "in-kind," which means investors get baskets of the underlying stocks in the ETF's target index instead of cash when they redeem their shares. It takes deep pockets and considerable scale to have the wherewithal to traffic in creation units directly with fund companies. (They typically are large Wall Street brokerages, specialists, and market makers.) That's why

## ETF Creation/Redemption Process

most average investors use a broker to trade ETF shares on the secondary market.

ETF shares should trade at or close to the net asset value of their underlying portfolios, but they don't always. Because ETF shares trade actively on an exchange, the laws of supply and demand influence their market prices. As a result, the shares can trade at a discount or premium to the fund's underlying NAV.

The ability of large investors to buy or sell shares in-kind helps minimize discounts or premiums, however. The process can be complicated, but here are a couple of simple examples. If a particular ETF was selling at a big discount to the value of its underlying securities, a large institutional investor could buy the ETF shares in the open market, swap them for the underlying securities, and sell the stocks for a profit. The presence of a big investor snapping up discounted ETF shares should generate enough demand for the issues to close the gap between its market price and the value of its underlying holdings.

Naturally, this arbitrage mechanism would work in the opposite direction, too. If an ETF's shares were trading at a premium to the fund's NAV, institutional investors would swap baskets of the underlying securities for the fund's creation units and break them up into individual ETF shares to be sold for a profit, which should help reduce the premium.

### Tax Advantages
Because most ETFs are index funds with low turnover rates, they save money on transaction costs and tend to be more tax efficient than actively managed traditional funds. ETFs' in-kind redemption feature also gives them an added tax advantage. Traditional mutual fund managers often have to sell securities to meet redemptions, in the process realizing capital gains that must be distributed to shareholders. Because ETFs satisfy redemptions with shares of stock, they don't have to sell any of their holdings to redeem shareholders.

ETFs are not immune from capital gains. They could make distributions if the indexes they track delete or add stocks. Like some other traditional fund managers, ETF skippers try to harvest losses that can be used to offset future gains. But they have other tools, too. Traditional fund managers often try to manage taxes by selling the shares that cost them the most to buy first because those shares have the smallest potential capital gains. That method, however, may only forestall taxable distributions because it leaves the least costly shares (the ones with the biggest potential gains) in the portfolio. In contrast, many ETF managers can use the in-kind redemption process to get rid of their lowest cost-basis shares first without selling securities. That keeps the unrealized gains in their funds low and reduces the probability of future distributions.

### Alphabet Soup
The average investor doesn't see what happens under an ETF's hood, though. What they see are SPDRs, VIPERs, Qubes, iShares, PowerShares, StreetTracks, and HOLDRs. Indeed, the variety of creatively spelled ETF names can bewilder. Other articles in this book will profile the major families in detail. Until then here's a quick key to the alphabet soup.

Among the most popular and heavily traded ETFs are the SPDRs (pronounced "spiders"); **Diamonds** DIA, which track the Dow Jones Industrial Average; and Qubes (pronounced "cubes"), or **NASDAQ 100 Trust Shares** QQQQ, which follow the NASDAQ 100 Index. The SPDRs and Diamonds trade on the American Stock Exchange. The Qubes trade on the NASDAQ Stock Market.

As noted earlier, the SPDR is the oldest and largest ETF in terms of net assets. It offers cheap (but not the cheapest) exposure to the venerable S&P 500 Index, which represents 82% of the U.S. market (based on market capitalization). The Qubes, however, are easily the most frequently traded ETF shares. The fund, which tracks the NASDAQ Composite's biggest nonfinancial companies, is a favorite of traders because of its concentration in volatile technology, biotechnology, Internet, and telecommunication stocks.

While those are the biggest individual ETFs, Barclays Global Investors has the largest ETF family with its iShares lineup. As of this writing Barclays had more than 100 funds and more than $150 billion in assets (or the lion's share of total domestic ETF assets). State Street Global Advisors was present at the creation of the ETF industry (it is the SPDR's trustee), but it's a distant second to Barclays in terms of size. The firm manages more than $70 billion in more than 20 ETFs. The SPDR accounts for most of those assets, but the firm also offers the Select Sector SPDRs, which track nine S&P 500 sectors, the StreetTracks series, and the Diamonds. Bank of New York is the third-largest ETF sponsor with about $30 billion. It runs the Qubes, Mid Cap SPDRs, and the BLDRS portfolios.

In recent years, Vanguard, which popularized conventional index funds, has launched its own lineup of ETFs—nearly two dozen VIPER shares for its domestic and foreign index funds. Vanguard's VIPERs, which total about $9 billion in assets, have one peculiarity: They're actually share classes of existing Vanguard index funds.

PowerShares has been the industry upstart. It has launched or proposed scads of ETFs since opening for business in 2002. Many of the firm's funds track enhanced indexes that use quantitative models to select stocks in an effort to beat traditional bogies. Others track bogies in hot-dot areas such as China or dividend-paying stocks.

Close cousins to ETFs are Merrill Lynch's HOLDRs, or Holding Company Depositary Receipts. They can be bought and sold on the American Stock Exchange and have relatively low expenses. However, HOLDRs don't track indexes. They are baskets of about 20 stocks usually picked by Merrill Lynch to represent narrow industry groups, such as biotechnology or semiconductors.

To sum up, ETFs offer a viable alternative to traditional mutual funds, especially for tax- and cost-conscious investors who prefer passive management. They are becoming more and more popular among investors and make up a larger part of the investment universe than ever before. Still, investors should shop carefully before jumping on the bandwagon. ▮▮

# Mutual Funds vs. ETFs

Is a traditional or exchange-traded fund right for you?

by Dan Culloton, Editor,
Morningstar ETFs 100

ETFs have a lot to offer investors. They're versatile, cheap, and their underlying portfolios are protected from the impact of investor trading. Beware, though: Many ETFs are too narrowly focused and concentrated to be of much use to the average investor. Moreover, transaction costs can add up quickly and erode returns. Let's take a closer look at some of these pros and cons.

### ETF Strengths

Low expenses are an obvious benefit. Because ETF sponsors deal directly with just a few, very large investors, they save money on many administrative costs. For example, they don't need call centers to handle scores of calls from retail investors and don't have to take care of hundreds of small accounts. On average, ETFs have large expense ratio advantages over the typical passive and actively managed mutual funds in many Morningstar categories.

ETFs also can be tax friendly. ETFs are not immune from capital gains distributions: They have to sell stocks to adjust for changes to their underlying benchmarks. But their structure allows them to greatly minimize their tax impact. Currently all ETFs are index funds, which usually trade less than the average actively managed fund and therefore generate fewer capital gains.

| Types of ETF | Average Expense Ratio % |
|---|---|
| U.S. Equity ETF | 0.39 |
| International ETF | 0.68 |
| Fixed Income ETF | 0.17 |
| Traditional Actively Managed U.S. Equity Fund | 1.48 |
| Traditional U.S. Equity Index Fund | 0.76 |
| Traditional Actively managed International Equity Fund | 1.75 |
| Traditional International Index Fund | 0.84 |
| Traditional Actively Managed Taxable Fixed income fund | 1.13 |
| Traditional Index Taxable Fixed Income Fund | 0.49 |

Data as of October 31, 2005

ETFs' tax efficiency is also helped by the fact that only large institutional investors (known as author-ized participants) are allowed to trade directly with the fund—everyone else buys or sells shares from each other over an exchange—so the ETF portfolio is largely insulated from the need to sell securities (and possibly realize capital gains) to raise cash to meet redemptions from small investors. Further, when an authorized participant redeems a block of ETF shares, the ETF manager gives it a basket of the underlying securities owned by the ETF, not cash. This allows the ETF manager to continually offload its lowest-cost-basis shares of securities, thus reducing the fund's potential capital gains exposure. It also shields the fund from having to sell securities—and potentially realize capital gains—to raise cash to meet redemptions from these large investors.

ETFs also offer greater trading flexibility than mutual funds. Mutual fund share prices are set once a day at the close of trading, and any purchases or sales placed after their prices are set are supposed to be executed at the next day's price. By contrast, ETF investors can buy or sell their shares without limit throughout the trading day, and ETFs, like stocks, are priced continuously, enabling ETF investors to know the price of the fund at the time they are trading. As proponents of long-term investing, we don't view this intraday trading ability as an advantage, but some may find it useful.

ETFs offer choices where traditional funds don't. It may be that you favor index investing and want to focus on a specific part of the market such as health care or telecommunications. There simply aren't any index funds that track those sectors but there are ETFs that do. Similarly, there are many more ETFs than mutual funds that focus on single foreign countries. It's hard to make the case that such narrowly focused investments are essential to any portfolio, but there are often ETFs for them.

Just as they can with stocks, investors also can set market, limit, stop loss, or stop buy orders on ETFs. They also can sell them short (sell borrowed shares with the intention of buying them back at lower prices and pocketing the difference), buy them on margin, and buy and write options on ETF shares. These are tricky tactics that can do more harm than good in the hands of novice investors. Many professionals argue, however, that such trading techniques allow them to hedge their portfolios against sudden losses.

Finally, the fact that ETFs are not susceptible to the kind of trading abuses uncovered in 2003 in the mutual fund industry has won a few converts among scandal-weary investors. Simply put, because ETF prices are set throughout the day by the market, there is no opportunity for late trading or NAV arbitrage.

### ETF Drawbacks

Commission costs are ETFs' nemesis. Brokerage costs can range from a few dollars at some cut-rate online brokers to as much as $30 per trade at full-service brokerages. Even at the discount brokers, though, transaction costs can pile up quickly and negate ETFs' expense advantage for investors who trade frequently or make regular investments. Many brokerages also saddle account holders with additional account maintenance, inactivity, and minimum balance fees.

Gaps can open between ETF prices and NAVs. Unlike traditional open-end mutual funds, ETFs don't always trade exactly at the net asset values of their portfolios. Some infrequently traded, highly specialized ETFs can trade at discounts or premiums to their NAVs, often to their shareholders' disadvantage.

Dividends can be a drag. Some older ETFs that are organized as unit investment trusts instead of open-end funds cannot reinvest the dividends they receive from their holdings and must hold them as cash until they are distributed quarterly. That can provide a cushion in down markets but can also restrain the fund when stocks rise. Also, some brokerages don't let investors automatically reinvest dividends in their ETF portfolios, and those that do may charge a fee for the service.

ETFs are ripe for misuse. Some of the broadly diversified, low-cost ETFs can be decent core holdings, but many of the more specialized offerings are concentrated and narrowly focused and are therefore extremely volatile. Indeed many sector and region ETFs seem of marginal use in building a diversified portfolio. They often are marketed to those who wish to speculate on certain industry groups or geographic areas, which, at best, can be extremely costly and difficult to do successfully over the long term.

Finally, not all index managers are created equal. There is evidence that skilled open-end index fund managers, such as Vanguard's indexing team lead by Gus Sauter, can outperform their underlying index and be very competitive with ETFs tracking the same bogy, despite the ETFs' lower costs.

For example, through Nov. 25, 2005, the **Vanguard 500 Index's** VFINX trailing five-year gain of 0.41% was within 2 or 3 basis points, or hundredths of a percent, of the returns of the **S&P 500 SPDR** SPY and the **iShares S&P 500 Index** IW. Not bad when you consider the Vanguard 500's expense ratio is nearly twice that of those ETF competitors. Clearly an index fund manager's ability to minimize tracking error, the amount by which an index fund trails its benchmark, matters.

### Which Is Right for You?

An ETF's performance and tracking error records are important, but they can't predict the future. Indeed, costs remain an important indicator of future performance. It's impossible to predict with absolute certainty the course of specific indexes as well as whether even a skilled index manager will be able to keep tracking error low over the long run. It is possible, however, to figure out how much an investor will surrender to costs. That makes choosing relatively simple. Because the spread between the returns of most index funds and ETFs tracking similar bogies is small, the lowest-cost option has a good chance of winning, especially over longer time horizons.

At first glance, ETFs may have it all over mutual funds on the cost front. Consider this: The SPDR charges 0.11% in expenses. The iShares S&P 500 Index is even cheaper at 0.09%. That's just $0.09 for each $100 you have invested—a small fraction of the typical mutual fund expense ratio. Even ultra-cheap Vanguard 500 Index charges more, with 0.18% in annual expenses. Plus Vanguard charges a $10 annual maintenance fee for account balances below $10,000. On a $3,000 investment, that effectively boosts your annual expense ratio from 0.18% to 0.51%.

The advantages aren't all on the side of ETFs, though. For starters, not all ETFs are as cheap as the SPDR and iShares S&P 500. Before buying, be sure to check the expense ratio. And as with a stock, trading boosts the cost of investing in any ETF. Unless you use a cheap broker, invest a large amount of money, and hold for the long term, an exchange-traded fund isn't likely to have a big cost advantage over a plain-vanilla index fund. Be sure to compare the total cost of investing in a fund or ETF. (As part of your purchase of the ETFs 100, you can receive a 14-day Research Pass on Morningstar.com, which provides access to the Cost Analyzer tool, as well as to all of our ETF analysis and research. Registration details can be found on the inside front cover of this book.)

The total cost of a fund or ETF depends on the size of the initial purchase, the frequency of additional investments, the length of the holding period, and the expected return. For example, assume you made a one-time, lump sum $10,000 investment in four core equity funds: **Selected American Shares** SLASX, Vanguard 500, SDPR, and iShares S&P 500 Index. If you paid no commission on the mutual funds and a $29.95 brokerage fee on the ETFs, made no additional investments, and got a 7% annualized return over 10 years, the iShares would be the cheapest option by a slim margin.

| ETF Name | Expense Ratio % | Return % | Total Cost $ |
| --- | --- | --- | --- |
| iShares S&P500 Index | 0.09 | 6.86 | 187.53 |
| SPDR | 0.1 | 6.83 | 215.72 |
| Vanguard 500 | 0.18 | 6.81 | 254.77 |
| Selected American | 0.93 | 6.02 | 1,250.59 |

Source: Morningstar Cost Analyzer

The decision then becomes whether you think Selected American and the Vanguard index fund can add enough value over the next decade to close the expense gap. On smaller investments, ETFs' cost advantage shrink. On a $5,000 lump sum investment made with the same assumptions as above, the iShares would be cheaper than the Vanguard 500 by less than $4.

| ETF Name | Expense Ratio % | Return % | Total Cost $ |
| --- | --- | --- | --- |
| iShares S&P 500 | 0.09 | 6.81 | 123.52 |
| Vanguard 500 | 0.18 | 6.81 | 127.38 |
| SPDR | 0.1 | 6.79 | 137.58 |
| Selected American | 0.93 | 6.02 | 625.29 |

Source: Morningstar Cost Analyzer

There are cut-rate online brokers, such as Sharebuilder or Foliofn, that charge as little as $4 per trade, and using them to make a lump sum investment could make the costs of owning ETFs significantly more attractive—unless you plan on making regular monthly investments. Even at a discount broker charging $4 per trade, the lowest cost S&P 500 ETF would be much more expensive than the Vanguard 500 fund if you followed up a $10,000 initial investment with monthly additions of $100 for 10 years and assumed a 7% annualize return.

| ETF Name | Expense Ratio % | Return % | Total Cost $ |
| --- | --- | --- | --- |
| Vanguard 500 | 0.18 | 6.81 | 389.70 |
| iShares S&P 500 | 0.09 | 6.65 | 680.94 |
| SPDR | 0.1 | 6.62 | 723.59 |
| Selected American | 0.93 | 6.02 | 1,921.98 |

Source: Morningstar Cost Analyzer

The bottom line is from a cost standpoint, ETFs can be an attractive choice for investors who are putting sizable lump sums to work for the long term, but they have not yet supplanted traditional index mutual funds as the best option for small investors who want to dollar-cost average. ▋

Disclosure: Barclays Global Investors (BGI), which is owned by Barclays, currently licenses Morningstar's 16 style-based indexes for use in BGI's iShares exchange-traded funds. iShares are not sponsored, issued, or sold by Morningstar. Morningstar does not make any representation regarding the advisability of investing in iShares that are based on Morningstar indexes.

# Using ETFs in a Fund Portfolio

How to best exploit ETF's low costs and flexibility.

**by Dan Culloton, Editor,
Morningstar ETFs 100**

Legendary college Ohio State University football coach Woody Hayes famously explained his aversion to the forward pass by saying, "Only three things can happen to you when you pass, and two of them are bad." A similar aphorism applies to ETFs: You can do a lot of things with them, but many of them can be counterproductive.

You can trade ETFs, short them, buy them on margin, and buy and write options on them. But that doesn't mean you should. These tactics are exciting and potentially potent tools, but they're also fraught with complexity and risk.

Day traders love ETFs because the funds enable quick bets on whole markets, sectors, industries, and geographic regions. Frequent trading and market-timing is a tough way to make a living, though. Studies by Morningstar and others have shown that, over the long haul, market-timing strategies lose to a buy-and-hold approach most of the time. Factor in brokerage fees and capital gains taxes, and market-timing looks even more perilous.

The ability to sell ETFs short also is oversold. Short selling, or betting a security's price will decline by selling borrowed shares with the intent of buying them back at lower prices, offers finite upside but infinite downside potential.

Here's a simple example. You think Hypothetical-Shares Small Cap Growth ETF is overpriced at $50 per share, so you decide to short it. On your behalf, your broker borrows 100 shares of the ETF from another investor and then sells the shares, netting you about $5,000. If you were right about the ETF and it falls to $20 per share, you can buy 100 shares for just $2,000 and return them to your broker; keeping $3,000 (the $5,000 sale minus the $2,000 purchase), minus whatever you have to pay for the broker's services.

If you're mistaken, however, and its shares soar from $50 to $150, you're in trouble. You have to buy back the shares, and it'll cost you $15,000.

You've lost $10,000, but theoretically, you could lose more if you are not able to cover your short position, because there's no limit on how high HypotheticalShares Small Growth's market price can rise.

Judicious short selling can control a portfolio's volatility, but it's a risky strategy if not properly. The same applies to buying stocks or ETFs on margin. When buying on margin, an investor puts up a certain percentage of the purchase price (at least half, according to current regulations) and borrows the rest from a broker. That can magnify your returns as well as your losses. For an example, the now infamous hedge fund Long-Term Capital Management posted eye-popping gains when the market was soaring, but suffered spectacular losses that imperiled the global financial system when markets turned south in September 1998. Its successes and near catastrophic failure were fueled, in part, by excessive borrowing.

You can also buy and write options ETFs. Options give their owners the right, but not the obligation, to buy or sell a specific item at a specific price (the "strike price") over a specific span of time. The owner can choose when to exercise an option, or he or she can choose not to exercise the option at all. The option then expires worthless, and the investor's only loss is what he or she paid for the option. Thus, options have less downside risk than other financial derivatives, such as futures, which are contractual agreements to buy something at a specific time and price in the future.

There are two types of options: calls and puts. Anyone can buy or sell them on exchanges, such as the Chicago Board of Options Exchange. A call option gives you the right (but not the obligation) to buy an ETF at a specified price (the strike price); you would buy calls if you think an ETF's price will rise above the strike price. A call option is said to be "in the money" if the ETF's market price is above the strike price.

A put option gives you the right (but not the obligation) to sell a stock at a specified price; you would buy puts if you think an ETF's price will go down. A put option is in the money if the market price of the ETF underlying the option is below the strike price.

Calls and puts may not be as risky as futures—because you're not obligated to do anything, your greatest loss will be the loss of the cost of the call or put. But options are leveraged on the upside. For example, buying call options requires far less outlay than buying stocks would.

Yet calls and puts are inappropriate for most investors, too. Why? Because few investors make money with options. In fact, 80% of all options expire worthless. Even if you're buying puts to protect your portfolio, you're still betting on the direction of a stock's price or the market during a specific period of time. That's not investing. It's gambling. And for the majority of investors, it's not profitable.

### Buying and Holding ETFs
Trading ETFs is expensive and most likely wasteful. Shorting them, leveraging them, or writing options on them is risky. So how can an investor use ETFs?

Try buying and holding. Because you must pay a brokerage commission every time you buy (or sell) shares in an ETF, they're poor vehicles for investors making regular purchases. However, broadly diversified ETFs are hard to beat as an option for lump sum investing.

The first step is to determine an appropriate asset allocation for your goals. One way to do that is to consult with a financial advisor. Another is to use online portfolio allocation tools, such as Morningstar's Asset Allocator, or those provided by online brokers, such as Amerivest and Sharebuilder.

Then it's time to choose ETFs. The easiest way is to stick with broadly diversified offerings. For example, if you've decided to go aggressive and put 80% of your money in stocks and 20% in bonds, you could use a U.S. total stock market ETFs, such as the **iShares Russell 3000 Index** IWV or **Vanguard Total Stock Market VIPERs** VTI. For your fixed-income allocation you could use the **iShares Lehman Aggregate Bond** AGG, which tracks virtually the entire bond market. For international exposure, you could employ the **iShares MSCI EAFE Index** EFA, which tracks most of the major developed markets outside of the United States. If you want exposure to emerging economies, throw in a smidgen of the **Vanguard Emerging Markets Stock VIPER** VWO. Many investors devote about 20% to 30% of their total stock portfolios to international stocks, but you may want to go higher or lower depending on your goals and risk tolerance.

The growing number of ETFs allow you to further break down both the international and domestic portions of your portfolio by style, market cap,

country, and sector. Remember, however, that the more ETFs you own the more commissions you will incur. It's better to keep it simple.

### The All-Sector Portfolio
Not everyone wants to keep it simple, though. Investors who want near-total control over their sector exposure can use ETFs like building blocks.

Want to dedicate certain portions of your portfolio to technology, utilities, and a variety of other sectors? If you invest in diversified stock funds, trying to maintain those allocations would be nearly impossible. Maybe your growth fund has 40% of its assets in technology today, but the manager's favor might shift to health-care or communications stocks tomorrow. Instead, you could buy a group of sector ETFs and control your sector weights.

There are a couple of serious drawbacks to the all-sector-ETF portfolio, though. For starters, it's expensive. You'd pay more in commissions maintaining your target allocations than you would buying a diversified offering that did it for you. Worse yet, an all-sector-fund portfolio can be tax inefficient. As you tweak your portfolio, you could incur capital gains along the way. It's also worth noting that many sector ETFs are highly concentrated in their top holdings, so you may not be getting as much diversification as you think.

### Portfolio Enhancers
If you already have a well-rounded portfolio, but want to emphasize a particular part of the market—such as communications companies or dividend-paying stocks—you could use a sector or style ETF. You also could use Morningstar's price/fair value measure for ETFs to help identify opportunities. The measure tries to offer a bottom-up assessment of whether an ETF portfolio is cheap or expensive by gauging if its holdings, on average, are trading above or below Morningstar stock analysts' fair value estimates. Regard "plays" such as these as speculative investments, though, and limit them to 5% or 10% of your portfolio. That way, you'll limit the damage if that sector or style disappoints.

### Tax Strategies
Some investors and financial planners use tax swaps to try to reduce the tax collector's cut. One form of swap consists of looking at your fund lineup for offerings that are about to make big distributions, then selling those funds before they make their payouts. Once distribution season is over, you swap

into another fund with a similar mandate, thereby maintaining your asset allocation. (You can't buy the same fund back within 31 days without running afoul of IRS rules.) ETFs can be useful in this role. For example, you could sell **Fidelity Low-Priced Stock** FLPSX before it makes a distribution, and then buy **Vanguard Small Cap VIPERs** VB.

If you try this, however, don't forget about your own tax position in a fund: If you have a taxable gain in the fund (if it has appreciated since you purchased it, for example), you'll be forced to pay taxes on that gain, and the swap could end up costing you more than its worth. Keep transaction costs in mind too. Brokerage fees or conventional fund redemption charges may make the swap counterproductive.

Tax swaps can be much more effective if you're holding a losing investment. You can sell your loser and use up to $3,000 of net investment losses to offset income in the current year and capital gains indefinitely. (There's no limit on the amount of losses you can use to offset capital gains.) Then you can swap into a similar ETF. For example, at the end of 2005 many large-growth funds—even decent ones—were in the red over the past five years. If you find yourself in that position, you can sell, book a loss to offset gains elsewhere in your portfolio, then buy an ETF, such as **Vanguard Growth VIPERs** VUG.

ETFs are potentially powerful tools and viable alternatives to conventional mutual funds (especially high-cost traditional funds). You can use them to manage risk, taxes and style, region and sector exposures. Be careful, though. Like a well-honed kitchen knife, you can also use ETFs to hurt yourself. Before embarking on a strategy, consider the costs and risks involved. Once you settle on a course, be sure to keep turnover and commission costs under control. ⦚

**Commentary**

# Using ETFs in a Stock Portfolio

Exchange-traded funds can diversify your holdings.

**by Dan Culloton, Editor, Morningstar ETFs 100**

Some investors buy funds and others buy stocks, and never the twain shall meet. That has been the conventional wisdom. But the rising popularity of exchange-traded funds, especially among those who prefer to pick their own equities, proves what we at Morningstar have known for a long time: Investing doesn't have to be a choice between investing directly in stocks or indirectly through mutual funds. Investors can—and many should—do both. The trick is determining how your portfolio can benefit most from each type of investment.

It's pretty clear why stock investors are warming to ETFs. Their low costs and ability to trade them throughout the day enable stock-pickers to diversify their portfolios on the fly, stay fully invested while they research new ideas, hedge their bets, and employ tax-management strategies. Be careful, though. As we mentioned in our article on building ETF portfolios, the more exotic the strategy the higher the potential costs and risks. That's why we favor using ETFs to provide stability and diversity to a stock portfolio. Here are a few of the many ways to use ETFs in a stock portfolio.

## ETFs as Stabilizers
Adding a broad equity ETF to your holdings can smooth your portfolio's flight path. The chance of an individual stock taking a big plunge is greater than that of a diversified ETF. For example in the 12 months ending Oct. 31, 2005, more than one fifth of the nearly 6,000 domestic stocks in Morningstar's database fell by more than 20%, while none of nearly 100 domestic equity ETFs dropped that hard. If you only have enough money to buy a couple of stocks and funds, a broad market ETF such as the **iShares S&P 500** IVV or the **Vanguard Total Stock Market VIPERs** VTI could be a cheap and easy way help control portfolio volatility.

## ETFs as Trailblazers
Many stock investors favor household names, such as software titan **Microsoft** MFST, industrial conglomerate **General Electric** GE, or health-care giant, **Johnson & Johnson** JNJ. It's pretty easy to find

annual reports, financial data, and other research on those mega-cap stocks.

But what about micro-caps such as **International Shipholding** ISH or foreign companies such as Japan's **Nippon Telegraph & Telephone** NTT? Such off-the-beaten-path securities aren't in most stock investors' comfort zones. Such stocks are also not easy to analyze, buy, or sell. That's where an ETF can help. Some funds, such as the **First Trust Dow Jones Select MicroCap** FDM, invest in tiny stocks; others invest around the globe, and still others focus on markets, such as real estate, that have their own quirks. These ETFs can give stock investors affordable, diversified exposure to hard-to-reach areas like these without forcing them to learn a whole new set of analytical skills.

## ETFs as Balancers
Just like personalities, everyone has a unique investment style. Perhaps you have a job in the health-care industry and thus are familiar with and own a number of pharmaceutical and biotechnology stocks. Or maybe you're a devotee of Warren Buffett and stick to dominant, easy-to-understand businesses such as **Home Depot** HD and **Coca-Cola** KO. Or you could be a true believer in the broadband revolution with a portfolio full of tech and wireless stocks.

No matter how convinced you are that time will prove your predilections are prescient, there will be periods when your style falters, at least temporarily. Biotech underwent a fierce correction in early 2000. Investors who stashed their money in Buffett-like businesses found it tough to profit in 1999. And new economy tech and telecom stocks have eaten the dust of old economy energy and utility shares in the past five years.

The market is constantly shifting. No one style remains in favor forever. There is an alternative, though, to frantically trying to master value investing, or growth investing, or whatever styles you don't use and happen to be in favor at the moment. You could use an ETF designed to track the territory with which you're not familiar. That way, your portfolio will have some protection when your style slumps.

Take the health-care worker with a portfolio full of biotech names, for instance. A diversified stock ETF is a natural first choice, adding some variety in one swoop. A value ETF, such as **iShares Russell 3000 Value Index** IWW or **Vanguard Value VIPERs**

VTV, probably won't have much biotech exposure, so you could get diversity with little overlap with what you already own.

### ETFs for Tax Swaps

Like mutual funds, ETFs can be used to maintain exposure to a portion of the market while harvesting tax losses to use as offsets to any realized gains or up to $3,000 in ordinary income. Say you're holding **Dell** DELL with an unrealized loss (a loss on paper only) but still like the computer maker's long-term prospects. If you sell the stock to book the losses, you can't buy the shares, or any "substantially similar" security, back for 31 days, or you'll violate the IRS' "wash sale rules" and the agency won't let you use the loss to cancel out gains. To maintain some exposure to Dell, and other tech stocks, you could move into a technology sector ETF, such as **Technology Select Sector SPDR** XLK. The SPDR is similar enough to keep your asset allocation in line, but different enough to keep you out of trouble with the IRS. Of course, as with all tax-related decisions, it's a good idea to consult with a professional tax advisor before attempting a tactic like this. As always, you should also pay attention to transaction costs. They can wipe out any benefit if you aren't careful. ▥

Disclosure: Barclays Global Investors (BGI), which is owned by Barclays, currently licenses Morningstar's 16 style-based indexes for use in BGI's iShares exchange-traded funds. iShares are not sponsored, issued, or sold by Morningstar.
Morningstar does not make any representation regarding the advisability of investing in iShares that are based on Morningstar indexes.

# The Cheap, the Dear, and the Fairly Valued

Funds our stock analysts would and wouldn't buy in today's market.

**by Dan Culloton, Editor, Morningstar ETFs 100**

It's been about seven months since we first used Morningstar's ETF price/fair value measure to take the temperature of the market and various sectors. As 2005 draws to a close, the song remains the same: Energy and basic-materials ETFs still look expensive, while consumer-goods and financial ETFs look undervalued.

Before we tackle the specifics, let's review the mechanics of the price/fair value ratio. This statistic is Morningstar's way of tapping the research of its 85 in-house equity analysts who research and estimate fair values on more than 1,600 stocks to help evaluate the attractiveness of ETF fund portfolios. The measure basically tries to offer a bottom-up assessment of whether an ETF portfolio is cheap or expensive by gauging whether its holdings, on average, are trading above or below their Morningstar fair value estimates.

To get the price/fair value ratio, we calculate the market value of all the holdings in the ETF for which we have fair value estimates. Then we use the fair value estimates of those stocks to calculate what we believe is the fair value of the same portfolio. Finally, we compare the two numbers and calculate the percentage premium or discount of the market value relative to the fair value estimate. When that difference is expressed as a ratio, a number more than one means the ETF's portfolio is overvalued; less than one indicates it is undervalued.

Morningstar does not estimate a fair value for every stock an ETF might own, so the relevance of the results of the price/fair value depends on how many stocks in a given portfolio have received a fair value estimate and the percentage of that portfolio's assets these stocks represent. Our coverage is pretty comprehensive for the vast majority of domestic large-cap ETFs: Morningstar analysts have assigned fair value estimates to stocks representing 75% or more of the asset values of most ETFs in that space.

## Broad Market vs. Large Growth

At the end of November 2005, the price/fair value ratio showed broad-market index ETFs were fairly valued. **Vanguard Total Stock Market VIPERs** VTI, **iShares Dow Jones Total Market** IYY, **StreetTracks Total Market** TMW, and **iShares Russell 3000 Index** IWV all had fair values within shouting distance of the total market values of their holdings.

| Broad Market ETFs<br>ETF Name | % of Assets<br>w/ FV Estimates | Price/<br>Fair Value |
|---|---|---|
| iShares Russell 3000 Index IWV | 90.0 | 0.99 |
| iShares DJ US Total Market Idx IYY | 93.3 | 0.99 |
| Vanguard Total Stk Mkt VIPERs VTI | 88.0 | 0.99 |

Data as of Dec. 9, 2005

Surprisingly, large-cap growth ETFs looked fair, too. Given the way large-growth stocks have lagged the rest of the market in recent years, one might expect ETFs focused on them, such as **Vanguard Growth VIPERs** VUG, **iShares S&P 500/Barra Growth Index** IVW, and **StreetTracks Dow Jones Wilshire Large Cap Growth** ELG, to look relatively undervalued. Despite this group's underperformance, however, the funds actually are mixed bags valuation-wise. There are some attractively priced stocks in there, such as software giant **Microsoft** MSFT, heart device maker **Boston Scientific** BSX, and computer maker **Dell** DELL. To even things out, though, there are a good number of richly priced shares, such as Internet search firm **Google** GOOG, health insurer **UnitedHealth Group** UNH, and oil services company **Schlumberger** SLB, which have all enjoyed very strong runs in the past year.

## Energy

As they were in the spring, the differences are more obvious among sector funds. Energy ETFs, which were the most overvalued funds when we first applied the price/fair value measure in May 2005, still look overvalued. Though energy prices moderated somewhat in the fall and took some of the wind out of the stocks' sails, the energy sector is still up smartly for 2005. Large integrated oil companies, such as **ExxonMobil** XOM and **BP** BP, which usually gobble up a lot of natural-resources ETFs' assets, look neither cheap nor expensive. But oil-services companies, such as Schlumberger and **Halliburton** HAL, as well as refiners and exploration and production companies, such as **Valero Energy** VLO, are way over their fair values after posting eye-popping returns in the past year. These stocks are big constituents of **iShares Goldman Sachs Natural Resources** IGE, **Energy Select Sector SPDR** XLE, **Vanguard Energy VIPERs** VDE, and **iShares S&P Global Energy Sector** IXC. Each of these ETFs was among the most overpriced large-cap ETFs at the end of November 2005, with their shares trading about 20% higher than the value of their underlying components.

## Real Estate

After five years of strong performance, real estate ETFs look overvalued, according to their Price/Fair Value measures. Each of the offerings in this area—**iShares Cohen & Steers Realty Majors** ICF, **iShares Dow Jones U.S. Real Estate** IYR, **StreetTracks Dow Jones Wilshire REIT** RWR, and **Vanguard REIT Viper** VNQ—were trading above their fair values at the end of 2005 (their Price/Fair Value ratios ranged from 1.1 to 1.2). Investors searching for yield and better absolute returns have helped fuel the years-long rally in real estate stocks. The problem is that real estate equities currently are priced at historic highs on many measures, including price to cash flows, yield relative to the 10-year Treasury bond, and earnings relative to the S&P 500. Though REITs are showing some growth and little evidence of overbuilding, it's still not clear how long real estate can sustain its recent performance, especially if interest rates rise.

| Undervalued ETFs ETF Name | % of Assets w/ FV Estimates | Price/ Fair Value |
|---|---|---|
| Consumer Staples Sector SPDR XLP | 98.9 | 0.91 |
| Vanguard Cons Staples VIPERs VDC | 89.7 | 0.91 |
| iShares DJ US Consumer Goods IYK | 89.7 | 0.92 |
| streetTRACKS Global Titans DGT | 92.9 | 0.92 |
| iShares DJ US Telecom IYZ | 91.8 | 0.93 |

Data as of Dec. 9, 2005

## Materials

Robust global demand for copper, gold, coal, and other commodities has boosted performance and valuations of mining and other hard-asset stocks, such as **Phelps Dodge** PD, **Newmont Mining** NEM, and **Peabody Energy** BTU. That, in turn, has kept the prices of basic-materials ETFs—**iShares Dow Jones US Basic Materials** IYM, **Vanguard Materials VIPERs** VAW, and **Materials Select Sector SPDR** XLB—above their fair values.

## Technology

A glance at broad technology ETFs, such as **Technology Select Sector SPDR** XLK and the **Vanguard Information Technology VIPERs** VGT, reveals a fairly valued sector. Drill down, however, and you find bigger disparities. ETFs focused on chip and communications-equipment makers, such as **iShares Goldman Sachs Networking** IGN and **iShares Goldman Sachs Semiconductor** IGW, were about 15% overvalued on Nov. 30, 2005. Speculative names,

such as network chipmakers **Marvell Technology** MRVL and **Broadcom** BRCM, were trading far above their fair values. Meanwhile, uncertainty about information technology spending and the product cycles of individual companies has restrained the performance and valuations of software stocks in **iShares Goldman Sachs Software Index** IGV. Some of its biggest components—Microsoft, **Oracle** ORCL, and **Symantec** SYMC—were trading at steep discounts to their fair values, which helped make the software ETF look undervalued as well.

## Consumer Goods

Concerns about the effect of rising energy prices on sales and raw materials costs, as well as stock-specific worries about competition and earnings growth, have kept a lid on returns in the consumer-goods sector. Nevertheless, a number of leading companies, such as **Procter & Gamble** PG, have still managed to generate decent earnings. As a result, consumer-goods ETFs still showed the biggest discounts to their fair values among large-cap ETFs. About three fourths of the 115 consumer-goods stocks covered by Morningstar analysts carried ratings of 3 or more stars (3 stars indicates the stock is trading near its fair value, 4 or 5 stars means the stock is priced below fair value). Shares of **Wal-Mart** WMT, which is trying to expand already-thin margins; **Coca-Cola** KO, which is still trying to re-energize growth; **Anheuser-Busch** BUD, which is contending with slower beer consumption and price competition; and **Avon Products** AVP, which is still quaking from series of summer earnings warnings; look particularly cheap. These are big positions in **Consumer Staples Select Sector SPDR** XLP and **Vanguard Consumer Staples VIPERs** VDC, so it's not surprising that the ETFs' shares were trading about 10% below their portfolios' fair value. **iShares Dow Jones US Consumer Goods** IYK showed a smaller discount, in part, because it doesn't include Wal-Mart.

| Overvalued ETFs ETF Name | % of Assets w/ FV Estimates | Price/ Fair Value |
|---|---|---|
| iShares GS Natural Resources IGE | 96.5 | 1.29 |
| Energy Select Sector SPDR XLE | 100.0 | 1.24 |
| Vanguard Energy VIPERs VDE | 94.1 | 1.23 |
| iShares S&P Global Energy IXC | 64.7 | 1.22 |
| iShares DJ US Energy IYE | 99.3 | 1.20 |

Data as of Dec. 9, 2005

## Telecom

Telecommunications ETFs also showed varying levels of discounts to fair value, depending on how much they packed into traditional phone-service providers, such as **Verizon Communications** VZ, which has taken a beating in 2005 as it tries to restructure its business and update its network to compete with high-tech competitors. **IShares Dow Jones US Telecommunications** IYZ and **iShares S&P Global Telecommunications** IXP, both of which have significant stakes in Verizon and other Baby Bells, were trading about 8% below their fair values. The shares of **Vanguard Telecom Services VIPERs** VOX, which also owns a big helping of the Bells, were closer to the fund's fair value because the portfolio devotes more money to more richly valued wireless services stocks, such as **American Tower** AMT and **Crown Castle International** CCI.

### Financial Services

Finally, worries about rising interest rates and a peaking real estate market have pressured stocks, such as **National City** NCC, that make their living off of spread income and mortgages. That and the still-modestly valued insurance giant **American International Group** AIG have kept financial-services ETFs, such as **iShares Dow Jones US Financial Services** IYG, **Financial Select Sector SPDR** XLF, and **Vanguard Financials VIPERs** VFH, below the fair value of their holdings.

### What to Do?

The data still paints a risky picture for energy and materials ETFs. The funds continued to gain ground after we last said they were overvalued, and there's no telling how long the momentum will last. Nevertheless, it still could be time to reap some winnings and redistribute the money among more attractively priced offerings in the financial and consumer-staples areas. Because cheap stocks can stay that way for a while, it is best to make these moves in a small part of a diversified portfolio. ▥

Disclosure: Barclays Global Investors BGI, which is owned by Barclays, currently licenses Morningstar's 16 style-based indexes for use in BGI's iShares exchange-traded funds. iShares are not sponsored, issued, or sold by Morningstar. Morningstar does not make any representation regarding the advisability of investing in iShares that are based on Morningstar indexes.

# Giants, Upstarts, and Also-Rans

A look at the major ETF families.

by Dan Culloton, Editor,
Morningstar ETFs 100
and Sonya Morris,
Fund Analyst

The world of exchange-traded funds is filled with cute sobriquets: iShares and PowerShares, SPDRs and Vipers, StreetTracks and Qubes. Smart investors know there's more to an investment than a catchy name, though. There are investment advisors of varying sizes and expertise behind those monikers. To help investors put these firms and their places in the industry into context, we've profiled the major ETF purveyors and compiled our information here.

## Barclays

Barclays Global Investors has become almost synonymous with exchange-traded funds. In a sense, San Francisco-based Barclays is the **McDonald's** MCD of the ETF world. Hamburgers weren't invented under the golden arches and Barclays didn't create ETFs, but the companies each exploited and popularized their industry niches to a greater degree than anyone else. Barclays' family of more than 100 iShares is the undisputed 800-pound gorilla of the growing ETF market. IShares has grown from a few funds and $2 billion in assets in 2000 to a complex of 102 domestically available ETFs that cover virtually every major asset class and, collectively, have about $150 billion in assets. The firm claims the lion's share of all ETF flows.

That's not an accident. Barclays' strategy has been simple: Launch ETFs tied to as many of the most popular benchmarks available and market them relentlessly. It doesn't ask if nine broad-based large-blend funds or six technology offerings are too many for one category or sector, and it doesn't try to tell investors which of the indexes are the best. The firm just wants to make it impossible for investors who want a broad-based, style-specific, regional, or sector ETF to ignore iShares.

Because of their low costs and trading flexibility it seems natural to pitch ETFs to do-it-yourself individual investors. Barclays takes its cues from financial planners, though. Demand from financial advisors, which Barclays considers iShares' primary market, determines what kind of ETFs the firm

launches as much as anything else. Advisors also indirectly influence iShare expense ratios. When pricing its funds, Barclays factors in the costs of spreading the gospel of ETFs through seminars, white papers, and other services. This is not a build-it-and-they-will-come business model. The firm is an aggressive evangelizer.

This is not to say iShares is all shake and no bake. The more than 30-year-old Barclays Global Investors is one of the largest institutional asset managers in the world with more than 2,000 employees and more than $1.3 trillion in assets under management in index funds. It obviously has some redoubtable resources and capabilities.

About a dozen portfolio managers work on iShares. Five split up the family's 63 domestic-equity iShares, four run its 33 international ETFs, and three managers are dedicated to the fixed-income ETFs. While not graybeards, most of the managers have at least five years of experience with Barclays as well as prior industry experience.

Like most index-fund managers, the iShares jockeys play close attention to tracking error, transaction costs, and taxes. Unlike some rivals, such as Vanguard's Gus Sauter, however, the iShares managers will not attempt to add value at the margins by opportunistically buying futures contracts, or by employing other tactics. Even though the risks of such stratagems are small, the iShares managers argue they would rather not chance increasing tracking error. Furthermore, they contend that many iShares clients use ETFs to hedge their portfolios and are more interested in replication than outperformance. The managers, however, are willing to diverge slightly from their benchmarks to harvest tax losses. When **Hewlett-Packard** HPQ bought Compaq a couple of years ago, for example, the iShares funds sold Compaq and bought Hewlett-Packard just before the deal consummated, giving them almost the same returns and tax losses because Compaq performed poorly even after the merger was announced.

It's clear Barclays knows how to run an ETF. Most of its largest funds trail their benchmarks by no more than their expense ratios, which indicates they're doing a good job tracking their bogies. Also, it has been a few years since any iShares ETF has distributed a capital gain (though the funds have paid out dividend income), which shows the firm has delivered tax efficiency.

The low costs, tax efficiency, and competent management of iShares make many of them compelling choices, but competition is increasing. State Street Global Advisors is a distant second in terms of assets under management, but in 2004 cut the expense ratio of its **S&P 500 SPDR** SPY and some of its sector ETFs. Its **StreetTracks Gold** GLD fund also was one of the most successful ETF launches ever and SSgA launched several new stock ETFs in 2005. Vanguard now offers a family of ETFs with compelling costs and methodologies. And, by cutting their traditional index-fund expenses, traditional fund families such as Fidelity Investments are making it harder to justify switching to ETFs.

Barclays claims it feels no pressure to enter into a price war with Fidelity. Even with the cuts, **iShares S&P 500 Index** IVY remains one of the cheapest index funds tracking that bogy. And even though Barclays doesn't price its funds at the level of their costs (as rival Vanguard does), iShares remain a pretty good deal with a weighted average expense ratio of about 0.30%.

To be sure, Barclays still sets the pace for the industry. Though growth in terms of new offerings will be slower in the future, the firm still plans to roll out more ETFs. In 2005, for instance, it launched micro-cap and international growth and value ETFs. The firm also sought regulatory approval for an ETF that would track a broad basket of commodities. It offers most flavors of equity funds several times over, but iShares hopes to expand its fixed-income lineup, which now consists of six funds. It also wants to extend ETFs to other asset classes such as real estate, energy, metals, and timber. Barclays is also interested in actively managed ETFs. Commodity and active ETFs won't get regulatory approval as easily as equity funds. Each commodity, for example, has its own unique pricing and settlement issues to work out. If the approval process for iShares' recently launched gold fund is any indication, it could take years to secure the SEC's blessing. It's also not clear how an actively managed ETF would work or who would be interested in one.

Barclays' may resemble McDonald's in another way. The restaurant's founder, Ray Kroc, once said, "I don't know what we'll be selling in the year 2000, I just know we want to be selling more of it than anyone else." There's a good chance that whatever ETFs are popular in the future, iShares will be selling a lot of them. That's a source of strength and a concern. Many of Barclays' ETFs are good for the firm's business, but not necessarily good for the average investor's portfolio. An ill-considered bet on a single country or sector offering, for example, could do a lot of damage to one's wealth. The iShares family has a lot to offer, but investors don't have to buy everything Barclays is selling.

**State Street**
There might not be any ETFs without State Street Global Advisors. SSgA created the first U.S. ETF, the S&P 500 SPDR, with the American Stock Exchange nearly 13 years ago. Though the grand-daddy of ETFs has a lot more competition now from both exchange-traded and conventional mutual funds, it's still the largest ETF and the core of SSgA's franchise, accounting for nearly $50 billion of the firm's $70 billion in ETF assets, and attracting more trading volume than all but one other ETF: **Nasdaq 100 Trust Shares** QQQQ.

While SSgA was the first to the ETF party, it has not been the life of it in recent years. That title goes to Barclays' iShares family, whose aggressive expansion and evangelization has overshadowed SSgA's ETFs in recent years. While Barclays has rolled out a steady stream of new iShares and now has more than 100 ETFs and $150 billion in assets, SSgA has been slower to issue new funds. It has more than 30 ETFs in its stable and $70 billion under management and, until recently, struggled to expand its success beyond the SPDRs.

SSgA, however, has been more assertive in the past year. Its late 2004 launch of the first ETF to hold gold bullion, StreetTracks Gold Shares, was perhaps the biggest ETF launch ever. The fund now has more than $3 billion in assets. The firm also introduced nine new ETFs under the StreetTracks and SPDR brands in November, has plans to launch new SPDRs tracking the biotech, homebuilder, and semiconductor industries. What's more, the firm has expressed as much interest as anyone in stretching the ETF format to more commodities, fixed-income, and actively managed strategies.

Several domestic ETF families actually fall under SSgA's umbrella. As noted before, the firm manages the S&P 500 SPDR, the series of Select Sector SPDRs, the group of 20 StreetTracks ETFs, and the Dow Industrial Diamonds, which track the poplar Dow Jones Industrial Average. The funds are priced competitively. With the exception of **StreetTracks Morgan Stanley Technology** MTK and **StreetTracks Dow Jones Global Titans** DGT, they all boast expense ratios smaller than the average for ETFs. SSgA's ETF fees are rarely the lowest available, though.

Indeed, expense-ratio cuts by conventional mutual funds, such as **Fidelity Spartan 500** FSMKX, and other large-blend ETFs such as **Vanguard Large Cap Vipers** W, have made it harder to make a strong case for the S&P 500 SPDR.

SSgA's lineup cannot match the breadth of iShares', its main rival. It has a broad range of domestic-equity offerings, and perhaps the most popular suite of sector funds in its Select Sector SPDRs. The complex, however, has just two international ETFs and no fixed-income funds. Some of its offerings, notably the SPDR, Diamonds, and Select Sector SPDRs also are hindered somewhat by their structure. Unlike most ETFs, which are organized as open-end mutual funds, the SPDRs and Diamonds are unit-investment trusts, which means they can't reinvest dividends paid by their holdings until the payouts can be distributed to shareholders. Rather, UITs must hold the dividends as cash, which can drag on returns over the long term.

SSgA did make some improvements to its family in the last year. It rounded out its lineup of style-specific equity funds with a batch of new ETFs tracking the Dow Jones Wilshire mid-cap value, core, and growth indexes; and new large- and small-cap blend offerings. The family also added a quality broad-market ETF when it switched the benchmark of its StreetTracks Fortune 500 to the Wilshire 5000, renaming the fund **StreetTracks Total Market ETF** TMW in the process.

SSgA, like other ETF purveyors and traditional fund firms, has not been immune to trend-hopping or overspecialization. The firm launched its **SPDR Dividend ETF** SDY, which tracks the S&P Dividend Aristocrats Index, after other dividend-oriented ETFs from iShares, and PowerShares received considerable attention and assets (Vanguard, as we shall see below, also jumped on the dividend bandwagon). For investors who think financial-sector funds are not focused enough (and we hope that is a very small group), SSgA rolled out three funds

tracking indexes that further divide financials into bank, capital-markets, and insurance segments. Ironically, the very day SSgA filed a preliminary prospectus with federal regulators for an ETF tracking one of hottest areas of the stock market in the last five years—homebuilders—luxury-house titan **Toll Brothers** TOL issued an earnings warning that sent the industry into a sell-off. That doesn't mean the proposed ETF will be a disaster, but it is a reminder of what can happen when you chase hot returns with new funds.

SSgA has the capability to ably track its funds' benchmarks whether broadly or narrowly focused. The firm not only was present at the creation of ETFs, but it has been managing index funds since 1978. With $1.4 trillion under its supervision in passive and actively managed accounts, it is the largest institutional asset manager in the world and, next to Barclays, the second-largest manager of indexed assets. Besides its domestic-ETF family, SSgA runs ETFs in Australia, Europe, China, and Singapore. The firm has about $70 billion in ETF assets under management domestically and nearly $80 billion in ETF assets worldwide. It should know how to run an index fund.

Indeed, the members of the firm's ETF-management team all have experience that is at least comparable to their counterparts at Barclays. SSgA's ETF prospectuses and Web site list five members on its ETF-management team, though officials say as many as nine are involved in the day-to-day management of the funds. There are no household names such as Vanguard's Gus Sauter, but the managers all have at least six years of experience with SSgA and 10 or more years of experience in investment business. The ETF squad is embedded in SSgA's Global Structured Products Group, which runs index and enhanced index strategies for institutional and private clients, and share the group's resources.

## ETF Purveyors from Large to Small

| ETF Family | Total Assets ($billions) | # of ETFs | Oldest ETF (Years) | Average Expense Ratio |
|---|---|---|---|---|
| **iShares** | 163.6 | 101 | 10 | 0.45 |
| **State Street Global Advisors** | 80.3 | 31 | 13 | 0.27 |
| **Bank of New York** | 29.8 | 6 | 9 | 0.28 |
| **Vanguard** | 10.6 | 23 | 5 | 0.22 |
| **Powershares** | 2.7 | 31 | 3 | 0.63 |
| **Rydex** | 1.4 | 2 | 3 | 0.30 |
| **Fidelity** | 0.1 | 1 | 2 | 0.30 |
| **First Trust** | 0.04 | 1 | 0 | 0.60 |

Sources: Morningstar, Barclays Global Investors. Data as of Nov. 30, 2005

**Commentary**

Overall, SSgA offers most everything an advisor or investor would need for a domestic-equity portfolio. It is possible, however, to find options just as compelling elsewhere—options with lower expense ratios.

**Vanguard**

For years, Vanguard and index funds have practically been synonymous. Founded in 1974 as the first (and to date only) mutually owned fund company, Vanguard was the first fund shop to bring indexing to the public when it introduced the first retail index fund, **Vanguard 500** VFINX in 1976. Since then, it has gathered far more assets than any other index fund and presently tops the scales at a whopping $106 billion. Through the years, Vanguard has supplemented that flagship offering with index funds that fit in nearly every square of the style box.

Given that resume, one would have expected Vanguard to dominate the ETF market, but the firm was slow to get in the game. It launched its first ETF, **Vanguard Total Stock Market VIPERs** VTI (VIPERs stands for "Vanguard Index Participation Equity Receipts"), in May 2001, over four years after Barclays' iShares debut and eight years behind SPDR's unveiling. Because of that delay, Vanguard's share of the ETF market is a fraction of industry-leader Barclays' stake: Vanguard has 23 ETFs with $10 billion in assets, while Barclays offers more than 100 ETFs and has amassed $164 billion in assets. Furthermore, VIPERs haven't captured the kind of attention that its competitors have enjoyed. Vanguard Total Stock Market, the most popular VIPER, registers average daily volume of 138,933 and has total assets of $5 billion. But that looks positively puny compared with SPDRs, which trades nearly 62.6 million shares per day on average and has $47.7 billion in assets. Moreover, that data likely overstates the popularity of VIPERs because Vanguard's open-end offerings use VIPERs to manage cash flows.

Although it ceded some ground to the competition, Vanguard is working hard to catch up. It launched several sector and international VIPERs in 2004 and 2005. In addition, the firm plans to roll out Vanguard Dividend Achievers Index VIPERs, which will increase the number of VIPER offerings to 24. As of September 2005, options trade on 20 of those funds. Previously, investors could only trade options on Vanguard Total Stock Market Fund. Vanguard's decision to add options trading on its VIPERs is a bid to attract more volume to these funds because many active ETF investors value the trading flexibility that options provide. The firm has also been pitching VIPERs to fee-only financial advisors, who have increasingly been using ETFs to build investors' portfolios. And in a break from tradition, Vanguard has also begun to lobby full-service brokers to offer VIPERs to their clients.

In an attempt to stake out its ground, Vanguard has patented its VIPER share-class structure. All other ETFs are stand-alone entities, but VIPERs are organized as separate share classes of open-ended index funds. The firm contends that this structure confers many advantages, even though some have argued that ETFs organized as separate share classes won't be as tax-efficient as traditional ETFs. Although we think those concerns are overblown, only time will tell for sure. However, our confidence is bolstered by the strong tax-adjusted performance of its open-ended index funds. For instance, Vanguard 500's long-term tax-adjusted returns are better than all of its ETF rivals.

That performance underscores the firm's reputation as the premier index-fund shop. CIO Gus Sauter and his team of quantitative analysts have proven adept at closely tracking benchmarks. Furthermore, the fund's mutual-ownership structure helps give it a low-cost advantage, which is a major leg up in the world of indexing, where cost is king. Excluding sector and country-specific funds, expenses on VIPERs range from 0.07% to 0.22% compared with 0.09% to 0.60% for iShares. In fact, many of

| Largest ETF | Largest ETF's Net Assets ($ millions) | Comment |
| --- | --- | --- |
| iShares MSCI EAFE Index EFA | 21,732.30 | The family with the most ETF, assets and inflows. |
| SPDRs SPY | 57,063.60 | Created the first ETF, but now plays second fiddle. |
| Nasdaq 100 QQQQ | 20,458.30 | Has the most actively traded ETF in the Qubes. |
| Vanguard Total Stock Market VTI | 5,433.20 | Indexing champion excels where you'd expect: on costs. |
| PowerShares Dynamic Market PWC | 654.10 | No sector is too narrow, or index too odd for this family. |
| Rydex S&P Equal Weight RSP | 1,250.40 | Expect more off beat ETFs from this firm. |
| Fidelity Nasdaq Composite Index ONEQ | 123.60 | Fidelity's index fund fee cuts undermine its own ETF. |
| First Trust Dow Jones Select MicroCap Index FDM | 35.40 | A small broker dealer trying to jump on the ETF wagon. |

Vanguard's open-ended funds are cheaper than ETF offerings from other firms. Vanguard's reputation for low costs and skillful management make it a player to contend with, despite its late entry into the ETF market.

### PowerShares

PowerShares Capital Management isn't breathing down the necks of the ETF industry's behemoths yet, but it's huffing and puffing to catch up. Based in Wheaton, Ill., PowerShares was founded in August 2002 by former Nuveen Investments sales and marketing executive H. Bruce Bond. With more than $2 billion in assets at the start of the fourth quarter of 2005, PowerShares is still miniscule compared with industry-leader Barclays Global Investors and its more-than-$150 billion iShares family. However, it has attracted attention with its unorthodox offerings: Whereas all other ETFs track traditional indexes, PowerShares' strategy is to offer ETFs that track specialized indexes designed specifically to beat the usual benchmarks.

PowerShares' first two funds, **PowerShares Dynamic Market** PWC and **PowerShares Dynamic OTC** PWO, track the American Stock Exchange's Intellidex indexes. Amex reconstructs these benchmarks once per quarter based on a quantitative stock-picking model that trolls for the most promising securities in the broad U.S. stock market and the NASDAQ Composite, respectively. So far, the funds have been able to beat their respective benchmarks and post strong absolute returns.

PowerShares has not been shy. The firm has since launched dozens of additional ETFs, including a microcap ETF, and style- and sector-based funds that track bogeys using the Intellidex methodology. In terms of number of funds, PowerShares is the second-largest family behind Barclays.

Clearly, PowerShares is focused on growth, and has no compunction about launching trendy funds and chasing hot money. PowerShares launched its dividend-focused and China ETFs in 2004 (after iShares rolled out its own versions) when interest in such strategies was boosted by strong recent performance and other trends, such as favorable dividend tax law changes and rapid Chinese economic growth. The family has since launched four more dividend ETFs as well as offerings following a variety of emerging industries, such as alternative energy and nanotechnology.

PowerShares has turned some heads. The firm still has a lot to prove, though. Its oldest funds, the Dynamic Market and Dynamic OTC ETFs, have fared well and have avoided costly capital-gains distributions even though their portfolio-turnover rates resemble those of actively managed funds. Nevertheless, their records remain short, and it's unknown whether Intellidex indexes will be able to thrive in all market environments. Indeed, the market has a way of catching up with quantitative models, lessening their effectiveness over time.

The biggest hurdle facing PowerShares, however, is distribution. It's hard for new ETFs to grab assets from established players, but the firm has sought approval from the SEC for a novel and controversial remedy. It wants to charge a 2% load on ETF shares sold during their initial subscription period. The loads, which would include break points for larger investors, are designed to induce brokers and financial advisors to sell PowerShares ETFs and increase their economies of scale, Bond argues.

No ETF has charged a load before, not even PowerShares, as the SEC has yet to give its blessing. If it does, it would be cheaper for many investors, especially those who use discount brokers, to avoid the sales charge by buying the ETFs in the secondary market after their initial public offerings. Bond says his firm many not need or use the loads, and we hope they don't. PowerShares' expense ratios already are above average for ETFs. The loads would add a layer of cost and complexity and detract from one of the central appeals of ETFs: The affordability and transparency of their fee structures.

Finally, PowerShares is thinly staffed and faces competition from above and below. The company still consists of a handful of partners and employees. Lead portfolio manager John W. Southard is a former senior analyst of Chicago Investment Analytics, a quantitative-research firm bought by Charles Schwab in 2000. He also worked as an analyst and portfolio manager at a unit-investment-trust firm, First Trust Portfolios, of Lisle, IL. But he has a short track record as a retail mutual fund or ETF manager.

The firm still lacks the resources of established ETF players such as Barclays or SSgA, as well as other recent entries into the ETF market, such as Vanguard, Fidelity Investments, and Rydex. Still, PowerShares is sure to add people and capabilities as it grows. In fact, San Francisco venture-capital firm FTVentures last year made a $10 million commitment to the shop.

So far, PowerShares has proved that it is worth keeping an eye on. It's not clear whether it will succeed at playing David to the ETF industry's Goliaths, though, and it has developed a worrisome habit of rolling out gimmicky funds. Investors should consider its relative inexperience, lack of scale, and marketing focus before making any decisions.

### Other Players

ETFs are not Bank of New York's main line of business. It makes most of its money in securities servicing and by acting as a custodian for financial institutions, including mutual funds and brokerage firms. It has more than $10 trillion in assets under custody around the globe. Yet Bank of New York also serves as the trustee for two of the larger and more popular ETFs on the market: the NASDAQ 100 Trust, which tracks the 100 largest non-financial stocks in the NASDAQ Composite and is the most actively traded ETF; and the MidCap SPDRs, which track the S&P MidCap 400 Index. Together, both funds have nearly $28 billion in assets. The bank also is the sponsor of the nearly $330 million in assets held by the BLDRS series of ETFs. BLDRS track indexes of international stocks whose shares trade as American Depository Receipts on U.S. exchanges.

They are not exactly ETFs, but Merrill Lynch's Holding Company Depository Receipts, or HOLDRs, are often viewed as such. HOLDRs are baskets of securities arbitrarily selected by Merrill Lynch to represent a narrow industry group such as biotechnology or semiconductors. They aren't organized as open-end funds or unit-investment trusts, but rather as grantor trusts. Each HOLDR is initially composed of 20 stocks, but because the vehicles aren't managed and new stocks are never added, they can grow more concentrated due to mergers, liquidations, or the disparate performance of their holdings. Unlike other ETFs, HOLDRs can only be bought and sold in 100-share increments. HOLDRs do not have creation units like other ETFs, but investors may exchange 100 shares of a HOLDR for its underlying stocks at any time for a fee. This round-lot requirement makes them unattractive to smaller investors, as it means they have to commit many thousands of dollars at a time to offerings that follow narrow market sectors.

Rydex, a firm more widely known for its family of sector and leveraged index funds, has attracted more than $1 billion to its two ETFs, the **Rydex Russell Top 50** XLG, which tracks megacap stocks; and the **Rydex S&P Equal Weight** RSP, which follows a version of the S&P 500 in which all the holdings are kept roughly the same size, rather than weighted by their market capitalization. The latter fund has gained popularity in recent years as more investors have started to question whether market-cap-weighted indexes are the best way to go. The equal-weighted index's strong performance versus the traditional S&P 500 hasn't hurt the ETF either.

Rydex is getting more serious about ETFs. Late in 2005 the firm launched its **Euro Currency Trust** FXE, which will track the price of the Euro. Rydex also plans to roll out ETFs that track a series of six pure equity style indexes developed by Standard & Poor's and **Citigroup** C.

First Trust Portfolios is another small firm trying to break into the ETF arena. The Lisle, IL.-based broker dealer's main business is unit investment trust and closed-end funds. In 2005, however, it launched the **First Trust Dow Jones Select MicroCap Index Fund** FDM, and filed plans with the Securities and Exchange Commission to introduce another ETF (full disclosure: the new ETF is based on a Morningstar dividend index). A five-person investment committee, whose members' have been with the firm anywhere from one to 13 years, run First Trust's ETFs, but the family is still a relative unknown.

Finally, ETFs may be one of the few realms in which Fidelity Investments, one of the world's largest mutual fund companies, is barely even an also-ran. The firm's **Fidelity Nasdaq Composite ETF** ONEQ has failed to get much traction since its 2003 inception, and the firm has not moved to launch any more ETFs. Instead, it appear to be trying to compete by slashing the expense ratios of its index mutual funds, some of which now charge as little as 0.07% a year for large investors, and 0.10% for others. ∎

Disclosure: Barclays Global Investors (BGI), which is owned by Barclays, currently licenses Morningstar's 16 style-based indexes for use in BGI's iShares exchange-traded funds. iShares are not sponsored, issued, or sold by Morningstar. Morningstar does not make any representation regarding the advisability of investing in iShares that are based on Morningstar indexes.

# ETFs With an Edge

Exchange-traded funds that trump traditional funds.

by Dan Culloton, Editor,
Morningstar ETFs 100

The exchange-traded fund toolbox is now almost fully equipped. The nearly 200 offerings available in the United States cover most major asset classes several times over, making it possible to craft a well-diversified portfolio consisting exclusively of exchange-traded funds. That wouldn't be a wise choice for most investors, however. Not only would they incur high tax and transaction costs if they ditched their traditional mutual fund holdings for all-ETF portfolios, but it's also worth noting that traditional mutual funds are perfectly service-able options for covering many market segments. For most investors, the best strategy for mixing ETFs into their portfolios is to use them to plug portfolio holes, especially in areas where the list of topnotch traditional funds is short.

---

### Reasons to Consider an ETF

- You plan to make a lump-sum investment and hold it for the long term.
- The traditional mutual fund options in a category are expensive.
- Options are limited in a category.
- There are few traditional funds with experienced managers in a category.
- You want to minimize capital gains distributions.

---

Not just any ETF will do, though. When selecting an exchange-traded fund, investors should consider a few important factors.

### Expenses

Currently all ETFs are index funds, which aim to match the gross returns of a given market segment and then rely on low costs to differentiate themselves. So for ETFs, the lower the expense ratio the better. Keep in mind, however, that with any ETF you will need to pay brokerage commissions when you buy and sell shares of the fund. If you trade even a few times a year, these extra costs can easily wipe out any expense ratio advantage the ETF has over a regular index mutual fund. The following recommendations assume that your trading level will be very low, and that you will hold your shares for a reasonably long period of time. If this doesn't apply to you, you may well be better off from a total cost perspective with a mutual fund, regardless of ETFs' low annual expense ratios.

### Taxes and Turnover

ETFs have the potential to be more tax-efficient than traditional mutual funds. Because ETFs trade on an exchange, you don't sell your shares back to the fund company for cash when you want to redeem them. Instead, you sell ETF shares just like a stock: through a broker to another investor. That means that ETF managers don't have to sell stocks or bonds from their portfolios to raise money to meet redemptions. Some large institutional investors, known as authorized participants, do buy and sell ETF shares directly with the fund company, but they deal in baskets of securities from the underlying portfolios, not cash, which also allows ETFs to avoid realizing capital gains. Many ETF managers use that process, known as in-kind redemptions, to unload their portfolios' lowest-cost-basis shares, which can help avoid distributions, too.

That said, it's possible for ETFs to issue capital gains. An ETF that tracks an index that frequently changes its constituents, such as some of the style- or market-cap-based benchmarks, can realize gains and transaction costs as it changes its portfolio to keep up with its benchmark. So treat ETF turnover like expenses: the lower the better.

### The Benchmark

You want to make sure the ETF is tracking a diversified index that does a good job of capturing the gross returns of the asset class it hopes to measure. If it's too narrow, top-heavy, or concentrated in one or more industries, the benchmark could fail to accurately represent its market segment.

### Management

Look for management firms with a lot of experience running index funds. Seasoned skippers know how to reduce tracking error and turnover and thereby enhance the total return and tax efficiency of their offerings. Applying these criteria, we've discussed a number of ETFs that could be good portfolio gap-fillers for a variety of needs.

### Low-Cost Options in High-Cost Categories

ETFs offer a clear advantage for investors looking to make a play on certain niche fund categories that are typically plagued by high expenses, short-tenured management teams, and limited options. (Granted, most investors don't need funds this specialized, but for those who think they do, an ETF may well be the best way to go.) A good example is the Japan stock group. There are only 20 distinct tradi-

## Our Favorite ETFs

| Name | YTD Total Return (%) | 12-Mo Total Return (%) | Expense Ratio (%) | Cat Avg Exp (%) |
|---|---|---|---|---|
| **iShares DJ Sel Dividend** DVY | -3.05 | 12.30 | 0.40 | 1.54 |
| **Vanguard TSM VIPERs** TSM | 1.89 | 10.53 | 0.07 | 1.21 |
| **Vanguard Large Cap VIPERs** VV | 2.10 | 10.24 | 0.07 | 1.21 |
| **Vanguard Growth VIPERs** VUG | 1.25 | 9.07 | 0.11 | 1.49 |
| **Vanguard Emerg Mkts Vpr*** EEM | 15.19 | 33.66 | 0.30 | 1.99 |
| **iShares NASD Biotech** IBB | -1.80 | 0.50 | 0.50 | 1.83 |
| **iShares Japan Index** EWJ | 10.13 | 21.30 | 0.59 | 1.65 |
| **iShares DJ Sel Dividend** DVY | 2.24 | 8.48 | 0.40 | 1.46 |
| **iShares S&P Latin 40** ILF | 43.73 | 69.13 | 0.40 | 2.10 |

Data through October 31, 2005. *YTD and 12-month return are for traditional share class.

tional Japan funds, and most of their managers have short and unimpressive records. On average the funds have been riskier than the MSCI Japan Index without offering much better returns than the index over the past five years.

The dearth of compelling alternatives in this group is why we're fans of **iShares MSCI Japan Index** EWJ. Its 0.59% expense ratio is about a third of the typical Japan fund's levy. While this fund's single-country focus is a recipe for high volatility, at least investors know what they're getting: exposure to large, well-known Japanese stocks.

A couple of other ETFs are worth a look for similar reasons. **Vanguard Emerging Markets Stock VIPERs** VWO tracks a modified version of the MSCI Emerging Markets Index and offers broad ownership of stocks from 18 emerging economies. Its 0.30% expense ratio is less than one sixth of the 2% levy for the typical diversified emerging-markets fund, and it is 50% less expensive than the only other ETF that tracks a similar benchmark. The Emerging Market VIPERs are new, and their bogy omits stocks from certain countries that are not as liquid or as open to foreign investment, such as Russia. Over the long term, though, the VIPERs' much older clone, **Vanguard Emerging Markets Stock Index** VEIEX, has correlated closely with the complete MSCI Emerging Markets Index.

IShares S&P Latin America 40 Index has its shortcomings (namely its sector and issue concentration), but its 0.50% expense ratio is far lower than all of the other Latin America stock funds. And while everyone can live a long and happy life without a biotech fund, those seeking to devote a slice of their portfolios to the risky industry can use iShares NASDAQ Biotechnology for affordable and low-turnover exposure in a category fraught with high-turnover strategies.

## Core Strength Builders

Broad diversification, low costs, and tax efficiency make ETFs enticing options for core holdings. It's getting harder to make a strong case for them as Fidelity Investments and other financial services firms, such as USAA and E-Trade, upped the ante in the index fund price wars in 2005 by slashing expenses on their traditional broad-based stock index funds. However, the Vanguard Total Stock Market Vipers and Vanguard Large Cap Vipers still have lower annual expense ratios than any large-blend fund (exchange-traded or not) that retail investors with less than $100,000 in assets can buy.

That gives these offerings a slight edge in the crowded market for core equity index funds because, all else being equal, costs are the best predictor of long-term performance among index funds and ETFs that track similar benchmarks.

Furthermore, taxable investors are likely to prefer the ETF due to the vehicle's more tax-efficient structure. (ETFs redeem shares with baskets of securities, rather than with cash, which lets them avoid realizing capital gains.) So, ETFs are remain a viable choice for those who want to buy the entire market in one fell swoop in a taxable account. We favor Vanguard Total Stock Market Vipers. The fund has switched its benchmark from the Wilshire 5000 to the MSCI U.S. Broad Market Index, but its risk/reward profile should stay pretty much the same.

## ETFs for Special Situations

We've been encouraging investors to take a look at the large-growth category, which has one of the worst recent performance records among domestic-stock fund groups but also cheaper valuation multiples than it has had in years. While there is no shortage of decent traditional large-growth funds, ETFs offer a simple, low-cost, and pure way to access the asset class. There are several choices, but we lean toward Vanguard Growth Vipers. Its 0.11% expense ratio is the lowest among large-growth ETFs and is a fraction of the typical large-growth mutual fund's.

This ETF also tracks an MSCI benchmark (the MSCI U.S. Prime Market Growth Index) that relies on multiple valuation and growth factors to determine its constituents and includes buffer zones between indexes. It may do a better job of mimicking the gross returns of the large-growth market than more widely followed benchmarks. The Russell 1000 Growth Index's annual reconstitution has been susceptible to front running, which occurs when traders try to exploit advance knowledge of large upcoming transactions. If Vanguard Growth Vipers' bogy proves to be a better representation of the large-growth segment, the fund should pull ahead on costs over the long run.

You also can make a strong argument for paying more attention to dividend-paying stocks. More companies have increased or started paying dividends since the 2003 dividend tax cut. And if we face an era of subdued equity performance, which many sophisticated investors say we do, yield will play a bigger role in total returns. In such an environment, the iShares Dow Jones Select Dividend Index has appeal. It owns 100 stocks that have increased their dividends per share over the previous five years without distributing too much of their earnings. The Powershares High Yield Dividend Achievers Index has a higher yield, but the iShares ETF is less concentrated in terms of number of holdings and, with a 0.4% expense ratio, is cheaper. ▥

# The Quest for the Holy Grail of ETFs Continues

Will actively managed ETFs become a reality?
Should you care?

by Dan Culloton, Editor,
Morningstar ETFs 100

Reports of the arrival of actively managed exchange-trade funds have been greatly exaggerated. Sure, there are some ETFs of recent vintage that come close, such as the PowerShares that track the quantitatively constructed Amex Intellidexes. Firms also have filed applications for active ETFs with the Securities and Exchange Commission, and it's a good bet there are others with their own plans out there, biding their time while someone else bears the expense and hassles of being the first one to brave regulatory review.

Don't expect to see a fully active ETF on an exchange near you any time soon, though. They still have too much to prove to regulators, money managers, and investors before they become widely available. In the four years since the SEC first sought comments on actively managed ETFs, we've often heard predictions of their imminent launch, but nothing has yet materialized. Even those involved in the development of what many in the industry consider the Holy Grail of products, concede it still could be a long time before the SEC decides whether to allow active ETFs.

Yet, someone eventually will figure out a way to offer actively managed ETFs. The market opportunity is simply too vast to ignore and ETFs have grown at a torrid pace on the backs of index funds. Most of the $8.6 trillion in conventional funds, however, is in actively managed offerings. The prospect of converting even a fraction of those assets to active ETFs is enough to make fund company and stock exchange executives drool. There is more than enough incentive for ETF sponsors to keep trying until they get it right.

Should you care when they do? After studying some of the more promising (or at least public) proposals, I can think of a couple attractions, but I'm still firmly in the skeptics camp. Here's why.

### Under the Hood

Index ETFs, as they are currently structured, work because everyone involved knows exactly what is in their portfolios and how to value their shares throughout the day. Indeed, the current crop of ETFs publishes per share portfolio values every 15 seconds throughout the trading day. That allows the market makers who assemble the baskets of securities required to create ETF shares to hedge their positions. If the specialists didn't have that information or received it less frequently, they might not be as willing to create or redeem ETF shares, which could lead the ETFs to trade at wider bid/ask spreads and bigger discounts or premiums to their net asset values. Active fund managers, however, often balk at disclosing their portfolios more than the four times per year required by the SEC. They fear doing so would tip off other investors about the funds' latest moves.

Let's look at a couple of the most widely discussed proposals for solving this conundrum. The American Stock Exchange, which launched the first ETF in 1993, has been working on a solution for several years. Instead of disclosing an actively managed portfolio's precise holdings, the AMEX plan would use quantitative models to construct a proxy portfolio that closely mimics the fund's risk characteristics. The proxy portfolio would be designed to give specialists and market makers enough information, including a intraday share value based on the proxy portfolio every 15 seconds, to hedge their trading positions without exposing the manager's trades. The proxy portfolio value won't exactly track the actual portfolio value, but AMEX argues the error would be small. Officials at the exchange also say the odds of other investors reverse engineering the actual portfolio from the proxy is infinitesimal.

For a more complicated approach, consider New Jersey-based Managed ETFs' proposal. The firm, which was cofounded by former AMEX and Nuveen Investments executive Gary Gastineau, plans to tell market participants each day what securities they need to compile creation or redemption baskets for its active ETFs, only it will hide its recent buys and sells until they are complete. If the fund is in the process of liquidating a position the stock or bond will stay in the creation/redemption basket at its original weight until the manager is done selling. If the offering is buying a holding it won't show up in the basket until the transaction is complete.

Managed ETFs also plans to give the market not one, but two intraday values for its portfolios. It will provide the precise value at 9:30 A.M. EST and update it on the hour from then until the market closes at 4 P.M. EST. The firm's funds also would reveal every 15 seconds a version of the precise portfolio value that has been modified by adding or subtracting a number drawn randomly from a disclosed probability distribution. The idea is to give market participants an idea of which way the portfolio value is trending between the hourly disclosures of the precise value.

**Potential Benefits**

Advocates say active ETF shareholders would enjoy many of the same benefits of index ETFs. Because only authorized participants would deal directly with the funds, managed ETFs would shed the administrative costs of maintaining individual investor accounts and thus have lower expense ratios than conventional actively managed funds. The funds will be able to use the in-kind redemption mechanism to avoid capital gains distributions, so they could be more tax efficient than regular mutual funds. And, of course, investors would be able to trade, short, and perhaps write options on actively managed ETFs all day, which gives them the flexibility to employ tax loss and risk control strategies they can't use with traditional funds (as well as the opportunity to rack up commission costs).

The most compelling argument in favor of active ETFs, though, is the protection they could provide from the trading of other shareholders. Traditional fund managers often have to hold cash or sell securities to pay off investors who redeem their shares. That can erode returns, especially if the manager would rather keep the fund fully invested. This isn't as big a problem with ETFs because investors buy and sell their shares from each other on the secondary market, so their trading has no significant effect on the portfolios' management. Managed ETFs plans to add another layer of protection by cutting off creation and redemption orders at 2:30 P.M. EST, even from authorized participants who deal directly with the fund.

**Persistent Cons**

It's far from clear active ETFs will live up to the hype, though. While they may be less expensive than old school mutual funds, they probably will be more expensive than index ETFs. Managed ETFs already has proposed creating ETF share classes with front- and back-end sales charges and 12b-1 fees.

It's also clear actively managed ETF portfolios will be less transparent than their index ETF counterparts; less transparency means wider bid/ask spreads and possibly larger premiums and discounts, which increase transaction costs. The opacity also might impair active offerings' tax efficiency. To answer these questions those pushing for active ETFs trot out a tired argument that traditional fund managers have often used to justify high fees: The offerings will make up for the higher costs and bigger spreads with superior performance. Most active fund managers fail to beat their benchmark indexes over the long term, though. The ETF format might help them eke out some extra performance via lower fees and reduced transaction costs, but it won't make them better investors.

There are a host of other issues. What happens if an actively managed ETF manager wants to close the fund to control its asset base? Will the ETF then act like a closed-end fund, which tends to trade at bigger premiums and discounts? What caliber of managers will have enough confidence in the proposed format to make their services available in an ETF? I could be wrong, but it seems doubtful there will be ETF versions of **American Funds Growth Fund of America** AGTHX or **Selected American Shares** SLASX.

In the end actively managed ETFs may sacrifice too much of what has made index ETFs successful. Who wants more expensive, and less tax efficient and transparent ETFs? Once actively managed ETFs arrive, they will bear the burden of proof to deliver what they promise before long-term investors can regard them as viable alternatives. ▮

# ETFs vs. Closed End Funds

## Which are best for you?

by David Kathman,
Fund Analyst

Some firms out there would have you believe exchange-traded funds and closed-end funds are the same thing. Don't buy it.

Though there are some key similarities between ETFs and closed-end funds, there are some crucial differences. Understanding these differences can make you a better investor and help ensure that you choose the type of fund that's right for you.

### How They're Similar

Both ETFs and closed-end funds represent portfolios of securities (stocks, bonds, cash, etc.), just like open-end mutual funds. These portfolios can represent many different styles and combinations of asset classes, also like open-end mutual funds. There are ETFs and closed-end funds representing all the areas of the domestic-equity style box, as well as many foreign markets, many specific sectors (such as telecommunications), and various types of bonds. However, the distribution of the two types of funds among categories is rather different; whereas almost half of closed-end funds are bond funds, there are currently only a handful of bond ETFs.

Another similarity between ETFs and closed-end funds—and a key way they differ from open-end mutual funds—is that they are traded on an exchange. About three quarters of ETFs are traded on the American Stock Exchange (though iShares plans to move the listings of 81 of its ETFs to the New York Stock Exchange or ArcaEx by 2007), while most closed-end funds are traded on the New York Stock Exchange. That means you can sell them short, buy them on margin, or do anything else you could do with a stock. At least, that's true in theory; in practice, many ETFs and closed-end funds are so thinly traded that it may be hard to find shares to borrow in order to sell them short.

Closed-end funds and ETFs share at least one advantage over conventional mutual funds due to their exchange listings. Because individual investors buy their shares in the secondary market instead of directly from the fund, closed-end fund and ETF managers don't need to hold cash or sell securities to meet sudden redemption requests from panicky shareholders or market-timers, nor can they be forced to invest vast new inflows of cash in a market that already seems pricey.

However, the fact that these funds are traded on an exchange also means that you have to pay brokerage commissions every time you buy or sell them, on top of whatever fees the funds charge. That means that they're not good for investors looking to do a significant amount of trading, or planning to buy more shares on a regular basis for dollar-cost averaging purposes. Some ETFs have recently tried to make dollar-cost averaging more feasible, but in general, anyone wishing to make regular additions to their investments will find open-end funds a cheaper option.

### And How They're Different

The most obvious difference between ETFs and closed-end funds is cost. The average ETF in Morningstar's database has an expense ratio of 0.43%, while the average closed-end fund has an expense ratio of 1.27%. Why the discrepancy? It's mainly due to the fact that all ETFs are index funds, whereas most closed-end funds are actively managed. Actively managed funds cost more in general, because they require analysts and other kinds of research.

The reason there are no actively managed ETFs has to do with another key difference between ETFs and closed-end funds—namely how their shares are issued. A closed-end fund issues a set number of shares in an initial public offering, just like a stock, and it only issues more shares if it makes a secondary offering, also like a stock. After the IPO, the fund's shares can only be traded on the secondary market.

Because there are a set number of shares to go around, there can be a difference—either a discount or a premium—between the market price of a closed-end fund and the net asset value (NAV) of the securities in its portfolio. For example, as of Aug. 31, 2005, closed-end **Spain Fund** SNF traded at a 26.3% premium to its NAV, while **Brazil Fund** BZF traded at a 7.5% discount to its NAV.

ETFs, on the other hand, are designed to avoid such discounts and premiums as much as possible. With most ETFs, large investors called "authorized participants" can buy or redeem shares directly from the fund company, but only in blocks of 50,000 shares, which they then break up and sell on the open market to retail investors. Furthermore, when these authorized participants redeem one of these 50,000-share blocks, they get not cash, but the equivalent value in the underlying stocks. That means that the fund's holdings will always be known, unlike in open-end mutual funds, which have to disclose their holdings only once a quarter. Such transparency is possible and often desirable for index funds, but is virtually unheard of in actively managed funds.

Such "in-kind" transactions result in an arbitrage mechanism that keeps the ETF's market price from deviating too far from the value of its underlying securities. If the ETF shares trade at a discount, the authorized participants can trade the cheaper ETF shares for the more valuable stocks; if the ETF shares trade at a premium to their NAV, the authorized participants can trade the cheaper stocks for the more valuable ETF shares. The process actually can be quite a bit more complicated than this simple example, but you get the picture. This mechanism isn't perfect, so there can still be differences, but nothing like the double-digit discounts and premiums one often finds with closed-end funds.

There are other differences. Closed-end funds have been around longer. The oldest ETF was born in 1993, while the eldest closed-end fund predates The Great Depression and 1929 stock market crash.

Index ETFs also just try to match the returns of their benchmarks, which commonly focus on large, frequently traded stocks. Many closed-end funds, however, engage in more esoteric strategies. They often dabble in illiquid securities that can be hard to sell in a pinch. Many closed-end funds also use leverage; which means they invest with borrowed money. That pumps up the funds' income, but it also increases the offerings' volatility and therefore risk. When interest rates fall, the returns on leveraged closed-end bond funds are superior. When interest rates rise, leveraged bond funds get slammed.

**Pluses and Minuses**

There are advantages and disadvantages to each type of investment. If you buy a closed-end fund at a significant discount to its NAV, and that discount narrows or becomes a premium in a rally, then you'll make extra gains that you wouldn't get in an equivalent ETF or open-end fund. On the other hand, the discount could persist or even get worse, which isn't likely to sit well with shareholders. In fact, one of the factors in the explosive growth of ETFs in recent years was shareholder dissatisfaction over closed-end fund discounts. ▥

# Think Twice Before Buying Bond ETFs

Despite the hype, bond ETFs face stiff competition from mutual funds.

**by Paul Herbert, CFA,
Senior Fund Analyst**

Click on any investing Web site or leaf through the pages of your daily copy of *The Wall Street Journal* and you'll find an article about or advertisement for an exchange-traded fund. And there are good reasons why ETFs have become nearly ubiquitous: their liquidity, low costs, and tax advantages have helped to make them useful tools for investors.

But while equity ETFs have certainly earned a seat at the investing table, it's not as clear that the few fixed-income ETFs make as much sense as owning mutual funds that hold bonds. The reasons for our skepticism range from more or less minor details (such as the fact that you'll have to contact your broker separately to request that the monthly dividend payouts you receive from owning a bond ETF are reinvested) to three more-concrete points that we've detailed below.

### Cost Benefits of ETFs Aren't So Clear
Bond ETFs are cheap—there's no doubt about that. You only have to pay 0.20% in annual operating expenses for **iShares Lehman Brothers Aggregate Bond** AGG and **iShares Lehman TIPS Bond** TIP, and those are the most expensive of the six fixed-income ETF offerings available today. But investors can find several bond-index mutual funds in the same price range. You would expect Vanguard to offer some cheap funds in this arena, and they deliver on that expectation, by offering, as just one example, **Vanguard Total Bond Market Index** VBMFX for 0.20%. For **Dreyfus Bond Market Index Basic** DBIRX, shareholders pay just 0.15% in expenses.

Brokerage commissions are another fact of ETF life. Commissions on ETF trades have dropped in recent years, bringing the average charge for an online trade to $12. But depending on how you access them, you could trade traditional mutual funds for free. The negative effect that commissions have on returns becomes magnified for those who want to make regular investments into their ETFs.

### Tax Advantages of ETFs Are Less Relevant
Both index mutual funds and ETFs are very tax-friendly because they feature low-turnover strategies.

The structure of ETFs makes them more tax-efficient than mutual funds, though. Mutual fund redemptions may force a fund manager to sell securities at a gain to raise cash, but ETF sales occur on the exchange and don't force a manager to do anything. Plus, if an ETF manager has to sell stocks to meet redemptions from major shareholders (or "authorized participants" in ETF lingo), he or she can offload securities with the lowest cost basis on them, thereby limiting unrealized gains.

Funds simply can't compete with ETFs in this regard. But while ETFs' tax edge gives them a leg up in the arena of stock funds, bond funds don't typically rack up sizeable capital gains. For example, while **Vanguard 500 Index** VFINX paid out some large distributions in the late 1990s, Vanguard Total Bond Market Index has distributed just nine cents of capital gains in the past decade. As such, you're usually making out all right after taxes with a bond mutual fund, so the advantages of ETFs don't come into play to the same extent.

### Rekindling the Passive vs. Active Debate
The argument over bond indexing is by no means an open-and-shut case, but a number of active managers have been able to outperform their indexes over time. That's because enough inefficiencies exist in the bond market for active managers to get ahead of indexes such as the Lehman Brothers Aggregate Bond Index. Rather consistently, a small group of funds such as **PIMCO Total Return** PTTDX have been able to find undervalued securities, such as the German government bonds it picked up in 2004, and employ other return-boosting tactics to beat the bogy. As of Oct. 31, 2005, 37 out of 338 distinct funds in the intermediate-term bond fund category have produced 10-year returns that top the Aggregate Bond index's gain. That's not a long list, but low-cost bond funds with experienced managers are out there.

All in all, we still think there can be a place for ETFs—and most other cheap, tax-efficient funds—in investors' portfolios. And truly sophisticated investors may get some benefits from trading ETFs intraday or short-selling them. But given the strengths of traditional bond mutual funds, we continue to think that they serve most investors very well. M

# Do ETFs Live up to the Tax Efficiency Hype?

They do, with a few exceptions.

by Dan Culloton, Editor, Morningstar ETFs 100

Exchange-traded fund purveyors hawk their wares as the cure for the common capital gains distribution. For a while, it was hard to assess the claim because few ETFs had significant track records. Now that about 40% of them have been around for five years or more, we can assess if ETFs have delivered the tax efficiency they promised. Overall the answer is yes. ETFs have been much more tax-efficient, as measured by Morningstar's tax cost ratio, than the typical conventional mutual fund. A few exceptions, however, show that ETFs' tax advantage, while large, is not unassailable.

## Tax Advantaged

Before we examine the particulars, lets review why ETFs should be more tax efficient than traditional mutual funds. ETFs are not immune from capital gains distributions; they may make them, for example, if the indexes they track change or if a constituent is acquired at a premium. A variety of factors should make distributions rare, though: ETFs are currently all index funds that—for the most part—have lower turnover than actively managed funds. This helps limit their realization of capital gains. ETF investors also trade shares among themselves, not with the fund, so ETF managers don't have to sell securities to pay off redeeming shareholders. Only large investors, known as authorized participants, deal directly with the funds, and ETFs can satisfy those redemptions with baskets of their underlying portfolios' stocks instead of cash. Finally, savvy ETF managers also can use that in-kind redemption process to get rid of the stock shares with the biggest unrealized gains, thereby limiting the ETF's potential for distributing gains.

The system seems to work. Capital gains distributions have been rare in recent years at most ETF shops. Indeed, we looked at the tax cost ratios (which measures how much a fund's annualized return is reduced by the taxes investors pay on distributions) of ETFs that have been around for at least five years and found the following: In eight of the nine diversified domestic-stock fund categories the average ETF had a lower five-year tax cost ratio through the end of November 2005 than the typical conventional open-end mutual fund. ETFs showed the biggest advantages in the mid- and small-cap blend and growth segments, where high-turnover strategies that can generate a lot of capital gains are common among traditional funds. The sole exception was the large-value category, where the average traditional fund's tax cost ratio of 0.72 was slightly lower than the 0.75 tax cost ratio of the typical ETF. Lower expense ratios may be working against ETFs here, because like regular funds, ETFs tap their income to pay expenses. Because large-value ETF expense ratios are a fraction of those charged by the average conventional offering in the category, the ETFs had more income to distribute.

When you rank the tax cost ratios of individual ETFs with traditional mutual funds, they look pretty good, too. The tax cost ratios of the vast majority of domestic and international ETFs with five-year records ranked in the top half of their respective categories and broad asset classes. There were just a couple of funds, such as **StreetTracks Dow Jones Wilshire Small Cap Value** DSV and **iShares Dow Jones US Real Estate Index** IYR, with below-average tax cost ratios.

## Exceptions to the Rule

StreetTracks Dow Jones Wilshire Small Cap Value has issued capital gains distributions in nearly every year of its existence, including one that amounted to 4% of its NAV in 2004. This is due, in part, to the ETF's unusually high turnover rate for an index fund: It reached 54% in 2004. The offering's turnover could be lower and tax efficiency better in the future, though. In 2005 it adopted a new benchmark that has rules designed to keep the fund from automatically kicking out stocks on the benchmark's size and style borders.

iShares Dow Jones US Real Estate Index hasn't made any capital gains distributions, but it has made payments consisting of return of capital, essentially a giving back all or part of an original investment, and dividend income, neither of which qualifies for the lower 15% tax on dividends enacted in 2003. In general, the government treats REIT distributions as regular income for tax purposes.

There are other, less obvious exceptions. Many investors who flocked to buy shares of **iShares Dow Jones Select Dividend Index** DVY after it was launched in November 2003 did so to take advantage of the dividend tax cut enacted that same year. A year later, however, they learned just 86% of the dividends this ETF paid out in 2004 were qualified for the corporate dividend tax break—a small but unpleasant surprise. To qualify for the lower rate, funds have to hold income-paying stocks for more than 60 of the 121 days surrounding the companies' ex-dividend date. However, this ETF ran afoul of that rule due to heavy inflows and outflows and the index's year-end reconstitution. Because this fund, like all ETFs, swaps fund shares for baskets of stocks and vice versa, it wound up accepting some securities that didn't qualify and chucking others before they did.

As tax-friendly as ETFs are, it also pays to compare their records with similar conventional mutual fund competitors. For instance, **Vanguard 500 Index's** VFINX tax cost ratios for the trailing one-, three-, and five-year periods ended Nov. 30, 2005, are lower than those of both of its ETF rivals: **SPDR** SPY and **iShares S&P 500 Index** IW. That means Vanguard shareholders lost less of their returns to taxes than investors in the ETFs. Vanguard 500's actual aftertax returns (assuming an investor doesn't sell the fund at the end of the time period) also are better than its exchanged-traded rivals. Similarly, at the end of November, the five-year tax cost ratios and tax-adjusted returns of traditional index funds such as the **Schwab 1000** SNXFX and the **TIAA-CREF Equity Index** TCEIX were a bit better than their ETFs' counterparts **iShares Russell 1000** IWB and **iShares Russell 3000** IWV, respectively. This shows traditional fund managers who pay attention to taxes can be more than competitive with ETFs.

**Tax Takeaways**

These examples, however, may be exceptions that prove the rule: In most cases ETFs are more tax efficient than conventional mutual funds in the same asset classes or categories. Nevertheless, ETFs can surprise you. We'd be wary of those tracking benchmarks that require a lot of turnover, such as **Rydex S&P Equal Weight** RSP, which has a turnover rate of 55%, or **PowerShares Dynamic OTC** PWO, which has a turnover rate of 112%. These ETFs have been successful at avoiding capital gains thus far, but it's not certain they can keep that up indefinitely. High-income ETFs, such as those focused on REITs or dividend-paying stocks, also might be better off in tax-deferred accounts. ▌▌

# The Folly of Funds of ETFs

High costs and poor strategies make these vehicles a poor choice.

**by Dan Culloton, Editor, Morningstar ETFs 100**

Beware of mutual funds promising to let the average investor in on the ETF (exchange-traded fund) revolution. Their pledges are most likely siren songs.

The rapid growth and attractions (low expense ratios and flexibility, for example) of ETFs have been well documented. One of the big knocks against them, however, is that commission and trading costs can quickly turn ETFs' low-cost advantage into a disadvantage, especially for rapid traders or small investors who want to make regular, monthly contributions to their portfolios. In recent years some fund firms have launched funds of funds that at first glance appear to put ETFs within the reach of small investors. A closer look, however, shows these offerings have several strikes against them. In fact in most cases they are no more desirable than an account at a cut-rate online broker, and considerably worse from a cost perspective than a good old-fashioned, low-cost open-ended index fund.

## Questionable Strategies

The funds of ETFs currently on the market are few, young, small, and, until recently, managed by people who have little or no prior track record of running mutual funds. Their strategies and performance so far have left much to be desired.

Among the first was the now defunct Everest3 fund. It distributed its money among three ETFs: **SPDRs** SPY, which track the S&P 500; **Diamonds** DIA, which follow the Dow Jones Industrial Average; and **Qubes** QQQQ, which ape the NASDAQ 100. However, with about half of its money concentrated in giant-cap stocks and virtually none in smaller equities, this three-indexes-in-one fund was not really as diversified as it looked. Its track record was pretty poor, too. The fund, which shifted its asset allocation according to market conditions, never cracked the top half of the large-blend category and liquidated in August 2004.

Another early entry was the now two-year-old **PMFM Managed Portfolio Trust** ETFGX, which has less than $100 million in assets. It uses a computer

model to help it select ETFs on the basis of technical measures, such as market breadth, trend lines, interest rates, and relative strength. Turnover clocks in at more than 400%. It's hard to succeed over the long term with such a frenetic strategy and the fund's frequent trading could generate enough trading costs and capital gains to negate the expense and tax benefits of the ETFs it owns.

Recently, more well-known fund families have launched asset-allocation and target-retirement funds that use ETFs. A close look proves reputation isn't everything.

Early in 2005 USAA, a fund family known for selling staid, reasonably priced mutual funds to American servicemen and servicewomen, launched **USAA Total Return Strategy** USTRX. It uses a proprietary model to opportunistically shift its assets among equity ETFs, investment-grade bonds, and cash. The fund's goal is to earn positive returns each year and beat the S&P 500 on a risk-adjusted basis over the long term.

This isn't the place to go if you simply want a prepackaged, buy-and-hold ETF portfolio, though. Sometimes this fund will own them, and sometimes it won't. In the first six months of 2005, for example, the offering kept its assets in money market instruments two thirds of the time, according to the offering's 2005 semiannual report.

Money management boutique J.W. Seligman's three new ETF-based lifecycle funds also don't impress. The Seligman TargETFund series, which consist of **Core** SHVAX, **2015** STJAX, and **2025** STKAX funds, are typical target-retirement funds. The risk profiles of their holdings gradually shift from riskier asset classes (small-cap and emerging-markets equities, for example) toward steadier ones (like blue-chip stocks and government bonds) as the funds approach their goal dates. These funds' big selling points, however, are the fact that they use equity, fixed-income, and REIT ETFs to fulfill their asset-allocation schemes.

## High Costs

But the real kicker for the Seligman funds and the others is costs. Like most funds of funds, these offerings charge expense ratios on top of the levies of the underlying ETFs. The A shares of the Seligman TargETFunds, for example charge a 4.75% front-end load and a 1.09% expense ratio. Once you factor in the expense ratios of the underlying ETFs in an offering such as Seligman TargETFund 2015, however, the expenses jump

**Commentary**

to 1.35%. The PMFM ETF Portfolio Trust's expenses, including the underlying ETFs' are nearly 2%, and the USAA Total Return fund caps expenses at 1%.

Once you factor in the costs of buying and selling ETFs for the portfolio, its hard to imagine these funds being cheaper on a total cost basis than an ETF portfolio assembled at an low-cost broker such as Sharebuilder or Foliofn (where you can get $4 trades). Even that will probably be more expensive for those that dollar-cost average than using low-cost, no-load conventional index funds, such as **Vanguard Total Stock Market Index** VTSMX over the same period.

For those without the time or inclination to construct and maintain their own ETF or traditional fund portfolios, there are lower-cost options. Some target-retirement funds, such as those offered by American Century and T. Rowe Price, charge no management fee on top of the expense ratios of their underlying funds.

The bottom line is this: You can lead a conventional fund to ETFs, but that doesn't make it a good investment. A fund of ETFs' worth depends on how it uses the ETFs and what it charges for its services. The funds of ETFs we've seen so far don't look like they're worth much. ▮▮

# A Day at the ETF Forum

Answers to questions from Morningstar.com's discussion forums.

by Dan Culloton, Editor,
Morningstar ETFs 100

You can usually find some lively debates and interesting questions posed in Morningstar's ETF discussion forums. Here are some common questions found in the "Discuss" area of Morningstar.com, along with answers we've crafted specifically to help readers of this book.

**Q. I'm trying to decide which of these ETFs is better: iShares Dow Jones US Total Market Index (IYY) or Vanguard Total Stock Market VIPERs (VTI). I know that the Vanguard ETF is broader based and has a lower expense ratio. What others things should I be looking at?**

A. Though these two funds track the entire U.S. stock market via different indexes, their returns should correlate closely over the long term. That means expenses will be the biggest differentiating factor between them. The questioner has good instincts, though. There are other attributes to consider and compare, including the quality of the ETFs' benchmark, the competence of its manager, and the risk profile and tax efficiency of its portfolio.

On most of these counts, these ETFs are pretty even. Both indexes cover about 95% of the domestic-stock market by tracking float-adjusted market-cap-weighted benchmarks. (That means each constituent's position in the indexes is adjusted for the number of shares that actually trade on the open market.) The ETFs' advisors, Barclays Global Investors for the iShares and Vanguard for the VIPERs, both have a wealth of experience running index funds with a minimum of tracking error. And because the sector and stock exposures are virtually the same, the ETFs' risk characteristics are all but indistinguishable.

You could quibble about taxes. Both ETFs should be tax efficient because of their low turnover and ability to meet redemptions with baskets of securities rather than cash. But the Vanguard fund is a share class of **Vanguard Total Stock Market Index** VTSMX, so it shares the existing conventional mutual fund's unrealized capital gains. If the traditional fund ever had to sell securities to satisfy

a rush of redemptions it might realize capital gains that would be distributed to investors in all share classes, exchange-traded or otherwise. That said, we think the possibility of that scenario is remote. Even during the throes of the 2000 to 2002 bear market (a likely time for a rush for the exit) Vanguard's Total Stock Market and other funds in the family didn't have to liquidate large blocks of securities to meet redemptions. Furthermore, Vanguard's quantitative equity group has proven adept in the past at realizing losses to offset gains in the firm's index funds.

That brings us back to expenses, where it is no contest. The 0.20% expense ratio of iShares U.S. Total Market Index is nearly three times the 0.07% levy of Vanguard Total Stock Market VIPERs. All things being equal, and they are pretty close with these ETFs, we recommend that investors go with the cheaper option.

**Q. What is the difference between iShares Comex Gold Trust (IAU) and StreetTracks Gold Shares (GLD)?**

A. Besides having different advisors, these ETFs are very similar. Barclays Global Advisors sponsors iShares Comex Gold and State Street Global Advisors runs StreetTracks Gold. The State Street fund was first to market (November 2004) and has a larger asset base and higher trading volume. Both ETFs have traded at very narrow discounts/premiums to the underlying value of their portfolios, so there has been little problem with liquidity thus far.

Beyond that, they share many of the same qualities. Instead of investing in the shares of mining companies (like most open-end precious-metals mutual funds), these funds buy gold bullion and store it at a bank in London. Initially, each share represents one tenth of an ounce of gold, but that could decline as the ETFs sell some of the gold to pay expenses. Both ETFs provide relatively convenient exposure to the gold bullion market for a 0.40% expense ratio, which is a fraction of that of the conventional precious metals mutual fund. The ETFs eliminate the hassle of finding dealers that sell to retail customers as well as concerns about transporting, storing, or insuring gold. Furthermore, while still highly volatile, these ETFs may provide relatively quieter rides than many precious-metals mutual funds; the prices of mining company stocks tend to be more volatile than gold itself.

48     Commentary

Remember what they say about all that glitters, though. If the fund sells gold to pay expenses or investors sell their ETF shares, the proceeds of those sales are taxed at a maximum rate of 28% instead of the 15% rate assessed on long-term capital gains on stocks and bonds. That's because gold is considered a collectible under U.S. tax laws.

And while the price of gold may be less volatile than mining company stocks are, it's still extremely volatile relative to the broad U.S. equity market. These ETFs should thus be used sparingly, if at all, and investors need to make sure that adding gold to their portfolios is part of a sound long-term investment plan, not just a bet on the flavor of the month.

**Q. Vanguard allows investors to shift money among its funds. Does that apply to their exchange-traded VIPERs share classes, and are exchanges among funds considered taxable events?**

A. Vanguard's exchange policy does not apply to its exchange-traded VIPERs share class. Exchanges among Vanguard funds also, like redemptions, may be taxable events. The family, however, does allow investors to move from an index fund's non-ETF shares to the same fund's ETF share class with no tax consequences. So, if you sell **Vanguard Large Cap Index** VLACX and buy a Vanguard Large Cap VIPER, it can be considered a share-class conversion with no tax implications. Some brokerages may not be able to convert fractional shares, so the transaction may not be totally capital gains free. Vanguard also charges clients with accounts of less than $1 million $50 for the conversion and doesn't allow ETF shareholders to convert to conventional share classes.

**Q. Are ETFs better in taxable or tax-deferred accounts?**

A. There is nothing about ETFs that make them a bad choice for tax-deferred accounts, but their tax-efficient structure can make them uniquely well-suited for taxable accounts. Because ETF investors buy and sell shares to and from each other instead of the fund company, ETF managers don't have to realize capital gains to raise cash to meet redemptions. Furthermore, the large institutional shareholders that are permitted to redeem ETF shares directly from the fund company do not receive cash in exchange for their shares. Instead they are given a basket of the stocks held in the ETF's portfolio. This allows the ETF to continu-

ally hand off its lowest-cost-basis shares to redeeming institutions, helping ETFs keep their potential capital gains exposure low.

Not all ETFs are suitable for taxable accounts, though. There have been a handful of instances when ETFs have made sizable capital gains distributions. All ETFs are index funds, which are often more tax-efficient due to their low turnover, but some of them follow benchmarks that require a lot of turnover to track. For example small-cap indexes often have to make substantive changes to their holdings as stocks move in and out of the benchmarks' market capitalization ranges. They may be no better for your taxable account than actively managed funds. ▥

Disclosure: Barclays Global Investors (BGI), which is owned by Barclays, currently licenses Morningstar's 16 style-based indexes for use in BGI's iShares exchange-traded funds. iShares are not sponsored, issued, or sold by Morningstar. Morningstar does not make any representation regarding the advisability of investing in iShares that are based on Morningstar indexes.

# Commission Control

## Some tips on keeping ETF brokerage costs in check

**by Emiko Kurotsu,
Associate Analyst**

ETFs are cheap, but not if brokerage costs get out of hand. Frequent trading and high commissions can negate any savings you would have realized from ETFs' low expenses. Here are some pointers to help you avoid that trap.

### A Brokerage Taxonomy

There are two types of brokers: full-service and transaction-based. Full-service firms, such as Morgan Stanley and UBS, can require account minimums of $25,000 or more, and often levy asset-based charges for brokerage activity and advice. Transaction-based brokers cater more to DIY or newer investors and include premium discount brokers like Charles Schwab, Fidelity, and E*Trade, as well as discount brokers such as Scottrade and Ameritrade. Because full-service providers offer professional advice as part of their services, we'll focus on transaction-based brokerage firms that offer less guidance.

We surveyed the 16 largest U.S. transaction-based brokerage firms to determine an average brokerage fee. It turns out that charges vary greatly depending on trading activity and asset level, so we calculated an average minimum and maximum fee. Maximum fees apply to investors who don't have a lot of money in their accounts ($50,000 was a common minimum), and who don't trade a lot. For them, the average fee was $14.63. Minimum fees apply to investors with a bundle to invest (say more than $500,000) or who buy and sell frequently (usually more than 30 times a quarter). Their average trade cost about $10.17.

Fees also differ according to service level. Premium discount brokers offering online research, advice, and better service, can run from $12.99 (E*Trade) to $25 a trade at Vanguard. Discount brokers that have more-basic operations range from Brown & Co's $5, to TD Waterhouse's $17.95. There's a catch at Brown & Co, though: The firm requires clients to have at least four years investment experience and accounts of at least $15,000. No-strings-attached deals include Firstrade's $6.95 and Scottrade's $7.

Other hidden costs can bite. E*Trade will sock you with a $40 inactivity fee if you don't make one trade per quarter. Other firms charge account-maintenance fees ranging from $15 per quarter (Ameritrade) to $30 annually (Vanguard). Brokerages will waive such fees for large investors. Others, such as Sharebuilder.com and Muriel Siebert, don't charge maintenance fees. Finally, ETF options cost about $40 per trade with a nominal fee for each contract.

### Dollar-Cost Averaging Deals

If you are willing to surrender flexibility or to commit to a regular investment program, there are other alternatives. Foliofn lets investors compile ETF baskets and make hundreds of trades for flat rates ranging from $19.95 to $39.95 per month, or $199 to $399 annually. The firm also offers a la carte transactions for as low as $4 if investors agree to submit their orders only during two designated daily trading windows.

Meanwhile at Amerivest, a unit of Ameritrade, investors can create ETF portfolios and buy and sell them commission free for an asset-based fee. The service charges 0.35% on top of the expenses of the underlying ETFs for accounts with balances above $100,000, 0.50% for $20,000 balances, and the lesser of $100 or 2.95% for small accounts. Sharebuilder.com also offers $4 trades for investors who agree to make regular weekly or monthly investments and only trade at specific times.

These programs can be more affordable than traditional mutual funds and brokerage accounts, but it still depends on your situation. For example, you'd need about $20,000 to get the percentage cost of Foliofn's lowest annual fee down to 1% of assets, not counting the expense ratios of the ETFs in the basket.

Bare-bones brokerage or restrictive regular investment plans might not satisfy everyone, but investors who want more bells and whistles also may have to pay more or agree to other conditions, such as a minimum number of trades. Bottom line: pay attention to brokerage fees and rules. They could make or break your results. ▮

# Are the New Commodity ETFs a Good Idea?

A look at proposed exchange-traded funds for hot asset classes.

by Dan Culloton, Editor,
Morningstar ETFs 100
and Karen Wallace,
Managing Editor

StreetTracks Gold Shares, the first exchange-traded fund tracking a commodity, was one of the most successful ETF launches in history. Within weeks of its November 2004 launch it amassed more than $1.5 billion in assets. Is it any wonder that other financial firms are scrambling to introduce their own commodity ETFs?

ETF purveyors are much like traditional mutual fund companies in that they aren't above launching new funds in asset classes that have enjoyed strong recent performance and have gotten a lot of attention. Not all of the new commodity ETF proposals, which include offerings tracking silver, oil, and the euro, are without merit. In many cases, however, they sacrifice the tax efficiency and transparency of stock ETFs and should be approached with caution. Nevertheless, here's a look at the commodity funds that started it all and an early line on some new ideas.

### The Midas Touch?

There are currently two commodity ETFs on the market: **StreetTracks Gold Shares** GLD and **iShares COMEX Gold Trust** IAU. Unlike traditional precious-meals mutual funds, which invest in the stocks of mining companies, these offerings invest directly in gold bullion. Initially, an investment in each share of either fund is equivalent to one tenth of an ounce of gold (and sometimes cash). That's a lot more convenient than investing directly in gold; ETF shares are more liquid, or easy to sell, than an actual chunk of gold bullion. Gold also has to be insured, stored, and guarded, which can be expensive. The ETF shares are also cheap. Their 0.40% expense ratio is a fraction of the 1.67% charged by the typical precious-metals fund.

Another potential positive of investing directly in gold is that the price of bullion tends to be less volatile than the price of gold itself. (Mining gold comes with very high capital expenditures; thus, a gold producer's profits are often drastically reduced by the cost of extracting the gold from the mine.)

There are several downsides, though. The funds pay their expenses by selling some of the gold they hold. So the amount of physical gold that a share in these ETFs represents will decline over time as some is sold at the then-current prices to pay those expenses. Any gain on that sale, by the way, even if the full amount goes to pay expenses, is a taxable event for U.S. investors. And the tax bite on gains from this fund could be quite noticeable. For tax purposes, investors of this ETF are treated as though they own "collectibles," which means any long-term gains will be taxed at a maximum 28% tax rate rather than the current 15% tax rate for long-term capital gains.

Volatility is the biggest downside. In November 2005 gold was trading at about $490 per ounce—a 17-year high. Investors took notice, especially because the new price of gold represented an almost 90% increase in dollar terms from a low of $253 per ounce in mid-July 1999. Potential investors in either of these funds need to make sure that adding gold to their portfolios is part of a long-term investment plan, not just a bet on the flavor of the month. Some risk-averse investors can use gold as an inflation hedge due to its countercyclical nature and low correlation to the broad stock market. Even if you have the stomach to handle gold's volatility, though, it should make up only a small percentage of a portfolio (no more than 5% of assets). Most investors can live without it.

### Silver Warning Bells

Barclays Global Investors, which was second to market with its gold ETF, is first in line with a fund that tracks the price of silver. Like the gold ETFs, iShares Silver Trust will hold the actual metal in an account with JP Morgan Chase's London branch. It will allow small investors to share the costs and hassles of owning silver directly (storage, assaying, and insurance expenses, for example) with other shareholders and will charge a 0.50% management fee, according to SEC filings.

The silver ETF, however, is like its gold counterparts in other, less appealing ways. It will sell silver to pay its expenses, so the amount of the metal represented by the ETF's shares will decline over time. If the price of silver doesn't rise enough to compensate for those sales, the share price will decline. Those silver sales, by the way, will be a big taxable event for U.S. investors. Silver, like gold, is considered a collectible.

The fund will be able to hurt you in other ways, too. It's harder to make a case for silver as an inflation hedge because it's notoriously volatile. The metal's price fell for seven straight years after 1985. Increased demand from industrial users, as well as investors looking for an alternative to erratic stock market returns over the last five years, has propelled silver prices from less than $3 per ounce to nearly $8 recently. The best time to discover this metal's virtues as a diversifier was when it was still in the doldrums, not when it is coming off a rally. You're better off dodging this silver bullet.

### Strange Currencies

Rydex Investments thinks investors should be able use an ETF to speculate on the price of the euro or to hedge foreign currency exposure. The Rydex Euro Currency Trust will track the price of the European Union's currency versus the dollar. This fund, which will trade on the New York Stock Exchange, could make a market that has been the province of large investors accessible.

The ETF, however, has many of the same drawbacks as the metals funds. It will tap interest earned on the euros it buys to pay expenses, but if that income isn't sufficient it will have to sell euros. Those sales could erode the ETF's share price if the currency doesn't appreciate enough and would be taxable events for U.S. shareholders.

This fund's biggest bugaboo, however, is the unpredictable nature of foreign exchange rates. Even outgoing Federal Reserve Chairman Alan Greenspan has likened attempts to predict the course of currencies to a coin toss. And as for currency hedging, most studies show over the long term it has minimal effect on returns. Small investors would do more harm to themselves than good with this fund.

### Oil ETF Gusher

A couple of small firms have decided that now is a good time to introduce oil ETFs. We're wary of these, though, and not just because they were conceived as energy prices hit record highs. Macro Securities Depositor LLC of Morristown, N.J. wants to offer two ETFs that would use derivatives to track the price of Brent crude oil. One will allow investors to bet that the price of Brent crude is going up, and the other will let them wager it is going down. Such calls are difficult, if not impossible, to get right consistently over the long term with broad stock and bond-market funds, and much more so with narrowly focused portfolios, such as one that focuses on oil.

Alameda, Calif.-based Ameristock Funds' New York Oil ETF will try to track the price of light, sweet crude oil by investing in oil futures contracts on the New York Mercantile Exchange. It will charge a fairly reasonable management fee of 0.4% on the first $1 billion in assets and 0.2% thereafter, according to the prospectus.

Manager Nicholas D. Gerber, longtime manager of the **Ameristock Fund** AMSTX, has no experience running a commodity pool, though. Gerber also has a history of floating trial balloons that sink. For example, he liquidated Ameristock Focused Value after a scheme to convert it into a publicly traded holding company flopped. It's hard to get too excited about either of these offerings.

### The Basket Approach

Deutsche Bank's and Barclay's proposed broad commodity funds are more promising. Rather than focusing on one commodity, both the DB Commodity Index Tracking Fund and the iShares GSCI Commodity-Indexed Trust will use futures to track indexes. Deutsche's ETF will ape the Deutsche Bank Liquid Commodity Index while iShares' will track the Goldman Sachs Commodity Index. Both benchmarks include a range of goods, such as crude oil, heating oil, aluminum, gold, corn, soybeans, and wheat. That offers investors more diversified commodities exposure.

Still, they are not as diversified as at least one other traditional mutual fund option. The Deutsche ETF would devote more than half its assets to crude and heating oil. The iShares GSCI fund also would keep about 75% of money in some form of oil or gas. Contrast those allocations with that of **PIMCO Commodity Real Return** PCRDX, which caps energy exposure at a third of assets.

At least the iShares ETF keeps fees simple with an expense ratio of 0.75%. The Deutsche fund estimates total costs (including management fee, operating expenses, and sales charges) of 4.9% for investors who buy it during its initial offering (during which it plans to charge a 3% load) and of 1.9% for those who buy it in the secondary market. The portfolio expects to earn interest income that can be used to offset much or all of those expenses, depending on how you buy it and the performance of the fund, but that's not the level of fee transparency to which ETF investors are accustomed. ▥

Disclosure: Barclays Global Investors BGI, which is owned by Barclays, currently licenses Morningstar's 16 style-based indexes for use in BGI's iShares exchange-traded funds. iShares are not sponsored, issued, or sold by Morningstar. Morningstar does not make any representation regarding the advisability of investing in iShares that are based on Morningstar indexes.

# Selecting the Right Dividend ETF

Does iShares or PowerShares offer the best?

by Dan Culloton, Editor,
Morningstar ETFs 100

All but forgotten in the go-go growth market of the late 1990s, dividends have returned to the spotlight in recent years. A 2003 dividend-tax cut, low bond yields, prospects for desultory returns, and an aging, more income-focused population have boosted investor interest in dividend-paying stocks. Fund companies, especially those with exchange-traded fund lineups, have responded with a slew of new dividend-focused funds.

We usually counsel investors to avoid trendy funds because in the past their sponsors have shown an uncanny knack for launching the offerings at precisely the wrong time. A rash of Internet funds rolled out just before the tech-stock bubble burst in 2000, for instance. Though it's easier to make a long-term investment case for a dividend focused fund than a sector offering, it still pays to approach these funds cautiously since their real-world track records are so short. (The oldest one has been around for just two years and has gone through a significant change in that time.) That doesn't stop people from asking which one of these new offerings is the best, however, so let's look at how the yield-centric ETFs stack up so far.

In terms of asset size and fund flows, **iShares Dow Jones Select Dividend Index** DVY looks dominant. Its biggest rival so far, **PowerShares HighYield Dividend Achievers** PEY, had amassed a respectable $461 million in net assets between its December 2004 launch and Sept. 30, 2005. However, that's still only a fraction of the more than $7 billion in assets in the iShares offering. Other competitors have entered the field since these funds launched. PowerShares launched three more dividend funds late in 2005, State Street Global Advisors rolled out a SPDR Dividend ETF shortly after, and Vanguard is waiting in the wings with plans for its own dividend focused fund and ETF. For now, though, the iShares ETF remains the biggest.

Asset size doesn't tell the whole story, though. You have to consider a fund's benchmark, expenses, management, and available track record, too.

On the surface, the funds look similar: They all try to offer exposure to stocks that have above-average yields and the ability to continue paying and increasing their dividends. The benchmarks they track, however, use different methodologies, and the funds' price tags and management expertise vary.

## The Landscape

The Select Dividend Index was created in 2003 as a 50-stock index. At first, Dow Jones screened the Dow Jones U.S. Total Market Index for companies that had increased their dividends over the last five years without ever missing or cutting a payout. Dow Jones then ranked qualifying stocks by their indicated annual yield and took the highest 50. In 2004 Dow Jones decided to broaden the index to 100 stocks in order to make the benchmark more diversified by industry and stock size. To ensure its constituents are liquid and financially viable, the Select Dividend Index requires its members to have three-month average daily trading volumes of at least 200,000 shares and to have retained an average of 40% of their earnings in the previous five years.

Meanwhile, the folks over at PowerShares apparently decided that if one dividend ETF was good, four would be even better. They now offer PowerShares HighYield Dividend Achievers, **PowerShares Dividend Achievers** PFM, **PowerShares International Dividend Achievers** PID, and **PowerShares High Growth Rate Dividend Achievers** PHJ. The oldest of the bunch, the HighYield Dividend Achievers, tracks the Mergent Dividend Achievers 50 Index. That benchmark includes the 50 highest-yielding members of the Dividend Achievers, a list of stocks that have increased their dividends in each of the last 10 years. Equity data and research firm Mergent has compiled the list for more than 20 years, but the Dividend Achievers 50 has been published only since late 2004. The index's quality screen is its insistence on a consistent record of dividend increases. It arranges its holdings by yield and rebalances quarterly.

The other PowerShares offerings track different versions of Mergent's Dividend Achievers universe. PowerShares Dividend Achievers mimics all 300 or so stocks. PowerShares High Growth Dividend Achievers tracks the 100 constituents with highest 10-year annualized dividend growth rates. The International Dividend Achievers apes the performance of dividend-paying American Depositary Receipts (ADRs) and foreign common stocks trading on major U.S. exchanges that have increased their annual dividends for five or more straight years.

The international index weights its components by yield, while the broader Dividend Achievers and High Growth benchmarks are market-cap weighted.

PowerShares isn't the only place to go for Dividend Achievers, though. Vanguard planned to launch its own Vanguard Dividend Achievers Index fund and Viper ETF in December. The offerings will track a version of the broad Dividend Achievers Index, and given Vanguard's reputation for low costs and indexing expertise, should be very competitive.

Not to be outdone, the recently launched **SPDR Dividend ETF** SDY tracks Standard & Poor's Dividend Aristocrats Index. That bogy includes the 50 highest-yielding members of the S&P Composite 1500 that have increased their dividends 25 years straight.

### Comparison Shopping

It's hard to compare funds with such short track records, so let's focus on the two that have been around the longest: The PowerShares High-Yield Dividend Achievers and the iShares Dow Jones Select Dividend Index.

More than half of the HighYield Dividend Achiever's holdings can be found in the Dow Jones Select Dividend Index, and both ETFs tend to concentrate their assets in the same yield-rich sectors—financial, utilities, and consumer-goods stocks. There are still significant differences, though. The Dividend Achiever 50 Index includes many utility and regional bank stocks that don't make the Select Dividend Index's cut, such as **Consolidated Edison** ED and **First Commonwealth Financial** FCF. The Select Dividend's liquidity and quality screens also cause it to lean more toward large-cap stocks.

Although both funds focus most of their money in a couple of sectors, the Dividend Achievers is the more concentrated of the two. It owns half as many stocks as the Select Dividend Index and keeps more than 85% of its stocks in utilities and financial issues. The Select Dividend Index puts about 60% in those areas. The difference gives the Dividend Achievers index a slightly higher yield—3.9% compared with about 3% for the iShares. The extra income could come with extra volatility, though.

These are index funds, but management still matters. It's not hard to figure out who's David and who's Goliath. PowerShares is about three years old and has a handful of employees. Barclays Global Investors, the advisor to iShares, has been managing index funds since they were first conceived about 30 years ago and now is the largest manager of index

assets in the world. PowerShares' crew very well may acquit themselves in the long run, but right now, Barclays has the better credentials.

Finally, the iShares fund is cheaper. PowerShares HighYield Dividend Achievers, which has capped its expense ratio at 0.50%, isn't expensive relative to traditional mutual funds, but its levy is still higher than the 0.40% charged by iShares Dow Jones Select Dividend Index.

### The Way to Go?

All these ETFs still have a lot to prove. If pressed to choose among them, though, I'd lean toward iShares Dow Jones Select Dividend Index because it has the longer track record, more established and accomplished advisor, lower expense ratio, and more diversified portfolio. Investors should be careful, though. These funds have a whiff of the Dogs of Dow about them. That once-popular strategy, which involves buying the highest-yielding stocks in the Dow Jones Industrial Average, has been discredited in recent years because it failed to avoid stocks that had high yields because their businesses were in peril and their stocks plummeting. Requiring histories of dividend increases may help these ETFs avoid such pratfalls, but, before considering any of these ETFs, income-seeking investors still might want to investigate funds that apply more rigorous qualitative research in their search for yield.

For example, **Vanguard Equity-Income** VEIPX offers investors a portfolio crafted by two seasoned subadvisors practicing time-tested strategies for identifying cheap stocks with above-average dividend payouts. It also charges a lower expense ratio than both of these ETFs. Meanwhile, **Franklin Rising Dividends** FRDPX has used strict dividend-growth and valuation screens, rigorous fundamental research, and a buy-and-hold approach to produce competitive absolute returns with below-average volatility over the last 15 years. Ⅲ

Disclosure: Barclays Global Investors BGI, which is owned by Barclays, currently licenses Morningstar's 16 style-based indexes for use in BGI's iShares exchange-traded funds. iShares are not sponsored, issued, or sold by Morningstar. Morningstar does not make any representation regarding the advisability of investing in iShares that are based on Morningstar indexes.

# Microcap ETFs Under the Microscope

These new micro-cap ETFs are intriguing, but unproven.

by Dan Culloton, Editor, Morningstar ETFs 100

The sponsors of three new micro-cap exchange-traded funds would have investors believe that if small is good, micro must be better. That certainly has been the case in recent years as tiny stocks have rallied. There is also considerable research suggesting smaller stocks can produce bigger returns than their larger-cap brethren over the long term. That's not likely to occur without some gut-wrenching performance swings in this volatile asset class, though. It's also not clear if the recently launched micro-cap ETFs will be the best way to maximize any micro-cap strength.

## Welcome Competition

Three micro-cap ETFs—**iShares Russell Microcap Index** IWC, **PowerShares Zacks Micro Cap Portfolio** PZI, and **First Trust Dow Jones Select MicroCap Index** FDM—launched in August and September, and others tracking a recently created MSCI micro-cap benchmark could emerge in the future. Although launching micro-cap funds after five years of strong small- and micro-cap stock performance is questionable, the new funds do introduce some welcome price competition. Traditional micro-cap funds tend to be costly, with an average no-load expense ratio of 1.6% and broker-sold levy of 2.3%. As if that wasn't bad enough, the cheapest micro-cap option, **DFA U.S. Micro Cap** DFSCX, is difficult for small investors to get at due to its $2 million minimum investment. With expense ratios of 0.6% and wide availability through online brokerages, the micro-cap ETFs make the asset class more affordable and accessible.

## Better Mousetraps?

I also think a couple of the offerings have intriguing approaches. The iShares Russell Microcap fund tracks its namesake index, which includes the smallest 1,000 denizens of the Russell 2000 along with the next 2,000 smallest stocks. The fund, however, won't own all of those securities, whose market caps range from $50 million to $550 million. Instead it follows a modified version of the Russell Microcap that tosses out companies whose stocks fail to maintain cumulative monthly trading volumes of

125,000 shares for six consecutive months. That and representative sampling whittles the ETF's holdings down to about 1,200 companies, which advisor Barclays Global Investors contends is enough to ensure liquidity and diversification. (As I'll discuss below, liquidity is a major concern for micro-cap ETFs.)

The PowerShares ETF, like most of the family's other offerings, tracks an index that has a twist of active management. The fund apes a benchmark assembled by Zacks Investment Research that relies on value and momentum factors to select stocks that will outperform the broader micro-cap universe. The index, which reconstitutes itself based on its screens four times a year and kicks out on a weekly basis constituents that cease to meet its standards, should have pretty high turnover for an index fund.

First Trust's ETF also filters its constituents through fundamental screens. The 30-year-old unit investment trust firm in Lisle, Ill., linked its ETF to the Dow Jones Select MicroCap Index. The benchmark, first published in June 2005, focuses on stocks in the two smallest deciles of the broad domestic stock market and then screens out shares that score poorly on five measures: operating profit margin, earnings momentum, trailing six-month return, P/E, and price/sales ratio. The idea is to produce an index whose constituents are more liquid and viable than the notoriously perilous microcap universe. Unlike the Zacks index, the Dow Jones bogy reconstitutes once a year in August.

It's hard to assess the merit of the PowerShares ETF, because Zacks guards the inputs to its quantitative model closely. The methodology behind the iShares ETF's benchmark, however, is more transparent and easier to understand. So are the construction rules of the Dow Jones index used by First Trust, though that bogy's reliance on quality screens probably would hold the fund back when more speculative micro-caps rally.

## Curb Your Enthusiasm

At the end of the day, however, not only are these offerings unproven, but it's also not clear how they will handle liquidity in what historically has been one of the less-liquid corners of the market. Because of the way ETFs are structured, it's easier for large discrepancies to emerge between an ETF's market price and the net asset value of its holdings when the ETF owns thinly traded stocks. That's because ETFs rely on large institutional strength investors (otherwise known as "authorized partici-

Commentary

pants") to use the funds' in-kind creation/redemption process to arbitrage away premiums and discounts by opportunistically trading baskets of the portfolio's securities for ETF shares and vice versa. It's easier to do that for large, frequently traded stocks, such as members of the S&P 500, than it is for micro-caps, which tend to have weaker trading volumes.

Capacity could be an issue, too. Most index funds don't face size constraints because their low turnover and broad diversification allow them to manage a lot of money. It's hard to say if, as these funds grow larger, they will be able to continue to invest in micro-caps without incurring progressively higher trading costs.

The ETF sponsors, of course, contend their funds have liquidity screens in place that ensure authorized participants will have no problem assembling creation units to match their fund's holdings. They also argue there is plenty of capacity, pointing out there is about $500 billion in total market capitalization in the micro-cap space and about $10 billion in micro-cap funds. Both hold up DFA U.S. Micro Cap, which has $3.8 billion, as proof that it's possible to run a big, passive micro-cap fund.

That may be true in the current environment, which has seen micro-cap trading volumes increase and bid/ask spreads narrow as strong performance has attracted money to the asset class. What happens if or when volume and spreads return to historical norms? Will there be enough liquidity to keep the funds from experiencing big premiums and discounts to NAV? Time and the trading ability of the funds' advisors will tell. Until we learn more about how these funds will behave, I'd steer clear of them. ▌▌▌

Disclosure: Barclays Global Investors BGI, which is owned by Barclays, currently licenses Morningstar's 16 style-based indexes for use in BGI's iShares exchange-traded funds. iShares are not sponsored, issued, or sold by Morningstar. Morningstar does not make any representation regarding the advisability of investing in iShares that are based on Morningstar indexes.

# Vipers vs. iShares

## How do Barclay's and Vanguard's ETF lineups compare?

by Dan Culloton, Editor, Morningstar ETFs 100

Barclays Global Investors was the first big asset manager to market ETFs to the masses, and the firm's iShares family of ETFs is easily the best known brand in the business. Vanguard is nipping at Barclays' heels, though. Since launching its first ETF, the Viper share class of the **Vanguard Total Stock Market Index fund** VTI, in 2001, the firm has gone on to roll out more than 20 other ETFs. Moreover, the firm's reputation as the indexing king among retail investors and its uniquely low cost structure may give it an edge going forward. As it stands, many iShares and Vipers ETFs compete head to head for assets. That's great for investors: It gives them additional choices, and it should help keep fees low. But whose lineup has the edge?

### Variety

This isn't much of a contest. There are a couple of dozen Vipers covering most of the domestic-equity style range and market-cap spectrum, as well as several sectors. Investors also can cobble together total international stock exposure with three foreign-equity Vipers.

Nobody, however, has more ETFs tracking more stock markets, styles, regions, or industries than iShares. It's also the only ETF family with fixed-income offerings and is branching out into commodities with its **iShares Comex Gold** IAU and proposed silver and broad commodity ETFs. Vanguard offers a tidy tool kit for ETF investors, but iShares is like the Craftsman super-sized, multidrawer implement chest.

This isn't a real advantage, though. With traditional mutual funds, you might want to aggregate your investments in a single family to ensure you only receive a single statement, or you might like the privilege of exchanging one fund in the family for another. But none of this applies to ETFs: You can buy an ETF from any family through your brokerage account, and they all can be tracked on the statement for that account. There are also no exchange privileges with ETFs.

### Expenses

This also isn't a close call. IShares are cheap, but Vipers are even cheaper. The average iShares ETF has an expense ratio of 0.43%. The typical Viper charges less than half that: 0.20%. No Viper charges more than 0.28%, and the cheapest of the lot, **Vanguard Total Stock Market Vipers** VTI and **Vanguard Large Cap Vipers** VV, exact just 0.07%, making them the lowest-cost large-blend funds available. As with its traditional funds, Vanguard's mutual-ownership structure allows it to deliver services at cost. Meanwhile Barclays bakes into iShares' expense ratios the price of marketing to financial planners and advisors.

### Tax Efficiency

Both iShares and Vipers should be more tax-efficient than traditional funds because they are all low-turnover index offerings. ETFs, however, have an added advantage. Small investors buy and sell shares among themselves through a broker on an exchange, and the large ones that deal directly with the funds use an in-kind purchase and redemption process. That means they trade baskets of securities, not cash, for fund shares and vice versa. So ETF managers don't have to sell securities to raise cash to accommodate investor behavior. Furthermore, they can use the in-kind redemption process to purge their funds of low-cost-basis stocks, or those with the biggest potential capital gains.

Vanguard's ETFs are different, though, and a bit controversial. They are share classes of conventional funds, not stand-alone entities. This could be a disadvantage at tax time, some critics argue, because an ETF share class still might have to distribute capital gains if its parent fund has to sell holdings to meet redemptions in the traditional share classes.

Vanguard contends conventional share classes can help Viper tax efficiency by realizing losses that can be used to offset gains for all share classes. We've examined this issue in the past and decided that, while the stand-alone ETFs could have a tax edge over exchange-traded share classes in certain cases, such as when the conventional share classes of the fund have more assets than the exchange-traded class, it wasn't a big or definitive advantage.

So far, Vanguard's oldest and largest Vipers, Vanguard Total Stock Market Vipers and **Vanguard Extended Stock Market Index Vipers** VXF, have never made capital gains distributions. Two of the newer Vipers, however, **Vanguard REIT Index Vipers** VNQ and **Vanguard Consumer Staples Vipers**

VDC, have paid out gains in the last year. Meanwhile, no iShares ETF has distributed a capital gain since 2001, though in prior years a number of funds, including **iShares S&P 500 Index** IVV, had issued occasional capital gains. Call this one even.

**Benchmarks**

What Vanguard lacks in selection, it makes up for in quality. The construction methods of the MSCI Indexes favored by the firm make them arguably more representative of the stock universes they represent than are many of the benchmarks tracked by iShares, such as the Russell growth and value indexes.

For example, Vanguard's Total Stock Market Viper includes stocks that are based overseas but conduct most of their business domestically, unlike offerings such as the **iShares Russell 3000 Index** IVV. The MSCI sector indexes are often less concentrated than similar iShares. MSCI's style-based equity indexes also use eight growth and valuation factors to determine what belongs in the growth and value indexes, as well as buffer zones to limit migration and turnover between styles and market-cap ranges.

It's telling that S&P, which used to rely on one factor to figure out a stock's style, is switching its style methodology from Barra to one fashioned by Citigroup that is similar to MSCI's. By mid-December 2005, when S&P made the switch, there were more iShares tracking indexes that employ multifactor construction models, but not at Vanguard's costs. This is a photo finish, but it's Vanguard by a nose.

**Conclusion**

If having access to all flavors of ETF from one place is important to you, iShares is that place. Since there are no discernable advantages to going with a single ETF provider, though, it's difficult to see why that should be a paramount concern. Nevertheless, Barclays clearly has the scale, skill, and expertise to run a big family of index funds, and its family is large and includes some tried-and-true benchmarks, as well as several novelties. Don't go with Barclays on reputation alone, though. Vanguard's rock-bottom costs, well-designed benchmarks, and indexing expertise make it an extremely competitive and, at times, better, alternative. ▮▮▮

Disclosure: Barclays Global Investors BGI, which is owned by Barclays, currently licenses Morningstar's 16 style-based indexes for use in BGI's iShares exchange-traded funds. iShares are not sponsored, issued, or sold by Morningstar. Morningstar does not make any representation regarding the advisability of investing in iShares that are based on Morningstar indexes.

# Managers Still Don't Earn Their Keep

They lose to indexes on a risk-adjusted basis, too.

by Christopher Davis,
Fund Analyst

The combatants are familiar by now. In one corner stand index-fund proponents, who argue that active managers' inability to best the major market indexes over the long haul is proof of the market's efficiency. They could point to the fact that 74% of actively managed large-blend funds lagged the s&p 500 Index over the trailing 10 years through the end of 2005's third quarter as an example. In the other corner, some indexing critics contend that argument is incomplete, as it ignores the valuable role active managers can play in reducing risk. The debate has direct bearing exchange-traded funds since all ETFs currently are index funds.

Active managers do indeed boast some potent weapons in their risk-reduction arsenal. They can retreat to cash in turbulent markets, for one. By contrast, because index funds seek to replicate their benchmark's returns, they must remain fully invested. Active managers also can limit price risk by avoiding pockets of the market with unjustifiable valuations. For instance, price-conscious investors had the flexibility to steer their portfolios away from expensive technology and telecommunications highfliers in 2000, just as those names were becoming an ever-larger part of the prevailing market indexes.

So do active managers really fare better once risk is factored into the equation? To answer that question, we compared the average risk-adjusted return for actively managed funds in each of the nine Morningstar U.S. equity style-box categories with those of the corresponding Russell Index for its style. In other words, we measured large-growth funds against the Russell 1000 Growth Index, pitted small-blend funds against the Russell 2000 Index, and so forth. The one exception to the rule was the large-blend group, which we compared with the s&p 500, the standard by which most funds in the category are judged.

We measured risk-adjusted returns using the Sharpe and Treynor ratios, comparing the average Sharpe and Treynor ratios for each fund category (weighting the performance of each fund in the group equally), with those of their corresponding benchmarks. The Sharpe ratio measures the trade-off between a security's excess returns (the portfolio return less the risk-free return of the 90-day T-bill) and its standard deviation, the most common measure of volatility. The Treynor ratio is similar to the Sharpe ratio, though it substitutes market risk, or beta, for standard deviation. By replacing standard deviation with beta, the Treynor ratio doesn't incorporate systemic risks such as business risk, financial risk, and default risk that the Sharpe ratio, with its use of standard deviation, does.

For the purposes of our study, we examined risk-adjusted returns for the trailing five- and 10-year periods through March 2005. And to help ensure our findings weren't an anomaly relating to the time frames we chose, we turned back the clock five years, also examining risk-adjusted returns for the five- and 10-year periods ending March 2000. To rid our data of survivorship bias, we added back the results of funds that were either liquidated or merged out of existence.

## Findings

Even on a risk-adjusted basis, indexing generally still wins out. That's especially true in the large-cap realm. In fact, in the two 10-year periods we studied—1990 through 2000 and 1995 through 2005—the risk-adjusted returns from the large-cap indexes, as measured by the Sharpe and Treynor ratios, were higher than the risk-adjusted returns of the average actively managed large-value, large-blend, and large-growth funds. The picture barely improves when you look at risk-adjusted returns from 2000 through 2005, an exceptionally volatile period that should have given active managers the opportunity to add value over their benchmarks' risk-adjusted returns. Only active large-blend fund managers had an edge, and a slight one at that. The average Sharpe ratio in the large-blend group matched the s&p 500's, but the average Treynor ratio modestly edged past the index's. Overall, though, the data strongly argue in favor of indexing large caps.

The case for indexing in the mid-cap arena is about as compelling. In just one of the four periods we looked at—1995 to 2000—did the average actively managed mid-blend fund outpace the Russell Midcap Index, but only as measured by the Treynor ratio. (Over that period, the Sharpe ratio of the average actively managed mid-blend fund was even with that of the benchmark.) Versus the Russell

Midcap Growth Index, active mid-growth funds succeeded in just one of four periods, the 10 years ending March 2005. The average active mid-value fund didn't post better risk-adjusted returns relative to the Russell Midcap Value Index in any period.

The argument for small-cap indexing isn't so cut and dried, however. It should be easier for active small-cap managers to beat their bogies. After all, they invest in a more thinly traded area of the market that is much less closely followed by Wall Street. And in contrast to small-cap index funds, whose best performers eventually graduate to mid-cap indexes, active managers can let their winners run. Finally, while many stocks get placed in small-cap indexes after they've enjoyed a big run, active small-cap investors are free to dabble in the IPO market.

Our findings suggest active small-cap managers do indeed stand a better chance of adding value. In two of the four periods we looked at—2000 to 2005 and 1995 to 2005—actively managed small-blend managers prevailed over the Russell 2000. Even small-cap indexing stalwarts like **Vanguard Small Cap Index** NAESX trailed their actively managed rivals. The justification for active management is strongest in the small-growth sphere. Regardless of the time period we looked at, the average active manager in the category topped the Russell 2000 Growth Index on an absolute and risk-adjusted basis. Our research also indicates that active small-cap managers of all stripes stand a better chance succeeding in rough environments than in up markets. In the five years through March 2005—a period that encompasses the brutal 2000 to 2002 bear market—active managers in the three small-cap style-box categories edged past their corresponding index's Sharpe ratio. (The average actively managed mid-blend fund also outpaced the Russell Midcap Growth's Treynor ratio over the period.)

As stocks raced ahead from 1995 through 2000, though, active managers of all stripes lagged their respective benchmarks on a risk-adjusted basis as measured by the Sharpe ratio, except for the small-growth category. Indexing also led by larger margins in the five years ending March 2000 in both absolute and risk-adjusted terms than in the succeeding five years. Indexing's edge appears to be greater in bull markets. That the active managers' risk-adjusted returns were better during the bear market than in the bull market brings to mind Dunn's Law. The theory, coined by researcher Steven Dunn, holds that when an asset class does well, the index tracking that class will outperform active

funds investing in the same universe. The theory also posits the opposite; indexes are likely to lag actively managed funds when the benchmark's target stocks are out of favor. That's because active managers generally don't offer pure exposure to an asset class like an index does. For instance, many value investors have recently eyed depressed technology names, which mostly reside in growth indexes.

Dunn's research originally referred to raw, rather than risk-adjusted, returns. Applied to risk-adjusted returns, the principles behind Dunn's Law don't work in every instance. With large-growth stocks decidedly out of favor in the past five years, one might have expected active large-growth managers to beat the Russell 1000 Growth Index over that stretch. That wasn't the case, though. Another anomaly: Active small-value managers topped the Russell 2000 Value Index for the trailing five years through March 2005 even as small-value stocks generally ruled the roost.

**Conclusion**
To be sure, there are areas of the U.S. market where active management appears to have an edge. Investors betting on active small-cap managers—especially those focused on small-growth stocks—have better odds of achieving index-beating risk-adjusted returns than those choosing active large-cap managers.

However, indexing enjoys a number of advantages, including style purity and ease of monitoring. (Regardless of who's at the helm of **Vanguard 500 Index** VFINX, its fundamental traits remain the same.) And with expenses the most effective predictor of a fund's long-term prospects, lower costs seal conventional index funds' and ETFs' appeal. Even where traditional index funds and ETFs may not be the ideal choice, investing in them is a sound option. ▥

# Our ETF Screener Narrows the Field

Search the exchange-traded fund universe quickly and easily.

by Dan Culloton, Editor, Morningstar ETFs 100

It's easy to lose your bearings in the rapidly expanding exchange-traded fund universe. Barely a week goes by without word of new ETF launches. To help navigate this changing terrain, Morningstar last year launched an ETF Screener (http://screen.morningstar.com/ETFScreener/Selector.htm) on its Web site. As part of your purchase of the ETFs 100, you can receive a 14-day Research Pass on Morningstar.com, which provides access to the ETF Screener, as well as to all of our ETF analysis and research. Registration details can be found on the inside front cover of this book.

The screener is a pretty simple tool. It allows investors to sift through the 200 currently available ETFs by asset class, category, expense ratio, fund family, performance, or any combination of those criteria.

You can narrow the field down quickly. Let's say you're interested in a financial sector ETF. First you select "Specialty Domestic" on the Fund Group drop-down menu; then "Specialty-Financial" in the Morningstar Category box. At the end of 2005, that search winnowed your choices to seven ETFs. You can add a cost screen by selecting one of the ranges in the Expense Ratio field. Adding "Less than or equal to 0.30%" to your criteria leaves you with two choices: **Financial Select Sector SPDR** XLF and **Vanguard Financials VIPERs** VFH. You'd get similar results by picking "Specialty-Technology" instead of "Specialty-Financial" in the Morningstar Category box and leaving the other settings alone: **Technology Select Sector SPDR** XLK and **Vanguard Information Technology VIPERs** VGT would be the only ETFs left standing.

Only interested in iShares, StreetTracks, or VIPERs? The screener's fund family field allows you to limit your search to one ETF purveyor. Thus, you can easily find iShares in the large-blend category with expense ratios of 0.20% or less. Or you could find the answer to broader questions, such as which ETF family doesn't offer any funds with expense ratios lower than 0.50%. You can discover the answer by choosing "Less than or equal to 0.50%" in the Expense Ratio box, selecting each ETF family in turn in the Fund Family area, and checking the results. (The answer is PowerShares.)

The screener can aid in other scavenger hunts, as well. For instance, it can locate diversified domestic-stock ETFs that have gained more than 10% in each of the trailing one-, three-, and five-year periods. Pick "Diversified Domestic" in the Fund Group menu and "Greater than 10%" in each of the performance fields. As of early January 2005, **iShares Russell 2000 Value Index** IWN and **iShares S&P SmallCap 600 Index** IJR passed the screen.

Once you get your results, you can conduct further research by ranking and sorting ETFs by a number of data points related to performance, risk, taxes, portfolio, and fund operations. You could, for example, see how concentrated sector ETFs can get. Select "Specialty Domestic" on the Fund Group menu to get a full list. On the results page chose "Portfolio" in the "View" box in the upper left corner. Rank the funds by percent of assets in top-10 holdings by clicking on that column's header. You'll find that many of the available sector ETFs keep more than 50% of their assets in their top-10 stocks. The **iShares Dow Jones US Telecom Index** IYZ has more than three fourths of its money packed in its biggest holdings. Energy ETFs, such as Energy **Select Sector SPDR** XLE and **iShares Dow Jones US Energy** IYE, bunch as much as two thirds of their assets in their top-10 positions. Funds that concentrated aren't providing diversified exposure to the sectors they track.

If you narrowed the field by more than you wanted, go back and change one of the screening measures to its original "Any" designation and you should get more funds. Happy screening. ▐▌

Disclosure: Barclays Global Investors BGI, which is owned by Barclays, currently licenses Morningstar's 16 style-based indexes for use in BGI's iShares exchange-traded funds. iShares are not sponsored, issued, or sold by Morningstar. Morningstar does not make any representation regarding the advisability of investing in iShares that are based on Morningstar indexes.

# Report Pages

This section offers a full-page report on each of the 100 ETFs.

# Consumer Staple SPDR

| | Ticker | NAV | Market Price | 52 wk High/Low | Yield | Mstar Category |
|---|---|---|---|---|---|---|
| | XLP | $23.30 | $23.55 | $23.90 - $22.48 | 1.9% | Large Blend |

## Management

### Portfolio Manager(s)

State Street Global Advisors serves as advisor to the trust, but the creation of the index tracked by the portfolio falls to Merrill Lynch, Pierce, Fenner & Smith. It allocates stocks in the S&P 500 to the sector it thinks is appropriate. The American Stock Exchange Index Services Group rebalances holdings based on periodic index adjustments and diversification requirements.

### Strategy

This exchange-traded offering owns the consumer-goods companies in the S&P 500. It also throws in a few retailers, such as Wal-Mart, that sell the stuff made by the likes of Procter & Gamble. This provides an initial screen for quality, as holdings meet the standards of the S&P's selection committee. Constituents usually have to be leading U.S. companies that meet S&P's profitability criteria. Unfortunately, the criteria eliminate large international companies, including Unilever and Diageo.

**Growth of $10,000**

— Investment Value of ETF
— Investment Value of Index S&P 500

| 1996 | 1997 | 1998 | 1999 | 2000 | 2001 | 2002 | 2003 | 2004 | 2005 | History |
|---|---|---|---|---|---|---|---|---|---|---|
| — | — | 27.24 | 22.98 | 28.56 | 25.40 | 19.96 | 21.76 | 23.09 | 23.30 | NAV $ |
| — | — | 27.16 | 23.03 | 28.56 | 25.40 | 19.94 | 21.78 | 23.08 | 23.29 | Market Price $ |
| — | — | -0.30* | -14.70 | 25.83 | -9.91 | -20.02 | 10.95 | 7.79 | 2.84 | NAV Return% |
| — | — | -0.33* | -14.27 | 25.56 | -9.91 | -20.10 | 11.16 | 7.65 | 2.84 | Market Price Return% |
| — | — | -0.29 | 0.04 | -0.06 | -0.25 | -0.10 | 0.06 | 0.03 | 0.01 | Avg Premium/Discount% |
| — | — | -0.30 | -35.74 | 34.93 | 1.97 | 2.07 | -17.72 | -3.08 | -2.07 | NAV Rtrn% +/-S&P 500 |
| — | — | -0.30 | -35.61 | 33.62 | 2.54 | 1.63 | -18.94 | -3.61 | -3.43 | NAV Rtrn% +/-Russ 1000 |
| — | — | — | 4 | 4 | 13 | 15 | 15 | 17 | 23 | NAV Return% Rank in Cat |
| — | — | — | 1.00 | 1.29 | 1.13 | 1.52 | 1.81 | 1.65 | 1.93 | Income Return % |
| — | — | — | -15.70 | 24.54 | -11.04 | -21.54 | 9.14 | 6.14 | 0.91 | Capital Return % |
| — | — | 0.00 | 0.27 | 0.30 | 0.32 | 0.38 | 0.36 | 0.36 | 0.44 | Income $ |
| — | — | 0.00 | 0.00 | 0.00 | 0.00 | 0.00 | 0.00 | 0.00 | 0.00 | Capital Gains $ |
| — | — | — | 0.57 | 0.42 | 0.28 | 0.28 | 0.27 | 0.27 | 0.26 | Expense Ratio % |
| — | — | — | 1.10 | 1.20 | 1.21 | 1.48 | 1.87 | 1.62 | 1.84 | Income Ratio % |
| — | — | — | 3 | 10 | 6 | 60 | 37 | 3 | 24 | Turnover Rate % |
| — | — | — | — | — | — | 230 | 305 | 761 | 785 | Net Assets $mil |

## Performance

### Historic Quarterly NAV Returns

| | 1st Qtr | 2nd Qtr | 3rd Qtr | 4th Qtr | Total |
|---|---|---|---|---|---|
| 2001 | -12.63 | -1.58 | 3.17 | 1.55 | -9.91 |
| 2002 | 2.89 | -14.16 | -10.50 | 1.19 | -20.02 |
| 2003 | -6.56 | 8.96 | 1.25 | 7.64 | 10.95 |
| 2004 | 5.39 | 1.30 | -5.69 | 7.06 | 7.79 |
| 2005 | 0.20 | -0.79 | 2.84 | 0.60 | 2.84 |

| Trailing | NAV Return% | Market Return% | NAV Rtrn% +/-S&P 500 | %Rank Cat.(NAV) |
|---|---|---|---|---|
| 3 Mo | 0.60 | 0.55 | -1.48 | 27 |
| 6 Mo | 3.46 | 3.40 | -2.30 | 27 |
| 1 Yr | 2.84 | 2.84 | -2.07 | 23 |
| 3 Yr Avg | 7.14 | 7.16 | -7.24 | 14 |
| 5 Yr Avg | -2.39 | -2.39 | -2.93 | 13 |
| 10 Yr Avg | — | — | — | 0 |

| Tax Analysis | Tax-Adj Return% | Tax-Cost Ratio |
|---|---|---|
| 3 Yr (estimated) | 6.49 | 0.61 |
| 5 Yr (estimated) | -2.97 | 0.59 |
| 10 Yr (estimated) | — | — |

### Risk Profile

| | Standard Index S&P 500 | Best Fit Index Russ 1000 |
|---|---|---|
| Alpha | -2.1 | -2.6 |
| Beta | 0.62 | 0.62 |
| R-Squared | 50 | 50 |
| Standard Deviation | 8.03 | |
| Mean | 7.14 | |
| Sharpe Ratio | 0.66 | |

### Morningstar Fair Value

| Price/Fair Value Ratio | Fair Value Estimate ($) | Hit Rate % |
|---|---|---|
| 0.9 Undervalued | 44.18 | 99 Good |

## Morningstar's Take by Dan Culloton

Consumer Staples Select Sector SPDR offers an interesting but risky deal.

For a low expense ratio, this ETF provides exposure to the shares of market-leading purveyors of everyday stuff. Since its bogy draws its constituents from the S&P 500, holdings tend to be established domestic names that investors know well. Large, global companies, such as Altria, Procter & Gamble, and Wal-Mart, play huge roles among the portfolio's nearly 40 stocks.

Yet there are considerable risks here. The ETF concentrates more than half of its assets in its top five holdings, which leaves it vulnerable to individual stock blowups. The portfolio's preponderance of giant- and large-cap stocks can hold it back at times. Indeed, the fund has suffered in recent years as small caps have rallied. The ETF has lost money in about 45% of the 70 rolling one-year periods from its 1998 inception through the end of September 2005.

You could argue that, due to its recent performance, the ETF is undervalued. Morningstar's stock analysts cover and have set fair values for stocks representing 95% of this ETF's total asset value. We took an asset-weighted average of all the fair values at of the end of October and compared it with an asset-weighted average of their share values. By that measure, this ETF's holdings were trading about 12% below fair value. A variety of factors have held this ETF's top holdings back, including slipping beer sales at Anheuser-Busch and labor challenges at Wal-Mart. However, Morningstar stock analysts think many of this fund's top holdings are dominant franchises that are worth more than their current market prices.

This fund's focus will be a plus if the valuations of mega-cap consumer-goods stocks rise, but it is reliant on a handful of companies. It also ignores foreign-based firms with big U.S. presences, such as Unilever. A more diversified rival would be a better investment.

| Address: | c/o State Street Bk&Tr, 225 Franklin St |
| | Boston MA 02210 |
| | 800-843-2639 |
| Web Address: | www.spdrindex.com |
| Inception: | 12-22-98 * |
| Advisor: | SSGA Funds Management, Inc. |

| Management Fee: | 0.05% | | |
| Expense Projections: | 3Yr:$87 | 5Yr:$152 | 10Yr:$345 |
| Income Distrib: | Quarterly | | |
| Exchange: | AMEX | | |

## Portfolio Analysis 12-31-05

Share change since 11-05 Total Stocks:38

| | Sector | PE | Tot Ret% | % Assets |
|---|---|---|---|---|
| ⊖ Procter & Gamble | Goods | 21.2 | 7.18 | 17.93 |
| ⊖ Altria Group | Goods | 15.0 | 27.72 | 14.38 |
| ⊖ Wal-Mart Stores | Consumer | 18.2 | -10.30 | 10.81 |
| ⊖ PepsiCo | Goods | 25.8 | 15.24 | 4.55 |
| ⊖ Coca-Cola | Goods | 18.6 | -0.66 | 4.52 |
| ⊖ Walgreen | Consumer | 29.1 | 15.94 | 4.38 |
| ⊖ Anheuser-Busch Companies | Goods | 17.1 | -13.38 | 3.32 |
| ⊖ Colgate-Palmolive | Goods | 24.1 | 9.55 | 2.87 |
| ⊖ Kimberly-Clark | Goods | 17.5 | -6.73 | 2.81 |
| ⊖ Costco Wholesale | Consumer | 22.7 | 3.19 | 2.40 |
| ⊕ CVS | Consumer | 20.8 | 17.89 | 2.23 |
| ⊕ Sysco | Consumer | 21.7 | -17.25 | 2.02 |
| ⊖ General Mills | Goods | 15.1 | 1.88 | 1.86 |
| ⊕ Archer Daniels Midland | Ind Mtrls | 16.8 | 12.25 | 1.73 |
| ⊕ Sara Lee | Goods | 23.3 | -18.56 | 1.57 |
| ⊕ Kroger | Consumer | — | 7.64 | 1.51 |
| ⊕ Avon Products | Goods | 14.3 | -24.77 | 1.44 |
| ⊕ Wm. Wrigley Jr. | Goods | 27.8 | -2.37 | 1.34 |
| ⊕ H.J. Heinz | Goods | 17.6 | -10.55 | 1.28 |
| ⊕ Kellogg | Goods | 18.5 | -0.92 | 1.26 |

### Current Investment Style

Value Blnd Growth — Large Mid Small

| Market Cap | % |
|---|---|
| Giant | 57.2 |
| Large | 35.5 |
| Mid | 7.3 |
| Small | 0.0 |
| Micro | 0.0 |

Avg $mil: 57,285

| Value Measures | | Rel Category |
|---|---|---|
| Price/Earnings | 18.40 | 1.08 |
| Price/Book | 4.37 | 1.62 |
| Price/Sales | 1.05 | 0.82 |
| Price/Cash Flow | 7.00 | 0.97 |
| Dividend Yield % | 2.25 | 1.27 |

| Growth Measures | % | Rel Category |
|---|---|---|
| Long-Term Erngs | 10.18 | 0.92 |
| Book Value | 12.19 | 1.30 |
| Sales | 8.83 | 1.10 |
| Cash Flow | 5.55 | 0.54 |
| Historical Erngs | 10.35 | 0.73 |

| Profitability | % | Rel Category |
|---|---|---|
| Return on Equity | 33.24 | 1.63 |
| Return on Assets | 10.50 | 1.13 |
| Net Margin | 9.54 | 0.88 |

| Sector Weightings | % of Stocks | Rel S&P 500 | 3 Year High | Low |
|---|---|---|---|---|
| ↻ Info | 0.00 | 0.00 | | |
| 📀 Software | 0.00 | 0.00 | 0 | 0 |
| 💻 Hardware | 0.00 | 0.00 | 0 | 0 |
| 🎤 Media | 0.00 | 0.00 | 0 | 0 |
| 📶 Telecom | 0.00 | 0.00 | 0 | 0 |
| ⊂ Service | 26.18 | 0.56 | | |
| ⚕ Health | 0.00 | 0.00 | 0 | 0 |
| 🛒 Consumer | 26.18 | 3.22 | 37 | 12 |
| 📊 Business | 0.00 | 0.00 | 0 | 0 |
| 💲 Financial | 0.00 | 0.00 | 0 | 0 |
| ⊔ Mfg | 73.82 | 2.21 | | |
| 🏭 Goods | 72.28 | 8.44 | 87 | 62 |
| ⚙ Ind Mtrls | 1.54 | 0.13 | 2 | 1 |
| 🔥 Energy | 0.00 | 0.00 | 0 | 0 |
| 💡 Utilities | 0.00 | 0.00 | 0 | 0 |

### Composition

| | |
|---|---|
| ● Cash | 0.6 |
| ● Stocks | 99.4 |
| ● Bonds | 0.0 |
| ● Other | 0.0 |
| Foreign | 0.0 |
| (% of Stock) | |

**MORNINGSTAR® ETFs 100**

# DIAMONDS Trust

| | Ticker | NAV | Market Price | 52 wk High/Low | Yield | Mstar Category |
|---|---|---|---|---|---|---|
| | DIA | $107.08 | $110.08 | $110.08 - $100.14 | 2.9% | Large Value |

## Management

### Portfolio Manager(s)

State Street Bank and Trust Company, whose subsidiary, State Street Global Advisors, is the second-largest manager of index assets in the world, serves as the trustee of Diamonds, which is a unit-investment trust.

### Strategy

This exchange-traded fund mimics the composition and performance of the Dow Jones Industrial Average, a 30-member index maintained by the editors of The Wall Street Journal. The selection committee looks for nonutility stocks with exceptional reputations and wide interest from individual and institutional investors. The committee has tried to add new economy stocks such as Microsoft in recent years, but, by and large, the Dow is made up of true-blue mega-cap firms, with a focus on industrial stocks. The index is price-weighted rather than capitalization-weighted.

## Performance

### Historic Quarterly NAV Returns

| | 1st Qtr | 2nd Qtr | 3rd Qtr | 4th Qtr | Total |
|---|---|---|---|---|---|
| 2001 | -8.01 | 6.66 | -15.35 | 13.75 | -5.52 |
| 2002 | 4.20 | -10.73 | -17.44 | 10.55 | -15.10 |
| 2003 | -3.69 | 13.05 | 3.72 | 13.35 | 28.00 |
| 2004 | -0.47 | 1.20 | -2.94 | 7.53 | 5.12 |
| 2005 | -1.27 | -1.67 | 3.39 | 2.02 | 2.40 |

| Trailing | NAV Return% | Market Return% | NAV Rtrn% +/-S&P 500 | %Rank Cat.(NAV) |
|---|---|---|---|---|
| 3 Mo | 2.02 | 1.76 | -0.06 | 13 |
| 6 Mo | 5.48 | 5.28 | -0.28 | 11 |
| 1 Yr | 2.40 | 2.47 | -2.51 | 10 |
| 3 Yr Avg | 11.28 | 11.23 | -3.10 | 7 |
| 5 Yr Avg | 2.02 | 2.19 | 1.48 | 7 |
| 10 Yr Avg | — | — | — | 0 |

| Tax Analysis | Tax-Adj Return% | Tax-Cost Ratio |
|---|---|---|
| 3 Yr (estimated) | 10.34 | 0.84 |
| 5 Yr (estimated) | 1.23 | 0.77 |
| 10 Yr (estimated) | — | — |

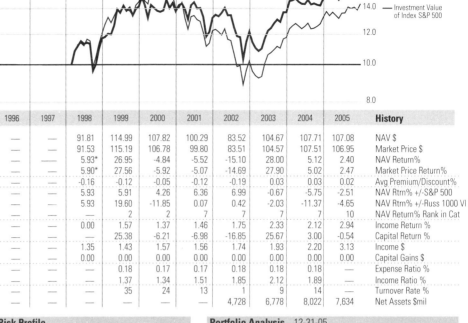

Growth of $10,000

— Investment Value of ETF
— Investment Value of Index S&P 500

| | 1996 | 1997 | 1998 | 1999 | 2000 | 2001 | 2002 | 2003 | 2004 | 2005 | History |
|---|---|---|---|---|---|---|---|---|---|---|---|
| | — | — | 91.81 | 114.99 | 107.82 | 100.29 | 83.52 | 104.67 | 107.71 | 107.08 | NAV $ |
| | — | — | 91.53 | 115.19 | 106.78 | 99.80 | 83.51 | 104.57 | 107.51 | 106.95 | Market Price $ |
| | — | — | 5.93* | 26.95 | -4.84 | -5.52 | -15.10 | 28.00 | 5.12 | 2.40 | NAV Return% |
| | — | — | 5.90* | 27.56 | -5.92 | -5.07 | -14.69 | 27.90 | 5.02 | 2.47 | Market Price Return% |
| | — | — | -0.16 | -0.12 | -0.05 | -0.12 | -0.19 | 0.03 | 0.03 | 0.02 | Avg Premium/Discount% |
| | — | — | 5.93 | 5.91 | 4.26 | 6.36 | 6.99 | -0.67 | -5.75 | -2.51 | NAV Rtrn% +/-S&P 500 |
| | — | — | 5.93 | 19.60 | -11.85 | 0.07 | 0.42 | -2.03 | -11.37 | -4.65 | NAV Rtrn% +/-Russ 1000 Vl |
| | — | — | — | 2 | 2 | 7 | 7 | 7 | 7 | 10 | NAV Return% Rank in Cat |
| | — | — | 0.00 | 1.57 | 1.37 | 1.46 | 1.75 | 2.33 | 2.12 | 2.94 | Income Return % |
| | — | — | — | 25.38 | -6.21 | -6.98 | -16.85 | 25.67 | 3.00 | -0.54 | Capital Return % |
| | — | — | 1.35 | 1.43 | 1.57 | 1.56 | 1.74 | 1.93 | 2.20 | 3.13 | Income $ |
| | — | — | 0.00 | 0.00 | 0.00 | 0.00 | 0.00 | 0.00 | 0.00 | 0.00 | Capital Gains $ |
| | — | — | — | 0.18 | 0.17 | 0.17 | 0.18 | 0.18 | 0.18 | — | Expense Ratio % |
| | — | — | — | 1.37 | 1.34 | 1.51 | 1.85 | 2.12 | 1.89 | — | Income Ratio % |
| | — | — | — | 35 | 24 | 13 | 1 | 9 | 14 | — | Turnover Rate % |
| | — | — | — | — | — | — | 4,728 | 6,778 | 8,022 | 7,634 | Net Assets $mil |

## Risk Profile

| | Standard Index S&P 500 | Best Fit Index S&P 500 |
|---|---|---|
| Alpha | -2.6 | -2.6 |
| Beta | 0.99 | 0.99 |
| R-Squared | 90 | 90 |
| Standard Deviation | 9.60 | |
| Mean | 11.28 | |
| Sharpe Ratio | 0.96 | |

## Morningstar Fair Value

| Price/Fair Value Ratio | Fair Value Estimate ($) | Hit Rate % |
|---|---|---|
| 0.9 Undervalued | 45.86 | 100 Good |

## Portfolio Analysis 12-31-05

Share change since 11-05   Total Stocks:30

| | Sector | PE | Tot Ret% | % Assets |
|---|---|---|---|---|
| ⊕ IBM | Hardware | 16.0 | -15.83 | 6.13 |
| ⊕ 3M Company | Ind Mtrls | 19.2 | -3.51 | 5.78 |
| ⊕ Altria Group | Goods | 15.0 | 27.72 | 5.57 |
| ⊕ Boeing | Ind Mtrls | 24.8 | 37.92 | 5.23 |
| ⊕ American International G | Financial | 15.6 | 4.83 | 5.08 |
| ⊕ Johnson & Johnson | Health | 19.1 | -3.36 | 4.48 |
| ⊕ Procter & Gamble | Goods | 21.2 | 7.18 | 4.31 |
| ⊕ Caterpillar | Ind Mtrls | 16.0 | 20.68 | 4.31 |
| ⊕ ExxonMobil | Energy | 10.6 | 11.76 | 4.19 |
| ⊕ United Technologies | Ind Mtrls | 17.9 | 10.03 | 4.17 |
| ⊕ American Express | Financial | 16.4 | 5.31 | 3.83 |
| ⊕ Citigroup | Financial | 12.1 | 4.63 | 3.62 |
| ⊕ Wal-Mart Stores | Consumer | 18.2 | -10.30 | 3.49 |
| ⊕ DuPont De Nemours E.I. | Ind Mtrls | 19.6 | -10.52 | 3.17 |
| ⊕ Home Depot | Consumer | 15.6 | -4.35 | 3.02 |
| ⊕ Coca-Cola | Goods | 18.6 | -0.66 | 3.00 |
| ⊕ J.P. Morgan Chase & Co. | Financial | 18.8 | 5.74 | 2.96 |
| ⊕ Honeywell International | Ind Mtrls | 24.0 | 7.52 | 2.78 |
| ⊕ General Electric | Ind Mtrls | 19.9 | -1.43 | 2.61 |
| ⊕ McDonald's | Consumer | 18.0 | 7.30 | 2.51 |

### Current Investment Style

Value Blnd Growth — Large Mid Small

| | Market Cap | % |
|---|---|---|
| | Giant | 83.7 |
| | Large | 16.3 |
| | Mid | 0.0 |
| | Small | 0.0 |
| | Micro | 0.0 |
| | Avg $mil: | 98,554 |

| Value Measures | | Rel Category |
|---|---|---|
| Price/Earnings | 16.23 | 1.13 |
| Price/Book | 2.60 | 1.17 |
| Price/Sales | 1.13 | 0.86 |
| Price/Cash Flow | 6.26 | 1.22 |
| Dividend Yield % | 2.29 | 0.94 |

| Growth Measures | % | Rel Category |
|---|---|---|
| Long-Term Erngs | 10.09 | 1.06 |
| Book Value | 14.95 | 1.24 |
| Sales | 6.60 | 0.82 |
| Cash Flow | 18.01 | 1.47 |
| Historical Erngs | 12.86 | 0.78 |

| Profitability | % | Rel Category |
|---|---|---|
| Return on Equity | 23.56 | 1.28 |
| Return on Assets | 11.06 | 1.12 |
| Net Margin | 11.63 | 0.90 |

| Sector Weightings | % of Stocks | Rel S&P 500 | 3 Year High | Low |
|---|---|---|---|---|
| ↷ Info | 18.87 | 0.93 | | |
| ▭ Software | 2.05 | 0.58 | 4 | 2 |
| ▭ Hardware | 10.76 | 1.07 | 11 | 9 |
| ▭ Media | 1.85 | 0.52 | 2 | 1 |
| ▭ Telecom | 4.21 | 1.40 | 5 | 3 |
| ⊂ Service | 32.73 | 0.71 | | |
| ▭ Health | 8.32 | 0.63 | 10 | 7 |
| ▭ Consumer | 9.20 | 1.13 | 9 | 7 |
| ▭ Business | 0.00 | 0.00 | 0 | 0 |
| ▭ Financial | 15.21 | 0.72 | 16 | 8 |
| ▭ Mfg | 48.39 | 1.45 | | |
| ▭ Goods | 14.41 | 1.68 | 20 | 13 |
| ▭ Ind Mtrls | 29.68 | 2.44 | 38 | 29 |
| ▭ Energy | 4.30 | 0.46 | 5 | 3 |
| ▭ Utilities | 0.00 | 0.00 | 0 | 0 |

### Composition

| | | % |
|---|---|---|
| ● | Cash | 0.2 |
| ● | Stocks | 99.8 |
| ● | Bonds | 0.0 |
| ● | Other | 0.0 |
| | Foreign | 0.0 |
| | (% of Stock) | |

## Morningstar's Take by Dan Culloton

These Diamonds aren't necessarily an investor's best friend.

The Diamonds don't look so rough. The exchange-traded fund has one of the lowest expense ratios among large value funds, exchange traded or otherwise. The ETF also has one of the highest yields among all offerings in this group and is focused on the bluest of U.S. blue-chip stocks, including established companies such as Procter & Gamble and Citigroup. Who wouldn't want a portfolio of large, profitable, dividend-paying stocks, especially in what could be an era of modest equity returns?

Certainly you can make an argument for holding the shares of giant, income-producing, globe-spanning enterprises. This vehicle still has some flaws as a portfolio linchpin, though. The construction methodology of the ETF's index, The Dow Jones Industrial Average, is subjective. The editors of The Wall Street Journal select and maintain the average's components. So, the ETF probably wouldn't appeal to investors who like their indexes based on more scientific, quantitative methods.

The portfolio's concentration also makes it hard to use. Not only is it disproportionately focused on giant stocks, but by definition it also holds just 30 issues. While the committee that assembles the average tries to insure it represents a broad swath of the U.S. commerce and industry, the benchmark still has heavy concentrations in hardware and industrial stocks. Furthermore, because the average's components are price-weighted, individual constituents with high nominal share prices, such as IBM, can assume large positions.

This ETF is a tempting choice for a pure, undiluted shot of mega-cap stocks with decent yields. Its many idiosyncrasies, however, render it less desirable than other more diversified options in the large-value category.

| Address: | PDR Services, 86 Trinity Place New York NY 10006 800-843-2639 |
|---|---|
| Web Address: | www.amex.com |
| Inception: | 01-20-98* |
| Advisor: | PDR Services |

| Management Fee: | 0.07% | | | |
|---|---|---|---|---|
| Expense Projections: | 3Yr: — | 5Yr: — | 10Yr: — | |
| Income Distrib: | Monthly | | | |
| Exchange: | AMEX | | | |

MORNINGSTAR® ETFs 100

# Energy SPDR

| | Ticker | NAV | Market Price | 52 wk High/Low | Yield | Mstar Category |
|---|---|---|---|---|---|---|
| | XLE | $50.28 | $53.98 | $54.52 - $35.23 | 1.1% | Specialty-Natural Res |

## Management

### Portfolio Manager(s)

State Street Global Advisors serves as advisor to the trust, but the creation of the index tracked by the portfolio falls to Merrill Lynch, Pierce, Fenner & Smith. It allocates stocks in the S&P 500 to the sector it thinks is appropriate. The American Stock Exchange Index Services Group rebalances holdings based on periodic index adjustments and diversification requirements.

### Strategy

This exchange-traded offering owns the oil & gas and energy-services companies in the S&P 500. (Power companies fall into the Utilities Select Sector SPDR.) This provides an initial screen for quality, as holdings meet the standards of the S&P's selection committee. Constituents usually have to be leading U.S. companies that meet S&P's profitability criteria. Unfortunately, the criteria eliminate large international oil companies, including Royal Dutch Petroleum, BP, and Total SA. This leaves the fund concentrated on the likes of ExxonMobil.

**Growth of $10,000**
— Investment Value of ETF
— Investment Value of Index S&P 500

| 1996 | 1997 | 1998 | 1999 | 2000 | 2001 | 2002 | 2003 | 2004 | 2005 | History |
|---|---|---|---|---|---|---|---|---|---|---|
| — | — | 23.20 | 27.18 | 33.27 | 26.70 | 22.30 | 27.62 | 36.29 | 50.28 | NAV $ |
| — | — | 23.34 | 27.09 | 33.19 | 26.70 | 22.33 | 27.55 | 36.32 | 50.31 | Market Price $ |
| — | — | 13.48* | 19.07 | 24.30 | -18.33 | -14.81 | 26.32 | 33.47 | 40.20 | NAV Return% |
| — | — | 13.46* | 17.96 | 24.41 | -19.14 | -14.69 | 25.82 | 33.93 | 40.17 | Market Price Return% |
| — | — | — | 0.60 | -0.04 | -0.11 | -0.03 | 0.01 | 0.04 | -0.01 | 0.01 | Avg Premium/Discount% |
| — | — | — | 13.48 | -1.97 | 33.40 | -6.45 | 7.28 | -2.35 | 22.60 | 35.29 | NAV Rtrn% +/-S&P 500 |
| — | — | — | 13.48 | -8.15 | 8.49 | -2.74 | -1.55 | -7.69 | 8.90 | 3.72 | NAV Rtrn% +/-GS NATR RES |
| — | — | — | 1 | 1 | 2 | 4 | 4 | 4 | 6 | NAV Return% Rank in Cat |
| — | — | — | 1.94 | 1.78 | 1.50 | 1.82 | 2.17 | 1.87 | 1.58 | Income Return % |
| — | — | — | 17.13 | 22.52 | -19.83 | -16.63 | 24.15 | 31.60 | 38.62 | Capital Return % |
| — | — | 0.00 | 0.45 | 0.43 | 0.49 | 0.48 | 0.48 | 0.51 | 0.57 | Income $ |
| — | — | 0.00 | 0.00 | 0.00 | 0.00 | 0.00 | 0.00 | 0.00 | 0.00 | Capital Gains $ |
| — | — | — | 0.56 | 0.41 | 0.28 | 0.27 | 0.28 | 0.27 | 0.26 | Expense Ratio % |
| — | — | — | 1.73 | 1.71 | 1.56 | 1.82 | 2.06 | 1.70 | 1.36 | Income Ratio % |
| — | — | — | 20 | 31 | 17 | 39 | 7 | 10 | 10 | Turnover Rate % |
| — | — | — | — | — | — | 289 | 635 | 1,572 | 3,526 | Net Assets $mil |

## Performance

### Historic Quarterly NAV Returns

| | 1st Qtr | 2nd Qtr | 3rd Qtr | 4th Qtr | Total |
|---|---|---|---|---|---|
| 2001 | -7.17 | -0.71 | -14.44 | 3.55 | -18.33 |
| 2002 | 8.64 | -8.79 | -18.90 | 6.02 | -14.81 |
| 2003 | 0.67 | 8.18 | 0.30 | 15.65 | 26.32 |
| 2004 | 6.66 | 7.80 | 11.56 | 4.05 | 33.47 |
| 2005 | 18.48 | 4.11 | 20.96 | -6.04 | 40.20 |

| Trailing | NAV Return% | Market Return% | NAV Rtrn% +/-S&P 500 | %Rank Cat(NAV) |
|---|---|---|---|---|
| 3 Mo | -6.04 | -6.01 | -8.12 | 7 |
| 6 Mo | 13.65 | 13.81 | 7.89 | 7 |
| 1 Yr | 40.20 | 40.17 | 35.29 | 6 |
| 3 Yr Avg | 33.21 | 33.18 | 18.83 | 4 |
| 5 Yr Avg | 10.46 | 10.53 | 9.92 | 2 |
| 10 Yr Avg | — | — | — | 0 |

| Tax Analysis | Tax-Adj Return% | Tax-Cost Ratio |
|---|---|---|
| 3 Yr (estimated) | 32.48 | 0.55 |
| 5 Yr (estimated) | 9.78 | 0.62 |
| 10 Yr (estimated) | — | — |

## Risk Profile

| | Standard Index S&P 500 | Best Fit Index GS NATR RES |
|---|---|---|
| Alpha | 20.5 | 0.5 |
| Beta | 0.68 | 1.03 |
| R-Squared | 12 | 92 |
| Standard Deviation | 18.39 | |
| Mean | 33.21 | |
| Sharpe Ratio | 1.56 | |

## Morningstar Fair Value

| Price/Fair Value Ratio | Fair Value Estimate ($) | Hit Rate % |
|---|---|---|
| 1.2 Overvalued | 64.05 | 100 Good |

## Portfolio Analysis 12-31-05

Share change since 11-05 Total Stocks:29

| | Sector | PE | Tot Ret% | % Assets |
|---|---|---|---|---|
| ⊕ ExxonMobil | Energy | 10.6 | 11.76 | 16.17 |
| ⊕ Chevron | Energy | 9.0 | 11.51 | 12.03 |
| ⊕ ConocoPhillips | Energy | 6.7 | 36.89 | 8.07 |
| ⊕ Burlington Resources | Energy | 15.4 | 99.35 | 4.48 |
| ⊕ Halliburton | Energy | 21.7 | 59.46 | 4.28 |
| ⊕ Occidental Petroleum | Energy | 6.7 | 39.15 | 3.96 |
| ⊕ Schlumberger | Energy | 31.1 | 46.62 | 3.91 |
| ⊕ Devon Energy | Energy | 11.4 | 61.57 | 3.72 |
| ⊕ EOG Resources | Energy | 17.9 | 106.26 | 3.61 |
| ⊕ Transocean | Energy | 48.1 | 64.40 | 3.53 |
| ⊕ Marathon Oil | Energy | 9.8 | 66.01 | 3.19 |
| ⊕ Anadarko Petroleum | Energy | 11.4 | 44.09 | 3.02 |
| ⊕ Apache | Energy | 9.8 | 36.28 | 2.98 |
| ⊕ Baker Hughes | Energy | 25.9 | 43.78 | 2.87 |
| ⊕ Valero Energy | Energy | 10.7 | 128.46 | 2.82 |
| ⊕ Sunoco | Energy | 12.6 | 94.37 | 2.27 |
| ⊕ Kerr-McGee | Energy | 15.3 | 58.41 | 2.16 |
| ⊕ Nabors Industries | Energy | 22.2 | 47.69 | 2.14 |
| ⊕ BJ Services | Energy | 26.6 | 58.54 | 2.08 |
| ⊕ Noble | Energy | 39.0 | 42.05 | 1.96 |

### Current Investment Style

Value Blnd Growth — Large Mid Small

| | Market Cap | % |
|---|---|---|
| | Giant | 42.2 |
| | Large | 55.0 |
| | Mid | 2.8 |
| | Small | 0.0 |
| | Micro | 0.0 |

Avg $mil: 45,938

| Value Measures | | Rel Category |
|---|---|---|
| Price/Earnings | 10.89 | 0.72 |
| Price/Book | 2.79 | 1.02 |
| Price/Sales | 1.04 | 0.75 |
| Price/Cash Flow | 7.23 | 0.77 |
| Dividend Yield % | 1.27 | 1.06 |

| Growth Measures | % | Rel Category |
|---|---|---|
| Long-Term Erngs | 8.07 | 0.77 |
| Book Value | 12.01 | 1.72 |
| Sales | 17.96 | 1.29 |
| Cash Flow | 24.91 | 1.31 |
| Historical Erngs | 44.71 | 1.35 |

| Profitability | % | Rel Category |
|---|---|---|
| Return on Equity | 23.90 | 1.51 |
| Return on Assets | 11.00 | 1.57 |
| Net Margin | 14.24 | 1.52 |

| Industry Weightings | % of Stocks | Rel Cat |
|---|---|---|
| Oil & Gas | 69.9 | 1.8 |
| Oil/Gas Products | 5.1 | 1.3 |
| Oil & Gas Srv | 22.3 | 0.8 |
| Pipelines | 2.7 | 1.8 |
| Utilities | 0.0 | 0.0 |
| Hard Commd | 0.0 | 0.0 |
| Soft Commd | 0.0 | 0.0 |
| Misc. Indstrl | 0.0 | 0.0 |
| Other | 0.0 | 0.0 |

**Composition**

| | | |
|---|---|---|
| ● Cash | 0.4 | |
| ● Stocks | 99.6 | |
| ● Bonds | 0.0 | |
| ● Other | 0.0 | |
| Foreign | 0.0 | (% of Stock) |

## Morningstar's Take by Dan Culloton

Energy Select Sector SPDR suffers from an oil glut.

It's the oldest and largest natural-resources index fund in terms of net assets. There are no surprises in the portfolio. Because its benchmark draws its constituents from the S&P 500, they all tend to be well-known domestic companies. Large integrated oil companies, such as ExxonMobil and Chevron, play huge roles among the nearly 30 stocks in this portfolio. Its 0.27% expense ratio also is the cheapest among its traditional and exchange-traded peers.

The fund also is coming off a tremendous run. It gained nearly 33% annualized in the three-year period ending in October 2005 as rising crude prices fueled an oil industry rally. Furthermore, increased consumption in China and the U.S. as well as depleted reserves and the need for new exploration and production could continue to buoy this fund's holdings.

Closer inspection, though, shows the fund is a concentrated bet on big domestic oil companies. It keeps nearly two thirds of its assets in its top 10 holdings, and virtually all of those positions are devoted to major U.S.-based oil and oil-services stocks. ExxonMobil and ChevronTexaco take up one fourth of the portfolio's assets.

The fund also is less global and diversified by sector than its peers are. The typical natural resources fund has leeway to own stocks outside of the U.S. and the energy sector. Large foreign energy firms such as London-based BP and France's Total SA play a bigger role in other portfolios. So do industrial-material stocks, which make up 21% of the average natural resources fund's assets. Focusing on huge oil companies is great when conditions favor them, but the sector is volatile and this fund's concentration has hampered it over time.

Furthermore, many of the ETF's largest holdings are widely held by more diversified stock funds. Investors should check their energy exposure before considering this ETF.

| Address: | c/o State Street Bk&Tr, 225 Franklin St Boston MA 02210 800-843-2639 | Management Fee: | 0.05% | | |
|---|---|---|---|---|---|
| | | Expense Projections: | 3Yr:$87 | 5Yr:$152 | 10Yr:$345 |
| Web Address: | www.spdrindex.com | Income Distrib: | Quarterly | | |
| Inception: | 12-22-98 * | Exchange: | AMEX | | |
| Advisor: | SSGA Funds Management, Inc. | | | | |

# Fidelity Nasdaq Comp Trac

| Ticker | NAV | Market Price | 52 wk High/Low | Yield | Mstar Category |
|---|---|---|---|---|---|
| ONEQ | $86.62 | $91.12 | $91.12 - $75.00 | 0.4% | Large Growth |

## Management

### Portfolio Manager(s)

Geode Capital Management, which manages five other conventional Fidelity stock and bond index funds since August of 2003, has managed the fund since its inception. Geode is a four-year-old Boston-based quantitative money manager. It was spun off from Fidelity to develop and manage quantitative investment strategies for stock funds. Jeffrey Adams, head of indexing for Geode, leads this fund's management team. Adams has been with Geode since 2003. Before that he worked for State Street Global advisors, including seven years as a portfolio manager.

### Strategy

This fund tracks the Nasdaq Composite Index, which includes all of the domestic- and foreign-based stocks listed on the Nasdaq stock market. The bogy includes more than 3,000 stocks but still has large concentrations of technology and cutting edge health-care companies. The Nasdaq Composite differs from the more popular Nasdaq 100 in two ways: The composite includes financial stocks and owns more small-cap securities. The overall sector exposures are similar, though. This ETF uses a representative sampling approach to tracking the benchmark. That means it doesn't own every security in the bogy.

### Growth of $10,000

— Investment Value of ETF
— Investment Value of Index S&P 500

| | 1996 | 1997 | 1998 | 1999 | 2000 | 2001 | 2002 | 2003 | 2004 | 2005 | History |
|---|---|---|---|---|---|---|---|---|---|---|---|
| | — | — | — | — | — | — | — | 80.06 | 85.82 | 86.62 | NAV $ |
| | — | — | — | — | — | — | — | 79.81 | 85.84 | 86.62 | Market Price $ |
| | — | — | — | — | — | — | — | 9.14* | 8.52 | 1.92 | NAV Return% |
| | — | — | — | — | — | — | — | 9.14* | 8.89 | 1.89 | Market Price Return% |
| | — | — | — | — | — | — | — | -0.15 | -0.06 | -0.07 | Avg Premium/Discount% |
| | — | — | — | — | — | — | — | 9.14 | -2.35 | -2.99 | NAV Rtrn% +/-S&P 500 |
| | — | — | — | — | — | — | — | 9.14 | 2.22 | -3.34 | NAV Rtrn% +/-Russ 1000Gr |
| | — | — | — | — | — | — | — | — | 6 | 9 | NAV Return% Rank in Cat |
| | — | — | — | — | — | — | — | 0.00 | 1.29 | 0.40 | Income Return % |
| | — | — | — | — | — | — | — | — | 7.23 | 1.52 | Capital Return % |
| | — | — | — | — | — | — | — | 0.07 | 1.03 | 0.34 | Income $ |
| | — | — | — | — | — | — | — | 0.00 | 0.00 | 0.50 | Capital Gains $ |
| | — | — | — | — | — | — | — | 0.45 | 0.30 | — | Expense Ratio % |
| | — | — | — | — | — | — | — | 0.31 | 1.26 | — | Income Ratio % |
| | — | — | — | — | — | — | — | 55 | 8 | — | Turnover Rate % |
| | — | — | — | — | — | — | — | 184 | 137 | 121 | Net Assets $mil |

## Performance

### Historic Quarterly NAV Returns

| | 1st Qtr | 2nd Qtr | 3rd Qtr | 4th Qtr | Total |
|---|---|---|---|---|---|
| 2001 | — | — | — | — | — |
| 2002 | — | — | — | — | — |
| 2003 | — | — | — | 12.10 | —* |
| 2004 | -0.59 | 2.83 | -7.36 | 14.59 | 8.52 |
| 2005 | -8.05 | 3.03 | 4.81 | 2.65 | 1.92 |

| Trailing | NAV Return% | Market Return% | NAV Rtrn% +/-S&P 500 | %Rank Cat.(NAV) |
|---|---|---|---|---|
| 3 Mo | 2.65 | 2.77 | 0.57 | 10 |
| 6 Mo | 7.58 | 7.72 | 1.82 | 10 |
| 1 Yr | 1.92 | 1.89 | -2.99 | 9 |
| 3 Yr Avg | — | — | — | 0 |
| 5 Yr Avg | — | — | — | 0 |
| 10 Yr Avg | — | — | — | 0 |

| Tax Analysis | Tax-Adj Return% | Tax-Cost Ratio |
|---|---|---|
| 3 Yr (estimated) | — | — |
| 5 Yr (estimated) | — | — |
| 10 Yr (estimated) | — | — |

## Risk Profile

| | Standard Index S&P 500 | Best Fit Index |
|---|---|---|
| Alpha | — | — |
| Beta | — | — |
| R-Squared | — | — |
| Standard Deviation | — | |
| Mean | — | |
| Sharpe Ratio | — | |

## Morningstar Fair Value

| Price/Fair Value Ratio | Fair Value Estimate ($) | Hit Rate % |
|---|---|---|
| 1.0 Fairly valued | 26.90 | 73 Fair |

## Portfolio Analysis 08-31-05

Share change since 05-05  Total Stocks:1891

| | Sector | PE | Tot Ret% | % Assets |
|---|---|---|---|---|
| ⊖ Microsoft | Software | 22.2 | -0.95 | 9.02 |
| ⊖ Intel | Hardware | 18.6 | 8.12 | 4.83 |
| ⊖ Cisco Systems | Hardware | 19.9 | -11.39 | 3.43 |
| ⊖ Amgen | Health | 28.3 | 22.93 | 3.01 |
| ⊖ Dell | Hardware | 23.2 | -28.93 | 2.63 |
| ⊖ Oracle | Software | 22.2 | -11.01 | 2.03 |
| ⊖ Qualcomm | Hardware | 34.2 | 2.50 | 1.98 |
| ⊖ eBay | Consumer | 59.2 | -25.70 | 1.67 |
| ⊖ Google | Business | — | 115.19 | 1.56 |
| ⊖ Yahoo | Media | 36.3 | 3.98 | 1.42 |
| ⊖ Comcast A | Media | 47.1 | -22.12 | 1.29 |
| ⊖ Apple Computer | Hardware | 46.1 | 123.26 | 1.17 |
| ⊖ Applied Materials | Hardware | 24.6 | 5.46 | 0.92 |
| ⊖ Comcast | Media | — | — | 0.76 |
| ⊕ Symantec | Software | 53.0 | -32.07 | 0.76 |
| ⊖ Fifth Third Bancorp | Financial | 15.2 | -17.26 | 0.69 |
| ⊖ Sears Holdings | Consumer | 22.7 | 16.76 | 0.67 |
| ⊖ Costco Wholesale | Consumer | 22.7 | 3.09 | 0.63 |
| ⊖ Gilead Sciences | Health | 38.1 | 50.24 | 0.59 |
| ⊖ Starbucks | Consumer | 49.2 | -3.75 | 0.59 |

### Current Investment Style

Value Blnd Growth — Large Mid Small

| Market Cap | % |
|---|---|
| Giant | 33.8 |
| Large | 16.9 |
| Mid | 23.2 |
| Small | 16.4 |
| Micro | 9.6 |

Avg $mil: 9,598

| Value Measures | | Rel Category |
|---|---|---|
| Price/Earnings | 21.96 | 1.04 |
| Price/Book | 2.99 | 0.89 |
| Price/Sales | 2.10 | 1.08 |
| Price/Cash Flow | 9.72 | 0.93 |
| Dividend Yield % | 0.56 | 0.63 |

| Growth Measures | % | Rel Category |
|---|---|---|
| Long-Term Erngs | 15.17 | 1.08 |
| Book Value | 5.58 | 0.68 |
| Sales | 6.06 | 0.54 |
| Cash Flow | 16.43 | 1.01 |
| Historical Erngs | 16.47 | 0.86 |

| Profitability | % | Rel Category |
|---|---|---|
| Return on Equity | 15.72 | 0.78 |
| Return on Assets | 9.73 | 0.90 |
| Net Margin | 15.94 | 1.14 |

| Sector Weightings | % of Stocks | Rel S&P 500 | 3 Year High Low | |
|---|---|---|---|---|
| ⌒ Info | 51.27 | 2.54 | | |
| Software | 17.83 | 5.01 | 19 | 18 |
| Hardware | 25.90 | 2.58 | 32 | 26 |
| Media | 5.49 | 1.53 | 6 | 5 |
| Telecom | 2.05 | 0.68 | 3 | 2 |
| ⌒ Service | 42.57 | 0.92 | | |
| Health | 14.04 | 1.06 | 14 | 12 |
| Consumer | 10.19 | 1.25 | 11 | 9 |
| Business | 7.63 | 1.97 | 8 | 6 |
| Financial | 10.71 | 0.51 | 12 | 10 |
| ⌒ Mfg | 6.17 | 0.18 | | |
| Goods | 1.49 | 0.17 | 2 | 1 |
| Ind Mtrls | 3.48 | 0.29 | 4 | 3 |
| Energy | 1.02 | 0.11 | 1 | 0 |
| Utilities | 0.18 | 0.05 | 0 | 0 |

### Composition

| | |
|---|---|
| ● Cash | 0.5 |
| ● Stocks | 98.9 |
| ● Bonds | 0.0 |
| ● Other | 0.6 |
| Foreign | 4.1 |
| (% of Stock) | |

## Morningstar's Take  by Dan Culloton

This exchange-traded fund doesn't get any love. Should it?

Fidelity Nasdaq Composite Tracking ETF offers exposure to nearly 1,800 stocks in one transaction. Its 0.30% expense ratio is a sliver of the median levy for conventional no-load large-cap growth funds. The six-letter acronym in its name usually draws aggressive investors like kids to an ice cream truck. A fund this cheap, diversified, and well branded should be an easy sell.

It hasn't been, though, and with good reason. This offering, sponsored by one of the world's biggest money managers, is small and infrequently traded. The problem is this vehicle, which is billed as a less intense way to get exposure to the Nasdaq than offered by the Qubes, isn't really that much different. The offering, which is the only ETF that tries to replicate the returns of the whole Nasdaq Composite, owns more stocks, but its exposures and attendant risks are similar to the Qubes. This ETF owns financial stocks, which the

Qubes exclude, but it still keeps nearly half its assets in hardware and software stocks and maintains a healthy biotech weighting. That makes the ETF prone to dips when tech is out of favor.

Other traits make this ETF a less than perfect core growth holding. It only owns securities listed on the Nasdaq stock market. Most indexes and active managers don't limit themselves to one exchange. Indeed, the restriction excludes widely held growth stocks, such as UnitedHealth Group, Medtronic and Texas Instruments. So this ETF offers an incomplete representation of the growth stock universe.

Furthermore, the ETF's expense ratio doesn't look so cheap next to exchange-traded rivals. Its levy is 50% more expensive than that of the Qubes and 100% more costly than the expense ratio of the lowest-cost large-growth ETF.

There's no sense in loving a fund like that.

| Address: | 82 Devonshire St Boston MA 02109 800-544-6666 |
|---|---|
| Web Address: | www.fidelity.com |
| Inception: | 09-25-03* |
| Advisor: | Fidelity Management & Research (FMR) |

| Management Fee: | 0.24% | | |
|---|---|---|---|
| Expense Projections: | 3Yr:$97 | 5Yr:$169 | 10Yr:$381 |
| Income Distrib: | Quarterly | | |
| Exchange: | AMEX | | |

MORNINGSTAR® ETFs 100

# Financial SPDR

| | Ticker | NAV | Market Price | 52 wk High/Low | Yield | Mstar Category |
|---|---|---|---|---|---|---|
| | XLF | $31.69 | $32.59 | $32.59 - $27.65 | 2.2% | Specialty-Financial |

## Management

### Portfolio Manager(s)

State Street Global Advisors serves as advisor to the trust, but the creation of the index tracked by the portfolio falls to Merrill Lynch Pierce Fenner & Smith. They allocate stocks in the S&P 500 to the sector they think is appropriate. The American Stock Exchange Index Services Group rebalances holdings based on periodic index adjustments and diversification requirements.

### Strategy

This fund contains all the financial companies in the S&P 500 Index, which screens its components for profitability, industry leadership, and certain trading criteria. The index is limited to U.S. companies, which eliminates some big international players. The fund holds more than 80 stocks, giving it a certain level of diversification, but it is top-heavy: nearly half of its assets are in its largest 10 positions. The S&P 500 committee rebalances the index every quarter and on special occasions.

**Growth of $10,000**

— Investment Value of ETF
— Investment Value of Index S&P 500

| 1996 | 1997 | 1998 | 1999 | 2000 | 2001 | 2002 | 2003 | 2004 | 2005 | History |
|---|---|---|---|---|---|---|---|---|---|---|
| — | — | 23.33 | 23.84 | 29.50 | 26.40 | 22.05 | 28.22 | 30.55 | 31.69 | NAV $ |
| — | — | 23.44 | 23.77 | 29.50 | 26.30 | 22.00 | 28.13 | 30.53 | 31.67 | Market Price $ |
| — | — | 6.42* | 3.46 | 25.50 | -9.07 | -14.88 | 30.60 | 10.58 | 6.20 | NAV Return% |
| — | — | 6.35* | 2.67 | 25.87 | -9.42 | -14.75 | 30.48 | 10.87 | 6.20 | Market Price Return% |
| — | — | 0.47 | 0.02 | 0.42 | -0.10 | -0.06 | -0.04 | -0.06 | -0.00 | Avg Premium/Discount% |
| — | — | 6.42 | -17.58 | 34.60 | 2.81 | 7.21 | 1.93 | -0.29 | 1.29 | NAV Rtrn% +/-S&P 500 |
| — | — | 6.42 | 1.94 | -1.44 | -2.69 | -2.53 | -1.63 | -2.81 | -0.25 | NAV Rtrn% +/-DJ Finance |
| — | — | — | 1 | 1 | 3 | 4 | 5 | 5 | 5 | NAV Return% Rank in Cat |
| — | — | — | 1.29 | 1.53 | 1.37 | 1.70 | 2.36 | 2.23 | 2.35 | Income Return % |
| — | — | — | 2.17 | 23.97 | -10.44 | -16.58 | 28.24 | 8.35 | 3.85 | Capital Return % |
| — | — | 0.00 | 0.30 | 0.36 | 0.40 | 0.45 | 0.52 | 0.63 | 0.71 | Income $ |
| — | — | 0.00 | 0.00 | 0.00 | 0.00 | 0.00 | 0.00 | 0.00 | 0.00 | Capital Gains $ |
| — | — | — | 0.57 | 0.44 | 0.27 | 0.27 | 0.28 | 0.26 | 0.26 | Expense Ratio % |
| — | — | — | 1.14 | 1.45 | 1.43 | 1.70 | 2.09 | 2.14 | 2.30 | Income Ratio % |
| — | — | — | 6 | 7 | 9 | 11 | 6 | 9 | 9 | Turnover Rate % |
| — | — | — | — | — | — | 451 | 802 | 1,140 | 1,872 | Net Assets $mil |

## Performance

### Historic Quarterly NAV Returns

| | 1st Qtr | 2nd Qtr | 3rd Qtr | 4th Qtr | Total |
|---|---|---|---|---|---|
| 2001 | -9.63 | 7.81 | -13.07 | 7.35 | -9.07 |
| 2002 | 3.40 | -7.49 | -17.11 | 7.36 | -14.88 |
| 2003 | -5.16 | 18.37 | 4.12 | 11.74 | 30.60 |
| 2004 | 4.79 | -2.43 | 0.31 | 7.82 | 10.58 |
| 2005 | -6.42 | 4.25 | 0.67 | 8.15 | 6.20 |

| Trailing | NAV Return% | Market Return% | NAV Rtrn% +/-S&P 500 | %Rank Cat.(NAV) |
|---|---|---|---|---|
| 3 Mo | 8.15 | 7.98 | 6.07 | 5 |
| 6 Mo | 8.87 | 8.79 | 3.11 | 5 |
| 1 Yr | 6.20 | 6.20 | 1.29 | 5 |
| 3 Yr Avg | 15.32 | 15.39 | 0.94 | 4 |
| 5 Yr Avg | 3.49 | 3.48 | 2.95 | 3 |
| 10 Yr Avg | — | — | — | 0 |

| Tax Analysis | Tax-Adj Return% | Tax-Cost Ratio |
|---|---|---|
| 3 Yr (estimated) | 14.45 | 0.75 |
| 5 Yr (estimated) | 2.74 | 0.72 |
| 10 Yr (estimated) | — | — |

## Risk Profile

| | Standard Index S&P 500 | Best Fit Index DJ Finance |
|---|---|---|
| Alpha | 0.8 | -1.5 |
| Beta | 1.02 | 1.01 |
| R-Squared | 68 | 99 |
| Standard Deviation | 11.40 | |
| Mean | 15.32 | |
| Sharpe Ratio | 1.14 | |

## Morningstar Fair Value

| Price/Fair Value Ratio | Fair Value Estimate ($) | Hit Rate % |
|---|---|---|
| 0.9 Undervalued | 50.62 | 94 Good |

## Portfolio Analysis 12-31-05

Share change since 11-05  Total Stocks:85

| | Sector | PE | Tot Ret% | % Assets |
|---|---|---|---|---|
| ⊕ Citigroup | Financial | 12.1 | 4.63 | 10.20 |
| ⊕ Bank of America | Financial | 11.1 | 2.39 | 7.68 |
| ⊕ American International G | Financial | 15.6 | 4.83 | 7.35 |
| ⊕ J.P. Morgan Chase & Co. | Financial | 18.8 | 5.74 | 5.77 |
| ⊕ Wells Fargo | Financial | 14.3 | 4.47 | 4.36 |
| ⊕ Wachovia | Financial | 13.0 | 4.29 | 3.40 |
| ⊕ American Express | Financial | 16.4 | 5.31 | 2.64 |
| ⊕ Merrill Lynch & Company | Financial | 13.7 | 14.77 | 2.58 |
| ⊕ Morgan Stanley | Financial | 13.3 | 4.28 | 2.54 |
| ⊕ Goldman Sachs Group | Financial | 12.4 | 23.89 | 2.39 |
| ⊕ US Bancorp | Financial | 12.7 | -0.46 | 2.25 |
| ⊕ Fannie Mae | Financial | — | -30.14 | 1.95 |
| ⊕ Freddie Mac | Financial | 16.6 | -9.16 | 1.87 |
| ⊕ Washington Mutual | Financial | 11.9 | 7.79 | 1.78 |
| ⊕ Metropolitan Life Insura | Financial | 11.8 | 22.22 | 1.53 |
| ⊕ Prudential Financial | Financial | 11.7 | 34.54 | 1.53 |
| ⊕ Allstate | Financial | 18.2 | 6.93 | 1.45 |
| ⊕ Lehman Brothers Holdings | Financial | 12.7 | 47.67 | 1.42 |
| ⊕ MBNA | Financial | — | — | 1.41 |
| ⊕ St. Paul Travelers Compa | Financial | 13.9 | 23.20 | 1.28 |

### Current Investment Style

Value Blnd Growth — Large Mid Small

| Market Cap | % |
|---|---|
| Giant | 51.7 |
| Large | 41.8 |
| Mid | 6.5 |
| Small | 0.0 |
| Micro | 0.0 |

Avg $mil: 51,985

| Value Measures | | Rel Category |
|---|---|---|
| Price/Earnings | 13.20 | 1.02 |
| Price/Book | 1.71 | 1.01 |
| Price/Sales | 2.37 | 0.94 |
| Price/Cash Flow | 2.17 | 0.57 |
| Dividend Yield % | 2.62 | 0.89 |

| Growth Measures | % | Rel Category |
|---|---|---|
| Long-Term Erngs | 10.46 | 1.01 |
| Book Value | 15.21 | 1.01 |
| Sales | 6.81 | 1.16 |
| Cash Flow | 31.54 | 2.51 |
| Historical Erngs | 12.00 | 1.00 |

| Profitability | % | Rel Category |
|---|---|---|
| Return on Equity | 16.42 | 1.03 |
| Return on Assets | 15.87 | 1.13 |
| Net Margin | 21.05 | 0.97 |

| Industry Weightings | % of Stocks | Rel Cat |
|---|---|---|
| Intl Banks | 27.6 | 1.7 |
| Banks | 19.1 | 0.9 |
| Real Estate | 3.4 | 1.0 |
| Sec Mgmt | 12.3 | 1.0 |
| S & Ls | 3.7 | 0.5 |
| Prop & Reins | 15.6 | 1.0 |
| Life Ins | 6.3 | 1.2 |
| Misc. Ins | 2.0 | 0.7 |
| Other | 10.0 | 0.7 |

### Composition

| | % |
|---|---|
| ● Cash | 0.6 |
| ● Stocks | 99.4 |
| ● Bonds | 0.0 |
| Other | 0.0 |
| Foreign (% of Stock) | 0.0 |

## Morningstar's Take  by Dan Culloton

Financial Select Sector SPDR is a convenient, but imperfect way to get exposure to financial services stocks.

Like other members of the Select Sector exchange-traded fund family, this offering carves out a sector's stocks from the S&P 500 Index and groups them together in one package. In this case the ETF holds the venerable index's financial services denizens. Sector bellwethers, such as Citigroup, Bank of America, and American International Group, play prominent roles among the 82 stocks in this portfolio.

Because this fund's benchmark is an offspring of the S&P 500, you know you're getting exposure to established domestic companies. The S&P index selection committee requires constituents to be profitable and headquartered in the U.S. That explains the fund's bias toward the sector's established giants (where it keeps more than half of its assets) and illuminates its lagging performance relative to other traditional financial services funds

that have the liberty to own more small cap and international stocks in recent years.

Indeed, this ETF's concentration is one of its main drawbacks. Although it owns plenty of stocks, it clusters its assets at the top of the portfolio and places a lot of weight on individual positions. More than a third of the fund's money is packed into its top five holdings including a nearly 11% weighting in Citigroup. It's not surprising that this ETF's volatility, as measured by standard deviation, has been above the specialty-financial category average and its risk adjusted returns, as gauged by its Sharpe ratio, are below average.

To its credit, this ETF is cheap. Its 0.26% expense ratio is a fraction of the average traditional financial services mutual fund and competitive with the most affordable ETFs in the sector. However, it's possible to get broader exposure to this area of the market elsewhere.

| Address: | c/o State Street Bk&Tr, 225 Franklin St Boston MA 02210 800-843-2639 |
|---|---|
| Web Address: | www.spdrindex.com |
| Inception: | 12-22-98 * |
| Advisor: | SSGA Funds Management, Inc. |

| Management Fee: | 0.05% | | |
|---|---|---|---|
| Expense Projections: | 3Yr:$84 | 5Yr:$147 | 10Yr:$333 |
| Income Distrib: | Quarterly | | |
| Exchange: | AMEX | | |

**MORNINGSTAR® ETFs 100**

Data through December 31, 2005

# Health Care Sel SPDR

| | Ticker | NAV | Market Price | 52 wk High/Low | Yield | Mstar Category |
|---|---|---|---|---|---|---|
| | XLV | $31.72 | $32.59 | $32.71 - $29.12 | 1.3% | Specialty-Health |

## Management

### Portfolio Manager(s)

State Street Global Advisors serves as advisor to the trust, but the creation of the index tracked by the portfolio falls to Merrill Lynch, Pierce, Fenner & Smith. It allocates stocks in the S&P 500 to the sector it thinks is appropriate. The American Stock Exchange Index Services Group rebalances holdings based on periodic index adjustments and diversification requirements.

### Strategy

This ETF owns the health-care companies in the S&P 500. The bogy includes companies from a number of industries, including health equipment and supplies, hospitals and health-care providers, medical devices, health insurers, biotechnology, and drugs. Because the index draws its constituents from the broader S&P 500, it has an inherent quality screen. S&P 500 holdings have to meet the standards of the S&P's selection committee, and this includes profitability and status as a leading U.S. company. Unfortunately, the criteria eliminate large foreign-based health-care companies.

**Growth of $10,000**

— Investment Value of ETF
— Investment Value of Index S&P 500

| | 1996 | 1997 | 1998 | 1999 | 2000 | 2001 | 2002 | 2003 | 2004 | 2005 | History |
|---|---|---|---|---|---|---|---|---|---|---|---|
| | — | — | 25.93 | 30.96 | 27.32 | 27.19 | 26.54 | 30.09 | 30.18 | 31.72 | NAV $ |
| | — | — | 26.00 | 30.89 | 27.25 | 26.95 | 26.55 | 30.15 | 30.19 | 31.72 | Market Price $ |
| | — | — | 4.24* | 20.10 | -11.57 | -0.20 | -1.66 | 14.75 | 1.44 | 6.44 | NAV Return% |
| | — | — | 4.23* | 19.51 | -11.60 | -0.82 | -0.75 | 14.92 | 1.28 | 6.41 | Market Price Return% |
| | — | — | 0.27 | -0.08 | -0.09 | -0.24 | 0.10 | 0.01 | 0.10 | 0.01 | Avg Premium/Discount% |
| | — | — | 4.24 | -0.94 | -2.47 | 11.68 | 20.43 | -13.92 | -9.43 | 1.53 | NAV Rtrn% +/-S&P 500 |
| | — | — | 4.24 | 24.13 | -49.04 | 12.41 | 19.15 | -4.68 | -3.11 | -1.88 | NAV Rtrn% +/-DJ Hlthcare |
| | — | — | — | 1 | 1 | 2 | 4 | 5 | 5 | 5 | NAV Return% Rank in Cat |
| | — | — | — | 0.00 | 0.17 | 0.27 | 0.73 | 1.31 | 1.14 | 1.32 | Income Return % |
| | — | — | — | 20.10 | -11.74 | -0.47 | -2.39 | 13.44 | 0.30 | 5.12 | Capital Return % |
| | — | — | 0.00 | 0.00 | 0.05 | 0.07 | 0.20 | 0.35 | 0.34 | 0.40 | Income $ |
| | — | — | 0.00 | 0.18 | 0.01 | 0.00 | 0.00 | 0.00 | 0.00 | 0.00 | Capital Gains $ |
| | — | — | — | 0.57 | 0.42 | 0.28 | 0.28 | 0.28 | 0.27 | 0.26 | Expense Ratio % |
| | — | — | — | -0.11 | 0.10 | 0.26 | 0.49 | 1.21 | 1.20 | 1.20 | Income Ratio % |
| | — | — | — | 15 | 22 | 28 | 103 | 6 | 7 | 3 | Turnover Rate % |
| | — | — | — | — | — | — | 158 | 454 | 1,053 | 1,787 | Net Assets $mil |

## Performance

**Historic Quarterly NAV Returns**

| | 1st Qtr | 2nd Qtr | 3rd Qtr | 4th Qtr | Total |
|---|---|---|---|---|---|
| 2001 | -1.15 | 9.49 | -20.27 | 15.66 | -0.20 |
| 2002 | 8.50 | -6.93 | -7.29 | 5.04 | -1.66 |
| 2003 | 0.94 | 9.86 | -4.51 | 8.37 | 14.75 |
| 2004 | -0.49 | 2.61 | -5.51 | 5.14 | 1.44 |
| 2005 | -0.68 | 4.08 | 1.50 | 1.44 | 6.44 |

| Trailing | NAV Return% | Market Return% | NAV Rtrn% +/-S&P 500 | %Rank Cat.(NAV) |
|---|---|---|---|---|
| 3 Mo | 1.44 | 1.51 | -0.64 | 7 |
| 6 Mo | 2.96 | 2.86 | -2.80 | 7 |
| 1 Yr | 6.44 | 6.41 | 1.53 | 5 |
| 3 Yr Avg | 7.40 | 7.39 | -6.98 | 4 |
| 5 Yr Avg | 3.99 | 4.04 | 3.45 | 2 |
| 10 Yr Avg | — | — | — | 0 |

| Tax Analysis | Tax-Adj Return% | Tax-Cost Ratio |
|---|---|---|
| 3 Yr (estimated) | 6.95 | 0.42 |
| 5 Yr (estimated) | 3.64 | 0.34 |
| 10 Yr (estimated) | — | — |

## Risk Profile

| | Standard Index S&P 500 | Best Fit Index DJ Hlthcare |
|---|---|---|
| Alpha | -0.6 | -3.0 |
| Beta | 0.52 | 1.01 |
| R-Squared | 26 | 98 |
| Standard Deviation | 9.39 | |
| Mean | 7.40 | |
| Sharpe Ratio | 0.60 | |

## Morningstar Fair Value

| Price/Fair Value Ratio | Fair Value Estimate ($) | Hit Rate % |
|---|---|---|
| 1.0 Fairly valued | 43.61 | 99 Good |

## Portfolio Analysis 12-31-05

| Share change since 11-05 Total Stocks:57 | Sector | PE | Tot Ret% | % Assets |
|---|---|---|---|---|
| ⊖ Johnson & Johnson | Health | 19.1 | -3.36 | 11.82 |
| ⊖ Pfizer | Health | 21.2 | -10.62 | 11.36 |
| ⊖ Amgen | Health | 28.3 | 22.93 | 6.44 |
| ⊕ UnitedHealth Group | Health | 26.2 | 41.22 | 5.65 |
| ⊖ Medtronic | Health | 37.4 | 16.72 | 4.63 |
| ⊖ Merck | Health | 15.2 | 4.04 | 4.60 |
| ⊖ Eli Lilly & Company | Health | 48.4 | 2.52 | 4.25 |
| ⊖ Wyeth | Health | 54.2 | 10.54 | 4.11 |
| ⊕ WellPoint | Health | 24.7 | 38.77 | 3.57 |
| ⊕ Abbott Laboratories | Health | 18.3 | -13.47 | 3.43 |
| ⊖ Bristol-Myers Squibb | Health | 17.1 | -6.16 | 2.99 |
| ⊖ Schering-Plough | Health | — | 0.95 | 2.06 |
| ⊖ Cardinal Health | Health | 28.3 | 18.63 | 1.97 |
| ⊖ Aetna | Health | 18.9 | 51.27 | 1.83 |
| ⊕ Gilead Sciences | Health | 38.1 | 50.24 | 1.60 |
| ⊖ Baxter International | Health | 30.6 | 10.63 | 1.58 |
| ⊖ Caremark RX | Health | 27.7 | 31.35 | 1.54 |
| ⊕ Guidant | Health | 44.4 | -9.68 | 1.44 |
| ⊕ HCA | Health | 16.0 | 27.87 | 1.44 |
| ⊖ St. Jude Medical | Health | 36.9 | 19.72 | 1.25 |

**Current Investment Style**

Value Blnd Growth — Large/Mid/Small

| Market Cap | % |
|---|---|
| Giant | 59.3 |
| Large | 31.6 |
| Mid | 9.1 |
| Small | 0.0 |
| Micro | 0.0 |

Avg $mil: 46,240

| Value Measures | | Rel Category |
|---|---|---|
| Price/Earnings | 18.08 | 0.78 |
| Price/Book | 2.57 | 0.79 |
| Price/Sales | 1.65 | 0.45 |
| Price/Cash Flow | 11.84 | 0.77 |
| Dividend Yield % | 1.48 | 1.45 |

| Growth Measures | % | Rel Category |
|---|---|---|
| Long-Term Erngs | 11.85 | 0.81 |
| Book Value | 20.35 | 1.66 |
| Sales | 13.30 | 0.92 |
| Cash Flow | 17.49 | 1.15 |
| Historical Erngs | 11.82 | 1.01 |

| Profitability | % | Rel Category |
|---|---|---|
| Return on Equity | 17.37 | 1.36 |
| Return on Assets | 9.47 | 1.70 |
| Net Margin | 13.20 | 1.09 |

| Industry Weightings | % of Stocks | Rel Cat |
|---|---|---|
| Biotech | 12.3 | 0.4 |
| Drugs | 47.5 | 1.8 |
| Mgd Care | 11.2 | 1.5 |
| Hospitals | 2.2 | 1.0 |
| Other HC Srv | 0.2 | 0.1 |
| Diagnostics | 1.1 | 0.9 |
| Equipment | 15.6 | 1.1 |
| Good/Srv | 9.2 | 1.0 |
| Other | 0.6 | 0.3 |

**Composition**

| | | |
|---|---|---|
| ● Cash | 0.3 | |
| ● Stocks | 99.7 | |
| ● Bonds | 0.0 | |
| ● Other | 0.0 | |
| Foreign (% of Stock) | 0.0 | |

## Morningstar's Take by Dan Culloton

Health-care stocks may look attractive, but Health Care Select Sector SPDR still has some warts.

Morningstar research indicates this fund was slightly undervalued at the end of October 2005. Morningstar's stock analysts cover and have set fair values for stocks representing 96% of this ETF's total asset value. We compared an average of all the fair values in the fund at the end of October 2005 with an average of their share prices. By that measure this ETF's holdings were trading about 9% below fair value.

That's not surprising given the fact that some of this fund's top holdings in the drug industry have been out of favor due to patent problems, thin product pipelines, regulatory uncertainty, and safety concerns. Six of this fund's top-five holdings were trading more than 10% below their Morningstar fair value estimates on Oct. 31, 2005.

That doesn't make this fund a sure thing. The challenges confronting the undervalued denizens of this portfolio could weigh on them for some time.

For instance, Merck faces years of litigation in the wake of its decision to yank its Vioxx painkiller from the market due to potentially deadly side effects.

That's why a more diversified offering may be in order. This ETF tracks a concentrated index of the health-care stocks in the S&P 500. It owns about 50 stocks and packs 60% of its money in its top-10 holdings. The ETF also is heavily reliant on U.S.-based mega-cap stocks in the sector, particularly pharmaceutical stocks such as Johnson & Johnson and Pfizer, which together take up one fourth of the ETF's assets.

So this fund is risky. It has lost money in 13 of the 27 quarters since its inception. The typical health-care fund has shed money in 11 of those same periods.

Similarly priced funds could offer a smoother ride. Vanguard Health Care Vipers, for example, owns more stocks across the market-cap spectrum.

| Address: | c/o State Street Bk&Tr, 225 Franklin St Boston MA 02210 800-843-2639 |
|---|---|
| Web Address: | www.spdrindex.com |
| Inception: | 12-22-98* |
| Advisor: | SSGA Funds Management, Inc. |

| Management Fee: | 0.05% | | |
|---|---|---|---|
| Expense Projections: | 3Yr:$87 | 5Yr:$152 | 10Yr:$345 |
| Income Distrib: | Quarterly | | |
| Exchange: | AMEX | | |

**MORNINGSTAR® ETFs 100**

# Industrial SPDR

| | Ticker | NAV | Market Price | 52 wk High/Low | Yield | Mstar Category |
|---|---|---|---|---|---|---|
| | XLI | $31.43 | $31.95 | $32.04 - $28.87 | 1.6% | Large Blend |

## Management

### Portfolio Manager(s)

State Street Global Advisors serves as advisor to the trust, but the creation of the index tracked by the portfolio falls to Merrill Lynch, Pierce, Fenner & Smith. It allocates stocks in the S&P 500 to the sector it thinks is appropriate. The American Stock Exchange Index Services Group rebalances holdings based on periodic index adjustments and diversification requirements.

### Strategy

This exchange-traded offering owns industrial companies in the S&P 500. The bogy includes companies from a number of areas, including manufacturers, builders, railroads, package delivery companies, and aerospace and defense contractors. Because the index draws its constituents from the broader S&P 500 it has an inherent quality screen. S&P 500 holdings have to meet the standards of the S&P's selection committee that include profitability and status as a leading U.S. company.

**Growth of $10,000**
— Investment Value of ETF
— Investment Value of Index S&P 500

| | 1996 | 1997 | 1998 | 1999 | 2000 | 2001 | 2002 | 2003 | 2004 | 2005 | History |
|---|---|---|---|---|---|---|---|---|---|---|---|
| | — | — | 24.37 | 29.58 | 31.29 | 27.73 | 20.55 | 26.84 | 31.08 | 31.43 | NAV $ |
| | — | — | 24.56 | 29.61 | 31.25 | 27.70 | 20.59 | 26.76 | 31.07 | 31.42 | Market Price $ |
| | — | — | 5.80* | 23.06 | 6.97 | -10.21 | -24.81 | 32.50 | 17.44 | 2.75 | NAV Return% |
| | — | — | 5.81* | 22.23 | 6.73 | -10.19 | -24.58 | 31.85 | 17.75 | 2.74 | Market Price Return% |
| | — | — | 0.78 | 0.10 | 0.08 | 0.01 | 0.10 | 0.03 | 0.02 | 0.03 | Avg Premium/Discount% |
| | — | — | 5.80 | 2.02 | 16.07 | 1.67 | -2.72 | 3.83 | 6.57 | -2.16 | NAV Rtrn% +/-S&P 500 |
| | — | — | 5.80 | 2.15 | 14.76 | 2.24 | -3.16 | 2.61 | 6.04 | -3.52 | NAV Rtrn% +/-Russ 1000 |
| | — | — | — | 4 | 4 | 13 | 15 | 15 | 17 | 23 | NAV Return% Rank in Cat |
| | — | — | — | 1.22 | 1.13 | 1.09 | 1.20 | 1.68 | 1.51 | 1.58 | Income Return % |
| | — | — | — | 21.84 | 5.84 | -11.30 | -26.01 | 30.82 | 15.93 | 1.17 | Capital Return % |
| | — | — | 0.00 | 0.30 | 0.33 | 0.34 | 0.33 | 0.34 | 0.40 | 0.49 | Income $ |
| | — | — | 0.00 | 0.08 | 0.00 | 0.00 | 0.00 | 0.00 | 0.00 | 0.00 | Capital Gains $ |
| | — | — | — | 0.57 | 0.44 | 0.28 | 0.28 | 0.27 | 0.28 | 0.25 | Expense Ratio % |
| | — | — | — | 0.94 | 1.10 | 1.25 | 1.26 | 1.59 | 1.44 | 1.54 | Income Ratio % |
| | — | — | — | 12 | 42 | 7 | 58 | 15 | 3 | 6 | Turnover Rate % |
| | — | — | — | — | — | — | 235 | 586 | 780 | 886 | Net Assets $mil |

## Performance

### Historic Quarterly NAV Returns

| | 1st Qtr | 2nd Qtr | 3rd Qtr | 4th Qtr | Total |
|---|---|---|---|---|---|
| 2001 | -14.96 | 9.70 | -18.39 | 17.95 | -10.21 |
| 2002 | -1.59 | -12.13 | -17.93 | 5.96 | -24.81 |
| 2003 | -5.88 | 16.18 | 4.48 | 15.97 | 32.50 |
| 2004 | -1.00 | 8.41 | -0.64 | 10.13 | 17.44 |
| 2005 | -1.81 | -3.10 | 2.92 | 4.93 | 2.75 |

| Trailing | NAV Return% | Market Return% | NAV Rtrn% +/-S&P 500 | %Rank Cat.(NAV) |
|---|---|---|---|---|
| 3 Mo | 4.93 | 4.80 | 2.85 | 27 |
| 6 Mo | 7.99 | 8.01 | 2.23 | 27 |
| 1 Yr | 2.75 | 2.74 | -2.16 | 23 |
| 3 Yr Avg | 16.93 | 16.84 | 2.55 | 14 |
| 5 Yr Avg | 1.54 | 1.56 | 1.00 | 13 |
| 10 Yr Avg | — | — | — | 0 |

| Tax Analysis | Tax-Adj Return% | Tax-Cost Ratio |
|---|---|---|
| 3 Yr (estimated) | 16.33 | 0.51 |
| 5 Yr (estimated) | 1.01 | 0.52 |
| 10 Yr (estimated) | — | — |

## Risk Profile

| | Standard Index S&P 500 | Best Fit Index S&P 500 |
|---|---|---|
| Alpha | 0.5 | 0.5 |
| Beta | 1.17 | 1.17 |
| R-Squared | 82 | 82 |
| Standard Deviation | 11.83 | |
| Mean | 16.93 | |
| Sharpe Ratio | 1.22 | |

## Morningstar Fair Value

| Price/Fair Value Ratio | Fair Value Estimate ($) | Hit Rate % |
|---|---|---|
| 1.0 Fairly valued | 46.58 | 100 Good |

## Portfolio Analysis 12-31-05

| Share change since 11-05 Total Stocks:53 | Sector | PE | Tot Ret% | % Assets |
|---|---|---|---|---|
| ⊕ General Electric | Ind Mtrls | 19.9 | -1.43 | 21.24 |
| ⊕ United Parcel Service B | Business | 22.9 | -10.51 | 6.54 |
| ⊖ 3M Company | Ind Mtrls | 19.2 | -3.51 | 4.68 |
| ⊖ Tyco International | Ind Mtrls | 19.1 | -18.17 | 4.66 |
| ⊖ Boeing | Ind Mtrls | 24.8 | 37.92 | 4.59 |
| ⊖ United Technologies | Ind Mtrls | 17.9 | 10.03 | 4.59 |
| ⊕ Caterpillar | Ind Mtrls | 16.0 | 20.68 | 3.25 |
| ⊕ FedEx | Business | 21.8 | 5.33 | 2.59 |
| ⊕ Honeywell International | Ind Mtrls | 24.0 | 7.52 | 2.57 |
| ⊕ Emerson Electric | Ind Mtrls | 22.0 | 9.22 | 2.53 |
| ⊕ Burlington Northern Sant | Business | 18.7 | 51.72 | 2.30 |
| ⊕ General Dynamics | Ind Mtrls | 16.6 | 10.60 | 1.93 |
| ⊕ Lockheed Martin | Ind Mtrls | 17.5 | 16.50 | 1.87 |
| ⊕ Northrop Grumman | Ind Mtrls | 16.6 | 12.62 | 1.79 |
| ⊕ Union Pacific | Business | 26.4 | 21.82 | 1.79 |
| ⊕ Norfolk Southern | Business | 15.5 | 25.52 | 1.65 |
| ⊖ Raytheon | Ind Mtrls | 20.1 | 5.76 | 1.52 |
| ⊖ Illinois Tool Works | Ind Mtrls | 17.7 | -3.69 | 1.49 |
| ⊖ Cendant | Business | 14.6 | -21.05 | 1.47 |
| ⊖ Waste Management | Business | 14.9 | 4.19 | 1.42 |

### Current Investment Style

Value Blnd Growth — Large / Mid / Small

| Market Cap | % |
|---|---|
| Giant | 47.1 |
| Large | 41.2 |
| Mid | 11.7 |
| Small | 0.0 |
| Micro | 0.0 |

Avg $mil: 43,947

| Value Measures | | Rel Category |
|---|---|---|
| Price/Earnings | 17.67 | 1.04 |
| Price/Book | 2.66 | 0.99 |
| Price/Sales | 1.38 | 1.08 |
| Price/Cash Flow | 9.57 | 1.32 |
| Dividend Yield % | 2.38 | 1.34 |

| Growth Measures | % | Rel Category |
|---|---|---|
| Long-Term Erngs | 12.22 | 1.10 |
| Book Value | 12.29 | 1.31 |
| Sales | 7.99 | 0.99 |
| Cash Flow | 11.06 | 1.07 |
| Historical Erngs | 14.40 | 1.02 |

| Profitability | % | Rel Category |
|---|---|---|
| Return on Equity | 18.45 | 0.90 |
| Return on Assets | 6.37 | 0.68 |
| Net Margin | 8.58 | 0.79 |

### Sector Weightings

| | % of Stocks | Rel S&P 500 | 3 Year High Low |
|---|---|---|---|
| ↻ Info | 0.69 | 0.03 | |
| 🖥 Software | 0.00 | 0.00 | 0 0 |
| 💾 Hardware | 0.69 | 0.07 | 1 0 |
| 🎬 Media | 0.00 | 0.00 | 0 0 |
| 📞 Telecom | 0.00 | 0.00 | 0 0 |
| ⊂ Service | 25.91 | 0.56 | |
| ⚕ Health | 0.39 | 0.03 | 0 0 |
| 🛒 Consumer | 0.67 | 0.08 | 3 1 |
| 📋 Business | 24.85 | 6.42 | 31 23 |
| 💲 Financial | 0.00 | 0.00 | 0 0 |
| ☐ Mfg | 73.40 | 2.20 | |
| ⛽ Goods | 0.00 | 0.00 | 0 0 |
| ⚙ Ind Mtrls | 73.40 | 6.04 | 75 65 |
| 🔋 Energy | 0.00 | 0.00 | 0 0 |
| 💡 Utilities | 0.00 | 0.00 | 0 0 |

### Composition

| | |
|---|---|
| ● Cash | 0.6 |
| ● Stocks | 99.4 |
| ● Bonds | 0.0 |
| ● Other | 0.0 |
| Foreign | 0.0 |
| (% of Stock) | |

## Morningstar's Take by Dan Culloton

You can't get what Industrial Select Sector SPDR offers in too many other places. Good thing you can live without it.

This ETF offers cheap exposure to industrial stocks, a sector on which few funds focus. There are only about a dozen regular mutual funds and five ETFs that focus explicitly on industrial or basic materials stocks and this ETF's 0.28% expense ratio is less than a third of that of the cheapest.

Like its siblings in the Select SPDR family, however, this fund has some drawbacks. The fund tracks a subset of the S&P 500 that includes all of the industrial stocks in the benchmark. That means the ETF holds the sectors' established moneymakers because S&P constituents have to meet the quality standards of the bogy's selection committee.

Quality is good, but even too much of a good thing can be bad. This fund and its target index focus almost exclusively on large-cap stocks (nearly 90% of assets). It also holds 56 stocks and heaps most of its money in its top 10. More than a fifth of the fund's assets rest on one stock: General Electric. Such focus invites volatility. Indeed, the ETF has been more risky, as measured by standard deviation, than most funds with above-average stakes in industrial materials stocks. It also lost money in 13 of 27 quarters through September 2005.

The fund has taken a breather in 2005 after posting robust returns for two straight years. Still the ETF is no screaming bargain. Using Morningstar's equity research to take the offering's temperature, it looks slightly undervalued. Morningstar's stock analysts cover and have set fair values for every stock in this ETF. We took an average of all the fair values as of the end of October 2005 and compared it with an average of the stocks' share prices. By that measure this ETF was 4% below fair value. That's still not enough to compensate for its risks.

| Address: | c/o State Street Bk&Tr, 225 Franklin St Boston MA 02210 800-843-2639 |
|---|---|
| Web Address: | www.spdrindex.com |
| Inception: | 12-22-98* |
| Advisor: | SSGA Funds Management, Inc. |

| Management Fee: | 0.05% | | |
|---|---|---|---|
| Expense Projections: | 3Yr:$90 | 5Yr:$158 | 10Yr:$358 |
| Income Distrib: | Quarterly | | |
| Exchange: | AMEX | | |

# iShares C&S Realty

| | Ticker | NAV | Market Price | 52 wk High/Low | Yield | Mstar Category |
|---|---|---|---|---|---|---|
| | ICF | $74.72 | $79.50 | $79.50 - $61.58 | 4.0% | Specialty-Real Estate |

## Management

### Portfolio Manager(s)

Barclays Global Fund Advisors is the advisor. The firm is the world's largest manager of indexed portfolios. Patrick O'Connor, the head of Barclay's U.S. iShares portfolio management group leads a team of a half dozen managers in running this and about 60 other ETFs. IShares' domestic portfolio-management group is responsible for about $75 billion in assets. Most of the managers have at least five years of experience with Barclays as well as prior industry experience.

### Strategy

This exchange-traded fund tracks the Cohen & Steers Realty Majors Index. The benchmark includes office, industrial, apartments, and retail REITs that meet the liquidity and quality standards of real estate investment firm Cohen & Steers' investment committee--usually about 30 stocks. Index constituents can't exceed 8% of assets. The bogey is rebalanced quarterly.

**Growth of $10,000**

— Investment Value of ETF
— Investment Value of Index S&P 500

| 1996 | 1997 | 1998 | 1999 | 2000 | 2001 | 2002 | 2003 | 2004 | 2005 | History |
|---|---|---|---|---|---|---|---|---|---|---|
| — | — | — | — | — | 42.19 | 40.70 | 52.95 | 68.31 | 74.72 | NAV $ |
| — | — | — | — | — | 42.15 | 40.77 | 53.04 | 68.16 | 74.84 | Market Price $ |
| — | — | — | — | — | 19.68* | 2.96 | 36.78 | 35.21 | 14.13 | NAV Return% |
| — | — | — | — | — | 19.72* | 3.25 | 36.74 | 34.68 | 14.57 | Market Price Return% |
| — | — | — | — | — | 0.06 | 0.04 | -0.03 | 0.01 | 0.10 | Avg Premium/Discount% |
| — | — | — | — | — | 19.68 | 25.05 | 8.11 | 24.34 | 9.22 | NAV Rtrn% +/-S&P 500 |
| — | — | — | — | — | 19.68 | -0.64 | 0.72 | 2.07 | 0.13 | NAV Rtrn% +/-DJ Wilshire REIT |
| — | — | — | — | — | — | 3 | 3 | 3 | 4 | NAV Return% Rank in Cat |
| — | — | — | — | — | 0.00 | 6.61 | 5.91 | 5.47 | 4.43 | Income Return % |
| — | — | — | — | — | — | -3.65 | 30.87 | 29.74 | 9.70 | Capital Return % |
| — | — | — | — | — | 2.18 | 2.72 | 2.36 | 2.84 | 2.98 | Income $ |
| — | — | — | — | — | 0.00 | 0.10 | 0.00 | 0.00 | 0.00 | Capital Gains $ |
| — | — | — | — | — | 0.35 | 0.35 | 0.35 | 0.35 | 0.35 | Expense Ratio % |
| — | — | — | — | — | 6.01 | 5.80 | 6.17 | 5.28 | 4.97 | Income Ratio % |
| — | — | — | — | — | 2 | 15 | 13 | 15 | 28 | Turnover Rate % |
| — | — | — | — | — | — | 208 | 614 | 1,298 | 1,666 | Net Assets $mil |

## Performance

**Historic Quarterly NAV Returns**

| | 1st Qtr | 2nd Qtr | 3rd Qtr | 4th Qtr | Total |
|---|---|---|---|---|---|
| 2001 | — | 10.25 | -1.42 | 4.04 | —* |
| 2002 | 7.87 | 4.63 | -8.82 | 0.05 | 2.96 |
| 2003 | 1.43 | 11.73 | 10.88 | 8.85 | 36.78 |
| 2004 | 13.03 | -5.98 | 9.19 | 16.52 | 35.21 |
| 2005 | -7.39 | 14.80 | 4.28 | 2.94 | 14.13 |

| Trailing | NAV Return% | Market Return% | NAV Rtrn% +/-S&P 500 | %Rank Cat.(NAV) |
|---|---|---|---|---|
| 3 Mo | 2.94 | 2.92 | 0.86 | 4 |
| 6 Mo | 7.34 | 7.30 | 1.58 | 4 |
| 1 Yr | 14.13 | 14.57 | 9.22 | 4 |
| 3 Yr Avg | 28.28 | 28.26 | 13.90 | 3 |
| 5 Yr Avg | — | — | — | 0 |
| 10 Yr Avg | — | — | — | 0 |

| Tax Analysis | Tax-Adj Return% | Tax-Cost Ratio |
|---|---|---|
| 3 Yr (estimated) | 26.21 | 1.61 |
| 5 Yr (estimated) | — | — |
| 10 Yr (estimated) | — | — |

## Risk Profile

| | Standard Index S&P 500 | Best Fit Index DJ Wilshire REIT |
|---|---|---|
| Alpha | 15.5 | 0.2 |
| Beta | 0.75 | 1.02 |
| R-Squared | 18 | 99 |
| Standard Deviation | 16.14 | |
| Mean | 28.28 | |
| Sharpe Ratio | 1.52 | |

## Morningstar Fair Value

| Price/Fair Value Ratio | Fair Value Estimate ($) | Hit Rate % |
|---|---|---|
| 1.2 Overvalued | 48.60 | 96 Good |

## Portfolio Analysis 12-31-05

Share change since 11-05  Total Stocks:30

| | Sector | PE | Tot Ret% | % Assets |
|---|---|---|---|---|
| ⊖ Simon Property Group | Financial | 57.2 | 23.30 | 8.04 |
| ⊖ Equity Office Properties | Financial | — | 10.93 | 7.01 |
| ⊖ Vornado Realty Trust | Financial | 19.4 | 15.15 | 6.61 |
| ⊖ ProLogis Trust | Financial | 32.0 | 11.73 | 6.28 |
| ⊖ General Growth Propertie | Financial | NMF | 35.15 | 6.24 |
| ⊖ Equity Residential | Financial | 75.2 | 13.37 | 6.19 |
| ⊖ Public Storage | Financial | 36.2 | 25.10 | 5.01 |
| ⊖ Archstone-Smith Trust | Financial | 55.1 | 14.47 | 4.82 |
| ⊖ Boston Properties | Financial | 24.8 | 23.57 | 4.78 |
| ⊖ Kimco Realty | Financial | 24.5 | 15.41 | 4.23 |
| ⊖ AvalonBay Communities | Financial | 60.7 | 22.84 | 3.88 |
| ⊖ Host Marriott | Financial | 94.8 | 12.16 | 3.72 |
| ⊖ Developers Diversified R | Financial | 20.4 | 11.07 | 2.74 |
| ⊖ AMB Property | Financial | 47.7 | 26.78 | 2.55 |
| ⊖ Duke Realty | Financial | 41.8 | 6.98 | 2.52 |
| ⊖ Regency Centers | Financial | 33.1 | 10.80 | 2.33 |
| ⊖ Liberty Property Trust | Financial | 25.4 | 5.19 | 2.28 |
| ⊖ Macerich | Financial | 79.9 | 11.47 | 2.12 |
| ⊖ SL Green Realty | Financial | 35.2 | 30.54 | 1.96 |
| ⊖ Reckson Associates Realt | Financial | 19.1 | 15.38 | 1.85 |

**Current Investment Style**

Value Blnd Growth — Large/Mid/Small

| Market Cap | % |
|---|---|
| Giant | 0.0 |
| Large | 40.4 |
| Mid | 58.7 |
| Small | 0.9 |
| Micro | 0.0 |

Avg $mil: 7,125

| Value Measures | | Rel Category |
|---|---|---|
| Price/Earnings | 16.70 | 1.05 |
| Price/Book | 2.81 | 1.10 |
| Price/Sales | 5.78 | 1.21 |
| Price/Cash Flow | 14.26 | 1.07 |
| Dividend Yield % | 3.97 | 0.92 |

| Growth Measures | % | Rel Category |
|---|---|---|
| Long-Term Erngs | 7.13 | 1.07 |
| Book Value | -0.16 | NMF |
| Sales | 4.00 | 0.89 |
| Cash Flow | 4.00 | 0.43 |
| Historical Erngs | 1.39 | 139.00 |

| Profitability | % | Rel Category |
|---|---|---|
| Return on Equity | 10.92 | 1.06 |
| Return on Assets | 9.66 | 1.06 |
| Net Margin | 28.19 | 1.13 |

| Sector Weightings | % of Stocks | Rel S&P 500 | 3 Year High Low | |
|---|---|---|---|---|
| ☌ Info | 0.00 | 0.00 | | |
| 🖳 Software | 0.00 | 0.00 | 0 | 0 |
| 🖥 Hardware | 0.00 | 0.00 | 0 | 0 |
| 🎙 Media | 0.00 | 0.00 | 0 | 0 |
| 📶 Telecom | 0.00 | 0.00 | 0 | 0 |
| ☞ Service | 100.00 | 2.16 | | |
| 🏥 Health | 0.00 | 0.00 | 0 | 0 |
| 🛒 Consumer | 0.00 | 0.00 | 0 | 0 |
| 📋 Business | 0.00 | 0.00 | 0 | 0 |
| 💲 Financial | 100.00 | 4.74 | 100 | 100 |
| ⚒ Mfg | 0.00 | 0.00 | | |
| 🏭 Goods | 0.00 | 0.00 | 0 | 0 |
| ⚙ Ind Mtrls | 0.00 | 0.00 | 0 | 0 |
| 🔋 Energy | 0.00 | 0.00 | 0 | 0 |
| 💧 Utilities | 0.00 | 0.00 | 0 | 0 |

**Composition**

| | | % |
|---|---|---|
| ● | Cash | 0.1 |
| ● | Stocks | 99.9 |
| ● | Bonds | 0.0 |
| ● | Other | 0.0 |
| | Foreign | 0.0 |
| | (% of Stock) | |

## Morningstar's Take by Dan Culloton

iShares Cohen & Steers Realty Majors has handicaps.

An ETF such as this one can add diversification to a portfolio, but this fund still has drawbacks. The ETF is fairly concentrated. The fund tracks the Cohen & Steers Realty Majors Index, which consists of 30 office, industrial, apartment, and retail REITs that meet the liquidity and quality standards set by real estate investment firm and index author Cohen & Steer's investment committee. The index caps each constituent's weight at 8% of assets, but it still packs more than half of its money in its top-10 holdings. That has made the offering more volatile, as measured by standard deviation, than the average real estate fund and all other real estate index funds over the three-year period ending Sept. 30, 2005.

Furthermore, while index funds and ETFs can be cheap and easy ways to access this asset class, they don't have a very long and illustrious record in this category. The oldest passive funds have been around for less than nine years, and the typical actively managed fund has beaten the average index real estate fund in seven of the last eight full calendar years. This ETFs results have been mixed, too. The ETF has posted strong absolute returns, but has lagged typical real estate fund in 40% the 45 rolling one-year periods from its inception through September 2005.

Finally, this fund, while cheap, isn't the cheapest real estate ETF available. That may seem like hairsplitting, but the results of all of the competing ETFs and index funds in this category have correlated closely over the last three years. So, the biggest difference among them in the future may be expenses. On that front this fund suffers. Its 0.35% expense ratio is a fraction of that of the typical specialty real estate offering, but it's still nearly double that of the lowest cost ETF available. So, this fund is far from a slam-dunk.

| | | | | |
|---|---|---|---|---|
| Address: | 45 Fremont Street San Francisco CA 94105 800-474-2737 | Management Fee: | 0.35% | |
| | | Expense Projections: | 3Yr:$113 5Yr:$197 10Yr:$443 | |
| | | Income Distrib: | Annually | |
| Web Address: | www.ishares.com | Exchange: | AMEX | |
| Inception: | 01-29-01* | | | |
| Advisor: | Barclays Global Fund Advisers | | | |

**M⊙RNINGSTAR® ETFs 100**

# iShares DJ Health

| | Ticker | NAV | Market Price | 52 wk High/Low | Yield | Mstar Category |
|---|---|---|---|---|---|---|
| | IYH | $62.96 | $65.12 | $65.12 - $56.82 | 0.7% | Specialty-Health |

## Management

### Portfolio Manager(s)

Barclays Global Investors runs this fund. It is the world's largest advisor of indexed assets. It also is the sponsor of the world's largest ETF family. Patrick O'Connor, the head of Barclay's U.S. iShares portfolio management group leads a team of a half dozen managers in running this and 57 other ETFs. iShares domestic portfolio management group is responsible for about $75 billion in assets. Most of the managers have at least five or more years of experience with Barclays as well as prior industry experience.

### Strategy

This exchange-traded fund tracks a subset of the Dow Jones U.S. Total Market Index that includes the health-care stocks in that broad market benchmark. That usually includes nearly 200 companies. Still, the fund's bogy is market-cap weighted and extremely concentrated, with most of its assets in its top holdings. The free-float-adjusted, market-capitalization-weighted index is rebalanced quarterly.

Growth of $10,000
— Investment Value of ETF
— Investment Value of Index S&P 500

| | 1996 | 1997 | 1998 | 1999 | 2000 | 2001 | 2002 | 2003 | 2004 | 2005 | History |
|---|---|---|---|---|---|---|---|---|---|---|---|
| | — | — | — | — | 71.77 | 61.95 | 48.47 | 57.08 | 58.92 | 62.96 | NAV $ |
| | — | — | — | — | 71.91 | 62.10 | 48.53 | 56.98 | 58.99 | 63.04 | Market Price $ |
| | — | — | — | — | 1.66* | -13.34 | -21.20 | 18.70 | 3.91 | 7.65 | NAV Return% |
| | — | — | — | — | 1.68* | -13.30 | -21.29 | 18.35 | 4.22 | 7.66 | Market Price Return% |
| | — | — | — | — | -0.13 | 0.14 | 0.15 | 0.05 | 0.05 | -0.02 | Avg Premium/Discount% |
| | — | — | — | — | 1.66 | -1.46 | 0.89 | -9.97 | -6.96 | 2.74 | NAV Rtrn% +/-S&P 500 |
| | — | — | — | — | 1.66 | -0.73 | -0.39 | -0.73 | -0.64 | -0.67 | NAV Rtrn% +/-DJ Hlthcare |
| | — | — | — | — | — | 2 | 4 | 5 | 5 | 5 | NAV Return% Rank in Cat |
| | — | — | — | — | 0.00 | 0.34 | 0.60 | 0.87 | 0.67 | 0.78 | Income Return % |
| | — | — | — | — | — | -13.68 | -21.80 | 17.83 | 3.24 | 6.87 | Capital Return % |
| | — | — | — | — | 0.07 | 0.24 | 0.37 | 0.42 | 0.38 | 0.46 | Income $ |
| | — | — | — | — | 0.09 | 0.00 | 0.00 | 0.00 | 0.00 | 0.00 | Capital Gains $ |
| | — | — | — | — | — | 0.60 | 0.60 | 0.60 | 0.60 | 0.60 | Expense Ratio % |
| | — | — | — | — | — | 0.29 | 0.45 | 0.80 | 0.71 | 0.74 | Income Ratio % |
| | — | — | — | — | — | 5 | 3 | 9 | 4 | 4 | Turnover Rate % |
| | — | — | — | — | — | 351 | 491 | 934 | 1,300 | | Net Assets $mil |

## Performance

### Historic Quarterly NAV Returns

| | 1st Qtr | 2nd Qtr | 3rd Qtr | 4th Qtr | Total |
|---|---|---|---|---|---|
| 2001 | -16.96 | 2.13 | -0.49 | 2.69 | -13.34 |
| 2002 | -1.80 | -16.70 | -7.65 | 4.30 | -21.20 |
| 2003 | 1.29 | 11.23 | -3.05 | 8.67 | 18.70 |
| 2004 | 0.67 | 2.53 | -4.78 | 5.73 | 3.91 |
| 2005 | -0.62 | 4.85 | 1.84 | 1.44 | 7.65 |

| Trailing | NAV Return% | Market Return% | NAV Rtrn% +/-S&P 500 | %Rank Cat.(NAV) |
|---|---|---|---|---|
| 3 Mo | 1.44 | 1.57 | -0.64 | 7 |
| 6 Mo | 3.31 | 3.54 | -2.45 | 7 |
| 1 Yr | 7.65 | 7.66 | 2.74 | 5 |
| 3 Yr Avg | 9.91 | 9.91 | -4.47 | 4 |
| 5 Yr Avg | -1.94 | -1.95 | -2.48 | 2 |
| 10 Yr Avg | — | — | — | 0 |

| Tax Analysis | Tax-Adj Return% | Tax-Cost Ratio |
|---|---|---|
| 3 Yr (estimated) | 9.63 | 0.25 |
| 5 Yr (estimated) | -2.17 | 0.23 |
| 10 Yr (estimated) | — | — |

## Risk Profile

| | Standard Index S&P 500 | Best Fit Index DJ Hlthcare |
|---|---|---|
| Alpha | 1.3 | -0.6 |
| Beta | 0.56 | 1.00 |
| R-Squared | 32 | 100 |
| Standard Deviation | 9.13 | |
| Mean | 9.91 | |
| Sharpe Ratio | 0.87 | |

## Morningstar Fair Value

| Price/Fair Value Ratio | Fair Value Estimate ($) | Hit Rate % |
|---|---|---|
| 1.0 Fairly valued | 43.10 | 93 Good |

## Portfolio Analysis 12-31-05

| Share change since 11-05 Total Stocks:171 | Sector | PE | Tot Ret% | % Assets |
|---|---|---|---|---|
| ⊕ Johnson & Johnson | Health | 19.1 | -3.36 | 10.45 |
| ⊕ Pfizer | Health | 21.2 | -10.62 | 10.14 |
| ⊕ Amgen | Health | 28.3 | 22.93 | 5.69 |
| ⊕ UnitedHealth Group | Health | 26.2 | 41.22 | 4.95 |
| ⊕ Merck | Health | 15.2 | 4.04 | 4.10 |
| ⊕ Medtronic | Health | 37.4 | 16.72 | 4.07 |
| ⊕ Wyeth | Health | 54.2 | 10.54 | 3.59 |
| ⊕ Abbott Laboratories | Health | 18.3 | -13.47 | 3.59 |
| ⊕ Eli Lilly & Company | Health | 48.4 | 2.52 | 3.20 |
| ⊕ WellPoint | Health | 24.7 | 38.77 | 3.06 |
| ⊕ Bristol-Myers Squibb | Health | 17.1 | -6.16 | 2.63 |
| ⊕ Genentech | Health | 86.5 | 69.91 | 2.51 |
| ⊕ Schering-Plough | Health | — | 0.95 | 1.80 |
| ⊕ Aetna | Health | 18.9 | 51.27 | 1.58 |
| ⊕ Gilead Sciences | Health | 38.1 | 50.24 | 1.41 |
| ⊕ Baxter International | Health | 30.6 | 10.63 | 1.36 |
| ⊕ Caremark RX | Health | 27.7 | 31.35 | 1.36 |
| ⊕ Guidant | Health | 44.4 | -9.68 | 1.25 |
| ⊕ HCA | Health | 16.0 | 27.87 | 1.19 |
| ⊕ St. Jude Medical | Health | 36.9 | 19.72 | 1.07 |

### Current Investment Style

Value Blnd Growth — Large Mid Small

| | Market Cap | % |
|---|---|---|
| | Giant | 55.4 |
| | Large | 25.4 |
| | Mid | 16.1 |
| | Small | 2.9 |
| | Micro | 0.2 |

Avg $mil: 35,313

| Value Measures | | Rel Category |
|---|---|---|
| Price/Earnings | 19.65 | 0.85 |
| Price/Book | 2.77 | 0.85 |
| Price/Sales | 2.32 | 0.63 |
| Price/Cash Flow | 12.95 | 0.85 |
| Dividend Yield % | 1.26 | 1.24 |

| Growth Measures | % | Rel Category |
|---|---|---|
| Long-Term Erngs | 12.26 | 0.84 |
| Book Value | 19.30 | 1.58 |
| Sales | 12.81 | 0.89 |
| Cash Flow | 15.78 | 1.04 |
| Historical Erngs | 12.84 | 1.09 |

| Profitability | % | Rel Category |
|---|---|---|
| Return on Equity | 16.66 | 1.30 |
| Return on Assets | 8.79 | 1.58 |
| Net Margin | 12.78 | 1.06 |

| Industry Weightings | % of Stocks | Rel Cat |
|---|---|---|
| Biotech | 16.4 | 0.5 |
| Drugs | 44.6 | 1.7 |
| Mgd Care | 10.4 | 1.4 |
| Hospitals | 2.5 | 1.1 |
| Other HC Srv | 1.4 | 0.9 |
| Diagnostics | 1.4 | 1.1 |
| Equipment | 17.1 | 1.2 |
| Good/Srv | 6.0 | 0.7 |
| Other | 0.2 | 0.1 |

### Composition

| | | % |
|---|---|---|
| ● | Cash | 0.1 |
| ● | Stocks | 99.9 |
| ● | Bonds | 0.0 |
| | Other | 0.0 |
| | Foreign | 0.0 |
| | (% of Stock) | |

## Morningstar's Take by Dan Culloton

iShares Dow Jones U.S. Healthcare lacks appeal.

This exchange-traded fund is cheap and supplies exposure to a broad swath of health-care stocks. However, it is neither the cheapest nor the most diversified option in its category.

The offering's 0.6% expense ratio is about one third of that of the typical traditional health-care mutual fund. Over the long term, that should help it stay competitive with the pack. The ETF cedes ground to its closest competitors, though. Its levy is more than twice the expense ratios of the lowest-cost options: Health Care Select Sector SPDR and Vanguard Healthcare VIPERs.

This fund, which tracks an index of all the health-care stocks in the Dow Jones U.S. Total Market Index, also courts more risk than its below-average standard deviation (a statistical measure of volatility) implies. Like other sector ETFs, this one is more concentrated in terms of individual positions, subsectors, and regions than the average traditional health-care fund. Though it owns 175 stocks, it keeps more than half of its assets in its top-10 holdings. It's also heavily reliant on large-cap pharmaceutical companies. More than one fourth of its assets rest on Johnson & Johnson and Pfizer alone. Traditional portfolios in the health-care category also keep more money in cash and overseas stock than this fund.

It's not too surprising then, that this ETF's road has been rocky and not as rewarding as its average traditional rival. The fund has had more down periods than usual in the health-care group. It has lost money in 46% of the 52 rolling one-year periods and 78% of the 28 rolling three-year periods from inception through September 2005.

Large-cap drug stocks, which have been besieged by patent and litigation woes, won't always be out of favor. When they revive, this fund will benefit. Shop around before investing here, though. There are cheaper and more diversified options.

| Address: | 45 Fremont Street San Francisco CA 94105 800-474-2737 |
|---|---|
| Web Address: | www.ishares.com |
| Inception: | 06-12-00 * |
| Advisor: | Barclays Global Fund Advisers |

| Management Fee: | 0.60% |
|---|---|
| Expense Projections: | 3Yr:$192  5Yr:$335  10Yr:$750 |
| Income Distrib: | Quarterly |
| Exchange: | NYSE |

# iShares DJ RE Index

| Ticker | NAV | Market Price | 52 wk High/Low | Yield | Mstar Category |
|---|---|---|---|---|---|
| IYR | $64.36 | $68.35 | $68.37 - $55.56 | 4.4% | Specialty-Real Estate |

## Management

### Portfolio Manager(s)

Barclays Global Fund Advisors is the advisor. The firm is the world's largest manager of indexed portfolios. Patrick O'Connor, the head of Barclay's U.S. iShares portfolio management group leads a team of a half dozen managers in running this and about 60 other ETFs. IShares' domestic portfolio-management group is responsible for about $75 billion in assets. Most of the managers have at least five years of experience with Barclays as well as prior industry experience.

### Strategy

This fund tracks the Dow Jones U.S. Real Estate Index, which includes the REITs and the real estate operating and holding companies in the Dow Jones U.S. Financials Index. It is market-cap weighted and adjusted for insider ownership, cross ownership, and other factors that could limit the number of stock shares that actually trade. The fund's advisor uses representative sampling to mirror the benchmark's return, which means the offering owns most but not every single stock in the index.

**Growth of $10,000**

- Investment Value of ETF
- Investment Value of Index S&P 500

| | 1996 | 1997 | 1998 | 1999 | 2000 | 2001 | 2002 | 2003 | 2004 | 2005 | History |
|---|---|---|---|---|---|---|---|---|---|---|---|
| | — | — | — | — | 37.89 | 39.92 | 38.52 | 49.60 | 61.66 | 64.36 | NAV $ |
| | — | — | — | — | 37.98 | 39.90 | 38.65 | 49.63 | 61.60 | 64.15 | Market Price $ |
| | — | — | — | — | 18.05* | 10.87 | 3.05 | 35.73 | 30.36 | 9.19 | NAV Return% |
| | — | — | — | — | 17.98* | 10.55 | 3.46 | 35.37 | 30.14 | 8.94 | Market Price Return% |
| | — | — | — | — | 0.34 | -0.06 | 0.08 | -0.07 | -0.14 | -0.21 | Avg Premium/Discount% |
| | — | — | — | — | 18.05 | 22.75 | 25.14 | 7.06 | 19.49 | 4.28 | NAV Rtrn% +/-S&P 500 |
| | — | — | — | — | 18.05 | -1.49 | -0.55 | -0.33 | -2.78 | -4.81 | NAV Rtrn% +/-DJ Wilshire REIT |
| | — | — | — | — | — | 1 | 3 | 3 | 3 | 4 | NAV Return% Rank in Cat |
| | — | — | — | — | 0.00 | 5.37 | 6.44 | 3.93 | 5.35 | 4.64 | Income Return % |
| | — | — | — | — | — | 5.50 | -3.39 | 31.80 | 25.01 | 4.55 | Capital Return % |
| | — | — | — | — | 1.21 | 2.00 | 2.51 | 1.47 | 2.60 | 2.81 | Income $ |
| | — | — | — | — | 0.07 | 0.00 | 0.18 | 0.86 | 0.00 | 0.00 | Capital Gains $ |
| | — | — | — | — | — | 0.60 | 0.60 | 0.60 | 0.60 | 0.60 | Expense Ratio % |
| | — | — | — | — | — | 6.37 | 5.97 | 6.40 | 5.58 | 5.35 | Income Ratio % |
| | — | — | — | — | 30 | 10 | 21 | 20 | 16 | Turnover Rate % |
| | — | — | — | — | — | 166 | 382 | 1,295 | 1,046 | Net Assets $mil |

## Performance

**Historic Quarterly NAV Returns**

| | 1st Qtr | 2nd Qtr | 3rd Qtr | 4th Qtr | Total |
|---|---|---|---|---|---|
| 2001 | -0.42 | 10.98 | -4.18 | 4.71 | 10.87 |
| 2002 | 7.99 | 4.36 | -9.07 | 0.55 | 3.05 |
| 2003 | 0.15 | 12.66 | 9.20 | 10.17 | 35.73 |
| 2004 | 12.02 | -6.57 | 8.25 | 15.05 | 30.36 |
| 2005 | -7.71 | 14.28 | 1.93 | 1.57 | 9.19 |

| Trailing | NAV Return% | Market Return% | NAV Rtrn% +/-S&P 500 | %Rank Cat.(NAV) |
|---|---|---|---|---|
| 3 Mo | 1.57 | 1.13 | -0.51 | 4 |
| 6 Mo | 3.53 | 3.28 | -2.23 | 4 |
| 1 Yr | 9.19 | 8.94 | 4.28 | 4 |
| 3 Yr Avg | 24.55 | 24.27 | 10.17 | 3 |
| 5 Yr Avg | 17.16 | 17.03 | 16.62 | 1 |
| 10 Yr Avg | — | — | — | 0 |

| Tax Analysis | Tax-Adj Return% | Tax-Cost Ratio |
|---|---|---|
| 3 Yr (estimated) | 22.76 | 1.44 |
| 5 Yr (estimated) | 15.14 | 1.72 |
| 10 Yr (estimated) | — | — |

## Risk Profile

| | Standard Index S&P 500 | Best Fit Index DJ Wilshire REIT |
|---|---|---|
| Alpha | 11.5 | -2.0 |
| Beta | 0.83 | 0.99 |
| R-Squared | 24 | 99 |
| Standard Deviation | 15.60 | |
| Mean | 24.55 | |
| Sharpe Ratio | 1.37 | |

## Morningstar Fair Value

| Price/Fair Value Ratio | Fair Value Estimate ($) | Hit Rate % |
|---|---|---|
| 1.2 Overvalued | 41.81 | 86 Good |

## Portfolio Analysis  12-31-05

Share change since 11-05  Total Stocks:83

| | Sector | PE | Tot Ret% | % Assets |
|---|---|---|---|---|
| ⊕ Simon Property Group | Financial | 57.2 | 23.30 | 6.16 |
| ⊕ Equity Office Properties | Financial | | 10.93 | 4.46 |
| ⊕ General Growth Propertie | Financial | NMF | 35.15 | 4.01 |
| ⊕ Equity Residential | Financial | 75.2 | 13.37 | 3.98 |
| ⊕ ProLogis Trust | Financial | 32.0 | 11.73 | 3.96 |
| ⊕ Vornado Realty Trust | Financial | 19.4 | 15.15 | 3.76 |
| ⊕ Archstone-Smith Trust | Financial | 55.1 | 14.47 | 3.08 |
| ⊕ Boston Properties | Financial | 24.8 | 23.57 | 2.88 |
| ⊕ Plum Creek Timber Compan | Ind Mtrls | 21.0 | -2.26 | 2.46 |
| ⊕ AvalonBay Communities | Financial | 60.7 | 22.84 | 2.37 |
| ⊕ Host Marriott | Financial | 94.8 | 12.16 | 2.32 |
| ⊕ Kimco Realty | Financial | 24.5 | 15.41 | 2.26 |
| ⊕ Public Storage | Financial | 36.2 | 25.10 | 2.15 |
| ⊕ Developers Diversified R | Financial | 20.4 | 11.07 | 1.84 |
| ⊕ St. Joe | Financial | 47.0 | 5.58 | 1.79 |
| ⊕ Duke Realty | Financial | 41.8 | 6.98 | 1.75 |
| ⊕ AMB Property | Financial | 47.7 | 26.78 | 1.50 |
| ⊕ iStar Financial | Financial | 14.1 | -15.09 | 1.47 |
| ⊕ Macerich | Financial | 79.9 | 11.47 | 1.46 |
| ⊕ Liberty Property Trust | Financial | 25.4 | 5.19 | 1.34 |

### Current Investment Style

Value Blnd Growth — Large/Mid/Small

| Market Cap | % |
|---|---|
| Giant | 0.0 |
| Large | 26.4 |
| Mid | 65.5 |
| Small | 8.1 |
| Micro | 0.0 |

Avg $mil: 4,803

| Value Measures | | Rel Category |
|---|---|---|
| Price/Earnings | 15.28 | 0.96 |
| Price/Book | 2.34 | 0.92 |
| Price/Sales | 4.32 | 0.90 |
| Price/Cash Flow | 12.57 | 0.95 |
| Dividend Yield % | 4.73 | 1.09 |

| Growth Measures | % | Rel Category |
|---|---|---|
| Long-Term Erngs | 6.34 | 0.95 |
| Book Value | 0.52 | 0.66 |
| Sales | 6.46 | 1.44 |
| Cash Flow | 26.19 | 2.80 |
| Historical Erngs | 4.01 | 401.00 |

| Profitability | % | Rel Category |
|---|---|---|
| Return on Equity | 11.06 | 1.07 |
| Return on Assets | 9.63 | 1.06 |
| Net Margin | 25.32 | 1.02 |

| Sector Weightings | % of Stocks | Rel S&P 500 | 3 Year High Low |
|---|---|---|---|
| ↻ Info | 0.00 | 0.00 | |
| 🔲 Software | 0.00 | 0.00 | 0  0 |
| 💻 Hardware | 0.00 | 0.00 | 0  0 |
| 🎤 Media | 0.00 | 0.00 | 0  0 |
| 📶 Telecom | 0.00 | 0.00 | 0  0 |
| ⊛ Service | 96.45 | 2.08 | |
| 🏥 Health | 0.00 | 0.00 | 0  0 |
| 🛒 Consumer | 0.36 | 0.04 | 0  0 |
| 📋 Business | 0.00 | 0.00 | 0  0 |
| 💲 Financial | 96.09 | 4.56 | 97  96 |
| 🏭 Mfg | 3.55 | 0.11 | |
| 🔩 Goods | 0.00 | 0.00 | 0  0 |
| ⚙ Ind Mtrls | 3.55 | 0.29 | 4  3 |
| 🔋 Energy | 0.00 | 0.00 | 0  0 |
| 💡 Utilities | 0.00 | 0.00 | 0  0 |

**Composition**

| Composition | % |
|---|---|
| ● Cash | 0.1 |
| ● Stocks | 99.9 |
| ● Bonds | 0.0 |
| ● Other | 0.0 |
| Foreign | 0.0 |
(% of Stock)

## Morningstar's Take  by Dan Culloton

This exchange traded fund offers broad real estate exposure, but it's pricier than it looks.

IShares Dow Jones U.S. Real Estate Index tracks an index of REITs and real estate operating and holding companies in the Dow Jones U.S. Financials Index. It's well-diversified for a sector fund. For example, it has about a third of its assets in its top-10 holdings, which is less than most real estate sector funds. That includes ETFs such as iShares Cohen & Steers Realty Majors and StreetTracks Wilshire REIT, which have close to 60% and 40% of their respective assets in their top-10 holdings. That diversification has kept a lid on volatility. The fund's standard deviation is no higher than its traditional and ETF rivals.

This still may not be the best option. First, this fund is the most expensive real estate ETF available. The offering's 0.60% expense ratio may not seem like a lot compared with traditional funds, but that levy is nearly four times that of the cheapest ETF in this area and almost three times

the cost of the largest traditional index fund contender, Vanguard REIT Index. Sure we're only talking about 40 or so hundredths of a percent, but every little bit counts over the long run when it comes to index funds. The difference between the expense ratios of the REIT index funds with the poorest and the best five-year returns through Aug. 22, 2005 accounts for more than half of their performance gap.

Price isn't the only thing that's not right. The time also may be wrong for this fund. It has posted attractive absolute returns over its life as the real estate category has boomed, but now REIT yields have contracted and earnings growth in many real estate subsectors has slowed, which makes the sector look pricey and risky. Real estate still has a place in many portfolios, but it may be time to rebalance and lower expectations. This fund can provide broad real estate exposure, but there are better deals out there.

| | | | |
|---|---|---|---|
| Address: | 45 Fremont Street San Francisco CA 94105 800-474-2737 | Management Fee: | 0.60% |
| | | Expense Projections: | 3Yr:$192    5Yr:$335    10Yr:$750 |
| Web Address: | www.ishares.com | Income Distrib: | Quarterly |
| Inception: | 06-12-00* | Exchange: | NYSE |
| Advisor: | Barclays Global Fund Advisers | | |

**MORNINGSTAR® ETFs 100**

# iShares DJ Sel Dividend

| | Ticker | NAV | Market Price | 52 wk High/Low | Yield | Mstar Category |
|---|---|---|---|---|---|---|
| | DVY | $61.30 | $63.05 | $64.50 - $58.11 | 3.0% | Mid-Cap Value |

## Management

### Portfolio Manager(s)

Barclays Global Fund Advisors is the advisor. The firm is the world's largest manager of indexed portfolios. Patrick O'Connor, the head of Barclay's U.S. iShares portfolio management group, leads a team of a half dozen managers in running this and about 60 other ETFs. IShares' domestic-portfolio-management group is responsible for about $75 billion in assets. Most of the managers have at least five years of experience with Barclays as well as prior industry experience.

### Strategy

Dow Jones created its Select Dividend Index for this fund. The benchmark screens the 1,600-member Dow Jones Total Market Index for 100 stocks that have three-month average daily trading volumes of 200,000 shares, have increased and never cut their dividends over the last five years, and that have paid out less than 60% of their earnings. The index screens out REITs because they do not qualify for the dividend tax cut passed in 2003. Dow Jones weights constituent stocks based on their indicated annual dividend and rebalances annually in December.

**Growth of $10,000**

— Investment Value of ETF
— Investment Value of Index S&P 500

| | 1996 | 1997 | 1998 | 1999 | 2000 | 2001 | 2002 | 2003 | 2004 | 2005 | History |
|---|---|---|---|---|---|---|---|---|---|---|---|
| | — | — | — | — | — | — | — | 53.80 | 61.34 | 61.30 | NAV $ |
| | — | — | — | — | — | — | — | 53.84 | 61.40 | 61.26 | Market Price $ |
| | — | — | — | — | — | — | — | 12.93* | 17.90 | 2.98 | NAV Return% |
| | — | — | — | — | — | — | — | 12.90* | 17.93 | 2.81 | Market Price Return% |
| | — | — | — | — | — | — | — | 0.14 | 0.11 | 0.03 | Avg Premium/Discount% |
| | — | — | — | — | — | — | — | 12.93 | 7.03 | -1.93 | NAV Rtrn% +/-S&P 500 |
| | — | — | — | — | — | — | — | 12.93 | -5.81 | -9.67 | NAV Rtrn% +/-Russ MV |
| | — | — | — | — | — | — | — | — | 3 | 5 | NAV Return% Rank in Cat |
| | — | — | — | — | — | — | — | 0.00 | 3.59 | 3.05 | Income Return % |
| | — | — | — | — | — | — | — | — | 14.31 | -0.07 | Capital Return % |
| | — | — | — | — | — | — | — | 0.29 | 1.91 | 1.85 | Income $ |
| | — | — | — | — | — | — | — | 0.00 | 0.00 | 0.00 | Capital Gains $ |
| | — | — | — | — | — | — | — | — | 0.40 | 0.40 | Expense Ratio % |
| | — | — | — | — | — | — | — | — | 3.43 | 3.39 | Income Ratio % |
| | — | — | — | — | — | — | — | — | 2 | 20 | Turnover Rate % |
| | — | — | — | — | — | — | — | 460 | 5,009 | 7,252 | Net Assets $mil |

## Performance

### Historic Quarterly NAV Returns

| | 1st Qtr | 2nd Qtr | 3rd Qtr | 4th Qtr | Total |
|---|---|---|---|---|---|
| 2001 | — | — | — | — | — |
| 2002 | — | — | — | — | — |
| 2003 | — | — | — | — | —* |
| 2004 | 3.58 | 1.47 | 4.01 | 7.85 | 17.90 |
| 2005 | -1.59 | 3.78 | 1.62 | -0.78 | 2.98 |

| Trailing | NAV Return% | Market Return% | NAV Rtrn% +/-S&P 500 | %Rank Cat.(NAV) |
|---|---|---|---|---|
| 3 Mo | -0.78 | -0.90 | -2.86 | 6 |
| 6 Mo | 0.83 | 0.73 | -4.93 | 6 |
| 1 Yr | 2.98 | 2.81 | -1.93 | 5 |
| 3 Yr Avg | — | — | — | 0 |
| 5 Yr Avg | — | — | — | 0 |
| 10 Yr Avg | — | — | — | 0 |

| Tax Analysis | Tax-Adj Return% | Tax-Cost Ratio |
|---|---|---|
| 3 Yr (estimated) | — | — |
| 5 Yr (estimated) | — | — |
| 10 Yr (estimated) | — | — |

## Risk Profile

| | Standard Index S&P 500 | Best Fit Index |
|---|---|---|
| Alpha | — | — |
| Beta | — | — |
| R-Squared | — | — |
| Standard Deviation | — | |
| Mean | — | |
| Sharpe Ratio | — | |

## Morningstar Fair Value

| Price/Fair Value Ratio | Fair Value Estimate ($) | Hit Rate % |
|---|---|---|
| 1.0 Fairly valued | 38.08 | 85 Good |

## Portfolio Analysis 12-31-05

| Share change since 11-05 Total Stocks:113 | Sector | PE | Tot Ret% | % Assets |
|---|---|---|---|---|
| ⊕ Altria Group | Goods | 15.0 | 27.72 | 4.09 |
| ⊕ Bank of America | Financial | 11.1 | 2.39 | 3.06 |
| ⊖ FPL Group | Utilities | 18.5 | 15.05 | 2.77 |
| ⊕ DTE Energy Holding | Utilities | 26.0 | 4.73 | 2.75 |
| ⊕ PNC Financial Services G | Financial | 14.0 | 11.66 | 2.60 |
| ⊕ Pinnacle West Capital | Utilities | 17.4 | -2.58 | 2.29 |
| ⊕ Comerica | Financial | 11.2 | -3.37 | 2.27 |
| ⊕ FirstEnergy | Utilities | 18.8 | 28.72 | 2.16 |
| ⊕ Kinder Morgan | Energy | 20.3 | 30.29 | 2.11 |
| ⊕ Unitrin | Financial | 12.9 | 2.73 | 2.08 |
| ⊕ Merck | Health | 15.2 | 4.04 | 2.06 |
| ⊕ KeyCorp | Financial | 13.0 | 1.02 | 1.88 |
| ⊕ Lincoln National | Financial | 11.7 | 17.15 | 1.82 |
| ⊕ AT&T | Telecom | 21.1 | 0 25 | 1.78 |
| ⊕ National City | Financial | 8.6 | -6.77 | 1.74 |
| ⊕ Bristol-Myers Squibb | Health | 17.1 | -6.16 | 1.68 |
| ⊕ Washington Mutual | Financial | 11.9 | 7.79 | 1.65 |
| ⊕ AmSouth Bancorporation | Financial | 13.0 | 5.18 | 1.57 |
| ⊖ People's Bank | Financial | — | 23.38 | 1.55 |
| ⊕ Eastman Chemical | Ind Mtrls | 7.7 | -7.68 | 1.54 |

### Current Investment Style

Value Blnd Growth — Large Mid Small

| Market Cap | % |
|---|---|
| Giant | 19.8 |
| Large | 32.4 |
| Mid | 41.1 |
| Small | 6.7 |
| Micro | 0.0 |

Avg $mil: 11,837

| Value Measures | | Rel Category |
|---|---|---|
| Price/Earnings | 13.72 | 0.94 |
| Price/Book | 1.83 | 0.99 |
| Price/Sales | 1.22 | 1.18 |
| Price/Cash Flow | 6.20 | 1.06 |
| Dividend Yield % | 4.03 | 1.50 |

| Growth Measures | % | Rel Category |
|---|---|---|
| Long-Term Erngs | 7.58 | 0.87 |
| Book Value | 9.77 | 1.28 |
| Sales | 6.05 | 0.96 |
| Cash Flow | 7.72 | 1.99 |
| Historical Erngs | 5.81 | 0.57 |

| Profitability | % | Rel Category |
|---|---|---|
| Return on Equity | 15.82 | 1.13 |
| Return on Assets | 9.44 | 1.10 |
| Net Margin | 15.45 | 1.22 |

| Sector Weightings | % of Stocks | Rel S&P 500 | 3 Year High | Low |
|---|---|---|---|---|
| ↻ Info | 3.36 | 0.17 | | |
| Software | 0.00 | 0.00 | 0 | 0 |
| Hardware | 0.00 | 0.00 | 0 | 0 |
| Media | 0.00 | 0.00 | 0 | 0 |
| Telecom | 3.36 | 1.12 | 4 | 3 |
| ⊂ Service | 52.05 | 1.12 | | |
| Health | 5.25 | 0.40 | 5 | 1 |
| Consumer | 1.99 | 0.24 | 3 | 2 |
| Business | 2.37 | 0.61 | 3 | 2 |
| Financial | 42.44 | 2.01 | 45 | 37 |
| ⊃ Mfg | 44.59 | 1.33 | | |
| Goods | 10.61 | 1.24 | 12 | 10 |
| Ind Mtrls | 6.44 | 0.53 | 10 | 6 |
| Energy | 6.37 | 0.68 | 10 | 6 |
| Utilities | 21.17 | 6.30 | 23 | 20 |

### Composition

| | | |
|---|---|---|
| ⬤ Cash | | 0.1 |
| ⬤ Stocks | | 99.9 |
| ⬤ Bonds | | 0.0 |
| ⬤ Other | | 0.0 |
| Foreign | | 0.0 |
| (% of Stock) | | |

## Morningstar's Take by Dan Culloton

Success hasn't spoiled this fund, but it has exposed some wrinkles.

IShares Dow Jones Select Dividend Index is the largest and best selling dividend-focused exchange-traded fund. Its niche is getting crowded, with rival PowerShares launching three more dividend ETFs in 2005 and Vanguard planning one, too. Despite the competition, this fund is still a viable option.

The ETF tracks a dividend-weighted bogy of 100 stocks that have increased their payouts for at least five years without distributing too much of their earnings. The portfolio sports a healthy yield and isn't reliant on a handful of stocks. There also are good reasons to make a long-term commitment to a portfolio of income-producing stocks like this one, including the chance to reinvest and compound those dividends over time.

The fund isn't perfect, though. Its 0.4% expense ratio is the lowest among ETFs with above-market yields but average for ETFs in general. The ETF also isn't diversified by sector. It shuns tech stocks and focuses on financial, utility, and consumer-goods firms.

This fund's biggest letdown, however, has been its tax efficiency. Just 86% of the dividends this ETF paid out in 2004 werc qualified for the two-year old corporate dividend tax break. That was a small but unpleasant surprise for those who bought this offering hoping to capitalize on the dividend tax cut. To qualify funds have to hold income-paying stocks for more than 60 of the 121 days surrounding the companies' ex-dividend date. However, this ETF ran afoul of that rule due to heavy creation/redemption activity and the index's year-end reconstitution. Since this fund, like all ETFs, swaps fund shares for baskets of stocks and vice versa, it wound up accepting some securities that didn't qualify and chucking others before they did.

This doesn't disqualify this ETF, though it may be better used in tax-deferred accounts.

| | | | | |
|---|---|---|---|---|
| Address: | 45 Fremont Street | Management Fee: | 0.40% | |
| | San Francisco CA 94105 | Expense Projections: | 3Yr:$128 | 5Yr: — 10Yr: — |
| | 800-474-2737 | Income Distrib: | Quarterly | |
| Web Address: | www.ishares.com | Exchange: | NYSE | |
| Inception: | 11-03-03 * | | | |
| Advisor: | Barclays Global Fund Advisers | | | |

# iShares DJ Tech

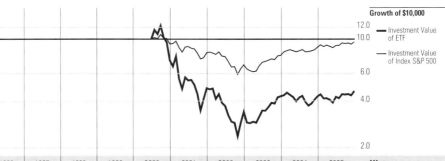

| | Ticker | NAV | Market Price | 52 wk High/Low | Yield | Mstar Category |
|---|---|---|---|---|---|---|
| | IYW | $49.76 | $53.22 | $53.22 - $41.98 | 0.1% | Specialty-Technology |

## Management

### Portfolio Manager(s)

Barclays Global Fund Advisors is the advisor. The firm is the world's largest manager of indexed portfolios. Patrick O'Connor, the head of Barclay's U.S. iShares portfolio management group leads a team of a half dozen managers in running this and about 60 other ETFs. iShares' domestic portfolio-management group is responsible for about $75 billion in assets. Most of the managers have at least five years of experience with Barclays as well as prior industry experience.

### Strategy

This exchange-traded fund tracks a subset of the Dow Jones U.S. Total Market Index that includes the technology stocks in that broad market benchmark. That usually amounts to the shares of about 260 companies. The fund's bogy is market-cap weighted, so it's still concentrated on its top holdings.

**Growth of $10,000**

— Investment Value of ETF
— Investment Value of Index S&P 500

| | 1996 | 1997 | 1998 | 1999 | 2000 | 2001 | 2002 | 2003 | 2004 | 2005 | History |
|---|---|---|---|---|---|---|---|---|---|---|---|
| | — | — | — | — | 74.57 | 53.15 | 32.41 | 48.66 | 48.52 | 49.76 | NAV $ |
| | — | — | — | — | 74.56 | 53.20 | 32.50 | 48.51 | 48.46 | 49.72 | Market Price $ |
| | — | — | — | — | -13.79* | -28.72 | -39.02 | 50.14 | 1.15 | 2.72 | NAV Return% |
| | — | — | — | — | -13.80* | -28.65 | -38.91 | 49.26 | 1.34 | 2.77 | Market Price Return% |
| | — | — | — | — | 0.44 | 0.30 | 0.21 | 0.04 | 0.04 | -0.06 | Avg Premium/Discount% |
| | — | — | — | — | -13.79 | -16.84 | -16.93 | 21.47 | -9.72 | -2.19 | NAV Rtrn% +/-S&P 500 |
| | — | — | — | — | -13.79 | -13.13 | -5.69 | -2.00 | -10.58 | -4.64 | NAV Rtrn% +/-ArcaEx Tech 100 |
| | — | — | — | — | | 3 | 8 | 8 | 8 | 9 | NAV Return% Rank in Cat |
| | — | — | — | — | 0.00 | 0.00 | 0.00 | 0.00 | 1.43 | 0.15 | Income Return % |
| | — | — | — | — | — | -28.72 | -39.02 | 50.14 | -0.28 | 2.57 | Capital Return % |
| | — | — | — | — | 0.00 | 0.00 | 0.00 | 0.00 | 0.70 | 0.07 | Income $ |
| | — | — | — | — | 0.00 | 0.00 | 0.00 | 0.00 | 0.00 | 0.00 | Capital Gains $ |
| | — | — | — | — | — | 0.60 | 0.60 | 0.60 | 0.60 | 0.60 | Expense Ratio % |
| | — | — | — | — | — | -0.47 | -0.41 | -0.22 | -0.22 | 1.78 | Income Ratio % |
| | — | — | — | — | — | 11 | 8 | 15 | 5 | 9 | Turnover Rate % |
| | — | — | — | — | — | 152 | 363 | 468 | 513 | | Net Assets $mil |

## Performance

### Historic Quarterly NAV Returns

| | 1st Qtr | 2nd Qtr | 3rd Qtr | 4th Qtr | Total |
|---|---|---|---|---|---|
| 2001 | -28.30 | 14.21 | -36.47 | 36.98 | -28.72 |
| 2002 | -6.85 | -27.25 | -26.68 | 22.72 | -39.02 |
| 2003 | -0.31 | 19.56 | 11.39 | 13.08 | 50.14 |
| 2004 | -2.63 | 1.67 | -10.75 | 14.49 | 1.15 |
| 2005 | -7.54 | 2.22 | 6.33 | 2.22 | 2.72 |

| Trailing | NAV Return% | Market Return% | NAV Rtrn% +/-S&P 500 | %Rank Cat.(NAV) |
|---|---|---|---|---|
| 3 Mo | 2.22 | 2.22 | 0.14 | 12 |
| 6 Mo | 8.69 | 8.63 | 2.93 | 12 |
| 1 Yr | 2.72 | 2.77 | -2.19 | 9 |
| 3 Yr Avg | 15.98 | 15.84 | 1.60 | 8 |
| 5 Yr Avg | -7.48 | -7.49 | -8.02 | 3 |
| 10 Yr Avg | — | — | — | 0 |

| Tax Analysis | Tax-Adj Return% | Tax-Cost Ratio |
|---|---|---|
| 3 Yr (estimated) | 15.76 | 0.19 |
| 5 Yr (estimated) | -7.58 | 0.11 |
| 10 Yr (estimated) | — | — |

## Risk Profile

| | Standard Index S&P 500 | Best Fit Index ArcaEx Tech 100 |
|---|---|---|
| Alpha | -3.3 | -5.8 |
| Beta | 1.47 | 1.03 |
| R-Squared | 65 | 94 |
| Standard Deviation | 16.71 | |
| Mean | 15.98 | |
| Sharpe Ratio | 0.86 | |

## Morningstar Fair Value

| Price/Fair Value Ratio | Fair Value Estimate ($) | Hit Rate % |
|---|---|---|
| 1.1 Fairly valued | 24.62 | 95 Good |

## Portfolio Analysis 12-31-05

Share change since 11-05 Total Stocks:244

| | | Sector | PE | Tot Ret% | % Assets |
|---|---|---|---|---|---|
| ⊕ | Microsoft | Software | 22.2 | -0.95 | 12.62 |
| ⊕ | Intel | Hardware | 18.6 | 8.12 | 7.74 |
| ⊕ | IBM | Hardware | 16.0 | -15.83 | 6.68 |
| ⊕ | Cisco Systems | Hardware | 19.9 | -11.39 | 5.74 |
| ⊕ | Google | Business | — | 115.19 | 4.21 |
| ⊕ | Hewlett-Packard | Hardware | 27.3 | 38.29 | 4.18 |
| ⊕ | Qualcomm | Hardware | 34.2 | 2.50 | 3.61 |
| ⊕ | Dell | Hardware | 23.2 | -28.93 | 3.34 |
| ⊕ | Apple Computer | Hardware | 46.1 | 123.26 | 3.06 |
| ⊕ | Motorola | Hardware | 13.9 | 32.43 | 2.86 |
| ⊕ | Texas Instruments | Hardware | 25.3 | 30.78 | 2.78 |
| ⊕ | Yahoo | Media | 36.3 | 3.98 | 2.65 |
| ⊕ | Oracle | Software | 22.2 | -11.01 | 2.44 |
| ⊕ | EMC | Hardware | 25.7 | -8.41 | 1.66 |
| ⊕ | Corning | Hardware | 36.4 | 67.03 | 1.52 |
| ⊕ | Applied Materials | Hardware | 24.6 | 5.46 | 1.48 |
| ⊕ | Adobe Systems | Software | 33.3 | 17.84 | 1.13 |
| ⊕ | Symantec | Software | 53.0 | -32.07 | 1.06 |
| ⊕ | Sun Microsystems | Hardware | — | -22.26 | 0.73 |
| ⊕ | Xerox | Ind Mtrls | 17.2 | -13.87 | 0.71 |

### Current Investment Style

Value Blnd Growth — Large/Mid/Small

| Market Cap | % |
|---|---|
| Giant | 62.2 |
| Large | 19.3 |
| Mid | 13.9 |
| Small | 4.1 |
| Micro | 0.5 |

Avg $mil: 39,262

| Value Measures | | Rel Category |
|---|---|---|
| Price/Earnings | 21.50 | 0.90 |
| Price/Book | 3.75 | 1.13 |
| Price/Sales | 2.50 | 0.83 |
| Price/Cash Flow | 11.62 | 1.06 |
| Dividend Yield % | 0.66 | 1.18 |

| Growth Measures | % | Rel Category |
|---|---|---|
| Long-Term Erngs | 13.95 | 0.94 |
| Book Value | 2.92 | 0.91 |
| Sales | 7.00 | 1.22 |
| Cash Flow | 15.30 | 0.77 |
| Historical Erngs | 24.26 | 0.94 |

| Profitability | % | Rel Category |
|---|---|---|
| Return on Equity | 19.86 | 1.28 |
| Return on Assets | 11.73 | 1.24 |
| Net Margin | 17.09 | 1.21 |

| Industry Weightings | % of Stocks | Rel Cat |
|---|---|---|
| Software | 23.9 | 1.2 |
| Hardware | 22.5 | 1.9 |
| Networking Eq | 8.8 | 1.3 |
| Semis | 20.0 | 1.0 |
| Semi Equip | 3.1 | 0.7 |
| Comp/Data Sv | 5.0 | 0.6 |
| Telecom | 1.1 | 0.4 |
| Health Care | 0.0 | 0.0 |
| Other | 15.6 | 0.7 |

### Composition

| | | % |
|---|---|---|
| ● | Cash | 0.1 |
| ● | Stocks | 99.9 |
| ● | Bonds | 0.0 |
| | Other | 0.0 |
| | Foreign (% of Stock) | 0.0 |

## Morningstar's Take by Dan Culloton

iShares Dow Jones U.S. Technology has some, but not all, of the pieces in place.

The fund tracks tech stocks in the Dow Jones U.S. Total Market Index. That gives investors in this offering exposure to about 260, mostly hardware and software, stocks. That's nearly quadruple the number of holdings in the typical tech fund, and the added diversification has helped keep a lid on this offering's volatility relative to other tech funds.

Nevertheless, the offering courts its share of risk. It's one of the more concentrated technology index funds in the bunch. It keeps more than 55% of its assets in its top-10 holdings even though it owns about 260 stocks. Microsoft and IBM take up more than a fifth of the ETF's assets alone. That leaves the portfolio more reliant on large-cap tech bellwethers than most funds in this category. Such a stance could prove to be a boon if large-cap growth stocks, which have been out of favor in recent years, regain the market's favor, but it also can be a drag when such issues are on the outs.

And of course, the offering's focus on one notoriously volatile sector is likely to keep it risky. Indeed it has lost money in about two thirds of the 54 rolling one-year periods between June 1, 2000, (roughly the fund's inception date) and Oct. 31, 2005.

There are also more affordable options. The fund is very cheap when compared with traditional actively managed tech funds, which, on average, carry a more than 2% expense ratio. This ETF's 0.60% levy is not exactly cheap among index funds and ETFs in this category, though. In fact, most of the 12 distinct passively managed mutual funds and ETFs in this area have lower expense ratios.

In general this fund offers investors relatively cheap, easy, and pure exposure to technology stocks, but there are cheaper and more diversified options. Be sure to shop around before committing money here.

| | |
|---|---|
| Address: | 45 Fremont Street |
| | San Francisco CA 94105 |
| | 800-474-2737 |
| Web Address: | www.ishares.com |
| Inception: | 05-15-00* |
| Advisor: | Barclays Global Fund Advisers |

| | |
|---|---|
| Management Fee: | 0.60% |
| Expense Projections: | 3Yr:$192  5Yr:$335  10Yr:$750 |
| Income Distrib: | Quarterly |
| Exchange: | NYSE |

**MORNINGSTAR® ETFs 100**

# iShares DJ Telecom

| | Ticker | NAV | Market Price | 52 wk High/Low | Yield | Mstar Category |
|---|---|---|---|---|---|---|
| | IYZ | $22.87 | $23.44 | $24.39 - $22.02 | 3.6% | Specialty-Communications |

## Management

### Portfolio Manager(s)

Barclays Global Fund Advisors is the advisor. The firm is the world's largest manager of indexed portfolios. Patrick O'Connor, the head of Barclay's U.S. iShares portfolio management group leads a team of a half dozen managers in running this and about 60 other ETFs. iShares' domestic portfolio-management group is responsible for about $75 billion in assets. Most of the managers have at least five years of experience with Barclays as well as prior industry experience.

### Strategy

This exchange-traded fund tracks a subset of the Dow Jones U.S. Total Market Index that includes the telecom service provider stocks in that broad market benchmark. That usually amounts to the shares of fewer than two dozen companies. The fund's bogy is market-cap weighted and extremely concentrated, with most of its assets in its top holdings.

### Growth of $10,000

— Investment Value of ETF
— Investment Value of Index S&P 500

| | 1996 | 1997 | 1998 | 1999 | 2000 | 2001 | 2002 | 2003 | 2004 | 2005 | History |
|---|---|---|---|---|---|---|---|---|---|---|---|
| | — | — | — | — | 38.81 | 31.35 | 19.09 | 21.05 | 24.27 | 22.87 | NAV $ |
| | — | — | — | — | 38.81 | 31.53 | 19.06 | 21.05 | 24.30 | 22.86 | Market Price $ |
| | — | — | — | — | -13.05* | -18.66 | -38.13 | 12.85 | 18.13 | -2.42 | NAV Return% |
| | — | — | — | — | -13.06* | -18.19 | -38.58 | 13.02 | 18.28 | -2.58 | Market Price Return% |
| | — | — | — | — | 0.15 | 0.05 | -0.02 | 0.14 | -0.02 | -0.03 | Avg Premium/Discount% |
| | — | — | — | — | -13.05 | -6.78 | -16.04 | -15.82 | 7.26 | -7.33 | NAV Rtrn% +/-S&P 500 |
| | — | — | — | — | -13.05 | -5.89 | -3.58 | 5.52 | -0.57 | 1.58 | NAV Rtrn% +/-DJ Telecom |
| | — | — | — | — | — | 1 | 2 | 2 | 3 | 3 | NAV Return% Rank in Cat |
| | — | — | — | — | 0.00 | 0.63 | 1.03 | 2.37 | 2.65 | 3.39 | Income Return % |
| | — | — | — | — | — | -19.29 | -39.16 | 10.48 | 15.48 | -5.81 | Capital Return % |
| | — | — | — | — | 0.22 | 0.24 | 0.32 | 0.45 | 0.55 | 0.81 | Income $ |
| | — | — | — | — | 0.59 | 0.00 | 0.00 | 0.00 | 0.00 | 0.00 | Capital Gains $ |
| | — | — | — | — | — | 0.60 | 0.60 | 0.60 | 0.60 | 0.60 | Expense Ratio % |
| | — | — | — | — | — | 0.80 | 1.05 | 2.27 | 2.27 | 2.97 | Income Ratio % |
| | — | — | — | — | — | 43 | 43 | 23 | 22 | 10 | Turnover Rate % |
| | — | — | — | — | — | 104 | 144 | 352 | 497 | Net Assets $mil |

## Performance

### Historic Quarterly NAV Returns

| | 1st Qtr | 2nd Qtr | 3rd Qtr | 4th Qtr | Total |
|---|---|---|---|---|---|
| 2001 | -4.34 | -1.33 | -7.26 | -7.08 | -18.66 |
| 2002 | -16.22 | -27.17 | -24.69 | 34.65 | -38.13 |
| 2003 | -10.86 | 22.40 | -7.32 | 11.60 | 12.85 |
| 2004 | 3.35 | -1.26 | 7.17 | 8.01 | 18.13 |
| 2005 | -4.98 | 2.71 | 1.50 | -1.49 | -2.42 |

| Trailing | NAV Return% | Market Return% | NAV Rtrn% +/-S&P 500 | %Rank Cat.(NAV) |
|---|---|---|---|---|
| 3 Mo | -1.49 | -1.58 | -3.57 | 4 |
| 6 Mo | -0.02 | 0.03 | -5.78 | 4 |
| 1 Yr | -2.42 | -2.58 | -7.33 | 3 |
| 3 Yr Avg | 9.16 | 9.20 | -5.22 | 2 |
| 5 Yr Avg | -8.12 | -8.13 | -8.66 | 1 |
| 10 Yr Avg | — | — | — | 0 |

| Tax Analysis | Tax-Adj Return% | Tax-Cost Ratio |
|---|---|---|
| 3 Yr (estimated) | 8.12 | 0.95 |
| 5 Yr (estimated) | -8.81 | 0.75 |
| 10 Yr (estimated) | — | — |

## Risk Profile

| | Standard Index S&P 500 | Best Fit Index DJ Telecom |
|---|---|---|
| Alpha | -4.7 | 2.7 |
| Beta | 1.03 | 0.85 |
| R-Squared | 56 | 96 |
| Standard Deviation | 12.58 | |
| Mean | 9.16 | |
| Sharpe Ratio | 0.61 | |

## Morningstar Fair Value

| Price/Fair Value Ratio | Fair Value Estimate ($) | Hit Rate % |
|---|---|---|
| 0.9 Undervalued | 23.11 | 91 Good |

## Portfolio Analysis 12-31-05

Share change since 11-05  Total Stocks:26

| | Sector | PE | Tot Ret% | % Assets |
|---|---|---|---|---|
| ⊖ AT&T | Telcom | 21.1 | 0.25 | 20.30 |
| ⊕ Verizon Communications | Telecom | 10.2 | -22.18 | 17.85 |
| ⊕ Sprint Nextel | Telecom | 19.1 | -4.81 | 14.57 |
| ⊕ Alltel | Telecom | 15.5 | 10.12 | 4.96 |
| ⊕ BellSouth | Telecom | 18.1 | 1.77 | 4.94 |
| ⊕ BCE | Telecom | 20.1 | 3.79 | 4.15 |
| ⊕ Centurytel | Telecom | 13.1 | -5.85 | 3.75 |
| ⊕ MCI | Telecom | 37.2 | 27.68 | 3.01 |
| ⊕ NII Holdings | Telecom | 37.8 | 84.11 | 3.00 |
| ⊕ Vodafone Group PLC ADR | Telecom | — | -18.96 | 2.81 |
| ⊕ Qwest Communications Int | Telecom | — | 27.25 | 2.72 |
| ⊕ United States Cellular | Telecom | 36.6 | 10.37 | 2.39 |
| ⊕ Citizens Communications | Telecom | 29.1 | -4.31 | 2.19 |
| ⊕ Telephone and Data Syste | Telecom | 41.6 | -5.55 | 1.74 |
| ⊕ NTL | Telecom | — | -6.69 | 1.72 |
| ⊕ Leucadia National | Ind Mtrls | 4.0 | 3.01 | 1.67 |
| ⊕ Tele & Data Sys | Telecom | — | — | 1.67 |
| ⊕ Nextel Partners A | Telecom | 14.3 | 42.99 | 1.28 |
| ⊕ Alamosa Holdings | Telecom | — | 49.24 | 1.17 |
| ⊕ American Tower A | Telecom | — | 47.28 | 0.71 |

### Current Investment Style

Value Blnd Growth — Large Mid Small

| Market Cap | % |
|---|---|
| Giant | 66.3 |
| Large | 8.6 |
| Mid | 23.7 |
| Small | 1.5 |
| Micro | 0.0 |

Avg $mil: 31,588

| Value Measures | | Rel Category |
|---|---|---|
| Price/Earnings | 16.46 | 0.90 |
| Price/Book | 2.13 | 0.89 |
| Price/Sales | 1.33 | 0.86 |
| Price/Cash Flow | 6.17 | 1.13 |
| Dividend Yield % | 3.08 | 1.26 |

| Growth Measures | % | Rel Category |
|---|---|---|
| Long-Term Erngs | 5.36 | 0.58 |
| Book Value | 2.49 | 1.09 |
| Sales | -3.77 | NMF |
| Cash Flow | -8.40 | NMF |
| Historical Erngs | -1.53 | NMF |

| Profitability | % | Rel Category |
|---|---|---|
| Return on Equity | 12.20 | 1.05 |
| Return on Assets | 3.90 | 0.79 |
| Net Margin | 8.39 | 0.84 |

| Industry Weightings | % of Stocks | Rel Cat |
|---|---|---|
| Telecom Srv | 64.0 | 2.5 |
| Wireless Srv | 34.1 | 1.0 |
| Network Eq | 0.0 | 0.0 |
| Semis | 0.0 | -0.0 |
| Big Media | 0.0 | 0.0 |
| Cable TV | 0.0 | 0.0 |
| Other Media | 0.0 | 0.0 |
| Soft/Hardwr | 0.0 | 0.0 |
| Other | 1.9 | 0.2 |

### Composition

| | | |
|---|---|---|
| ● Cash | 0.1 |
| ● Stocks | 99.9 |
| ● Bonds | 0.0 |
| ● Other | 0.0 |
| Foreign | 7.0 |
| (% of Stock) | |

## Morningstar's Take by Dan Culloton

This exchange-traded fund's appeal is less than skin deep.

iShares Dow Jones U.S. Telecommunications Index would seem to have some advantages over the traditional telecom sector funds. Its 0.60% expense ratio is nearly two thirds of that of the typical telecom fund. Its advisor is the largest manager of index assets in the world and it offers an undiluted shot of wireless and traditional telecom service providers. Furthermore, the telecom category is filled with some wacky offerings that are too narrowly focused and fraught with risk for most investors to allow in the same area code as their portfolios.

The fact is most investors can live long and happy lives without a telecom fund because they already get exposure to this sector through more diversified offerings. If you must have a telecom fund you can make an argument for using an ETF, but probably not this one. The fund is concentrated both in terms of number of equity holdings (fewer than two dozen) and individual position sizes. More than 40% of its assets are in two stocks, Verizon Communications and SBC Communications. So it has been volatile. The ETF lost money in nearly half of the 54 rolling one-year periods from June 1, 2000, through the end of October 2005 and fell by more than 25% in most of those downdrafts.

Finally, while this ETF's expense ratio is cheap relative to traditional funds, it's not the cheapest telecom ETF available. Vanguard Telecommunications Services Vipers' levy is less than half that of this fund. The Vanguard fund also keeps less money in its top-10 holdings and owns more mid- and small-cap telecom stocks, so it's more diversified. Actively managed Analyst Pick T. Rowe Price Media & Telecom owns more stocks outside of the sector but also has delivered better returns with less volatility.

If you can't live without a telecom fund, there are better options than this ETF.

| | |
|---|---|
| Address: | 45 Fremont Street San Francisco CA 94105 800-474-2737 |
| Web Address: | www.ishares.com |
| Inception: | 05-22-00 * |
| Advisor: | Barclays Global Fund Advisers |

| | |
|---|---|
| Management Fee: | 0.60% |
| Expense Projections: | 3Yr:$192  5Yr:$335  10Yr:$750 |
| Income Distrib: | Quarterly |
| Exchange: | NYSE |

MORNINGSTAR® ETFs 100

# iShares DJ Total Mkt

| Ticker | NAV | Market Price | 52 wk High/Low | Yield | Mstar Category |
|---|---|---|---|---|---|
| IYY | $60.53 | $62.69 | $62.76 - $54.60 | 1.6% | Large Blend |

## Management

### Portfolio Manager(s)

Barclays Global Fund Advisors is the advisor. The firm is the world's largest manager of indexed portfolios. Patrick O'Connor, the head of Barclay's U.S. iShares portfolio management group, leads a team of a half dozen managers in running this and about 60 other ETFs. IShares' domestic portfolio-management group is responsible for about $75 billion in assets. Most of the managers have at least five years of experience with Barclays as well as prior industry experience.

### Strategy

This fund tracks the Dow Jones U.S. Total Market Index, which includes about 95% of the domestic-stock market capitalization. It is market-cap-weighted and adjusted for insider ownership, cross ownership, and other factors that could limit the number of stock shares that actually trade. The fund's advisor uses representative sampling to mirror the benchmark's return, which means the offering owns most, but not every, stock in the index.

### Growth of $10,000

— Investment Value of ETF
— Investment Value of Index S&P 500

| | 1996 | 1997 | 1998 | 1999 | 2000 | 2001 | 2002 | 2003 | 2004 | 2005 | History |
|---|---|---|---|---|---|---|---|---|---|---|---|
| | — | — | — | — | 61.42 | 53.39 | 41.00 | 52.71 | 57.94 | 60.53 | NAV $ |
| | — | — | — | — | 61.53 | 53.57 | 41.02 | 52.71 | 58.00 | 60.51 | Market Price $ |
| | — | — | — | — | -0.51* | -12.13 | -22.17 | 30.42 | 11.78 | 6.14 | NAV Return% |
| | — | — | — | — | -0.52* | -12.00 | -22.40 | 30.36 | 11.90 | 6.00 | Market Price Return% |
| | — | — | — | — | 0.13 | 0.02 | 0.10 | 0.12 | 0.04 | 0.01 | Avg Premium/Discount% |
| | — | — | — | — | -0.51 | -0.25 | -0.08 | 1.75 | 0.91 | 1.23 | NAV Rtrn% +/-S&P 500 |
| | — | — | — | — | -0.51 | 0.32 | -0.52 | 0.53 | 0.38 | -0.13 | NAV Rtrn% +/-Russ 1000 |
| | — | — | — | — | — | 13 | 15 | 15 | 17 | 23 | NAV Return% Rank in Cat |
| | — | — | — | — | 0.00 | 0.94 | 1.13 | 1.64 | 1.76 | 1.63 | Income Return % |
| | — | — | — | — | — | -13.07 | -23.30 | 28.78 | 10.02 | 4.51 | Capital Return % |
| | — | — | — | — | 0.24 | 0.57 | 0.60 | 0.67 | 0.92 | 0.94 | Income $ |
| | — | — | — | — | 0.01 | 0.00 | 0.00 | 0.00 | 0.00 | 0.00 | Capital Gains $ |
| | — | — | — | — | — | 0.20 | 0.20 | 0.20 | 0.20 | 0.20 | Expense Ratio % |
| | — | — | — | — | — | 0.98 | 1.15 | 1.57 | 1.49 | 1.81 | Income Ratio % |
| | — | — | — | — | — | 5 | 5 | 14 | 5 | 6 | Turnover Rate % |
| | — | — | — | — | — | 143 | 335 | 435 | 472 | | Net Assets $mil |

## Performance

### Historic Quarterly NAV Returns

| | 1st Qtr | 2nd Qtr | 3rd Qtr | 4th Qtr | Total |
|---|---|---|---|---|---|
| 2001 | -12.75 | 6.88 | -15.75 | 11.84 | -12.13 |
| 2002 | 0.37 | -13.57 | -17.07 | 8.18 | -22.17 |
| 2003 | -3.09 | 16.12 | 3.16 | 12.35 | 30.42 |
| 2004 | 2.15 | 1.46 | -1.93 | 9.98 | 11.78 |
| 2005 | -2.12 | 2.10 | 3.92 | 2.20 | 6.14 |

| Trailing | NAV Return% | Market Return% | NAV Rtrn% +/-S&P 500 | %Rank Cat.(NAV) |
|---|---|---|---|---|
| 3 Mo | 2.20 | 2.13 | 0.12 | 27 |
| 6 Mo | 6.21 | 6.02 | 0.45 | 27 |
| 1 Yr | 6.14 | 6.00 | 1.23 | 23 |
| 3 Yr Avg | 15.67 | 15.63 | 1.29 | 14 |
| 5 Yr Avg | 1.14 | 1.09 | 0.60 | 13 |
| 10 Yr Avg | — | — | — | 0 |

| Tax Analysis | Tax-Adj Return% | Tax-Cost Ratio |
|---|---|---|
| 3 Yr (estimated) | 15.03 | 0.55 |
| 5 Yr (estimated) | 0.62 | 0.51 |
| 10 Yr (estimated) | — | — |

## Risk Profile

| | Standard Index S&P 500 | Best Fit Index Russ 1000 |
|---|---|---|
| Alpha | 0.7 | -0.1 |
| Beta | 1.04 | 1.03 |
| R-Squared | 99 | 100 |
| Standard Deviation | 9.53 | |
| Mean | 15.67 | |
| Sharpe Ratio | 1.37 | |

## Morningstar Fair Value

| Price/Fair Value Ratio | Fair Value Estimate ($) | Hit Rate % |
|---|---|---|
| 1.0 Fairly valued | 37.19 | 93 Good |

## Portfolio Analysis 12-31-05

Share change since 11-05  Total Stocks:1627

| | Sector | PE | Tot Ret% | % Assets |
|---|---|---|---|---|
| ⊖ General Electric | Ind Mtrls | 19.9 | -1.43 | 2.73 |
| ⊖ ExxonMobil | Energy | 10.6 | 11.76 | 2.63 |
| ⊖ Citigroup | Financial | 12.1 | 4.63 | 1.86 |
| ⊖ Microsoft | Software | 22.2 | -0.95 | 1.82 |
| ⊖ Procter & Gamble | Goods | 21.2 | 7.18 | 1.45 |
| ⊖ Bank of America | Financial | 11.1 | 2.39 | 1.37 |
| ⊖ Johnson & Johnson | Health | 19.1 | -3.36 | 1.31 |
| ⊖ Pfizer | Health | 21.2 | -10.62 | 1.27 |
| ⊖ American International G | Financial | 15.6 | 4.83 | 1.14 |
| ⊖ Altria Group | Goods | 15.0 | 27.72 | 1.14 |
| ⊖ Intel | Hardware | 18.6 | 8.12 | 1.12 |
| ⊖ J.P. Morgan Chase & Co. | Financial | 18.8 | 5.74 | 1.03 |
| ⊖ IBM | Hardware | 16.0 | -15.83 | 0.96 |
| ⊖ Chevron | Energy | 9.0 | 11.51 | 0.94 |
| ⊖ Wal-Mart Stores | Consumer | 18.2 | -10.30 | 0.89 |
| ⊖ Cisco Systems | Hardware | 19.9 | -11.39 | 0.83 |
| ⊖ Wells Fargo | Financial | 14.3 | 4.47 | 0.77 |
| ⊖ PepsiCo | Goods | 25.8 | 15.24 | 0.72 |
| ⊖ Amgen | Health | 28.3 | 22.93 | 0.71 |
| ⊖ AT&T | Telecom | 21.1 | 0.25 | 0.71 |

### Current Investment Style

Value Blnd Growth — Large / Mid / Small

| Market Cap | % |
|---|---|
| Giant | 45.0 |
| Large | 32.3 |
| Mid | 19.2 |
| Small | 3.3 |
| Micro | 0.2 |

Avg $mil: 29,879

| Value Measures | | Rel Category |
|---|---|---|
| Price/Earnings | 16.45 | 0.97 |
| Price/Book | 2.49 | 0.92 |
| Price/Sales | 1.46 | 1.14 |
| Price/Cash Flow | 6.41 | 0.89 |
| Dividend Yield % | 1.78 | 1.01 |

| Growth Measures | | Rel Category |
|---|---|---|
| Long-Term Erngs | 10.81 | 0.97 |
| Book Value | 10.07 | 1.07 |
| Sales | 8.54 | 1.06 |
| Cash Flow | 11.56 | 1.12 |
| Historical Erngs | 15.13 | 1.07 |

| Profitability | % | Rel Category |
|---|---|---|
| Return on Equity | 18.67 | 0.92 |
| Return on Assets | 9.93 | 1.06 |
| Net Margin | 13.16 | 1.21 |

| Sector Weightings | % of Stocks | Rel S&P 500 | 3 Year High Low | |
|---|---|---|---|---|
| ↻ Info | 20.13 | 1.00 | | |
| Software | 3.71 | 1.04 | 5 | 4 |
| Hardware | 9.82 | 0.98 | 12 | 9 |
| Media | 3.72 | 1.04 | 4 | 4 |
| Telecom | 2.88 | 0.96 | 4 | 3 |
| ⊕ Service | 47.75 | 1.03 | | |
| Health | 13.08 | 0.98 | 16 | 12 |
| Consumer | 8.56 | 1.05 | 9 | 8 |
| Business | 5.24 | 1.35 | 5 | 4 |
| Financial | 20.87 | 0.99 | 22 | 20 |
| ⊟ Mfg | 32.12 | 0.96 | | |
| Goods | 7.98 | 0.93 | 9 | 8 |
| Ind Mtrls | 11.44 | 0.94 | 12 | 10 |
| Energy | 9.32 | 1.00 | 10 | 6 |
| Utilities | 3.38 | 1.01 | 4 | 3 |

### Composition

| | % |
|---|---|
| ● Cash | 0.1 |
| ● Stocks | 99.9 |
| ● Bonds | 0.0 |
| Other | 0.0 |
| Foreign | 0.2 |
| (% of Stock) | |

## Morningstar's Take  by Dan Culloton

This exchange-traded fund gets the job done, but it is possible to do better.

IShares Dow Jones U.S. Total Market Index offers one-stop domestic-stock exposure by tracking an index that includes 95% of the free-float U.S. stock market capitalization. Like other index funds that try to ape the performance of the entire stock market, it is diversified across the size and sector spectrums. Not surprisingly, its volatility, as measured by standard deviation, is close to the average large-blend offering and other total-market index funds.

This fund's long-term performance should correlate with its market-tracking index-fund peers because the vast majority of their holdings are the same. They won't always move in lockstep over shorter periods, though. For example, this ETF has lagged Vanguard Total Stock Market Index over the past five years because its benchmark doesn't include as many small-cap stocks, which have rallied in recent years. The tables could turn in this fund's favor, however, when the market favors large caps.

Execution and expenses usually distinguish a fund like this. The offering has done its job, trailing its benchmark by the size of its expense ratio since inception, which indicates competent management. The problem is the ETF's 0.2% expense ratio. While that's cheap compared with the typical traditional large-blend fund, its more than twice that of the lowest-cost all-market ETF and higher than some traditional index funds, as well. It may seem silly to quibble over a few hundredths of a percent, but every little bit counts among index funds. Expense ratios can explain about 30% of the difference in returns between this offering and the top-performing large-blend index fund for the five years ending Aug. 22, 2005.

This fund won't kill you, but you can find offerings with similar risk and reward profiles and even lower expense ratios.

| Address: | 45 Fremont Street San Francisco CA 94105 800-474-2737 | Management Fee: | 0.20% |
|---|---|---|---|
| | | Expense Projections: | 3Yr:$64  5Yr:$113  10Yr:$255 |
| Web Address: | www.ishares.com | Income Distrib: | Quarterly |
| Inception: | 06-12-00* | Exchange: | NYSE |
| Advisor: | Barclays Global Fund Advisers | | |

MORNINGSTAR® ETFs 100

# iShares DJ US Energy

| Ticker | NAV | Market Price | 52 wk High/Low | Yield | Mstar Category |
|---|---|---|---|---|---|
| IYE | $85.52 | $91.49 | $92.70 - $62.49 | 0.9% | Specialty-Natural Res |

## Management

### Portfolio Manager(s)

Barclays Global Fund Advisors is the advisor. The firm is the world's largest manager of indexed portfolios. Patrick O'Connor, the head of Barclay's U.S. iShares portfolio management group leads a team of a half dozen managers in running this and about 60 other ETFs. IShares' domestic portfolio-management group is responsible for about $75 billion in assets. Most of the managers have at least five years of experience with Barclays as well as prior industry experience.

### Strategy

This exchange-traded fund tracks a subset of the Dow Jones U.S. Total Market Index: The Dow Jones U.S. Oil & Gas Index. The bogy includes the oil- and gas-company stocks from the broader-market benchmark. The index includes more than 80 stocks, but this fund typically owns fewer than that because it uses representative sampling to track the benchmark. The fund is extremely concentrated, with most of its assets in its top holdings.

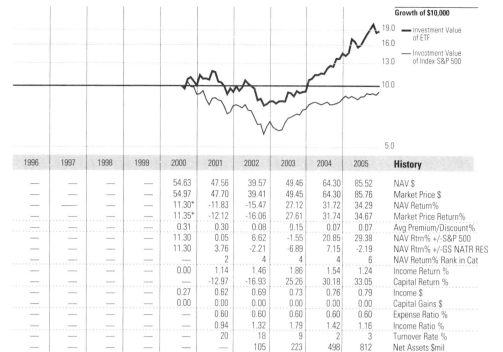

Growth of $10,000
— Investment Value of ETF
— Investment Value of Index S&P 500

| | 1996 | 1997 | 1998 | 1999 | 2000 | 2001 | 2002 | 2003 | 2004 | 2005 | History |
|---|---|---|---|---|---|---|---|---|---|---|---|
| | — | — | — | — | 54.63 | 47.56 | 39.57 | 49.46 | 64.30 | 85.52 | NAV $ |
| | — | — | — | — | 54.97 | 47.70 | 39.41 | 49.45 | 64.30 | 85.76 | Market Price $ |
| | — | — | — | — | 11.30* | -11.83 | -15.47 | 27.12 | 31.72 | 34.29 | NAV Return% |
| | — | — | — | — | 11.35* | -12.12 | -16.06 | 27.61 | 31.74 | 34.67 | Market Price Return% |
| | — | — | — | — | 0.31 | 0.30 | 0.08 | 0.15 | 0.07 | 0.07 | Avg Premium/Discount% |
| | — | — | — | — | 11.30 | 0.05 | 6.62 | -1.55 | 20.85 | 29.38 | NAV Rtrn% +/-S&P 500 |
| | — | — | — | — | 11.30 | 3.76 | -2.21 | -6.89 | 7.15 | -2.19 | NAV Rtrn% +/-GS NATR RES |
| | — | — | — | — | — | 2 | 4 | 4 | 4 | 6 | NAV Return% Rank in Cat |
| | — | — | — | — | 0.00 | 1.14 | 1.46 | 1.86 | 1.54 | 1.24 | Income Return % |
| | — | — | — | — | — | -12.97 | -16.93 | 25.26 | 30.18 | 33.05 | Capital Return % |
| | — | — | — | — | 0.27 | 0.62 | 0.69 | 0.73 | 0.76 | 0.79 | Income $ |
| | — | — | — | — | 0.00 | 0.00 | 0.00 | 0.00 | 0.00 | 0.00 | Capital Gains $ |
| | — | — | — | — | 0.60 | 0.60 | 0.60 | 0.60 | 0.60 | 0.60 | Expense Ratio % |
| | — | — | — | — | 0.94 | 1.32 | 1.79 | 1.42 | 1.16 | | Income Ratio % |
| | — | — | — | — | 20 | 18 | 9 | 2 | 3 | | Turnover Rate % |
| | — | — | — | — | — | 105 | 223 | 498 | 812 | | Net Assets $mil |

## Performance

### Historic Quarterly NAV Returns

| | 1st Qtr | 2nd Qtr | 3rd Qtr | 4th Qtr | Total |
|---|---|---|---|---|---|
| 2001 | -5.02 | -2.16 | -13.15 | 9.24 | -11.83 |
| 2002 | 6.95 | -8.97 | -17.55 | 5.30 | -15.47 |
| 2003 | 0.12 | 9.41 | 0.23 | 15.79 | 27.12 |
| 2004 | 5.84 | 7.74 | 11.74 | 3.37 | 31.72 |
| 2005 | 17.20 | 2.70 | 18.79 | -6.07 | 34.29 |

| Trailing | NAV Return% | Market Return% | NAV Rtrn% +/-S&P 500 | %Rank Cat.(NAV) |
|---|---|---|---|---|
| 3 Mo | -6.07 | -5.76 | -8.15 | 7 |
| 6 Mo | 11.58 | 11.85 | 5.82 | 7 |
| 1 Yr | 34.29 | 34.67 | 29.38 | 6 |
| 3 Yr Avg | 31.01 | 31.31 | 16.63 | 4 |
| 5 Yr Avg | 10.88 | 10.80 | 10.34 | 2 |
| 10 Yr Avg | — | — | — | 0 |

| Tax Analysis | Tax-Adj Return% | Tax-Cost Ratio |
|---|---|---|
| 3 Yr (estimated) | 30.41 | 0.46 |
| 5 Yr (estimated) | 10.33 | 0.50 |
| 10 Yr (estimated) | — | — |

## Risk Profile

| | Standard Index S&P 500 | Best Fit Index GS NATR RES |
|---|---|---|
| Alpha | 18.4 | -1.0 |
| Beta | 0.71 | 1.03 |
| R-Squared | 13 | 92 |
| Standard Deviation | 18.25 | |
| Mean | 31.01 | |
| Sharpe Ratio | 1.48 | |

## Morningstar Fair Value

| Price/Fair Value Ratio | Fair Value Estimate ($) | Hit Rate % |
|---|---|---|
| 1.2 Overvalued | 63.62 | 99 Good |

## Morningstar's Take by Dan Culloton

The tide is high for the exchange-traded iShares Dow Jones US Energy. Don't get swamped.

Despite slipping some in the 2005's fourth quarter, this fund has been on a roll. Record-high oil prices have fueled a rally among this fund's holdings sending it up by more than 35% in the 12-month period ending Nov. 11, 2005. Talk about a sustained period of higher oil prices has investors excited about the prospects for the oil patch.

The big question is whether all that excitement is priced into the stocks. The answer is open to debate, but there are signs that valuations are getting full. For example, the stock prices relative to earnings, book value, and sales of the average energy firm are above their five-year average.

Furthermore, oil prices can be fickle and wreak havoc on the earnings and stock performance of the companies included in this portfolio. This ETF has been down often during its lifetime, losing money in 43% of the 53 rolling one-year periods between July 2000 and the end of October 2005. Most of

those declines were by double digits.

There's more behind the fund's variability than its reliance on oil patch stocks, though. It is concentrated, with close to 70% of its assets in its top-10 holdings and about 56 stocks in the portfolio overall. Its top-two holdings, ExxonMobil and ChevronTexaco, claim nearly half of the ETF's assets.

This is not to say that energy stocks are too volatile for a portfolio. However, you should see how much exposure your portfolio already has to the sector through more-diversified funds before adding a sector fund like this to the mix. Even then you can find more-diversified and more-affordable options than this one, which has an expense ratio that, while cheap relative to traditional natural-resources funds, is more than double that of the cheapest ETF alternatives in the category.

## Portfolio Analysis 12-31-05

| Share change since 11-05 Total Stocks:54 | Sector | PE | Tot Ret% | % Assets |
|---|---|---|---|---|
| ⊕ ExxonMobil | Energy | 10.6 | 11.76 | 20.56 |
| ⊕ Chevron | Energy | 9.0 | 11.51 | 16.82 |
| ⊕ ConocoPhillips | Energy | 6.7 | 36.89 | 5.43 |
| ⊕ Schlumberger | Energy | 31.1 | 46.62 | 5.26 |
| ⊕ Burlington Resources | Energy | 15.4 | 99.35 | 4.70 |
| ⊕ Occidental Petroleum | Energy | 6.7 | 39.15 | 4.65 |
| ⊕ Devon Energy | Energy | 11.4 | 61.57 | 2.93 |
| ⊕ Baker Hughes | Energy | 25.9 | 43.78 | 2.60 |
| ⊕ Halliburton | Energy | 21.7 | 59.46 | 2.59 |
| ⊕ Anadarko Petroleum | Energy | 11.4 | 47.42 | 2.58 |
| ⊕ Apache | Energy | 9.8 | 36.28 | 2.42 |
| ⊕ EOG Resources | Energy | 17.9 | 106.26 | 2.18 |
| ⊕ Murphy Oil | Energy | 12.4 | 35.48 | 2.16 |
| ⊕ Transocean | Energy | 48.1 | 64.40 | 2.11 |
| ⊕ Marathon Oil | Energy | 9.8 | 66.01 | 1.98 |
| ⊕ Valero Energy | Energy | 10.7 | 128.46 | 1.81 |
| ⊕ Kerr-McGee | Energy | 15.3 | 58.41 | 1.37 |
| ⊕ Amerada Hess | Energy | 12.9 | 55.55 | 1.33 |
| ⊕ Williams Companies | Energy | 38.0 | 43.97 | 1.31 |
| ⊕ Kinder Morgan | Energy | 20.3 | 30.29 | 1.19 |

### Current Investment Style

Value Blnd Growth — Large Mid Small

| Market Cap | % |
|---|---|
| Giant | 48.1 |
| Large | 45.2 |
| Mid | 6.3 |
| Small | 0.4 |
| Micro | 0.0 |

Avg $mil: 51,380

| Value Measures | | Rel Category |
|---|---|---|
| Price/Earnings | 11.14 | 0.73 |
| Price/Book | 2.83 | 1.04 |
| Price/Sales | 1.10 | 0.79 |
| Price/Cash Flow | 7.28 | 0.78 |
| Dividend Yield % | 1.42 | 1.18 |

| Growth Measures | % | Rel Category |
|---|---|---|
| Long-Term Erngs | 7.01 | 0.67 |
| Book Value | 13.47 | 1.93 |
| Sales | 18.20 | 1.30 |
| Cash Flow | 25.25 | 1.38 |
| Historical Erngs | 45.81 | 1.38 |

| Profitability | % | Rel Category |
|---|---|---|
| Return on Equity | 24.21 | 1.53 |
| Return on Assets | 11.38 | 1.62 |
| Net Margin | 14.50 | 1.55 |

| Industry Weightings | % of Stocks | Rel Cat |
|---|---|---|
| Oil & Gas | 73.4 | 1.9 |
| Oil/Gas Products | 2.8 | 0.7 |
| Oil & Gas Srv | 20.9 | 0.7 |
| Pipelines | 2.7 | 1.8 |
| Utilities | 0.0 | 0.0 |
| Hard Commd | 0.1 | 0.0 |
| Soft Commd | 0.0 | 0.0 |
| Misc. Indstrl | 0.0 | 0.0 |
| Other | 0.0 | 0.0 |

### Composition

| | | |
|---|---|---|
| ● Cash | 0.1 | |
| ● Stocks | 99.9 | |
| ● Bonds | 0.0 | |
| ● Other | 0.0 | |
| Foreign | 0.0 | (% of Stock) |

| Address: | 45 Fremont Street San Francisco CA 94105 800-474-2737 | Management Fee: | 0.60% |
|---|---|---|---|
| | | Expense Projections: | 3Yr:$192  5Yr:$335  10Yr:$750 |
| Web Address: | www.ishares.com | Income Distrib: | Quarterly |
| Inception: | 06-12-00* | Exchange: | NYSE |
| Advisor: | Barclays Global Fund Advisers | | |

MᴏRNINGSTAR® ETFs 100

# iShares DJ Utilities

| | Ticker | NAV | Market Price | 52 wk High/Low | Yield | Mstar Category |
|---|---|---|---|---|---|---|
| | IDU | $76.47 | $77.99 | $83.12 - $66.76 | 2.9% | Specialty-Utilities |

## Management

### Portfolio Manager(s)

Barclays Global Fund Advisors is the advisor. The firm is the world's largest manager of indexed portfolios. Patrick O'Connor, the head of Barclay's U.S. iShares portfolio management group leads a team of a half dozen managers in running this and about 60 other ETFs. iShares' domestic portfolio-management group is responsible for about $75 billion in assets. Most of the managers have at least five years of experience with Barclays as well as prior industry experience.

### Strategy

This fund tracks the Dow Jones U.S. Utilities Index, which includes the power, gas, water, and other utility stocks from the Dow Jones U.S. Total Market Index. It's market-cap-weighted and adjusted for insider ownership, cross ownership, and other factors that could limit the number of stock shares that actually trade. The fund's advisor uses representative sampling to mirror the benchmark's return, which means the offering owns most, but not all, the stocks in the index.

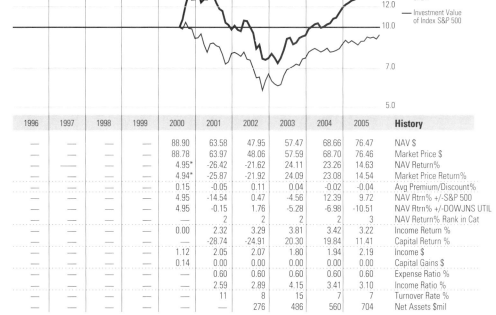

Growth of $10,000
— Investment Value of ETF
— Investment Value of Index S&P 500

| | 1996 | 1997 | 1998 | 1999 | 2000 | 2001 | 2002 | 2003 | 2004 | 2005 | History |
|---|---|---|---|---|---|---|---|---|---|---|---|
| | — | — | — | — | 88.90 | 63.58 | 47.95 | 57.47 | 68.66 | 76.47 | NAV $ |
| | — | — | — | — | 88.78 | 63.97 | 48.06 | 57.59 | 68.70 | 76.46 | Market Price $ |
| | — | — | — | — | 4.95* | -26.42 | -21.62 | 24.11 | 23.26 | 14.63 | NAV Return% |
| | — | — | — | — | 4.94* | -25.87 | -21.92 | 24.09 | 23.08 | 14.54 | Market Price Return% |
| | — | — | — | — | 0.15 | -0.05 | 0.11 | 0.04 | -0.02 | -0.04 | Avg Premium/Discount% |
| | — | — | — | — | 4.95 | -14.54 | 0.47 | -4.56 | 12.39 | 9.72 | NAV Rtrn% +/-S&P 500 |
| | — | — | — | — | 4.95 | -0.15 | 1.76 | -5.28 | -6.98 | -10.51 | NAV Rtrn% +/-DOWJNS UTIL |
| | — | — | — | — | — | 2 | 2 | 2 | 2 | 3 | NAV Return% Rank in Cat |
| | — | — | — | — | 0.00 | 2.32 | 3.29 | 3.81 | 3.42 | 3.22 | Income Return % |
| | — | — | — | — | — | -28.74 | -24.91 | 20.30 | 19.84 | 11.41 | Capital Return % |
| | — | — | — | — | 1.12 | 2.05 | 2.07 | 1.80 | 1.94 | 2.19 | Income $ |
| | — | — | — | — | 0.14 | 0.00 | 0.00 | 0.00 | 0.00 | 0.00 | Capital Gains $ |
| | — | — | — | — | — | 0.60 | 0.60 | 0.60 | 0.60 | 0.60 | Expense Ratio % |
| | — | — | — | — | — | 2.59 | 2.89 | 4.15 | 3.41 | 3.10 | Income Ratio % |
| | — | — | — | — | — | 11 | 8 | 15 | 7 | 7 | Turnover Rate % |
| | — | — | — | — | — | 276 | 486 | 560 | 704 | Net Assets $mil |

## Performance

### Historic Quarterly NAV Returns

| | 1st Qtr | 2nd Qtr | 3rd Qtr | 4th Qtr | Total |
|---|---|---|---|---|---|
| 2001 | -7.62 | -3.07 | -15.63 | -2.61 | -26.42 |
| 2002 | 4.54 | -10.20 | -20.04 | 4.42 | -21.62 |
| 2003 | -3.68 | 19.33 | -0.24 | 8.24 | 24.11 |
| 2004 | 5.01 | -1.00 | 6.00 | 11.85 | 23.26 |
| 2005 | 4.62 | 9.24 | 6.88 | -6.16 | 14.63 |

| Trailing | NAV Return% | Market Return% | NAV Rtrn% +/-S&P 500 | %Rank Cat.(NAV) |
|---|---|---|---|---|
| 3 Mo | -6.16 | -6.22 | -8.24 | 3 |
| 6 Mo | 0.30 | 0.26 | -5.46 | 3 |
| 1 Yr | 14.63 | 14.54 | 9.72 | 3 |
| 3 Yr Avg | 20.59 | 20.49 | 6.21 | 2 |
| 5 Yr Avg | 0.23 | 0.25 | -0.31 | 2 |
| 10 Yr Avg | — | — | — | 0 |

| Tax Analysis | Tax-Adj Return% | Tax-Cost Ratio |
|---|---|---|
| 3 Yr (estimated) | 19.26 | 1.10 |
| 5 Yr (estimated) | -0.95 | 1.18 |
| 10 Yr (estimated) | — | — |

## Risk Profile

| | Standard Index S&P 500 | Best Fit Index DOWJNS UTIL |
|---|---|---|
| Alpha | 9.6 | -3.9 |
| Beta | 0.67 | 0.89 |
| R-Squared | 27 | 94 |
| Standard Deviation | 11.72 | |
| Mean | 20.59 | |
| Sharpe Ratio | 1.50 | |

## Morningstar Fair Value

| Price/Fair Value Ratio | Fair Value Estimate ($) | Hit Rate % |
|---|---|---|
| 1.0 Fairly valued | 36.04 | 96 Good |

## Portfolio Analysis  12-31-05

| Share change since 11-05  Total Stocks:72 | Sector | PE | Tot Ret% | % Assets |
|---|---|---|---|---|
| ⊕ Exelon | Utilities | 17.0 | 24.58 | 7.66 |
| ⊕ Dominion Resources | Utilities | 26.5 | 18.19 | 5.65 |
| ⊕ Southern | Utilities | 15.8 | 7.57 | 5.51 |
| ⊕ Duke Energy | Utilities | 11.2 | 13.11 | 5.16 |
| ⊕ TXU | Utilities | — | 59.98 | 4.89 |
| ⊕ FirstEnergy | Utilities | 18.8 | 28.72 | 3.47 |
| ⊕ Public Service Enterpris | Utilities | 22.2 | 30.22 | 3.33 |
| ⊕ FPL Group | Utilities | 18.5 | 15.05 | 3.23 |
| ⊖ American Electric Power | Utilities | 12.0 | 12.33 | 3.07 |
| ⊖ Entergy | Utilities | 15.5 | 4.67 | 3.06 |
| ⊕ PG & E | Utilities | 16.3 | 15.32 | 2.95 |
| ⊕ Edison International | Utilities | 13.5 | 39.63 | 2.80 |
| ⊕ Consolidated Edison | Utilities | 17.8 | 11.32 | 2.42 |
| ⊕ PPL | Utilities | 15.8 | 14.03 | 2.40 |
| ⊕ Progress Energy | Utilities | 13.8 | 2.47 | 2.38 |
| ⊕ Constellation Energy Gro | Utilities | 18.1 | 35.05 | 2.21 |
| ⊕ AES | Utilities | 24.4 | 15.80 | 2.21 |
| ⊕ Sempra Energy | Utilities | 12.1 | 25.62 | 2.18 |
| ⊕ Ameren | Utilities | 15.3 | 7.18 | 2.14 |
| ⊕ Cinergy | Utilities | 18.5 | 6.90 | 1.68 |

### Current Investment Style

Value Blnd Growth — Large / Mid / Small

| | Market Cap | % |
|---|---|---|
| | Giant | 0.0 |
| | Large | 66.8 |
| | Mid | 30.0 |
| | Small | 3.2 |
| | Micro | 0.0 |
| | Avg $mil: | 10,592 |

| Value Measures | | Rel Category |
|---|---|---|
| Price/Earnings | 16.16 | 0.99 |
| Price/Book | 1.96 | 0.97 |
| Price/Sales | 1.21 | 0.95 |
| Price/Cash Flow | 5.94 | 0.88 |
| Dividend Yield % | 3.13 | 1.04 |

| Growth Measures | % | Rel Category |
|---|---|---|
| Long-Term Erngs | 5.99 | 1.04 |
| Book Value | 1.14 | 2.24 |
| Sales | 2.01 | 1.40 |
| Cash Flow | -2.44 | NMF |
| Historical Erngs | 7.55 | 0.93 |

| Profitability | % | Rel Category |
|---|---|---|
| Return on Equity | 15.89 | 1.14 |
| Return on Assets | 3.03 | 1.00 |
| Net Margin | 7.92 | 0.99 |

### Industry Weightings

| | % of Stocks | Rel Cat |
|---|---|---|
| Telecom Srv | 0.0 | 0.0 |
| Electric Utls | 86.6 | 1.4 |
| Nat Gas Utls | 9.7 | 1.0 |
| Wireless Srv | 0.0 | 0.0 |
| Energy | 3.0 | 0.3 |
| Media | 0.0 | 0.0 |
| Network Eq | 0.0 | 0.0 |
| Water | 0.8 | 1.1 |
| Other | 0.0 | 0.0 |

### Composition

| | % |
|---|---|
| ● Cash | 0.1 |
| ● Stocks | 99.9 |
| ● Bonds | 0.0 |
| ● Other | 0.0 |
| Foreign | 0.0 |
| (% of Stock) | |

## Morningstar's Take  by Dan Culloton

This exchange-traded fund has some advantages, but one key disadvantage.

iShares Dow Jones U.S. Utilities Index is a pure play on utilities stocks. The fund tracks the power, gas, and water companies in the Dow Jones U.S. Total Market Index. Unlike many traditional mutual funds in the utilities category, this portfolio shuns stocks outside of its sector. Because it hasn't been hampered by the telecom stocks often found in its actively managed rivals, this ETF has capitalized on utilities' recent rally to best the category average.

This ETF also presents a more diversified alternative to its largest rival: Utilities Select Sector SPDR. This fund spreads its money out over more stocks than the concentrated SPDR. This fund is no shrinking violet. It has 44% of its assets in its top-10 holdings, and more than 7% in top holding Exelon alone. But the SPDR has nearly 60% of its assets in its top 10. While this ETF's volatility, as measured by standard deviation, is higher than the category average, it's lower than that of the SPDR.

That's not to say this portfolio is without some tough competition. There is at least one ETF with a similar portfolio and risk profile but with an expense ratio that is less than half of this fund's 0.6% levy: Vanguard Utilities VIPERs. The 35 basis-point (0.35%) difference between the expenses of the two ETFs may seem small, but it can make a big difference over the long run, especially among index funds that cover substantially the same ground and whose returns should correlate fairly closely over the long term.

Overall, we'd approach this offering with caution, if at all. After a couple of years of strong performance, the utilities sector is arguably pricier and riskier than it has been in some time. Utilities historically have been pretty cheap relative to the broad market, but this fund now sports a P/E ratio close to that of the S&P 500. Despite owning more than 70 stocks, this portfolio is still pretty concentrated, too. Finally, you can buy a portfolio that covers the same ground for less.

| | |
|---|---|
| Address: | 45 Fremont Street<br>San Francisco CA 94105<br>800-474-2737 |
| Web Address: | www.ishares.com |
| Inception: | 06-12-00* |
| Advisor: | Barclays Global Fund Advisers |

| | |
|---|---|
| Management Fee: | 0.60% |
| Expense Projections: | 3Yr:$192  5Yr:$335  10Yr:$750 |
| Income Distrib: | Quarterly |
| Exchange: | NYSE |

MORNINGSTAR® ETFs 100

# iShares EMU Index

| | Ticker | NAV | Market Price | 52 wk High/Low | Yield | Mstar Category |
|---|---|---|---|---|---|---|
| | EZU | $77.23 | $81.48 | $81.89 - $68.89 | 1.7% | Europe Stock |

## Management

### Portfolio Manager(s)

The fund's advisor, Barclays Global Fund Advisors, is one of the world's largest and most experienced managers of index-tracking portfolios.

### Strategy

This exchange-traded offering is a passive fund that simply attempts to match the performance of the MSCI EMU Index. The benchmark is a free float-adjusted market-capitalization index designed to track the stocks in member nations of the European Monetary Union. It includes companies based in Austria, Belgium, Finland, France, Germany, Greece, Ireland, Italy, the Netherlands, Portugal, and Spain. It uses a representative sampling method of tracking the index.

**Growth of $10,000**

- Investment Value of ETF
- Investment Value of Index MSCI EAFE

| 1996 | 1997 | 1998 | 1999 | 2000 | 2001 | 2002 | 2003 | 2004 | 2005 | History |
|---|---|---|---|---|---|---|---|---|---|---|
| — | — | — | — | 73.22 | 55.78 | 43.28 | 60.81 | 72.31 | 77.23 | NAV $ |
| — | — | — | — | 73.25 | 55.99 | 43.50 | 61.25 | 72.60 | 77.65 | Market Price $ |
| — | — | — | — | 0.47* | -22.96 | -21.60 | 42.39 | 21.06 | 8.61 | NAV Return% |
| — | — | — | — | 0.57* | -22.70 | -21.50 | 42.69 | 20.68 | 8.77 | Market Price Return% |
| — | — | — | — | 0.62 | 0.59 | 0.16 | 0.30 | 0.57 | 0.12 | Avg Premium/Discount% |
| — | — | — | — | 0.47 | -1.54 | -5.66 | 3.80 | 0.81 | -4.93 | NAV Rtrn% +/-MSCI EAFE |
| — | — | — | — | 0.47 | -3.06 | -3.22 | 3.85 | 0.18 | -0.81 | NAV Rtrn% +/-MSCI Eur |
| — | — | — | — | — | 12 | 12 | 15 | 15 | 15 | NAV Return% Rank in Cat |
| — | — | — | — | 0.00 | 0.56 | 0.81 | 1.83 | 2.14 | 1.83 | Income Return % |
| — | — | — | — | — | -23.52 | -22.41 | 40.56 | 18.92 | 6.78 | Capital Return % |
| — | — | — | — | 0.01 | 0.41 | 0.45 | 0.79 | 1.30 | 1.32 | Income $ |
| — | — | — | — | 0.00 | 0.26 | 0.00 | 0.00 | 0.00 | 0.00 | Capital Gains $ |
| — | — | — | — | — | 0.84 | 0.84 | 0.84 | 0.79 | 0.58 | Expense Ratio % |
| — | — | — | — | — | 1.13 | 1.44 | 2.08 | 2.29 | 2.50 | Income Ratio % |
| — | — | — | — | — | 24 | 3 | 7 | 11 | 8 | Turnover Rate % |
| — | — | — | — | — | — | 143 | 234 | 456 | 552 | Net Assets $mil |

## Performance

### Historic Quarterly NAV Returns

| | 1st Qtr | 2nd Qtr | 3rd Qtr | 4th Qtr | Total |
|---|---|---|---|---|---|
| 2001 | -16.29 | -2.81 | -16.13 | 12.91 | -22.96 |
| 2002 | -0.32 | -4.30 | -28.17 | 14.42 | -21.60 |
| 2003 | -10.24 | 26.00 | 2.51 | 22.81 | 42.39 |
| 2004 | -0.59 | 2.43 | 0.18 | 18.68 | 21.06 |
| 2005 | -0.10 | -1.22 | 7.83 | 2.06 | 8.61 |

| Trailing | NAV Return% | Market Return%+/-MSCI EAFE | NAV Rtrn% | %Rank Cat.(NAV) |
|---|---|---|---|---|
| 3 Mo | 2.06 | 2.66 | -2.02 | 16 |
| 6 Mo | 10.06 | 11.00 | -4.82 | 16 |
| 1 Yr | 8.61 | 8.77 | -4.93 | 15 |
| 3 Yr Avg | 23.25 | 23.27 | -0.43 | 15 |
| 5 Yr Avg | 2.49 | 2.59 | -2.07 | 12 |
| 10 Yr Avg | — | — | — | 0 |

| Tax Analysis | Tax-Adj Return% | Tax-Cost Ratio |
|---|---|---|
| 3 Yr (estimated) | 22.57 | 0.55 |
| 5 Yr (estimated) | 2.01 | 0.47 |
| 10 Yr (estimated) | — | — |

## Risk Profile

| | Standard Index S&P 500 | Best Fit Index MSCI Eur |
|---|---|---|
| Alpha | -4.3 | -1.6 |
| Beta | 1.22 | 1.14 |
| R-Squared | 85 | 97 |
| Standard Deviation | 15.29 | |
| Mean | 23.25 | |
| Sharpe Ratio | 1.32 | |

## Morningstar Fair Value

| Price/Fair Value Ratio | Fair Value Estimate ($) | Hit Rate % |
|---|---|---|
| — | — | — |

## Portfolio Analysis 12-31-05

Share change since 11-05 Total Stocks:286

| | Sector | Country | % Assets |
|---|---|---|---|
| ⊕ TOTAL | Energy | France | 4.36 |
| ⊕ Sanofi-Synthelabo | Health | France | 2.81 |
| ⊕ Banco Santander Central | Financial | Spain | 2.43 |
| ⊕ Nokia | Hardware | Finland | 2.39 |
| ⊕ Eni | Energy | Italy | 2.25 |
| ⊕ Siemens | Hardware | Germany | 2.11 |
| ⊕ Telefonica | Telecom | Spain | 2.04 |
| ⊕ ING Groep | Financial | Netherlands | 2.00 |
| ⊕ E.ON | Utilities | Germany | 1.98 |
| ⊕ BNP Paribas | Financial | France | 1.97 |
| ⊕ BBVA | Financial | Spain | 1.87 |
| ⊕ Allianz | Financial | Germany | 1.75 |
| ⊕ UniCredito Italiano Grp | Financial | Italy | 1.70 |
| ⊕ Deutsche Bank | Financial | Germany | 1.48 |
| ⊕ ABN AMRO Holding | Financial | Netherlands | 1.44 |
| ⊕ AXA | Financial | France | 1.44 |
| ⊕ DaimlerChrysler | Goods | Germany | 1.44 |
| ⊕ Deutsche Telekom | Telecom | Germany | 1.40 |
| ⊕ Societe Generale Grp | Financial | France | 1.33 |
| ⊕ France Telecom | Telecom | France | 1.29 |

### Current Investment Style

Value Blnd Growth — Large Mid Small

| Market Cap | % |
|---|---|
| Giant | 54.5 |
| Large | 33.0 |
| Mid | 11.9 |
| Small | 0.6 |
| Micro | 0.0 |

Avg $mil: 29,647

| Value Measures | | Rel Category |
|---|---|---|
| Price/Earnings | 13.44 | 1.00 |
| Price/Book | 2.25 | 0.95 |
| Price/Sales | 0.97 | 0.82 |
| Price/Cash Flow | 6.97 | 0.96 |
| Dividend Yield % | 2.83 | 0.97 |

| Growth Measures | % | Rel Category |
|---|---|---|
| Long-Term Erngs | 11.37 | 1.00 |
| Book Value | 1.54 | 0.69 |
| Sales | 0.93 | 0.36 |
| Cash Flow | -2.69 | NMF |
| Historical Erngs | 10.87 | 0.68 |

### Composition

| Cash | 0.2 | Bonds | 0.0 |
|---|---|---|---|
| Stocks | 99.1 | Other | 0.7 |
| Foreign (% of Stock) | | | 100.0 |

### Sector Weightings

| | % of Stocks | Rel MSCI EAFE | 3 Year High | Low |
|---|---|---|---|---|
| ↗ Info | 18.60 | 1.33 | | |
| Software | 1.45 | 1.36 | 2 | 0 |
| Hardware | 6.03 | 1.67 | 10 | 6 |
| Media | 2.81 | 1.34 | 3 | 2 |
| Telecom | 8.31 | 1.15 | 11 | 8 |
| Service | 43.64 | 0.95 | | |
| Health | 4.28 | 0.60 | 6 | 4 |
| Consumer | 2.88 | 0.66 | 4 | 3 |
| Business | 4.68 | 0.77 | 5 | 3 |
| Financial | 31.80 | 1.13 | 32 | 24 |
| Mfg | 37.77 | 0.94 | | |
| Goods | 10.96 | 0.80 | 13 | 10 |
| Ind Mtrls | 10.98 | 0.78 | 11 | 9 |
| Energy | 8.51 | 1.08 | 14 | 9 |
| Utilities | 7.32 | 1.59 | 8 | 5 |

### Regional Exposure

| | % Stock | | % Stock |
|---|---|---|---|
| UK/W. Europe | 100 | N. America | 0 |
| Japan | 0 | Latn America | 0 |
| Asia X Japan | 0 | Other | 0 |

### Country Exposure

| | % Stock | | % Stock |
|---|---|---|---|
| France | 30 | Spain | 12 |
| Germany | 21 | Netherlands | 12 |
| Italy | 12 | | |

## Morningstar's Take by Dan Culloton

This fund provides affordable, but flawed, exposure to European stocks.

The iShares EMU Index tracks leading companies in the European Monetary Union, as measured by the MSCI EMU Index, which currently includes nearly 300 companies in a variety of industries and sectors from the 11 nations that have adopted the euro. With a recently reduced expense ratio of 0.59% it is one of the cheapest offerings among traditional and exchange-traded rivals.

Hedge funds and traders may have their uses for a fund that contains only EMU stocks. Most long-term investors, however, should ask themselves why they would need a fund like this. This offering takes in a broad swath of Europe but leaves out important developed economies, such as Britain and Switzerland, and developing ones, such as the Czech Republic. Given the interplay and interdependence among EMU and non-EMU countries and companies, it probably makes more sense to seek exposure to Europe from a fund that invests more widely across the continent.

Although the Europe stock fund category doesn't have a wealth of alternatives with long-tenured managers or attractive expenses, options do exist. For index investors, the obvious choice is Vanguard European Stock Index. The Vanguard offering tracks a more diversified index (it too leaves out emerging Europe, but includes the U.K. and Switzerland), and its expense ratio is 45% lower (the exchange-traded Viper shares are even cheaper). Furthermore, this ETF has been more volatile, as measured by standard deviation, than the Vanguard option and the average traditional Europe fund and hasn't compensated investors. The ETF gained 1.6% annualized over the trailing five years ending Nov. 11, 2005, while the Vanguard fund rose 3.2%. Bottom line: There are better ways to capture the returns of the European bourses.

| Address: | 45 Fremont Street San Francisco CA 94105 800-474-2737 | Management Fee: | 0.59% | | |
|---|---|---|---|---|---|
| | | Expense Projections: | 3Yr:$189 | 5Yr:$329 | 10Yr:$738 |
| | | Income Distrib: | Annually | | |
| Web Address: | www.ishares.com | Exchange: | AMEX | | |
| Inception: | 07-25-00* | | | | |
| Advisor: | Barclays Global Fund Advisers | | | | |

# iShares FTSE/Xinhua China

| | Ticker | NAV | Market Price | 52 wk High/Low | Yield | Mstar Category |
|---|---|---|---|---|---|---|
| | FXI | $61.44 | $66.14 | $66.79 - $52.00 | 2.0% | Pacific/Asia ex-Japan Stk |

## Management

### Portfolio Manager(s)

The fund is managed by Barclays Global Investors, one of the world's largest and most experienced managers of index-tracking portfolios.

### Strategy

This fund tracks the FTSE/Xinhua China 25 Index. The bogy tracks the stocks of 25 large Chinese companies whose shares trade on the Hong Kong Stock Exchange and are available to international investors (some share classes of Chinese companies restrict foreign investment). The index is rebalanced quarterly.

**Growth of $10,000**

— Investment Value of ETF
— Investment Value of Index MSCI EAFE

| | 1996 | 1997 | 1998 | 1999 | 2000 | 2001 | 2002 | 2003 | 2004 | 2005 | History |
|---|---|---|---|---|---|---|---|---|---|---|---|
| | — | — | — | — | — | — | — | — | 54.91 | 61.44 | NAV $ |
| | — | — | — | — | — | — | — | — | 55.47 | 61.62 | Market Price $ |
| | — | — | — | — | — | — | — | — | 13.48* | 14.15 | NAV Return% |
| | — | — | — | — | — | — | — | — | 14.68* | 13.33 | Market Price Return% |
| | — | — | — | — | — | — | — | — | 0.65 | 0.44 | Avg Premium/Discount% |
| | — | — | — | — | — | — | — | — | 13.48 | 0.61 | NAV Rtrn% +/-MSCI EAFE |
| | — | — | — | — | — | — | — | — | 13.48 | -3.71 | NAV Rtrn% +/-MSCIAC FExJ |
| | — | — | — | — | — | — | — | — | — | 9 | NAV Return% Rank in Cat |
| | — | — | — | — | — | — | — | — | 0.00 | 2.28 | Income Return % |
| | — | — | — | — | — | — | — | — | — | 11.87 | Capital Return % |
| | — | — | — | — | — | — | — | — | 0.00 | 1.25 | Income $ |
| | — | — | — | — | — | — | — | — | 0.00 | 0.00 | Capital Gains $ |
| | — | — | — | — | — | — | — | — | — | 0.74 | Expense Ratio % |
| | — | — | — | — | — | — | — | — | — | 2.97 | Income Ratio % |
| | — | — | — | — | — | — | — | — | — | 13 | Turnover Rate % |
| | — | — | — | — | — | — | — | — | 568 | 1,352 | Net Assets $mil |

## Performance

**Historic Quarterly NAV Returns**

| | 1st Qtr | 2nd Qtr | 3rd Qtr | 4th Qtr | Total |
|---|---|---|---|---|---|
| 2001 | — | — | — | — | — |
| 2002 | — | — | — | — | — |
| 2003 | — | — | — | — | — |
| 2004 | — | — | — | — | —* |
| 2005 | -0.97 | 5.42 | 11.53 | -1.97 | 14.15 |

| Trailing | NAV Return% | Market Return% | NAV Rtrn% +/-MSCI EAFE | %Rank Cat.(NAV) |
|---|---|---|---|---|
| 3 Mo | -1.97 | -2.14 | -6.05 | 9 |
| 6 Mo | 9.33 | 10.07 | -5.55 | 9 |
| 1 Yr | 14.15 | 13.33 | 0.61 | 9 |
| 3 Yr Avg | — | — | — | 0 |
| 5 Yr Avg | — | — | — | 0 |
| 10 Yr Avg | — | — | — | 0 |

| Tax Analysis | Tax-Adj Return% | Tax-Cost Ratio |
|---|---|---|
| 3 Yr (estimated) | — | — |
| 5 Yr (estimated) | — | — |
| 10 Yr (estimated) | — | — |

### Risk Profile

| | Standard Index S&P 500 | Best Fit Index |
|---|---|---|
| Alpha | — | — |
| Beta | — | — |
| R-Squared | — | — |
| Standard Deviation | — | |
| Mean | — | |
| Sharpe Ratio | — | |

### Morningstar Fair Value

| Price/Fair Value Ratio | Fair Value Estimate ($) | Hit Rate % |
|---|---|---|
| — | — | — |

## Portfolio Analysis 12-31-05

| Share change since 11-05 Total Stocks:25 | Sector | Country | % Assets |
|---|---|---|---|
| ⊕ China Mobile | Telecom | Hong Kong | 9.78 |
| ⊖ PetroChina | Energy | Hong Kong | 8.85 |
| ⊕ CNOOC Ltd | Energy | Hong Kong | 7.67 |
| ⊖ Sinopec | Business | Hong Kong | 6.66 |
| ⊖ Bank of China (Hong Kong) | Financial | Hong Kong | 6.56 |
| ⊕ China Life Insurance | Financial | Hong Kong | 4.43 |
| ⊕ China Construction Bank | Financial | Hong Kong | 4.25 |
| ⊕ Ping An Insurance Grp Co | Financial | Hong Kong | 4.14 |
| ⊖ China Telecom | Telecom | Hong Kong | 4.07 |
| Citic Pacific | Ind Mtrls | Hong Kong | 3.87 |
| ⊕ China Unicom Ltd | Telecom | Hong Kong | 3.86 |
| ⊖ China Merchants Hldgs (I | Ind Mtrls | Hong Kong | 3.68 |
| ⊕ Bank of Communications | Financial | Hong Kong | 3.61 |
| ⊖ China Shenhua Energy | Energy | Hong Kong | 3.59 |
| ⊕ China Netcom Grp | Telecom | Hong Kong | 3.34 |
| ⊕ Huaneng Power Int'l | Utilities | China | 3.17 |
| ⊕ China Resources Enterpri | Financial | Hong Kong | 3.14 |
| ⊖ COSCO Pacific Ltd | Business | Hong Kong | 3.10 |
| ⊕ Aluminum Corp of China | Ind Mtrls | Hong Kong | 2.67 |
| ⊕ Yanzhou Coal Mining | Energy | China | 1.96 |

### Current Investment Style

| Market Cap | % |
|---|---|
| Giant | 63.7 |
| Large | 36.3 |
| Mid | 0.0 |
| Small | 0.0 |
| Micro | 0.0 |

Avg $mil: 19,961

| Value Measures | | Rel Category |
|---|---|---|
| Price/Earnings | 11.20 | 0.84 |
| Price/Book | 1.86 | 1.02 |
| Price/Sales | 1.35 | 0.80 |
| Price/Cash Flow | 5.82 | 0.89 |
| Dividend Yield % | 4.56 | 0.99 |

| Growth Measures | % | Rel Category |
|---|---|---|
| Long-Term Erngs | 15.58 | 1.13 |
| Book Value | 9.93 | 1.37 |
| Sales | 23.67 | 1.75 |
| Cash Flow | 15.82 | 0.99 |
| Historical Erngs | 24.79 | 1.17 |

### Composition

| | | | |
|---|---|---|---|
| Cash | 0.1 | Bonds | 0.0 |
| Stocks | 99.8 | Other | 0.0 |
| Foreign (% of Stock) | | | 100.0 |

| Sector Weightings | % of Stocks | Rel MSCI EAFE | 3 Year High Low |
|---|---|---|---|
| ☎ Info | 21.08 | 1.51 | |
| ▣ Software | 0.00 | 0.00 | — — |
| ▣ Hardware | 0.00 | 0.00 | — — |
| ▣ Media | 0.00 | 0.00 | — — |
| ▣ Telecom | 21.08 | 2.92 | — — |
| ☞ Service | 40.25 | 0.88 | |
| ⚕ Health | 0.00 | 0.00 | — — |
| ⚘ Consumer | 0.00 | 0.00 | — — |
| ▤ Business | 12.57 | 2.08 | — — |
| $ Financial | 27.68 | 0.98 | — — |
| ↗ Mfg | 38.67 | 0.96 | |
| ⚒ Goods | 0.00 | 0.00 | — — |
| ✿ Ind Mtrls | 10.24 | 0.72 | — — |
| ⛽ Energy | 23.49 | 2.97 | — — |
| ⚡ Utilities | 4.94 | 1.07 | — — |

### Regional Exposure % Stock

| | | | |
|---|---|---|---|
| UK/W. Europe | 0 | N. America | 0 |
| Japan | 0 | Latn America | 0 |
| Asia X Japan | 100 | Other | 0 |

### Country Exposure % Stock

| | |
|---|---|
| Hong Kong | 92 |
| China | 8 |

## Morningstar's Take by Arijit Dutta

Investors should think long and hard before signing on to iShares FTSE/Xinhua China 25 Index.

This ETF is one of the latest investment vehicles aimed at the fast-growing and enormously influential Chinese economy. Besides the dozen or so China-focused mutual funds, PowerShares Golden Dragon Halter USX China, which also launched in 2004, is the other ETF choice.

The iShares fund's best feature is that it simplifies things for investors looking to brave the Chinese market. In communist China, the government owns large chunks of most companies, many of which suffer from terrible management, trade thinly, and do little to protect the rights of small shareholders. This ETF includes only the 25 largest companies that have listed on the Hong Kong exchange, however, which ensures that investors here are in the most liquid Chinese stocks, ones that have been earmarked by the government to showcase the country's best corporate citizens. It is also very cheap, costing about half the cheapest mutual fund option.

The flip side of the fund's approach, though, is that it has the potential to magnify the already unsettling volatility that a single-country emerging-markets vehicle brings to the table. With only 25 stocks and 60% of assets in the top 10 holdings, we'd expect this portfolio to be rocked violently and often. Moreover, as the fund's more than 22% energy stake indicates, it has lumpy sector weightings that add risk.

Therefore, this ETF's appeal as a cheap way to gain access to arguably the best companies in a rapidly growing economic powerhouse is not without serious drawbacks. Investors should consider the PowerShares ETF and mutual funds such as Fidelity China Region that are more diversified. Even better would be a broad emerging-markets fund that can invest in firms across the globe that directly or indirectly benefit from the booming Chinese economy, while sparing investors some of the volatility.

| Address: | 45 Fremont Street San Francisco CA 94105 800-474-2737 | Management Fee: | 0.74% |
|---|---|---|---|
| | | Expense Projections: | 3Yr:$237  5Yr:$411  10Yr:$918 |
| Web Address: | www.ishares.com | Income Distrib: | Annually |
| Inception: | 10-05-04 * | Exchange: | NYSE |
| Advisor: | Barclays Global Fund Advisers | | |

MORNINGSTAR® ETFs 100

# iShares GS$ InvesTop

| | Ticker | NAV | Market Price | 52 wk High/Low | Yield | Mstar Category |
|---|---|---|---|---|---|---|
| | LQD | $107.50 | $107.93 | $113.70 - $106.24 | 4.8% | Long-Term Bond |

## Management

### Portfolio Manager(s)

Three managers are in charge of the six fixed-income ETFs offered by Barclays Global Investors. Matthew Tucker and Lee Sterne, who both joined BGI in 1996, and Christopher Mosellen who came on board in 2003. Recently, Trevor Whelan was also added as a backup.

### Strategy

The fund's benchmark, the Goldman Sachs $ InvesTop Corporate Index, uses sampling techniques to mimic the corporate-bond market. The index includes bonds from companies that meet Goldman Sachs' definition of liquid, long-term corporate debt. The issuers must have headquarters in the U.S., Canada, Western Europe, or Japan; have investment-grade ratings; have at least $500 million in outstanding debt; be less than five years old; and have at least three years until maturity. The managers can also differ from the index by up to 10%, to add value on the margins.

### Growth of $10,000

— Investment Value of ETF
— Investment Value of Index LB Aggr

| 1996 | 1997 | 1998 | 1999 | 2000 | 2001 | 2002 | 2003 | 2004 | 2005 | History |
|---|---|---|---|---|---|---|---|---|---|---|
| — | — | — | — | — | — | 107.99 | 110.38 | 111.53 | 107.50 | NAV $ |
| — | — | — | — | — | — | 109.69 | 110.57 | 111.53 | 107.69 | Market Price $ |
| — | — | — | — | — | — | 6.27* | 7.43 | 5.91 | 1.00 | NAV Return% |
| — | — | — | — | — | — | 6.32* | 5.94 | 5.73 | 1.18 | Market Price Return% |
| — | — | — | — | — | — | 0.92 | 0.24 | 0.25 | 0.09 | Avg Premium/Discount% |
| — | — | — | — | — | — | 6.27 | 3.33 | 1.57 | -1.43 | NAV Rtrn% +/-LB Aggr |
| — | — | — | — | — | — | 6.27 | 1.56 | -2.65 | -4.33 | NAV Rtrn% +/-LB LongTerm |
| — | — | — | — | — | — | | 1 | 1 | 1 | NAV Return% Rank in Cat |
| — | — | — | — | — | — | 0.00 | 5.20 | 4.81 | 4.70 | Income Return % |
| — | — | — | — | — | — | | 2.23 | 1.10 | -3.70 | Capital Return % |
| — | — | — | — | — | — | 2.48 | 5.48 | 5.19 | 5.13 | Income $ |
| — | — | — | — | — | — | 0.00 | 0.00 | 0.00 | 0.00 | Capital Gains $ |
| — | — | — | — | — | — | | 0.15 | 0.15 | 0.15 | Expense Ratio % |
| — | — | — | — | — | — | | 5.38 | 5.38 | 4.71 | Income Ratio % |
| — | — | — | — | — | — | | 20 | 20 | 32 | Turnover Rate % |
| — | — | — | — | — | — | 1,857 | 2,307 | 2,520 | 2,419 | Net Assets $mil |

## Performance

### Historic Quarterly NAV Returns

| | 1st Qtr | 2nd Qtr | 3rd Qtr | 4th Qtr | Total |
|---|---|---|---|---|---|
| 2001 | — | | | | — |
| 2002 | — | — | — | 3.33 | —* |
| 2003 | 2.60 | 5.26 | -0.82 | 0.29 | 7.43 |
| 2004 | 3.71 | -4.26 | 5.04 | 1.55 | 5.91 |
| 2005 | -1.52 | 4.03 | -1.66 | 0.25 | 1.00 |

| Trailing | NAV Return% | Market Return% | NAV Rtrn% +/-LB Aggr | %Rank Cat.(NAV) |
|---|---|---|---|---|
| 3 Mo | 0.25 | 0.33 | -0.34 | 1 |
| 6 Mo | -1.41 | -0.90 | -1.33 | 1 |
| 1 Yr | 1.00 | 1.18 | -1.43 | 1 |
| 3 Yr Avg | 4.74 | 4.26 | 1.12 | 1 |
| 5 Yr Avg | — | — | — | 0 |
| 10 Yr Avg | — | — | — | 0 |

| Tax Analysis | Tax-Adj Return% | Tax-Cost Ratio |
|---|---|---|
| 3 Yr (estimated) | 3.01 | 1.65 |
| 5 Yr (estimated) | — | — |
| 10 Yr (estimated) | — | — |

## Risk Profile

| | Standard Index S&P 500 | Best Fit Index LB Credit |
|---|---|---|
| Alpha | 0.2 | -0.8 |
| Beta | 1.58 | 1.21 |
| R-Squared | 98 | 99 |
| Standard Deviation | 6.58 | |
| Mean | 4.74 | |
| Sharpe Ratio | 0.44 | |

## Morningstar Fair Value

| Price/Fair Value Ratio | Fair Value Estimate ($) | Hit Rate % |
|---|---|---|
| — | — | — |

## Morningstar's Take by Dieter Bardy

This ETF provides decent, if imperfect, exposure to long-term corporate bonds.

iShares GS $ InvesTop Corporate Bond has first-mover advantage, as it's the only long-term corporate-bond ETF on the market. The index that it matches takes a 100-bond sample of the most liquid, long-term bonds in the corporate universe. The bonds are selected to mimic the universe's sector representation and maturity positioning.

We're concerned about a few facets of the fund's strategy, though. For one, it seems quite concentrated, considering that there are nearly 700 bonds in its universe. If a problem arises with one of the fund's bonds, it would have a big impact on results. Moreover, unlike other ETFs, there is a hands-on aspect to this offering. The fund's advisor, Barclays Global Investors, may devote up to 10% of assets to bonds that aren't in the benchmark to try to reflect corporate actions and index additions and deletions. Although the managers haven't yet used this flexibility, doing so would add an uncertain

active hand to the mix.

So far, the fund has tracked its index well--depending on how you look at it. Since the fund's July 2002 inception, it gained 7.52% per year, right in line with its index's gain through Aug. 31, 2005. However that's just the fund's gain on an NAV basis. A better reflection of an investor's results is an ETF's market-price return, which is impacted by demand for its shares. (Investors trade ETF shares at market prices, and buy and sell mutual fund shares at NAV.) The fund's market return for the same stretch was 7.83%, meaning LQD's owners have done better than its holdings. Based on the fund's history, expect similar variations between the fund's NAV and market-price.

The biggest advantage here is costs. At 0.15%, the ETF easily beats its closest mutual fund rival on fees. Still, investors' returns can differ, sometimes by a lot, from this fund's NAV return.

| Address: | 45 Fremont Street San Francisco CA 94105 800-474-2737 |
|---|---|
| Web Address: | www.ishares.com |
| Inception: | 07-22-02* |
| Advisor: | Barclays Global Fund Advisers |

| Management Fee: | 0.15% | | |
|---|---|---|---|
| Expense Projections: | 3Yr:$48 | 5Yr:$85 | 10Yr:$192 |
| Income Distrib: | Monthly | | |
| Exchange: | AMEX | | |

## Portfolio Analysis 12-31-05

| Total Fixed-Income:98 | Date of Maturity | Amount $000 | Value $000 | % Net Assets |
|---|---|---|---|---|
| At&T Wireless Svcs 8.125 | 05-01-12 | 24,750 | 28,613 | 1.19 |
| General Elec Cap 6.75% | 03-15-32 | 23,625 | 27,858 | 1.16 |
| Sprint Cap 8.375% | 03-15-12 | 23,625 | 27,382 | 1.14 |
| Deere John Cap 7% | 03-15-12 | 24,750 | 27,301 | 1.14 |
| Weyerhaeuser 7.375% | 03-15-32 | 23,625 | 26,236 | 1.10 |
| United Tech 4.375% | 05-01-10 | 25,875 | 25,392 | 1.06 |
| Kinder Morgan Engy Partn | 11-15-14 | 25,875 | 25,342 | 1.06 |
| Bellsouth 6.55% | 06-15-34 | 23,625 | 25,333 | 1.06 |
| Txu Engy 7% | 03-15-13 | 23,625 | 25,242 | 1.05 |
| Wells Fargo 4.2% | 01-15-10 | 25,875 | 25,217 | 1.05 |
| Bk Of Amer 4.75% | 08-01-15 | 25,875 | 25,138 | 1.05 |
| Procter & Gamble 5.8% | 08-15-34 | 23,625 | 25,133 | 1.05 |
| Weyerhaeuser 6.75% | 03-15-12 | 23,625 | 25,092 | 1.05 |
| United Tech 5.4% | 05-01-35 | 24,750 | 24,781 | 1.03 |
| Daimler Chrysler North A | 11-15-13 | 23,625 | 24,763 | 1.03 |
| Kinder Morgan Engy Partn | 03-15-35 | 25,875 | 24,749 | 1.03 |
| Citigroup 5.85% | 12-11-34 | 23,625 | 24,723 | 1.03 |
| Jpmorgan Chase Cap Xv 5. | 03-15-35 | 24,750 | 24,641 | 1.03 |
| Sbc Comms 6.45% | 06-15-34 | 23,625 | 24,584 | 1.03 |
| Marsh & Mclennan Cos 5.1 | 09-15-10 | 24,750 | 24,567 | 1.03 |

### Current Investment Style

Duration: Short Int Long
Quality: High Med Low

1 figure provided by fund

| Avg Eff Duration1 | 6.5 Yrs |
|---|---|
| Avg Eff Maturity | 10.0 Yrs |
| Avg Credit Quality | A |
| Avg Wtd Coupon | 5.21% |
| Avg Wtd Price | 101.48% of par |

| Coupon Range | % of Bonds | Rel Cat |
|---|---|---|
| 0% PIK | 0.0 | 0.0 |
| 0% to 6% | 83.3 | 1.0 |
| 6% to 8% | 14.2 | 1.0 |
| 8% to 10% | 2.5 | 1.0 |
| More than 10% | 0.0 | 0.0 |
1.00=Category Average

| Credit Analysis | % bonds 12-31-05 | | |
|---|---|---|---|
| US Govt | 0 | BB | 0 |
| AAA | 3 | B | 0 |
| AA | 32 | Below B | 0 |
| A | 37 | NR/NA | 1 |
| BBB | 28 | | |

### Sector Breakdown
| | % of assets |
|---|---|
| US Treasuries | 0 |
| TIPS | 0 |
| US Agency | 0 |
| Mortgage Pass-Throughs | 0 |
| Mortgage CMO | 0 |
| Mortgage ARM | 0 |
| US Corporate | 98 |
| Asset-Backed | 0 |
| Convertible | 1 |
| Municipal | 0 |
| Corporate Inflation-Protected | 0 |
| Foreign Corporate | 0 |
| Foreign Govt | 0 |

### Composition
| Cash | 0.6 | Bonds | 97.4 |
|---|---|---|---|
| Stocks | 0.0 | Other | 2.0 |

### Special Securities
| Restricted/Illiquid Secs | 0 |
|---|---|
| Exotic Mortgage-Backed | — |
| Emerging-Markets Secs | 0 |
| Options/Futures/Warrants | No |

# iShares GS Tech

| | Ticker | NAV | Market Price | 52 wk High/Low | Yield | Mstar Category |
|---|---|---|---|---|---|---|
| | IGM | $47.39 | $50.51 | $50.51 - $39.60 | 0.1% | Specialty-Technology |

## Management

### Portfolio Manager(s)

Barclays Global Fund Advisors is the advisor. The firm is the world's largest manager of indexed portfolios. Patrick O'Connor, the head of Barclay's U.S. iShares portfolio management group leads a team of a half dozen managers in running this and about 60 other ETFs. IShares' domestic portfolio-management group is responsible for about $75 billion in assets. Most of the managers have at least five years of experience with Barclays as well as prior industry experience.

### Strategy

Management attempts to track the performance of the Goldman Sachs Technology Index, which covers six tech subsectors ranging from software to semiconductors to the Internet. The index's holdings are weighted by market cap, but some position sizes are limited to improve diversification. Even so, it is dominated by the stocks with the largest market caps.

**Growth of $10,000**

— Investment Value of ETF
— Investment Value of Index S&P 500

| | 1996 | 1997 | 1998 | 1999 | 2000 | 2001 | 2002 | 2003 | 2004 | 2005 | History |
|---|---|---|---|---|---|---|---|---|---|---|---|
| | — | — | — | — | — | 50.44 | 29.97 | 46.04 | 46.74 | 47.39 | NAV $ |
| | — | — | — | — | — | 50.69 | 30.04 | 45.85 | 46.71 | 47.35 | Market Price $ |
| | — | — | — | — | — | -3.50* | -40.58 | 53.62 | 2.24 | 1.54 | NAV Return% |
| | — | — | — | — | — | -3.51* | -40.74 | 52.63 | 2.60 | 1.52 | Market Price Return% |
| | — | — | — | — | — | 0.37 | -0.11 | 0.06 | 0.04 | -0.10 | Avg Premium/Discount% |
| | — | — | — | — | — | -3.50 | -18.49 | 24.95 | -8.63 | -3.37 | NAV Rtrn% +/-S&P 500 |
| | — | — | — | — | — | -3.50 | -7.25 | 1.48 | -9.49 | -5.82 | NAV Rtrn% +/-ArcaEx Tech 100 |
| | — | — | — | — | — | — | 8 | 8 | 8 | 9 | NAV Return% Rank in Cat |
| | — | — | — | — | — | 0.00 | 0.00 | 0.00 | 0.71 | 0.14 | Income Return % |
| | — | — | — | — | — | — | -40.58 | 53.62 | 1.53 | 1.40 | Capital Return % |
| | — | — | — | — | — | 0.00 | 0.00 | 0.00 | 0.33 | 0.07 | Income $ |
| | — | — | — | — | — | 0.00 | 0.00 | 0.00 | 0.00 | 0.00 | Capital Gains $ |
| | — | — | — | — | — | — | 0.50 | 0.50 | 0.50 | 0.50 | Expense Ratio % |
| | — | — | — | — | — | — | -0.30 | -0.18 | -0.20 | 0.81 | Income Ratio % |
| | — | — | — | — | — | — | 8 | 11 | 5 | 7 | Turnover Rate % |
| | — | — | — | — | — | 39 | 147 | 194 | 280 | | Net Assets $mil |

## Performance

**Historic Quarterly NAV Returns**

| | 1st Qtr | 2nd Qtr | 3rd Qtr | 4th Qtr | Total |
|---|---|---|---|---|---|
| 2001 | — | 14.45 | -35.59 | 33.26 | —* |
| 2002 | -7.41 | -27.84 | -27.18 | 22.13 | -40.58 |
| 2003 | -0.63 | 22.20 | 11.27 | 13.71 | 53.62 |
| 2004 | -1.30 | 1.69 | -11.15 | 14.64 | 2.24 |
| 2005 | -8.83 | 1.42 | 6.85 | 2.78 | 1.54 |

| Trailing | NAV Return% | Market Return% | NAV Rtrn% +/-S&P 500 | %Rank Cat.(NAV) |
|---|---|---|---|---|
| 3 Mo | 2.78 | 2.98 | 0.70 | 12 |
| 6 Mo | 9.82 | 9.88 | 4.06 | 12 |
| 1 Yr | 1.54 | 1.52 | -3.37 | 9 |
| 3 Yr Avg | 16.84 | 16.71 | 2.46 | 8 |
| 5 Yr Avg | — | — | — | 0 |
| 10 Yr Avg | — | — | — | 0 |

| Tax Analysis | Tax-Adj Return% | Tax-Cost Ratio |
|---|---|---|
| 3 Yr (estimated) | 16.72 | 0.10 |
| 5 Yr (estimated) | — | — |
| 10 Yr (estimated) | — | — |

## Risk Profile

| | Standard Index S&P 500 | Best Fit Index ArcaEx Tech 100 |
|---|---|---|
| Alpha | -3.9 | -6.3 |
| Beta | 1.60 | 1.10 |
| R-Squared | 69 | 96 |
| Standard Deviation | 17.68 | |
| Mean | 16.84 | |
| Sharpe Ratio | 0.86 | |

## Morningstar Fair Value

| Price/Fair Value Ratio | Fair Value Estimate ($) | Hit Rate % |
|---|---|---|
| 1.1 Overvalued | 24.21 | 96 Good |

## Morningstar's Take  by Dan Culloton

You don't need this exchange-traded fund.

IShares Goldman Sachs Technology Index tracks a benchmark of domestic software, hardware, Internet, and related stocks assembled by the Goldman Sachs Research Department. Like a lot of other market-cap-weighted technology indexes, it has a lot of money in bellwethers such as Microsoft, Intel, IBM, Cisco Systems, and Dell. Indeed, even though the bogy includes hundreds of other stocks and caps the positions of its constituents in an effort to keep from relying too heavily on a few holdings, the fund remains top-heavy, with more than 30% of its assets in those five brand-name tech stocks.

Focusing on the shares of established, profitable businesses may seem like decent idea, especially if you think growth stocks are due for a resurgence after lagging value equities in recent years and you don't have the stomach for some of the style's racier fare. It might be a good idea if you owned these stocks in a more diversified portfolio, but

emphasizing the biggest names in one sector hasn't afforded this fund any more protection than the typical traditional tech fund. This ETF's standard deviation, a measure of volatility, is about average for the category, and its 15% gain for the three-year period ending Aug. 31, 2005, trails the 17% advance of the typical traditional tech fund.

The fund hasn't been worth its bumps and probably isn't necessary if you own a diversified portfolio. This ETF's top holdings are often found in broad-based large-cap funds. Adding this ETF to the mix would likely create redundancy.

Finally, if you must have a technology ETF, there are cheaper options. Yes, this fund's 0.50% expense ratio is far below the levy for the typical traditional tech fund. But it's also about twice as expensive as the cheapest tech ETF option. You can live without this one.

| Address: | 45 Fremont Street |
|---|---|
| | San Francisco CA 94105 |
| | 800-474-2737 |
| Web Address: | www.ishares.com |
| Inception: | 03-13-01 * |
| Advisor: | Barclays Global Fund Advisers |

| Management Fee: | 0.50% | | |
|---|---|---|---|
| Expense Projections: | 3Yr:$160 | 5Yr:$280 | 10Yr:$628 |
| Income Distrib: | Quarterly | | |
| Exchange: | AMEX | | |

## Portfolio Analysis  12-31-05

Share change since 11-05 Total Stocks:236

| | Sector | PE | Tot Ret% | % Assets |
|---|---|---|---|---|
| ⊖ Microsoft | Software | 22.2 | -0.95 | 8.13 |
| ⊖ Intel | Hardware | 18.6 | 8.12 | 6.79 |
| ⊖ IBM | Hardware | 16.0 | -15.83 | 5.84 |
| ⊖ Cisco Systems | Hardware | 19.9 | -11.39 | 4.82 |
| ⊖ Hewlett-Packard | Hardware | 27.3 | 38.29 | 3.64 |
| ⊖ Dell | Hardware | 23.2 | -28.93 | 3.20 |
| ⊖ Google | Business | — | 115.19 | 3.13 |
| ⊖ Qualcomm | Hardware | 34.2 | 2.50 | 3.10 |
| ⊖ Oracle | Software | 22.2 | -11.01 | 2.76 |
| ⊖ Apple Computer | Hardware | 46.1 | 123.26 | 2.61 |
| ⊖ eBay | Consumer | 59.2 | -25.70 | 2.57 |
| ⊖ Motorola | Hardware | 13.9 | 32.43 | 2.44 |
| ⊖ Yahoo | Media | 36.3 | 3.98 | 2.41 |
| ⊖ Texas Instruments | Hardware | 25.3 | 30.78 | 2.35 |
| ⊖ First Data | Business | 20.8 | 1.70 | 1.47 |
| ⊖ EMC | Hardware | 25.7 | -8.41 | 1.44 |
| ⊖ Applied Materials | Hardware | 24.6 | 5.46 | 1.30 |
| ⊖ Corning | Hardware | 36.4 | 67.03 | 1.23 |
| ⊖ Automatic Data Processin | Business | 25.2 | 5.03 | 1.18 |
| ⊕ Adobe Systems | Software | 33.3 | 17.84 | 0.95 |

**Current Investment Style**

Value Blnd Growth — Large Mid Small

| | Market Cap | % |
|---|---|---|
| | Giant | 54.0 |
| | Large | 24.2 |
| | Mid | 18.3 |
| | Small | 3.5 |
| | Micro | 0.0 |
| | Avg $mil: 31,915 | |

| Value Measures | | Rel Category |
|---|---|---|
| Price/Earnings | 22.25 | 0.94 |
| Price/Book | 3.64 | 1.10 |
| Price/Sales | 2.42 | 0.80 |
| Price/Cash Flow | 11.69 | 1.07 |
| Dividend Yield % | 0.54 | 0.96 |

| Growth Measures | % | Rel Category |
|---|---|---|
| Long-Term Erngs | 14.48 | 0.97 |
| Book Value | 4.20 | 1.31 |
| Sales | 7.44 | 1.29 |
| Cash Flow | 15.46 | 0.78 |
| Historical Erngs | 21.52 | 0.83 |

| Profitability | % | Rel Category |
|---|---|---|
| Return on Equity | 19.15 | 1.23 |
| Return on Assets | 11.17 | 1.18 |
| Net Margin | 16.16 | 1.15 |

| Industry Weightings | % of Stocks | Rel Cat |
|---|---|---|
| Software | 20.3 | 1.0 |
| Hardware | 21.0 | 1.7 |
| Networking Eq | 8.4 | 1.3 |
| Semis | 18.1 | 0.9 |
| Semi Equip | 2.6 | 0.6 |
| Comp/Data Sv | 8.7 | 1.1 |
| Telecom | 0.4 | 0.1 |
| Health Care | 0.0 | 0.0 |
| Other | 20.4 | 1.0 |

**Composition**

| | | % |
|---|---|---|
| ● Cash | | 0.1 |
| ● Stocks | | 99.9 |
| ● Bonds | | 0.0 |
| ● Other | | 0.0 |
| Foreign (% of Stock) | | 3.2 |

MORNINGSTAR® ETFs 100

# iShares Japan Index

| | Ticker | NAV | Market Price | 52 wk High/Low | Yield | Mstar Category |
|---|---|---|---|---|---|---|
| | EWJ | $13.48 | $14.00 | $14.26 - $9.94 | 0.4% | Japan Stock |

## Management

### Portfolio Manager(s)

The fund's advisor, Barclays Global Fund Advisors, is one of the world's largest and most experienced managers of index-tracking portfolios.

### Strategy

This exchange-traded fund attempts to track the performance of the MSCI Japan Index, which focuses primarily on the largest companies in the Japanese market. It is passively managed.

**Growth of $10,000**

— Investment Value of ETF
— Investment Value of Index MSCI EAFE

| 1996 | 1997 | 1998 | 1999 | 2000 | 2001 | 2002 | 2003 | 2004 | 2005 | History |
|---|---|---|---|---|---|---|---|---|---|---|
| 13.10 | 10.00 | 10.34 | 16.15 | 11.17 | 7.83 | 7.01 | 9.50 | 10.86 | 13.48 | NAV $ |
| 13.06 | 9.88 | 10.25 | 16.31 | 11.06 | 7.71 | 6.95 | 9.64 | 10.92 | 13.52 | Market Price $ |
| -0.40* | -23.63 | 3.53 | 57.89 | -28.57 | -29.90 | -10.47 | 35.54 | 14.78 | 24.65 | NAV Return% |
| -0.37* | -24.32 | 3.87 | 60.86 | -29.97 | -30.29 | -9.86 | 38.73 | 13.74 | 24.34 | Market Price Return% |
| 0.25 | 0.03 | -0.07 | 0.31 | 0.53 | 0.37 | -0.08 | 0.61 | 0.24 | 0.00 | Avg Premium/Discount% |
| -0.40 | -25.41 | -16.40 | 30.86 | -14.38 | -8.48 | 5.47 | -3.05 | -5.47 | 11.11 | NAV Rtrn% +/-MSCI EAFE |
| -0.40 | 0.04 | -1.52 | -3.64 | -0.40 | -0.51 | -0.19 | -0.37 | -1.08 | -0.87 | NAV Rtrn% +/-MSCI JP NDT |
| — | 1 | 1 | 1 | 1 | 1 | 2 | 2 | 2 | 2 | NAV Return% Rank in Cat |
| 0.00 | 0.00 | 0.00 | 0.43 | 0.01 | 0.00 | 0.00 | 0.02 | 0.45 | 0.53 | Income Return % |
| — | -23.63 | 3.53 | 57.46 | -28.58 | -29.90 | -10.47 | 35.52 | 14.33 | 24.12 | Capital Return % |
| 0.01 | 0.00 | 0.00 | 0.04 | 0.00 | 0.00 | 0.00 | 0.00 | 0.04 | 0.06 | Income $ |
| 0.00 | 0.01 | 0.01 | 0.11 | 0.45 | 0.00 | 0.00 | 0.00 | 0.00 | 0.00 | Capital Gains $ |
| — | — | — | — | 0.88 | 0.84 | 0.84 | 0.84 | 0.64 | 0.57 | Expense Ratio % |
| — | — | — | — | -0.32 | -0.11 | -0.12 | 0.03 | 0.28 | 0.59 | Income Ratio % |
| — | — | — | — | 22 | 21 | 2 | 2 | 5 | 6 | Turnover Rate % |
| — | — | — | — | — | — | 542 | 2,890 | 6,624 | 13,042 | Net Assets $mil |

## Performance

### Historic Quarterly NAV Returns

| | 1st Qtr | 2nd Qtr | 3rd Qtr | 4th Qtr | Total |
|---|---|---|---|---|---|
| 2001 | -8.77 | 0.49 | -18.75 | -5.89 | -29.90 |
| 2002 | 3.32 | 4.45 | -12.19 | -5.53 | -10.47 |
| 2003 | -7.56 | 11.42 | 21.47 | 8.34 | 35.54 |
| 2004 | 14.63 | -3.95 | -7.65 | 12.88 | 14.78 |
| 2005 | -2.58 | -3.69 | 18.94 | 11.69 | 24.65 |

| Trailing | NAV Return% | Market Return%+/-MSCI EAFE | NAV Rtrn% | %Rank Cat.(NAV) |
|---|---|---|---|---|
| 3 Mo | 11.69 | 11.38 | 7.61 | 3 |
| 6 Mo | 32.85 | 33.90 | 17.97 | 3 |
| 1 Yr | 24.65 | 24.34 | 11.11 | 2 |
| 3 Yr Avg | 24.71 | 25.19 | 1.03 | 2 |
| 5 Yr Avg | 4.01 | 4.28 | -0.55 | 1 |
| 10 Yr Avg | — | — | — | 0 |

| Tax Analysis | Tax-Adj Return% | Tax-Cost Ratio |
|---|---|---|
| 3 Yr (estimated) | 24.58 | 0.10 |
| 5 Yr (estimated) | 3.95 | 0.06 |
| 10 Yr (estimated) | — | — |

## Risk Profile

| | Standard Index S&P 500 | Best Fit Index MSCI JP NDT |
|---|---|---|
| Alpha | 5.6 | -0.5 |
| Beta | 0.80 | 0.99 |
| R-Squared | 30 | 100 |
| Standard Deviation | 16.78 | |
| Mean | 24.71 | |
| Sharpe Ratio | 1.29 | |

## Morningstar Fair Value

| Price/Fair Value Ratio | Fair Value Estimate ($) | Hit Rate % |
|---|---|---|
| — | — | — |

## Portfolio Analysis 12-31-05

Share change since 11-05  Total Stocks:278

| | Sector | Country | % Assets |
|---|---|---|---|
| ⊕ Toyota Motor | Goods | Japan | 5.71 |
| ⊕ Mitsubishi Tokyo Fin. Gr | Financial | Japan | 3.69 |
| ⊕ Mizuho Financial Grp | Financial | Japan | 2.94 |
| ⊕ Sumitomo Mitsui Financia | Financial | Japan | 1.83 |
| ⊕ Takeda Chemical Industri | Health | Japan | 1.80 |
| ⊕ Honda Motor | Goods | Japan | 1.76 |
| ⊕ Canon | Goods | Japan | 1.66 |
| ⊕ Sony | Goods | Japan | 1.57 |
| ⊕ Matsushita Electric Indu | Ind Mtrls | Japan | 1.43 |
| ⊕ Nomura Hldgs | Financial | Japan | 1.35 |
| ⊕ Seven & I Hldgs | — | Japan | 1.33 |
| ⊕ SOFTBANK CORP. | Financial | Japan | 1.25 |
| ⊕ The Tokyo Electric Power | Utilities | Japan | 1.08 |
| ⊕ Millea Hldgs | Financial | Japan | 1.06 |
| ⊕ Mitsubishi | Ind Mtrls | Japan | 1.04 |
| ⊕ NTT DoCoMo | Telecom | Japan | 0.98 |
| ⊕ East Japan Railway | Business | Japan | 0.93 |
| ⊕ Nippon Telegraph & Telep | Telecom | Japan | 0.90 |
| ⊕ Nissan Motor | Goods | Japan | 0.89 |
| ⊕ Nippon Steel | Ind Mtrls | Japan | 0.84 |

### Current Investment Style

Value Blnd Growth — Large/Mid/Small

| Market Cap | % |
|---|---|
| Giant | 54.7 |
| Large | 37.0 |
| Mid | 8.2 |
| Small | 0.0 |
| Micro | 0.0 |

Avg $mil: 18,181

| Value Measures | | Rel Category |
|---|---|---|
| Price/Earnings | 20.51 | 1.07 |
| Price/Book | 1.93 | 1.05 |
| Price/Sales | 1.01 | 1.01 |
| Price/Cash Flow | 7.61 | 1.04 |
| Dividend Yield % | 1.04 | 0.72 |

| Growth Measures | % | Rel Category |
|---|---|---|
| Long-Term Erngs | 9.80 | 1.03 |
| Book Value | 6.36 | 1.02 |
| Sales | 0.02 | 0.08 |
| Cash Flow | 2.62 | 0.78 |
| Historical Erngs | 21.04 | 1.06 |

### Composition

| | | | |
|---|---|---|---|
| Cash | 0.2 | Bonds | 0.0 |
| Stocks | 99.8 | Other | 0.0 |
| Foreign (% of Stock) | | | 100.0 |

### Sector Weightings

| | % of Stocks | Rel MSCI EAFE | 3 Year High | Low |
|---|---|---|---|---|
| ↻ Info | 10.17 | 0.73 | | |
| Software | 0.80 | 0.75 | 1 | 0 |
| Hardware | 5.81 | 1.61 | 9 | 5 |
| Media | 0.97 | 0.46 | 1 | 1 |
| Telecom | 2.59 | 0.36 | 6 | 3 |
| ☞ Service | 39.91 | 0.87 | | |
| Health | 4.26 | 0.59 | 7 | 3 |
| Consumer | 4.31 | 0.98 | 6 | 4 |
| Business | 8.09 | 1.34 | 8 | 7 |
| Financial | 23.25 | 0.83 | 23 | 8 |
| Mfg | 49.90 | 1.24 | | |
| Goods | 22.30 | 1.63 | 30 | 22 |
| Ind Mtrls | 22.76 | 1.61 | 24 | 19 |
| Energy | 0.81 | 0.10 | 1 | 1 |
| Utilities | 4.03 | 0.88 | 8 | 4 |

### Regional Exposure

| | % Stock | | % Stock |
|---|---|---|---|
| UK/W. Europe | 0 | N. America | 0 |
| Japan | 100 | Latn America | 0 |
| Asia X Japan | 0 | Other | 0 |

### Country Exposure

| | % Stock |
|---|---|
| Japan | 100 |

## Morningstar's Take by Dan Culloton

The shortfalls of the Japan-stock fund category are iShares MSCI Japan Index's gain.

Single country exchange-traded funds are inappropriate for most investors, because more and more the geographic homes of stocks matter less than their individual merits and sector trends. Japan, however, may be the exception because its market is so big and independent. The problem is there's a scarcity of traditional Japan funds with long-tenured managers, attractive risk/reward profiles, and affordable expense ratios.

Consequently, this ETF's low-priced, diversified exposure to leading Japanese companies looks good. Its 0.59% expense ratio is more than 66% lower than that of the average Japan fund. For that price this ETF offers exposure to large, well-known stocks, such as Toyota Motor, Canon, Sony, and Honda Motor. There are cheaper index funds in the category, but Vanguard Pacific Stock Index and TD Waterhouse Asian Index include stocks from Australia, Hong Kong, and Singapore. IShares

S&P/TOPIX 150 Index provides similar exposure, but it's a bit less diversified.

This ETF has done a decent job tracking its benchmark, but it has its risks. Its shares have been known to trade at discounts and premiums of more than 1% to its net asset value for short periods. Buying at the latter and selling at the former can hurt returns.

This fund also is capable of both staggering gains and losses. It posted market gains of more than 60% in 1999 and nearly 38% in 2003. But it fell by double digits in four of the last 10 years. Although there is hope that the Japan market has finally shaken off its long miasma, the country is still susceptible to fears of an economic slowdown in China as well as rising interest rates in the United States.

Nevertheless, the lack of other viable Japan options make this ETF an appealing one for those who want to venture into the Japanese market. Just use it in measured doses.

| | | | | |
|---|---|---|---|---|
| Address: | 45 Fremont Street USA 800-474-2737 | Management Fee: | 0.59% | |
| | | Expense Projections: | 3Yr:$189 5Yr:$329 | 10Yr:$738 |
| Web Address: | www.ishares.com | Income Distrib: | Annually | |
| Inception: | 03-12-96 * | Exchange: | NYSE | |
| Advisor: | Barclays Global Fund Advisers | | | |

**MORNINGSTAR® ETFs 100**

# iShares KLD Sel Soc Idx

| Ticker | NAV | Market Price | 52 wk High/Low | Yield | Mstar Category |
|---|---|---|---|---|---|
| KLD | $53.14 | $54.89 | $55.10 - $48.35 | 0.0% | Large Blend |

## Management

### Portfolio Manager(s)

Ed Corallo and Patrick O'Connor are responsible for the day-to-day management of this fund, along with several other iShares index funds. They work for Barclays Global Fund Advisors, the fund's advisor and an indirect subsidiary of Barclays Bank.

### Strategy

This fund tracks the KLD Select Social Index, which includes 230 mostly large-cap companies drawn from the Russell 1000 and S&P 500 indexes. This index is designed to have risk and return characteristics similar to the Russell 1000 while limiting itself to companies with positive social and environmental characteristics. It overweights stocks with good social scores relative to their weight in the Russell 1000 and underweights or cuts those with low scores. KLD uses similar social criteria for the Domini 400 Social Index, which is the basis for Domini Social Equity.

**Growth of $10,000**

— Investment Value of ETF
— Investment Value of Index S&P 500

| | 1996 | 1997 | 1998 | 1999 | 2000 | 2001 | 2002 | 2003 | 2004 | 2005 | History |
|---|---|---|---|---|---|---|---|---|---|---|---|
| | — | — | — | — | — | — | — | — | — | 53.14 | NAV $ |
| | — | — | — | — | — | — | — | — | — | 53.17 | Market Price $ |
| | — | — | — | — | — | — | — | — | — | 8.21* | NAV Return% |
| | — | — | — | — | — | — | — | — | — | 8.27* | Market Price Return% |
| | — | — | — | — | — | — | — | — | — | -0.09 | Avg Premium/Discount% |
| | — | — | — | — | — | — | — | — | — | 8.21 | NAV Rtrn% +/-S&P 500 |
| | — | — | — | — | — | — | — | — | — | 8.21 | NAV Rtrn% +/-Russ 1000 |
| | — | — | — | — | — | — | — | — | — | — | NAV Return% Rank in Cat |
| | — | — | — | — | — | — | — | — | — | — | Income Return % |
| | — | — | — | — | — | — | — | — | — | — | Capital Return % |
| | — | — | — | — | — | — | — | — | — | 0.61 | Income $ |
| | — | — | — | — | — | — | — | — | — | 0.00 | Capital Gains $ |
| | — | — | — | — | — | — | — | — | — | 0.50 | Expense Ratio % |
| | — | — | — | — | — | — | — | — | — | 1.16 | Income Ratio % |
| | — | — | — | — | — | — | — | — | — | 3 | Turnover Rate % |
| | — | — | — | — | — | — | — | — | — | 117 | Net Assets $mil |

## Performance

### Historic Quarterly NAV Returns

| | 1st Qtr | 2nd Qtr | 3rd Qtr | 4th Qtr | Total |
|---|---|---|---|---|---|
| 2001 | — | — | — | — | — |
| 2002 | — | — | — | — | — |
| 2003 | — | — | — | — | — |
| 2004 | — | — | — | — | — |
| 2005 | — | 2.38 | 2.49 | 2.57 | —* |

| Trailing | NAV Return% | Market Return% | NAV Rtrn% +/-S&P 500 | %Rank Cat.(NAV) |
|---|---|---|---|---|
| 3 Mo | 2.57 | 2.69 | 0.49 | 27 |
| 6 Mo | 5.13 | 5.08 | -0.63 | 27 |
| 1 Yr | — | — | — | 0 |
| 3 Yr Avg | — | — | — | 0 |
| 5 Yr Avg | — | — | — | 0 |
| 10 Yr Avg | — | — | — | 0 |

| Tax Analysis | Tax-Adj Return% | Tax-Cost Ratio |
|---|---|---|
| 3 Yr (estimated) | — | — |
| 5 Yr (estimated) | — | — |
| 10 Yr (estimated) | — | — |

## Risk Profile

| | Standard Index S&P 500 | Best Fit Index |
|---|---|---|
| Alpha | — | — |
| Beta | — | — |
| R-Squared | — | — |
| Standard Deviation | — | |
| Mean | — | |
| Sharpe Ratio | — | |

## Morningstar Fair Value

| Price/Fair Value Ratio | Fair Value Estimate ($) | Hit Rate % |
|---|---|---|
| 1.0 Fairly valued | 36.68 | 96 Good |

## Portfolio Analysis 12-31-05

| Share change since 11-05 Total Stocks:226 | Sector | PE | Tot Ret% | % Assets |
|---|---|---|---|---|
| ⊕ Johnson & Johnson | Health | 19.1 | -3.36 | 5.09 |
| ⊖ Wells Fargo | Financial | 14.3 | 4.47 | 5.00 |
| ⊕ American Express | Financial | 16.4 | 5.31 | 4.48 |
| ⊕ Microsoft | Software | 22.2 | -0.95 | 4.19 |
| ⊕ General Mills | Goods | 15.1 | 1.88 | 3.68 |
| ⊕ Intel | Hardware | 18.6 | 8.12 | 3.37 |
| ⊖ Bristol-Myers Squibb | Health | 17.1 | -6.16 | 2.89 |
| ⊕ Progress Energy | Utilities | 13.8 | 2.47 | 2.50 |
| ⊕ 3M Company | Ind Mtrls | 19.2 | -3.51 | 2.15 |
| ⊖ Nike B | Goods | 17.8 | -3.09 | 2.01 |
| ⊖ General Electric | Ind Mtrls | 19.9 | -1.43 | 2.00 |
| ⊖ Hewlett-Packard | Hardware | 27.3 | 38.29 | 1.71 |
| ⊖ Synovus Financial | Financial | 17.1 | -3.00 | 1.62 |
| ⊕ St. Paul Travelers Compa | Financial | 13.9 | 23.20 | 1.54 |
| ⊖ Ecolab | Ind Mtrls | 28.1 | 4.37 | 1.46 |
| ⊕ IBM | Hardware | 16.0 | -15.83 | 1.40 |
| ⊖ Cisco Systems | Hardware | 19.9 | -11.39 | 1.34 |
| ⊖ ExxonMobil | Energy | 10.6 | 11.76 | 1.25 |
| ⊕ Rockwell Collins | Ind Mtrls | 21.1 | 19.05 | 1.25 |
| ⊖ Fannie Mae | Financial | — | -30.14 | 1.10 |

### Current Investment Style

Value Blnd Growth — Large / Mid / Small

| Market Cap | % |
|---|---|
| Giant | 45.0 |
| Large | 35.9 |
| Mid | 18.9 |
| Small | 0.2 |
| Micro | 0.0 |

Avg $mil: 33,449

| Value Measures | | Rel Category |
|---|---|---|
| Price/Earnings | 16.49 | 0.97 |
| Price/Book | 2.91 | 1.08 |
| Price/Sales | 1.80 | 1.41 |
| Price/Cash Flow | 5.64 | 0.78 |
| Dividend Yield % | 1.71 | 0.97 |

| Growth Measures | % | Rel Category |
|---|---|---|
| Long-Term Erngs | 10.90 | 0.98 |
| Book Value | 9.03 | 0.96 |
| Sales | 8.36 | 1.04 |
| Cash Flow | 11.66 | 1.13 |
| Historical Erngs | 15.48 | 1.09 |

| Profitability | % | Rel Category |
|---|---|---|
| Return on Equity | 21.18 | 1.04 |
| Return on Assets | 12.50 | 1.34 |
| Net Margin | 14.70 | 1.35 |

| Sector Weightings | % of Stocks | Rel S&P 500 | 3 Year High Low |
|---|---|---|---|
| ↻ Info | 23.17 | 1.15 | |
| 🖥 Software | 6.36 | 1.79 | — — |
| 💻 Hardware | 13.50 | 1.34 | — — |
| 🎤 Media | 2.85 | 0.80 | — — |
| 📶 Telecom | 0.46 | 0.15 | — — |
| ⊂ Service | 44.90 | 0.97 | |
| ✚ Health | 14.39 | 1.08 | — — |
| 🛒 Consumer | 4.71 | 0.58 | — — |
| 📋 Business | 2.06 | 0.53 | — — |
| $ Financial | 23.74 | 1.13 | — — |
| ⊐ Mfg | 31.92 | 0.96 | |
| 🛋 Goods | 10.56 | 1.23 | — — |
| ⚙ Ind Mtrls | 12.68 | 1.04 | — — |
| ◊ Energy | 5.86 | 0.63 | — — |
| ♀ Utilities | 2.82 | 0.84 | — — |

### Composition

| | | % |
|---|---|---|
| ● Cash | | 0.1 |
| ● Stocks | | 99.9 |
| ● Bonds | | 0.0 |
| Other | | 0.0 |
| Foreign | | 0.0 |
| (% of Stock) | | |

## Morningstar's Take by David Kathman

iShares KLD Select Social Index ably fills a niche among exchange-traded funds, though investors still have other options.

This is the only exchange-traded fund with a diversified, socially responsible strategy. It tracks the KLD Select Social Index, which aims to mimic the characteristics of the Russell 1000 Index while limiting itself to companies that pass its social and environmental criteria. It's similar in many ways to the Domini 400 Social Index, also maintained by KLD Research & Analytics, which mimics the characteristics of the S&P 500 and is the basis for the Domini Social Equity.

Both indexes try to avoid companies in the alcohol, tobacco, gambling, military weapons, and nuclear power businesses and prefer those with good relationships to employees, shareholders, and the environment. The KLD Select Social Index consists of about 230 stocks with positive scores on these criteria, drawn from the Russell 1000 and S&P 500 indexes. The resulting portfolio is about 80% large-cap stocks, with the rest mid-caps.

Because the screening criteria are especially hard on industrial and energy stocks, those sectors are underrepresented in this fund relative to their weights in the Russell 1000, and technology and financial stocks are overweighted. That energy underweight is one reason the fund has trailed the Russell 1000 and the large-blend category since its inception in January 2005, though it will likely do better in a technology-led rally like those of 1999 and 2003.

Although this is the only option for investors seeking a socially responsible ETF, it's not a bad one; we've always been impressed with the thoroughness of KLD's screening and research for the Domini fund. However, its 0.50% expense ratio is just so-so for an ETF, and there are some cheaper options among the ranks of socially responsible mutual funds, such as Vanguard Calvert Social Index and its 0.25% expense ratio.

| | | | |
|---|---|---|---|
| Address: | 45 Fremont Street San Francisco CA 94105 800-474-2737 | Management Fee: | 0.50% |
| | | Expense Projections: | 3Yr:$160   5Yr: —   10Yr: — |
| | | Income Distrib: | Quarterly |
| Web Address: | www.ishares.com | Exchange: | AMEX |
| Inception: | 01-24-05* | | |
| Advisor: | Barclays Global Fund Advisers | | |

MORNINGSTAR® ETFs 100

# iShares Lehman 1-3 T

| Ticker | NAV | Market Price | 52 wk High/Low | Yield | Mstar Category |
|---|---|---|---|---|---|
| SHY | $80.16 | $80.28 | $81.50 - $80.06 | 3.0% | Short Government |

## Management

### Portfolio Manager(s)

Three managers are in charge of the six ETFs offered by Barclays Global Investors. Matthew Tucker and Lee Sterne, who both joined BGI in 1996, and Christopher Mosellen who came on board in 2003. Recently, Trevor Whelan was also added as a backup.

### Strategy

The fund tries to match the returns and yield of its index, the Lehman Brothers U.S. Treasury: 1-3 Year Index. The index includes bonds that are less than three years old; have at least one year until maturity; at least $250 million in par outstanding; and must be a U.S. Treasury security. On the margins, the managers can also differ from the index by up to 10%, to add a little extra value.

**Growth of $10,000**

— Investment Value of ETF
— Investment Value of Index LB Aggr

| 1996 | 1997 | 1998 | 1999 | 2000 | 2001 | 2002 | 2003 | 2004 | 2005 | History |
|---|---|---|---|---|---|---|---|---|---|---|
| — | — | — | — | — | — | 82.21 | 82.35 | 81.42 | 80.16 | NAV $ |
| — | — | — | — | — | — | 82.27 | 82.47 | 81.43 | 80.21 | Market Price $ |
| — | — | — | — | — | — | 1.84* | 1.78 | 0.80 | 1.48 | NAV Return% |
| — | — | — | — | — | — | 1.86* | 1.86 | 0.66 | 1.53 | Market Price Return% |
| — | — | — | — | — | — | 0.06 | 0.07 | 0.04 | -0.09 | Avg Premium/Discount% |
| — | — | — | — | — | — | 1.84 | -2.32 | -3.54 | -0.95 | NAV Rtrn% +/-LB Aggr |
| — | — | — | — | — | — | 1.84 | -0.38 | -0.74 | -0.95 | NAV Rtrn% +/-LB 1-5 YR GOVT |
| — | — | — | — | — | — | — | 1 | 1 | 1 | NAV Return% Rank in Cat |
| — | — | — | — | — | — | 0.00 | 1.61 | 1.94 | 3.05 | Income Return % |
| — | — | — | — | — | — | — | 0.17 | -1.14 | -1.57 | Capital Return % |
| — | — | — | — | — | — | 0.64 | 1.31 | 1.58 | 2.45 | Income $ |
| — | — | — | — | — | — | 0.00 | 0.00 | 0.00 | 0.00 | Capital Gains $ |
| — | — | — | — | — | — | — | 0.15 | 0.15 | 0.15 | Expense Ratio % |
| — | — | — | — | — | — | — | 1.80 | 1.63 | 2.11 | Income Ratio % |
| — | — | — | — | — | — | — | 44 | 21 | 106 | Turnover Rate % |
| — | — | — | — | — | — | 896 | 1,326 | 2,247 | 4,401 | Net Assets $mil |

## Performance

### Historic Quarterly NAV Returns

| | 1st Qtr | 2nd Qtr | 3rd Qtr | 4th Qtr | Total |
|---|---|---|---|---|---|
| 2001 | — | — | — | — | — |
| 2002 | — | — | — | 0.82 | —* |
| 2003 | 0.57 | 0.68 | 0.40 | 0.12 | 1.78 |
| 2004 | 1.00 | -1.16 | 0.98 | -0.01 | 0.80 |
| 2005 | -0.33 | 1.12 | 0.03 | 0.66 | 1.48 |

| Trailing | NAV Return% | Market Return% | NAV Rtrn% +/-LB Aggr | %Rank Cat.(NAV) |
|---|---|---|---|---|
| 3 Mo | 0.66 | 0.95 | 0.07 | 1 |
| 6 Mo | 0.69 | 0.87 | 0.77 | 1 |
| 1 Yr | 1.48 | 1.53 | -0.95 | 1 |
| 3 Yr Avg | 1.35 | 1.35 | -2.27 | 1 |
| 5 Yr Avg | — | — | — | 0 |
| 10 Yr Avg | — | — | — | 0 |

| Tax Analysis | Tax-Adj Return% | Tax-Cost Ratio |
|---|---|---|
| 3 Yr (estimated) | 0.58 | 0.76 |
| 5 Yr (estimated) | — | — |
| 10 Yr (estimated) | — | — |

## Risk Profile

| | Standard Index S&P 500 | Best Fit Index LB 1-5 YR GOVT |
|---|---|---|
| Alpha | -1.1 | -0.5 |
| Beta | 0.30 | 0.61 |
| R-Squared | 82 | 96 |
| Standard Deviation | 1.37 | |
| Mean | 1.35 | |
| Sharpe Ratio | -0.41 | |

## Morningstar Fair Value

| Price/Fair Value Ratio | Fair Value Estimate ($) | Hit Rate % |
|---|---|---|
| — | — | — |

## Portfolio Analysis 12-31-05

| Total Fixed-Income:15 | Date of Maturity | Amount $000 | Value $000 | % Net Assets |
|---|---|---|---|---|
| US Treasury Note 3.75% | 05-15-08 | 516,060 | 508,804 | 11.62 |
| US Treasury Note 3.125% | 05-15-07 | 485,865 | 477,479 | 10.91 |
| US Treasury Note 2.75% | 08-15-07 | 473,238 | 461,057 | 10.53 |
| US Treasury Note 3.375% | 02-28-07 | 413,397 | 408,345 | 9.33 |
| US Treasury Note 2.25% | 02-15-07 | 388,692 | 379,422 | 8.67 |
| US Treasury Note 3% | 02-15-08 | 356,301 | 346,335 | 7.91 |
| US Treasury Note 3% | 11-15-07 | 338,733 | 330,329 | 7.55 |
| US Treasury Note 4.125% | 08-15-08 | 275,598 | 274,124 | 6.26 |
| US Treasury Note 4% | 09-30-07 | 238,815 | 237,177 | 5.42 |
| US Treasury Note 4.75% | 11-15-08 | 192,699 | 194,572 | 4.45 |
| US Treasury Note 4.25% | 10-31-07 | 164,700 | 164,237 | 3.75 |
| US Treasury Note 3.625% | 06-30-07 | 160,857 | 159,039 | 3.63 |
| US Treasury Note 2.625% | 05-15-08 | 126,270 | 121,320 | 2.77 |
| US Treasury Note 3.125% | 09-15-08 | 125,172 | 121,200 | 2.77 |
| US Treasury Note 3.125% | 10-15-08 | 115,290 | 111,544 | 2.55 |

## Morningstar's Take by Dieter Bardy

This fund is a worthy option for short-term goals.

The job of iShares Lehman 1-3 Year Treasury Bond Index is to ape the performance of the Lehman Brothers U.S. Treasury: 1-3 Year Index. Unlike for one of its siblings, iShares Lehman Aggregate Bond AGG, the job here is easier because the index is smaller and more easily reproduced. The index holds just three-dozen issues. And even then, the fund doesn't need to hold all of the bonds, because there are few differences between various U.S. Treasury issues besides maturity and yield. The fund's advisor, Barclays Global Investors, thinks that a sample of bonds, 12 as of Sept. 30, 2005, will best match the performance of the index.

So far, the fund has accomplished its goal. Since its inception in July 2002, the ETF gained an annualized 1.77%, versus 1.92% for the index through Sept. 30, 2005. The reason it has gained little less than the index is due to expenses. Because ETFs trade like stocks and market demand can affect their share price, this fund's market performance can sink or rise more than its portfolio value, though that has not been a problem here.

The most attractive advantage here is its low costs. At 0.15%, it's just a fifth as much as its typical category rival's 0.74% ratio. That said, it's only a smidgeon cheaper than its least expensive mutual fund rival (Vanguard Short-Term Treasury). Once you factor in transaction costs, it might be less costly overall to buy a low-cost retail fund.

Investors who want a dedicated short-term U.S. Treasury offering should do fine here. Its hands-off approach and low fees will keep it competitive with rivals. And finally, because it only invests in U.S. Treasuries (many of its category rivals hold some mortgage and other agency debt), credit quality isn't an issue.

| Address: | 45 Fremont Street San Francisco CA 94105 800-474-2737 |
|---|---|
| Web Address: | www.ishares.com |
| Inception: | 07-22-02* |
| Advisor: | Barclays Global Fund Advisers |

| Management Fee: | 0.15% | | |
|---|---|---|---|
| Expense Projections: | 3Yr:$48 | 5Yr:$85 | 10Yr:$192 |
| Income Distrib: | Monthly | | |
| Exchange: | AMEX | | |

### Current Investment Style

Duration: Short Int Long

Quality: High Med Low

1 figure provided by fund

| Avg Eff Duration | 1.7 Yrs |
|---|---|
| Avg Eff Maturity | 1.8 Yrs |
| Avg Credit Quality | AAA |
| Avg Wtd Coupon | 3.33% |
| Avg Wtd Price | 98.55% of par |

| Coupon Range | % of Bonds | Rel Cat |
|---|---|---|
| 0% PIK | 0.0 | 0.0 |
| 0% to 6% | 93.2 | 1.0 |
| 6% to 8% | 6.8 | 1.0 |
| 8% to 10% | 0.0 | 0.0 |
| More than 10% | 0.0 | 0.0 |

1.00=Category Average

### Credit Analysis

% bonds 12-31-05

| US Govt | 0 | BB | 0 |
|---|---|---|---|
| AAA | 100 | B | 0 |
| AA | 0 | Below B | 0 |
| A | 0 | NR/NA | 0 |
| BBB | 0 | | |

### Sector Breakdown

% of assets

| US Treasuries | 100 |
|---|---|
| TIPS | 0 |
| US Agency | 0 |
| Mortgage Pass-Throughs | 0 |
| Mortgage CMO | 0 |
| Mortgage ARM | 0 |
| US Corporate | 0 |
| Asset-Backed | 0 |
| Convertible | 0 |
| Municipal | 0 |
| Corporate Inflation-Protected | 0 |
| Foreign Corporate | 0 |
| Foreign Govt | 0 |

### Composition

| Cash | 1.9 | Bonds | 98.1 |
|---|---|---|---|
| Stocks | 0.0 | Other | 0.0 |

### Special Securities

| Restricted/Illiquid Secs | 0 |
|---|---|
| Exotic Mortgage-Backed | — |
| Emerging-Markets Secs | 0 |
| Options/Futures/Warrants | No |

MORNINGSTAR® ETFs 100

# iShares Lehman Aggregate

| | Ticker | NAV | Market Price | 52 wk High/Low | Yield | Mstar Category |
|---|---|---|---|---|---|---|
| | AGG | $100.13 | $100.56 | $103.44 - $99.45 | 4.1% | Intermediate-Term Bond |

## Management

### Portfolio Manager(s)

Barclays Global Investors is the world's biggest index investor with more than $1 trillion in passively managed assets under management globally. It also is the largest purveyor of exchange-traded funds. Three managers are in charge of the six bond ETFs offered by Barclays Global Investors. Matthew Tucker and Lee Sterne, who both joined BGI in 1996, and Christopher Mosellen who came on board in 2003. Recently, Trevor Whelan was also added as a backup.

### Strategy

The fund strives to approximate the performance of the Lehman Brothers Aggregate Bond Index, which is a commonly used proxy for the broad, investment-grade U.S. bond market. It uses representative sampling to do this because owning every fixed income security in the domestic market would be unwieldy and costly because some of the issues are illiquid.

**Growth of $10,000**

— Investment Value of ETF
— Investment Value of Index LB Aggr

| 1996 | 1997 | 1998 | 1999 | 2000 | 2001 | 2002 | 2003 | 2004 | 2005 | History |
|---|---|---|---|---|---|---|---|---|---|---|
| — | — | — | — | — | — | — | 101.61 | 102.05 | 100.13 | NAV $ |
| — | — | — | — | — | — | — | 102.15 | 102.40 | 100.59 | Market Price $ |
| — | — | — | — | — | — | — | 3.42* | 3.99 | 2.16 | NAV Return% |
| — | — | — | — | — | — | — | 3.62* | 3.79 | 2.28 | Market Price Return% |
| — | — | — | — | — | — | — | 0.50 | 0.25 | 0.12 | Avg Premium/Discount% |
| — | — | — | — | — | — | — | 3.42 | -0.35 | -0.27 | NAV Rtrn% +/-LB Aggr |
| — | — | — | — | — | — | — | 3.42 | -1.31 | 0.33 | NAV Rtrn% +/-LB 5-10YR |
| — | — | — | — | — | — | — | — | 1 | 1 | NAV Return% Rank in Cat |
| — | — | — | — | — | — | — | 0.00 | 3.54 | 4.08 | Income Return % |
| — | — | — | — | — | — | — | — | 0.45 | -1.92 | Capital Return % |
| — | — | — | — | — | — | — | 0.92 | 3.54 | 4.09 | Income $ |
| — | — | — | — | — | — | — | 0.00 | 0.00 | 0.00 | Capital Gains $ |
| — | — | — | — | — | — | — | — | 0.20 | 0.20 | Expense Ratio % |
| — | — | — | — | — | — | — | — | 2.47 | 2.90 | Income Ratio % |
| — | — | — | — | — | — | — | — | 165 | 457 | Turnover Rate % |
| — | — | — | — | — | — | — | 213 | 990 | 2,894 | Net Assets $mil |

## Performance

### Historic Quarterly NAV Returns

| | 1st Qtr | 2nd Qtr | 3rd Qtr | 4th Qtr | Total |
|---|---|---|---|---|---|
| 2001 | — | — | — | — | — |
| 2002 | — | — | — | — | — |
| 2003 | — | — | — | 0.28 | —* |
| 2004 | 2.59 | -2.66 | 3.22 | 0.88 | 3.99 |
| 2005 | -0.60 | 3.01 | -0.74 | 0.51 | 2.16 |

| Trailing | NAV Return% | Market Return% | NAV Rtrn% +/-LB Aggr | %Rank Cat.(NAV) |
|---|---|---|---|---|
| 3 Mo | 0.51 | 0.85 | -0.08 | 1 |
| 6 Mo | -0.23 | 0.03 | -0.15 | 1 |
| 1 Yr | 2.16 | 2.28 | -0.27 | 1 |
| 3 Yr Avg | — | — | — | 0 |
| 5 Yr Avg | — | — | — | 0 |
| 10 Yr Avg | — | — | — | 0 |

| Tax Analysis | Tax-Adj Return% | Tax-Cost Ratio |
|---|---|---|
| 3 Yr (estimated) | — | — |
| 5 Yr (estimated) | — | — |
| 10 Yr (estimated) | — | — |

## Risk Profile

| | Standard Index S&P 500 | Best Fit Index |
|---|---|---|
| Alpha | — | — |
| Beta | — | — |
| R-Squared | — | — |
| Standard Deviation | — | |
| Mean | — | |
| Sharpe Ratio | — | |

## Morningstar Fair Value

| Price/Fair Value Ratio | Fair Value Estimate ($) | Hit Rate % |
|---|---|---|
| — | — | — |

## Portfolio Analysis 12-31-05

| Total Fixed-Income:123 | Date of Maturity | Amount $000 | Value $000 | % Net Assets |
|---|---|---|---|---|
| US Treasury Note 6% | 08-15-09 | 145,367 | 153,239 | 3.97 |
| US Treasury Note 3.875% | 07-31-07 | 141,610 | 140,466 | 3.64 |
| FNMA 5.5% | 01-01-36 | 133,229 | 131,897 | 3.41 |
| FNMA 5% | 01-01-36 | 128,605 | 124,586 | 3.22 |
| US Treasury Note 3% | 11-15-07 | 104,329 | 101,741 | 2.63 |
| FHLMC 5% | 01-01-36 | 100,283 | 97,055 | 2.51 |
| US Treasury Bond 8.125% | 08-15-19 | 68,782 | 93,336 | 2.42 |
| FHLMC 2.75% | 03-15-08 | 95,948 | 92,168 | 2.39 |
| FHLMC 5.5% | 01-01-36 | 89,590 | 88,750 | 2.30 |
| US Treasury Bond 7.625% | 02-15-25 | 61,268 | 84,443 | 2.19 |
| FNMA 4% | 02-28-07 | 80,920 | 80,250 | 2.08 |
| FNMA 6% | 01-01-36 | 63,580 | 64,156 | 1.66 |
| US Treasury Note 4.75% | 05-15-14 | 59,823 | 61,308 | 1.59 |
| FHLMC 4.5% | 01-15-13 | 59,245 | 58,206 | 1.51 |
| US Treasury Note 3.5% | 02-15-10 | 52,598 | 50,891 | 1.32 |
| FNMA 5% | 01-01-21 | 47,685 | 47,163 | 1.22 |
| FHLMC 4.5% | 01-01-21 | 46,818 | 45,545 | 1.18 |
| FNMA 7.25% | 01-15-10 | 41,616 | 45,415 | 1.18 |
| FNMA 6.5% | 01-01-36 | 39,882 | 40,904 | 1.06 |
| GNMA 5.5% | 01-01-36 | 39,015 | 39,247 | 1.02 |

### Current Investment Style

Duration: Short Int Long
Quality: High Med Low

1 figure provided by fund

| Avg Eff Duration1 | 4.6 Yrs |
|---|---|
| Avg Eff Maturity | 6.4 Yrs |
| Avg Credit Quality | AA |
| Avg Wtd Coupon | 5.24% |
| Avg Wtd Price | 103.74% of par |

| Coupon Range | % of Bonds | Rel Cat |
|---|---|---|
| 0% PIK | 0.0 | 0.0 |
| 0% to 6% | 78.9 | 1.0 |
| 6% to 8% | 17.6 | 1.0 |
| 8% to 10% | 3.5 | 1.0 |
| More than 10% | 0.0 | 0.0 |

1.00=Category Average

| Credit Analysis | | % bonds 12-31-05 | |
|---|---|---|---|
| US Govt | 0 | BB | 0 |
| AAA | 73 | B | 0 |
| AA | 8 | Below B | 0 |
| A | 11 | NR/NA | 1 |
| BBB | 8 | | |

### Sector Breakdown % of assets

| | |
|---|---|
| US Treasuries | 19 |
| TIPS | 0 |
| US Agency | 8 |
| Mortgage Pass-Throughs | 26 |
| Mortgage CMO | 0 |
| Mortgage ARM | 0 |
| US Corporate | 20 |
| Asset-Backed | 0 |
| Convertible | 0 |
| Municipal | 0 |
| Corporate Inflation-Protected | 0 |
| Foreign Corporate | 1 |
| Foreign Govt | 0 |

### Composition

| | | | |
|---|---|---|---|
| Cash | 26.5 | Bonds | 73.5 |
| Stocks | 0.0 | Other | 0.0 |

### Special Securities

| | |
|---|---|
| Restricted/Illiquid Secs | 0 |
| Exotic Mortgage-Backed | 0 |
| Emerging-Markets Secs | Trace |
| Options/Futures/Warrants | No |

## Morningstar's Take by Dan Culloton

If you want to own the broad bond market through an ETF, this is the only choice.

The iShares Lehman Aggregate Bond Index currently is the only all-bond-market ETF in town. It's the sole exchange-traded fund tracking the Lehman Aggregate, which is used by many as a proxy for the investment grade domestic bond universe. The fund doesn't own all of the securities in the index. That wouldn't be cost effective because some of the bogy's constituents are small and thinly traded. Rather, the ETF uses a sampling technique to replicate the index's major characteristics, such as maturity and interest-rate sensitivity.

The fund is not the cheapest way to own the entire bond market. That distinction goes to Dreyfus Bond Market Index Basic, a traditional open-end index fund. The Dreyfus fund is unappealing for other reasons, though. When an index fund trails its benchmark by the size of its expense ratio or less, it's a good sign it's doing its job, but Dreyfus Bond

Market often has failed to do that.

The jury is still out on the ability of this two-year-old ETF to consistently ape its benchmark as well as older bond index funds, such as Fidelity U.S. Bond Index or Vanguard Total Bond Market Index. On Oct. 31, 2005, the ETF's returns since inception trailed the bogy by 26 basis points, or hundredths of a percent. That's six basis points more than its expense ratio. However, this fund's advisor, Barclays Global Fund Advisors, is the world's largest manager of index assets. It should be able to do a better job managing tracking error.

Despite its youth, this ETF offers broad, cheap fixed-income exposure and would be a good complement to a total stock market fund in a low maintenance ETF portfolio. Things could get rough for this fund if interest rates move higher, but long-term investors should do all right here as long as they keep an eye on transaction costs, which could negate this fund's advantages.

| | | | | |
|---|---|---|---|---|
| Address: | 45 Fremont Street San Francisco CA 94105 800-474-2737 | Management Fee: | 0.20% | |
| | | Expense Projections: | 3Yr:$64 | 5Yr:$113  10Yr:$255 |
| | | Income Distrib: | Monthly | |
| Web Address: | www.ishares.com | Exchange: | AMEX | |
| Inception: | 09-22-03* | | | |
| Advisor: | Barclays Global Fund Advisers | | | |

MORNINGSTAR® ETFs 100

# iShares Lehman TIPS Bond

| Ticker | NAV | Market Price | 52 wk High/Low | Yield | Mstar Category |
|---|---|---|---|---|---|
| TIP | $102.80 | $102.59 | $107.72 - $101.79 | 5.4% | Long Government |

## Management

**Portfolio Manager(s)**

Three managers are in charge of the six ETFs offered by Barclays Global Investors. Matthew Tucker and Lee Sterne both joined BGI in 1996, and Christopher Mosellen came on board in 2003. Recently, Trevor Whelan was also added as a backup.

**Strategy**

The fund's index, the Lehman Brothers U.S. Treasury Inflation Notes Index, holds all TIPs that currently trade: 17 individual issues, as of Aug. 31, 2005. The index includes bonds that have at least one year until maturity, and that have at least $250 million par outstanding. The managers can also differ from the index by up to 5%, in order to add value on the margins.

**Growth of $10,000**

— Investment Value of ETF
— Investment Value of Index LB Aggr

| 1996 | 1997 | 1998 | 1999 | 2000 | 2001 | 2002 | 2003 | 2004 | 2005 | History |
|---|---|---|---|---|---|---|---|---|---|---|
| — | — | — | — | — | — | — | 101.61 | 105.64 | 102.80 | NAV $ |
| — | — | — | — | — | — | — | 101.71 | 105.81 | 102.82 | Market Price $ |
| — | — | — | — | — | — | — | 5.60* | 8.21 | 2.65 | NAV Return% |
| — | — | — | — | — | — | — | 5.61* | 8.28 | 2.50 | Market Price Return% |
| — | — | — | — | — | — | — | 0.10 | 0.18 | 0.06 | Avg Premium/Discount% |
| — | — | — | — | — | — | — | 5.60 | 3.87 | 0.22 | NAV Rtrn% +/-LB Aggr |
| — | — | — | — | — | — | — | 5.60 | 0.27 | -3.96 | NAV Rtrn% +/-LB LTGvtBd |
| — | — | — | — | — | — | — | — | 2 | 2 | NAV Return% Rank in Cat |
| — | — | — | — | — | — | — | — | 4.15 | 5.41 | Income Return % |
| — | — | — | — | — | — | — | — | 4.06 | -2.76 | Capital Return % |
| — | — | — | — | — | — | — | 0.12 | 4.14 | 5.58 | Income $ |
| — | — | — | — | — | — | — | 0.00 | 0.00 | 0.00 | Capital Gains $ |
| — | — | — | — | — | — | — | — | 0.20 | 0.20 | Expense Ratio % |
| — | — | — | — | — | — | — | — | -0.25 | 3.60 | Income Ratio % |
| — | — | — | — | — | — | — | — | 2 | 32 | Turnover Rate % |
| — | — | — | — | — | — | — | 142 | 1,511 | 3,310 | Net Assets $mil |

## Performance

**Historic Quarterly NAV Returns**

| | 1st Qtr | 2nd Qtr | 3rd Qtr | 4th Qtr | Total |
|---|---|---|---|---|---|
| 2001 | — | — | — | — | — |
| 2002 | — | — | — | — | — |
| 2003 | — | — | — | — | —* |
| 2004 | 5.07 | -3.14 | 3.79 | 2.44 | 8.21 |
| 2005 | -0.37 | 2.98 | -0.02 | 0.06 | 2.65 |

| Trailing | NAV Return% | Market Return% | NAV Rtrn% +/-LB Aggr | %Rank Cat.(NAV) |
|---|---|---|---|---|
| 3 Mo | 0.06 | -0.11 | -0.53 | 2 |
| 6 Mo | 0.05 | -0.26 | 0.13 | 2 |
| 1 Yr | 2.65 | 2.50 | 0.22 | 2 |
| 3 Yr Avg | — | — | — | 0 |
| 5 Yr Avg | — | — | — | 0 |
| 10 Yr Avg | — | — | — | 0 |

| Tax Analysis | Tax-Adj Return% | Tax-Cost Ratio |
|---|---|---|
| 3 Yr (estimated) | — | — |
| 5 Yr (estimated) | — | — |
| 10 Yr (estimated) | — | — |

## Risk Profile

| | Standard Index S&P 500 | Best Fit Index |
|---|---|---|
| Alpha | — | — |
| Beta | — | — |
| R-Squared | — | — |
| Standard Deviation | — | |
| Mean | — | |
| Sharpe Ratio | — | |

## Morningstar Fair Value

| Price/Fair Value Ratio | Fair Value Estimate ($) | Hit Rate % |
|---|---|---|
| — | — | — |

## Portfolio Analysis 12-31-05

| Total Fixed-Income:17 | Date of Maturity | Amount $000 | Value $000 | % Net Assets |
|---|---|---|---|---|
| US Treasury Bond 2.375% | 01-15-25 | 272,193 | 286,649 | 8.71 |
| US Treasury Bond 3.875% | 04-15-29 | 208,327 | 281,631 | 8.56 |
| US Treasury Note 0.875% | 04-15-10 | 284,710 | 270,740 | 8.23 |
| US Treasury Note 3% | 07-15-12 | 244,336 | 258,481 | 7.86 |
| US Treasury Note 2% | 01-15-14 | 233,247 | 232,099 | 7.06 |
| US Treasury Bond 3.625% | 04-15-28 | 179,230 | 231,684 | 7.04 |
| US Treasury Note 1.875% | 07-15-13 | 213,008 | 210,196 | 6.39 |
| US Treasury Note 2% | 07-15-14 | 203,805 | 202,849 | 6.17 |
| US Treasury Note 1.625% | 01-15-15 | 210,260 | 202,720 | 6.16 |
| US Treasury Note 3.625% | 01-15-08 | 188,566 | 193,693 | 5.89 |
| US Treasury Note 3.875% | 01-15-09 | 167,375 | 176,005 | 5.35 |
| US Treasury Note 3.375% | 01-15-07 | 174,467 | 175,830 | 5.35 |
| US Treasury Note 1.875% | 07-15-15 | 156,618 | 154,121 | 4.69 |
| US Treasury Note 3.5% | 01-15-11 | 127,866 | 136,709 | 4.16 |
| US Treasury Note 4.25% | 01-15-10 | 125,794 | 136,388 | 4.15 |
| US Treasury Bond 3.375% | 04-15-32 | 49,501 | 64,533 | 1.96 |
| US Treasury Note 3.375% | 01-15-12 | 57,429 | 61,763 | 1.88 |

## Morningstar's Take by Dieter Bardy

The exchange-traded iShares Lehman TIPS Bond provides decent exposure to the TIPS market, but it's not the best of its kind.

The fund plays a solo role in the ETF world. It's the only ETF that invests in Treasury inflation-protected securities. Because the TIPS market is still fairly narrow at this point, it's entirely possible to own every issue. As of Aug. 31, 2005, only 17 individual issues existed in the marketplace, and this fund owned a piece of each one. Going forward, this index fund can also dedicate up to 5% of its assets to securities outside of the TIPS realm to better mimic the results of its bogy, although we don't expect that to occur often.

Although the fund is unique among ETFs, better mutual fund options exist. The fund charges a reasonable 0.20%. However, two actively managed open-end mutual funds, including Vanguard Inflation-Protected Securities, charge less (0.17%). A small difference can have a big impact on total performance. Moreover, an index fund's costs should be more competitive with its actively managed peers'.

Still, the fund has delivered decent returns. Since the fund's Dec. 4, 2003, inception through the year-to-date period ending Aug. 31, 2005, it had gained an annualized 6.76%, which runs behind its index's 6.99% gain. Part of the reason for this lag is the fund's expense ratio, where we would expect to see the fund trail by its annual levy. Contender Vanguard Inflation-Protected Securities is right there with them though, earning 6.79% over the same time period.

Most investors will not gain much by investing in this ETF over a traditional mutual fund. Those buying into the TIPS market now should consider dollar-cost averaging, as TIPS are fairly expensive at this point and are more at risk as interest rates rise. And making regular investments into an ETF can be costly, since investors must pay commissions.

| Address: | 45 Fremont Street San Francisco CA 94105 800-474-2737 |
|---|---|
| Web Address: | www.ishares.com |
| Inception: | 12-04-03 * |
| Advisor: | Barclays Global Fund Advisers |

| Management Fee: | 0.20% | | |
|---|---|---|---|
| Expense Projections: | 3Yr:$64 | 5Yr:$113 | 10Yr:$255 |
| Income Distrib: | Monthly | | |
| Exchange: | NYSE | | |

**Current Investment Style**

Duration: Short Int Long
Quality: High Med Low

1 figure provided by fund

| Avg Eff Duration1 | 6.0 Yrs |
|---|---|
| Avg Eff Maturity | 10.9 Yrs |
| Avg Credit Quality | AAA |
| Avg Wtd Coupon | 2.83% |
| Avg Wtd Price | 110.06% of par |

| Coupon Range | % of Bonds | Rel Cat |
|---|---|---|
| 0% PIK | 0.0 | 0.0 |
| 0% to 6% | 100.0 | 1.4 |
| 6% to 8% | 0.0 | 0.0 |
| 8% to 10% | 0.0 | 0.0 |
| More than 10% | 0.0 | 0.0 |
| 1.00=Category Average | | |

| Credit Analysis | % bonds 12-31-05 | | |
|---|---|---|---|
| US Govt | 0 | BB | 0 |
| AAA | 100 | B | 0 |
| AA | 0 | Below B | 0 |
| A | 0 | NR/NA | 0 |
| BBB | 0 | | |

| Sector Breakdown | % of assets |
|---|---|
| US Treasuries | 31 |
| TIPS | 69 |
| US Agency | 0 |
| Mortgage Pass-Throughs | 0 |
| Mortgage CMO | 0 |
| Mortgage ARM | 0 |
| US Corporate | 0 |
| Asset-Backed | 0 |
| Convertible | 0 |
| Municipal | 0 |
| Corporate Inflation-Protected | 0 |
| Foreign Corporate | 0 |
| Foreign Govt | 0 |

**Composition**

| Cash | 0.4 | Bonds | 99.6 |
|---|---|---|---|
| Stocks | 0.0 | Other | 0.0 |

| Special Securities | |
|---|---|
| Restricted/Illiquid Secs | 0 |
| Exotic Mortgage-Backed | — |
| Emerging-Markets Secs | 0 |
| Options/Futures/Warrants | No |

Morningstar ETFs 100

# iShares MSCI EAFE

| Ticker | NAV | Market Price | 52 wk High/Low | Yield | Mstar Category |
|---|---|---|---|---|---|
| EFA | $59.12 | $61.92 | $62.48 - $51.26 | 1.9% | Foreign Large Blend |

## Management

### Portfolio Manager(s)

The fund's advisor, Barclays Global Fund Advisors, is one of the world's largest and most experienced managers of index-tracking portfolios.

### Strategy

This exchange-traded offering is a passive fund that simply attempts to match the performance of the MSCI EAFE Index. The benchmark is a free float-adjusted market-capitalization index designed to track the developed world's stock markets outside Canada and the U.S. The index includes equities from Australia, Western Europe, Hong Kong, Japan, New Zealand, and Singapore. It uses a representative sampling method of tracking the index, so it doesn't own the thousands of the securities in the benchmark. Rather it invest in a portion of the bogy that is quantitatively constructed to match the index.

**Growth of $10,000**

— Investment Value of ETF
— Investment Value of Index MSCI EAFE

| | 1996 | 1997 | 1998 | 1999 | 2000 | 2001 | 2002 | 2003 | 2004 | 2005 | History |
|---|---|---|---|---|---|---|---|---|---|---|---|
| | — | — | — | — | — | 39.76 | 32.92 | 45.03 | 53.11 | 59.12 | NAV $ |
| | — | — | — | — | — | 39.77 | 33.00 | 45.59 | 53.42 | 59.43 | Market Price $ |
| | — | — | — | — | — | 9.46* | -15.61 | 38.45 | 19.75 | 13.39 | NAV Return% |
| | — | — | — | — | — | 9.59* | -15.41 | 39.80 | 18.96 | 13.34 | Market Price Return% |
| | — | — | — | — | — | 0.30 | 0.12 | 0.32 | 0.58 | 0.24 | Avg Premium/Discount% |
| | — | — | — | — | — | 9.46 | 0.33 | -0.14 | -0.50 | -0.15 | NAV Rtrn% +/-MSCI EAFE |
| | — | — | — | — | — | 9.46 | 0.19 | -0.97 | -0.63 | -1.08 | NAV Rtrn% +/-MSCI Wd xUS |
| | — | — | — | — | — | — | 1 | 2 | 2 | 2 | NAV Return% Rank in Cat |
| | — | — | — | — | — | 0.00 | 1.58 | 1.59 | 1.78 | 2.09 | Income Return % |
| | — | — | — | — | — | — | -17.19 | 36.86 | 17.97 | 11.30 | Capital Return % |
| | — | — | — | — | — | 0.08 | 0.63 | 0.52 | 0.80 | 1.11 | Income $ |
| | — | — | — | — | — | 0.00 | 0.00 | 0.00 | 0.00 | 0.00 | Capital Gains $ |
| | — | — | — | — | — | — | 0.35 | 0.35 | 0.35 | 0.36 | Expense Ratio % |
| | — | — | — | — | — | — | 1.87 | 2.31 | 2.34 | 2.57 | Income Ratio % |
| | — | — | — | — | — | — | 8 | 8 | 7 | 8 | Turnover Rate % |
| | — | — | — | — | — | — | 2,192 | 5,404 | 13,639 | 22,739 | Net Assets $mil |

## Performance

### Historic Quarterly NAV Returns

| | 1st Qtr | 2nd Qtr | 3rd Qtr | 4th Qtr | Total |
|---|---|---|---|---|---|
| 2001 | — | — | — | 6.71 | —* |
| 2002 | 1.06 | -2.18 | -19.69 | 6.30 | -15.61 |
| 2003 | -8.18 | 19.16 | 8.10 | 17.06 | 38.45 |
| 2004 | 4.21 | 0.20 | -0.32 | 15.05 | 19.75 |
| 2005 | -0.18 | -1.14 | 10.44 | 4.05 | 13.39 |

| Trailing | NAV Return% | Market Return%+/-MSCI EAFE | NAV Rtrn% +/-MSCI EAFE | %Rank Cat.(NAV) |
|---|---|---|---|---|
| 3 Mo | 4.05 | 4.20 | -0.03 | 2 |
| 6 Mo | 14.91 | 15.56 | 0.03 | 2 |
| 1 Yr | 13.39 | 13.34 | -0.15 | 2 |
| 3 Yr Avg | 23.42 | 23.52 | -0.26 | 2 |
| 5 Yr Avg | — | — | — | 0 |
| 10 Yr Avg | — | — | — | 0 |

| Tax Analysis | Tax-Adj Return% | Tax-Cost Ratio |
|---|---|---|
| 3 Yr (estimated) | 22.77 | 0.53 |
| 5 Yr (estimated) | — | — |
| 10 Yr (estimated) | — | — |

## Risk Profile

| | Standard Index S&P 500 | Best Fit Index MSCI EAFE |
|---|---|---|
| Alpha | -0.1 | -0.1 |
| Beta | 1.00 | 1.00 |
| R-Squared | 100 | 100 |
| Standard Deviation | 11.51 | |
| Mean | 23.42 | |
| Sharpe Ratio | 1.73 | |

## Morningstar Fair Value

| Price/Fair Value Ratio | Fair Value Estimate ($) | Hit Rate % |
|---|---|---|
| — | — | — |

## Portfolio Analysis 12-31-05

| Share change since 11-05  Total Stocks:807 | Sector | Country | % Assets |
|---|---|---|---|
| ⊖ BP | Energy | U.K. | 2.18 |
| ⊕ HSBC Hldgs | Financial | U.K. | 1.74 |
| ⊕ Toyota Motor | Goods | Japan | 1.43 |
| ⊕ GlaxoSmithKline | Health | U.K. | 1.43 |
| ⊖ TOTAL | Energy | France | 1.38 |
| ⊕ Vodafone Grp | Telecom | U.K. | 1.35 |
| ⊖ Royal Dutch Shell | Energy | U.K. | 1.22 |
| ⊖ Novartis | Health | Switzerland | 1.19 |
| ⊖ Nestle | Goods | Switzerland | 1.14 |
| ⊖ Roche Holding | Health | Switzerland | 1.01 |
| ⊕ Mitsubishi Tokyo Fin. Gr | Financial | Japan | 0.99 |
| ⊖ UBS | Financial | Switzerland | 0.97 |
| ⊖ Royal Bank Of Scotland G | Financial | U.K. | 0.94 |
| ⊕ Sanofi-Synthelabo | Health | France | 0.90 |
| ⊖ Royal Dutch Shell | Energy | U.K. | 0.87 |
| ⊕ Nokia | Hardware | Finland | 0.79 |
| ⊕ AstraZeneca | Health | U.K. | 0.77 |
| ⊕ Banco Santander Central | Financial | Spain | 0.76 |
| ⊕ Mizuho Financial Grp | Financial | Japan | 0.76 |
| ⊖ Eni | Energy | Italy | 0.73 |

### Current Investment Style

Value Blnd Growth (Large Mid Small)

| Market Cap | % |
|---|---|
| Giant | 56.1 |
| Large | 31.8 |
| Mid | 11.7 |
| Small | 0.4 |
| Micro | 0.0 |

Avg $mil: 27,646

| Value Measures | | Rel Category |
|---|---|---|
| Price/Earnings | 15.11 | 1.12 |
| Price/Book | 2.23 | 1.07 |
| Price/Sales | 1.13 | 1.13 |
| Price/Cash Flow | 7.81 | 1.20 |
| Dividend Yield % | 2.70 | 0.93 |

| Growth Measures | % | Rel Category |
|---|---|---|
| Long-Term Erngs | 11.21 | 0.92 |
| Book Value | 3.14 | 5.41 |
| Sales | 1.83 | 2.51 |
| Cash Flow | 4.73 | 0.42 |
| Historical Erngs | 15.10 | 0.87 |

### Composition

| | | | |
|---|---|---|---|
| Cash | 0.2 | Bonds | 0.0 |
| Stocks | 99.5 | Other | 0.2 |
| Foreign (% of Stock) | | | 100.0 |

| Sector Weightings | % of Stocks | Rel MSCI EAFE | 3 Year High | Low |
|---|---|---|---|---|
| ☎ Info | 12.46 | 0.89 | | |
| 🖥 Software | 0.70 | 0.65 | 1 | 0 |
| 📠 Hardware | 3.94 | 1.09 | 6 | 4 |
| 🎤 Media | 2.11 | 1.00 | 3 | 2 |
| 📱 Telecom | 5.71 | 0.79 | 10 | 6 |
| ⊡ Service | 45.96 | 1.01 | | |
| 🩺 Health | 7.49 | 1.05 | 10 | 7 |
| 🛒 Consumer | 4.42 | 1.01 | 5 | 4 |
| 🏢 Business | 5.17 | 0.86 | 5 | 5 |
| $ Financial | 28.88 | 1.03 | 29 | 19 |
| ⬛ Mfg | 41.57 | 1.03 | | |
| 🏭 Goods | 13.39 | 0.98 | 17 | 13 |
| ⚙ Ind Mtrls | 15.35 | 1.09 | 15 | 12 |
| 🔥 Energy | 8.30 | 1.05 | 10 | 7 |
| 💧 Utilities | 4.53 | 0.98 | 6 | 5 |

### Regional Exposure                                  % Stock

| | | | |
|---|---|---|---|
| UK/W. Europe | 67 | N. America | 0 |
| Japan | 26 | Latn America | 0 |
| Asia X Japan | 8 | Other | 0 |

### Country Exposure                                  % Stock

| | | | |
|---|---|---|---|
| Japan | 26 | Switzerland | 7 |
| U.K. | 24 | Germany | 7 |
| France | 9 | | |

## Morningstar's Take by Dan Culloton

A price war has dampened this fund's appeal somewhat.

This exchange-traded fund still provides cheap and diversified exposure to developed overseas markets. It follows the well-known MSCI EAFE Index which includes brand-name international stocks such as BP, Toyota and Nestle. The benchmark's renown (many active managers gauge themselves against it), as well as the liquidity of its constituents, make this one of the more actively traded international ETFs. That means buying and selling this fund's shares at a price close to its net asset value shouldn't be much of a problem.

The offering also has done a good job aping its bogy and staying competitive with other exchange-traded and traditional mutual fund portfolios in this category. Its 8.9% annualized gain from September 2001 (roughly its inception) through the end of October 2005 matches that of the index. That gain also beats the average actively managed foreign large blend fund, as well as the typical foreign large blend index fund, which gained 7.9% and 8.4%, respectively over the same time period (not all of the index funds in the group track the same benchmark).

This fund's biggest drawback, however, is its expense ratio. It's much lower than those of actively managed international funds, but it's not the cheapest index fund in its category. Investors have long been able to find similar exposure with lower expense ratios and no brokerage commissions from Vanguard's index offerings. However, now that Fidelity Investments, E-Trade and others have cut their index fund fees there are even more no-load index offerings in this group with lower costs. Once you factor in commissions, this ETF loses appeal. Be sure to factor in costs when deciding whether to use this in a portfolio.

| | | | | |
|---|---|---|---|---|
| Address: | 45 Fremont Street San Francisco CA 94105 800-474-2737 | Management Fee: | 0.35% | |
| | | Expense Projections: | 3Yr:$113 | 5Yr:$197  10Yr:$443 |
| | | Income Distrib: | Annually | |
| Web Address: | www.ishares.com | Exchange: | AMEX | |
| Inception: | 08-14-01* | | | |
| Advisor: | Barclays Global Fund Advisers | | | |

**MORNINGSTAR® ETFs 100**

# iShares MSCI EAFE Growth

| Ticker | NAV | Market Price | 52 wk High/Low | Yield | Mstar Category |
|---|---|---|---|---|---|
| EFG | $56.31 | $58.98 | $59.63 - $50.88 | 0.0% | Foreign Large Growth |

## Management

### Portfolio Manager(s)

The fund's advisor, Barclays Global Fund Advisors, is one of the world's largest and most experienced managers of index-tracking portfolios.

### Strategy

This exchange-traded fund tracks the MSCI Europe, Australasia, Far East Value Index, a free-float-adjusted market-capitalization index designed to track the developed world's stock markets outside Canada and the U.S. Like the standard EAFE Index, the fund is dominated by large-cap companies. This fund is skewed toward "growth" stocks, which MSCI classifies using an eight-factor model. MSCI also employs "buffer zones" to limit migration between growth and value camps. Because the stocks in this portfolio are denominated in foreign currency, the fund's U.S. dollar value is vulnerable to currency fluctuations.

### Growth of $10,000

— Investment Value of ETF
— Investment Value of Index MSCI EAFE

| | 1996 | 1997 | 1998 | 1999 | 2000 | 2001 | 2002 | 2003 | 2004 | 2005 | History |
|---|---|---|---|---|---|---|---|---|---|---|---|
| | — | — | — | — | — | — | — | — | — | 56.31 | NAV $ |
| | — | — | — | — | — | — | — | — | — | 56.60 | Market Price $ |
| | — | — | — | — | — | — | — | — | — | 11.13* | NAV Return% |
| | — | — | — | — | — | — | — | — | — | 11.70* | Market Price Return% |
| | — | — | — | — | — | — | — | — | — | 0.36 | Avg Premium/Discount% |
| | — | — | — | — | — | — | — | — | — | 11.13 | NAV Rtrn% +/-MSCI EAFE |
| | — | — | — | — | — | — | — | — | — | 11.13 | NAV Rtrn% +/-MSCI Wd xUS |
| | — | — | — | — | — | — | — | — | — | — | NAV Return% Rank in Cat |
| | — | — | — | — | — | — | — | — | — | — | Income Return % |
| | — | — | — | — | — | — | — | — | — | — | Capital Return % |
| | — | — | — | — | — | — | — | — | — | 0.23 | Income $ |
| | — | — | — | — | — | — | — | — | — | 0.00 | Capital Gains $ |
| | — | — | — | — | — | — | — | — | — | — | Expense Ratio % |
| | — | — | — | — | — | — | — | — | — | — | Income Ratio % |
| | — | — | — | — | — | — | — | — | — | — | Turnover Rate % |
| | — | — | — | — | — | — | — | — | — | 45 | Net Assets $mil |

## Performance

### Historic Quarterly NAV Returns

| | 1st Qtr | 2nd Qtr | 3rd Qtr | 4th Qtr | Total |
|---|---|---|---|---|---|
| 2001 | — | — | — | — | — |
| 2002 | — | — | — | — | — |
| 2003 | — | — | — | — | — |
| 2004 | — | — | — | — | — |
| 2005 | — | — | — | 4.24 | —* |

| Trailing | NAV Return% | Market Return%+/-MSCI EAFE | NAV Rtrn% +/-MSCI EAFE | %Rank Cat.(NAV) |
|---|---|---|---|---|
| 3 Mo | 4.24 | 4.78 | 0.16 | 1 |
| 6 Mo | — | — | — | 0 |
| 1 Yr | — | — | — | 0 |
| 3 Yr Avg | — | — | — | 0 |
| 5 Yr Avg | — | — | — | 0 |
| 10 Yr Avg | — | — | — | 0 |

| Tax Analysis | Tax-Adj Return% | Tax-Cost Ratio |
|---|---|---|
| 3 Yr (estimated) | — | — |
| 5 Yr (estimated) | — | — |
| 10 Yr (estimated) | — | — |

### Risk Profile

| | Standard Index S&P 500 | Best Fit Index |
|---|---|---|
| Alpha | — | — |
| Beta | — | — |
| R-Squared | — | — |
| Standard Deviation | — | |
| Mean | — | |
| Sharpe Ratio | — | |

### Morningstar Fair Value

| Price/Fair Value Ratio | Fair Value Estimate ($) | Hit Rate % |
|---|---|---|
| — | — | — |

## Portfolio Analysis 12-31-05

Share change since 11-05  Total Stocks:542

| | Sector | Country | % Assets |
|---|---|---|---|
| ⊕ BP | Energy | U.K. | 4.37 |
| ⊖ GlaxoSmithKline | Health | U.K. | 2.88 |
| ⊖ Novartis | Health | Switzerland | 2.40 |
| Roche Holding | Health | Switzerland | 2.07 |
| ⊖ Mitsubishi Tokyo Fin. Gr | Financial | Japan | 1.93 |
| ⊖ Sanofi-Synthelabo | Health | France | 1.78 |
| ⊖ AstraZeneca | Health | U.K. | 1.54 |
| ⊖ Vodafone Grp | Telecom | U.K. | 1.33 |
| Telefonica | Telecom | Spain | 1.32 |
| BHP Billiton Ltd | Ind Mtrls | Australia | 1.18 |
| ☼ Allianz | Financial | Germany | 1.12 |
| ⊖ Ericsson AB (publ) | Hardware | Sweden | 1.00 |
| Nokia | Hardware | Finland | 0.99 |
| Sumitomo Mitsui Financia | Financial | Japan | 0.99 |
| TOTAL | Energy | France | 0.98 |
| Rio Tinto | Ind Mtrls | U.K. | 0.96 |
| Tesco | Consumer | U.K. | 0.87 |
| ⊖ Canon | Goods | Japan | 0.86 |
| ⊕ Koninklijke Philips Elec | Goods | Netherlands | 0.81 |
| BHP Billiton | Ind Mtrls | U.K. | 0.80 |

### Current Investment Style

Value Blnd Growth — Large/Mid/Small

| | Market Cap | % |
|---|---|---|
| | Giant | 50.6 |
| | Large | 35.9 |
| | Mid | 13.2 |
| | Small | 0.3 |
| | Micro | 0.0 |

Avg $mil: 24,037

| Value Measures | | Rel Category |
|---|---|---|
| Price/Earnings | 17.55 | 1.00 |
| Price/Book | 2.78 | 1.00 |
| Price/Sales | 1.24 | 1.00 |
| Price/Cash Flow | 9.20 | 1.00 |
| Dividend Yield % | 2.25 | 1.00 |

| Growth Measures | % | Rel Category |
|---|---|---|
| Long-Term Erngs | 13.03 | 1.00 |
| Book Value | 2.69 | 1.00 |
| Sales | 4.86 | 1.00 |
| Cash Flow | 4.92 | 1.00 |
| Historical Erngs | 15.92 | 1.00 |

### Composition

| Cash | 0.1 | Bonds | 0.0 |
|---|---|---|---|
| Stocks | 99.7 | Other | 0.1 |
| Foreign | (% of Stock) | | 100.0 |

### Sector Weightings

| | % of Stocks | Rel MSCI EAFE | 3 Year High Low |
|---|---|---|---|
| ↻ Info | 14.32 | 1.02 | |
| 🖳 Software | 1.30 | 1.21 | — — |
| 🖥 Hardware | 4.85 | 1.34 | — — |
| 🎬 Media | 3.00 | 1.43 | — — |
| 📶 Telecom | 5.17 | 0.72 | — — |
| ☎ Service | 42.77 | 0.94 | |
| ⚕ Health | 14.03 | 1.96 | — — |
| 🛒 Consumer | 5.61 | 1.28 | — — |
| 🏢 Business | 6.38 | 1.06 | — — |
| $ Financial | 16.75 | 0.60 | — — |
| 🔧 Mfg | 42.89 | 1.06 | |
| 🏭 Goods | 14.30 | 1.05 | — — |
| ⚙ Ind Mtrls | 18.06 | 1.28 | — — |
| 🔋 Energy | 7.43 | 0.94 | — — |
| 💡 Utilities | 3.10 | 0.67 | — — |

### Regional Exposure

| | % Stock | | % Stock |
|---|---|---|---|
| UK/W. Europe | 66 | N. America | 0 |
| Japan | 26 | Latn America | 0 |
| Asia X Japan | 8 | Other | 0 |

### Country Exposure

| | % Stock | | % Stock |
|---|---|---|---|
| Japan | 26 | Germany | 7 |
| U.K. | 24 | Switzerland | 7 |
| France | 9 | | |

## Morningstar's Take by Dan Lefkovitz

IShares MSCI EAFE Growth Index Fund has some long-term appeal, but interested investors should consider a few things.

Investors looking to add a growth bias to their foreign portfolio will find a lot to like in this new exchange-traded fund that tracks a growth-leaning version of the popular MSCI Europe, Australasia, Far East Index. The fund's portfolio is dominated by many of the same developed-market blue chips that also populate EAFE. But it puts more emphasis on stocks in sectors, such as health care and telecom, that trade at high prices relative to metrics such as earnings, book value, and cash flow. Conversely, the fund goes lighter on cheaper sectors (e.g., energy and financials).

Like any ETF, this fund has built-in advantages, including tax efficiency and a low expense ratio. And, because MSCI uses a multifactor model to split the stock universe between growth and value, this fund will stick more predictably to its style than an active manager. Lately, many growth managers have been delving into traditional value sectors, which could lead to overlap between a foreign large-value fund. So, this fund could serve a useful function for investors looking to balance out a value bias in their foreign portfolios.

Some investors may look to this fund as a way to play a rebound in growth stocks, which many predict. But history has shown that market moves are extremely hard to time. Investors who trade in and out of ETFs risk paying so much in brokerage commissions that their cost advantage is undermined.

Also, investors should be aware that both Vanguard and Fidelity offer EAFE-tracking index funds for just 0.10% (compared with this fund's 0.40% price tag). We can't predict whether this index will outperform the more broad-based one over the long term. But we do know that the price differential will make a big impact over the years.

| | | | |
|---|---|---|---|
| Address: | 45 Fremont Street San Francisco CA 94105 800-474-2737 | Management Fee: | 0.40% |
| | | Expense Projections: | 3Yr:$128  5Yr: —  10Yr: — |
| | | Income Distrib: | Annually |
| Web Address: | www.ishares.com | Exchange: | NYSE |
| Inception: | 08-01-05* | | |
| Advisor: | Barclays Global Fund Advisers | | |

# iShares MSCI EAFE Value I

| Ticker | NAV | Market Price | 52 wk High/Low | Yield | Mstar Category |
|---|---|---|---|---|---|
| EFV | $56.00 | $59.32 | $59.38 - $51.00 | 0.0% | Foreign Large Value |

## Management

### Portfolio Manager(s)

The fund's advisor, Barclays Global Fund Advisors, is one of the world's largest and most experienced managers of index-tracking portfolios.

### Strategy

This exchange-traded fund tracks the MSCI Europe, Australasia, Far East Value Index, a free-float-adjusted market-capitalization index designed to track the developed world's stock markets outside Canada and the U.S. Like the EAFE Index, the fund is dominated by large-cap companies. This fund is skewed toward "value" stocks, which MSCI classifies using an eight-factor model. MSCI also employs "buffer zones" to limit migration between growth and value camps. Because the stocks in this portfolio are denominated in foreign currency, the fund's U.S. dollar value is vulnerable to currency fluctuations.

## Performance

### Historic Quarterly NAV Returns

| | 1st Qtr | 2nd Qtr | 3rd Qtr | 4th Qtr | Total |
|---|---|---|---|---|---|
| 2001 | — | — | — | — | — |
| 2002 | — | — | — | — | — |
| 2003 | — | — | — | — | — |
| 2004 | — | — | — | — | — |
| 2005 | — | — | — | 3.69 | —* |

| Trailing | NAV Return% | Market Return% | NAV Rtrn% +/-MSCI EAFE | %Rank Cat.(NAV) |
|---|---|---|---|---|
| 3 Mo | 3.69 | 4.13 | -0.39 | 3 |
| 6 Mo | — | — | — | 0 |
| 1 Yr | — | — | — | 0 |
| 3 Yr Avg | — | — | — | 0 |
| 5 Yr Avg | — | — | — | 0 |
| 10 Yr Avg | — | — | — | 0 |

| Tax Analysis | Tax-Adj Return% | Tax-Cost Ratio |
|---|---|---|
| 3 Yr (estimated) | — | — |
| 5 Yr (estimated) | — | — |
| 10 Yr (estimated) | — | — |

**Growth of $10,000**

— Investment Value of ETF
— Investment Value of Index MSCI EAFE

| | 1996 | 1997 | 1998 | 1999 | 2000 | 2001 | 2002 | 2003 | 2004 | 2005 | History |
|---|---|---|---|---|---|---|---|---|---|---|---|
| | — | — | — | — | — | — | — | — | — | 56.00 | NAV $ |
| | — | — | — | — | — | — | — | — | — | 56.32 | Market Price $ |
| | — | — | — | — | — | — | — | — | — | 10.30* | NAV Return% |
| | — | — | — | — | — | — | — | — | — | 10.93* | Market Price Return% |
| | — | — | — | — | — | — | — | — | — | 0.48 | Avg Premium/Discount% |
| | — | — | — | — | — | — | — | — | — | 10.30 | NAV Rtrn% +/-MSCI EAFE |
| | — | — | — | — | — | — | — | — | — | 10.30 | NAV Rtrn% +/-MSCI Wd xUS |
| | — | — | — | — | — | — | — | — | — | — | NAV Return% Rank in Cat |
| | — | — | — | — | — | — | — | — | — | — | Income Return % |
| | — | — | — | — | — | — | — | — | — | — | Capital Return % |
| | — | — | — | — | — | — | — | — | — | 0.25 | Income $ |
| | — | — | — | — | — | — | — | — | — | 0.00 | Capital Gains $ |
| | — | — | — | — | — | — | — | — | — | — | Expense Ratio % |
| | — | — | — | — | — | — | — | — | — | — | Income Ratio % |
| | — | — | — | — | — | — | — | — | — | — | Turnover Rate % |
| | — | — | — | — | — | — | — | — | — | 65 | Net Assets $mil |

## Risk Profile

| | Standard Index S&P 500 | Best Fit Index |
|---|---|---|
| Alpha | — | — |
| Beta | — | — |
| R-Squared | — | — |
| Standard Deviation | — | |
| Mean | — | |
| Sharpe Ratio | — | |

## Morningstar Fair Value

| Price/Fair Value Ratio | Fair Value Estimate ($) | Hit Rate % |
|---|---|---|
| — | — | — |

## Portfolio Analysis 12-31-05

Share change since 11-05 Total Stocks:520

| | Sector | Country | % Assets |
|---|---|---|---|
| ⊕ HSBC Hldgs | Financial | U.K. | 3.53 |
| ⊕ Toyota Motor | Goods | Japan | 2.92 |
| ⊕ Royal Dutch Shell | Energy | U.K. | 2.42 |
| ⊕ Nestle | Goods | Switzerland | 2.35 |
| ⊕ UBS | Financial | Switzerland | 1.92 |
| ⊕ Royal Bank Of Scotland G | Financial | U.K. | 1.87 |
| ⊕ TOTAL | Energy | France | 1.80 |
| ⊕ Royal Dutch Shell | Energy | U.K. | 1.72 |
| ⊕ Banco Santander Central | Financial | Spain | 1.57 |
| ⊕ Eni | Energy | Italy | 1.41 |
| ✳ Vodafone Grp | Telecom | U.K. | 1.33 |
| ⊕ Barclays | Financial | U.K. | 1.31 |
| ⊕ HBOS | Financial | U.K. | 1.29 |
| ⊕ ING Groep | Financial | Netherlands | 1.25 |
| ⊕ BNP Paribas | Financial | France | 1.25 |
| ⊕ E.ON | Utilities | Germany | 1.25 |
| ⊕ BBVA | Financial | Spain | 1.22 |
| ⊕ Credit Suisse Grp | Financial | Switzerland | 1.20 |
| ⊕ UniCredito Italiano Grp | Financial | Italy | 1.08 |
| ⊕ Mizuho Financial Grp | Financial | Japan | 0.96 |

### Current Investment Style

Value Blnd Growth — Large Mid Small

| Market Cap | % |
|---|---|
| Giant | 61.9 |
| Large | 26.6 |
| Mid | 10.8 |
| Small | 0.6 |
| Micro | 0.0 |

Avg $mil: 31,436

| Value Measures | | Rel Category |
|---|---|---|
| Price/Earnings | 13.31 | 0.98 |
| Price/Book | 1.86 | 0.90 |
| Price/Sales | 1.06 | 0.74 |
| Price/Cash Flow | 6.78 | 1.21 |
| Dividend Yield % | 3.05 | 1.27 |

| Growth Measures | % | Rel Category |
|---|---|---|
| Long-Term Erngs | 9.99 | 0.98 |
| Book Value | 3.47 | 0.56 |
| Sales | -0.76 | NMF |
| Cash Flow | 1.37 | 0.09 |
| Historical Erngs | 14.40 | 0.96 |

### Composition

| | | | | |
|---|---|---|---|---|
| Cash | 0.1 | Bonds | 0.0 | |
| Stocks | 99.5 | Other | 0.3 | |
| Foreign | (% of Stock) | | 100.0 | |

### Sector Weightings

| | % of Stocks | Rel MSCI EAFE | 3 Year High Low |
|---|---|---|---|
| ↻ Info | 10.42 | 0.74 | |
| Software | 0.04 | 0.04 | — — |
| Hardware | 3.24 | 0.90 | — — |
| Media | 1.12 | 0.53 | — — |
| Telecom | 6.02 | 0.83 | — — |
| ☰ Service | 49.48 | 1.08 | |
| Health | 1.41 | 0.20 | — — |
| Consumer | 3.04 | 0.69 | — — |
| Business | 4.10 | 0.68 | — — |
| Financial | 40.93 | 1.46 | — — |
| Mfg | 40.10 | 0.99 | |
| Goods | 12.49 | 0.91 | — — |
| Ind Mtrls | 12.49 | 0.88 | — — |
| Energy | 8.94 | 1.13 | — — |
| Utilities | 6.18 | 1.34 | — — |

### Regional Exposure

| | % Stock | | % Stock |
|---|---|---|---|
| UK/W. Europe | 67 | N. America | 0 |
| Japan | 25 | Latn America | 0 |
| Asia X Japan | 8 | Other | 0 |

### Country Exposure

| | % Stock | | % Stock |
|---|---|---|---|
| Japan | 25 | Switzerland | 7 |
| U.K. | 24 | Germany | 6 |
| France | 9 | | |

## Morningstar's Take by Dan Lefkovitz

There are reasons to own iShares MSCI EAFE Value, but past performance isn't one of them.

This exchange-traded fund is designed to track a value-leaning version of the popular MSCI Europe, Australasia, and Far East (EAFE) Index. Its portfolio is dominated by the same developed-market blue-chip stocks as EAFE, but it favors names trading at cheap prices relative to metrics such as earnings, book value, and cash flow. This leaves the fund with much more exposure to sectors such as financials, energy, and utilities than EAFE. On the flip side, it's lighter on tech and health-care stocks.

This ETF has several built-in advantages, including tax efficiency and a 0.40% expense ratio--well below the 1.26% charged by the typical large-cap-focused foreign fund. And, because MSCI uses a multifactor model to split the stock universe between growth and value, this fund will stick more predictably to its style than an active manager.

But we have concerns. For one thing, value stocks have outperformed growth (both in the U.S.

and abroad) for several years now. Investors should not look at this performance and assume that this fund will continue beating its broad-based sibling iShares MSCI EAFE or the growth-leaning iShares MSCI EAFE Growth.

For another, investors should be aware that this fund's expense ratio looks rather steep when compared with some EAFE-tracking alternatives. Even if you think value will beat growth over the long term, this fund will have to overcome an expense ratio that is 30 basis points higher than index funds Fidelity Spartan International Index and Vanguard Developed Markets Index. The brokerage commissions required for buying and selling ETFs put this fund at a further cost disadvantage.

Still, we can see the appeal of this fund for long-term investors who want to tilt their foreign portfolios to the value side.

| | | | | |
|---|---|---|---|---|
| Address: | 45 Fremont Street San Francisco CA 94105 800-474-2737 | Management Fee: | 0.40% | |
| | | Expense Projections: | 3Yr:$128 | 5Yr: — 10Yr: — |
| Web Address: | www.ishares.com | Income Distrib: | Annually | |
| Inception: | 08-01-05* | Exchange: | NYSE | |
| Advisor: | Barclays Global Advisors | | | |

**MORNINGSTAR® ETFs 100**

# iShares MSCI Emerg Mkts

| Ticker | NAV | Market Price | 52 wk High/Low | Yield | Mstar Category |
|---|---|---|---|---|---|
| EEM | $88.52 | $94.57 | $95.72 - $63.63 | 1.1% | Diversified Emerging Mkts |

## Management

### Portfolio Manager(s)

The fund is managed by Barclays Global Investors, one of the world's largest and most experienced managers of index-tracking portfolios.

### Strategy

This fund tracks the MSCI Emerging Markets Free Index, which includes stocks from the markets of 26 developing countries, including South Korea, South Africa, Taiwan, and China. The fund doesn't own all of the stocks in the index; rather, it uses quantitative tools to help it own a representative sample of the stocks in the index.

**Growth of $10,000**
- Investment Value of ETF
- Investment Value of Index MSCI EAFE

| | 1996 | 1997 | 1998 | 1999 | 2000 | 2001 | 2002 | 2003 | 2004 | 2005 | History |
|---|---|---|---|---|---|---|---|---|---|---|---|
| | — | — | — | — | — | — | — | 53.95 | 66.91 | 88.52 | NAV $ |
| | — | — | — | — | — | — | — | 54.64 | 67.28 | 88.25 | Market Price $ |
| | — | — | — | — | — | — | — | 43.75* | 25.53 | 33.78 | NAV Return% |
| | — | — | — | — | — | — | — | 44.41* | 24.64 | 32.62 | Market Price Return% |
| | — | — | — | — | — | — | — | 0.53 | 0.25 | 0.07 | Avg Premium/Discount% |
| | — | — | — | — | — | — | — | 43.75 | 5.28 | 20.24 | NAV Rtrn% +/-MSCI EAFE |
| | — | — | — | — | — | — | — | 43.75 | 3.08 | 3.47 | NAV Rtrn% +/-MSCI EmrMkt |
| | — | — | — | — | — | — | — | — | 3 | 3 | NAV Return% Rank in Cat |
| | — | — | — | — | — | — | — | 0.00 | 1.49 | 1.48 | Income Return % |
| | — | — | — | — | — | — | — | — | 24.04 | 32.30 | Capital Return % |
| | — | — | — | — | — | — | — | 0.27 | 0.80 | 0.99 | Income $ |
| | — | — | — | — | — | — | — | 0.00 | 0.00 | 0.00 | Capital Gains $ |
| | — | — | — | — | — | — | — | 0.78 | 0.76 | 0.77 | Expense Ratio % |
| | — | — | — | — | — | — | — | 1.58 | 2.10 | 2.40 | Income Ratio % |
| | — | — | — | — | — | — | — | 10 | 8 | 9 | Turnover Rate % |
| | — | — | — | — | — | — | — | 1,076 | 3,894 | 10,264 | Net Assets $mil |

## Performance

### Historic Quarterly NAV Returns

| | 1st Qtr | 2nd Qtr | 3rd Qtr | 4th Qtr | Total |
|---|---|---|---|---|---|
| 2001 | — | — | — | — | — |
| 2002 | — | — | — | — | — |
| 2003 | — | — | 14.19 | 19.41 | —* |
| 2004 | 7.67 | -7.92 | 6.87 | 18.48 | 25.53 |
| 2005 | 1.73 | 4.96 | 18.30 | 5.91 | 33.78 |

| Trailing | NAV Return% | Market Return%+/-MSCI EAFE | NAV Rtrn% | %Rank Cat.(NAV) |
|---|---|---|---|---|
| 3 Mo | 5.91 | 5.13 | 1.83 | 4 |
| 6 Mo | 25.29 | 24.63 | 10.41 | 4 |
| 1 Yr | 33.78 | 32.62 | 20.24 | 3 |
| 3 Yr Avg | — | — | — | 0 |
| 5 Yr Avg | — | — | — | 0 |
| 10 Yr Avg | — | — | — | 0 |

| Tax Analysis | Tax-Adj Return% | Tax-Cost Ratio |
|---|---|---|
| 3 Yr (estimated) | — | — |
| 5 Yr (estimated) | — | — |
| 10 Yr (estimated) | — | — |

## Risk Profile

| | Standard Index S&P 500 | Best Fit Index |
|---|---|---|
| Alpha | — | — |
| Beta | — | — |
| R-Squared | — | — |
| Standard Deviation | — | |
| Mean | — | |
| Sharpe Ratio | — | |

## Morningstar Fair Value

| Price/Fair Value Ratio | Fair Value Estimate ($) | Hit Rate % |
|---|---|---|
| — | — | — |

## Portfolio Analysis 12-31-05

| Share change since 11-05 Total Stocks:257 | Sector | Country | % Assets |
|---|---|---|---|
| ⊕ Samsung Electnc GDR 144A | Goods | Korea | 6.63 |
| ⊕ Taiwan Semiconductor Man | Hardware | Taiwan | 3.76 |
| ⊕ Kookmin Bank ADR | Financial | Korea | 3.70 |
| ⊕ Posco ADR | Ind Mtrls | Korea | 2.40 |
| ⊕ Siliconware Precision In | Hardware | Taiwan | 2.22 |
| ⊖ Lukoil ADR | Energy | Russia | 2.19 |
| ⊕ Korea Electric Power ADR | Utilities | Korea | 2.18 |
| ⊕ America Movil S.A. de C. | Telecom | Mexico | 1.94 |
| ⊕ United Microelectronics | Hardware | Taiwan | 1.82 |
| ⊕ AU Optronics ADR | Hardware | Taiwan | 1.76 |
| ⊕ Teva Pharmaceutical Indu | Health | Israel | 1.61 |
| ⊖ China Mobile | Telecom | Hong Kong | 1.57 |
| ⊖ Chunghwa Telecom Company | Telecom | Taiwan | 1.53 |
| ⊕ Surgutneftegaz | Energy | Russia | 1.52 |
| ⊕ Sasol Ltd | Ind Mtrls | South Africa | 1.51 |
| ⊖ Petroleo Brasileiro S.A. | Energy | Brazil | 1.50 |
| ⊕ Banco Bradesco S.A. (ADR | Financial | Brazil | 1.45 |
| ⊖ Companhia Vale Do Rio Do | Ind Mtrls | Brazil | 1.43 |
| ⊖ Petroleo Brasileiro ADR | Energy | Brazil | 1.39 |
| ⊖ Companhia Vale Do Rio Do | Ind Mtrls | Brazil | 1.36 |

### Current Investment Style

| Value | Blnd | Growth | | Market Cap | % |
|---|---|---|---|---|---|
| | | | Large | Giant | 45.4 |
| | | ■ | | Large | 33.5 |
| | | | Mid | Mid | 17.8 |
| | | | | Small | 2.9 |
| | | | Small | Micro | 0.4 |

Avg $mil: 11,259

| Value Measures | | Rel Category |
|---|---|---|
| Price/Earnings | 12.80 | 1.06 |
| Price/Book | 1.97 | 0.93 |
| Price/Sales | 1.23 | 1.40 |
| Price/Cash Flow | 6.62 | 1.11 |
| Dividend Yield % | 3.46 | 0.86 |

| Growth Measures | % | Rel Category |
|---|---|---|
| Long-Term Erngs | 15.30 | 0.99 |
| Book Value | 10.95 | 1.43 |
| Sales | 12.23 | 1.30 |
| Cash Flow | 19.82 | 1.76 |
| Historical Erngs | 28.40 | 1.21 |

### Composition

| Cash | 0.2 | Bonds | 0.0 |
|---|---|---|---|
| Stocks | 99.7 | Other | 0.0 |
| Foreign (% of Stock) | | | 99.3 |

| Sector Weightings | % of Stocks | Rel MSCI EAFE | 3 Year High | 3 Year Low |
|---|---|---|---|---|
| ↻ Info | 28.91 | 2.06 | | |
| ▨ Software | 2.85 | 2.66 | 4 | 2 |
| ▦ Hardware | 10.87 | 3.01 | 14 | 8 |
| ▤ Media | 1.42 | 0.68 | 1 | 0 |
| ▥ Telecom | 13.77 | 1.91 | 16 | 12 |
| ⊂ϴ Service | 28.87 | 0.63 | | |
| ▧ Health | 2.84 | 0.40 | 4 | 3 |
| ▧ Consumer | 4.20 | 0.96 | 5 | 3 |
| ▨ Business | 1.95 | 0.32 | 2 | 1 |
| ⑤ Financial | 19.88 | 0.71 | 20 | 14 |
| ▱ Mfg | 42.22 | 1.05 | | |
| ▧ Goods | 10.07 | 0.74 | 13 | 9 |
| ✿ Ind Mtrls | 16.22 | 1.15 | 21 | 16 |
| ▧ Energy | 11.18 | 1.41 | 12 | 10 |
| ▨ Utilities | 4.75 | 1.03 | 5 | 4 |

### Regional Exposure % Stock

| UK/W. Europe | 1 | N. America | 1 |
|---|---|---|---|
| Japan | 0 | Latn America | 21 |
| Asia X Japan | 50 | Other | 27 |

### Country Exposure % Stock

| South Korea | 18 | Brazil | 10 |
|---|---|---|---|
| South Africa | 12 | Hong Kong | 8 |
| Taiwan | 11 | | |

## Morningstar's Take by Dan Culloton

The iShares MSCI Emerging Markets Index offers cheap exposure to the developing world, but it may not be the best alternative.

The fund tracks the MSCI Emerging Markets Index, which offers broad ownership of stocks from 26 rising countries. Its 0.75% expense ratio is about one third of the 2% levy for the typical mutual fund in the diversified emerging markets category. It's also been competitive with regard to performance since its April 2003 inception. The ETF's trailing 12-month gain of nearly 35% through Nov. 8, 2005, beats the 32% advance of the average traditional emerging markets fund over the same period.

That won't always be the case. Emerging markets are still fairly inefficient and actively managed funds can gain an edge on this ETF's bogy via savvy stock-picking. Nevertheless, low cost and diversification give this ETF a fighting chance over the long term.

This fund, however, isn't the cheapest offering of its kind. Vanguard Emerging Markets Stock Index, which apes a modified version of the MSCI emerging markets bogy (it excludes a few regions, such as Russia), offers pretty much the same thing for an expense ratio that is about 20 basis points, or hundredths of a percent, lower. The exchange-traded Viper share class of the Vanguard offering is even cheaper and doesn't charge a 0.50% entry and exit fees like its parent fund does.

Some other words of caution: Many of this fund's top holdings, such as Samsung and Infosys Technologies, are showing up more often in broad-based foreign funds. If you own one you may already have all of the emerging-markets exposure you need. Also, the emerging-markets group has been one of the best performing equity categories over the trailing three years, and this notoriously volatile asset class probably can't sustain that pace indefinitely. Shop around and carefully consider this fund's role in your portfolio before committing to it.

| | | | | |
|---|---|---|---|---|
| Address: | 45 Fremont Street | Management Fee: | 0.75% | |
| | San Francisco CA 94105 | Expense Projections: | 3Yr:$240 | 5Yr:$417 10Yr:$930 |
| | 800-474-2737 | Income Distrib: | Annually | |
| Web Address: | www.ishares.com | Exchange: | AMEX | |
| Inception: | 04-07-03 * | | | |
| Advisor: | Barclays Global Fund Advisers | | | |

# iShares MSCI ex-Japn

| | Ticker | NAV | Market Price | 52 wk High/Low | Yield | Mstar Category |
|---|---|---|---|---|---|---|
| | EPP | $98.55 | $102.76 | $103.95 - $86.88 | 3.8% | Pacific/Asia ex-Japan Stk |

## Management

### Portfolio Manager(s)

Barclays Global Fund Investors, the world's largest manager of passively run indexed assets, operates this fund. It offers nearly 100 exchange-traded funds, including individual country ETFs based on the major countries covered by this portfolio.

### Strategy

This fund tracks MSCI's Pacific Free ex-Japan Index. It uses representative sampling to own more than 160 large-cap stocks in a variety of industries and sectors from Australia, Hong Kong, New Zealand, and Singapore. More than two thirds of the market cap weighting bogy's assets are in Australia.

**Growth of $10,000**

— Investment Value of ETF
— Investment Value of Index MSCI EAFE

| 1996 | 1997 | 1998 | 1999 | 2000 | 2001 | 2002 | 2003 | 2004 | 2005 | History |
|---|---|---|---|---|---|---|---|---|---|---|
| — | — | — | — | — | 54.55 | 50.55 | 72.10 | 89.70 | 98.55 | NAV $ |
| — | — | — | — | — | 54.17 | 50.79 | 72.48 | 90.17 | 98.67 | Market Price $ |
| — | — | — | — | — | 20.86* | -5.73 | 45.73 | 28.68 | 14.03 | NAV Return% |
| — | — | — | — | — | 20.89* | -4.62 | 45.80 | 28.68 | 13.57 | Market Price Return% |
| — | — | — | — | — | 0.07 | 0.87 | 1.10 | 0.34 | 0.19 | Avg Premium/Discount% |
| — | — | — | — | — | 20.86 | 10.21 | 7.14 | 8.43 | 0.49 | NAV Rtrn% +/-MSCi EAFE |
| — | — | — | — | — | 20.86 | 5.32 | 4.96 | 14.45 | -3.83 | NAV Rtrn% +/-MSCIAC FExJ |
| — | — | — | — | — | — | 7 | 7 | 7 | 9 | NAV Return% Rank in Cat |
| — | — | — | — | — | 0.00 | 1.62 | 2.99 | 4.18 | 4.12 | Income Return % |
| — | — | — | — | — | — | -7.35 | 42.74 | 24.50 | 9.91 | Capital Return % |
| — | — | — | — | — | 0.27 | 0.88 | 1.51 | 3.01 | 3.70 | Income $ |
| — | — | — | — | — | 0.00 | 0.00 | 0.00 | 0.00 | 0.00 | Capital Gains $ |
| — | — | — | — | — | — | 0.50 | 0.50 | 0.50 | 0.50 | Expense Ratio % |
| — | — | — | — | — | — | 2.87 | 3.47 | 3.68 | 4.09 | Income Ratio % |
| — | — | — | — | — | — | 5 | 8 | 8 | 16 | Turnover Rate % |
| — | — | — | — | — | — | 157 | 490 | 996 | 1,675 | Net Assets $mil |

## Performance

### Historic Quarterly NAV Returns

| | 1st Qtr | 2nd Qtr | 3rd Qtr | 4th Qtr | Total |
|---|---|---|---|---|---|
| 2001 | — | — | — | — | —* |
| 2002 | 3.94 | -1.82 | -11.75 | 4.67 | -5.73 |
| 2003 | 0.65 | 14.86 | 10.76 | 13.80 | 45.73 |
| 2004 | 6.13 | -4.78 | 9.47 | 16.33 | 28.68 |
| 2005 | 0.52 | 4.57 | 9.26 | -0.72 | 14.03 |

| Trailing | NAV Return% | Market Return% | NAV Rtrn% +/-MSCI EAFE | %Rank Cat.(NAV) |
|---|---|---|---|---|
| 3 Mo | -0.72 | -0.72 | -4.80 | 9 |
| 6 Mo | 8.48 | 8.78 | -6.40 | 9 |
| 1 Yr | 14.03 | 13.57 | 0.49 | 9 |
| 3 Yr Avg | 28.83 | 28.68 | 5.15 | 7 |
| 5 Yr Avg | — | — | — | 0 |
| 10 Yr Avg | — | — | — | 0 |

| Tax Analysis | Tax-Adj Return% | Tax-Cost Ratio |
|---|---|---|
| 3 Yr (estimated) | 27.46 | 1.06 |
| 5 Yr (estimated) | — | — |
| 10 Yr (estimated) | — | — |

## Risk Profile

| | Standard Index S&P 500 | Best Fit Index MSCI Pac xJp |
|---|---|---|
| Alpha | 8.9 | 0.1 |
| Beta | 0.77 | 1.00 |
| R-Squared | 62 | 100 |
| Standard Deviation | 11.25 | |
| Mean | 28.83 | |
| Sharpe Ratio | 2.15 | |

## Morningstar Fair Value

| Price/Fair Value Ratio | Fair Value Estimate ($) | Hit Rate % |
|---|---|---|
| — | — | — |

## Morningstar's Take by Dan Culloton

IShares MSCI Pacific ex-Japan is a viable option, but still should be handled with care.

This fund offers cheap exposure to Pacific region stocks outside of Japan. This exchange-traded fund is the cheapest offering in the Pacific/Asia ex-Japan Stock fund category. Its 0.50% expense ratio is about one fourth the levy of the average traditional mutual fund in the group. And if you are a devoted indexer seeking exposure to the MSCI Pacific Free ex-Japan Index, this currently is your only option.

The fund, which owns leading, mostly large cap, stocks from Australia, Hong Kong, New Zealand and Singapore, has provided very competitive returns over its short lifetime. The ETF's 25.9% annualized gain over the trailing three-year period ending Nov. 9, 2005, is not only better than the average return of its own peer group but also of most other equity categories. Strong demand from China has fueled advances for firms such as Australian miner BHP Billiton.

Investors would be mistaken, however, to expect such strong performance to continue uninterrupted. Although this offering has been less volatile, as gauged by standard deviation, than its typical category competitor, it still courts a few risks. Developed and open economies, such as Australia and Singapore, comprise the bulk of this fund, but those economies depend on exports to developing and less open markets, such as China. The risk reward record of this ETF's benchmark also has a checkered past. It lost money in five of 10 years from 1995 to 2004.

There are reasons to own a fund that focuses on stocks from the other side of the Pacific except Japan. You may, for example, already own a Japan fund, or you may have a Japanese employer and own some company stock. Still, if investors own broad international funds or ETFs they should check to see if they have enough exposure to this area before buying this one.

| Address: | 45 Fremont Street USA 800-474-2737 |
|---|---|
| Web Address: | www.ishares.com |
| Inception: | 10-25-01 * |
| Advisor: | Barclays Global Fund Advisers |

| Management Fee: | 0.50% | | |
|---|---|---|---|
| Expense Projections: | 3Yr:$160 | 5Yr:$280 | 10Yr:$628 |
| Income Distrib: | Annually | | |
| Exchange: | AMEX | | |

## Portfolio Analysis 12-31-05

| Share change since 11-05 Total Stocks:177 | Sector | Country | % Assets |
|---|---|---|---|
| ⊕ BHP Billiton Ltd | Ind Mtrls | Australia | 7.40 |
| ⊕ Commonwealth Bank of Aus | Financial | Australia | 4.95 |
| ⊕ National Australia Bank | Financial | Australia | 4.60 |
| ⊖ Australia & New Zealand | Financial | Australia | 3.96 |
| ⊖ Westpac Banking | Financial | Australia | 3.76 |
| ⊖ Hutchison Whampoa Ltd | Telecom | Hong Kong | 2.52 |
| ⊕ Westfield Grp | Financial | Australia | 2.43 |
| ⊕ Cheung Kong (hldgs) Ltd | Financial | Hong Kong | 1.88 |
| ⊖ Rio Tinto Ltd | Ind Mtrls | Australia | 1.79 |
| ⊕ Woolworths Ltd | Consumer | Australia | 1.76 |
| ⊕ Woodside Petroleum Ltd | Energy | Australia | 1.65 |
| ⊕ Sun Hung Kai Properties | Financial | Hong Kong | 1.58 |
| ⊕ Macquarie Bank Ltd | Financial | Australia | 1.42 |
| ⊕ DBS Grp Hldgs Ltd | Financial | Singapore | 1.41 |
| ⊕ Rinker Grp Ltd | Ind Mtrls | Australia | 1.39 |
| ⊖ QBE Insurance Grp Ltd | Financial | Australia | 1.37 |
| ⊖ Singapore Telecommunicat | Telecom | Singapore | 1.31 |
| ⊖ AMP Ltd | Financial | Australia | 1.30 |
| ⊕ CLP Hldgs Ltd | Utilities | Hong Kong | 1.30 |
| ⊕ Wesfarmers Ltd | Ind Mtrls | Australia | 1.28 |

### Current Investment Style

Value Blnd Growth — Large/Mid/Small

| Market Cap | % |
|---|---|
| Giant | 49.5 |
| Large | 37.3 |
| Mid | 12.9 |
| Small | 0.3 |
| Micro | 0.0 |

Avg $mil: 12,075

| Value Measures | | Rel Category |
|---|---|---|
| Price/Earnings | 14.88 | 1.12 |
| Price/Book | 2.09 | 1.14 |
| Price/Sales | 1.81 | 1.07 |
| Price/Cash Flow | 8.38 | 1.29 |
| Dividend Yield % | 5.00 | 1.09 |

| Growth Measures | % | Rel Category |
|---|---|---|
| Long-Term Erngs | 11.33 | 0.83 |
| Book Value | 5.13 | 0.71 |
| Sales | 11.69 | 0.87 |
| Cash Flow | 14.18 | 0.88 |
| Historical Erngs | 18.25 | 0.86 |

### Composition

| | | | |
|---|---|---|---|
| Cash | 0.2 | Bonds | 0.0 |
| Stocks | 99.8 | Other | 0.0 |
| Foreign (% of Stock) | | | 100.0 |

| Sector Weightings | % of Stocks | Rel MSCI EAFE | 3 Year High | Low |
|---|---|---|---|---|
| ☎ Info | 8.96 | 0.64 | | |
| 🖥 Software | 0.25 | 0.23 | 0 | 0 |
| 💻 Hardware | 0.76 | 0.21 | 1 | 1 |
| 🎬 Media | 1.78 | 0.85 | 6 | 1 |
| ☏ Telecom | 6.17 | 0.85 | 9 | 6 |
| ⚙ Service | 60.55 | 1.32 | | |
| 🏥 Health | 2.04 | 0.28 | 2 | 1 |
| 🛒 Consumer | 6.34 | 1.45 | 7 | 5 |
| 💼 Business | 6.31 | 1.04 | 7 | 4 |
| 💲 Financial | 45.86 | 1.63 | 50 | 40 |
| 🏭 Mfg | 30.51 | 0.76 | | |
| 🏷 Goods | 3.27 | 0.24 | 5 | 2 |
| ⚙ Ind Mtrls | 19.83 | 1.40 | 22 | 15 |
| 🔆 Energy | 3.17 | 0.40 | 3 | 1 |
| 💡 Utilities | 4.24 | 0.92 | 6 | 4 |

### Regional Exposure % Stock

| | | | |
|---|---|---|---|
| UK/W. Europe | 0 | N. America | 0 |
| Japan | 0 | Latn America | 0 |
| Asia X Japan | 100 | Other | 0 |

### Country Exposure % Stock

| | | | |
|---|---|---|---|
| Australia | 66 | New Zealand | 2 |
| Hong Kong | 21 | | |
| Singapore | 11 | | |

MORNINGSTAR® ETFs 100

# iShares NASD Biotech

| | Ticker | NAV | Market Price | 52 wk High/Low | Yield | Mstar Category |
|---|---|---|---|---|---|---|
| | IBB | $77.46 | $81.84 | $81.84 - $63.00 | 0.0% | Specialty-Health |

## Management

### Portfolio Manager(s)

Barclays Global Investors runs this fund. It is the world's largest advisor of indexed assets. It also is the sponsor of the world's largest ETF family.

### Strategy

The fund uses representative sampling to track an index that includes biotech stocks from the NASDQ Composite. The index includes the shares of companies that meet the FTSE definition of Biotech, or companies that research, develop and sell drugs and diagnostic tools with "living material." The stocks also must meet liquidity and financial standards. They need market caps of $200 million, trading volume of 100,000 shares, and six months of trading history. Firms in bankruptcy or with any audit opinions stating their financial statements are unreliable are out.

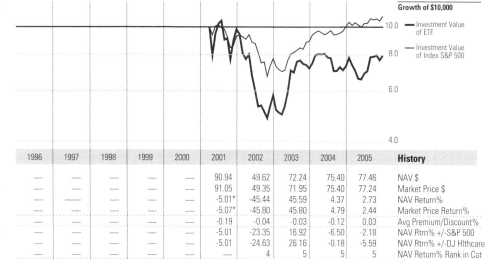

Growth of $10,000
— Investment Value of ETF
— Investment Value of Index S&P 500

| 1996 | 1997 | 1998 | 1999 | 2000 | 2001 | 2002 | 2003 | 2004 | 2005 | History |
|---|---|---|---|---|---|---|---|---|---|---|
| — | — | — | — | — | 90.94 | 49.62 | 72.24 | 75.40 | 77.46 | NAV $ |
| — | — | — | — | — | 91.05 | 49.35 | 71.95 | 75.40 | 77.24 | Market Price $ |
| — | — | — | — | — | -5.01* | -45.44 | 45.59 | 4.37 | 2.73 | NAV Return% |
| — | — | — | — | — | -5.07* | -45.80 | 45.80 | 4.79 | 2.44 | Market Price Return% |
| — | — | — | — | — | -0.19 | -0.04 | -0.03 | -0.12 | 0.03 | Avg Premium/Discount% |
| — | — | — | — | — | -5.01 | -23.35 | 16.92 | -6.50 | -2.18 | NAV Rtrn% +/-S&P 500 |
| — | — | — | — | — | -5.01 | -24.63 | 26.16 | -0.18 | -5.59 | NAV Rtrn% +/-DJ Hlthcare |
| — | — | — | — | — | — | 4 | 5 | 5 | 5 | NAV Return% Rank in Cat |
| — | — | — | — | — | 0.00 | 0.00 | 0.00 | 0.00 | 0.00 | Income Return % |
| — | — | — | — | — | — | -45.44 | 45.59 | 4.37 | 2.73 | Capital Return % |
| — | — | — | — | — | 0.00 | 0.00 | 0.00 | 0.00 | 0.00 | Income $ |
| — | — | — | — | — | 0.00 | 0.00 | 0.00 | 0.00 | 0.00 | Capital Gains $ |
| — | — | — | — | — | 0.50 | 0.50 | 0.50 | 0.50 | 0.50 | Expense Ratio % |
| — | — | — | — | — | -0.50 | -0.46 | -0.43 | -0.43 | -0.40 | Income Ratio % |
| — | — | — | — | — | 9 | 17 | 48 | 36 | 14 | Turnover Rate % |
| — | — | — | — | — | — | 486 | 708 | 1,493 | 1,607 | Net Assets $mil |

## Performance

### Historic Quarterly NAV Returns

| | 1st Qtr | 2nd Qtr | 3rd Qtr | 4th Qtr | Total |
|---|---|---|---|---|---|
| 2001 | — | 32.11 | -26.75 | 22.35 | —* |
| 2002 | -15.02 | -34.06 | -8.83 | 6.80 | -45.44 |
| 2003 | 2.96 | 31.16 | 7.07 | 0.68 | 45.59 |
| 2004 | 7.13 | -2.87 | -6.86 | 7.70 | 4.37 |
| 2005 | -15.31 | 6.14 | 13.60 | 0.60 | 2.73 |

| Trailing | NAV Return% | Market Return% | NAV Rtrn% +/-S&P 500 | %Rank Cat.(NAV) |
|---|---|---|---|---|
| 3 Mo | 0.60 | 0.31 | -1.48 | 7 |
| 6 Mo | 14.28 | 13.76 | 8.52 | 7 |
| 1 Yr | 2.73 | 2.44 | -2.18 | 5 |
| 3 Yr Avg | 16.00 | 16.11 | 1.62 | 4 |
| 5 Yr Avg | — | — | — | 0 |
| 10 Yr Avg | — | — | — | 0 |

| Tax Analysis | Tax-Adj Return% | Tax-Cost Ratio |
|---|---|---|
| 3 Yr (estimated) | 16.00 | 0.00 |
| 5 Yr (estimated) | — | — |
| 10 Yr (estimated) | — | — |

## Risk Profile

| | Standard Index S&P 500 | Best Fit Index ArcaEx Tech 100 |
|---|---|---|
| Alpha | -3.0 | -3.3 |
| Beta | 1.48 | 0.93 |
| R-Squared | 49 | 56 |
| Standard Deviation | 19.57 | |
| Mean | 16.00 | |
| Sharpe Ratio | 0.76 | |

## Morningstar Fair Value

| Price/Fair Value Ratio | Fair Value Estimate ($) | Hit Rate % |
|---|---|---|
| 1.1 Overvalued | 33.94 | 66 Poor |

## Portfolio Analysis 12-31-05

| Share change since 11-05 Total Stocks:160 | Sector | PE | Tot Ret% | % Assets |
|---|---|---|---|---|
| ⊖ Amgen | Health | 28.3 | 22.93 | 17.95 |
| ⊖ Gilead Sciences | Health | 38.1 | 50.24 | 4.90 |
| ⊖ Teva Pharmaceutical Indu | Health | 86.0 | 45.03 | 4.13 |
| ⊖ Genzyme | Health | NMF | 21.89 | 3.76 |
| ⊖ Biogen Idec | Health | NMF | -32.02 | 3.48 |
| ⊖ Celgene | Health | NMF | 144.34 | 2.81 |
| ⊖ MedImmune | Health | — | 29.18 | 1.88 |
| ⊖ Chiron | Health | — | 33.33 | 1.69 |
| ⊖ Sepracor | Health | — | -13.09 | 1.57 |
| ⊖ Vertex Pharmaceuticals | Health | — | 161.78 | 1.51 |
| ⊖ Protein Design Labs | Health | — | 37.56 | 1.38 |
| ⊖ Kos Pharmaceuticals | Health | 16.7 | 37.43 | 1.28 |
| ⊖ Medarex | Health | — | 28.48 | 1.27 |
| ⊖ Amylin Pharmaceuticals | Health | — | 70.89 | 1.22 |
| ⊖ Endo Pharmaceutical Hldg | Health | 25.4 | 44.03 | 1.18 |
| ⊖ Affymetrix | Health | 53.1 | 30.64 | 1.16 |
| ⊖ United Therapeutics | Health | 40.7 | 53.09 | 1.09 |
| ⊖ Abgenix | Health | — | 107.83 | 1.05 |
| ⊖ Nektar Therapeutics | Health | — | -18.68 | 1.03 |
| ⊕ Gen-Probe | Health | 46.0 | 7.92 | 1.01 |

### Current Investment Style

Value Blnd Growth / Large Mid Small

| Market Cap | % |
|---|---|
| Giant | 18.0 |
| Large | 19.1 |
| Mid | 25.2 |
| Small | 26.3 |
| Micro | 11.3 |

Avg $mil: 4,475

| Value Measures | | Rel Category |
|---|---|---|
| Price/Earnings | 29.51 | 1.27 |
| Price/Book | 3.40 | 1.04 |
| Price/Sales | 5.81 | 1.58 |
| Price/Cash Flow | 17.39 | 1.14 |
| Dividend Yield % | 0.01 | 0.01 |

| Growth Measures | % | Rel Category |
|---|---|---|
| Long-Term Erngs | 19.03 | 1.31 |
| Book Value | 3.56 | 0.29 |
| Sales | 19.00 | 1.31 |
| Cash Flow | 16.37 | 1.08 |
| Historical Erngs | 8.30 | 0.71 |

| Profitability | % | Rel Category |
|---|---|---|
| Return on Equity | -0.91 | NMF |
| Return on Assets | -5.51 | NMF |
| Net Margin | 7.02 | 0.58 |

| Industry Weightings | % of Stocks | Rel Cat |
|---|---|---|
| Biotech | 82.4 | 2.4 |
| Drugs | 13.2 | 0.5 |
| Mgd Care | 0.0 | 0.0 |
| Hospitals | 0.0 | 0.0 |
| Other HC Srv | 0.0 | 0.0 |
| Diagnostics | 1.9 | 1.5 |
| Equipment | 0.8 | 0.1 |
| Good/Srv | 1.8 | 0.2 |
| Other | 0.0 | 0.0 |

### Composition

| | |
|---|---|
| ● Cash | 0.0 |
| ● Stocks | 100.0 |
| ● Bonds | 0.0 |
| ● Other | 0.0 |
| Foreign (% of Stock) | 8.2 |

## Morningstar's Take by Dan Culloton

iShares Nasdaq Biotech is a viable choice in an iffy bunch, but that doesn't make it a great idea.

This fund offers affordable and transparent exposure to a health-care subsector that is fraught with expensive and erratic traditional mutual funds run by short-tenured managers. The average biotech fund has an expense ratio that approaches 2%, can count its manager's tenure on one hand, and has an affinity for high turnover strategies.

This exchange-traded fund, which tracks the Nasdaq Biotech Index, makes up for some of those shortcomings. Its 0.5% expense ratio is much cheaper than the typical traditional biotech fund. It's an index fund run by the world's largest advisor of indexed assets, so manager tenure is less of a concern. And while it's volatile, at least its shareholders know what they own.

You still need to be careful with this ETF, though. It's diversified in terms of number of holdings (150) and assets in its top 10 (about 38%). But the portfolio has a big stake in smaller companies whose the fortunes often rise and fall on the fortunes of a few products that may or may not have proved themselves commercially viable. Many of these firms engage in cutting-edge research and have tremendous growth potential, but they also carry high valuations. As a result the portfolio has significantly higher-than-average price-to-earnings, cash, and sales ratios.

You'd expect a portfolio like that to be volatile, and this one is. Its standard deviation is the highest among health-care ETFs and one of the highest among health-care funds overall. Although the fund is capable of huge gains, such as its 45% advance in 2003, it can be equally painful, as its 45% plunge in 2002 shows.

This ETF provides an option for investors who don't like their choices among traditional biotech funds. But it's best used sparingly, if at all, in a diversified portfolio.

| | | | | |
|---|---|---|---|---|
| Address: | 45 Fremont Street San Francisco CA 94105 800-474-2737 | Management Fee: | 0.50% | |
| | | Expense Projections: | 3Yr:$160 | 5Yr:$280 10Yr:$628 |
| Web Address: | www.ishares.com | Income Distrib: | Annually | |
| Inception: | 02-05-01* | Exchange: | AMEX | |
| Advisor: | Barclays Global Fund Advisers | | | |

# iShares NYSE Composite

| | Ticker | NAV | Market Price | 52 wk High/Low | Yield | Mstar Category |
|---|---|---|---|---|---|---|
| | NYC | $70.88 | $73.57 | $73.57 - $63.40 | 1.5% | Large Blend |

## Management

### Portfolio Manager(s)

Barclays Global Fund Advisors is the ETF's advisor. The firm is the world's largest manager of indexed portfolios. Patrick O'Connor, the head of Barclay's U.S. iShares portfolio management group leads a team of a half dozen managers in running this and about 60 other ETFs. IShares' domestic portfolio-management group is responsible for about $75 billion in assets. Most of the managers have at least five years of experience with Barclays as well as prior industry experience.

### Strategy

This exchange-traded fund tracks the NYSE Composite Index, which includes more than 2,000 stocks, REITs, ADRs, and tracking stocks listed on the New York Stock Exchange. Component stocks have to meet the listing requirements of NYSE, which include trading volume and profitability standards. About one third of the constituents are the securities of foreign-based companies, which gives this fund an international flavor. The index excludes preferred stocks, closed-end funds, exchange-traded funds, trust units, limited partnerships, and derivative securities. It is float-adjusted and market-cap-weighted.

## Performance

### Historic Quarterly NAV Returns

| | 1st Qtr | 2nd Qtr | 3rd Qtr | 4th Qtr | Total |
|---|---|---|---|---|---|
| 2001 | — | — | — | — | — |
| 2002 | — | — | — | — | — |
| 2003 | — | — | — | — | — |
| 2004 | — | 0.20 | -0.46 | 10.76 | —* |
| 2005 | -0.67 | 1.34 | 6.18 | 2.02 | 9.05 |

| Trailing | NAV Return% | Market Return% | NAV Rtrn% +/-S&P 500 | %Rank Cat.(NAV) |
|---|---|---|---|---|
| 3 Mo | 2.02 | 1.76 | -0.06 | 27 |
| 6 Mo | 8.32 | 6.63 | 2.56 | 27 |
| 1 Yr | 9.05 | 8.64 | 4.14 | 23 |
| 3 Yr Avg | — | — | — | 0 |
| 5 Yr Avg | — | — | — | 0 |
| 10 Yr Avg | — | — | — | 0 |

| Tax Analysis | Tax-Adj Return% | Tax-Cost Ratio |
|---|---|---|
| 3 Yr (estimated) | — | — |
| 5 Yr (estimated) | — | — |
| 10 Yr (estimated) | — | — |

Growth of $10,000

— Investment Value of ETF
— Investment Value of Index S&P 500

| 1996 | 1997 | 1998 | 1999 | 2000 | 2001 | 2002 | 2003 | 2004 | 2005 | History |
|---|---|---|---|---|---|---|---|---|---|---|
| — | — | — | — | — | — | — | — | 66.01 | 70.88 | NAV $ |
| — | — | — | — | — | — | — | — | 66.22 | 70.84 | Market Price $ |
| — | — | — | — | — | — | — | — | 11.33* | 9.05 | NAV Return% |
| — | — | — | — | — | — | — | — | 11.29* | 8.64 | Market Price Return% |
| — | — | — | — | — | — | — | — | -0.02 | 0.41 | Avg Premium/Discount% |
| — | — | — | — | — | — | — | — | 11.33 | 4.14 | NAV Rtrn% +/-S&P 500 |
| — | — | — | — | — | — | — | — | 11.33 | 2.78 | NAV Rtrn% +/-Russ 1000 |
| — | — | — | — | — | — | — | — | — | 23 | NAV Return% Rank in Cat |
| — | — | — | — | — | — | — | — | 0.00 | 1.60 | Income Return % |
| — | — | — | — | — | — | — | — | — | 7.45 | Capital Return % |
| — | — | — | — | — | — | — | — | 0.78 | 1.05 | Income $ |
| — | — | — | — | — | — | — | — | 0.00 | 0.00 | Capital Gains $ |
| — | — | — | — | — | — | — | — | 0.25 | 0.25 | Expense Ratio % |
| — | — | — | — | — | — | — | — | 1.98 | 2.01 | Income Ratio % |
| — | — | — | — | — | — | — | — | 1 | 5 | Turnover Rate % |
| — | — | — | — | — | — | — | — | 7 | 32 | Net Assets $mil |

## Risk Profile

| | Standard Index S&P 500 | Best Fit Index |
|---|---|---|
| Alpha | — | — |
| Beta | — | — |
| R-Squared | — | — |
| Standard Deviation | — | |
| Mean | — | |
| Sharpe Ratio | — | |

## Morningstar Fair Value

| Price/Fair Value Ratio | Fair Value Estimate ($) | Hit Rate % |
|---|---|---|
| 1.0 Fairly valued | 37.79 | 91 Good |

## Portfolio Analysis 12-31-05

Share change since 11-05  Total Stocks:1599

| | Sector | PE | Tot Ret% | % Assets |
|---|---|---|---|---|
| ⊕ General Electric | Ind Mtrls | 19.9 | -1.43 | 2.13 |
| ⊕ ExxonMobil | Energy | 10.6 | 11.76 | 2.04 |
| ⊕ Citigroup | Financial | 12.1 | 4.63 | 1.45 |
| ⊕ BP PLC ADR | Energy | 15.1 | 13.54 | 1.34 |
| ⊕ Procter & Gamble | Goods | 21.2 | 7.18 | 1.14 |
| ⊕ Bank of America | Financial | 11.1 | 2.39 | 1.07 |
| ⊕ HSBC Holdings PLC ADR | Financial | 15.0 | -1.39 | 1.03 |
| ⊕ Johnson & Johnson | Health | 19.1 | -3.36 | 1.01 |
| ⊕ Pfizer | Health | 21.2 | -10.62 | 1.00 |
| ⊕ Toyota Motor ADR | Goods | 15.8 | 29.66 | 0.93 |
| ⊕ American International G | Financial | 15.6 | 4.83 | 0.90 |
| ⊕ Altria Group | Goods | 15.0 | 27.72 | 0.88 |
| ⊕ GlaxoSmithKline PLC ADR | Health | 18.6 | 9.87 | 0.85 |
| ⊕ Total SA ADR | Energy | 13.0 | 18.78 | 0.85 |
| ⊕ J.P. Morgan Chase & Co. | Financial | 18.8 | 5.74 | 0.81 |
| ⊕ Vodafone Group PLC ADR | Telecom | — | -18.96 | 0.77 |
| ⊕ IBM | Hardware | 16.0 | -15.83 | 0.76 |
| ⊕ Mitsubishi UFJ Financial | Financial | 23.5 | 35.15 | 0.76 |
| ⊕ Chevron | Energy | 9.0 | 11.51 | 0.74 |
| ⊕ Novartis AG ADR | Health | 22.4 | 5.64 | 0.74 |

### Current Investment Style

Value Blnd Growth — Large Mid Small

| | Market Cap | % |
|---|---|---|
| | Giant | 55.4 |
| | Large | 29.1 |
| | Mid | 12.7 |
| | Small | 2.7 |
| | Micro | 0.2 |
| | Avg $mil: | 35,434 |

| Value Measures | | Rel Category |
|---|---|---|
| Price/Earnings | 15.28 | 0.90 |
| Price/Book | 2.32 | 0.86 |
| Price/Sales | 1.32 | 1.03 |
| Price/Cash Flow | 5.86 | 0.81 |
| Dividend Yield % | 2.01 | 1.14 |

| Growth Measures | % | Rel Category |
|---|---|---|
| Long-Term Erngs | 10.30 | 0.93 |
| Book Value | 10.09 | 1.07 |
| Sales | 8.19 | 1.02 |
| Cash Flow | 10.50 | 1.02 |
| Historical Erngs | 15.84 | 1.12 |

| Profitability | % | Rel Category |
|---|---|---|
| Return on Equity | 17.89 | 0.88 |
| Return on Assets | 9.21 | 0.99 |
| Net Margin | 11.90 | 1.09 |

| Sector Weightings | % of Stocks | Rel S&P 500 | 3 Year High Low |
|---|---|---|---|
| ↻ Info | 14.10 | 0.70 | |
| Software | 0.46 | 0.13 | — — |
| Hardware | 5.20 | 0.52 | — — |
| Media | 2.69 | 0.75 | — — |
| Telecom | 5.75 | 1.91 | — — |
| ⊂ Service | 46.06 | 0.99 | |
| Health | 11.27 | 0.85 | — — |
| Consumer | 5.70 | 0.70 | — — |
| Business | 3.52 | 0.91 | — — |
| Financial | 25.57 | 1.21 | — — |
| ⊐ Mfg | 39.85 | 1.19 | |
| Goods | 9.64 | 1.13 | — — |
| Ind Mtrls | 12.84 | 1.06 | — — |
| Energy | 13.20 | 1.41 | — — |
| Utilities | 4.17 | 1.24 | — — |

### Composition

| | | |
|---|---|---|
| ● Cash | 0.1 |
| ● Stocks | 100.0 |
| ● Bonds | 0.0 |
| ● Other | 0.0 |
| Foreign | 34.0 |
(% of Stock)

## Morningstar's Take by Dan Culloton

This exchange-traded fund is a decent core holding, but it won't always look this good.

IShares NYSE Composite Index is broadly diversified and cheap. The ETF, which owns most of more than 2,000 stocks traded on the NYSE and keeps 13.5% of its assets in its top 10 holdings, is one of the least concentrated offerings in the large-blend category. Since about one third of NYSE stocks are American Depository Receipts of foreign firms, this ETF also offers some exposure to overseas large caps.

The broad portfolio keeps the portfolio from being as volatile as most other core equity funds. The ETF also has done well since its March 2004 inception. That may have more to do with serendipity than any inherent advantage, though. This fund's benchmark excludes stocks listed on the Nasdaq Composite and other exchanges. That leaves the portfolio with lighter-than-average hardware and software stakes, and heavier-than-average energy, utility, and financial allocations. The big energy and utility stakes have been a boon as record-high oil prices and burgeoning energy needs have boosted returns in those sectors. The portfolio's lack of underperforming large-cap growth stocks like Cisco Systems and Dell has also helped. It's not clear, however, how long oil prices will stay high enough to support arguably rich valuations in the energy sector. The shares of big tech companies will also have their day in the sun eventually, and when they do, this fund's strong results could look weaker.

Due to its broad diversification and low costs (the fund's 0.25% expense ratio isn't the cheapest among ETFs, but it's a fraction of its typical conventional rival's), this offering won't blow up often. However, its omission of stocks from other U.S. exchanges and inclusion of ADRs mean it's not a perfect measure of the broad domestic market. We'd choose other core funds first.

| | | | | |
|---|---|---|---|---|
| Address: | 45 Fremont Street San Francisco CA 94105 800-474-2737 | Management Fee: | 0.25% | |
| | | Expense Projections: | 3Yr:$80 | 5Yr:$141  10Yr:$318 |
| | | Income Distrib: | Quarterly | |
| Web Address: | www.ishares.com | Exchange: | NYSE | |
| Inception: | 03-30-04 * | | | |
| Advisor: | Barclays Global Fund Advisers | | | |

 Morningstar® ETFs 100

# iShares R. Midcap

| | Ticker | NAV | Market Price | 52 wk High/Low | Yield | Mstar Category |
|---|---|---|---|---|---|---|
| | IWR | $88.08 | $91.65 | $91.65 - $75.71 | 1.4% | Mid-Cap Blend |

## Management

### Portfolio Manager(s)

Barclays Global Investors runs the show here. This fund is one of nearly 100 exchange-traded funds that the firm runs under the "iShares" banner. Barclays has more than $1 trillion in assets under management.

### Strategy

The strategy here is simple: Match the risk-adjusted performance of the Russell Midcap Index. To that end, management assembles a basket of securities corresponding to the benchmark and rebalances the portfolio as necessary. The Russell index spans the smallest 800 names in the Russell 1000 Index (which, in turn, represents the 1,000 largest publicly traded stocks in the U.S.). Unlike the S&P Midcap 400 Index, which is derived using a mix of qualitative and quantitative factors, the Russell bogy's methodology is wholly quantitative.

### Growth of $10,000

— Investment Value of ETF
— Investment Value of Index S&P 500

| | 1996 | 1997 | 1998 | 1999 | 2000 | 2001 | 2002 | 2003 | 2004 | 2005 | History |
|---|---|---|---|---|---|---|---|---|---|---|---|
| | — | — | — | — | — | 58.51 | 48.55 | 67.00 | 79.38 | 88.08 | NAV $ |
| | — | — | — | — | — | 58.92 | 48.63 | 67.12 | 79.33 | 87.93 | Market Price $ |
| | — | — | — | — | — | 10.56* | -16.17 | 39.74 | 19.93 | 12.60 | NAV Return% |
| | — | — | — | — | — | 10.52* | -16.62 | 39.76 | 19.64 | 12.48 | Market Price Return% |
| | — | — | — | — | — | 0.04 | 0.06 | 0.08 | 0.02 | 0.03 | Avg Premium/Discount% |
| | — | — | — | — | — | 10.56 | 5.92 | 11.07 | 9.06 | 7.69 | NAV Rtrn% +/-S&P 500 |
| | — | — | — | — | — | 10.56 | -1.64 | 4.15 | 3.46 | 0.05 | NAV Rtrn% +/-S&P Mid 400 |
| | — | — | — | — | — | — | 4 | 4 | 5 | 7 | NAV Return% Rank in Cat |
| | — | — | — | — | — | 0.00 | 0.90 | 1.50 | 1.32 | 1.56 | Income Return % |
| | — | — | — | — | — | — | -17.07 | 38.24 | 18.61 | 11.04 | Capital Return % |
| | — | — | — | — | — | 0.35 | 0.53 | 0.72 | 0.88 | 1.23 | Income $ |
| | — | — | — | — | — | 0.00 | 0.00 | 0.00 | 0.00 | 0.00 | Capital Gains $ |
| | — | — | — | — | — | — | 0.20 | 0.20 | 0.20 | 0.20 | Expense Ratio % |
| | — | — | — | — | — | — | 1.40 | 1.50 | 1.39 | 1.48 | Income Ratio % |
| | — | — | — | — | — | — | 7 | 15 | 7 | 15 | Turnover Rate % |
| | — | — | — | — | — | — | 165 | 415 | 1,131 | 1,696 | Net Assets $mil |

## Performance

### Historic Quarterly NAV Returns

| | 1st Qtr | 2nd Qtr | 3rd Qtr | 4th Qtr | Total |
|---|---|---|---|---|---|
| 2001 | — | — | — | 17.13 | —* |
| 2002 | 4.22 | -9.56 | -17.56 | 7.89 | -16.17 |
| 2003 | -2.41 | 18.19 | 6.37 | 13.89 | 39.74 |
| 2004 | 5.09 | 1.41 | -0.89 | 13.54 | 19.93 |
| 2005 | -0.23 | 4.18 | 5.90 | 2.29 | 12.60 |

| Trailing | NAV Return% | Market Return% | NAV Rtrn% +/-S&P 500 | %Rank Cat.(NAV) |
|---|---|---|---|---|
| 3 Mo | 2.29 | 2.07 | 0.21 | 7 |
| 6 Mo | 8.33 | 7.55 | 2.57 | 7 |
| 1 Yr | 12.60 | 12.48 | 7.69 | 7 |
| 3 Yr Avg | 23.58 | 23.44 | 9.20 | 4 |
| 5 Yr Avg | — | — | — | 0 |
| 10 Yr Avg | — | — | — | 0 |

| Tax Analysis | Tax-Adj Return% | Tax-Cost Ratio |
|---|---|---|
| 3 Yr (estimated) | 23.01 | 0.46 |
| 5 Yr (estimated) | — | — |
| 10 Yr (estimated) | — | — |

## Risk Profile

| | Standard Index S&P 500 | Best Fit Index S&P Mid 400 |
|---|---|---|
| Alpha | 6.4 | 2.7 |
| Beta | 1.14 | 0.96 |
| R-Squared | 85 | 97 |
| Standard Deviation | 11.35 | |
| Mean | 23.58 | |
| Sharpe Ratio | 1.76 | |

## Morningstar Fair Value

| Price/Fair Value Ratio | Fair Value Estimate ($) | Hit Rate % |
|---|---|---|
| 1.1 Overvalued | 32.00 | 89 Good |

## Portfolio Analysis 12-31-05

| Share change since 11-05 Total Stocks:785 | Sector | PE | Tot Ret% | % Assets |
|---|---|---|---|---|
| ⊕ Norfolk Southern | Business | 15.5 | 25.52 | 0.49 |
| ⊕ EOG Resources | Energy | 17.9 | 106.26 | 0.48 |
| ⊕ Federated Department Sto | Consumer | 11.0 | 15.68 | 0.47 |
| ⊕ Agilent Technologies | Hardware | 43.8 | 38.13 | 0.44 |
| ⊕ Archer Daniels Midland | Ind Mtrls | 16.8 | 12.25 | 0.44 |
| ⊕ XTO Energy | Energy | 22.7 | 66.57 | 0.43 |
| ⊕ Biogen Idec | Health | NMF | -32.02 | 0.42 |
| ⊕ Public Service Enterpris | Utilities | 22.2 | 30.22 | 0.42 |
| ⊕ McKesson | Health | — | 64.90 | 0.42 |
| ⊕ Moody's | Business | 35.4 | 41.96 | 0.42 |
| ⊕ Cigna | Health | 9.1 | 37.07 | 0.40 |
| ⊕ Mellon Financial | Financial | 16.1 | 13.05 | 0.39 |
| ⊕ Forest Laboratories | Health | 19.6 | -9.32 | 0.39 |
| ⊕ Sun Microsystems | Hardware | — | -22.26 | 0.39 |
| ⊕ American Electric Power | Utilities | 12.0 | 12.33 | 0.39 |
| ⊕ Edison International | Utilities | 13.5 | 39.63 | 0.38 |
| ⊕ Allergan | Health | 38.1 | 33.81 | 0.38 |
| ⊕ Xerox | Ind Mtrls | 17.2 | -13.87 | 0.38 |
| ⊕ Johnson Controls | Ind Mtrls | 18.7 | 16.87 | 0.38 |
| ⊕ Phelps Dodge | Ind Mtrls | 8.2 | 53.13 | 0.38 |

### Current Investment Style

Value Blnd Growth — Large Mid Small

| Market Cap | % |
|---|---|
| Giant | 0.0 |
| Large | 35.4 |
| Mid | 63.9 |
| Small | 0.7 |
| Micro | 0.0 |

Avg $mil: 6,382

| Value Measures | | Rel Category |
|---|---|---|
| Price/Earnings | 17.32 | 0.99 |
| Price/Book | 2.41 | 1.01 |
| Price/Sales | 1.21 | 1.05 |
| Price/Cash Flow | 7.10 | 0.95 |
| Dividend Yield % | 1.37 | 1.18 |

| Growth Measures | % | Rel Category |
|---|---|---|
| Long-Term Erngs | 11.38 | 0.90 |
| Book Value | 8.64 | 1.00 |
| Sales | 7.08 | 0.87 |
| Cash Flow | 7.68 | 0.77 |
| Historical Erngs | 15.29 | 0.95 |

| Profitability | % | Rel Category |
|---|---|---|
| Return on Equity | 16.30 | 1.08 |
| Return on Assets | 8.55 | 1.10 |
| Net Margin | 12.01 | 1.13 |

| Sector Weightings | % of Stocks | Rel S&P 500 | 3 Year High Low | |
|---|---|---|---|---|
| ↻ Info | 15.92 | 0.79 | | |
| Software | 2.56 | 0.72 | 4 | 2 |
| Hardware | 8.99 | 0.90 | 11 | 7 |
| Media | 2.51 | 0.70 | 3 | 2 |
| Telecom | 1.86 | 0.62 | 2 | 1 |
| ⊆ Service | 50.85 | 1.10 | | |
| Health | 10.37 | 0.78 | 13 | 10 |
| Consumer | 11.88 | 1.46 | 14 | 11 |
| Business | 8.39 | 2.17 | 8 | 7 |
| Financial | 20.21 | 0.96 | 22 | 19 |
| Mfg | 33.22 | 0.99 | | |
| Goods | 7.07 | 0.83 | 8 | 7 |
| Ind Mtrls | 10.92 | 0.90 | 12 | 10 |
| Energy | 7.99 | 0.85 | 8 | 4 |
| Utilities | 7.24 | 2.15 | 8 | 6 |

### Composition

| | | |
|---|---|---|
| ● Cash | | 0.1 |
| ● Stocks | | 99.8 |
| ● Bonds | | 0.0 |
| ● Other | | 0.0 |
| Foreign | | 0.2 |
| (% of Stock) | | |

## Morningstar's Take by Dan Culloton

This fund isn't a bad catch, but there are other fish in the sea, too.

The iShares Russell Midcap Index has many laudable traits. It's broadly diversified, with nearly 800 stocks and holdings in virtually every sector. The offering's advisor, Barclays Global Fund Advisors, also is an accomplished indexer that has managed this fund well. On an annualized basis the fund has trailed its benchmark by less than its expense ratio from its July 2001 inception through the end of October 2005. And the fund's 0.20% expense ratio is lower than most index funds and traditional actively managed offerings in the mid-cap blend category.

Like other segments of the exchange-traded fund industry, however, price competition among mid-cap ETFs is fierce. The iShares S&P Mid Cap 400 covers similar territory for the same price, while Vanguard Mid Cap VIPERs charges a 0.18% expense ratio.

It's also worth paying attention to fundamental differences between the Russell Midcap, this fund's benchmark, and those of its competitors. The Russell bogy defines mid-cap stocks as the 800 smallest companies in the Russell 1000 Index, which tracks the 1,000 largest U.S. stocks. Unlike the S&P MidCap 400, the Russell index also includes some companies that don't have profitable records.

That gives this fund a higher average market cap as well as a dose of speculative stocks, which can influence performance. For example, larger-cap stocks, such as Apple Computer, as well as stocks with losses, such as telecom gear maker Avaya and oil company Amerada Hess, have helped this fund beat those tracking the S&P Mid Cap 400 in the past three years. Over longer periods, though, the S&P Mid Cap has the edge on this fund's bogy.

None of these flaws are fatal, but they are reasons to weigh your options before buying this fund.

| | | | | |
|---|---|---|---|---|
| Address: | 45 Fremont Street San Francisco CA 94105 800-474-2737 | Management Fee: | 0.20% | |
| | | Expense Projections: | 3Yr:$64 | 5Yr:$113 10Yr:$255 |
| Web Address: | www.ishares.com | Income Distrib: | Quarterly | |
| Inception: | 07-17-01* | Exchange: | AMEX | |
| Advisor: | Barclays Global Fund Advisers | | | |

Data through December 31, 2005

# iShares R. Midcap Gr

| Ticker | NAV | Market Price | 52 wk High/Low | Yield | Mstar Category |
|---|---|---|---|---|---|
| IWP | $94.06 | $98.10 | $98.10 - $79.15 | 0.5% | Mid-Cap Growth |

## Management

### Portfolio Manager(s)

Barclays Global Fund Advisors is the advisor. The firm is the world's largest manager of indexed portfolios. Patrick O'Connor, the head of Barclay's U.S. iShares portfolio management group leads a team of a half dozen managers in running this and about 60 other ETFs. IShares domestic portfolio management group is responsible for about $75 billion in assets. Most of the managers have at least five or more years of experience with Barclays as well as prior industry experience.

### Strategy

The fund tracks a subset of the Russell Midcap Index, which consists of the smallest 800 stocks in the Russell 1000 Index (essentially the smallest of the big). The Russell Midcap Growth Index includes mid-cap stocks that show higher book values and forecasted growth. It represents about 40% of the Russell Midcap's market capitalization. The fund uses representative sampling to track the index. That means it doesn't own all of the stocks in the index but holds a quantitatively constructed sample of the benchmark designed to match its risk and return profile. The index reconstitutes just once a year, at the end of each May.

### Growth of $10,000

— Investment Value of ETF
— Investment Value of Index S&P 500

| | 1996 | 1997 | 1998 | 1999 | 2000 | 2001 | 2002 | 2003 | 2004 | 2005 | History |
|---|---|---|---|---|---|---|---|---|---|---|---|
| | — | — | — | — | — | 71.61 | 51.82 | 73.63 | 84.53 | 94.06 | NAV $ |
| | — | — | — | — | — | 71.86 | 51.70 | 73.70 | 84.50 | 93.96 | Market Price $ |
| | — | — | — | — | — | 6.11* | -27.55 | 42.38 | 15.15 | 11.82 | NAV Return% |
| | — | — | — | — | — | 6.08* | -27.97 | 42.85 | 15.00 | 11.74 | Market Price Return% |
| | — | — | — | — | — | 0.43 | 0.16 | 0.07 | 0.09 | 0.01 | Avg Premium/Discount% |
| | — | — | — | — | — | 6.11 | -5.46 | 13.71 | 4.28 | 6.91 | NAV Rtrn% +/-S&P 500 |
| | — | — | — | — | — | 6.11 | -0.14 | -0.33 | -0.33 | -0.28 | NAV Rtrn% +/-Russ MG |
| | — | — | — | — | — | — | 2 | 2 | 3 | 4 | NAV Return% Rank in Cat |
| | — | — | — | — | — | 0.00 | 0.09 | 0.26 | 0.32 | 0.52 | Income Return % |
| | — | — | — | — | — | — | -27.64 | 42.12 | 14.83 | 11.30 | Capital Return % |
| | — | — | — | — | — | 0.02 | 0.06 | 0.14 | 0.23 | 0.44 | Income $ |
| | — | — | — | — | — | 0.00 | 0.00 | 0.00 | 0.00 | 0.00 | Capital Gains $ |
| | — | — | — | — | — | — | 0.25 | 0.25 | 0.25 | 0.25 | Expense Ratio % |
| | — | — | — | — | — | — | 0.08 | 0.20 | 0.27 | 0.38 | Income Ratio % |
| | — | — | — | — | — | — | 5 | 31 | 10 | 27 | Turnover Rate % |
| | — | — | — | — | — | — | 104 | 409 | 820 | 1,312 | Net Assets $mil |

## Performance

### Historic Quarterly NAV Returns

| | 1st Qtr | 2nd Qtr | 3rd Qtr | 4th Qtr | Total |
|---|---|---|---|---|---|
| 2001 | — | — | — | 26.99 | —* |
| 2002 | -1.83 | -18.29 | -17.21 | 9.10 | -27.55 |
| 2003 | -0.06 | 18.69 | 7.09 | 12.09 | 42.38 |
| 2004 | 4.76 | 0.99 | -4.40 | 13.84 | 15.15 |
| 2005 | -1.74 | 3.37 | 6.50 | 3.37 | 11.82 |

| Trailing | NAV Return% | Market Return% | NAV Rtrn% +/-S&P 500 | %Rank Cat.(NAV) |
|---|---|---|---|---|
| 3 Mo | 3.37 | 3.25 | 1.29 | 5 |
| 6 Mo | 10.09 | 10.04 | 4.33 | 5 |
| 1 Yr | 11.82 | 11.74 | 6.91 | 4 |
| 3 Yr Avg | 22.39 | 22.44 | 8.01 | 2 |
| 5 Yr Avg | — | — | — | 0 |
| 10 Yr Avg | — | — | — | 0 |

| Tax Analysis | Tax-Adj Return% | Tax-Cost Ratio |
|---|---|---|
| 3 Yr (estimated) | 22.25 | 0.11 |
| 5 Yr (estimated) | — | — |
| 10 Yr (estimated) | — | — |

## Risk Profile

| | Standard Index S&P 500 | Best Fit Index Russ MG |
|---|---|---|
| Alpha | 5.0 | -0.3 |
| Beta | 1.18 | 1.00 |
| R-Squared | 77 | 100 |
| Standard Deviation | 12.36 | |
| Mean | 22.39 | |
| Sharpe Ratio | 1.55 | |

## Morningstar Fair Value

| Price/Fair Value Ratio | Fair Value Estimate ($) | Hit Rate % |
|---|---|---|
| 1.1 Overvalued | 35.49 | 87 Good |

## Morningstar's Take by Dan Culloton

IShares Russell Midcap Growth Index is a strong alternative.

This fund offers a hard combination to beat: affordable, diversified exposure to fast-growing mid-cap stocks, as defined by the Russell Midcap Growth Index. Low and transparent fees are this exchange-traded fund's most obvious advantages. Its 0.25% expense ratio is a fraction of the average mid-cap growth fund and is among the lowest among diversified ETFs in this category. You still have to pay a broker to purchase or sell this offering, and those costs can negate this fund's price advantage for frequent traders or investors making regular deposits. However, at least you have a good idea of what you are paying: a management fee to the fund and a commission to the broker. There are no front- or back-end loads or 12b-1 fees that can make figuring out what you are paying for traditional mutual funds such a bewildering experience.

For that price the fund and its benchmark provide exposure to a broad swath of growth stocks across sectors. It does own a lot of technology, media, and telecommunications stocks, which has made it more volatile, as measured by standard deviation, than average. The bogy also has been susceptible to speculators who try to front run the Russell indexes' annual reconstitution, bidding up additions and selling off deletions to the bogies.

Despite those quirks the Russell Midcap still has correlated well with the movements of the typical mid-cap growth fund. It also has been difficult to surpass. This ETF's 4.9% annualized gain from August 2001 through the end of October 2005 beat the category's 2.7% annualized gain over the same time period. Over longer time spans, such as the 15 years ending Oct. 31, 2005, the average mid-cap growth fund still lags this fund's index.

As long as this fund continues to do a good job tracking its bogy it should put up competitive returns. It's a solid choice.

| Address: | 45 Fremont Street San Francisco CA 94105 800-474-2737 |
|---|---|
| Web Address: | www.ishares.com |
| Inception: | 07-17-01 * |
| Advisor: | Barclays Global Fund Advisers |

| Management Fee: | 0.25% | | |
|---|---|---|---|
| Expense Projections: | 3Yr:$80 | 5Yr:$141 | 10Yr:$318 |
| Income Distrib: | Quarterly | | |
| Exchange: | AMEX | | |

## Portfolio Analysis 12-31-05

Share change since 11-05 Total Stocks:501

| | Sector | PE | Tot Ret% | % Assets |
|---|---|---|---|---|
| ⊕ EOG Resources | Energy | 17.9 | 106.26 | 0.98 |
| ⊕ XTO Energy | Energy | 22.7 | 66.57 | 0.89 |
| ⊕ Moody's | Business | 35.4 | 41.96 | 0.87 |
| ⊕ Forest Laboratories | Health | 19.6 | -9.32 | 0.80 |
| ⊕ Allergan | Health | 38.1 | 33.81 | 0.79 |
| ⊕ Agilent Technologies | Hardware | 43.8 | 38.13 | 0.77 |
| ⊕ Legg Mason | Financial | 30.9 | 64.48 | 0.76 |
| ⊕ Analog Devices | Hardware | 33.2 | -1.84 | 0.74 |
| ⊕ Broadcom | Hardware | 58.9 | 46.07 | 0.73 |
| ⊕ Paychex | Business | 36.6 | 13.71 | 0.71 |
| ⊕ Chicago Mercantile Excha | Financial | 44.4 | 61.83 | 0.70 |
| ⊕ Coach | Goods | 30.9 | 18.23 | 0.70 |
| ⊕ Maxim Integrated Product | Hardware | 24.6 | -13.57 | 0.66 |
| ⊕ BJ Services | Energy | 26.6 | 58.54 | 0.66 |
| ⊕ Fortune Brands | Goods | 17.9 | 9.28 | 0.63 |
| ⊕ TJX Companies | Consumer | 18.4 | -6.65 | 0.62 |
| ⊕ Linear Technology | Hardware | 26.5 | -5.93 | 0.62 |
| ⊕ Rockwell Automation | Ind Mtrls | 21.4 | 21.29 | 0.61 |
| ⊕ Celgene | Health | NMF | 144.34 | 0.60 |
| ⊕ Peabody Energy | Energy | 33.1 | 104.95 | 0.60 |

### Current Investment Style

Value Blnd Growth / Large Mid Small

| Market Cap | % |
|---|---|
| Giant | 0.0 |
| Large | 34.2 |
| Mid | 65.0 |
| Small | 0.7 |
| Micro | 0.1 |

Avg $mil: 6,403

| Value Measures | | Rel Category |
|---|---|---|
| Price/Earnings | 20.33 | 0.91 |
| Price/Book | 3.62 | 0.99 |
| Price/Sales | 1.64 | 0.85 |
| Price/Cash Flow | 10.97 | 0.96 |
| Dividend Yield % | 0.70 | 1.56 |

| Growth Measures | % | Rel Category |
|---|---|---|
| Long-Term Erngs | 14.77 | 0.94 |
| Book Value | 9.87 | 0.99 |
| Sales | 11.34 | 1.01 |
| Cash Flow | 15.10 | 1.00 |
| Historical Erngs | 21.66 | 1.05 |

| Profitability | % | Rel Category |
|---|---|---|
| Return on Equity | 20.03 | 1.02 |
| Return on Assets | 9.62 | 0.93 |
| Net Margin | 11.70 | 0.99 |

| Sector Weightings | % of Stocks | Rel S&P 500 | 3 Year High Low | |
|---|---|---|---|---|
| Info | 22.14 | 1.10 | | |
| Software | 3.86 | 1.08 | 9 | 4 |
| Hardware | 13.51 | 1.35 | 17 | 10 |
| Media | 3.24 | 0.91 | 4 | 3 |
| Telecom | 1.53 | 0.51 | 3 | 1 |
| Service | 51.51 | 1.11 | | |
| Health | 16.03 | 1.21 | 25 | 16 |
| Consumer | 15.84 | 1.95 | 19 | 16 |
| Business | 11.61 | 3.00 | 12 | 10 |
| Financial | 8.03 | 0.38 | 8 | 4 |
| Mfg | 26.35 | 0.79 | | |
| Goods | 5.66 | 0.66 | 8 | 6 |
| Ind Mtrls | 9.60 | 0.79 | 10 | 5 |
| Energy | 10.49 | 1.12 | 11 | 3 |
| Utilities | 0.60 | 0.18 | 1 | 0 |

### Composition

| | |
|---|---|
| Cash | 0.1 |
| Stocks | 99.9 |
| Bonds | 0.0 |
| Other | 0.0 |
| Foreign | 0.0 |
| (% of Stock) | |

MORNINGSTAR® ETFs 100

Data through December 31, 2005

# iShares R. Midcap VI

| Ticker | NAV | Market Price | 52 wk High/Low | Yield | Mstar Category |
|---|---|---|---|---|---|
| IWS | $124.59 | $129.07 | $129.07 - $108.09 | 2.0% | Mid-Cap Value |

## Management

### Portfolio Manager(s)

Barclays Global Fund Advisors is the advisor. The firm is the world's largest manager of indexed portfolios. Patrick O'Connor, the head of Barclay's U.S. iShares portfolio management group leads a team of a half dozen managers in running this and about 60 other ETFs. iShares domestic portfolio management group is responsible for about $75 billion in assets. Most of the managers have at least five or more years of experience with Barclays as well as prior industry experience.

### Strategy

This fund tries to match the performance of the Russell Midcap Value Index. The index is a subset of the smallest 800 names in the Russell 1000 Index (which, in turn, represents the 1,000 largest publicly traded stocks in the U.S.). Unlike the S&P Midcap 400 Index, which is derived using a mix of qualitative and quantitative factors, the Russell bogy's methodology is wholly quantitative. This fund focuses on Russell Midcap stocks with lower price/book ratios and forecasted growth according to the Institutional Brokers Estimate System.

## Performance

### Historic Quarterly NAV Returns

| | 1st Qtr | 2nd Qtr | 3rd Qtr | 4th Qtr | Total |
|---|---|---|---|---|---|
| 2001 | — | — | — | 12.00 | —* |
| 2002 | 7.84 | -4.73 | -17.84 | 7.00 | -9.69 |
| 2003 | -4.11 | 17.79 | 5.88 | 15.14 | 37.70 |
| 2004 | 5.27 | 1.68 | 1.62 | 13.31 | 23.26 |
| 2005 | 0.83 | 4.70 | 5.34 | 1.31 | 12.68 |

| Trailing | NAV Return% | Market Return% | NAV Rtrn% +/-S&P 500 | %Rank Cat.(NAV) |
|---|---|---|---|---|
| 3 Mo | 1.31 | 1.15 | -0.77 | 6 |
| 6 Mo | 6.73 | 6.55 | 0.97 | 6 |
| 1 Yr | 12.68 | 12.54 | 7.77 | 5 |
| 3 Yr Avg | 24.12 | 24.26 | 9.74 | 2 |
| 5 Yr Avg | — | — | — | 0 |
| 10 Yr Avg | — | — | — | 0 |

| Tax Analysis | Tax-Adj Return% | Tax-Cost Ratio |
|---|---|---|
| 3 Yr (estimated) | 23.32 | 0.64 |
| 5 Yr (estimated) | — | — |
| 10 Yr (estimated) | — | — |

## Risk Profile

| | Standard Index S&P 500 | Best Fit Index Russ MV |
|---|---|---|
| Alpha | 7.1 | -0.1 |
| Beta | 1.11 | 1.00 |
| R-Squared | 85 | 100 |
| Standard Deviation | 11.04 | |
| Mean | 24.12 | |
| Sharpe Ratio | 1.85 | |

## Morningstar Fair Value

| Price/Fair Value Ratio | Fair Value Estimate ($) | Hit Rate % |
|---|---|---|
| 1.1 Overvalued | 29.33 | 90 Good |

### Growth of $10,000

— Investment Value of ETF
— Investment Value of Index S&P 500

| | 1996 | 1997 | 1998 | 1999 | 2000 | 2001 | 2002 | 2003 | 2004 | 2005 | History |
|---|---|---|---|---|---|---|---|---|---|---|---|
| | — | — | — | — | — | 77.62 | 68.87 | 93.11 | 112.83 | 124.59 | NAV $ |
| | — | — | — | — | — | 77.93 | 68.55 | 93.30 | 112.81 | 124.42 | Market Price $ |
| | — | — | — | — | — | 12.88* | -9.69 | 37.70 | 23.26 | 12.68 | NAV Return% |
| | — | — | — | — | — | 12.84* | -10.46 | 38.62 | 22.98 | 12.54 | Market Price Return% |
| | — | — | — | — | — | 0.13 | 0.05 | 0.20 | 0.00 | -0.00 | Avg Premium/Discount% |
| | — | — | — | — | — | 12.88 | 12.40 | 9.03 | 12.39 | 7.77 | NAV Rtrn% +/-S&P 500 |
| | — | — | — | — | — | 12.88 | -0.05 | -0.37 | -0.45 | 0.03 | NAV Rtrn% +/-Russ MV |
| | — | — | — | — | — | — | 2 | 2 | 3 | 5 | NAV Return% Rank in Cat |
| | — | — | — | — | — | 0.00 | 1.70 | 2.14 | 1.87 | 2.17 | Income Return % |
| | — | — | — | — | — | — | -11.39 | 35.56 | 21.39 | 10.51 | Capital Return % |
| | — | — | — | — | — | 0.67 | 1.31 | 1.46 | 1.73 | 2.43 | Income $ |
| | — | — | — | — | — | 0.00 | 0.00 | 0.00 | 0.00 | 0.00 | Capital Gains $ |
| | — | — | — | — | — | — | 0.25 | 0.25 | 0.25 | 0.25 | Expense Ratio % |
| | — | — | — | — | — | — | 1.91 | 2.24 | 2.05 | 2.20 | Income Ratio % |
| | — | — | — | — | — | — | 6 | 24 | 10 | 20 | Turnover Rate % |
| | — | — | — | — | — | — | 96 | 275 | 1,055 | 2,012 | Net Assets $mil |

## Portfolio Analysis 12-31-05

| Share change since 11-05 Total Stocks:521 | Sector | PE | Tot Ret% | % Assets |
|---|---|---|---|---|
| ⊕ Federated Department Sto | Consumer | 11.0 | 15.68 | 0.91 |
| ⊕ Archer Daniels Midland | Ind Mtrls | 16.8 | 12.25 | 0.86 |
| ⊕ Public Service Enterpris | Utilities | 22.2 | 30.22 | 0.82 |
| ⊕ Norfolk Southern | Business | 15.5 | 25.52 | 0.82 |
| ⊕ Cigna | Health | 9.1 | 37.07 | 0.77 |
| ⊕ American Electric Power | Utilities | 12.0 | 12.33 | 0.75 |
| ⊕ Edison International | Utilities | 13.5 | 39.63 | 0.75 |
| ⊕ Xerox | Ind Mtrls | 17.2 | -13.87 | 0.74 |
| ⊕ Principal Financial Grou | Financial | 16.5 | 17.36 | 0.74 |
| ⊕ Kroger | Consumer | — | 7.64 | 0.73 |
| ⊕ PG & E | Utilities | 16.3 | 15.32 | 0.73 |
| ⊕ KeyCorp | Financial | 13.0 | 1.02 | 0.71 |
| ⊕ Mellon Financial | Financial | 16.1 | 13.05 | 0.71 |
| ⊕ Bear Stearns Companies | Financial | 11.5 | 14.04 | 0.69 |
| ⊕ North Fork Bancorporatio | Financial | 13.5 | -2.02 | 0.69 |
| ⊕ Equity Office Properties | Financial | — | 10.93 | 0.65 |
| ⊕ Lucent Technologies | Hardware | 11.1 | -29.26 | 0.62 |
| ⊕ Sempra Energy | Utilities | 12.1 | 25.62 | 0.61 |
| ⊕ Aon | Financial | 20.1 | 54.33 | 0.60 |
| ⊕ Johnson Controls | Ind Mtrls | 18.7 | 16.87 | 0.60 |

### Current Investment Style

Value Blnd Growth — Large Mid Small

| Market Cap | % |
|---|---|
| Giant | 0.0 |
| Large | 36.5 |
| Mid | 62.9 |
| Small | 0.6 |
| Micro | 0.0 |

Avg $mil: 6,361

| Value Measures | | Rel Category |
|---|---|---|
| Price/Earnings | 15.21 | 1.05 |
| Price/Book | 1.84 | 1.00 |
| Price/Sales | 0.97 | 0.94 |
| Price/Cash Flow | 5.32 | 0.91 |
| Dividend Yield % | 2.01 | 0.75 |

| Growth Measures | % | Rel Category |
|---|---|---|
| Long-Term Erngs | 9.11 | 1.05 |
| Book Value | 8.12 | 1.06 |
| Sales | 5.02 | 0.80 |
| Cash Flow | 3.06 | 0.79 |
| Historical Erngs | 11.72 | 1.16 |

| Profitability | % | Rel Category |
|---|---|---|
| Return on Equity | 12.77 | 0.91 |
| Return on Assets | 7.53 | 0.88 |
| Net Margin | 12.30 | 0.97 |

### Sector Weightings

| | % of Stocks | Rel S&P 500 | 3 Year High | Low |
|---|---|---|---|---|
| ↻ Info | 10.04 | 0.50 | | |
| Software | 1.33 | 0.37 | 2 | 1 |
| Hardware | 4.72 | 0.47 | 8 | 3 |
| Media | 1.82 | 0.51 | 2 | 1 |
| Telecom | 2.17 | 0.72 | 2 | 1 |
| ⊂ Service | 50.21 | 1.08 | | |
| Health | 5.01 | 0.38 | 5 | 4 |
| Consumer | 8.13 | 1.00 | 11 | 7 |
| Business | 5.34 | 1.38 | 6 | 4 |
| Financial | 31.73 | 1.50 | 32 | 27 |
| ⊔ Mfg | 39.73 | 1.19 | | |
| Goods | 8.40 | 0.98 | 9 | 6 |
| Ind Mtrls | 12.18 | 1.00 | 16 | 12 |
| Energy | 5.62 | 0.60 | 9 | 5 |
| Utilities | 13.53 | 4.03 | 14 | 11 |

### Composition

| | | |
|---|---|---|
| ● Cash | 0.2 | |
| ● Stocks | 99.8 | |
| ● Bonds | 0.0 | |
| Other | 0.0 | |
| Foreign | 0.3 | (% of Stock) |

## Morningstar's Take by Dan Culloton

iShares Russell Midcap Value Index gets the job done, but others may do it better.

This ETF gives investors cheap exposure to mid-cap value stocks. It is one of the cheapest mid-value funds available to retail investors. Its 0.25% expense ratio is lower than all of its rivals' except that of the equally priced iShares S&P MidCap 400/Barra Value (which will soon change its benchmark and drop Barra from its name).

The fund has solid management. The advisor, Barclays Global Advisors, has a long track record running index funds and has done well here. The gap between the fund's 12.3% annualized gain from its July 2001 inception through the end of October 2005 and the return of its bogey is less than the ETF's expense ratio--a sign the fund is doing a good job tracking its index.

There are significant differences between this offering and its sister ETF, though. This fund's bogy, the Russell Midcap Value, defines mid-value stocks as those issues among the smallest 800 stocks in the Russell 1000 Index that have below-average growth rates and price/book ratios. Meanwhile, the S&P 400/Citigroup Value Index focuses on stocks with market caps between $1 billion and $4 billion and uses seven value and growth factors to determine what is a value stock. Unlike the S&P 400/Citigroup Value index, this ETF's bogy also doesn't use buffer zones to slow stocks' migration across style boundaries. So, this fund's benchmark might be less representative of the mid-value universe and require more turnover to track.

Moreover, speculators have been known to exploit the Russell Indexes annual reconstitution by bidding up additions to the benchmarks and selling deletions. This can drive up transaction and impact costs for Russell index funds like this one.

In the long run, this fund should correlate closely with rivals, such as its sibling. If all things are equal, though, investors should consider a fund tracking a more efficient benchmark first.

| | | |
|---|---|---|
| Address: | 45 Fremont Street San Francisco CA 94105 800-474-2737 | |
| Web Address: | www.ishares.com | |
| Inception: | 07-17-01 * | |
| Advisor: | Barclays Global Fund Advisers | |

| Management Fee: | 0.25% | | |
|---|---|---|---|
| Expense Projections: | 3Yr:$80 | 5Yr:$141 | 10Yr:$318 |
| Income Distrib: | Quarterly | | |
| Exchange: | AMEX | | |

Mᴏʀɴɪɴɢsᴛᴀʀ® ETFs 100

# iShares R1000 Growth

| Ticker | NAV | Market Price | 52 wk High/Low | Yield | Mstar Category |
|---|---|---|---|---|---|
| IWF | $51.11 | $52.94 | $52.94 - $45.33 | 0.9% | Large Growth |

## Management

### Portfolio Manager(s)

Barclays Global Fund Advisors is the advisor. The firm is the world's largest manager of indexed portfolios. Patrick O'Connor, the head of Barclay's U.S. iShares portfolio management group leads a team of a half dozen managers in running this and about 60 other ETFs. IShares' domestic portfolio-management group is responsible for about $75 billion in assets. Most of the managers have at least five years of experience with Barclays as well as prior industry experience.

### Strategy

This exchange-traded fund tracks the Russell 1000 Growth Index, which is a subset of the Russell 1000 Index of the largest 1,000 publicly traded U.S. stocks. As such, the portfolio spans hundreds of individual names and the full panoply of industries. This fund and its bogy focus on large-cap stocks in the Russell 1000 with higher book values and forecast earnings growth. Unlike conventional index mutual funds, shares in ETFs are bought and sold throughout the day on the secondary market (similar to closed-end funds). As such, management does not have to buy or sell shares depending on the flow of assets into the fund.

## Performance

### Historic Quarterly NAV Returns

| | 1st Qtr | 2nd Qtr | 3rd Qtr | 4th Qtr | Total |
|---|---|---|---|---|---|
| 2001 | -20.90 | 8.37 | -19.44 | 14.93 | -20.64 |
| 2002 | -2.63 | -18.70 | -15.07 | 7.10 | -27.99 |
| 2003 | -1.11 | 14.22 | 3.86 | 10.35 | 29.46 |
| 2004 | 0.74 | 1.90 | -5.26 | 9.10 | 6.10 |
| 2005 | -4.12 | 2.41 | 3.96 | 2.94 | 5.08 |

| Trailing | NAV Return% | Market Return% | NAV Rtrn% +/-S&P 500 | %Rank Cat.(NAV) |
|---|---|---|---|---|
| 3 Mo | 2.94 | 2.63 | 0.86 | 10 |
| 6 Mo | 7.02 | 6.76 | 1.26 | 10 |
| 1 Yr | 5.08 | 4.75 | 0.17 | 9 |
| 3 Yr Avg | 13.01 | 12.83 | -1.37 | 5 |
| 5 Yr Avg | -3.78 | -3.85 | -4.32 | 5 |
| 10 Yr Avg | — | — | — | 0 |

| Tax Analysis | Tax-Adj Return% | Tax-Cost Ratio |
|---|---|---|
| 3 Yr (estimated) | 12.63 | 0.34 |
| 5 Yr (estimated) | -4.06 | 0.29 |
| 10 Yr (estimated) | — | — |

## Risk Profile

| | Standard Index S&P 500 | Best Fit Index Russ 1000Gr |
|---|---|---|
| Alpha | -1.3 | -0.2 |
| Beta | 1.01 | 1.00 |
| R-Squared | 92 | 100 |
| Standard Deviation | 9.66 | |
| Mean | 13.01 | |
| Sharpe Ratio | 1.12 | |

## Morningstar Fair Value

| Price/Fair Value Ratio | Fair Value Estimate ($) | Hit Rate % |
|---|---|---|
| 1.0 Fairly valued | 39.28 | 96 Good |

### Growth of $10,000

- Investment Value of ETF
- Investment Value of Index S&P 500

| 1996 | 1997 | 1998 | 1999 | 2000 | 2001 | 2002 | 2003 | 2004 | 2005 | History |
|---|---|---|---|---|---|---|---|---|---|---|
| — | — | — | — | 64.52 | 50.99 | 36.45 | 46.77 | 49.09 | 51.11 | NAV $ |
| — | — | — | — | 64.62 | 50.94 | 36.55 | 46.80 | 49.15 | 51.01 | Market Price $ |
| — | — | — | — | -6.82* | -20.64 | -27.99 | 29.46 | 6.10 | 5.08 | NAV Return% |
| — | — | — | — | -6.85* | -20.84 | -27.73 | 29.19 | 6.16 | 4.75 | Market Price Return% |
| — | — | — | — | 0.08 | 0.01 | 0.02 | 0.01 | 0.12 | 0.02 | Avg Premium/Discount% |
| — | — | — | — | -6.82 | -8.76 | -5.90 | 0.79 | -4.77 | 0.17 | NAV Rtrn% +/-S&P 500 |
| — | — | — | — | -6.82 | -0.22 | -0.11 | -0.29 | -0.20 | -0.18 | NAV Rtrn% +/-Russ 1000Gr |
| — | — | — | — | | 5 | 5 | 5 | 6 | 9 | NAV Return% Rank in Cat |
| — | — | — | — | 0.00 | 0.32 | 0.58 | 1.02 | 1.10 | 0.93 | Income Return % |
| — | — | — | — | | -20.96 | -28.57 | 28.44 | 5.00 | 4.15 | Capital Return % |
| — | — | — | — | 0.09 | 0.21 | 0.29 | 0.37 | 0.51 | 0.45 | Income $ |
| — | — | — | — | 0.11 | 0.00 | 0.00 | 0.00 | 0.00 | 0.00 | Capital Gains $ |
| — | — | — | — | | 0.20 | 0.20 | 0.20 | 0.20 | 0.20 | Expense Ratio % |
| — | — | — | — | | 0.26 | 0.52 | 0.92 | 0.87 | 1.27 | Income Ratio % |
| — | — | — | — | | 11 | 22 | 13 | 9 | 14 | Turnover Rate % |
| — | — | — | — | | — | 744 | 1,455 | 3,071 | 5,399 | Net Assets $mil |

## Portfolio Analysis 12-31-05

| Share change since 11-05 Total Stocks:639 | Sector | PE | Tot Ret% | % Assets |
|---|---|---|---|---|
| ⊕ General Electric | Ind Mtrls | 19.9 | -1.43 | 4.39 |
| ⊕ Microsoft | Software | 22.2 | -0.95 | 3.77 |
| ⊕ Procter & Gamble | Goods | 21.2 | 7.18 | 3.04 |
| ⊕ Johnson & Johnson | Health | 19.1 | -3.36 | 2.78 |
| ⊕ Intel | Hardware | 18.6 | 8.12 | 2.40 |
| ⊕ Wal-Mart Stores | Consumer | 18.2 | -10.30 | 1.84 |
| ⊕ IBM | Hardware | 16.0 | -15.83 | 1.75 |
| ⊕ Cisco Systems | Hardware | 19.9 | -11.39 | 1.72 |
| ⊕ PepsiCo | Goods | 25.8 | 15.24 | 1.54 |
| ⊕ Amgen | Health | 28.3 | 22.93 | 1.52 |
| ⊕ Home Depot | Consumer | 15.6 | -4.35 | 1.36 |
| ⊕ UnitedHealth Group | Health | 26.2 | 41.22 | 1.32 |
| ⊕ Dell | Hardware | 23.2 | -28.93 | 1.15 |
| ⊕ Qualcomm | Hardware | 34.2 | 2.50 | 1.10 |
| ⊕ Medtronic | Health | 37.4 | 16.72 | 1.09 |
| ⊕ Google | Business | — | 115.19 | 1.07 |
| ⊕ Altria Group | Goods | 15.0 | 27.72 | 0.97 |
| ⊕ 3M Company | Ind Mtrls | 19.2 | -3.51 | 0.93 |
| ⊕ Apple Computer | Hardware | 46.1 | 123.26 | 0.92 |
| ⊕ Boeing | Ind Mtrls | 24.8 | 37.92 | 0.90 |

## Current Investment Style

Value Blnd Growth — Large Mid Small

| Market Cap | % |
|---|---|
| Giant | 49.8 |
| Large | 31.8 |
| Mid | 18.2 |
| Small | 0.2 |
| Micro | 0.0 |

Avg $mil: 35,858

| Value Measures | | Rel Category |
|---|---|---|
| Price/Earnings | 20.22 | 0.96 |
| Price/Book | 3.74 | 1.11 |
| Price/Sales | 1.86 | 0.95 |
| Price/Cash Flow | 11.51 | 1.10 |
| Dividend Yield % | 1.12 | 1.26 |

| Growth Measures | % | Rel Category |
|---|---|---|
| Long-Term Erngs | 13.38 | 0.95 |
| Book Value | 9.86 | 1.21 |
| Sales | 11.77 | 1.06 |
| Cash Flow | 14.34 | 0.88 |
| Historical Erngs | 18.01 | 0.94 |

| Profitability | % | Rel Category |
|---|---|---|
| Return on Equity | 22.79 | 1.13 |
| Return on Assets | 10.98 | 1.02 |
| Net Margin | 13.35 | 0.96 |

| Sector Weightings | % of Stocks | Rel S&P 500 | 3 Year High Low | |
|---|---|---|---|---|
| ↻ Info | 26.42 | 1.31 | | |
| Software | 6.53 | 1.83 | 8 | 6 |
| Hardware | 15.92 | 1.59 | 18 | 13 |
| Media | 3.32 | 0.93 | 4 | 3 |
| Telecom | 0.65 | 0.22 | 1 | 1 |
| Service | 46.15 | 0.99 | | |
| Health | 19.48 | 1.47 | 28 | 19 |
| Consumer | 13.61 | 1.67 | 15 | 12 |
| Business | 6.79 | 1.75 | 7 | 5 |
| Financial | 6.27 | 0.30 | 10 | 6 |
| Mfg | 27.43 | 0.82 | | |
| Goods | 10.03 | 1.17 | 11 | 9 |
| Ind Mtrls | 13.19 | 1.09 | 13 | 6 |
| Energy | 3.67 | 0.39 | 4 | 1 |
| Utilities | 0.54 | 0.16 | 1 | 0 |

### Composition

| Composition | % |
|---|---|
| ● Cash | 0.1 |
| ● Stocks | 99.9 |
| ● Bonds | 0.0 |
| ○ Other | 0.0 |
| Foreign (% of Stock) | 0.0 |

## Morningstar's Take by Dan Culloton

IShares Russell 1000 Growth Index has competition.

This exchange-traded fund is attractively priced at 0.20%. That's a fraction of the average large-growth fund's expense ratio and among the lowest levies for index funds in this category. It has rivals, though. At the end of 2005, retail investors could find three ETFs that use different indexes to cover similar ground and were as cheap if not cheaper.

The fund still has value. It tracks its index, the Russell 1000 Growth, well. The ETF's bogy also spreads its money across hundreds of large companies that have higher-than-average book values and forecasted growth, so it's diversified. Larger-than-average helpings of technology, media, and telecommunications shares give the ETF an edge, but it's been no more volatile than the average large-growth offering.

The ETF isn't a clear winner, though. Its bogy has been susceptible to speculators who try to front-run the Russell indexes' annual reconstitution, bidding up additions and selling off deletions to the bogies. And its record versus the average large-growth fund is mixed. The fund's 8.1% annualized loss from June 2000 (roughly its inception) through the end of October 2005 lags the 5.6% loss of the typical large-growth fund for the same period. The average offering in that group also edged the index over the 15 years ending Oct. 31, 2005, 10.8% to 10.3%.

These are not fatal flaws. Over time, this ETF and its benchmark have correlated well with the large-cap growth group. That combined with its low expense ratio should allow the fund to deliver competitive results, but you should still shop around before committing to this ETF. Other funds may do a better job of capturing the return of the large-cap growth universe at a better price.

| | | |
|---|---|---|
| Address: | 45 Fremont Street San Francisco CA 94105 800-474-2737 | |
| Web Address: | www.ishares.com | |
| Inception: | 05-22-00* | |
| Advisor: | Barclays Global Fund Advisers | |

| Management Fee: | 0.20% | | |
|---|---|---|---|
| Expense Projections: | 3Yr:$64 | 5Yr:$113 | 10Yr:$255 |
| Income Distrib: | Quarterly | | |
| Exchange: | AMEX | | |

MORNINGSTAR® ETFs 100

# iShares R1000 Index

| Ticker | NAV | Market Price | 52 wk High/Low | Yield | Mstar Category |
|---|---|---|---|---|---|
| IWB | $67.78 | $70.06 | $70.06 - $61.20 | 1.9% | Large Blend |

## Management

### Portfolio Manager(s)

Barclays Global Fund Advisors is the advisor. The firm is the world's largest manager of indexed portfolios. Patrick O'Connor, the head of Barclay's U.S. iShares portfolio management group leads a team of a half dozen managers in running this and about 60 other ETFs. IShares' domestic portfolio-management group is responsible for about $75 billion in assets. Most of the managers have at least five years of experience with Barclays as well as prior industry experience.

### Strategy

This exchange-traded fund (ETF) tracks the Russell 1000 Index, a collection of the largest 1,000 publicly traded U.S. stocks. As such, the portfolio spans hundreds of individual names and the full panoply of industries. Unlike conventional index mutual funds, shares in ETFs are bought and sold throughout the day on the secondary market (similar to closed-end funds). As such, management does not have to buy or sell shares depending on the flow of assets into the fund.

### Growth of $10,000

— Investment Value of ETF
— Investment Value of Index S&P 500

| | 1996 | 1997 | 1998 | 1999 | 2000 | 2001 | 2002 | 2003 | 2004 | 2005 | History |
|---|---|---|---|---|---|---|---|---|---|---|---|
| | — | — | — | — | 70.05 | 60.53 | 46.72 | 59.61 | 65.13 | 67.78 | NAV $ |
| | — | — | — | — | 70.20 | 60.98 | 46.72 | 59.59 | 64.94 | 67.70 | Market Price $ |
| | — | — | — | — | -0.69* | -12.59 | -21.72 | 29.64 | 11.27 | 6.15 | NAV Return% |
| | — | — | — | — | -0.72* | -12.13 | -22.30 | 29.60 | 10.98 | 6.34 | Market Price Return% |
| | — | — | — | — | -0.05 | 0.10 | -0.02 | 0.08 | 0.01 | 0.02 | Avg Premium/Discount% |
| | — | — | — | — | -0.69 | -0.71 | 0.37 | 0.97 | 0.40 | 1.24 | NAV Rtrn% +/-S&P 500 |
| | — | — | — | — | -0.69 | -0.14 | -0.07 | -0.25 | -0.13 | -0.12 | NAV Rtrn% +/-Russ 1000 |
| | — | — | — | — | — | 13 | 15 | 15 | 17 | 23 | NAV Return% Rank in Cat |
| | — | — | — | — | 0.00 | 0.99 | 1.20 | 1.82 | 1.90 | 2.01 | Income Return % |
| | — | — | — | — | — | -13.58 | -22.92 | 27.82 | 9.37 | 4.14 | Capital Return % |
| | — | — | — | — | 0.45 | 0.69 | 0.72 | 0.85 | 1.12 | 1.30 | Income $ |
| | — | — | — | — | 0.00 | 0.00 | 0.00 | 0.00 | 0.00 | 0.00 | Capital Gains $ |
| | — | — | — | — | — | 0.15 | 0.15 | 0.15 | 0.15 | 0.15 | Expense Ratio % |
| | — | — | — | — | — | 1.01 | 1.23 | 1.66 | 1.62 | 1.87 | Income Ratio % |
| | — | — | — | — | — | 9 | 8 | 5 | 5 | 5 | Turnover Rate % |
| | — | — | — | — | — | 691 | 1,860 | 1,869 | 2,413 | Net Assets $mil |

## Performance

### Historic Quarterly NAV Returns

| | 1st Qtr | 2nd Qtr | 3rd Qtr | 4th Qtr | Total |
|---|---|---|---|---|---|
| 2001 | -12.56 | 6.26 | -15.24 | 10.99 | -12.59 |
| 2002 | 0.71 | -13.49 | -16.89 | 8.10 | -21.72 |
| 2003 | -2.97 | 15.66 | 2.96 | 12.20 | 29.64 |
| 2004 | 1.87 | 1.37 | -1.82 | 9.75 | 11.27 |
| 2005 | -1.92 | 2.02 | 3.93 | 2.08 | 6.15 |

| Trailing | NAV Return% | Market Return% | NAV Rtrn% +/-S&P 500 | %Rank Cat.(NAV) |
|---|---|---|---|---|
| 3 Mo | 2.08 | 1.71 | 0.00 | 27 |
| 6 Mo | 6.09 | 6.06 | 0.33 | 27 |
| 1 Yr | 6.15 | 6.34 | 1.24 | 23 |
| 3 Yr Avg | 15.26 | 15.22 | 0.88 | 14 |
| 5 Yr Avg | 0.94 | 0.87 | 0.40 | 13 |
| 10 Yr Avg | — | — | — | 0 |

| Tax Analysis | Tax-Adj Return% | Tax-Cost Ratio |
|---|---|---|
| 3 Yr (estimated) | 14.54 | 0.62 |
| 5 Yr (estimated) | 0.36 | 0.57 |
| 10 Yr (estimated) | — | — |

## Risk Profile

| | Standard Index S&P 500 | Best Fit Index Russ 1000 |
|---|---|---|
| Alpha | 0.7 | -0.1 |
| Beta | 1.01 | 1.00 |
| R-Squared | 100 | 100 |
| Standard Deviation | 9.24 | |
| Mean | 15.26 | |
| Sharpe Ratio | 1.38 | |

## Morningstar Fair Value

| Price/Fair Value Ratio | Fair Value Estimate ($) | Hit Rate % |
|---|---|---|
| 1.0 Fairly valued | 38.14 | 95 Good |

## Portfolio Analysis 12-31-05

Share change since 11-05 Total Stocks:983

| | Sector | PE | Tot Ret% | % Assets |
|---|---|---|---|---|
| ⊕ General Electric | Ind Mtrls | 19.9 | -1.43 | 2.94 |
| ⊕ ExxonMobil | Energy | 10.6 | 11.76 | 2.83 |
| ⊕ Citigroup | Financial | 12.1 | 4.63 | 2.00 |
| ⊕ Microsoft | Software | 22.2 | -0.95 | 1.91 |
| ⊕ Procter & Gamble | Goods | 21.2 | 7.18 | 1.54 |
| ⊕ Bank of America | Financial | 11.1 | 2.39 | 1.47 |
| ⊕ Johnson & Johnson | Health | 19.1 | -3.36 | 1.41 |
| ⊕ Pfizer | Health | 21.2 | -10.62 | 1.37 |
| ⊕ American International G | Financial | 15.6 | 4.83 | 1.24 |
| ⊕ Altria Group | Goods | 15.0 | 27.72 | 1.22 |
| ⊕ Intel | Hardware | 18.6 | 8.12 | 1.22 |
| ⊕ J.P. Morgan Chase & Co. | Financial | 18.8 | 5.74 | 1.10 |
| ⊕ IBM | Hardware | 16.0 | -15.83 | 1.05 |
| ⊕ Chevron | Energy | 9.0 | 11.51 | 1.02 |
| ⊕ Wal-Mart Stores | Consumer | 18.2 | -10.30 | 0.93 |
| ⊕ Cisco Systems | Hardware | 19.9 | -11.39 | 0.87 |
| ⊕ Wells Fargo | Financial | 14.3 | 4.47 | 0.84 |
| ⊕ PepsiCo | Goods | 25.8 | 15.24 | 0.78 |
| ⊕ Amgen | Health | 28.3 | 22.93 | 0.77 |
| ⊕ AT&T | Telecom | 21.1 | 0.25 | 0.76 |

### Current Investment Style

Value Blnd Growth — Large Mid Small

| Market Cap | % |
|---|---|
| Giant | 47.6 |
| Large | 33.5 |
| Mid | 18.8 |
| Small | 0.2 |
| Micro | 0.0 |

Avg $mil: 35,376

| Value Measures | | Rel Category |
|---|---|---|
| Price/Earnings | 16.29 | 0.96 |
| Price/Book | 2.51 | 0.93 |
| Price/Sales | 1.48 | 1.16 |
| Price/Cash Flow | 6.30 | 0.87 |
| Dividend Yield % | 1.83 | 1.03 |

| Growth Measures | % | Rel Category |
|---|---|---|
| Long-Term Erngs | 10.63 | 0.96 |
| Book Value | 10.52 | 1.12 |
| Sales | 9.02 | 1.12 |
| Cash Flow | 12.18 | 1.18 |
| Historical Erngs | 15.29 | 1.08 |

| Profitability | % | Rel Category |
|---|---|---|
| Return on Equity | 19.17 | 0.94 |
| Return on Assets | 10.23 | 1.10 |
| Net Margin | 13.39 | 1.23 |

### Sector Weightings

| | % of Stocks | Rel S&P 500 | 3 Year High | Low |
|---|---|---|---|---|
| ↻ Info | 20.24 | 1.00 | | |
| 🖬 Software | 3.59 | 1.01 | 4 | 4 |
| 💻 Hardware | 9.71 | 0.97 | 12 | 9 |
| 🖵 Media | 3.89 | 1.09 | 5 | 4 |
| 🕾 Telecom | 3.05 | 1.01 | 4 | 3 |
| ⊆ Service | 48.25 | 1.04 | | |
| 🖾 Health | 13.35 | 1.00 | 16 | 13 |
| 🖻 Consumer | 8.65 | 1.06 | 9 | 8 |
| 🖹 Business | 4.85 | 1.25 | 5 | 4 |
| 💲 Financial | 21.40 | 1.01 | 22 | 20 |
| 🖳 Mfg | 31.51 | 0.94 | | |
| 🖤 Goods | 8.06 | 0.94 | 10 | 8 |
| ⚙ Ind Mtrls | 11.19 | 0.92 | 12 | 10 |
| ◐ Energy | 8.70 | 0.93 | 10 | 5 |
| ⬤ Utilities | 3.56 | 1.06 | 4 | 3 |

### Composition

| | | |
|---|---|---|
| ● Cash | | 0.1 |
| ● Stocks | | 99.9 |
| ● Bonds | | 0.0 |
| ● Other | | 0.0 |
| Foreign | | 0.1 |
| (% of Stock) | | |

## Morningstar's Take by Dan Culloton

This fund offers a lot, but not everything.

IShares Russell 1000 Index has many characteristics of a good core stock fund. It tracks the Russell 1000 Index of the 1,000 largest stocks based in the U.S., so it's broadly diversified. Since its May 2000 inception through the end of the end of October 2005, the fund's annualized loss of 1.41% trails its bogy by about 14 hundredths of a percent, or roughly the size of its expense ratio, so there's evidence it doing a good job tracking its index.

Furthermore, the fund's 0.15% expense ratio is lower than most large-blend exchange-traded funds and more than 90% of traditional large blend index mutual funds available to retail investors. The offering's bogy includes some of the most-liquid stocks in the world. You should have little trouble finding someone to buy or sell shares of this ETF when you need to trade.

Nevertheless, the fund has a few warts. First, despite its lower expense ratio and tax-efficient ETF structure, this fund's five-year annualized aftertax loss (assuming an investor still held the fund's shares at the end of the period) of 2.06% through Oct. 31, 2005, trails the 1.78% annualized aftertax loss of traditional mutual-fund rival, Schwab 1000.

Second, while this fund is cheap, it s not the cheapest fund in the category, and competition is heating up. Several traditional large-blend index funds, as well as the SPDRs, and Vanguard Total Stock Market and Vanguard Large Cap ETFs have cut their fees. That may seem like a quibble, but every basis point counts when comparing index funds, especially those that track indexes that track similar territory. Expenses remain the biggest differentiating factor among funds tracking closely correlated benchmarks.

These caveats keep this fund from being our first choice.

| Address: | 45 Fremont Street | Management Fee: | 0.15% | | |
|---|---|---|---|---|---|
| | San Francisco CA 94105 | Expense Projections: | 3Yr:$48 | 5Yr:$85 | 10Yr:$192 |
| | 800-474-2737 | Income Distrib: | Quarterly | | |
| Web Address: | www.ishares.com | Exchange: | AMEX | | |
| Inception: | 05-15-00* | | | | |
| Advisor: | Barclays Global Fund Advisers | | | | |

MORNINGSTAR® ETFs 100

# iShares R1000 Value

| | Ticker | NAV | Market Price | 52 wk High/Low | Yield | Mstar Category |
|---|---|---|---|---|---|---|
| | IWD | $69.22 | $71.59 | $71.59 - $63.49 | 2.5% | Large Value |

## Management

### Portfolio Manager(s)

Barclays Global Fund Advisors is the advisor. The firm is the world's largest manager of indexed portfolios. Patrick O'Connor, the head of Barclay's U.S. iShares portfolio management group leads a team of a half dozen managers in running this and about 60 other ETFs. iShares domestic portfolio management group is responsible for about $75 billion in assets. Most of the managers have at least five or more years of experience with Barclays as well as prior industry experience.

### Strategy

This fund tracks the Russell 1000 Value Index, which is a subset of the Russell 1000 Index of large-cap stocks that measures the performance of companies whose shares have lower price/book ratios and forecasted growth according the I/B/E/S. Russell uses a purely quantitative method to construct the index. It holds about 700 stocks. The index reconstitutes just once a year, at the end of each May.

**Growth of $10,000**

— Investment Value of ETF
— Investment Value of Index S&P 500

| 1996 | 1997 | 1998 | 1999 | 2000 | 2001 | 2002 | 2003 | 2004 | 2005 | History |
|---|---|---|---|---|---|---|---|---|---|---|
| — | — | — | — | 59.88 | 55.57 | 45.94 | 58.30 | 66.38 | 69.22 | NAV $ |
| — | — | — | — | 60.03 | 55.40 | 46.05 | 58.37 | 66.37 | 69.03 | Market Price $ |
| — | — | — | — | 5.89* | -5.73 | -15.68 | 29.70 | 16.28 | 6.92 | NAV Return% |
| — | — | — | — | 5.84* | -6.26 | -15.22 | 29.55 | 16.12 | 6.64 | Market Price Return% |
| — | — | — | — | 0.36 | -0.02 | -0.01 | -0.00 | 0.05 | -0.05 | Avg Premium/Discount% |
| — | — | — | — | 5.89 | 6.15 | 6.41 | 1.03 | 5.41 | 2.01 | NAV Rtrn% +/-S&P 500 |
| — | — | — | — | 5.89 | -0.14 | -0.16 | -0.33 | -0.21 | -0.13 | NAV Rtrn% +/-Russ 1000 VI |
| — | — | — | — | | 7 | 7 | 7 | 7 | 10 | NAV Return% Rank in Cat |
| — | — | — | — | 0.00 | 1.45 | 1.78 | 2.44 | 2.25 | 2.58 | Income Return % |
| — | — | — | — | | -7.18 | -17.46 | 27.26 | 14.03 | 4.34 | Capital Return % |
| — | — | — | — | 0.44 | 0.87 | 0.98 | 1.11 | 1.30 | 1.70 | Income $ |
| — | — | — | — | 0.00 | 0.00 | 0.00 | 0.00 | 0.00 | 0.00 | Capital Gains $ |
| — | — | — | — | 0.20 | 0.20 | 0.20 | 0.20 | 0.20 | 0.20 | Expense Ratio % |
| — | — | — | — | | 1.64 | 1.82 | 2.29 | 2.29 | 2.42 | Income Ratio % |
| — | — | — | — | | 9 | 16 | 20 | 12 | 15 | Turnover Rate % |
| — | — | — | — | — | 1,123 | 2,326 | 4,710 | 6,185 | | Net Assets $mil |

## Performance

### Historic Quarterly NAV Returns

| | 1st Qtr | 2nd Qtr | 3rd Qtr | 4th Qtr | Total |
|---|---|---|---|---|---|
| 2001 | -5.90 | 4.84 | -10.97 | 7.32 | -5.73 |
| 2002 | 4.04 | -8.58 | -18.76 | 9.11 | -15.68 |
| 2003 | -4.92 | 17.20 | 2.01 | 14.10 | 29.70 |
| 2004 | 2.98 | 0.84 | 1.51 | 10.31 | 16.28 |
| 2005 | 0.09 | 1.63 | 3.85 | 1.20 | 6.92 |

| Trailing | NAV Return% | Market Return% | NAV Rtrn% +/-S&P 500 | %Rank Cat.(NAV) |
|---|---|---|---|---|
| 3 Mo | 1.20 | 0.94 | -0.88 | 13 |
| 6 Mo | 5.10 | 4.92 | -0.66 | 11 |
| 1 Yr | 6.92 | 6.64 | 2.01 | 10 |
| 3 Yr Avg | 17.26 | 17.06 | 2.88 | 7 |
| 5 Yr Avg | 5.09 | 4.98 | 4.55 | 7 |
| 10 Yr Avg | — | — | — | 0 |

| Tax Analysis | Tax-Adj Return% | Tax-Cost Ratio |
|---|---|---|
| 3 Yr (estimated) | 16.34 | 0.78 |
| 5 Yr (estimated) | 4.31 | 0.74 |
| 10 Yr (estimated) | — | — |

## Risk Profile

| | Standard Index S&P 500 | Best Fit Index Russ 1000 VI |
|---|---|---|
| Alpha | 2.4 | -0.1 |
| Beta | 1.01 | 1.00 |
| R-Squared | 94 | 100 |
| Standard Deviation | 9.57 | |
| Mean | 17.26 | |
| Sharpe Ratio | 1.51 | |

## Morningstar Fair Value

| Price/Fair Value Ratio | Fair Value Estimate ($) | Hit Rate % |
|---|---|---|
| 1.0 Fairly valued | 37.00 | 94 Good |

## Portfolio Analysis  12-31-05

| Share change since 11-05  Total Stocks:646 | Sector | PE | Tot Ret% | % Assets |
|---|---|---|---|---|
| ⊕ ExxonMobil | Energy | 10.6 | 11.76 | 5.74 |
| ⊕ Citigroup | Financial | 12.1 | 4.63 | 4.05 |
| ⊕ Bank of America | Financial | 11.1 | 2.39 | 2.98 |
| ⊕ Pfizer | Health | 21.2 | -10.62 | 2.78 |
| ⊕ J.P. Morgan Chase & Co. | Financial | 18.8 | 5.74 | 2.24 |
| ⊕ Chevron | Energy | 9.0 | 11.51 | 2.06 |
| ⊕ American International G | Financial | 15.6 | 4.83 | 1.77 |
| ⊕ AT&T | Telecom | 21.1 | 0.25 | 1.54 |
| ⊕ Wells Fargo | Financial | 14.3 | 4.47 | 1.53 |
| ⊕ Altria Group | Goods | 15.0 | 27.72 | 1.48 |
| ⊕ General Electric | Ind Mtrls | 19.9 | -1.43 | 1.44 |
| ⊕ Verizon Communications | Telecom | 10.2 | -22.18 | 1.34 |
| ⊕ Wachovia | Financial | 13.0 | 4.29 | 1.34 |
| ⊕ Hewlett-Packard | Hardware | 27.3 | 38.29 | 1.33 |
| ⊕ ConocoPhillips | Energy | 6.7 | 36.89 | 1.30 |
| ⊕ Time Warner | Media | 30.6 | -9.83 | 1.21 |
| ⊕ Merrill Lynch & Company | Financial | 13.7 | 14.77 | 1.02 |
| ⊕ Morgan Stanley | Financial | 13.3 | 4.28 | 0.90 |
| ⊕ US Bancorp | Financial | 12.7 | -0.46 | 0.88 |
| ⊕ Merck | Health | 15.2 | 4.04 | 0.86 |

### Current Investment Style

Value Blnd Growth — Large Mid Small

| Market Cap | % |
|---|---|
| Giant | 45.3 |
| Large | 35.3 |
| Mid | 19.3 |
| Small | 0.2 |
| Micro | 0.0 |

Avg $mil: 34,914

| Value Measures | | Rel Category |
|---|---|---|
| Price/Earnings | 13.55 | 0.94 |
| Price/Book | 1.88 | 0.84 |
| Price/Sales | 1.22 | 0.92 |
| Price/Cash Flow | 4.07 | 0.79 |
| Dividend Yield % | 2.56 | 1.05 |

| Growth Measures | % | Rel Category |
|---|---|---|
| Long-Term Erngs | 8.74 | 0.91 |
| Book Value | 10.85 | 0.90 |
| Sales | 7.30 | 0.91 |
| Cash Flow | 10.53 | 0.86 |
| Historical Erngs | 13.66 | 0.83 |

| Profitability | % | Rel Category |
|---|---|---|
| Return on Equity | 15.40 | 0.83 |
| Return on Assets | 9.45 | 0.95 |
| Net Margin | 13.43 | 1.04 |

| Sector Weightings | % of Stocks | Rel S&P 500 | 3 Year High Low |
|---|---|---|---|
| ⌖ Info | 13.90 | 0.69 | |
| Software | 0.57 | 0.16 | 1  0 |
| Hardware | 3.32 | 0.33 | 6  3 |
| Media | 4.48 | 1.25 | 7  4 |
| Telecom | 5.53 | 1.84 | 7  5 |
| ⊆ Service | 50.42 | 1.09 | |
| Health | 7.03 | 0.53 | 8  3 |
| Consumer | 3.55 | 0.44 | 5  3 |
| Business | 2.85 | 0.74 | 3  3 |
| Financial | 36.99 | 1.75 | 37  31 |
| Mfg | 35.69 | 1.07 | |
| Goods | 6.03 | 0.70 | 9  6 |
| Ind Mtrls | 9.12 | 0.75 | 16  9 |
| Energy | 13.87 | 1.48 | 16  10 |
| Utilities | 6.67 | 1.99 | 7  6 |

### Composition

| | | |
|---|---|---|
| ● Cash | | 0.1 |
| ● Stocks | | 99.9 |
| ● Bonds | | 0.0 |
| ● Other | | 0.0 |
| Foreign | | 0.1 |
| (% of Stock) | | |

## Morningstar's Take  by Dan Culloton

This fund's advantages outweigh its quirks.

The iShares Russell 1000 Value Index offers affordable exposure to large, cheap stocks. This exchange-traded fund tracks an index composed of stocks with big market caps, low price/book ratios, and low earnings growth forecasts. That makes it diversified, with about 700 stocks in its portfolio, a little more than one fourth of its assets in its top-10 holdings, and assets spread out across all major sectors. Its breadth also limits bumps. The ETF's standard deviation, a measure of volatility, is in line with the average open-end, large-value fund.

Retail investors can find ETFs with cheaper expense ratios and different methods of tracking the large-value universe, such as Vanguard Value Vipers. However, this fund's levy is still less than one fifth of the average traditional large-cap value mutual fund, which gives it a big head start, assuming it isn't frittered away on trading commissions.

There are a couple of potential pitfalls, though.

The ETF has a very large helping of financial stocks (about one third of its assets), which can hurt relative performance in times when the financial sector lags. Speculators also often take advantage of this ETF's benchmark, which can affect its returns. They try to front run the Russell indexes' predictable annual reconstitution, bidding up additions and selling off deletions to the bogies.

Even with those issues, though, this fund's bogy has been a tough one for managers of traditional actively managed funds to beat over time. The annualized returns of the Russell 1000 Value Index have outdistanced the typical large-value fund in every trailing period up to 15 years. The benchmark's success has been consistent, too. It has bested the average large-value fund in 10 of the 15 calendar years from 1989 to 2003.

As long as this fund continues do a good job tracking its index, its low expenses give it a good chance of turning in competitive results over the long term.

| Address: | 45 Fremont Street San Francisco CA 94105 800-474-2737 | Management Fee: | 0.20% | | |
|---|---|---|---|---|---|
| | | Expense Projections: | 3Yr:$64 | 5Yr:$113 | 10Yr:$255 |
| Web Address: | www.ishares.com | Income Distrib: | Quarterly | | |
| Inception: | 05-22-00 * | Exchange: | AMEX | | |
| Advisor: | Barclays Global Fund Advisers | | | | |

MORNINGSTAR® ETFs 100

# iShares R2000 Growth

| Ticker | NAV | Market Price | 52 wk High/Low | Yield | Mstar Category |
|---|---|---|---|---|---|
| IWO | $69.86 | $74.11 | $74.11 - $58.22 | 0.5% | Small Growth |

## Management

### Portfolio Manager(s)

Barclays Global Fund Advisors is the advisor. The firm is the world's largest manager of indexed portfolios. Patrick O'Connor, the head of Barclay's U.S. iShares portfolio management group leads a team of a half dozen managers in running this and about 60 other ETFs. IShares' domestic portfolio-management group is responsible for about $75 billion in assets. Most of the managers have at least five years of experience with Barclays as well as prior industry experience.

### Strategy

This fund tracks the Russell 2000 Growth Index, which is a subset of the Russell 2000 Index that measures the performance of companies whose shares have higher price/book ratios and forecasted growth according the I/B/E/S. Russell uses a purely quantitative method to construct the index. It holds nearly 1,300 stocks. The index reconstitutes just once a year, at the end of each May.

### Growth of $10,000

— Investment Value of ETF
— Investment Value of Index S&P 500

| | 1996 | 1997 | 1998 | 1999 | 2000 | 2001 | 2002 | 2003 | 2004 | 2005 | History |
|---|---|---|---|---|---|---|---|---|---|---|---|
| | — | — | — | — | 64.27 | 57.84 | 40.16 | 59.28 | 67.48 | 69.86 | NAV $ |
| | — | — | — | — | 64.19 | 57.60 | 39.85 | 59.26 | 67.30 | 69.66 | Market Price $ |
| | — | — | — | — | -2.43* | -9.82 | -30.29 | 48.19 | 14.13 | 4.04 | NAV Return% |
| | — | — | — | — | -2.49* | -10.08 | -30.54 | 49.30 | 13.86 | 4.02 | Market Price Return% |
| | — | — | — | — | -0.09 | -0.14 | -0.20 | -0.09 | -0.13 | -0.11 | Avg Premium/Discount% |
| | — | — | — | — | -2.43 | 2.06 | -8.20 | 19.52 | 3.26 | -0.87 | NAV Rtrn% +/-S&P 500 |
| | — | — | — | — | -2.43 | -0.59 | -0.03 | -0.35 | -0.18 | -0.11 | NAV Rtrn% +/-Russ 2000 Gr |
| | — | — | — | — | — | 3 | 3 | 3 | 3 | 5 | NAV Return% Rank in Cat |
| | — | — | — | — | 0.00 | 0.17 | 0.30 | 0.50 | 0.27 | 0.49 | Income Return % |
| | — | — | — | — | — | -9.99 | -30.59 | 47.69 | 13.86 | 3.55 | Capital Return % |
| | — | — | — | — | 0.02 | 0.11 | 0.17 | 0.20 | 0.16 | 0.33 | Income $ |
| | — | — | — | — | 0.04 | 0.00 | 0.00 | 0.00 | 0.00 | 0.00 | Capital Gains $ |
| | — | — | — | — | 0.25 | 0.25 | 0.25 | 0.25 | 0.25 | Expense Ratio % |
| | — | — | — | — | 0.14 | 0.22 | 0.58 | 0.38 | 0.37 | Income Ratio % |
| | — | — | — | — | 9 | 28 | 41 | 37 | 22 | Turnover Rate % |
| | — | — | — | — | 608 | 1,515 | 2,203 | 2,620 | Net Assets $mil |

## Performance

### Historic Quarterly NAV Returns

| | 1st Qtr | 2nd Qtr | 3rd Qtr | 4th Qtr | Total |
|---|---|---|---|---|---|
| 2001 | -15.21 | 17.77 | -28.14 | 25.68 | -9.82 |
| 2002 | -1.99 | -15.70 | -21.47 | 7.45 | -30.29 |
| 2003 | -3.91 | 24.06 | 10.39 | 12.61 | 48.19 |
| 2004 | 5.54 | 0.09 | -6.04 | 14.98 | 14.13 |
| 2005 | -6.84 | 3.47 | 6.28 | 1.55 | 4.04 |

| Trailing | NAV Return% | Market Return% | NAV Rtrn% +/-S&P 500 | %Rank Cat.(NAV) |
|---|---|---|---|---|
| 3 Mo | 1.55 | 1.37 | -0.53 | 6 |
| 6 Mo | 7.94 | 7.69 | 2.18 | 6 |
| 1 Yr | 4.04 | 4.02 | -0.87 | 5 |
| 3 Yr Avg | 20.73 | 20.92 | 6.35 | 3 |
| 5 Yr Avg | 2.04 | 2.01 | 1.50 | 3 |
| 10 Yr Avg | — | — | — | 0 |

| Tax Analysis | Tax-Adj Return% | Tax-Cost Ratio |
|---|---|---|
| 3 Yr (estimated) | 20.57 | 0.13 |
| 5 Yr (estimated) | 1.91 | 0.13 |
| 10 Yr (estimated) | — | — |

## Risk Profile

| | Standard Index S&P 500 | Best Fit Index Russ 2000 Gr |
|---|---|---|
| Alpha | -0.3 | -0.2 |
| Beta | 1.56 | 1.00 |
| R-Squared | 73 | 100 |
| Standard Deviation | 16.74 | |
| Mean | 20.73 | |
| Sharpe Ratio | 1.10 | |

## Morningstar Fair Value

| Price/Fair Value Ratio | Fair Value Estimate ($) | Hit Rate % |
|---|---|---|
| | | |

## Portfolio Analysis 12-31-05

| Share change since 11-05 Total Stocks:1368 | Sector | PE | Tot Ret% | % Assets |
|---|---|---|---|---|
| ⊖ Amylin Pharmaceuticals | Health | — | 70.89 | 0.72 |
| ⊖ Intuitive Surgical | Health | 77.2 | 193.03 | 0.67 |
| ⊕ Cal Dive International | Energy | 24.0 | 76.15 | 0.45 |
| ⊖ JLG Industries | Ind Mtrls | 23.7 | 132.76 | 0.38 |
| ⊖ Neurocrine Biosciences | Health | — | 27.24 | 0.38 |
| ⊖ Eagle Materials | Consumer | 17.0 | 43.39 | 0.37 |
| ⊕ Pediatrix Medical Group | Health | 21.3 | 38.28 | 0.36 |
| ⊖ Frontier Oil | Energy | 10.1 | 189.81 | 0.34 |
| ⊕ Jarden | Goods | — | 4.11 | 0.33 |
| ⊖ Acxiom | Business | 41.8 | -11.68 | 0.33 |
| ⊖ Adtran | Hardware | 27.5 | 57.52 | 0.32 |
| ⊖ Cleveland-Cliffs | Ind Mtrls | 5.9 | 71.93 | 0.32 |
| ⊖ Abgenix | Health | — | 107.83 | 0.31 |
| ⊖ CNET Networks | Media | — | 30.81 | 0.31 |
| ⊖ Pacific Sunwear | Consumer | 15.9 | 11.95 | 0.31 |
| ⊖ Cypress Semiconductor | Hardware | — | 21.48 | 0.31 |
| ⊖ MoneyGram International | Financial | — | 23.73 | 0.31 |
| ⊖ National Financial Partn | Financial | 42.0 | 37.00 | 0.30 |
| ⊖ Micros Systems | Software | 34.5 | 23.80 | 0.30 |
| ⊖ Continental Airlines B | Business | — | 57.31 | 0.30 |

### Current Investment Style

Value Blnd Growth — Large Mid Small

| Market Cap | % |
|---|---|
| Giant | 0.0 |
| Large | 0.0 |
| Mid | 22.7 |
| Small | 63.4 |
| Micro | 14.0 |

Avg $mil: 970

| Value Measures | | Rel Category |
|---|---|---|
| Price/Earnings | 21.10 | 0.96 |
| Price/Book | 2.90 | 0.97 |
| Price/Sales | 1.35 | 0.91 |
| Price/Cash Flow | 7.88 | 0.93 |
| Dividend Yield % | 0.42 | 1.45 |

| Growth Measures | % | Rel Category |
|---|---|---|
| Long-Term Erngs | 17.03 | 0.98 |
| Book Value | 5.78 | 0.62 |
| Sales | 9.93 | 0.81 |
| Cash Flow | 13.35 | 0.82 |
| Historical Erngs | 16.42 | 0.81 |

| Profitability | % | Rel Category |
|---|---|---|
| Return on Equity | 11.96 | 0.87 |
| Return on Assets | 5.09 | 0.72 |
| Net Margin | 8.39 | 0.96 |

### Sector Weightings

| Sector Weightings | % of Stocks | Rel S&P 500 | 3 Year High | Low |
|---|---|---|---|---|
| ↻ Info | 21.80 | 1.08 | | |
| 🖳 Software | 6.90 | 1.94 | 10 | 7 |
| 💻 Hardware | 11.49 | 1.14 | 16 | 11 |
| 🎬 Media | 1.54 | 0.43 | 2 | 1 |
| 📞 Telecom | 1.87 | 0.62 | 2 | 2 |
| Ǥ Service | 53.25 | 1.15 | | |
| ⚕ Health | 18.96 | 1.43 | 24 | 18 |
| 🛒 Consumer | 10.37 | 1.27 | 12 | 9 |
| 📋 Business | 13.86 | 3.58 | 14 | 11 |
| 💲 Financial | 10.06 | 0.48 | 17 | 9 |
| 🏭 Mfg | 24.94 | 0.75 | | |
| 🏷 Goods | 5.02 | 0.59 | 5 | 3 |
| ⚙ Ind Mtrls | 13.13 | 1.08 | 14 | 9 |
| 🔥 Energy | 6.69 | 0.72 | 7 | 3 |
| 💡 Utilities | 0.10 | 0.03 | 1 | 0 |

### Composition

| | | |
|---|---|---|
| ● Cash | 0.1 | |
| ● Stocks | 99.8 | |
| ● Bonds | 0.0 | |
| ● Other | 0.0 | |
| Foreign | 0.2 | |
| (% of Stock) | | |

## Morningstar's Take by Dan Culloton

IShares Russell 2000 Growth Index doesn't hit on all cylinders.

This fund is diversified and cheap, but other factors detract from its appeal. The fund's 0.25% levy is among the lowest available to retail investors looking for small growth index fund. But it's not the lowest. The traditional and exchange-traded share classes of Vanguard Small Cap Growth Index are cheaper.

The fund covers a broad swath of stocks. It owns the members of the Russell 2000 Index that have higher-than-average price/book ratios and forecasted growth rates, regardless of their profitability. That includes more than 1,300 stocks across every major sector. The fund also owns more micro-cap and fewer mid-cap stocks than competing offerings that track indexes from S&P, Dow Jones and MSCI, which gives it a smaller-than-typical average market cap.

Because of its market-cap bias and indifference to profits, however, this ETF has been bumpier. Its leanings helped in 2003 and 2004 as smaller, more speculative stocks have outperformed their larger brethren. But the portfolio also has been more volatile, as measured by standard deviation, because many of the tiny equities it owns tend to be more variable.

Overall thc ride hasn't been worth it. The fund's annualized 2.4% loss from August 2000 (roughly its inception) through Oct. 31, 2005, was deeper than the 0.22% decline of the average small-cap growth fund. That's attributable to smaller, edgier stocks that were hit hard by the bear market. Over time, however, the average active manager has not had much trouble beating the Russell 2000 Growth Index; he or she has done so in eight of the 10 calendar years between 1995 and 2004. Over the last 15 years, the bogy's 9.8% annualized gain lags the 11.5% gain of its average peer.

So, while this fund offers cheap small-growth exposure, options with better risk/reward profiles are available.

| Address: | 45 Fremont Street San Francisco CA 94105 800-474-2737 | Management Fee: | 0.25% |
|---|---|---|---|
| | | Expense Projections: | 3Yr:$80   5Yr:$141   10Yr:$318 |
| Web Address: | www.ishares.com | Income Distrib: | Quarterly |
| Inception: | 07-24-00* | Exchange: | AMEX |
| Advisor: | Barclays Global Fund Advisers | | |

# iShares R2000 Index

| | Ticker | NAV | Market Price | 52 wk High/Low | Yield | Mstar Category |
|---|---|---|---|---|---|---|
| | IWM | $66.86 | $70.70 | $70.70 - $56.88 | 1.3% | Small Blend |

## Management

### Portfolio Manager(s)

Barclays Global Fund Advisors is the advisor. The firm is the world's largest manager of indexed portfolios. Patrick O'Connor, the head of Barclay's U.S. iShares portfolio management group leads a team of a half dozen managers in running this and about 60 other ETFs. IShares' domestic portfolio-management group is responsible for about $75 billion in assets. Most of the managers have at least five years of experience with Barclays as well as prior industry experience.

### Strategy

This fund tracks the Russell 2000 Index, which measures the performance of the 2,000 smallest companies in the Russell 3000 Index. The bogy represents about 7% of the U.S. stock market's total capitalization. The index reconstitutes just once a year, at the end of each May. The fund uses representative sampling to track the bogy.

**Growth of $10,000**

- Investment Value of ETF
- Investment Value of Index S&P 500

| | 1996 | 1997 | 1998 | 1999 | 2000 | 2001 | 2002 | 2003 | 2004 | 2005 | History |
|---|---|---|---|---|---|---|---|---|---|---|---|
| | — | — | — | — | 48.14 | 48.53 | 38.12 | 55.47 | 64.89 | 66.86 | NAV $ |
| | — | — | — | — | 47.88 | 48.17 | 37.91 | 55.40 | 64.75 | 66.72 | Market Price $ |
| | — | — | — | — | 7.66* | 1.97 | -20.51 | 46.94 | 18.15 | 4.46 | NAV Return% |
| | — | — | — | — | 7.62* | 1.78 | -20.37 | 47.58 | 18.05 | 4.46 | Market Price Return% |
| | — | — | — | — | -0.16 | -0.30 | -0.40 | -0.08 | -0.13 | -0.06 | Avg Premium/Discount% |
| | — | — | — | — | 7.66 | 13.85 | 1.58 | 18.27 | 7.28 | -0.45 | NAV Rtrn% +/-S&P 500 |
| | — | — | — | — | 7.66 | -0.52 | -0.03 | -0.31 | -0.18 | -0.09 | NAV Rtrn% +/-Russ 2000 |
| | — | — | — | — | — | 2 | 2 | 2 | 2 | 4 | NAV Return% Rank in Cat |
| | — | — | — | — | 0.00 | 1.09 | 1.03 | 1.16 | 1.08 | 1.36 | Income Return % |
| | — | — | — | — | — | 0.88 | -21.54 | 45.78 | 17.07 | 3.10 | Capital Return % |
| | — | — | — | — | 0.34 | 0.52 | 0.50 | 0.44 | 0.59 | 0.88 | Income $ |
| | — | — | — | — | 0.08 | 0.00 | 0.00 | 0.02 | 0.00 | 0.00 | Capital Gains $ |
| | — | — | — | — | 0.20 | 0.20 | 0.20 | 0.20 | 0.20 | 0.20 | Expense Ratio % |
| | — | — | — | — | 1.39 | 1.25 | 1.28 | 1.08 | 1.20 | | Income Ratio % |
| | — | — | — | — | 39 | 20 | 30 | 26 | 17 | | Turnover Rate % |
| | — | — | — | — | — | 2,127 | 4,515 | 6,988 | 7,432 | | Net Assets $mil |

## Performance

### Historic Quarterly NAV Returns

| | 1st Qtr | 2nd Qtr | 3rd Qtr | 4th Qtr | Total |
|---|---|---|---|---|---|
| 2001 | -6.53 | 14.15 | -20.87 | 20.78 | 1.97 |
| 2002 | 3.95 | -8.38 | -21.35 | 6.12 | -20.51 |
| 2003 | -4.52 | 23.34 | 9.01 | 14.46 | 46.94 |
| 2004 | 6.21 | 0.47 | -2.89 | 14.02 | 18.15 |
| 2005 | -5.36 | 4.30 | 4.66 | 1.11 | 4.46 |

| Trailing | NAV Return% | Market Return% | NAV Rtrn% +/-S&P 500 | %Rank Cat.(NAV) |
|---|---|---|---|---|
| 3 Mo | 1.11 | 0.88 | -0.97 | 7 |
| 6 Mo | 5.82 | 5.46 | 0.06 | 4 |
| 1 Yr | 4.46 | 4.46 | -0.45 | 4 |
| 3 Yr Avg | 21.95 | 22.09 | 7.57 | 2 |
| 5 Yr Avg | 8.01 | 8.08 | 7.47 | 2 |
| 10 Yr Avg | — | — | — | 0 |

| Tax Analysis | Tax-Adj Return% | Tax-Cost Ratio |
|---|---|---|
| 3 Yr (estimated) | 21.48 | 0.39 |
| 5 Yr (estimated) | 7.57 | 0.41 |
| 10 Yr (estimated) | — | — |

## Risk Profile

| | Standard Index S&P 500 | Best Fit Index Russ 2000 |
|---|---|---|
| Alpha | 1.6 | -0.1 |
| Beta | 1.47 | 1.00 |
| R-Squared | 78 | 100 |
| Standard Deviation | 15.27 | |
| Mean | 21.95 | |
| Sharpe Ratio | 1.25 | |

## Morningstar Fair Value

| Price/Fair Value Ratio | Fair Value Estimate ($) | Hit Rate % |
|---|---|---|
| — | — | — |

## Portfolio Analysis  12-31-05

| Share change since 11-05 Total Stocks:2007 | Sector | PE | Tot Ret% | % Assets |
|---|---|---|---|---|
| ⊖ Amylin Pharmaceuticals | Health | — | 70.89 | 0.36 |
| ⊖ Intuitive Surgical | Health | 77.2 | 193.03 | 0.34 |
| ⊖ Cimarex Energy | Energy | 11.5 | 13.48 | 0.29 |
| ⊕ Cal Dive International | Energy | 24.0 | 76.15 | 0.23 |
| ⊖ Vertex Pharmaceuticals | Health | — | 161.78 | 0.22 |
| ⊖ Integrated Device Techno | Hardware | — | 14.01 | 0.21 |
| ⊕ Sierra Pacific Resources | Utilities | 27.8 | 24.19 | 0.20 |
| ⊖ Hughes Supply | Business | 17.2 | 12.06 | 0.20 |
| ⊖ JLG Industries | Ind Mtrls | 23.7 | 132.76 | 0.19 |
| ⊖ Neurocrine Biosciences | Health | — | 27.24 | 0.19 |
| ⊖ Commercial Metals | Ind Mtrls | 8.1 | 49.76 | 0.19 |
| ⊖ Shaw Group | Ind Mtrls | NMF | 62.97 | 0.19 |
| ⊖ MoneyGram International | Financial | — | 23.73 | 0.19 |
| ⊖ La Quinta | Financial | — | 22.55 | 0.19 |
| ⊖ Eagle Materials | Consumer | 17.0 | 43.39 | 0.19 |
| ⊖ Cabot Oil & Gas A | Energy | 18.3 | 53.50 | 0.18 |
| ⊕ Pediatrix Medical Group | Health | 21.3 | 38.28 | 0.18 |
| ⊖ Flowserve | Ind Mtrls | — | 43.65 | 0.18 |
| ⊖ St. Mary Land & Explorat | Energy | 18.8 | 77.02 | 0.17 |
| ⊖ Frontier Oil | Energy | 10.1 | 189.81 | 0.17 |

### Current Investment Style

Value Blnd Growth — Large / Mid / Small

| Market Cap | % |
|---|---|
| Giant | 0.0 |
| Large | 0.0 |
| Mid | 20.2 |
| Small | 65.3 |
| Micro | 14.5 |

Avg $mil: 936

| Value Measures | | Rel Category |
|---|---|---|
| Price/Earnings | 17.83 | 1.04 |
| Price/Book | 2.02 | 1.05 |
| Price/Sales | 1.03 | 1.13 |
| Price/Cash Flow | 7.09 | 1.08 |
| Dividend Yield % | 1.03 | 1.14 |

| Growth Measures | % | Rel Category |
|---|---|---|
| Long-Term Erngs | 13.31 | 0.96 |
| Book Value | 4.80 | 1.33 |
| Sales | 6.94 | 1.32 |
| Cash Flow | 2.76 | 30.67 |
| Historical Erngs | 10.22 | 0.83 |

| Profitability | % | Rel Category |
|---|---|---|
| Return on Equity | 10.21 | 1.05 |
| Return on Assets | 5.14 | 1.00 |
| Net Margin | 9.00 | 1.11 |

| Sector Weightings | % of Stocks | Rel S&P 500 | 3 Year High Low | |
|---|---|---|---|---|
| ↻ Info | 17.67 | 0.88 | | |
| ▣ Software | 4.41 | 1.24 | 6 | 4 |
| ▣ Hardware | 9.57 | 0.95 | 11 | 7 |
| ▣ Media | 1.61 | 0.45 | 2 | 1 |
| ▣ Telecom | 2.08 | 0.69 | 2 | 2 |
| ☞ Service | 53.79 | 1.16 | | |
| ▣ Health | 11.84 | 0.89 | 14 | 11 |
| ▣ Consumer | 9.55 | 1.17 | 10 | 9 |
| ▣ Business | 10.75 | 2.78 | 11 | 10 |
| ▣ Financial | 21.65 | 1.03 | 23 | 21 |
| ⊔ Mfg | 28.55 | 0.85 | | |
| ▣ Goods | 5.17 | 0.60 | 6 | 4 |
| ▣ Ind Mtrls | 15.33 | 1.26 | 16 | 13 |
| ▣ Energy | 5.68 | 0.61 | 6 | 4 |
| ▣ Utilities | 2.37 | 0.71 | 4 | 2 |

### Composition

| | | % |
|---|---|---|
| ● | Cash | 0.2 |
| ● | Stocks | 99.8 |
| ● | Bonds | 0.0 |
| ● | Other | 0.0 |
| | Foreign | 0.1 |
| | (% of Stock) | |

## Morningstar's Take  by Dan Culloton

IShares Russell 2000 Index has keen competition.

This fund offers much. It provides diversified, low-cost exposure to small-cap stocks. Since it's a passively managed fund that tracks the Russell 2000 Index, it's less susceptible to asset bloat, which causes many good actively managed small-cap funds to close to new investors or to begin struggling. Like all ETFs that are bought and sold on an exchange rather than directly from the fund, it also offers protection from the trading of other investors (traditional fund managers often hold cash or sell securities to meet redemptions, which affects returns).

Those traits have helped this ETF become the biggest small-cap index fund in terms of assets. It still has some tough rivals, though. The ETF's 0.20% expense ratio is a fraction of the cost of the typical small-blend fund, but it's not the least expensive option. Vanguard has two offerings with lower expense ratios: an ETF, Vanguard Small Cap VIPERs, and a traditional fund, Vanguard Tax-Managed

Small Cap (the tax-managed fund requires a $10,000 minimum investment). A few hundredths of a percent may not seem like much, but over the long term it can make a big difference among index funds, which rely on low costs to beat their peers.

Other traits limit this fund's appeal. Its index is often targeted by speculators who try to take advantage of its annual reconstitution, bidding up additions and selling off deletions. That's part of the reason this ETF's index has been an easy one for active managers to beat. The returns of the ETF and its benchmark lag those of the average small-cap blend offering as well as those of other small-cap indexes, such as the S&P Smallcap 600, over most trailing periods.

It's hard to argue with broad, cheap equity exposure, but it's also hard to ignore that there are cheaper, more efficient options.

| Address: | 45 Fremont Street San Francisco CA 94105 800-474-2737 | Management Fee: | 0.20% | | |
|---|---|---|---|---|---|
| | | Expense Projections: | 3Yr:$64 | 5Yr:$113 | 10Yr:$255 |
| Web Address: | www.ishares.com | Income Distrib: | Quarterly | | |
| Inception: | 05-22-00* | Exchange: | AMEX | | |
| Advisor: | Barclays Global Fund Advisers | | | | |

 MORNINGSTAR® ETFs 100

# iShares R2000 Value

| Ticker | NAV | Market Price | 52 wk High/Low | Yield | Mstar Category |
|--------|-----|--------------|----------------|-------|----------------|
| IWN | $66.10 | $69.50 | $69.50 - $57.64 | 1.8% | Small Value |

## Management

### Portfolio Manager(s)

Barclays Global Fund Advisors is the advisor. The firm is the world's largest manager of indexed portfolios. Patrick O'Connor, the head of Barclay's U.S. iShares portfolio management group leads a team of a half dozen managers in running this and about 60 other ETFs. IShares' domestic portfolio-management group is responsible for about $75 billion in assets. Most of the managers have at least five years of experience with Barclays as well as prior industry experience.

### Strategy

This fund tracks the Russell 2000 Value Index, which is a subset of the Russell 2000 Index that measures the performance of companies whose shares have lower price/book ratios and lower forecasted growth according the I/B/E/S. Russell uses a purely quantitative method to construct the index, and this fund's advisor, Barclays Global Fund Advisors, uses representative sampling to track the index. It holds nearly 1,300 stocks. The index reconstitutes just once a year, at the end of each May.

### Growth of $10,000

— Investment Value of ETF
— Investment Value of Index S&P 500

| | 1996 | 1997 | 1998 | 1999 | 2000 | 2001 | 2002 | 2003 | 2004 | 2005 | History |
|---|------|------|------|------|------|------|------|------|------|------|---------|
| NAV $ | — | — | — | — | 38.61 | 42.93 | 37.34 | 53.58 | 64.40 | 66.10 | |
| Market Price $ | — | — | — | — | 38.54 | 42.93 | 37.17 | 53.47 | 64.32 | 65.93 | |
| NAV Return% | — | — | — | — | 14.67* | 13.42 | -11.52 | 45.60 | 22.02 | 4.49 | |
| Market Price Return% | — | — | — | — | 14.61* | 13.62 | -11.92 | 45.96 | 22.11 | 4.36 | |
| Avg Premium/Discount% | — | — | — | — | -0.05 | 0.02 | -0.30 | -0.14 | -0.00 | -0.13 | |
| NAV Rtrn% +/-S&P 500 | — | — | — | — | 14.67 | 25.30 | 10.57 | 16.93 | 11.15 | -0.42 | |
| NAV Rtrn% +/-Russ 2000 VL | — | — | — | — | 14.67 | -0.60 | -0.09 | -0.43 | -0.23 | -0.22 | |
| NAV Return% Rank in Cat | — | — | — | — | — | 3 | 3 | 3 | 3 | 5 | |
| Income Return % | — | — | — | — | 0.00 | 2.05 | 1.65 | 1.16 | 1.66 | 1.81 | |
| Capital Return % | — | — | — | — | — | 11.37 | -13.17 | 44.44 | 20.36 | 2.68 | |
| Income $ | — | — | — | — | 0.29 | 0.79 | 0.70 | 0.43 | 0.88 | 1.16 | |
| Capital Gains $ | — | — | — | — | 0.01 | 0.00 | 0.00 | 0.23 | 0.00 | 0.00 | |
| Expense Ratio % | — | — | — | — | — | 0.25 | 0.25 | 0.25 | 0.25 | 0.25 | |
| Income Ratio % | — | — | — | — | — | 2.40 | 2.07 | 1.85 | 1.64 | 1.84 | |
| Turnover Rate % | — | — | — | — | — | 9 | 26 | 45 | 16 | 23 | |
| Net Assets $mil | — | — | — | — | — | 790 | 1,607 | 2,908 | 3,014 | | |

## Performance

### Historic Quarterly NAV Returns

| | 1st Qtr | 2nd Qtr | 3rd Qtr | 4th Qtr | Total |
|------|---------|---------|---------|---------|-------|
| 2001 | 0.94 | 11.56 | -13.43 | 16.34 | 13.42 |
| 2002 | 9.51 | -2.20 | -21.22 | 4.86 | -11.52 |
| 2003 | -5.13 | 22.62 | 7.64 | 16.28 | 45.60 |
| 2004 | 6.85 | 0.85 | 0.11 | 13.11 | 22.02 |
| 2005 | -4.03 | 5.01 | 3.05 | 0.62 | 4.49 |

| Trailing | NAV Return% | Market Return% | NAV Rtrn% +/-S&P 500 | %Rank Cat.(NAV) |
|----------|-------------|----------------|----------------------|-----------------|
| 3 Mo | 0.62 | 0.51 | -1.46 | 6 |
| 6 Mo | 3.68 | 3.49 | -2.08 | 6 |
| 1 Yr | 4.49 | 4.36 | -0.42 | 5 |
| 3 Yr Avg | 22.90 | 22.98 | 8.52 | 3 |
| 5 Yr Avg | 13.25 | 13.23 | 12.71 | 3 |
| 10 Yr Avg | — | — | — | 0 |

| Tax Analysis | Tax-Adj Return% | Tax-Cost Ratio |
|--------------|-----------------|----------------|
| 3 Yr (estimated) | 22.31 | 0.48 |
| 5 Yr (estimated) | 12.60 | 0.57 |
| 10 Yr (estimated) | — | — |

## Risk Profile

| | Standard Index S&P 500 | Best Fit Index Russ 2000 VL |
|---|---|---|
| Alpha | 3.2 | -0.2 |
| Beta | 1.39 | 1.00 |
| R-Squared | 79 | 100 |
| Standard Deviation | 14.26 | |
| Mean | 22.90 | |
| Sharpe Ratio | 1.39 | |

## Morningstar Fair Value

| Price/Fair Value Ratio | Fair Value Estimate ($) | Hit Rate % |
|---|---|---|
| — | — | — |

## Portfolio Analysis 12-31-05

| Share change since 11-05 Total Stocks:1320 | Sector | PE | Tot Ret% | % Assets |
|---|---|---|---|---|
| ⊕ Cimarex Energy | Energy | 11.5 | 13.48 | 0.58 |
| ⊕ Vertex Pharmaceuticals | Health | — | 161.78 | 0.44 |
| ⊕ Sierra Pacific Resources | Utilities | 27.8 | 24.19 | 0.40 |
| ⊕ Commercial Metals | Ind Mtrls | 8.1 | 49.76 | 0.38 |
| ⊕ Shaw Group | Ind Mtrls | NMF | 62.97 | 0.38 |
| ⊕ La Quinta | Financial | — | 22.55 | 0.38 |
| ⊕ Flowserve | Ind Mtrls | — | 43.65 | 0.37 |
| ⊕ Briggs & Stratton | Ind Mtrls | 16.4 | -4.67 | 0.33 |
| ⊕ Level 3 Communications | Telecom | — | -15.34 | 0.33 |
| ⊕ Hughes Supply | Business | 17.2 | 12.06 | 0.33 |
| ⊕ Kennametal | Ind Mtrls | 15.8 | 4.08 | 0.32 |
| ⊕ Colonial Properties Trus | Financial | — | 14.28 | 0.31 |
| ⊕ Prentiss Properties Trus | Financial | — | — | 0.31 |
| ⊕ Crane | Ind Mtrls | 14.4 | 24.21 | 0.31 |
| ⊕ Trinity Industries | Ind Mtrls | 39.4 | 30.35 | 0.30 |
| ⊕ Corn Products Internatio | Goods | 22.8 | -9.70 | 0.30 |
| ⊕ Ohio Casualty | Financial | 10.0 | 22.87 | 0.30 |
| ⊕ Nicor | Utilities | 14.3 | 11.50 | 0.29 |
| ⊕ Carpenter Technology | Ind Mtrls | 11.5 | 21.62 | 0.29 |
| ⊕ BancorpSouth | Financial | 16.5 | -6.31 | 0.29 |

### Current Investment Style

Value Blnd Growth — Large Mid Small

| Market Cap | % |
|---|---|
| Giant | 0.0 |
| Large | 0.0 |
| Mid | 17.7 |
| Small | 67.2 |
| Micro | 15.1 |

Avg $mil: 902

| Value Measures | | Rel Category |
|---|---|---|
| Price/Earnings | 15.52 | 1.05 |
| Price/Book | 1.56 | 0.89 |
| Price/Sales | 0.83 | 1.02 |
| Price/Cash Flow | 6.48 | 0.98 |
| Dividend Yield % | 1.65 | 0.86 |

| Growth Measures | % | Rel Category |
|---|---|---|
| Long-Term Erngs | 10.73 | 1.01 |
| Book Value | 4.45 | 0.80 |
| Sales | 5.32 | 1.17 |
| Cash Flow | -3.32 | NMF |
| Historical Erngs | 6.86 | 0.69 |

| Profitability | % | Rel Category |
|---|---|---|
| Return on Equity | 8.44 | 0.73 |
| Return on Assets | 5.18 | 0.74 |
| Net Margin | 9.61 | 0.92 |

### Sector Weightings

| | % of Stocks | Rel S&P 500 | 3 Year High | Low |
|---|---|---|---|---|
| ↻ Info | 13.44 | 0.67 | | |
| 🔲 Software | 1.86 | 0.52 | 2 | 1 |
| 💻 Hardware | 7.60 | 0.76 | 8 | 4 |
| 🎙 Media | 1.69 | 0.47 | 2 | 1 |
| 📶 Telecom | 2.29 | 0.76 | 2 | 1 |
| Ⅾ Service | 54.35 | 1.17 | | |
| 🏥 Health | 4.54 | 0.34 | 8 | 4 |
| 🛒 Consumer | 8.70 | 1.07 | 11 | 8 |
| 📋 Business | 7.56 | 1.95 | 10 | 7 |
| 💲 Financial | 33.55 | 1.59 | 35 | 29 |
| ⊑ Mfg | 32.23 | 0.96 | | |
| 🏭 Goods | 5.32 | 0.62 | 6 | 5 |
| ⚙ Ind Mtrls | 17.57 | 1.45 | 19 | 16 |
| 🔋 Energy | 4.64 | 0.50 | 7 | 4 |
| 💡 Utilities | 4.70 | 1.40 | 7 | 5 |

### Composition

| | |
|---|---|
| ● Cash | 0.2 |
| ● Stocks | 99.7 |
| ● Bonds | 0.0 |
| Other | 0.1 |
| Foreign | 0.1 |
| (% of Stock) | |

## Morningstar's Take by Dan Culloton

This exchange-traded fund is adequate.

IShares Russell 2000 Value Index is a cheap option for investors tired of battling bloat. Good, actively managed small-cap value funds can be hard to find. Many of the best ones close early to control asset growth, while those that remain open risk getting too big to sustain their performance. Asset growth is less of a concern with this exchange-traded fund, because it's an index fund.

The fund has competition, though. Its 0.25% levy is a fraction of the typical small-value fund's cost. That gives a head start to long-term investors who don't plan to rack up commission costs by trading. But the exchange-traded and traditional share classes of Vanguard Small Cap Value Index are cheaper than this one.

The ETF also spreads its assets across all major sectors and owns more individual stocks than any other small-value index fund, but keeps about one third of its assets in financial stocks. The typical small-value offering puts about a fifth of its money in that sector. That could hurt the ETF's returns when financial stocks suffer. Furthermore, the fund's index is often targeted by speculators who try to take advantage of its annual reconstitution, bidding up additions and selling off deletions.

The fund has beaten the average small-value fund, so far. Its 14.4% annualized gain for the five years ending Oct. 31, 2005 edges the category's 14.2% advance. That time period has been favorable for small-value stocks, though, and the fund's results may not look as good when the market favors another style.

The movements of this ETF's benchmark correlate closely with the average small-value fund. If it does a good job tracking the bogy, its low turnover and expenses give it a shot at achieving above-average results over the long term. Success is not a sure thing, though and there are cheaper options, so this fund isn't an obvious choice.

| Address: | 45 Fremont Street San Francisco CA 94105 800-474-2737 | Management Fee: | 0.25% |
|---|---|---|---|
| | | Expense Projections: | 3Yr:$80  5Yr:$141  10Yr:$318 |
| | | Income Distrib: | Quarterly |
| Web Address: | www.ishares.com | Exchange: | AMEX |
| Inception: | 07-24-00* | | |
| Advisor: | Barclays Global Fund Advisers | | |

**M⊙RNINGSTAR® ETFs 100**

# iShares R3000 Growth

| | Ticker | NAV | Market Price | 52 wk High/Low | Yield | Mstar Category |
|---|---|---|---|---|---|---|
| | IWZ | $41.48 | $43.00 | $43.00 - $36.75 | 0.8% | Large Growth |

## Management

### Portfolio Manager(s)

Barclays Global Fund Advisors is the advisor. The firm is the world's largest manager of indexed portfolios. Patrick O'Connor, the head of Barclay's U.S. iShares portfolio management group leads a team of a half dozen managers in running this and about 60 other ETFs. iShares' domestic portfolio-management group is responsible for about $75 billion in assets. Most of the managers have at least five years of experience with Barclays as well as prior industry experience.

### Strategy

This exchange-traded fund tracks the Russell 3000 Growth Index, which is a subset of the Russell 3000 Index. As such, the portfolio spans hundreds of individual names and the full panoply of industries. This fund and its bogy focus on stocks in the all-market Russell 3000 that have higher book values and forecast earnings growth. The fund's bogy rebalances once a year in May.

Growth of $10,000
— Investment Value of ETF
— Investment Value of Index S&P 500

| 1996 | 1997 | 1998 | 1999 | 2000 | 2001 | 2002 | 2003 | 2004 | 2005 | History |
|---|---|---|---|---|---|---|---|---|---|---|
| — | — | — | — | 51.23 | 40.85 | 29.14 | 37.79 | 39.88 | 41.48 | NAV $ |
| — | — | — | — | 51.78 | 40.89 | 29.22 | 37.80 | 39.80 | 41.45 | Market Price $ |
| — | — | — | — | -8.20* | -19.96 | -28.15 | 30.66 | 6.65 | 4.92 | NAV Return% |
| — | — | — | — | -8.21* | -20.73 | -28.02 | 30.34 | 6.41 | 5.06 | Market Price Return% |
| — | — | — | — | 0.10 | 0.14 | 0.25 | 0.21 | 0.01 | -0.00 | Avg Premium/Discount% |
| — | — | — | — | -8.20 | -8.08 | -6.06 | 1.99 | -4.22 | 0.01 | NAV Rtrn% +/-S&P 500 |
| — | — | — | — | -8.20 | 0.46 | -0.27 | 0.91 | 0.35 | -0.34 | NAV Rtrn% +/-Russ 1000Gr |
| — | — | — | — | — | 5 | 5 | 5 | 6 | 9 | NAV Return% Rank in Cat |
| — | — | — | — | 0.00 | 0.29 | 0.58 | 0.86 | 1.08 | 0.87 | Income Return % |
| — | — | — | — | — | -20.25 | -28.73 | 29.80 | 5.57 | 4.05 | Capital Return % |
| — | — | — | — | 0.03 | 0.15 | 0.24 | 0.25 | 0.41 | 0.35 | Income $ |
| — | — | — | — | 0.00 | 0.00 | 0.00 | 0.00 | 0.00 | 0.00 | Capital Gains $ |
| — | — | — | — | — | 0.25 | 0.25 | 0.25 | 0.25 | 0.25 | Expense Ratio % |
| — | — | — | — | — | 0.20 | 0.47 | 0.83 | 0.78 | 1.12 | Income Ratio % |
| — | — | — | — | — | 3 | 18 | 15 | 11 | 16 | Turnover Rate % |
| — | — | — | — | — | 58 | 128 | 132 | 214 | Net Assets $mil |

## Performance

### Historic Quarterly NAV Returns

| | 1st Qtr | 2nd Qtr | 3rd Qtr | 4th Qtr | Total |
|---|---|---|---|---|---|
| 2001 | -20.49 | 9.03 | -20.04 | 15.47 | -19.96 |
| 2002 | -2.60 | -18.49 | -15.53 | 7.13 | -28.15 |
| 2003 | -1.33 | 14.86 | 4.33 | 10.50 | 30.66 |
| 2004 | 1.07 | 1.74 | -5.36 | 9.58 | 6.65 |
| 2005 | -4.37 | 2.47 | 4.16 | 2.79 | 4.92 |

| Trailing | NAV Return% | Market Return% | NAV Rtrn% +/-S&P 500 | %Rank Cat.(NAV) |
|---|---|---|---|---|
| 3 Mo | 2.79 | 2.92 | 0.71 | 10 |
| 6 Mo | 7.07 | 6.93 | 1.31 | 10 |
| 1 Yr | 4.92 | 5.06 | 0.01 | 9 |
| 3 Yr Avg | 13.50 | 13.37 | -0.88 | 5 |
| 5 Yr Avg | -3.41 | -3.63 | -3.95 | 5 |
| 10 Yr Avg | — | — | — | 0 |

| Tax Analysis | Tax-Adj Return% | Tax-Cost Ratio |
|---|---|---|
| 3 Yr (estimated) | 13.15 | 0.31 |
| 5 Yr (estimated) | -3.67 | 0.27 |
| 10 Yr (estimated) | — | — |

## Risk Profile

| | Standard Index S&P 500 | Best Fit Index Russ 1000Gr |
|---|---|---|
| Alpha | -1.3 | -0.2 |
| Beta | 1.05 | 1.04 |
| R-Squared | 91 | 100 |
| Standard Deviation | 10.08 | |
| Mean | 13.50 | |
| Sharpe Ratio | 1.12 | |

## Morningstar Fair Value

| Price/Fair Value Ratio | Fair Value Estimate ($) | Hit Rate % |
|---|---|---|
| 1.0 Fairly valued | 38.02 | 90 Good |

## Portfolio Analysis 12-31-05

| Share change since 11-05 Total Stocks:2007 | Sector | PE | Tot Ret% | % Assets |
|---|---|---|---|---|
| ⊕ General Electric | Ind Mtrls | 19.9 | -1.43 | 4.01 |
| ⊕ Microsoft | Software | 22.2 | -0.95 | 3.45 |
| ⊕ Procter & Gamble | Goods | 21.2 | 7.18 | 2.77 |
| ⊕ Johnson & Johnson | Health | 19.1 | -3.36 | 2.54 |
| ⊕ Intel | Hardware | 18.6 | 8.12 | 2.19 |
| ⊕ Wal-Mart Stores | Consumer | 18.2 | -10.30 | 1.68 |
| ⊕ IBM | Hardware | 16.0 | -15.83 | 1.60 |
| ⊕ Cisco Systems | Hardware | 19.9 | -11.39 | 1.57 |
| ⊕ PepsiCo | Goods | 25.8 | 15.24 | 1.41 |
| ⊕ Amgen | Health | 28.3 | 22.93 | 1.39 |
| ⊕ Home Depot | Consumer | 15.6 | -4.35 | 1.24 |
| ⊕ UnitedHealth Group | Health | 26.2 | 41.22 | 1.20 |
| ⊕ Dell | Hardware | 23.2 | -28.93 | 1.05 |
| ⊕ Qualcomm | Hardware | 34.2 | 2.50 | 1.00 |
| ⊕ Medtronic | Health | 37.4 | 16.72 | 0.99 |
| ⊕ Google | Business | — | 115.19 | 0.97 |
| ⊕ Altria Group | Goods | 15.0 | 27.72 | 0.89 |
| ⊕ 3M Company | Ind Mtrls | 19.2 | -3.51 | 0.85 |
| ⊕ Apple Computer | Hardware | 46.1 | 123.26 | 0.84 |
| ⊕ Boeing | Ind Mtrls | 24.8 | 37.92 | 0.83 |

### Current Investment Style

Value Blnd Growth — Large Mid Small

| Market Cap | % |
|---|---|
| Giant | 45.5 |
| Large | 29.0 |
| Mid | 18.6 |
| Small | 5.6 |
| Micro | 1.3 |

Avg $mil: 26,209

| Value Measures | | Rel Category |
|---|---|---|
| Price/Earnings | 20.29 | 0.96 |
| Price/Book | 3.66 | 1.09 |
| Price/Sales | 1.79 | 0.92 |
| Price/Cash Flow | 11.15 | 1.06 |
| Dividend Yield % | 1.06 | 1.19 |

| Growth Measures | % | Rel Category |
|---|---|---|
| Long-Term Erngs | 13.59 | 0.96 |
| Book Value | 9.41 | 1.15 |
| Sales | 11.56 | 1.04 |
| Cash Flow | 14.26 | 0.87 |
| Historical Erngs | 17.89 | 0.93 |

| Profitability | % | Rel Category |
|---|---|---|
| Return on Equity | 21.90 | 1.09 |
| Return on Assets | 10.47 | 0.97 |
| Net Margin | 12.95 | 0.93 |

| Sector Weightings | % of Stocks | Rel S&P 500 | 3 Year High | Low |
|---|---|---|---|---|
| ⓘ Info | 26.04 | 1.29 | | |
| Software | 6.57 | 1.85 | 8 | 7 |
| Hardware | 15.53 | 1.55 | 18 | 13 |
| Media | 3.18 | 0.89 | 3 | 2 |
| Telecom | 0.76 | 0.25 | 1 | 1 |
| ⓒ Service | 46.76 | 1.01 | | |
| Health | 19.41 | 1.46 | 27 | 19 |
| Consumer | 13.32 | 1.64 | 14 | 12 |
| Business | 7.43 | 1.92 | 7 | 5 |
| Financial | 6.60 | 0.31 | 10 | 6 |
| ⓜ Mfg | 27.20 | 0.81 | | |
| Goods | 9.60 | 1.12 | 11 | 9 |
| Ind Mtrls | 13.17 | 1.08 | 13 | 7 |
| Energy | 3.93 | 0.42 | 4 | 1 |
| Utilities | 0.50 | 0.15 | 1 | 0 |

### Composition

| | | |
|---|---|---|
| ● Cash | 0.1 | |
| ● Stocks | 99.9 | |
| ● Bonds | 0.0 | |
| Other | 0.0 | |
| Foreign | 0.0 | |
| (% of Stock) | | |

## Morningstar's Take by Dan Culloton

IShares Russell 3000 Growth Index's expansive appetite won't always help it.

This exchange-traded fund tracks the stocks in the all-market Russell 3000 Index that have higher book values and forecast growth. Because this fund's bogy, the Russell 3000 Growth Index, is market-cap weighted the top holdings of the portfolio look a lot like those of its sibling, the iShares Russell 1000 Growth Index, which draws growth stocks from the largest 1,000 stocks in the market. However, this ETF owns more mid-and small-cap stocks because its benchmark is a subset of the entire stock market, rather than the biggest 1,000 firms.

The difference can matter. The extra diversification has made this fund less volatile, as measured by standard deviation, than many of its index fund and ETF peers. This ETF also has bested Russell 1000 Growth over the five year period ending Oct. 31, 2005 as small-cap stocks have performed better than larger ones. Offerings that

focus more on bigger stocks could turn the tables on this ETF, though, when small-cap momentum begins to flag and large-cap shares take their turn. So, investors who expect this relative performance to continue could be in for a surprise.

Other factors keep this fund from being a clear winner. Its bogy has been susceptible to speculators who try to front run the Russell indexes' annual reconstitution, bidding up additions and selling off deletions to the bogies. Also there is a lot of competition. This fund's 0.25% expense ratio is low, but not the lowest available among large-growth ETFs. The exchange-traded and traditional share classes of Vanguard Growth Index are cheaper, for instance.

None of these caveats is a killer. The ETF is still an affordable, broadly diversified offering that has correlated well with the average large-growth fund. Its low expenses give it a fighting chance of putting up competitive long-term results, but other options may have better odds.

| | | | | |
|---|---|---|---|---|
| Address: | 45 Fremont Street San Francisco CA 94105 800-474-2737 | Management Fee: | 0.25% | |
| | | Expense Projections: | 3Yr:$80 | 5Yr:$141 10Yr:$318 |
| Web Address: | www.ishares.com | Income Distrib: | Quarterly | |
| Inception: | 07-24-00* | Exchange: | AMEX | |
| Advisor: | Barclays Global Fund Advisers | | | |

MORNINGSTAR® ETFs 100

# iShares R3000 Index

| | Ticker | NAV | Market Price | 52 wk High/Low | Yield | Mstar Category |
|---|---|---|---|---|---|---|
| | IWV | $72.01 | $74.55 | $74.55 - $64.83 | 1.8% | Large Blend |

## Management

### Portfolio Manager(s)

Barclays Global Fund Advisors is the advisor. The firm is the world's largest manager of indexed portfolios. Patrick O'Connor, the head of Barclay's U.S. shares portfolio management group leads a team of a half dozen managers in running this and about 60 other ETFs. IShares' domestic portfolio-management group is responsible for about $75 billion in assets. Most of the managers have at least five years of experience with Barclays as well as prior industry experience.

### Strategy

This index offering mirrors the Russell 3000 Index, which is made up of the 3,000 largest U.S.-based companies. Thus, its huge portfolio holds a broadly diversified mix of large-, mid-, and small-cap names. The index reconstitutes just once a year, at the end of each May.

**Growth of $10,000**
— Investment Value of ETF
— Investment Value of Index S&P 500

| | 1996 | 1997 | 1998 | 1999 | 2000 | 2001 | 2002 | 2003 | 2004 | 2005 | History |
|---|---|---|---|---|---|---|---|---|---|---|---|
| | — | — | — | — | 72.65 | 63.45 | 48.93 | 62.98 | 69.21 | 72.01 | NAV $ |
| | — | — | — | — | 72.44 | 63.50 | 48.96 | 62.96 | 69.15 | 72.02 | Market Price $ |
| | — | — | — | — | 0.44* | -11.78 | -21.63 | 30.77 | 11.76 | 5.97 | NAV Return% |
| | — | — | — | — | 0.44* | -11.46 | -21.64 | 30.65 | 11.70 | 6.08 | Market Price Return% |
| | — | — | — | — | 0.16 | 0.10 | -0.19 | 0.02 | -0.01 | 0.02 | Avg Premium/Discount% |
| | — | — | — | — | 0.44 | 0.10 | 0.46 | 2.10 | 0.89 | 1.06 | NAV Rtrn% +/-S&P 500 |
| | — | — | — | — | 0.44 | 0.67 | 0.02 | 0.88 | 0.36 | -0.30 | NAV Rtrn% +/-Russ 1000 |
| | — | — | — | — | — | 13 | 15 | 15 | 17 | 23 | NAV Return% Rank in Cat |
| | — | — | — | — | 0.00 | 0.88 | 1.36 | 1.81 | 1.77 | 1.86 | Income Return % |
| | — | — | — | — | 0.00 | -12.66 | -22.99 | 28.96 | 9.99 | 4.11 | Capital Return % |
| | — | — | — | — | 0.34 | 0.64 | 0.86 | 0.88 | 1.11 | 1.28 | Income $ |
| | — | — | — | — | 0.01 | 0.00 | 0.00 | 0.00 | 0.00 | 0.00 | Capital Gains $ |
| | — | — | — | — | — | 0.20 | 0.20 | 0.20 | 0.20 | 0.20 | Expense Ratio % |
| | — | — | — | — | — | 1.09 | 1.20 | 1.53 | 1.54 | 1.81 | Income Ratio % |
| | — | — | — | — | — | 3 | 6 | 5 | 4 | 5 | Turnover Rate % |
| | — | — | — | — | — | — | 1,236 | 1,316 | 1,754 | 1,955 | Net Assets $mil |

## Performance

### Historic Quarterly NAV Returns

| | 1st Qtr | 2nd Qtr | 3rd Qtr | 4th Qtr | Total |
|---|---|---|---|---|---|
| 2001 | -12.15 | 6.81 | -15.63 | 11.44 | -11.78 |
| 2002 | 0.92 | -13.09 | -17.22 | 7.94 | -21.63 |
| 2003 | -3.08 | 16.16 | 3.37 | 12.36 | 30.77 |
| 2004 | 2.17 | 1.30 | -1.92 | 10.09 | 11.76 |
| 2005 | -2.23 | 2.22 | 3.96 | 1.99 | 5.97 |

| Trailing | NAV Return% | Market Return% | NAV Rtrn% +/-S&P 500 | %Rank Cat.(NAV) |
|---|---|---|---|---|
| 3 Mo | 1.99 | 1.81 | -0.09 | 27 |
| 6 Mo | 6.03 | 6.16 | 0.27 | 27 |
| 1 Yr | 5.97 | 6.08 | 1.06 | 23 |
| 3 Yr Avg | 15.70 | 15.68 | 1.32 | 14 |
| 5 Yr Avg | 1.38 | 1.44 | 0.84 | 13 |
| 10 Yr Avg | — | — | — | 0 |

| Tax Analysis | Tax-Adj Return% | Tax-Cost Ratio |
|---|---|---|
| 3 Yr (estimated) | 15.01 | 0.60 |
| 5 Yr (estimated) | 0.81 | 0.56 |
| 10 Yr (estimated) | — | — |

## Risk Profile

| | Standard Index S&P 500 | Best Fit Index Russ 1000 |
|---|---|---|
| Alpha | 0.7 | -0.2 |
| Beta | 1.04 | 1.03 |
| R-Squared | 99 | 100 |
| Standard Deviation | 9.60 | |
| Mean | 15.70 | |
| Sharpe Ratio | 1.37 | |

## Morningstar Fair Value

| Price/Fair Value Ratio | Fair Value Estimate ($) | Hit Rate % |
|---|---|---|
| 1.0 Fairly valued | 36.78 | 90 Good |

## Portfolio Analysis 12-31-05

| Share change since 11-05 Total Stocks:2990 | Sector | PE | Tot Ret% | % Assets |
|---|---|---|---|---|
| ⊖ General Electric | Ind Mtrls | 19.9 | -1.43 | 2.68 |
| ⊖ ExxonMobil | Energy | 10.6 | 11.76 | 2.58 |
| ⊖ Citigroup | Financial | 12.1 | 4.63 | 1.82 |
| ⊖ Microsoft | Software | 22.2 | -0.95 | 1.75 |
| ⊖ Procter & Gamble | Goods | 21.2 | 7.18 | 1.41 |
| ⊖ Bank of America | Financial | 11.1 | 2.39 | 1.34 |
| ⊖ Johnson & Johnson | Health | 19.1 | -3.36 | 1.29 |
| ⊖ Pfizer | Health | 21.2 | -10.62 | 1.25 |
| ⊖ American International G | Financial | 15.6 | 4.83 | 1.13 |
| ⊖ Altria Group | Goods | 15.0 | 27.72 | 1.12 |
| ⊖ Intel | Hardware | 18.6 | 8.12 | 1.11 |
| ⊖ J.P. Morgan Chase & Co. | Financial | 18.8 | 5.74 | 1.01 |
| ⊖ IBM | Hardware | 16.0 | -15.83 | 0.96 |
| ⊖ Chevron | Energy | 9.0 | 11.51 | 0.93 |
| ⊖ Wal-Mart Stores | Consumer | 18.2 | -10.30 | 0.85 |
| ⊖ Cisco Systems | Hardware | 19.9 | -11.39 | 0.80 |
| ⊖ Wells Fargo | Financial | 14.3 | 4.47 | 0.76 |
| ⊖ PepsiCo | Goods | 25.8 | 15.24 | 0.71 |
| ⊖ Amgen | Health | 28.3 | 22.93 | 0.70 |
| ⊖ AT&T | Telecom | 21.1 | 0.25 | 0.69 |

### Current Investment Style

Value Blnd Growth — Large Mid Small

| Market Cap | % |
|---|---|
| Giant | 43.4 |
| Large | 30.6 |
| Mid | 18.9 |
| Small | 5.9 |
| Micro | 1.3 |

Avg $mil: 25,793

| Value Measures | | Rel Category |
|---|---|---|
| Price/Earnings | 16.40 | 0.97 |
| Price/Book | 2.46 | 0.91 |
| Price/Sales | 1.42 | 1.11 |
| Price/Cash Flow | 6.35 | 0.88 |
| Dividend Yield % | 1.76 | 0.99 |

| Growth Measures | % | Rel Category |
|---|---|---|
| Long-Term Erngs | 10.79 | 0.97 |
| Book Value | 9.91 | 1.05 |
| Sales | 8.77 | 1.09 |
| Cash Flow | 11.42 | 1.11 |
| Historical Erngs | 14.95 | 1.06 |

| Profitability | % | Rel Category |
|---|---|---|
| Return on Equity | 18.42 | 0.90 |
| Return on Assets | 9.79 | 1.05 |
| Net Margin | 13.02 | 1.19 |

| Sector Weightings | % of Stocks | Rel S&P 500 | 3 Year High | Low |
|---|---|---|---|---|
| ↻ Info | 20.02 | 0.99 | | |
| Software | 3.67 | 1.03 | 4 | 4 |
| Hardware | 9.69 | 0.97 | 12 | 9 |
| Media | 3.69 | 1.03 | 4 | 4 |
| Telecom | 2.97 | 0.99 | 4 | 3 |
| ☞ Service | 48.72 | 1.05 | | |
| Health | 13.21 | 0.99 | 16 | 13 |
| Consumer | 8.73 | 1.07 | 9 | 8 |
| Business | 5.36 | 1.39 | 5 | 4 |
| Financial | 21.42 | 1.02 | 22 | 20 |
| Mfg | 31.25 | 0.94 | | |
| Goods | 7.81 | 0.91 | 9 | 8 |
| Ind Mtrls | 11.55 | 0.95 | 12 | 10 |
| Energy | 8.43 | 0.90 | 9 | 5 |
| Utilities | 3.46 | 1.03 | 4 | 3 |

### Composition

| | | |
|---|---|---|
| ● Cash | 0.2 | |
| ● Stocks | 99.8 | |
| ● Bonds | 0.0 | |
| ● Other | 0.0 | |
| Foreign | 0.1 | |
| (% of Stock) | | |

## Morningstar's Take by Dan Culloton

This is a fine core fund, but maybe not the finest.

IShares Russell 3000 Index is diversified. It tracks the Russell 3000 Index, which includes the stocks of the biggest 3,000 companies in the U.S. and represents 98% of the domestic equity market. The fund's 0.20% expense ratio is lower than the average traditional large blend mutual fund, including offerings that track the same bogy. Furthermore, because investors buy and sell this exchange-traded fund among themselves, rather than with the fund company, it offers tax efficiency and protection from the effects other investors' trading.

There are distinctions between this fund and other all-stock-market options, though. First it excludes some of the smaller, less liquid stocks in the U.S. market, so its average market capitalization is a bit higher than that of funds that track benchmarks that own more small caps. That could cause this fund to lag behind those offerings when small cap stocks rally, as they have in recent years. That and other characteristics (the Russell 3000 Index omits stocks incorporated outside of U.S., such as Tyco and Carnival) have caused this fund to trail funds like Vanguard Total Stock Market Index on an annualized basis over the trailing five-year period ending Nov. 14, 2005. Another drawback is the Russell indexes have been vulnerable to speculators who try to front run the benchmarks' annual reconstitution, which can increase transaction costs for funds tracking the bogies.

Those differences may be small in a fund this diversified over the long run, though. Indeed, the real reason to choose another offering over this one is costs. You can get similar exposure for the same expense ratio and no broker's commission from Vanguard Total Stock Market Index, which also offers ETF shares.

There's nothing wrong with using this fund for the stock portion of a simple portfolio, but there are offerings that are more right.

| Address: | 45 Fremont Street San Francisco CA 94105 800-474-2737 | Management Fee: | 0.20% |
|---|---|---|---|
| | | Expense Projections: | 3Yr:$64  5Yr:$113  10Yr:$255 |
| Web Address: | www.ishares.com | Income Distrib: | Quarterly |
| Inception: | 05-22-00* | Exchange: | AMEX |
| Advisor: | Barclays Global Fund Advisers | | |

M⊙RNINGSTAR® ETFs 100

# iShares R3000 Value

| | Ticker | NAV | Market Price | 52 wk High/Low | Yield | Mstar Category |
|---|---|---|---|---|---|---|
| | IWW | $90.21 | $93.46 | $93.46 - $82.58 | 2.3% | Large Value |

## Management

### Portfolio Manager(s)

Barclays Global Fund Advisors is the advisor. The firm is the world's largest manager of indexed portfolios. Patrick O'Connor, the head of Barclay's U.S. iShares portfolio management group leads a team of a half dozen managers in running this and about 60 other ETFs. iShares' domestic portfolio-management group is responsible for about $75 billion in assets. Most of the managers have at least five years of experience with Barclays as well as prior industry experience.

### Strategy

This ETF tracks the Russell 3000 Value Index, which is a subset of the Russell 3000 Index of the broad stock market. The index measures the performance of Russell 3000 companies whose shares have below-average price/book ratios and forecasted growth according the I/B/E/S. Russell uses a purely quantitative method to construct the index. It holds about half the stocks in the Russell 3000. The index reconstitutes just once a year, at the end of May, and rebalances in June.

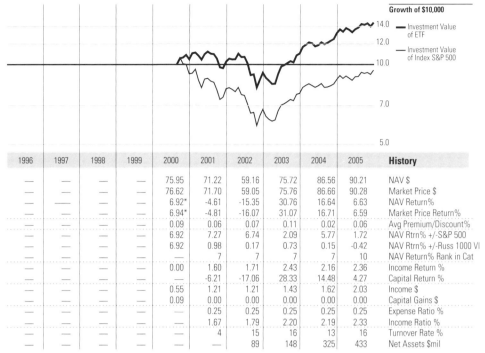

Growth of $10,000
— Investment Value of ETF
— Investment Value of Index S&P 500

| 1996 | 1997 | 1998 | 1999 | 2000 | 2001 | 2002 | 2003 | 2004 | 2005 | History |
|---|---|---|---|---|---|---|---|---|---|---|
| — | — | — | — | 75.95 | 71.22 | 59.16 | 75.72 | 86.56 | 90.21 | NAV $ |
| — | — | — | — | 76.62 | 71.70 | 59.05 | 75.76 | 86.66 | 90.28 | Market Price $ |
| — | — | — | — | 6.92* | -4.61 | -15.35 | 30.76 | 16.64 | 6.63 | NAV Return% |
| — | — | — | — | 6.94* | -4.81 | -16.07 | 31.07 | 16.71 | 6.59 | Market Price Return% |
| — | — | — | — | 0.09 | 0.06 | 0.07 | 0.11 | 0.02 | 0.06 | Avg Premium/Discount% |
| — | — | — | — | 6.92 | 7.27 | 6.74 | 2.09 | 5.77 | 1.72 | NAV Rtrn% +/-S&P 500 |
| — | — | — | — | 6.92 | 0.98 | 0.17 | 0.73 | 0.15 | -0.42 | NAV Rtrn% +/-Russ 1000 Vl |
| — | — | — | — | | 7 | 7 | 7 | 7 | 10 | NAV Return% Rank in Cat |
| — | — | — | — | 0.00 | 1.60 | 1.71 | 2.43 | 2.16 | 2.36 | Income Return % |
| — | — | — | — | | -6.21 | -17.06 | 28.33 | 14.48 | 4.27 | Capital Return % |
| — | — | — | — | 0.55 | 1.21 | 1.21 | 1.43 | 1.62 | 2.03 | Income $ |
| — | — | — | — | 0.09 | 0.00 | 0.00 | 0.00 | 0.00 | 0.00 | Capital Gains $ |
| — | — | — | — | 0.25 | 0.25 | 0.25 | 0.25 | 0.25 | 0.25 | Expense Ratio % |
| — | — | — | — | 1.67 | 1.79 | 2.20 | 2.19 | 2.33 | | Income Ratio % |
| — | — | — | — | 4 | 15 | 16 | 13 | 16 | | Turnover Rate % |
| — | — | — | — | | 89 | 148 | 325 | 433 | | Net Assets $mil |

## Performance

### Historic Quarterly NAV Returns

| | 1st Qtr | 2nd Qtr | 3rd Qtr | 4th Qtr | Total |
|---|---|---|---|---|---|
| 2001 | -5.46 | 5.29 | -11.13 | 7.83 | -4.61 |
| 2002 | 4.41 | -8.07 | -18.93 | 8.79 | -15.35 |
| 2003 | -4.94 | 17.54 | 2.43 | 14.25 | 30.76 |
| 2004 | 3.26 | 0.83 | 1.37 | 10.51 | 16.64 |
| 2005 | -0.31 | 1.89 | 3.78 | 1.15 | 6.63 |

| Trailing | NAV Return% | Market Return% | NAV Rtrn% +/-S&P 500 | %Rank Cat.(NAV) |
|---|---|---|---|---|
| 3 Mo | 1.15 | 1.22 | -0.93 | 13 |
| 6 Mo | 4.97 | 4.93 | -0.79 | 11 |
| 1 Yr | 6.63 | 6.59 | 1.72 | 10 |
| 3 Yr Avg | 17.60 | 17.70 | 3.22 | 7 |
| 5 Yr Avg | 5.60 | 5.43 | 5.06 | 7 |
| 10 Yr Avg | — | — | — | 0 |

| Tax Analysis | Tax-Adj Return% | Tax-Cost Ratio |
|---|---|---|
| 3 Yr (estimated) | 16.72 | 0.75 |
| 5 Yr (estimated) | 4.83 | 0.73 |
| 10 Yr (estimated) | — | — |

## Risk Profile

| | Standard Index S&P 500 | Best Fit Index Russ 1000 Vl |
|---|---|---|
| Alpha | 2.4 | -0.2 |
| Beta | 1.04 | 1.02 |
| R-Squared | 94 | 100 |
| Standard Deviation | 9.82 | |
| Mean | 17.60 | |
| Sharpe Ratio | 1.51 | |

## Morningstar Fair Value

| Price/Fair Value Ratio | Fair Value Estimate ($) | Hit Rate % |
|---|---|---|
| 1.0 Fairly valued | 35.56 | 89 Good |

## Portfolio Analysis  12-31-05

| Share change since 11-05  Total Stocks:1966 | Sector | PE | Tot Ret% | % Assets |
|---|---|---|---|---|
| ⊖ ExxonMobil | Energy | 10.6 | 11.76 | 5.23 |
| ⊖ Citigroup | Financial | 12.1 | 4.63 | 3.70 |
| ⊖ Bank of America | Financial | 11.1 | 2.39 | 2.72 |
| ⊖ Pfizer | Health | 21.2 | -10.62 | 2.54 |
| ⊖ J.P. Morgan Chase & Co. | Financial | 18.8 | 5.74 | 2.04 |
| ⊖ Chevron | Energy | 9.0 | 11.51 | 1.88 |
| ⊖ American International G | Financial | 15.6 | 4.83 | 1.61 |
| ⊖ AT&T | Telecom | 21.1 | 0.25 | 1.41 |
| ⊖ Wells Fargo | Financial | 14.3 | 4.47 | 1.39 |
| ⊖ Altria Group | Goods | 15.0 | 27.72 | 1.35 |
| ⊖ General Electric | Ind Mtrls | 19.9 | -1.43 | 1.32 |
| ⊖ Verizon Communications | Telecom | 10.2 | -22.18 | 1.22 |
| ⊖ Wachovia | Financial | 13.0 | 4.29 | 1.22 |
| ⊖ Hewlett-Packard | Hardware | 27.3 | 38.29 | 1.21 |
| ⊖ ConocoPhillips | Energy | 6.7 | 36.89 | 1.19 |
| ⊖ Time Warner | Media | 30.6 | -9.83 | 1.11 |
| ⊖ Merrill Lynch & Company | Financial | 13.7 | 14.77 | 0.93 |
| ⊖ Morgan Stanley | Financial | 13.3 | 4.28 | 0.82 |
| ⊖ US Bancorp | Financial | 12.7 | -0.46 | 0.80 |
| ⊖ Merck | Health | 15.2 | 4.04 | 0.79 |

### Current Investment Style

Value Blnd Growth — Large Mid Small

| Market Cap | % |
|---|---|
| Giant | 41.3 |
| Large | 32.2 |
| Mid | 19.2 |
| Small | 6.1 |
| Micro | 1.3 |

Avg $mil: 25,322

| Value Measures | | Rel Category |
|---|---|---|
| Price/Earnings | 13.70 | 0.95 |
| Price/Book | 1.85 | 0.83 |
| Price/Sales | 1.17 | 0.89 |
| Price/Cash Flow | 4.22 | 0.82 |
| Dividend Yield % | 2.48 | 1.02 |

| Growth Measures | % | Rel Category |
|---|---|---|
| Long-Term Erngs | 8.86 | 0.93 |
| Book Value | 10.16 | 0.84 |
| Sales | 7.05 | 0.88 |
| Cash Flow | 9.25 | 0.75 |
| Historical Erngs | 13.20 | 0.80 |

| Profitability | % | Rel Category |
|---|---|---|
| Return on Equity | 14.81 | 0.80 |
| Return on Assets | 9.08 | 0.92 |
| Net Margin | 13.10 | 1.01 |

| Sector Weightings | % of Stocks | Rel S&P 500 | 3 Year High Low | |
|---|---|---|---|---|
| ☍ Info | 13.85 | 0.69 | | |
| ▣ Software | 0.68 | 0.19 | 1 | 0 |
| ⬚ Hardware | 3.69 | 0.37 | 6 | 3 |
| ⬤ Media | 4.23 | 1.18 | 6 | 4 |
| ▤ Telecom | 5.25 | 1.74 | 7 | 5 |
| ☞ Service | 50.75 | 1.09 | | |
| ▥ Health | 6.81 | 0.51 | 7 | 3 |
| ▧ Consumer | 4.00 | 0.49 | 5 | 4 |
| ▨ Business | 3.26 | 0.84 | 3 | 3 |
| $ Financial | 36.68 | 1.74 | 37 | 31 |
| ⊔ Mfg | 35.41 | 1.06 | | |
| ▩ Goods | 5.97 | 0.70 | 9 | 6 |
| ⚙ Ind Mtrls | 9.87 | 0.81 | 16 | 10 |
| ◈ Energy | 13.07 | 1.40 | 15 | 10 |
| ▪ Utilities | 6.50 | 1.93 | 7 | 6 |

### Composition

| | | |
|---|---|---|
| ● Cash | 0.1 | |
| ● Stocks | 99.9 | |
| ○ Bonds | 0.0 | |
| | Other | 0.0 |
| | Foreign | 0.1 |
| | (% of Stock) | |

## Morningstar's Take  by Dan Culloton

This ETF has a monopoly of sorts.

iShares Russell 3000 Value is the only exchange-traded or traditional mutual fund tracking the Russell 3000 Value Index. That benchmark gauges the performance of all of the value stocks in the Russell 3000 Index, which includes 98% of total domestic-equity market capitalization. Essentially this is the only fund that gives you exposure to all the value stocks (as defined by Russell) in the U.S. market in one fell swoop.

The fund has other unique traits. Since the ETF's index draws its holdings from the broad market, it has a lower average market capitalization and keeps less money tied up in its top 10 holdings than its typical competitor. So while all of the usual large-value portfolio subjects show up here, the ETF is more diversified, with more than one fourth of its assets in small and mid-caps.

The fund's breadth has kept volatility, as measured by standard deviation, below average. It also has given the fund an edge over many of its

peers in the last five years.

Don't expect that performance to last, though. One style of investing never rules the roost indefinitely, and value has been on top for a long time. And there are other aspects of this fund that may cause it to behave differently than other large-value offerings. For example, it doesn't include the shares of foreign-based companies, even if they list their stock on U.S. exchanges and conduct most of their business here.

Further, the fund's index uses two factors (price/book value and forecasted earnings growth) to define a stock's style. Many other value indexes, not to mention active managers, use several other factors to evaluate equities. Finally, the fund's expense ratio isn't the most costly in its peer group, but it isn't the cheapest either. This ETF is a viable, value-leaning core holding, but it's not perfect, and given its recent run you should curb your expectations.

| Address: | 45 Fremont Street San Francisco CA 94105 800-474-2737 | Management Fee: | 0.25% | | |
|---|---|---|---|---|---|
| | | Expense Projections: | 3Yr:$80 | 5Yr:$141 | 10Yr:$318 |
| Web Address: | www.ishares.com | Income Distrib: | Quarterly | | |
| Inception: | 07-24-00* | Exchange: | AMEX | | |
| Advisor: | Barclays Global Fund Advisers | | | | |

MORNINGSTAR® ETFs 100

# iShares Russell Microcap

| | Ticker | NAV | Market Price | 52 wk High/Low | Yield | Mstar Category |
|---|---|---|---|---|---|---|
| | IWC | $51.31 | $54.03 | $54.03 - $47.51 | 0.0% | Small Blend |

## Management

### Portfolio Manager(s)

Barclays Global Fund Advisors is the advisor. The firm is the world's largest manager of indexed portfolios. Patrick O'Connor, the head of Barclay's U.S. iShares portfolio management group leads a team of a half dozen managers in running this and about 60 other ETFs. IShares' domestic portfolio-management group is responsible for about $75 billion in assets. Most of the managers have at least five years of experience with Barclays as well as prior industry experience.

### Strategy

Management tracks the Russell MicrocapX Index, a modified version of the Russell Microcap Index. The normal index includes the 1,000 smallest stocks from the Russell 2000 index, plus the next 1,000 smallest stocks from outside the benchmark. It excludes stocks from the OTC bulletin board and Pink Sheets. Barclays uses a customized version of this index, the Russell MicrocapX, that tosses out securities that have not maintained cumulative monthly trading volumes of 125,000 shares for six consecutive months. The fund uses a representative sampling to track the index, which rebalances annually in June.

### Growth of $10,000

— Investment Value of ETF
— Investment Value of Index S&P 500

| 1996 | 1997 | 1998 | 1999 | 2000 | 2001 | 2002 | 2003 | 2004 | 2005 | History |
|---|---|---|---|---|---|---|---|---|---|---|
| — | — | — | — | — | — | — | — | — | 51.31 | NAV $ |
| — | — | — | — | — | — | — | — | — | 51.15 | Market Price $ |
| — | — | — | — | — | — | — | — | — | 2.81* | NAV Return% |
| — | — | — | — | — | — | — | — | — | 2.49* | Market Price Return% |
| — | — | — | — | — | — | — | — | — | -0.23 | Avg Premium/Discount% |
| — | — | — | — | — | — | — | — | — | 2.81 | NAV Rtrn% +/-S&P 500 |
| — | — | — | — | — | — | — | — | — | 2.81 | NAV Rtrn% +/-Russ 2000 |
| — | — | — | — | — | — | — | — | — | — | NAV Return% Rank in Cat |
| — | — | — | — | — | — | — | — | — | — | Income Return % |
| — | — | — | — | — | — | — | — | — | — | Capital Return % |
| — | — | — | — | — | — | — | — | — | 0.10 | Income $ |
| — | — | — | — | — | — | — | — | — | 0.00 | Capital Gains $ |
| — | — | — | — | — | — | — | — | — | — | Expense Ratio % |
| — | — | — | — | — | — | — | — | — | — | Income Ratio % |
| — | — | — | — | — | — | — | — | — | — | Turnover Rate % |
| — | — | — | — | — | — | — | — | — | 103 | Net Assets $mil |

## Performance

### Historic Quarterly NAV Returns

| | 1st Qtr | 2nd Qtr | 3rd Qtr | 4th Qtr | Total |
|---|---|---|---|---|---|
| 2001 | — | — | — | — | — |
| 2002 | — | — | — | — | — |
| 2003 | — | — | — | — | — |
| 2004 | — | — | — | — | — |
| 2005 | — | — | — | 1.05 | —* |

| Trailing | NAV Return% | Market Return% | NAV Rtrn% +/-S&P 500 | %Rank Cat.(NAV) |
|---|---|---|---|---|
| 3 Mo | 1.05 | 0.72 | -1.03 | 7 |
| 6 Mo | — | — | — | 0 |
| 1 Yr | — | — | — | 0 |
| 3 Yr Avg | — | — | — | 0 |
| 5 Yr Avg | — | — | — | 0 |
| 10 Yr Avg | — | — | — | 0 |

| Tax Analysis | Tax-Adj Return% | Tax-Cost Ratio |
|---|---|---|
| 3 Yr (estimated) | — | — |
| 5 Yr (estimated) | — | — |
| 10 Yr (estimated) | — | — |

## Risk Profile

| | Standard Index S&P 500 | Best Fit Index |
|---|---|---|
| Alpha | — | — |
| Beta | — | — |
| R-Squared | — | — |
| Standard Deviation | — | |
| Mean | — | |
| Sharpe Ratio | — | |

## Morningstar Fair Value

| Price/Fair Value Ratio | Fair Value Estimate ($) | Hit Rate % |
|---|---|---|
| — | — | — |

## Portfolio Analysis 12-31-05

Share change since 11-05 Total Stocks:1233

| Sector | | PE | Tot Ret% | % Assets |
|---|---|---|---|---|
| Cubist Pharmaceuticals | Health | — | 79.54 | 0.31 |
| Royal Gold | Ind Mtrls | 62.0 | 92.37 | 0.28 |
| ViroPharma | Health | 18.7 | 469.23 | 0.26 |
| Trident Microsystems | Hardware | — | 115.31 | 0.26 |
| AAR | Ind Mtrls | 38.6 | 75.84 | 0.24 |
| IBERIABANK | Financial | 22.7 | -1.97 | 0.24 |
| Nuance Communications | Software | — | 82.10 | 0.23 |
| KNBT Bancorp | Financial | — | -2.08 | 0.23 |
| American States Water | Utilities | 21.5 | 22.35 | 0.22 |
| Town and Country Trust | Financial | 62.6 | 30.04 | 0.22 |
| EnergySouth | Energy | 15.4 | -1.56 | 0.22 |
| Orbital Sciences | Ind Mtrls | 4.4 | 8.54 | 0.22 |
| Myogen | Health | — | 272.99 | 0.22 |
| TierOne | Financial | 16.3 | 19.36 | 0.22 |
| Dobson Communications A | Telecom | — | 336.05 | 0.22 |
| Biomarin Pharmaceutical | Health | — | 68.70 | 0.22 |
| Brightpoint | Telecom | 26.6 | 112.86 | 0.22 |
| Micromuse | Software | — | 78.20 | 0.21 |
| Integra Bank | Financial | 13.5 | -4.92 | 0.21 |
| Atlas America | Energy | — | 68.45 | 0.21 |

### Current Investment Style

Value Blnd Growth — Large/Mid/Small

| Market Cap | % |
|---|---|
| Giant | 0.0 |
| Large | 0.0 |
| Mid | 0.0 |
| Small | 33.9 |
| Micro | 66.1 |

Avg $mil: 332

| Value Measures | | Rel Category |
|---|---|---|
| Price/Earnings | 17.94 | 1.04 |
| Price/Book | 1.78 | 0.92 |
| Price/Sales | 0.92 | 1.01 |
| Price/Cash Flow | 6.31 | 0.96 |
| Dividend Yield % | 1.07 | 1.19 |

| Growth Measures | % | Rel Category |
|---|---|---|
| Long-Term Erngs | 14.65 | 1.05 |
| Book Value | 0.58 | 0.16 |
| Sales | 3.83 | 0.73 |
| Cash Flow | -5.32 | NMF |
| Historical Erngs | 4.03 | 0.33 |

| Profitability | % | Rel Category |
|---|---|---|
| Return on Equity | 3.48 | 0.36 |
| Return on Assets | 0.61 | 0.12 |
| Net Margin | 5.83 | 0.72 |

### Sector Weightings

| | % of Stocks | Rel S&P 500 | 3 Year High Low |
|---|---|---|---|
| ⚙ Info | 20.41 | 1.01 | |
| Software | 5.71 | 1.60 | — — |
| Hardware | 11.63 | 1.16 | — — |
| Media | 1.01 | 0.28 | — — |
| Telecom | 2.06 | 0.68 | — — |
| ⚒ Service | 56.33 | 1.21 | |
| Health | 17.54 | 1.32 | — — |
| Consumer | 6.36 | 0.78 | — — |
| Business | 10.99 | 2.84 | — — |
| Financial | 21.44 | 1.02 | — — |
| ⚒ Mfg | 23.25 | 0.70 | |
| Goods | 4.83 | 0.56 | — — |
| Ind Mtrls | 13.07 | 1.08 | — — |
| Energy | 4.43 | 0.47 | — — |
| Utilities | 0.92 | 0.27 | — — |

### Composition

| | | |
|---|---|---|
| ● Cash | | 0.1 |
| ● Stocks | | 99.8 |
| ● Bonds | | 0.0 |
| ● Other | | 0.1 |
| Foreign | | 0.2 |
| (% of Stock) | | |

## Morningstar's Take by Dan Culloton

This one's still too new to get excited about.

IShares Russell Microcap Index catches the eye. The ETF tracks a version of the Russell Microcap Index that kicks out the bogy's least-active stocks. It's still diversified by individual stock and across sectors, though.

The ETF also is more affordable than many traditional micro-cap funds. The fund's 0.60% expense ratio is a fraction of that of the typical traditional micro-cap mutual fund (though it is high for an ETF). Low turnover and diversification may allow it to handle more money than actively managed options that often get too big.

Still, you should give this fund a wide berth. The burden of proof is on new funds to prove they can effectively execute their strategy (in this case tracking its index). That burden is heavier for funds in volatile asset classes like micro-caps. Investors should take little comfort in the fact that tiny stocks and funds that buy them have racked up strong performance in recent years. Performance trends are fickle and can turn quickly.

Don't expect this ETF to twist and turn the same way its rivals do, though. Micro-cap indexes define their universes and liquidity standards differently, so their holdings and sector allocations vary. This one has bigger weightings in financial services, health-care, technology, and consumer stocks.

There are other reasons to adopt a wait-and-see attitude. The fund and index have barely any real-world record. The shares of ETFs that track less-liquid market segments like this one also could trade at premiums or discounts to the net asset values of their underlying holdings. And Russell indexes have been susceptible to front-running during yearly rebalancing, making this fund's job harder.

It's too early to tell whether any of these issues are true flaws or just idle worries. Still there are enough questions to justify watching the ETF from afar until it builds a record.

| Address: | 45 Fremont Street | Management Fee: | 0.60% | | |
|---|---|---|---|---|---|
| | San Francisco CA 94105 | Expense Projections: | 3Yr:$192 | 5Yr: — | 10Yr: — |
| | 800-474-2737 | Income Distrib: | Quarterly | | |
| Web Address: | www.ishares.com | Exchange: | NYSE | | |
| Inception: | 08-12-05* | | | | |
| Advisor: | Barclays Global Fund Advisers | | | | |

Data through December 31, 2005

# iShares S&P 100 Ind.

| | Ticker | NAV | Market Price | 52 wk High/Low | Yield | Mstar Category |
|---|---|---|---|---|---|---|
| | OEF | $56.86 | $58.50 | $58.54 - $54.17 | 1.9% | Large Blend |

## Management

### Portfolio Manager(s)

Barclays Global Fund Advisors is the advisor. The firm is the world's largest manager of indexed portfolios. Patrick O'Connor, the head of Barclay's U.S. iShares portfolio management group leads a team of a half dozen managers in running this and about 60 other ETFs. IShares' domestic portfolio-management group is responsible for about $75 billion in assets. Most of the managers have at least five years of experience with Barclays as well as prior industry experience.

### Strategy

This exchange-traded offering is a passive fund that simply attempts to match the performance of the S&P 100 Index. The benchmark is a market-capitalization weighted index designed to track large liquid companies in the S&P 500 that also have options trading on the Chicago Board of Options Exchange. The bogy's sector exposures are similar to that of the S&P 500 and constituents have to meet the S&P index committee's profitability and index representation guidelines. The fund uses a representative sampling method of tracking the index.

## Performance

### Historic Quarterly NAV Returns

| | 1st Qtr | 2nd Qtr | 3rd Qtr | 4th Qtr | Total |
|---|---|---|---|---|---|
| 2001 | -13.62 | 7.05 | -15.39 | 9.94 | -13.99 |
| 2002 | -0.81 | -14.88 | -16.56 | 9.68 | -22.72 |
| 2003 | -3.08 | 14.72 | 2.08 | 10.98 | 25.97 |
| 2004 | 0.45 | 0.90 | -2.99 | 8.05 | 6.23 |
| 2005 | -1.85 | -0.23 | 2.04 | 1.07 | 1.00 |

| Trailing | NAV Return% | Market Return% | NAV Rtrn% +/-S&P 500 | %Rank Cat.(NAV) |
|---|---|---|---|---|
| 3 Mo | 1.07 | 0.85 | -1.01 | 27 |
| 6 Mo | 3.13 | 3.04 | -2.63 | 27 |
| 1 Yr | 1.00 | 1.03 | -3.91 | 23 |
| 3 Yr Avg | 10.56 | 10.67 | -3.82 | 14 |
| 5 Yr Avg | -2.12 | -2.15 | -2.66 | 13 |
| 10 Yr Avg | — | — | — | 0 |

| Tax Analysis | Tax-Adj Return% | Tax-Cost Ratio |
|---|---|---|
| 3 Yr (estimated) | 9.83 | 0.66 |
| 5 Yr (estimated) | -2.69 | 0.58 |
| 10 Yr (estimated) | — | — |

Growth of $10,000
— Investment Value of ETF
— Investment Value of Index S&P 500

| | 1996 | 1997 | 1998 | 1999 | 2000 | 2001 | 2002 | 2003 | 2004 | 2005 | History |
|---|---|---|---|---|---|---|---|---|---|---|---|
| | — | — | — | — | 68.67 | 58.46 | 44.56 | 55.21 | 57.36 | 56.86 | NAV $ |
| | — | — | — | — | 68.81 | 58.75 | 44.46 | 55.13 | 57.38 | 56.90 | Market Price $ |
| | — | — | — | — | -3.27* | -13.99 | -22.72 | 25.97 | 6.23 | 1.00 | NAV Return% |
| | — | — | — | — | -3.25* | -13.74 | -23.27 | 26.07 | 6.42 | 1.03 | Market Price Return% |
| | — | — | — | — | -0.67 | 0.20 | 0.02 | 0.01 | 0.06 | 0.09 | Avg Premium/Discount% |
| | — | — | — | — | -3.27 | -2.11 | -0.63 | -2.70 | -4.64 | -3.91 | NAV Rtrn% +/-S&P 500 |
| | — | — | — | — | -3.27 | -1.54 | -1.07 | -3.92 | -5.17 | -5.27 | NAV Rtrn% +/-Russ 1000 |
| | — | — | — | — | — | 13 | 15 | 15 | 17 | 23 | NAV Return% Rank in Cat |
| | — | — | — | — | 0.00 | 0.87 | 1.17 | 1.87 | 2.27 | 1.86 | Income Return % |
| | — | — | — | — | — | -14.86 | -23.89 | 24.10 | 3.96 | -0.86 | Capital Return % |
| | — | — | — | — | 0.15 | 0.59 | 0.68 | 0.83 | 1.25 | 1.06 | Income $ |
| | — | — | — | — | 0.00 | 0.00 | 0.00 | 0.00 | 0.00 | 0.00 | Capital Gains $ |
| | — | — | — | — | — | 0.20 | 0.20 | 0.20 | 0.20 | 0.20 | Expense Ratio % |
| | — | — | — | — | — | 1.03 | 1.12 | 1.63 | 1.62 | 2.41 | Income Ratio % |
| | — | — | — | — | — | 5 | 13 | 4 | 5 | 6 | Turnover Rate % |
| | — | — | — | — | — | — | 178 | 378 | 608 | 685 | Net Assets $mil |

## Risk Profile

| | Standard Index S&P 500 | Best Fit Index S&P 500 |
|---|---|---|
| Alpha | -2.8 | -2.8 |
| Beta | 0.94 | 0.94 |
| R-Squared | 95 | 95 |
| Standard Deviation | 8.84 | |
| Mean | 10.56 | |
| Sharpe Ratio | 0.96 | |

## Morningstar Fair Value

| Price/Fair Value Ratio | Fair Value Estimate ($) | Hit Rate % |
|---|---|---|
| 0.9 Undervalued | 38.45 | 99 Good |

## Portfolio Analysis 12-31-05

Share change since 11-05 Total Stocks:101

| | Sector | PE | Tot Ret% | % Assets |
|---|---|---|---|---|
| ⊕ General Electric | Ind Mtrls | 19.9 | -1.43 | 5.98 |
| ⊕ ExxonMobil | Energy | 10.6 | 11.76 | 5.64 |
| ⊕ Citigroup | Financial | 12.1 | 4.63 | 3.97 |
| ⊕ Microsoft | Software | 22.2 | -0.95 | 3.87 |
| ⊕ Procter & Gamble | Goods | 21.2 | 7.18 | 3.13 |
| ⊕ Bank of America | Financial | 11.1 | 2.39 | 2.99 |
| ⊕ Johnson & Johnson | Health | 19.1 | -3.36 | 2.89 |
| ⊕ American International G | Financial | 15.6 | 4.83 | 2.86 |
| ⊕ Pfizer | Health | 21.2 | -10.62 | 2.78 |
| ⊕ Altria Group | Goods | 15.0 | 27.72 | 2.51 |
| ⊕ Intel | Hardware | 18.6 | 8.12 | 2.43 |
| ⊕ J.P. Morgan Chase & Co. | Financial | 18.8 | 5.74 | 2.24 |
| ⊕ IBM | Hardware | 16.0 | -15.83 | 2.10 |
| ⊕ Chevron | Energy | 9.0 | 11.51 | 2.06 |
| ⊕ Wal-Mart Stores | Consumer | 18.2 | -10.30 | 1.89 |
| ⊕ Cisco Systems | Hardware | 19.9 | -11.39 | 1.70 |
| ⊕ Wells Fargo | Financial | 14.3 | 4.47 | 1.70 |
| ⊕ PepsiCo | Goods | 25.8 | 15.24 | 1.58 |
| ⊕ Amgen | Health | 28.3 | 22.93 | 1.57 |
| ⊕ AT&T | Telecom | 21.1 | 0.25 | 1.55 |

### Current Investment Style

Value Blnd Growth — Large Mid Small

| Market Cap | % |
|---|---|
| Giant | 83.3 |
| Large | 15.8 |
| Mid | 0.9 |
| Small | 0.0 |
| Micro | 0.0 |

Avg $mil: 99,371

| Value Measures | | Rel Category |
|---|---|---|
| Price/Earnings | 15.60 | 0.92 |
| Price/Book | 2.65 | 0.98 |
| Price/Sales | 1.60 | 1.25 |
| Price/Cash Flow | 8.50 | 1.18 |
| Dividend Yield % | 2.20 | 1.24 |

| Growth Measures | % | Rel Category |
|---|---|---|
| Long-Term Erngs | 10.03 | 0.90 |
| Book Value | 10.18 | 1.08 |
| Sales | 8.49 | 1.05 |
| Cash Flow | 12.13 | 1.18 |
| Historical Erngs | 15.54 | 1.10 |

| Profitability | % | Rel Category |
|---|---|---|
| Return on Equity | 21.46 | 1.05 |
| Return on Assets | 11.00 | 1.18 |
| Net Margin | 13.29 | 1.22 |

### Sector Weightings

| | % of Stocks | Rel S&P 500 | 3 Year High | 3 Year Low |
|---|---|---|---|---|
| ☁ Info | 23.11 | 1.14 | | |
| Software | 4.61 | 1.29 | 7 | 5 |
| Hardware | 10.43 | 1.04 | 13 | 10 |
| Media | 4.06 | 1.13 | 5 | 3 |
| Telecom | 4.01 | 1.33 | 5 | 4 |
| ☞ Service | 40.31 | 0.87 | | |
| Health | 12.29 | 0.92 | 17 | 11 |
| Consumer | 5.16 | 0.63 | 8 | 5 |
| Business | 2.72 | 0.70 | 3 | 1 |
| Financial | 20.14 | 0.95 | 21 | 18 |
| Mfg | 36.58 | 1.09 | | |
| Goods | 10.81 | 1.26 | 12 | 11 |
| Ind Mtrls | 14.33 | 1.18 | 15 | 12 |
| Energy | 9.82 | 1.05 | 10 | 6 |
| Utilities | 1.62 | 0.48 | 2 | 1 |

### Composition

| | |
|---|---|
| ● Cash | 0.0 |
| ● Stocks | 100.0 |
| ● Bonds | 0.0 |
| ● Other | 0.0 |
| Foreign | 0.0 |
| (% of Stock) | |

## Morningstar's Take by Dan Culloton

Cheap, diversified, and focused on large, liquid domestic stocks; iShares S&P 100 Index could be a good way to play a large-cap rebound.

Small-cap stocks have been on top for quite a while. The small-blend category has beat the large-blend group in each of the last five years. This exchange-traded fund, which tracks the performance of some of the largest and most-liquid denizens of S&P 500 Index, has suffered as a result, lagging most other large-blend funds since its inception. Such runs don't last forever. It's hard to say when the tables will turn in favor of bigger, blue-chip stocks, but when they do this ETF will do a lot better.

It doesn't take a genius to figure out why. This portfolio has one of the highest average market capitalizations in the large-blend category. Because the ETF's benchmark is a subset of the S&P 500, its holdings tend to be established, profitable, brand-name companies based in the United States. Many of those stocks are arguably looking undervalued, such as Microsoft, Wal-Mart, and Johnson & Johnson.

Other factors work in this ETF's favor. Its 0.20% expense ratio, while not the cheapest in the large-blend category, is cheaper than the typical large-blend fund and a fraction of the levy of perhaps the only traditional fund tracking the same bogy: North Track S&P 100 Index. Although this offering does keep about one third of its assets in its top 10 holdings, it spreads its money across most sectors. That diversification keeps a lid on variability. The fund's standard deviation, a measure of volatility, has been about even with the category average and the S&P 500.

The ETF is not without its risks. If small caps continue to outperform, for instance, this offering will keep lagging. For those looking to add a diversified shot of blue-chip domestic stocks to their portfolios, though, this is an acceptable choice.

| Address: | 45 Fremont Street San Francisco CA 94105 800-474-2737 |
|---|---|
| Web Address: | www.ishares.com |
| Inception: | 10-23-00* |
| Advisor: | Barclays Global Fund Advisers |

| Management Fee: | 0.20% |
|---|---|
| Expense Projections: | 3Yr:$64  5Yr:$113  10Yr:$255 |
| Income Distrib: | Quarterly |
| Exchange: | CBOE |

MORNINGSTAR® ETFs 100

# iShares S&P 500

| | Ticker | NAV | Market Price | 52 wk High/Low | Yield | Mstar Category |
|---|---|---|---|---|---|---|
| | IVV | $124.87 | $129.15 | $129.15 - $113.66 | 1.7% | Large Blend |

## Management

### Portfolio Manager(s)

Barclays Global Fund Advisors is the advisor. The firm is the world's largest manager of indexed portfolios. Patrick O'Connor, the head of Barclay's U.S. shares portfolio management group leads a team of a half dozen managers in running this and about 60 other ETFs. IShares' domestic portfolio-management group is responsible for about $75 billion in assets. Most of the managers have at least five years of experience with Barclays as well as prior industry experience.

### Strategy

This fund owns all the stocks in the Standard & Poor's 500. The S&P 500 includes more than three fourths of the market's capitalization, but leaves out most mid- and virtually all small-cap equities. This fund's advisor will use futures, options, and other techniques to reduce tracking error. Unlike its largest traditional index fund rival, the Vanguard 500, however, this offering will not utilize those techniques to gain a basis point or two of an edge on its bogy. That's because traders and institutional investors who use this ETF to hedge their portfolios count on it to try to match the S&P 500's return, not beat it.

## Performance

### Historic Quarterly NAV Returns

| | 1st Qtr | 2nd Qtr | 3rd Qtr | 4th Qtr | Total |
|---|---|---|---|---|---|
| 2001 | -11.85 | 5.82 | -14.68 | 10.63 | -11.96 |
| 2002 | 0.25 | -13.41 | -17.26 | 8.39 | -22.15 |
| 2003 | -3.16 | 15.34 | 2.61 | 12.14 | 28.53 |
| 2004 | 1.66 | 1.70 | -1.89 | 9.20 | 10.77 |
| 2005 | -2.15 | 1.35 | 3.58 | 2.05 | 4.83 |

| Trailing | NAV Return% | Market Return% | NAV Rtrn% +/-S&P 500 | %Rank Cat.(NAV) |
|---|---|---|---|---|
| 3 Mo | 2.05 | 1.77 | -0.03 | 27 |
| 6 Mo | 5.71 | 5.53 | -0.05 | 27 |
| 1 Yr | 4.83 | 4.87 | -0.08 | 23 |
| 3 Yr Avg | 14.28 | 14.15 | -0.10 | 14 |
| 5 Yr Avg | 0.45 | 0.54 | -0.09 | 13 |
| 10 Yr Avg | — | — | — | 0 |

| Tax Analysis | Tax-Adj Return% | Tax-Cost Ratio |
|---|---|---|
| 3 Yr (estimated) | 13.58 | 0.61 |
| 5 Yr (estimated) | -0.12 | 0.57 |
| 10 Yr (estimated) | — | — |

### Growth of $10,000

— Investment Value of ETF
— Investment Value of Index S&P 500

| | 1996 | 1997 | 1998 | 1999 | 2000 | 2001 | 2002 | 2003 | 2004 | 2005 | History |
|---|---|---|---|---|---|---|---|---|---|---|---|
| | — | — | — | — | 132.14 | 115.00 | 88.18 | 111.46 | 121.24 | 124.87 | NAV $ |
| | — | — | — | — | 131.34 | 114.33 | 88.35 | 111.22 | 121.00 | 124.67 | Market Price $ |
| | — | — | — | — | -1.16* | -11.96 | -22.15 | 28.53 | 10.77 | 4.83 | NAV Return% |
| | — | — | — | — | -1.19* | -11.94 | -21.55 | 28.00 | 10.79 | 4.87 | Market Price Return% |
| | — | — | — | — | -0.03 | -0.07 | -0.15 | 0.03 | 0.07 | -0.01 | Avg Premium/Discount% |
| | — | — | — | — | -1.16 | -0.08 | -0.06 | -0.14 | -0.10 | -0.08 | NAV Rtrn% +/-S&P 500 |
| | — | — | — | — | -1.16 | 0.49 | -0.50 | -1.36 | -0.63 | -1.44 | NAV Rtrn% +/-Russ 1000 |
| | — | — | — | — | — | 13 | 15 | 15 | 17 | 23 | NAV Return% Rank in Cat |
| | — | — | — | — | 0.00 | 1.01 | 1.30 | 1.87 | 1.90 | 1.78 | Income Return % |
| | — | — | — | — | — | -12.97 | -23.45 | 26.66 | 8.87 | 3.05 | Capital Return % |
| | — | — | — | — | 0.77 | 1.33 | 1.48 | 1.64 | 2.10 | 2.15 | Income $ |
| | — | — | — | — | 0.07 | 0.00 | 0.00 | 0.00 | 0.00 | 0.00 | Capital Gains $ |
| | — | — | — | — | — | 0.09 | 0.09 | 0.09 | 0.09 | 0.09 | Expense Ratio % |
| | — | — | — | — | — | 1.06 | 1.27 | 1.67 | 1.66 | 2.02 | Income Ratio % |
| | — | — | — | — | — | 5 | 3 | 5 | 3 | 6 | Turnover Rate % |
| | — | — | — | — | — | 5,075 | 7,874 | 11,784 | 14,229 | Net Assets $mil |

## Risk Profile

| | Standard Index S&P 500 | Best Fit Index S&P 500 |
|---|---|---|
| Alpha | -0.1 | -0.1 |
| Beta | 1.00 | 1.00 |
| R-Squared | 100 | 100 |
| Standard Deviation | 9.15 | |
| Mean | 14.28 | |
| Sharpe Ratio | 1.29 | |

## Morningstar Fair Value

| Price/Fair Value Ratio | Fair Value Estimate ($) | Hit Rate % |
|---|---|---|
| 1.0 Fairly valued | 38.82 | 97 Good |

## Portfolio Analysis 12-31-05

| Share change since 11-05 Total Stocks:501 | Sector | PE | Tot Ret% | % Assets |
|---|---|---|---|---|
| ⊕ General Electric | Ind Mtrls | 19.9 | -1.43 | 3.29 |
| ⊕ ExxonMobil | Energy | 10.6 | 11.76 | 3.10 |
| ⊕ Citigroup | Financial | 12.1 | 4.63 | 2.18 |
| ⊕ Microsoft | Software | 22.2 | -0.95 | 2.13 |
| ⊕ Procter & Gamble | Goods | 21.2 | 7.18 | 1.72 |
| ⊕ Bank of America | Financial | 11.1 | 2.39 | 1.65 |
| ⊕ Johnson & Johnson | Health | 19.1 | -3.36 | 1.59 |
| ⊕ American International G | Financial | 15.6 | 4.83 | 1.57 |
| ⊕ Pfizer | Health | 21.2 | -10.62 | 1.53 |
| ⊕ Altria Group | Goods | 15.0 | 27.72 | 1.38 |
| ⊕ Intel | Hardware | 18.6 | 8.12 | 1.34 |
| ⊕ J.P. Morgan Chase & Co. | Financial | 18.8 | 5.74 | 1.23 |
| ⊕ IBM | Hardware | 16.0 | -15.83 | 1.15 |
| ⊕ Chevron | Energy | 9.0 | 11.51 | 1.13 |
| ⊕ Wal-Mart Stores | Consumer | 18.2 | -10.30 | 1.04 |
| ⊖ Cisco Systems | Hardware | 19.9 | -11.39 | 0.93 |
| ⊕ Wells Fargo | Financial | 14.3 | 4.47 | 0.93 |
| ⊕ PepsiCo | Goods | 25.8 | 15.24 | 0.87 |
| ⊕ Amgen | Health | 28.3 | 22.93 | 0.86 |
| ⊕ AT&T | Telecom | 21.1 | 0.25 | 0.85 |

### Current Investment Style

| Value Blnd Growth | | Market Cap | % |
|---|---|---|---|
| Large Mid Small | | Giant | 54.1 |
| | | Large | 37.3 |
| | | Mid | 8.5 |
| | | Small | 0.1 |
| | | Micro | 0.0 |
| | | Avg $mil: 46,962 | |

| Value Measures | | Rel Category |
|---|---|---|
| Price/Earnings | 15.97 | 0.94 |
| Price/Book | 2.50 | 0.93 |
| Price/Sales | 1.47 | 1.15 |
| Price/Cash Flow | 6.08 | 0.84 |
| Dividend Yield % | 1.92 | 1.08 |

| Growth Measures | % | Rel Category |
|---|---|---|
| Long-Term Erngs | 10.51 | 0.95 |
| Book Value | 10.67 | 1.14 |
| Sales | 8.91 | 1.11 |
| Cash Flow | 12.22 | 1.18 |
| Historical Erngs | 15.34 | 1.08 |

| Profitability | % | Rel Category |
|---|---|---|
| Return on Equity | 19.61 | 0.96 |
| Return on Assets | 10.42 | 1.12 |
| Net Margin | 13.34 | 1.22 |

| Sector Weightings | % of Stocks | Rel S&P 500 | 3 Year High | Low |
|---|---|---|---|---|
| ↻ Info | 20.19 | 1.00 | | |
| 🖳 Software | 3.56 | 1.00 | 5 | 4 |
| 💻 Hardware | 10.04 | 1.00 | 12 | 9 |
| 🔊 Media | 3.58 | 1.00 | 4 | 3 |
| 📱 Telecom | 3.01 | 1.00 | 4 | 3 |
| ☞ Service | 46.39 | 1.00 | | |
| ⚕ Health | 13.29 | 1.00 | 16 | 12 |
| 🛒 Consumer | 8.14 | 1.00 | 10 | 8 |
| 📋 Business | 3.87 | 1.00 | 4 | 4 |
| 💲 Financial | 21.09 | 1.00 | 21 | 20 |
| 🔧 Mfg | 33.42 | 1.00 | | |
| 🏭 Goods | 8.56 | 1.00 | 10 | 9 |
| ⚙ Ind Mtrls | 12.15 | 1.00 | 13 | 11 |
| 🔋 Energy | 9.35 | 1.00 | 10 | 6 |
| 💡 Utilities | 3.36 | 1.00 | 4 | 3 |

### Composition

| Composition | % |
|---|---|
| ● Cash | 0.1 |
| ● Stocks | 100.0 |
| ● Bonds | 0.0 |
| ○ Other | 0.0 |
| Foreign (% of Stock) | 0.0 |

## Morningstar's Take by Dan Culloton

This fund has stiffer competition than ever.

Until recently, iShares S&P 500 Index was not only the cheapest exchange-traded fund tracking the S&P 500, but also the cheapest S&P 500 index fund available to retail investors. That worked in this offering's favor because, all else being equal, costs are the best predictor of long-term performance among ETFs that track the same benchmark. That made the fund a viable option for investors who wanted to make a large, lump-sum investment into a large-blend fund and, in rare cases, very big initial investments followed by substantial regular purchases.

An index fund price war, however, has stolen some of this fund's thunder. ETF rivals in the large blend category, such as Vanguard Large Cap Vipers, now charge as little as 0.07%. Meanwhile, conventional funds, such as Fidelity Spartan 500 and E*Trade S&P 500 have slashed expense ratios to a level equal close to this ETF's 0.09% levy. As long as those expense ratios remain in place, they all but negate this ETF's cost advantage for most retail investors. Why pay a commission for S&P 500 exposure when you can get it for roughly the same expense ratio from a no-load fund?

That said, this ETF is not without merit. You can be reasonably sure that this fund's advisor, Barclays Global Investors (the world's largest manager of index funds), will capably track the fund's benchmark. Indeed, from the ETF's May 2000 inception through October 2005 the offering has trailed its index by less than its expense ratio, which is a good sign. In its lifetime, the ETF also has beaten its largest traditional index fund rival, Vanguard 500, in 28 of 30 rolling three-year periods, and in more than two thirds of the 54 rolling one-year periods.

While not a slam-dunk from a cost perspective anymore, this ETF remains a cheap and reliable core stock fund.

| Address: | 45 Fremont Street San Francisco CA 94105 800-474-2737 | Management Fee: | 0.09% |
|---|---|---|---|
| | | Expense Projections: | 3Yr:$30  5Yr:$53  10Yr:$121 |
| Web Address: | www.ishares.com | Income Distrib: | Quarterly |
| Inception: | 05-15-00* | Exchange: | NYSE |
| Advisor: | Barclays Global Fund Advisers | | |

# iShares S&P Euro-350

| | Ticker | NAV | Market Price | 52 wk High/Low | Yield | Mstar Category |
|---|---|---|---|---|---|---|
| | IEV | $80.15 | $84.52 | $85.01 - $72.44 | 2.3% | Europe Stock |

## Management

### Portfolio Manager(s)

The fund's advisor, Barclays Global Fund Advisors, is one of the world's largest and most experienced managers of index-tracking portfolios. Lisa Chen and Carl Gilchrist are the primary portfolio managers of this and Barclays other international and global iShares. Chen has been a portfolio manager with Barclays for six years. Gilchrist has been on board for a decade.

### Strategy

This exchange-traded offering is a passive fund that simply attempts to match the performance of the S&P Europe 350 Index. The benchmark is a market-capitalization index designed to track leading stocks from across Europe. It includes stocks from nations such as the United Kingdom, Austria, Belgium, Denmark, Finland, France, Germany, Greece, Ireland, Italy, the Netherlands, Norway, Portugal, Sweden, Switzerland, and Spain. It uses a representative sampling method of tracking the index.

**Growth of $10,000**

— Investment Value of ETF
— Investment Value of Index MSCI EAFE

| 1996 | 1997 | 1998 | 1999 | 2000 | 2001 | 2002 | 2003 | 2004 | 2005 | History |
|---|---|---|---|---|---|---|---|---|---|---|
| — | — | — | — | 75.09 | 59.12 | 47.34 | 64.04 | 75.13 | 80.15 | NAV $ |
| — | — | — | — | 76.69 | 59.09 | 47.48 | 64.15 | 75.25 | 80.77 | Market Price $ |
| — | — | — | — | 2.03* | -20.05 | -18.12 | 37.70 | 19.44 | 9.17 | NAV Return% |
| — | — | — | — | 2.18* | -21.76 | -17.84 | 37.53 | 19.42 | 9.84 | Market Price Return% |
| — | — | — | — | 2.12 | 0.94 | 0.37 | 0.30 | 0.74 | 0.29 | Avg Premium/Discount% |
| — | — | — | — | 2.03 | 1.37 | -2.18 | -0.89 | -0.81 | -4.37 | NAV Rtrn% +/-MSCI EAFE |
| — | — | — | — | 2.03 | -0.15 | 0.26 | -0.84 | -1.44 | -0.25 | NAV Rtrn% +/-MSCI Eur |
| — | — | — | — | — | 12 | 12 | 15 | 15 | 15 | NAV Return% Rank in Cat |
| — | — | — | — | 0.00 | 1.25 | 1.80 | 2.35 | 2.11 | 2.50 | Income Return % |
| — | — | — | — | — | -21.30 | -19.92 | 35.35 | 17.33 | 6.67 | Capital Return % |
| — | — | — | — | 0.18 | 0.93 | 1.06 | 1.11 | 1.35 | 1.88 | Income $ |
| — | — | — | — | 0.00 | 0.00 | 0.00 | 0.00 | 0.00 | 0.00 | Capital Gains $ |
| — | — | — | — | — | 0.60 | 0.60 | 0.60 | 0.60 | 0.60 | Expense Ratio % |
| — | — | — | — | — | 1.12 | 1.49 | 2.11 | 2.17 | 2.26 | Income Ratio % |
| — | — | — | — | — | 24 | 4 | 6 | 5 | 5 | Turnover Rate % |
| — | — | — | — | — | 428 | 647 | 1,082 | 1,270 | | Net Assets $mil |

## Performance

**Historic Quarterly NAV Returns**

| | 1st Qtr | 2nd Qtr | 3rd Qtr | 4th Qtr | Total |
|---|---|---|---|---|---|
| 2001 | -15.82 | -0.92 | -12.38 | 9.39 | -20.05 |
| 2002 | -0.14 | -4.15 | -22.88 | 10.93 | -18.12 |
| 2003 | -9.42 | 22.08 | 3.51 | 20.29 | 37.70 |
| 2004 | 0.55 | 1.86 | 1.08 | 15.37 | 19.44 |
| 2005 | 0.21 | -0.88 | 7.64 | 2.10 | 9.17 |

| Trailing | NAV Return% | Market Return%+/-MSCI EAFE | NAV Rtrn% | %Rank Cat.(NAV) |
|---|---|---|---|---|
| 3 Mo | 2.10 | 2.61 | -1.98 | 16 |
| 6 Mo | 9.90 | 10.94 | -4.98 | 16 |
| 1 Yr | 9.17 | 9.84 | -4.37 | 15 |
| 3 Yr Avg | 21.54 | 21.73 | -2.14 | 15 |
| 5 Yr Avg | 3.28 | 3.01 | -1.28 | 12 |
| 10 Yr Avg | — | — | — | 0 |

| Tax Analysis | Tax-Adj Return% | Tax-Cost Ratio |
|---|---|---|
| 3 Yr (estimated) | 20.72 | 0.67 |
| 5 Yr (estimated) | 2.56 | 0.70 |
| 10 Yr (estimated) | — | — |

## Risk Profile

| | Standard Index S&P 500 | Best Fit Index MSCI Eur |
|---|---|---|
| Alpha | -3.1 | -0.7 |
| Beta | 1.07 | 1.00 |
| R-Squared | 88 | 100 |
| Standard Deviation | 13.20 | |
| Mean | 21.54 | |
| Sharpe Ratio | 1.40 | |

## Morningstar Fair Value

| Price/Fair Value Ratio | Fair Value Estimate ($) | Hit Rate % |
|---|---|---|
| — | — | — |

## Portfolio Analysis  12-31-05

Share change since 11-05 Total Stocks:347

| | | Sector | Country | % Assets |
|---|---|---|---|---|
| ⊕ | BP | Energy | U.K. | 3.33 |
| ⊕ | HSBC Hldgs | Financial | U.K. | 2.75 |
| ⊕ | TOTAL | Energy | France | 2.33 |
| ⊕ | GlaxoSmithKline | Health | U.K. | 2.23 |
| ⊕ | Novartis | Health | Switzerland | 2.17 |
| ⊖ | Vodafone Grp | Telecom | U.K. | 2.02 |
| ⊕ | Nestle | Goods | Switzerland | 1.82 |
| ⊖ | Royal Dutch Shell | Energy | U.K. | 1.82 |
| ⊕ | Roche Holding | Health | Switzerland | 1.60 |
| ⊕ | UBS | Financial | Switzerland | 1.56 |
| ⊕ | Royal Bank Of Scotland G | Financial | U.K. | 1.45 |
| ⊕ | Royal Dutch Shell | Energy | U.K. | 1.33 |
| ⊕ | Sanofi-Synthelabo | Health | France | 1.33 |
| ⊕ | Banco Santander Central | Financial | Spain | 1.25 |
| ⊕ | Nokia | Hardware | Finland | 1.23 |
| ⊕ | AstraZeneca | Health | U.K. | 1.17 |
| ⊕ | ING Groep | Financial | Netherlands | 1.16 |
| ⊕ | Telefonica | Telecom | Spain | 1.12 |
| ⊕ | Eni | Energy | Italy | 1.08 |
| ⊕ | E.ON | Utilities | Germany | 1.08 |

### Current Investment Style

Value Blnd Growth — Large / Mid / Small

| Market Cap | % |
|---|---|
| Giant | 61.0 |
| Large | 30.8 |
| Mid | 8.1 |
| Small | 0.1 |
| Micro | 0.0 |

Avg $mil: 41,774

| Value Measures | | Rel Category |
|---|---|---|
| Price/Earnings | 13.59 | 1.01 |
| Price/Book | 2.38 | 1.00 |
| Price/Sales | 1.16 | 0.97 |
| Price/Cash Flow | 7.87 | 1.08 |
| Dividend Yield % | 3.04 | 1.04 |

| Growth Measures | % | Rel Category |
|---|---|---|
| Long-Term Erngs | 11.32 | 1.00 |
| Book Value | 1.49 | 0.67 |
| Sales | 1.67 | 0.64 |
| Cash Flow | 4.77 | 1.38 |
| Historical Erngs | 13.87 | 0.87 |

### Composition

| | | | |
|---|---|---|---|
| Cash | 0.2 | Bonds | 0.0 |
| Stocks | 99.3 | Other | 0.5 |
| Foreign (% of Stock) | | | 100.0 |

| Sector Weightings | % of Stocks | Rel MSCI EAFE | 3 Year High | Low |
|---|---|---|---|---|
| ☏ Info | 13.62 | 0.97 | | |
| Software | 0.68 | 0.64 | 1 | 0 |
| Hardware | 3.81 | 1.06 | 6 | 4 |
| Media | 2.36 | 1.12 | 3 | 2 |
| Telecom | 6.77 | 0.94 | 11 | 7 |
| ☞ Service | 46.66 | 1.02 | | |
| Health | 9.60 | 1.34 | 12 | 13 |
| Consumer | 3.56 | 0.81 | 5 | 3 |
| Business | 3.11 | 0.51 | 3 | 3 |
| Financial | 30.39 | 1.08 | 30 | 22 |
| ⎘ Mfg | 39.74 | 0.99 | | |
| Goods | 11.78 | 0.86 | 14 | 11 |
| Ind Mtrls | 10.76 | 0.76 | 11 | 9 |
| Energy | 11.82 | 1.49 | 14 | 10 |
| Utilities | 5.38 | 1.17 | 6 | 4 |

### Regional Exposure % Stock

| | | | |
|---|---|---|---|
| UK/W. Europe | 100 | N. America | 0 |
| Japan | 0 | Latn America | 0 |
| Asia X Japan | 0 | Other | 0 |

### Country Exposure % Stock

| | | | |
|---|---|---|---|
| U.K. | 37 | Germany | 11 |
| France | 15 | Netherlands | 6 |
| Switzerland | 11 | | |

## Morningstar's Take  by Dan Culloton

IShares S&P Europe 350 Index isn't a clear winner.

This fund offers diversified exposure to European large-cap stocks. Unlike its sibling, iShares MSCI EMU Index, the fund includes more than the countries in the European Monetary Union. It extends its reach to such markets as Britain, Denmark, Norway, Sweden, and Switzerland. That gives this ETF broader exposure to the continent than the EMU fund, which keeps close to half its assets in Germany and France. Ostensibly, this ETF should hold higher quality stocks, too, because Standard & Poor's only admits the stocks that meet its liquidity and profitability standards.

Consequently, this ETF, which keeps more than 90% of its assets in large-cap stocks, can fall behind more-inclusive funds when smaller and more-speculative stocks rally. For example, in 2003 this fund lagged the EMU ETF and Vanguard European Stock Index, which tracks the MSCI Europe Index. Both of those funds own more mid- and small-cap stocks. The lack of smaller-cap

stocks, however, has not held this fund's bogy back in the past. Over the 15-year period ending Oct. 31, 2005, the S&P Europe 350's 11% annualized gain has beaten the returns of MSCI's EMU and Europe indexes.

You can't count on the past to repeat itself, though. So, investors need to consider other factors, such as management and costs. This ETF's scores are mixed in those areas. Its advisor, Barclays Global Fund Advisors, is capable, but the fund's annualized return from inception through the end of October has lagged its benchmark by more than its expense ratio. Furthermore, that 0.60% expense ratio is lower than the typical European stock fund, but higher than the traditional index fund Vanguard European Stock Index. The no-load Vanguard fund has the added advantage of being available without a brokerage commission.

Despite those drawbacks, this ETF can provide reasonably priced exposure to big European companies.

| | | | | |
|---|---|---|---|---|
| Address: | 45 Fremont Street San Francisco CA 94105 800-474-2737 | Management Fee: | 0.60% | |
| | | Expense Projections: | 3Yr:$192  5Yr:$335  10Yr:$750 | |
| | | Income Distrib: | Annually | |
| Web Address: | www.ishares.com | Exchange: | NYSE | |
| Inception: | 07-25-00* | | | |
| Advisor: | Barclays Global Fund Advisers | | | |

**M‹RNINGSTAR® ETFs 100**

# iShares S&P Glob 100

| Ticker | NAV | Market Price | 52 wk High/Low | Yield | Mstar Category |
|---|---|---|---|---|---|
| IOO | $62.92 | $65.66 | $65.75 - $58.70 | 1.9% | World Stock |

## Management

### Portfolio Manager(s)

The fund's advisor, Barclays Global Fund Advisors, is one of the world's largest and most experienced managers of index-tracking portfolios. Lisa Chen and Carl Gilchrist are the primary portfolio managers of this and Barclays other international and global iShares. Chen has been a portfolio manager with Barclays for six years. Gilchrist has been on board for a decade.

### Strategy

This exchange-traded offering is a passive fund that simply attempts to match the performance of the S&P Global 100 Index. The benchmark is a market-capitalization weighted index designed to track multinational companies with market caps greater than $5 billion, regardless of their country of origin. The bogy includes companies from 15 developed countries, but it's really concentrated on firms from two nations: the United States and England, which comprise two thirds of the index's country exposure (Western European nations and Japan account for most of the balance). The fund uses representative sampling.

**Growth of $10,000**

— Investment Value of ETF
— Investment Value of Index MSCI EAFE

| | 1996 | 1997 | 1998 | 1999 | 2000 | 2001 | 2002 | 2003 | 2004 | 2005 | History |
|---|---|---|---|---|---|---|---|---|---|---|---|
| | — | — | — | — | 69.66 | 58.66 | 44.06 | 56.85 | 61.25 | 62.92 | NAV $ |
| | — | — | — | — | 69.68 | 59.00 | 44.30 | 57.40 | 61.50 | 62.95 | Market Price $ |
| | — | — | — | — | -1.40* | -14.90 | -23.96 | 30.53 | 9.55 | 4.66 | NAV Return% |
| | — | — | — | — | -1.39* | -14.43 | -23.99 | 31.08 | 8.94 | 4.29 | Market Price Return% |
| | — | — | — | — | 0.03 | 0.24 | -0.02 | 0.29 | 0.47 | 0.09 | Avg Premium/Discount% |
| | — | — | — | — | -1.40 | 6.52 | -8.02 | -8.06 | -10.70 | -8.88 | NAV Rtrn% +/-MSCI EAFE |
| | — | — | — | — | -1.40 | 1.90 | -4.07 | -2.58 | -5.17 | -4.83 | NAV Rtrn% +/-MSCI World |
| | — | — | — | — | — | 2 | 2 | 2 | 2 | 2 | NAV Return% Rank in Cat |
| | — | — | — | — | — | 0.90 | 0.94 | 1.47 | 1.80 | 1.96 | Income Return % |
| | — | — | — | — | — | -15.80 | -24.90 | 29.06 | 7.75 | 2.70 | Capital Return % |
| | — | — | — | — | 0.02 | 0.63 | 0.55 | 0.65 | 1.03 | 1.20 | Income $ |
| | — | — | — | — | 0.00 | 0.00 | 0.00 | 0.00 | 0.00 | 0.00 | Capital Gains $ |
| | — | — | — | — | — | 0.40 | 0.40 | 0.40 | 0.40 | 0.40 | Expense Ratio % |
| | — | — | — | — | — | 0.88 | 1.08 | 1.60 | 1.63 | 2.24 | Income Ratio % |
| | — | — | — | — | — | 5 | 4 | 5 | 4 | 4 | Turnover Rate % |
| | — | — | — | — | — | 46 | 122 | 279 | 374 | | Net Assets $mil |

## Performance

**Historic Quarterly NAV Returns**

| | 1st Qtr | 2nd Qtr | 3rd Qtr | 4th Qtr | Total |
|---|---|---|---|---|---|
| 2001 | -12.54 | 3.56 | -14.50 | 9.89 | -14.90 |
| 2002 | -2.69 | -12.30 | -18.56 | 9.40 | -23.96 |
| 2003 | -4.61 | 15.58 | 3.83 | 14.02 | 30.53 |
| 2004 | 0.62 | 0.96 | -2.15 | 10.21 | 9.55 |
| 2005 | -0.95 | -1.17 | 6.05 | 0.81 | 4.66 |

| Trailing | NAV Return% | Market Return%+/-MSCI EAFE | NAV Rtrn% +/-MSCI EAFE | %Rank Cat.(NAV) |
|---|---|---|---|---|
| 3 Mo | 0.81 | 0.95 | -3.27 | 2 |
| 6 Mo | 6.91 | 6.63 | -7.97 | 2 |
| 1 Yr | 4.66 | 4.29 | -8.88 | 2 |
| 3 Yr Avg | 14.38 | 14.20 | -9.30 | 2 |
| 5 Yr Avg | -0.64 | -0.64 | -5.20 | 2 |
| 10 Yr Avg | — | — | — | 0 |

| Tax Analysis | Tax-Adj Return% | Tax-Cost Ratio |
|---|---|---|
| 3 Yr (estimated) | 13.76 | 0.54 |
| 5 Yr (estimated) | -1.14 | 0.50 |
| 10 Yr (estimated) | — | — |

## Risk Profile

| | Standard Index S&P 500 | Best Fit Index MSCI World |
|---|---|---|
| Alpha | -3.7 | -3.2 |
| Beta | 0.78 | 0.96 |
| R-Squared | 86 | 94 |
| Standard Deviation | 9.71 | |
| Mean | 14.38 | |
| Sharpe Ratio | 1.23 | |

## Morningstar Fair Value

| Price/Fair Value Ratio | Fair Value Estimate ($) | Hit Rate % |
|---|---|---|
| 0.9 Undervalued | 36.95 | 58 Poor |

## Portfolio Analysis 12-31-05

Share change since 11-05 Total Stocks:100

| | Sector | Country | % Assets |
|---|---|---|---|
| ⊖ General Electric | Ind Mtrls | United States | 4.81 |
| ⊖ ExxonMobil | Energy | United States | 4.53 |
| ⊖ Citigroup | Financial | United States | 3.19 |
| ⊖ Microsoft | Software | United States | 3.11 |
| ⊖ BP | Energy | U.K. | 2.86 |
| ⊖ Procter & Gamble | Goods | United States | 2.51 |
| ⊖ HSBC Hldgs | Financial | U.K. | 2.34 |
| ⊖ Johnson & Johnson | Health | United States | 2.31 |
| ⊖ American International G | Financial | United States | 2.30 |
| ⊖ Pfizer | Health | United States | 2.22 |
| ⊖ TOTAL | Energy | France | 2.03 |
| ⊖ Altria Group | Goods | United States | 2.02 |
| ⊖ Intel | Hardware | United States | 1.96 |
| ⊖ GlaxoSmithKline | Health | U.K. | 1.91 |
| Novartis | Health | Switzerland | 1.83 |
| Toyota Motor | Goods | Japan | 1.81 |
| ⊖ J.P. Morgan Chase & Co. | Financial | United States | 1.81 |
| ⊖ Vodafone Grp | Telecom | U.K. | 1.73 |
| ⊖ IBM | Hardware | United States | 1.69 |
| Nestle | Goods | Switzerland | 1.58 |

### Current Investment Style

Value Blnd Growth — Large/Mid/Small

| | Market Cap | % |
|---|---|---|
| | Giant | 92.2 |
| | Large | 7.8 |
| | Mid | 0.0 |
| | Small | 0.0 |
| | Micro | 0.0 |

Avg $mil: 110,751

| Value Measures | | Rel Category |
|---|---|---|
| Price/Earnings | 14.40 | 1.00 |
| Price/Book | 2.46 | 0.96 |
| Price/Sales | 1.31 | 0.83 |
| Price/Cash Flow | 8.13 | 0.94 |
| Dividend Yield % | 2.55 | 1.00 |

| Growth Measures | % | Rel Category |
|---|---|---|
| Long-Term Erngs | 10.51 | 1.04 |
| Book Value | 6.43 | 0.67 |
| Sales | 5.66 | 0.68 |
| Cash Flow | 11.02 | 0.96 |
| Historical Erngs | 15.18 | 0.93 |

### Composition

| Cash | 0.3 | Bonds | 0.0 |
|---|---|---|---|
| Stocks | 99.8 | Other | 0.0 |
| Foreign (% of Stock) | | | 49.7 |

| Sector Weightings | % of Stocks | Rel MSCI EAFE | 3 Year High Low | |
|---|---|---|---|---|
| ☎ Info | 19.41 | 1.39 | | |
| Software | 3.13 | 2.93 | 6 | 3 |
| Hardware | 10.31 | 2.86 | 14 | 10 |
| Media | 2.17 | 1.03 | 2 | 2 |
| Telecom | 3.80 | 0.53 | 5 | 4 |
| ☞ Service | 36.32 | 0.79 | | |
| Health | 11.94 | 1.67 | 16 | 12 |
| Consumer | 2.46 | 0.56 | 4 | 2 |
| Business | 0.00 | 0.00 | 0 | 0 |
| Financial | 21.92 | 0.78 | 22 | 13 |
| ⊞ Mfg | 44.26 | 1.10 | | |
| Goods | 17.93 | 1.31 | 18 | 17 |
| Ind Mtrls | 10.75 | 0.76 | 12 | 10 |
| Energy | 14.19 | 1.79 | 16 | 10 |
| Utilities | 1.39 | 0.30 | 1 | 0 |

### Regional Exposure

| | % Stock | | |
|---|---|---|---|
| UK/W. Europe | 42 | N. America | 51 |
| Japan | 5 | Latn America | 0 |
| Asia X Japan | 2 | Other | 0 |

### Country Exposure

| | % Stock | | |
|---|---|---|---|
| United States | 50 | Switzerland | 6 |
| U.K. | 13 | Germany | 6 |
| France | 7 | | |

## Morningstar's Take by Dan Culloton

You won't find a cheaper, purer shot of massive multinational stocks than the iShares S&P Global 100 Index.

If you just look at expense ratios, this fund is the cheapest fund most retail investors can buy in the world-stock category. Its 0.40% levy is less than one fourth of the typical offering in the group. Brokerage commissions can quickly erode that advantage, however, if you plan to trade frequently or make regular investments. For a lump-sum investment, though, this exchange-traded fund's low expenses give it a big head start.

That doesn't make it a sure winner. The fund's returns so far show it's too concentrated on large-cap stocks to flourish in every market. The ETF's 1.4% loss from Jan. 1, 2001, through Oct. 31, 2004, lags the world stock average. Yet there are reasons to consider the offering.

The dominance of smaller, less-established stocks in recent years explains some of its poor results. Most world-stock funds include more mid-

and small-caps than this ETF. Indeed, the average market cap of this fund is nearly five times the category average.

If the shares of smaller firms keep rolling, this fund will keep lagging. Such runs don't last forever, though, and when the markets turn to large caps this ETF will benefit. It tracks Standard & Poor's index of the largest companies in the world. About 90% of its money is devoted to massive, globe-spanning businesses, such as General Electric, BP and HSBC Holdings.

The fund has its risks. Because the fund's market-cap-weighted bogy focuses on titanic firms, it's top heavy with a third of its money in its top 10 holdings. It also is heavily exposed to the United States and Britain. Still, many of this ETF's holdings are tied more to the ebb and flow of global sector trends than they are to their home economies. For affordable exposure to huge stocks this will do.

| | | | | |
|---|---|---|---|---|
| Address: | 45 Fremont Street San Francisco CA 94105 800-474-2737 | Management Fee: | 0.40% | |
| | | Expense Projections: | 3Yr:$128 5Yr:$224 10Yr:$505 | |
| Web Address: | www.ishares.com | Income Distrib: | Annually | |
| Inception: | 12-05-00* | Exchange: | NYSE | |
| Advisor: | Barclays Global Fund Advisers | | | |

**MORNINGSTAR® ETFs 100**

# iShares SP Latin 40

| | Ticker | NAV | Market Price | 52 wk High/Low | Yield | Mstar Category |
|---|---|---|---|---|---|---|
| | ILF | $123.00 | $133.10 | $134.17 - $75.05 | 1.4% | Latin America Stock |

## Management

### Portfolio Manager(s)

Barclays Global Fund Advisors manages the fund. The firm is the largest manager of indexed assets in the world, with more than $1 trillion in passive money under management.

### Strategy

This fund passively tracks the Standard & Poor's Latin 40 Index. Forty of the largest companies from Argentina, Brazil, Chile, and Mexico make up the benchmark. The fund's managers do not buy the shares of the constituents directly, though. Rather, they primarily buy American Depository Receipts, or ADRs, that trade on U.S. stock exchanges. ADRs are receipts of the shares of foreign-based companies that trade in the U.S. It does not hedge its currency exposure.

**Growth of $10,000**

— Investment Value of ETF
— Investment Value of Index MSCI EAFE

| 1996 | 1997 | 1998 | 1999 | 2000 | 2001 | 2002 | 2003 | 2004 | 2005 | History |
|---|---|---|---|---|---|---|---|---|---|---|
| — | — | — | — | — | 47.73 | 36.35 | 58.17 | 79.92 | 123.00 | NAV $ |
| — | — | — | — | — | 47.69 | 36.59 | 58.84 | 80.55 | 122.85 | Market Price $ |
| — | — | — | — | — | 31.78* | -21.96 | 62.12 | 39.03 | 56.00 | NAV Return% |
| — | — | — | — | — | 31.74* | -21.38 | 62.91 | 38.53 | 54.59 | Market Price Return% |
| — | — | — | — | — | -0.05 | -0.01 | 0.57 | 0.49 | 0.37 | Avg Premium/Discount% |
| — | — | — | — | — | 31.78 | -6.02 | 23.53 | 18.78 | 42.46 | NAV Rtrn% +/-MSCI EAFE |
| — | — | — | — | — | 31.78 | 2.83 | -4.94 | 4.26 | 11.08 | NAV Rtrn% +/-MSCI EMF LA |
| — | — | — | — | — | — | 3 | 3 | 3 | 3 | NAV Return% Rank in Cat |
| — | — | — | — | — | 0.00 | 1.93 | 2.04 | 1.61 | 2.11 | Income Return % |
| — | — | — | — | — | — | -23.89 | 60.08 | 37.42 | 53.89 | Capital Return % |
| — | — | — | — | — | 0.27 | 0.92 | 0.74 | 0.94 | 1.69 | Income $ |
| — | — | — | — | — | 0.00 | 0.00 | 0.00 | 0.00 | 0.00 | Capital Gains $ |
| — | — | — | — | — | — | 0.50 | 0.50 | 0.50 | 0.50 | Expense Ratio % |
| — | — | — | — | — | — | 2.94 | 2.42 | 2.61 | 2.00 | Income Ratio % |
| — | — | — | — | — | — | 2 | 9 | 13 | 6 | Turnover Rate % |
| — | — | — | — | — | — | 9 | 61 | 224 | 1,230 | Net Assets $mil |

## Performance

### Historic Quarterly NAV Returns

| | 1st Qtr | 2nd Qtr | 3rd Qtr | 4th Qtr | Total |
|---|---|---|---|---|---|
| 2001 | — | — | — | — | —* |
| 2002 | 9.97 | -21.76 | -23.59 | 18.70 | -21.96 |
| 2003 | -2.12 | 23.78 | 11.72 | 19.78 | 62.12 |
| 2004 | 6.91 | -6.54 | 13.99 | 22.07 | 39.03 |
| 2005 | 2.40 | 13.04 | 29.39 | 4.16 | 56.00 |

| Trailing | NAV Return% | Market Return%+/-MSCI EAFE | NAV Rtrn% +/-MSCI EAFE | %Rank Cat.(NAV) |
|---|---|---|---|---|
| 3 Mo | 4.16 | 3.46 | 0.08 | 3 |
| 6 Mo | 34.77 | 33.87 | 19.89 | 3 |
| 1 Yr | 56.00 | 54.59 | 42.46 | 3 |
| 3 Yr Avg | 52.06 | 51.67 | 28.38 | 3 |
| 5 Yr Avg | — | — | — | 0 |
| 10 Yr Avg | — | — | — | 0 |

| Tax Analysis | Tax-Adj Return% | Tax-Cost Ratio |
|---|---|---|
| 3 Yr (estimated) | 51.39 | 0.44 |
| 5 Yr (estimated) | — | — |
| 10 Yr (estimated) | — | — |

## Risk Profile

| | Standard Index S&P 500 | Best Fit Index MSCI EMF LA |
|---|---|---|
| Alpha | 17.0 | 4.6 |
| Beta | 1.27 | 0.95 |
| R-Squared | 56 | 97 |
| Standard Deviation | 19.72 | |
| Mean | 52.06 | |
| Sharpe Ratio | 2.16 | |

## Morningstar Fair Value

| Price/Fair Value Ratio | Fair Value Estimate ($) | Hit Rate % |
|---|---|---|
| 1.7 Overvalued | 34.25 | 54 Poor |

## Portfolio Analysis 12-31-05

Share change since 11-05 Total Stocks:37

| | Sector | Country | % Assets |
|---|---|---|---|
| ⊕ America Movil S.A. de C. | Telecom | Mexico | 11.10 |
| ⊕ Petroleo Brasileiro ADR | Energy | Brazil | 10.63 |
| ⊕ CEMEX | Ind Mtrls | Mexico | 9.23 |
| ⊕ Companhia Vale Do Rio Do | Ind Mtrls | Brazil | 6.59 |
| ⊕ Banco Bradesco S.A. (ADR | Financial | Brazil | 5.74 |
| ⊖ Telefonos de Mexico | Telecom | Mexico | 5.29 |
| ⊕ Companhia Vale Do Rio Do | Ind Mtrls | Brazil | 5.10 |
| ⊕ Banco Itau Holding Finan | Financial | Brazil | 4.83 |
| ⊕ Wal-Mart de Mexico | Consumer | Mexico | 3.99 |
| ⊕ Companhia de Bebidas das | Goods | Brazil | 3.53 |
| ⊕ Grupo Televisa | Media | Mexico | 2.98 |
| ⊕ Empresa Nacional De Elec | Utilities | Chile | 2.40 |
| ⊕ Unibanco Uniao de Bancos | Financial | Brazil | 2.22 |
| ⊕ Tenaris SA | Ind Mtrls | Luxembourg | 2.20 |
| ⊕ Banco Santander-Chile AD | Financial | Chile | 2.00 |
| ⊕ Tele Norte Leste Partici | Telecom | Brazil | 1.99 |
| ⊕ Fomento Economico Mexica | Goods | Mexico | 1.90 |
| ⊕ Gerdau SA ADR PN | Ind Mtrls | Brazil | 1.68 |
| ⊕ Empresa Brasileira ADR | Ind Mtrls | Brazil | 1.58 |
| ⊕ Companhia Siderurgica Na | Ind Mtrls | Brazil | 1.37 |

### Current Investment Style

Value Blnd Growth — Large Mid Small

| Market Cap | % |
|---|---|
| Giant | 69.1 |
| Large | 25.7 |
| Mid | 5.1 |
| Small | 0.1 |
| Micro | 0.0 |

Avg $mil: 21,382

| Value Measures | | Rel Category |
|---|---|---|
| Price/Earnings | 14.56 | 1.18 |
| Price/Book | 3.36 | 1.24 |
| Price/Sales | 2.04 | 1.32 |
| Price/Cash Flow | 7.43 | 1.15 |
| Dividend Yield % | 0.98 | 0.34 |

| Growth Measures | % | Rel Category |
|---|---|---|
| Long-Term Erngs | 12.73 | 0.93 |
| Book Value | 14.47 | 2.25 |
| Sales | 17.91 | 1.02 |
| Cash Flow | 36.22 | 1.63 |
| Historical Erngs | 32.58 | 1.54 |

### Composition

| | | | |
|---|---|---|---|
| Cash | 0.5 | Bonds | 0.0 |
| Stocks | 99.5 | Other | 0.0 |
| Foreign | (% of Stock) | | 100.0 |

### Sector Weightings

| | % of Stocks | Rel MSCI EAFE | 3 Year High | Low |
|---|---|---|---|---|
| Info | 23.16 | 1.65 | | |
| Software | 0.00 | 0.00 | 0 | 0 |
| Hardware | 0.00 | 0.00 | 0 | 0 |
| Media | 2.99 | 1.42 | 6 | 0 |
| Telecom | 20.17 | 2.79 | 42 | 20 |
| Service | 20.13 | 0.44 | | |
| Health | 0.00 | 0.00 | 0 | 0 |
| Consumer | 4.70 | 1.07 | 11 | 0 |
| Business | 0.00 | 0.00 | 0 | 0 |
| Financial | 15.43 | 0.55 | 20 | 2 |
| Mfg | 56.72 | 1.41 | | |
| Goods | 6.42 | 0.47 | 8 | 0 |
| Ind Mtrls | 32.46 | 2.30 | 34 | 17 |
| Energy | 11.21 | 1.42 | 18 | 10 |
| Utilities | 6.63 | 1.44 | 8 | 4 |

### Regional Exposure % Stock

| | | | |
|---|---|---|---|
| UK/W. Europe | 2 | N. America | 0 |
| Japan | 0 | Latn America | 98 |
| Asia X Japan | 0 | Other | 0 |

### Country Exposure % Stock

| | | | |
|---|---|---|---|
| Brazil | 50 | Luxembourg | 2 |
| Mexico | 38 | Argentina | 1 |
| Chile | 9 | | |

## Morningstar's Take by William Samuel Rocco

IShares S&P Latin America 40 Index's pros and cons remain the same.

This ETF's primary strength is its low cost. At just 0.50%, its expense ratio is roughly 30 to 45 basis points lower than those of the two other Latin America ETFs available and 65 to 150 basis points cheaper than those of the no-load and front-load Latin America mutual funds. That kind of cost advantage gives this fund a substantial edge over its rivals year in and year out.

Meanwhile, this offering is quite tax-efficient due to its passive strategy and ETF structure. It's also pretty easy for investors to know what securities they own through this vehicle, which tracks a focused index of Latin American blue chips that rarely changes.

The fact that this ETF mirrors a relatively narrow index of roughly three dozen well-established companies from Brazil, Mexico, Chile, and Argentina also has its downside, though. Since it owns little besides large- and giant-cap names--it

has the biggest average market cap of any Latin America offering by far--and it shuns Peruvian, Colombian, and Venezuelan issues, it is at a real disadvantage when smaller-cap and smaller-market stocks thrive. This ETF's concentrated purview also means it takes on even more issue-specific risk than its rivals. (It devotes almost two thirds of its assets to its top 10 names, while the typical Latin America fund devotes about half.)

Finally, despite its cost advantage, this ETF has been a middling rather than a superior performer. Since its late-2001 inception, it has posted a 25% annualized return, which is right in line with the Latin America norm. And it also looks pretty average from a volatility perspective.

All in all, we think this ETF is a worthy option for cost-conscious investors who will be satisfied with mainstream, rather than exciting, Latin America exposure and performance.

| Address: | 45 Fremont Street San Francisco CA 94105 800-474-2737 | Management Fee: | 0.50% |
|---|---|---|---|
| | | Expense Projections: | 3Yr:$160  5Yr:$280  10Yr:$628 |
| Web Address: | www.ishares.com | Income Distrib: | Annually |
| Inception: | 10-25-01 * | Exchange: | AMEX |
| Advisor: | Barclays Global Fund Advisers | | |

**MORNINGSTAR® ETFs 100**

# iShares SP 400 Growth

| | Ticker | NAV | Market Price | 52 wk High/Low | Yield | Mstar Category |
|---|---|---|---|---|---|---|
| | IJK | $75.73 | $79.23 | $79.23 - $63.69 | 0.6% | Mid-Cap Growth |

## Management

### Portfolio Manager(s)

Barclays Global Fund Advisors is the advisor. The firm is the world's largest manager of indexed portfolios. Patrick O'Connor, the head of Barclay's U.S. iShares portfolio management group, leads a team of a half dozen managers in running this and about 60 other ETFs. IShares domestic portfolio management group is responsible for about $75 billion in assets. Most of the managers have at least five or more years of experience with Barclays as well as prior industry experience.

### Strategy

This fund tracks the S&P MidCap 400/Citigroup Growth Index. The bogy relies on seven growth and valuation measures to classify stocks. The factors are dividend yield; price-book, -sales and -cash flow; and five-year earnings, sales, and internal growth rates. A third of the index's market capitalization ends up in each value, core or growth bucket, but stocks in the middle zone can end up in both style indexes in proportion to their style scores. The overlap should reduce turnover caused by stocks moving from one style to another. The index includes no buffer zones between market-cap ranges. It rebalances annually in December.

## Performance

### Historic Quarterly NAV Returns

| | 1st Qtr | 2nd Qtr | 3rd Qtr | 4th Qtr | Total |
|---|---|---|---|---|---|
| 2001 | -18.21 | 15.46 | -20.21 | 21.81 | -8.22 |
| 2002 | 3.39 | -13.10 | -14.61 | 5.05 | -19.40 |
| 2003 | -3.07 | 15.95 | 5.92 | 9.76 | 30.66 |
| 2004 | 4.50 | 0.71 | -3.48 | 11.94 | 13.71 |
| 2005 | -0.13 | 3.60 | 4.32 | 4.98 | 13.31 |

| Trailing | NAV Return% | Market Return% | NAV Rtrn% +/-S&P 500 | %Rank Cat.(NAV) |
|---|---|---|---|---|
| 3 Mo | 4.98 | 4.75 | 2.90 | 5 |
| 6 Mo | 9.52 | 9.17 | 3.76 | 5 |
| 1 Yr | 13.31 | 13.23 | 8.40 | 4 |
| 3 Yr Avg | 18.96 | 18.88 | 4.58 | 2 |
| 5 Yr Avg | 4.48 | 4.45 | 3.94 | 1 |
| 10 Yr Avg | — | — | — | 0 |

| Tax Analysis | Tax-Adj Return% | Tax-Cost Ratio |
|---|---|---|
| 3 Yr (estimated) | 18.75 | 0.18 |
| 5 Yr (estimated) | 4.35 | 0.12 |
| 10 Yr (estimated) | — | — |

### Growth of $10,000

— Investment Value of ETF
— Investment Value of Index S&P 500

| | 1996 | 1997 | 1998 | 1999 | 2000 | 2001 | 2002 | 2003 | 2004 | 2005 | History |
|---|---|---|---|---|---|---|---|---|---|---|---|
| | — | — | — | — | 61.95 | 56.79 | 45.66 | 59.42 | 67.25 | 75.73 | NAV $ |
| | — | — | — | — | 61.94 | 56.98 | 45.69 | 59.35 | 67.20 | 75.62 | Market Price $ |
| | — | — | — | — | 2.45* | -8.22 | -19.40 | 30.66 | 13.71 | 13.31 | NAV Return% |
| | — | — | — | — | 2.42* | -7.92 | -19.61 | 30.42 | 13.76 | 13.23 | Market Price Return% |
| | — | — | — | — | -0.08 | 0.10 | 0.09 | 0.05 | -0.00 | -0.03 | Avg Premium/Discount% |
| | — | — | — | — | 2.45 | 3.66 | 2.69 | 1.99 | 2.84 | 8.40 | NAV Rtrn% +/-S&P 500 |
| | — | — | — | — | 2.45 | 11.93 | 8.01 | -12.05 | -1.77 | 1.21 | NAV Rtrn% +/-Russ MG |
| | — | — | — | — | — | 1 | 2 | 2 | 3 | 4 | NAV Return% Rank in Cat |
| | — | — | — | — | 0.00 | 0.09 | 0.21 | 0.46 | 0.49 | 0.65 | Income Return % |
| | — | — | — | — | — | -8.31 | -19.61 | 30.20 | 13.22 | 12.66 | Capital Return % |
| | — | — | — | — | 0.00 | 0.05 | 0.12 | 0.21 | 0.29 | 0.44 | Income $ |
| | — | — | — | — | 0.23 | 0.00 | 0.00 | 0.00 | 0.00 | 0.00 | Capital Gains $ |
| | — | — | — | — | — | 0.25 | 0.25 | 0.25 | 0.25 | 0.25 | Expense Ratio % |
| | — | — | — | — | — | 0.06 | 0.15 | 0.31 | 0.45 | 0.56 | Income Ratio % |
| | — | — | — | — | — | 67 | 50 | 58 | 37 | 34 | Turnover Rate % |
| | — | — | — | — | — | — | 352 | 612 | 1,083 | 1,787 | Net Assets $mil |

## Risk Profile

| | Standard Index S&P 500 | Best Fit Index S&P Mid 400 |
|---|---|---|
| Alpha | 3.7 | -0.6 |
| Beta | 1.04 | 0.93 |
| R-Squared | 74 | 96 |
| Standard Deviation | 11.08 | |
| Mean | 18.96 | |
| Sharpe Ratio | 1.46 | |

## Morningstar Fair Value

| Price/Fair Value Ratio | Fair Value Estimate ($) | Hit Rate % |
|---|---|---|
| 1.2 Overvalued | 39.75 | 82 Fair |

## Portfolio Analysis 12-31-05

| Share change since 11-05 Total Stocks:235 | Sector | PE | Tot Ret% | % Assets |
|---|---|---|---|---|
| ⊕ Legg Mason | Financial | 30.9 | 64.48 | 2.63 |
| ✳ SanDisk | Hardware | 36.1 | 151.58 | 2.09 |
| ⊕ Whole Foods Market | Consumer | 78.2 | 63.73 | 1.92 |
| ⊕ Chico's FAS | Consumer | 43.9 | 92.97 | 1.43 |
| ⊕ Expeditors International | Business | 41.4 | 21.41 | 1.30 |
| ✳ Noble Energy | Energy | 11.3 | 31.24 | 1.27 |
| ⊕ Cognizant Technology Sol | Business | 52.9 | 18.76 | 1.26 |
| ⊕ Ivax | Health | 42.9 | 98.04 | 1.23 |
| ⊕ Barr Pharmaceuticals | Health | 26.9 | 36.78 | 1.21 |
| ⊕ Varian Medical Systems | Health | 33.6 | 16.42 | 1.19 |
| ✳ Pioneer Natural Resource | Energy | 18.6 | 46.75 | 1.19 |
| ⊕ Harman International Ind | Goods | 27.0 | -22.91 | 1.16 |
| ✳ Newfield Exploration | Energy | 24.9 | 69.59 | 1.15 |
| ⊕ CH Robinson Worldwide | Business | 35.1 | 34.89 | 1.14 |
| ✳ Southwestern Energy | Energy | 41.1 | 183.60 | 1.08 |
| ✳ Commerce Bancorp NJ | Financial | 19.1 | 8.40 | 1.08 |
| ⊕ Abercrombie & Fitch A | Consumer | 21.8 | 40.27 | 1.03 |
| ⊕ Patterson-UTI Energy | Energy | 20.0 | 70.37 | 1.03 |
| ⊕ Grant Prideco | Energy | 41.2 | 120.05 | 1.02 |
| ⊕ Sepracor | Health | — | -13.09 | 0.99 |

### Current Investment Style

Value Blnd Growth — Large Mid Small

| Market Cap | % |
|---|---|
| Giant | 0.0 |
| Large | 7.3 |
| Mid | 87.3 |
| Small | 5.4 |
| Micro | 0.0 |

Avg $mil: 4,150

| Value Measures | | Rel Category |
|---|---|---|
| Price/Earnings | 20.40 | 0.91 |
| Price/Book | 3.29 | 0.90 |
| Price/Sales | 1.90 | 0.98 |
| Price/Cash Flow | 10.14 | 0.89 |
| Dividend Yield % | 0.48 | 1.07 |

| Growth Measures | % | Rel Category |
|---|---|---|
| Long-Term Erngs | 15.05 | 0.96 |
| Book Value | 16.47 | 1.65 |
| Sales | 14.61 | 1.30 |
| Cash Flow | 17.86 | 1.18 |
| Historical Erngs | 19.83 | 0.96 |

| Profitability | % | Rel Category |
|---|---|---|
| Return on Equity | 17.53 | 0.89 |
| Return on Assets | 9.79 | 0.94 |
| Net Margin | 11.67 | 0.99 |

| Sector Weightings | % of Stocks | Rel S&P 500 | 3 Year High Low | |
|---|---|---|---|---|
| ↻ Info | 13.40 | 0.66 | | |
| 🖥 Software | 3.41 | 0.96 | 6 | 3 |
| 💻 Hardware | 8.91 | 0.89 | 12 | 5 |
| 🎙 Media | 1.08 | 0.30 | 7 | 1 |
| 📶 Telecom | 0.00 | 0.00 | 1 | 0 |
| 🖅 Service | 63.30 | 1.36 | | |
| 💊 Health | 17.94 | 1.35 | 24 | 15 |
| 🛒 Consumer | 19.05 | 2.34 | 23 | 14 |
| 💼 Business | 14.30 | 3.70 | 15 | 12 |
| 💲 Financial | 12.01 | 0.57 | 13 | 11 |
| 🏭 Mfg | 23.28 | 0.70 | | |
| 🔧 Goods | 5.51 | 0.64 | 10 | 5 |
| ⚙ Ind Mtrls | 4.03 | 0.33 | 7 | 3 |
| 🔋 Energy | 13.42 | 1.44 | 13 | 5 |
| 💡 Utilities | 0.32 | 0.10 | 1 | 0 |

### Composition

| | | % |
|---|---|---|
| ● Cash | | 0.1 |
| ● Stocks | | 99.9 |
| ● Bonds | | 0.0 |
| ● Other | | 0.0 |
| | Foreign | 0.0 |
| | (% of Stock) | |

## Morningstar's Take by Dan Culloton

We look forward to this exchange-traded fund's impending benchmark change.

Standard & Poor's, which publishes the benchmark for the iShares S&P MidCap 400/Barra Growth Index, will drop the style index methodology developed by risk-management firm Barra, which relied on a stock's price/book value to determine if it was growth or value. Instead, it will adopt bogies derived from a multifactor model created by Citigroup.

The switch will rearrange the guts of this fund. Barclays Global Investors, this fund's advisor, planned to make the switch to the new index on or about Dec. 16, 2005. The fund will change its name to iShares S&P MidCap 400 Growth Index Fund at that time. Barclays, however, doesn't expect the changeover to require much more turnover than a normal rebalancing of the old Barra index. It also said it would try to minimize transaction costs and capital gains, though there's no guarantee transition won't have an impact on those fronts.

More importantly this ETF's new index could help the fund keep turnover low on an ongoing basis and offer more realistic exposure to the mid-cap growth universe. The new S&P MidCap 400/Citigroup Growth Index will still draw its constituents from the S&P MidCap 400, but it will look at seven valuation and growth factors instead of one to figure out if a stock belongs. Unlike the Barra index, it also will allow some stocks that have both value and growth characteristics to live in both value and growth indexes. This addresses a few knocks against the old Barra index: that its refusal to allow style overlap and its reliance on one factor made it an unrealistic measure of the mid-growth universe; and that turnover was increased as stocks migrated based on their price/book values.

Much of the indexing world has adopted multifactor style indexes. It's about time S&P joined the party.

| Address: | 45 Fremont Street San Francisco CA 94105 800-474-2737 |
|---|---|
| Web Address: | www.ishares.com |
| Inception: | 07-24-00* |
| Advisor: | Barclays Global Fund Advisers |

| Management Fee: | 0.25% | | |
|---|---|---|---|
| Expense Projections: | 3Yr:$80 | 5Yr:$141 | 10Yr:$318 |
| Income Distrib: | Quarterly | | |
| Exchange: | NYSE | | |

# iShares SP 400 Value

| | Ticker | NAV | Market Price | 52 wk High/Low | Yield | Mstar Category |
|---|---|---|---|---|---|---|
| | IJJ | $70.60 | $73.35 | $73.35 - $60.67 | 1.6% | Mid-Cap Value |

## Management

### Portfolio Manager(s)

Barclays Global Fund Advisors is the advisor. The firm is the world's largest manager of indexed portfolios. Patrick O'Connor, the head of Barclay's U.S. iShares portfolio management group leads a team of a half dozen managers in running this and about 60 other ETFs. IShares domestic portfolio management group is responsible for about $75 billion in assets. Most of the managers have at least five or more years of experience with Barclays as well as prior industry experience.

### Strategy

This fund tracks the S&P MidCap 400/Citigroup Value Index. The bogy relies on seven growth and valuation measures to classify stocks. The factors are dividend yield; price-book, -sales and -cash flow; and five-year earnings, sales, and internal growth rates. A third of the index's market capitalization ends up in each value, core or growth bucket, but stocks in the middle zone can end up in both style indexes in proportion to their style scores. The overlap should reduce turnover caused by stocks moving from one style to another. The index includes no buffer zones between market-cap ranges. It rebalances annually in December.

## Performance

### Historic Quarterly NAV Returns

| | 1st Qtr | 2nd Qtr | 3rd Qtr | 4th Qtr | Total |
|---|---|---|---|---|---|
| 2001 | -3.51 | 11.40 | -13.06 | 14.55 | 7.05 |
| 2002 | 9.79 | -5.91 | -18.51 | 6.49 | -10.36 |
| 2003 | -5.86 | 19.11 | 7.09 | 16.42 | 39.79 |
| 2004 | 5.46 | 1.14 | -0.83 | 12.17 | 18.65 |
| 2005 | -0.76 | 5.04 | 5.36 | 1.50 | 11.47 |

| Trailing | NAV Return% | Market Return% | NAV Rtrn% +/-S&P 500 | %Rank Cat.(NAV) |
|---|---|---|---|---|
| 3 Mo | 1.50 | 1.25 | -0.58 | 6 |
| 6 Mo | 6.94 | 6.55 | 1.18 | 6 |
| 1 Yr | 11.47 | 11.59 | 6.56 | 5 |
| 3 Yr Avg | 22.74 | 22.61 | 8.36 | 2 |
| 5 Yr Avg | 12.15 | 12.08 | 11.61 | 1 |
| 10 Yr Avg | — | — | — | 0 |

| Tax Analysis | Tax-Adj Return% | Tax-Cost Ratio |
|---|---|---|
| 3 Yr (estimated) | 22.10 | 0.52 |
| 5 Yr (estimated) | 11.58 | 0.51 |
| 10 Yr (estimated) | — | — |

Growth of $10,000
— Investment Value of ETF
— Investment Value of Index S&P 500

| | 1996 | 1997 | 1998 | 1999 | 2000 | 2001 | 2002 | 2003 | 2004 | 2005 | History |
|---|---|---|---|---|---|---|---|---|---|---|---|
| | — | — | — | — | 42.69 | 45.13 | 39.94 | 55.01 | 64.42 | 70.60 | NAV $ |
| | — | — | — | — | 42.75 | 45.24 | 39.99 | 55.20 | 64.25 | 70.49 | Market Price $ |
| | — | — | — | — | 14.71* | 7.05 | -10.36 | 39.79 | 18.65 | 11.47 | NAV Return% |
| | — | — | — | — | 14.68* | 7.16 | -10.46 | 40.05 | 17.94 | 11.59 | Market Price Return% |
| | — | — | — | — | 0.28 | 0.01 | 0.15 | 0.10 | -0.07 | -0.01 | Avg Premium/Discount% |
| | — | — | — | — | 14.71 | 18.93 | 11.73 | 11.12 | 7.78 | 6.56 | NAV Rtrn% +/-S&P 500 |
| | — | — | — | — | 14.71 | 4.72 | -0.72 | 1.72 | -5.06 | -1.18 | NAV Rtrn% +/-Russ MV |
| | — | — | — | — | — | 1 | 2 | 2 | 3 | 5 | NAV Return% Rank in Cat |
| | — | — | — | — | 0.00 | 1.25 | 1.24 | 1.71 | 1.41 | 1.81 | Income Return % |
| | — | — | — | — | — | 5.80 | -11.60 | 38.08 | 17.24 | 9.66 | Capital Return % |
| | — | — | — | — | 0.25 | 0.53 | 0.56 | 0.68 | 0.77 | 1.16 | Income $ |
| | — | — | — | — | 0.07 | 0.00 | 0.00 | 0.00 | 0.00 | 0.00 | Capital Gains $ |
| | — | — | — | — | — | 0.25 | 0.25 | 0.25 | 0.25 | 0.25 | Expense Ratio % |
| | — | — | — | — | — | 1.58 | 1.43 | 1.50 | 1.47 | 1.78 | Income Ratio % |
| | — | — | — | — | — | 17 | 13 | 11 | 11 | 10 | Turnover Rate % |
| | — | — | — | — | — | 607 | 996 | 1,726 | 2,513 | | Net Assets $mil |

## Risk Profile

| | Standard Index S&P 500 | Best Fit Index S&P Mid 400 |
|---|---|---|
| Alpha | 4.4 | 0.2 |
| Beta | 1.26 | 1.07 |
| R-Squared | 84 | 97 |
| Standard Deviation | 12.64 | |
| Mean | 22.74 | |
| Sharpe Ratio | 1.54 | |

## Morningstar Fair Value

| Price/Fair Value Ratio | Fair Value Estimate ($) | Hit Rate % |
|---|---|---|
| 1.1 Overvalued | 29.82 | 77 Fair |

## Portfolio Analysis 12-31-05

| Share change since 11-05 Total Stocks:298 | Sector | PE | Tot Ret% | % Assets |
|---|---|---|---|---|
| ☼☼ Peabody Energy | Energy | 33.1 | 104.95 | 1.27 |
| ☼☼ Developers Diversified R | Financial | 20.4 | 11.07 | 0.94 |
| ⊖ Lyondell Chemical | Energy | 15.1 | -14.87 | 0.89 |
| ⊖ Pride International | Energy | — | 49.71 | 0.89 |
| ⊖ Old Republic Internation | Financial | 9.6 | 10.46 | 0.88 |
| ⊖ Mercantile Bankshares | Financial | 17.4 | 11.19 | 0.85 |
| ⊖ Wisconsin Energy | Utilities | 23.0 | 18.71 | 0.84 |
| ⊖ Scana | Utilities | 15.6 | 3.86 | 0.83 |
| ⊖ Associated Banc-Corp | Financial | 13.8 | 1.21 | 0.81 |
| ⊖ First American | Financial | 10.0 | 31.26 | 0.79 |
| ⊖ Pepco Holdings | Utilities | | 9.71 | 0.78 |
| ⊖ AMB Property | Financial | 47.7 | 26.78 | 0.77 |
| ☼☼ Precision Castparts | Ind Mtrls | 26.0 | 58.08 | 0.74 |
| ⊖ Manpower | Business | 17.8 | -2.67 | 0.74 |
| ☼☼ Regency Centers | Financial | 33.1 | 10.80 | 0.73 |
| ⊖ MDU Resources Group | Utilities | 15.3 | 25.75 | 0.72 |
| ⊖ New York Community Banco | Financial | 12.8 | -14.99 | 0.72 |
| ⊖ Intersil | Hardware | 50.8 | 50.19 | 0.70 |
| ⊖ Arrow Electronics | Hardware | 17.1 | 31.81 | 0.70 |
| ☼☼ Smith International | Energy | 27.9 | 37.41 | 0.70 |

### Current Investment Style

Value Blnd Growth — Large Mid Small

| Market Cap | % |
|---|---|
| Giant | 0.0 |
| Large | 1.3 |
| Mid | 84.4 |
| Small | 14.3 |
| Micro | 0.1 |

Avg $mil: 2,872

| Value Measures | | Rel Category |
|---|---|---|
| Price/Earnings | 17.08 | 1.17 |
| Price/Book | 1.87 | 1.02 |
| Price/Sales | 0.93 | 0.90 |
| Price/Cash Flow | 5.78 | 0.99 |
| Dividend Yield % | 1.88 | 0.70 |

| Growth Measures | % | Rel Category |
|---|---|---|
| Long-Term Erngs | 10.66 | 1.23 |
| Book Value | 6.65 | 0.87 |
| Sales | 7.19 | 1.14 |
| Cash Flow | 2.39 | 0.62 |
| Historical Erngs | 9.32 | 0.92 |

| Profitability | % | Rel Category |
|---|---|---|
| Return on Equity | 10.88 | 0.78 |
| Return on Assets | 6.12 | 0.71 |
| Net Margin | 8.98 | 0.71 |

| Sector Weightings | % of Stocks | Rel S&P 500 | 3 Year High | Low |
|---|---|---|---|---|
| ↻ Info | 14.67 | 0.73 | | |
| 🖥 Software | 2.33 | 0.65 | 3 | 2 |
| 🖳 Hardware | 8.91 | 0.89 | 10 | 7 |
| 🎤 Media | 2.43 | 0.68 | 3 | 2 |
| 📶 Telecom | 1.00 | 0.33 | 1 | 1 |
| ☞ Service | 43.63 | 0.94 | | |
| 🩺 Health | 4.87 | 0.37 | 7 | 4 |
| 🛒 Consumer | 7.15 | 0.88 | 14 | 6 |
| 💼 Business | 8.12 | 2.10 | 8 | 6 |
| $ Financial | 23.49 | 1.11 | 28 | 21 |
| 🏭 Mfg | 41.69 | 1.25 | | |
| 🛢 Goods | 5.49 | 0.64 | 9 | 5 |
| ✿ Ind Mtrls | 14.65 | 1.21 | 15 | 9 |
| 🔋 Energy | 8.92 | 0.95 | 12 | 7 |
| 💡 Utilities | 12.63 | 3.76 | 13 | 10 |

### Composition

| | |
|---|---|
| ● Cash | 0.1 |
| ● Stocks | 99.9 |
| ○ Bonds | 0.0 |
| ○ Other | 0.0 |
| Foreign | 0.0 |
| (% of Stock) | |

## Morningstar's Take by Dan Culloton

The exchange-traded iShares S&P MidCap 400/BARRA Value is getting a new, souped-up benchmark.

Standard & Poor's, which publishes the benchmark for this fund, will drop the style index methodology developed by risk management firm Barra that relied on a stock's price/book value to determine if it was growth or value. Instead, it will adopt bogies derived from a multi-factor model created by Citigroup.

The switch will rearrange the guts of this fund. Barclays Global Investors, this fund's advisor, planned to make the switch to the new index on or about Dec. 16, 2005. The fund will change its name to iShares S&P MidCap 400 Value Index Fund at that time. Barclays, however, doesn't expect the changeover to require much more turnover than a normal rebalancing of the old Barra index. It also said it would try to minimize transaction costs and capital gains, though there's no guarantee transition won't have an impact on either of those

fronts.

More importantly this ETF's new index could help the fund keep turnover low on an ongoing basis and offer more realistic exposure to the mid-cap-value universe. The new S&P MidCap 400/Citigroup Value Index will still draw its constituents from the S&P MidCap 400, but it will look at seven valuation and growth factors, instead of one, to figure out if a stock belongs. Unlike the Barra index, it also will allow some stocks that have both value and growth characteristics to live in both value and growth indexes. This addresses a few knocks against the old Barra index: that its refusal to allow style overlap and its reliance on one factor made it an unrealistic measure of the mid-value universe; and that turnover increased as stocks migrated based on their price/book values.

Much of the indexing world has adopted multifactor style indexes. It's about time S&P joined the party. Doing so will help keep this ETF competitive.

| Address: | 45 Fremont Street San Francisco CA 94105 800-474-2737 |
|---|---|
| Web Address: | www.ishares.com |
| Inception: | 07-24-00* |
| Advisor: | Barclays Global Fund Advisers |

| Management Fee: | 0.25% | | |
|---|---|---|---|
| Expense Projections: | 3Yr:$80 | 5Yr:$141 | 10Yr:$318 |
| Income Distrib: | Quarterly | | |
| Exchange: | NYSE | | |

MORNINGSTAR® ETFs 100

Data through December 31, 2005

# iShares SP 500 Growth

| Ticker | NAV | Market Price | 52 wk High/Low | Yield | Mstar Category |
|--------|-----|--------------|----------------|-------|----------------|
| IVW | $59.33 | $61.34 | $61.42 - $54.65 | 1.3% | Large Growth |

## Management

### Portfolio Manager(s)

Barclays Global Fund Advisors is the advisor. The firm is the world's largest manager of indexed portfolios. Patrick O'Connor, the head of Barclay's U.S. iShares portfolio management group leads a team of a half dozen managers in running this and about 60 other ETFs. IShares' domestic portfolio-management group is responsible for about $75 billion in assets. Most of the managers have at least five years of experience with Barclays as well as prior industry experience.

### Strategy

This fund tracks the S&P 500/Citigroup Growth Index. The bogy relies on seven growth and valuation measures to classify stocks. The factors are dividend yield; price-book, -sales and -cash flow; and five-year earnings, sales, and internal growth rates. A third of the index's market capitalization ends up in each value, core or growth bucket, but stocks in the middle zone can end up in both style indexes in proportion to their style scores. The overlap should reduce turnover caused by stocks moving from one style to another. The index includes no buffer zones between market-cap ranges. It rebalances annually in December.

## Performance

### Historic Quarterly NAV Returns

|  | 1st Qtr | 2nd Qtr | 3rd Qtr | 4th Qtr | Total |
|--|---------|---------|---------|---------|-------|
| 2001 | -17.43 | 7.66 | -13.24 | 12.97 | -12.87 |
| 2002 | -0.84 | -16.29 | -14.13 | 7.03 | -23.71 |
| 2003 | -0.85 | 12.09 | 2.70 | 9.88 | 25.42 |
| 2004 | -0.03 | 2.63 | -4.80 | 8.44 | 5.91 |
| 2005 | -1.89 | 0.08 | 3.74 | 1.92 | 3.81 |

| Trailing | NAV Return% | Market Return% | NAV Rtrn% +/-S&P 500 | %Rank Cat.(NAV) |
|----------|-------------|----------------|----------------------|------------------|
| 3 Mo | 1.92 | 1.49 | -0.16 | 10 |
| 6 Mo | 5.73 | 5.59 | -0.03 | 10 |
| 1 Yr | 3.81 | 3.99 | -1.10 | 9 |
| 3 Yr Avg | 11.30 | 11.26 | -3.08 | 5 |
| 5 Yr Avg | -1.73 | -1.62 | -2.27 | 5 |
| 10 Yr Avg | — | — | — | 0 |

| Tax Analysis | Tax-Adj Return% | Tax-Cost Ratio |
|--------------|-----------------|----------------|
| 3 Yr (estimated) | 10.76 | 0.49 |
| 5 Yr (estimated) | -2.15 | 0.43 |
| 10 Yr (estimated) | — | — |

### Growth of $10,000

— Investment Value of ETF
— Investment Value of Index S&P 500

| | 1996 | 1997 | 1998 | 1999 | 2000 | 2001 | 2002 | 2003 | 2004 | 2005 | History |
|--|------|------|------|------|------|------|------|------|------|------|---------|
| | — | — | — | — | 68.67 | 59.41 | 44.89 | 55.62 | 57.90 | 59.33 | NAV $ |
| | — | — | — | — | 68.25 | 59.31 | 44.91 | 55.60 | 57.75 | 59.28 | Market Price $ |
| | — | — | — | — | -4.58* | -12.87 | -23.71 | 25.42 | 5.91 | 3.81 | NAV Return% |
| | — | — | — | — | -4.59* | -12.48 | -23.55 | 25.32 | 5.68 | 3.99 | Market Price Return% |
| | — | — | — | — | -0.28 | -0.03 | 0.05 | 0.00 | 0.05 | 0.08 | Avg Premium/Discount% |
| | — | — | — | — | -4.58 | -0.99 | -1.62 | -3.25 | -4.96 | -1.10 | NAV Rtrn% +/-S&P 500 |
| | — | — | — | — | -4.58 | 7.55 | 4.17 | -4.33 | -0.39 | -1.45 | NAV Rtrn% +/-Russ 1000Gr |
| | — | — | — | — | — | 5 | 5 | 5 | 6 | 9 | NAV Return% Rank in Cat |
| | — | — | — | — | 0.00 | 0.59 | 0.81 | 1.36 | 1.77 | 1.30 | Income Return % |
| | — | — | — | — | — | -13.46 | -24.52 | 24.06 | 4.14 | 2.51 | Capital Return % |
| | — | — | — | — | 0.15 | 0.40 | 0.48 | 0.61 | 0.98 | 0.75 | Income $ |
| | — | — | — | — | 0.11 | 0.00 | 0.00 | 0.00 | 0.00 | 0.00 | Capital Gains $ |
| | — | — | — | — | — | 0.18 | 0.18 | 0.18 | 0.18 | 0.18 | Expense Ratio % |
| | — | — | — | — | — | 0.45 | 0.82 | 1.19 | 1.22 | 1.93 | Income Ratio % |
| | — | — | — | — | — | 31 | 28 | 17 | 14 | 22 | Turnover Rate % |
| | — | — | — | — | — | 637 | 1,296 | 2,157 | 3,242 | | Net Assets $mil |

## Risk Profile

| | Standard Index S&P 500 | Best Fit Index Russ 1000Gr |
|--|------------------------|----------------------------|
| Alpha | -1.5 | -0.3 |
| Beta | 0.89 | 0.86 |
| R-Squared | 92 | 95 |
| Standard Deviation | 8.51 | |
| Mean | 11.30 | |
| Sharpe Ratio | 1.08 | |

## Morningstar Fair Value

| Price/Fair Value Ratio | Fair Value Estimate ($) | Hit Rate % |
|------------------------|--------------------------|------------|
| 1.0 Fairly valued | 41.52 | 97 Good |

## Portfolio Analysis 12-31-05

Share change since 11-05 Total Stocks:298

| Sector | | PE | Tot Ret% | % Assets |
|--------|--|----|----------|----------|
| ⊖ Microsoft | Software | 22.2 | -0.95 | 4.20 |
| ⊖ ExxonMobil | Energy | 10.6 | 11.76 | 3.92 |
| ⊖ Procter & Gamble | Goods | 21.2 | 7.18 | 3.40 |
| ⊕ Johnson & Johnson | Health | 19.1 | -3.36 | 3.13 |
| ⊖ General Electric | Ind Mtrls | 19.9 | -1.43 | 3.12 |
| ✳ Pfizer | Health | 21.2 | -10.62 | 3.01 |
| ⊖ IBM | Hardware | 16.0 | -15.83 | 2.28 |
| ⊕ Wal-Mart Stores | Consumer | 18.2 | -10.30 | 2.05 |
| ⊖ Cisco Systems | Hardware | 19.9 | -11.39 | 1.84 |
| ✳ American International G | Financial | 15.6 | 4.83 | 1.80 |
| ⊖ PepsiCo | Goods | 25.8 | 15.24 | 1.72 |
| ⊕ Amgen | Health | 28.3 | 22.93 | 1.71 |
| ⊖ Altria Group | Goods | 15.0 | 27.72 | 1.69 |
| ⊖ Home Depot | Consumer | 15.6 | -4.35 | 1.51 |
| ⊕ UnitedHealth Group | Health | 26.2 | 41.22 | 1.49 |
| ⊖ Intel | Hardware | 18.6 | 8.12 | 1.37 |
| ✳ Chevron | Energy | 9.0 | 11.51 | 1.27 |
| ⊖ Dell | Hardware | 23.2 | -28.93 | 1.24 |
| ⊕ Medtronic | Health | 37.4 | 16.72 | 1.22 |
| ⊕ Eli Lilly & Company | Health | 48.4 | 2.52 | 1.13 |

### Current Investment Style

Value Blnd Growth — Large Mid Small

| Market Cap | % |
|------------|---|
| Giant | 57.9 |
| Large | 34.7 |
| Mid | 7.4 |
| Small | 0.0 |
| Micro | 0.0 |

Avg $mil: 53,584

| Value Measures | | Rel Category |
|----------------|--|--------------|
| Price/Earnings | 17.42 | 0.83 |
| Price/Book | 3.41 | 1.01 |
| Price/Sales | 1.80 | 0.92 |
| Price/Cash Flow | 5.91 | 0.56 |
| Dividend Yield % | 1.42 | 1.60 |

| Growth Measures | % | Rel Category |
|-----------------|---|--------------|
| Long-Term Erngs | 11.68 | 0.83 |
| Book Value | 11.64 | 1.42 |
| Sales | 12.34 | 1.11 |
| Cash Flow | 15.49 | 0.95 |
| Historical Erngs | 17.79 | 0.93 |

| Profitability | % | Rel Category |
|---------------|---|--------------|
| Return on Equity | 23.49 | 1.17 |
| Return on Assets | 11.73 | 1.09 |
| Net Margin | 14.52 | 1.04 |

| Sector Weightings | % of Stocks | Rel S&P 500 | 3 Year High Low | |
|-------------------|-------------|-------------|------|-----|
| ↗ Info | 21.25 | 1.05 | | |
| Software | 6.67 | 1.87 | 9 | 7 |
| Hardware | 11.82 | 1.18 | 19 | 12 |
| Media | 2.57 | 0.72 | 3 | 1 |
| Telecom | 0.19 | 0.06 | 3 | 0 |
| Service | 48.40 | 1.04 | | |
| Health | 22.14 | 1.67 | 28 | 17 |
| Consumer | 12.38 | 1.52 | 13 | 11 |
| Business | 3.97 | 1.03 | 5 | 4 |
| Financial | 9.91 | 0.47 | 10 | 2 |
| Mfg | 30.36 | 0.91 | | |
| Goods | 12.29 | 1.44 | 16 | 12 |
| Ind Mtrls | 6.62 | 0.54 | 16 | 7 |
| Energy | 10.72 | 1.15 | 11 | 0 |
| Utilities | 0.73 | 0.22 | 1 | 0 |

### Composition

| | % |
|--|---|
| Cash | 0.0 |
| Stocks | 100.0 |
| Bonds | 0.0 |
| Other | 0.0 |
| Foreign | 0.0 |

(% of Stock)

## Morningstar's Take by Dan Culloton

A new benchmark should make this an improved fund.

Standard & Poor's, which publishes the benchmark for iShares S&P 500/Barra Growth Index, will drop the style index methodology developed by risk-management firm Barra that relied on a stock's price/book value to determine whether it should be classified as growth or value. Instead, the firm will adopt bogies derived from a multifactor model created by Citigroup C.

The switch will rearrange the guts of this fund. Barclays Global Investors, this fund's advisor, planned to make the switch to the new index on or about Dec. 16, 2005. The fund will change its name to iShares S&P 500 Growth Index Fund at that time. Barclays, however, doesn't expect the changeover to require much more turnover than a normal rebalancing of the old Barra index. It also said it would try to minimize transaction costs and capital gains, though there's no guarantee transition won't have an impact on either of those fronts.

More importantly, this ETF's new index could help the fund keep turnover low on an ongoing basis and allow it to offer more complete exposure to the growth universe. The new S&P 500/Citigroup Growth Index will still draw its constituents from the S&P 500, but it will look at seven valuation and growth factors instead of one to figure out whether a stock belongs. Unlike the Barra index, it will also allow some stocks that have both value and growth characteristics to live in both value and growth indexes. This addresses a few knocks against the old Barra index: By refusing to allow style overlap and relying on only one factor, the index was an unrealistic measure of the value universe and it increased turnover as stocks migrated based on their price/book values.

Much of the indexing world has adopted multifactor style indexes. It's about time S&P joined the party. Doing so will help keep this ETF competitive.

| | |
|--|--|
| Address: | 45 Fremont Street |
| | San Francisco CA 94105 |
| | 800-474-2737 |
| Web Address: | www.ishares.com |
| Inception: | 05-22-00* |
| Advisor: | Barclays Global Fund Advisers |

| | |
|--|--|
| Management Fee: | 0.18% |
| Expense Projections: | 3Yr:$58  5Yr:$101  10Yr:$230 |
| Income Distrib: | Quarterly |
| Exchange: | NYSE |

© 2006 Morningstar, Inc. All rights reserved. The information herein is not represented or warranted to be accurate, correct, complete or timely.
Past performance is no guarantee of future results. Activate your free 14-day research pass at http://www.morningstar.com/goto/ETF1002006

MᴏRNINGSTAR® ETFs 100        117

# iShares SP 500 Value

| Ticker | NAV | Market Price | 52 wk High/Low | Yield | Mstar Category |
|---|---|---|---|---|---|
| IVE | $65.11 | $67.20 | $67.28 - $58.55 | 2.0% | Large Value |

## Management

### Portfolio Manager(s)

Barclays Global Fund Advisors is the advisor. The firm is the world's largest manager of indexed portfolios. Patrick O'Connor, the head of Barclay's U.S. iShares portfolio management group leads a team of a half dozen managers in running this and about 60 other ETFs. IShares domestic portfolio management group is responsible for about $75 billion in assets. Most of the managers have at least five or more years of experience with Barclays as well as prior industry experience.

### Strategy

This fund tracks the S&P MidCap 400/Citigroup Value Index. The bogy relies on seven growth and valuation measures to classify stocks. The factors are dividend yield; price-book, -sales and -cash flow; and five-year earnings, sales, and internal growth rates. A third of the index's market capitalization ends up in each value, core or growth bucket, but stocks in the middle zone can end up in both style indexes in proportion to their style scores. The overlap should reduce turnover caused by stocks moving from one style to another. The index includes no buffer zones between market-cap ranges. It rebalances annually in December.

### Growth of $10,000

| | | | | Investment Value of ETF |
| | | | | Investment Value of Index S&P 500 |

| 1996 | 1997 | 1998 | 1999 | 2000 | 2001 | 2002 | 2003 | 2004 | 2005 | History |
|---|---|---|---|---|---|---|---|---|---|---|
| — | — | — | — | 63.63 | 55.28 | 42.93 | 55.42 | 62.91 | 65.11 | NAV $ |
| — | — | — | — | 63.38 | 55.28 | 42.90 | 55.33 | 62.88 | 65.05 | Market Price $ |
| — | — | — | — | 3.20* | -11.85 | -20.98 | 31.51 | 15.51 | 5.67 | NAV Return% |
| — | — | — | — | 3.18* | -11.50 | -21.04 | 31.39 | 15.64 | 5.63 | Market Price Return% |
| — | — | — | — | 0.05 | -0.01 | -0.02 | 0.06 | 0.07 | 0.02 | Avg Premium/Discount% |
| — | — | — | — | 3.20 | 0.03 | 1.11 | 2.84 | 4.64 | 0.76 | NAV Rtrn% +/-S&P 500 |
| — | — | — | — | 3.20 | -6.26 | -5.46 | 1.48 | -0.98 | -1.38 | NAV Rtrn% +/-Russ 1000 VI |
| — | — | — | — | — | 7 | 7 | 7 | 7 | 10 | NAV Return% Rank in Cat |
| — | — | — | — | 0.00 | 1.31 | 1.50 | 2.08 | 1.85 | 2.10 | Income Return % |
| — | — | — | — | — | -13.16 | -22.48 | 29.43 | 13.66 | 3.57 | Capital Return % |
| — | — | — | — | 0.45 | 0.83 | 0.83 | 0.89 | 1.02 | 1.31 | Income $ |
| — | — | — | — | 0.15 | 0.00 | 0.00 | 0.00 | 0.00 | 0.00 | Capital Gains $ |
| — | — | — | — | — | 0.18 | 0.18 | 0.18 | 0.18 | 0.18 | Expense Ratio % |
| — | — | — | — | — | 1.51 | 1.56 | 2.01 | 1.91 | 1.95 | Income Ratio % |
| — | — | — | — | — | 9 | 17 | 22 | 5 | 5 | Turnover Rate % |
| — | — | — | — | — | 702 | 1,477 | 2,931 | 3,015 | | Net Assets $mil |

## Performance

### Historic Quarterly NAV Returns

| | 1st Qtr | 2nd Qtr | 3rd Qtr | 4th Qtr | Total |
|---|---|---|---|---|---|
| 2001 | -6.55 | 4.35 | -16.23 | 7.91 | -11.85 |
| 2002 | 1.26 | -10.67 | -20.45 | 9.81 | -20.98 |
| 2003 | -5.54 | 18.76 | 2.49 | 14.38 | 31.51 |
| 2004 | 3.29 | 0.76 | 1.00 | 9.88 | 15.51 |
| 2005 | -2.44 | 2.54 | 3.41 | 2.15 | 5.67 |

| Trailing | NAV Return% | Market Return% | NAV Rtrn% +/-S&P 500 | %Rank Cat.(NAV) |
|---|---|---|---|---|
| 3 Mo | 2.15 | 1.96 | 0.07 | 13 |
| 6 Mo | 5.63 | 5.35 | -0.13 | 11 |
| 1 Yr | 5.67 | 5.63 | 0.76 | 10 |
| 3 Yr Avg | 17.09 | 17.08 | 2.71 | 7 |
| 5 Yr Avg | 2.26 | 2.32 | 1.72 | 7 |
| 10 Yr Avg | — | — | — | 0 |

| Tax Analysis | Tax-Adj Return% | Tax-Cost Ratio |
|---|---|---|
| 3 Yr (estimated) | 16.32 | 0.66 |
| 5 Yr (estimated) | 1.60 | 0.65 |
| 10 Yr (estimated) | — | — |

## Risk Profile

| | Standard Index S&P 500 | Best Fit Index Russ 1000 VI |
|---|---|---|
| Alpha | 1.1 | -1.4 |
| Beta | 1.11 | 1.08 |
| R-Squared | 95 | 97 |
| Standard Deviation | 10.47 | |
| Mean | 17.09 | |
| Sharpe Ratio | 1.38 | |

## Morningstar Fair Value

| Price/Fair Value Ratio | Fair Value Estimate ($) | Hit Rate % |
|---|---|---|
| 1.0 Fairly valued | 36.38 | 97 Good |

## Portfolio Analysis 12-31-05

| Share change since 11-05 | Total Stocks:354 | Sector | PE | Tot Ret% | % Assets |
|---|---|---|---|---|---|
| ⊕ Citigroup | | Financial | 12.1 | 4.63 | 4.42 |
| ✕ General Electric | | Ind Mtrls | 19.9 | -1.43 | 3.46 |
| ⊕ Bank of America | | Financial | 11.1 | 2.39 | 3.33 |
| ⊕ J.P. Morgan Chase & Co. | | Financial | 18.8 | 5.74 | 2.50 |
| ✕ ExxonMobil | | Energy | 10.6 | 11.76 | 2.26 |
| ⊕ Wells Fargo | | Financial | 14.3 | 4.47 | 1.89 |
| ⊕ AT&T | | Telecom | 21.1 | 0.25 | 1.72 |
| ⊕ Verizon Communications | | Telecom | 10.2 | -22.18 | 1.50 |
| ⊕ Wachovia | | Financial | 13.0 | 4.29 | 1.48 |
| ⊕ Hewlett-Packard | | Hardware | 27.3 | 38.29 | 1.48 |
| ⊕ ConocoPhillips | | Energy | 6.7 | 36.89 | 1.45 |
| ⊖ American International G | | Financial | 15.6 | 4.83 | 1.34 |
| ✕ Intel | | Hardware | 18.6 | 8.12 | 1.30 |
| ⊕ Sprint Nextel | | Telecom | 19.1 | -4.81 | 1.24 |
| ⊕ Merrill Lynch & Company | | Financial | 13.7 | 14.77 | 1.12 |
| ⊕ Morgan Stanley | | Financial | 13.3 | 4.28 | 1.10 |
| ✕ Altria Group | | Goods | 15.0 | 27.72 | 1.06 |
| ⊕ Tyco International | | Ind Mtrls | 19.1 | -18.17 | 1.04 |
| ⊕ Goldman Sachs Group | | Financial | 12.4 | 23.89 | 1.04 |
| ✕ United Technologies | | Ind Mtrls | 17.9 | 10.03 | 1.02 |

### Current Investment Style

| Market Cap | % |
|---|---|
| Giant | 50.2 |
| Large | 40.0 |
| Mid | 9.7 |
| Small | 0.2 |
| Micro | 0.0 |

Avg $mil: 41,012

| Value Measures | | Rel Category |
|---|---|---|
| Price/Earnings | 14.70 | 1.02 |
| Price/Book | 1.96 | 0.88 |
| Price/Sales | 1.24 | 0.94 |
| Price/Cash Flow | 6.30 | 1.23 |
| Dividend Yield % | 2.44 | 1.00 |

| Growth Measures | % | Rel Category |
|---|---|---|
| Long-Term Erngs | 9.50 | 0.99 |
| Book Value | 10.15 | 0.84 |
| Sales | 6.73 | 0.84 |
| Cash Flow | 9.50 | 0.77 |
| Historical Erngs | 13.49 | 0.82 |

| Profitability | % | Rel Category |
|---|---|---|
| Return on Equity | 15.65 | 0.85 |
| Return on Assets | 9.07 | 0.92 |
| Net Margin | 12.12 | 0.94 |

| Sector Weightings | % of Stocks | Rel S&P 500 | 3 Year High | Low |
|---|---|---|---|---|
| ↻ Info | 19.12 | 0.95 | | |
| Software | 0.37 | 0.10 | 1 | 0 |
| Hardware | 8.21 | 0.82 | 8 | 4 |
| Media | 4.63 | 1.29 | 8 | 5 |
| Telecom | 5.91 | 1.96 | 7 | 5 |
| ☞ Service | 44.32 | 0.96 | | |
| Health | 4.20 | 0.32 | 8 | 2 |
| Consumer | 3.80 | 0.47 | 7 | 4 |
| Business | 3.76 | 0.97 | 4 | 3 |
| Financial | 32.56 | 1.54 | 39 | 33 |
| Mfg | 36.57 | 1.09 | | |
| Goods | 4.74 | 0.55 | 5 | 3 |
| Ind Mtrls | 17.83 | 1.47 | 18 | 9 |
| Energy | 7.94 | 0.85 | 13 | 7 |
| Utilities | 6.06 | 1.80 | 6 | 5 |

### Composition

| | |
|---|---|
| Cash | 0.1 |
| Stocks | 99.9 |
| Bonds | 0.0 |
| Other | 0.0 |
| Foreign | 0.0 |
| (% of Stock) | |

## Morningstar's Take by Dan Culloton

This exchange-traded fund is getting an extreme, and favorable, makeover.

Standard & Poor's, which publishes the benchmark for the iShares S&P 500/Barra Value Index, will drop the style-index methodology developed by risk-management firm Barra, which relied on a stock's price/book value to determine if it was growth or value. Instead, it will adopt bogies derived from a multifactor model created by Citigroup.

The switch will rearrange the guts of this fund. Barclays Global Investors, this fund's advisor, planned to make the switch to the new index on or about Dec. 16, 2005. The fund will change its name to iShares S&P 500 Value Index Fund at that time. Barclays, however, doesn't expect the changeover to require much more turnover than a normal rebalancing of the old Barra index. It also said it would try to minimize transaction costs and capital gains, though there's no guarantee transition won't have an impact on either of those fronts.

More importantly this ETF's new index could help the fund keep turnover low on an ongoing basis and offer more complete exposure to the value universe. The new S&P/Citigroup Large Value index will still draw its constituents from the S&P 500, but it will look at seven valuation and growth factors instead of one to figure out if a stock belongs. Unlike the Barra index, it also will allow some stocks that have both value and growth characteristics to live in both value and growth indexes. This addresses a few knocks against the old Barra index: By refusing to allow style overlap and relying on only one factor, the index was an unrealistic measure of the value universe, and it increased turnover as stocks migrated based on their price/book values.

Much of the indexing world has adopted multifactor style indexes. It's about time S&P joined the party. Doing so will help keep this ETF competitive.

| Address: | 45 Fremont Street San Francisco CA 94105 800-474-2737 |
|---|---|
| Web Address: | www.ishares.com |
| Inception: | 05-22-00* |
| Advisor: | Barclays Global Fund Advisers |

| Management Fee: | 0.18% | | |
|---|---|---|---|
| Expense Projections: | 3Yr:$58 | 5Yr:$101 | 10Yr:$230 |
| Income Distrib: | Quarterly | | |
| Exchange: | NYSE | | |

MORNINGSTAR® ETFs 100

Data through December 31, 2005

# iShares SP 600 Growth

| | Ticker | NAV | Market Price | 52 wk High/Low | Yield | Mstar Category |
|---|---|---|---|---|---|---|
| | IJT | $116.41 | $121.11 | $121.11 - $98.69 | 0.6% | Small Growth |

## Management

### Portfolio Manager(s)

Barclays Global Fund Advisors is the advisor. The firm is the world's largest manager of indexed portfolios. Patrick O'Connor, the head of Barclay's U.S. iShares portfolio management group leads a team of a half dozen managers in running this and about 60 other ETFs. IShares domestic portfolio management group is responsible for about $75 billion in assets. Most of the managers have at least five or more years of experience with Barclays as well as prior industry experience.

### Strategy

This fund tracks the S&P SmallCap 600/Citigroup Growth Index. The bogy relies on seven growth and valuation measures to classify stocks. The factors are dividend yield; price-book, -sales and -cash flow; and five-year earnings, sales, and internal growth rates. A third of the index's market capitalization ends up in each value, core or growth bucket, but stocks in the middle zone can end up in both style indexes in proportion to their style scores. The overlap should reduce turnover caused by stocks moving from one style to another. The index includes no buffer zones between market-cap ranges. It rebalances annually in December.

## Performance

### Historic Quarterly NAV Returns

| | 1st Qtr | 2nd Qtr | 3rd Qtr | 4th Qtr | Total |
|---|---|---|---|---|---|
| 2001 | -13.19 | 14.18 | -17.28 | 20.28 | -1.38 |
| 2002 | 3.53 | -8.99 | -14.68 | 5.06 | -15.55 |
| 2003 | -3.63 | 16.85 | 7.79 | 12.92 | 37.05 |
| 2004 | 5.65 | 4.37 | -3.08 | 13.80 | 21.61 |
| 2005 | -1.77 | 3.71 | 6.56 | 0.39 | 8.99 |

| Trailing | NAV Return% | Market Return% | NAV Rtrn% +/-S&P 500 | %Rank Cat.(NAV) |
|---|---|---|---|---|
| 3 Mo | 0.39 | 0.05 | -1.69 | 6 |
| 6 Mo | 6.98 | 6.74 | 1.22 | 6 |
| 1 Yr | 8.99 | 9.00 | 4.08 | 5 |
| 3 Yr Avg | 22.02 | 21.81 | 7.64 | 3 |
| 5 Yr Avg | 8.63 | 8.52 | 8.09 | 3 |
| 10 Yr Avg | — | — | — | 0 |

| Tax Analysis | Tax-Adj Return% | Tax-Cost Ratio |
|---|---|---|
| 3 Yr (estimated) | 21.82 | 0.16 |
| 5 Yr (estimated) | 8.50 | 0.12 |
| 10 Yr (estimated) | — | — |

### Growth of $10,000

— Investment Value of ETF
— Investment Value of Index S&P 500

| | 1996 | 1997 | 1998 | 1999 | 2000 | 2001 | 2002 | 2003 | 2004 | 2005 | History |
|---|---|---|---|---|---|---|---|---|---|---|---|
| | — | — | — | — | 78.24 | 77.09 | 64.96 | 88.67 | 107.43 | 116.41 | NAV $ |
| | — | — | — | — | 78.41 | 76.95 | 65.10 | 88.72 | 107.10 | 116.07 | Market Price $ |
| | — | — | — | — | 6.82* | -1.38 | -15.55 | 37.05 | 21.61 | 8.99 | NAV Return% |
| | — | — | — | — | 6.76* | -1.77 | -15.21 | 36.83 | 21.17 | 9.00 | Market Price Return% |
| | — | — | — | — | 0.07 | 0.22 | 0.07 | 0.10 | -0.06 | -0.08 | Avg Premium/Discount% |
| | — | — | — | — | 6.82 | 10.50 | 6.54 | 8.38 | 10.74 | 4.08 | NAV Rtrn% +/-S&P 500 |
| | — | — | — | — | 6.82 | 7.85 | 14.71 | -11.49 | 7.30 | 4.84 | NAV Rtrn% +/-Russ 2000 Gr |
| | — | — | — | — | — | 3 | 3 | 3 | 3 | 5 | NAV Return% Rank in Cat |
| | — | — | — | — | 0.00 | 0.08 | 0.20 | 0.48 | 0.41 | 0.60 | Income Return % |
| | — | — | — | — | — | -1.46 | -15.75 | 36.57 | 21.20 | 8.39 | Capital Return % |
| | — | — | — | — | 0.00 | 0.06 | 0.16 | 0.31 | 0.36 | 0.65 | Income $ |
| | — | — | — | — | 0.62 | 0.00 | 0.00 | 0.00 | 0.00 | 0.00 | Capital Gains $ |
| | — | — | — | — | — | 0.25 | 0.25 | 0.25 | 0.25 | 0.25 | Expense Ratio % |
| | — | — | — | — | — | 0.00 | 0.14 | 0.34 | 0.39 | 0.45 | Income Ratio % |
| | — | — | — | — | — | 77 | 49 | 57 | 37 | 45 | Turnover Rate % |
| | — | — | — | — | — | — | 513 | 625 | 1,064 | 1,280 | Net Assets $mil |

## Risk Profile

| | Standard Index S&P 500 | Best Fit Index Mstar Small Core |
|---|---|---|
| Alpha | 4.0 | 0.2 |
| Beta | 1.25 | 0.94 |
| R-Squared | 70 | 94 |
| Standard Deviation | 13.73 | |
| Mean | 22.02 | |
| Sharpe Ratio | 1.38 | |

## Morningstar Fair Value

| Price/Fair Value Ratio | Fair Value Estimate ($) | Hit Rate % |
|---|---|---|
| — | — | — |

## Portfolio Analysis 12-31-05

Share change since 11-05 Total Stocks:354

| | | Sector | PE | Tot Ret% | % Assets |
|---|---|---|---|---|---|
| ⊖ | NVR | Consumer | 8.8 | -8.76 | 1.42 |
| ⚡ | Cimarex Energy | Energy | 11.5 | 13.48 | 1.36 |
| ⊕ | Pharmaceutical Product D | Health | 29.1 | 52.84 | 1.20 |
| ⊕ | Global Payments | Business | 37.7 | 59.62 | 1.18 |
| ⊕ | Cerner | Software | 43.7 | 70.98 | 1.08 |
| ⊕ | Cal Dive International | Energy | 24.0 | 76.15 | 1.07 |
| ⊕ | ResMed | Health | 40.8 | 49.94 | 1.04 |
| ⊕ | Respironics | Health | 61.3 | 36.39 | 1.03 |
| ⊕ | Unit | Energy | 16.0 | 44.02 | 0.98 |
| ⊕ | Landstar System | Business | 25.1 | 13.52 | 0.94 |
| ⊕ | Idexx Laboratories | Health | 32.9 | 31.86 | 0.89 |
| ⚡ | Cooper Companies | Health | 18.9 | -27.25 | 0.87 |
| ⊕ | Cabot Oil & Gas A | Energy | 18.3 | 53.50 | 0.85 |
| ⊕ | Pediatrix Medical Group | Health | 21.3 | 38.28 | 0.84 |
| ⊕ | Frontier Oil | Energy | 10.1 | 189.81 | 0.82 |
| ⊕ | Polaris Industries | Goods | 15.1 | -24.69 | 0.80 |
| ⊕ | St. Mary Land & Explorat | Energy | 18.8 | 77.02 | 0.80 |
| ⊕ | East West Bancorp | Financial | 19.7 | -12.55 | 0.79 |
| ⊕ | Sierra Health Services | Health | 22.4 | 45.09 | 0.79 |
| ⊕ | Panera Bread | Consumer | 41.3 | 62.90 | 0.79 |

### Current Investment Style

Value Blnd Growth — Large/Mid/Small

| Market Cap | % |
|---|---|
| Giant | 0.0 |
| Large | 0.0 |
| Mid | 42.6 |
| Small | 54.2 |
| Micro | 3.2 |

Avg $mil: 1,388

| Value Measures | | Rel Category |
|---|---|---|
| Price/Earnings | 17.02 | 0.77 |
| Price/Book | 2.79 | 0.94 |
| Price/Sales | 1.48 | 1.00 |
| Price/Cash Flow | 9.40 | 1.11 |
| Dividend Yield % | 0.42 | 1.45 |

| Growth Measures | % | Rel Category |
|---|---|---|
| Long-Term Erngs | 15.18 | 0.87 |
| Book Value | 15.14 | 1.63 |
| Sales | 15.74 | 1.28 |
| Cash Flow | 20.57 | 1.26 |
| Historical Erngs | 21.67 | 1.07 |

| Profitability | % | Rel Category |
|---|---|---|
| Return on Equity | 17.90 | 1.31 |
| Return on Assets | 10.75 | 1.52 |
| Net Margin | 11.68 | 1.33 |

### Sector Weightings

| | % of Stocks | Rel S&P 500 | 3 Year High | Low |
|---|---|---|---|---|
| ↻ Info | 12.44 | 0.62 | | |
| 🖥 Software | 7.30 | 2.05 | 9 | 6 |
| 💾 Hardware | 4.09 | 0.41 | 10 | 3 |
| 🎙 Media | 0.00 | 0.00 | 0 | 0 |
| 📱 Telecom | 1.05 | 0.35 | 1 | 0 |
| ☞ Service | 55.29 | 1.19 | | |
| 🏥 Health | 18.42 | 1.39 | 21 | 16 |
| 🛒 Consumer | 12.52 | 1.54 | 16 | 11 |
| 💼 Business | 12.40 | 3.20 | 13 | 9 |
| $ Financial | 11.95 | 0.57 | 13 | 9 |
| 🏭 Mfg | 32.26 | 0.97 | | |
| 🏠 Goods | 6.04 | 0.71 | 8 | 6 |
| ⚙ Ind Mtrls | 14.46 | 1.19 | 20 | 14 |
| 🔋 Energy | 11.03 | 1.18 | 13 | 3 |
| 💡 Utilities | 0.73 | 0.22 | 2 | 0 |

### Composition

| | | |
|---|---|---|
| ● Cash | | 0.0 |
| ● Stocks | | 100.0 |
| ● Bonds | | 0.0 |
| ● Other | | 0.0 |
| Foreign | | 0.0 |
| (% of Stock) | | |

## Morningstar's Take by Dan Culloton

This exchange-traded fund is making some changes for the better.

Standard & Poor's, which publishes the benchmark for the iShares S&P SmallCap 600/Barra Growth Index, will drop the style index methodology developed by risk-management firm Barra, which relied on a stock's price/book value to determine if it was growth or value. Instead, it will adopt bogies derived from a multifactor model created by Citigroup C.

The switch will rearrange the guts of this fund. Barclays Global Investors, this fund's advisor, planned to make the switch to the new index on or about Dec. 16, 2005. The fund will change its name to iShares S&P SmallCap 600 Growth Index Fund at that time. Barclays, however, doesn't expect the changeover to require much more turnover than a normal rebalancing of the old Barra index. It also said it would try to minimize transaction costs and capital gains, though there's no guarantee transition won't have an impact on either of those

fronts.

More importantly this ETF's new index could help the fund keep turnover low on an ongoing basis and offer more realistic exposure to the small-cap growth universe. The new S&P SmallCap 600/Citigroup Growth Index will still draw its constituents from the S&P SmallCap 600, but it will look at seven valuation and growth factors instead of one to figure out if a stock belongs. Unlike the Barra index, it also will allow some stocks that have both value and growth characteristics to live in both value and growth indexes. This addresses a few knocks against the old Barra index: that its refusal to allow style overlap and its reliance on one factor made it an unrealistic measure of the small growth universe; and that turnover was increased as stocks migrated based on their price/book values.

Much of the indexing world has adopted multifactor style indexes. It's about time S&P joined the party.

| Address: | 45 Fremont Street San Francisco CA 94105 800-474-2737 |
|---|---|
| Web Address: | www.ishares.com |
| Inception: | 07-24-00* |
| Advisor: | Barclays Global Fund Advisers |

| Management Fee: | 0.25% | | |
|---|---|---|---|
| Expense Projections: | 3Yr:$80 | 5Yr:$141 | 10Yr:$318 |
| Income Distrib: | Quarterly | | |
| Exchange: | NYSE | | |

# iShares SP 600 Value

| Ticker | NAV | Market Price | 52 wk High/Low | Yield | Mstar Category |
|---|---|---|---|---|---|
| IJS | $63.99 | $67.52 | $67.52 - $55.55 | 1.0% | Small Value |

## Management

### Portfolio Manager(s)

Barclays Global Fund Advisors is the advisor. The firm is the world's largest manager of indexed portfolios. Patrick O'Connor, the head of Barclay's U.S. iShares portfolio management group, leads a team of a half dozen managers in running this and about 60 other ETFs. iShares domestic portfolio management group is responsible for about $75 billion in assets. Most of the managers have at least five or more years of experience with Barclays as well as prior industry experience.

### Strategy

This fund tracks the S&P SmallCap 600/Citigroup Value Index. The bogy relies on seven growth and valuation measures to classify stocks. The factors are dividend yield; price-book, -sales and -cash flow; and five-year earnings, sales, and internal growth rates. A third of the index's market capitalization ends up in each value, core or growth bucket, but stocks in the middle zone can end up in both style indexes in proportion to their style scores. The overlap should reduce turnover caused by stocks moving from one style to another. The index includes no buffer zones between market-cap ranges. It rebalances annually in December.

## Performance

### Historic Quarterly NAV Returns

| | 1st Qtr | 2nd Qtr | 3rd Qtr | 4th Qtr | Total |
|---|---|---|---|---|---|
| 2001 | -0.95 | 12.73 | -16.52 | 20.82 | 12.61 |
| 2002 | 10.19 | -4.39 | -22.54 | 4.59 | -14.65 |
| 2003 | -8.01 | 22.65 | 6.30 | 16.52 | 39.75 |
| 2004 | 6.58 | 2.83 | 0.21 | 11.97 | 22.96 |
| 2005 | -2.44 | 4.05 | 4.11 | 0.24 | 5.93 |

| Trailing | NAV Return% | Market Return% | NAV Rtrn% +/-S&P 500 | %Rank Cat.(NAV) |
|---|---|---|---|---|
| 3 Mo | 0.24 | 0.26 | -1.84 | 6 |
| 6 Mo | 4.36 | 4.18 | -1.40 | 6 |
| 1 Yr | 5.93 | 5.99 | 1.02 | 5 |
| 3 Yr Avg | 22.10 | 21.93 | 7.72 | 3 |
| 5 Yr Avg | 11.84 | 11.72 | 11.30 | 3 |
| 10 Yr Avg | — | — | — | 0 |

| Tax Analysis | Tax-Adj Return% | Tax-Cost Ratio |
|---|---|---|
| 3 Yr (estimated) | 21.65 | 0.37 |
| 5 Yr (estimated) | 11.45 | 0.35 |
| 10 Yr (estimated) | — | — |

## Growth of $10,000

— Investment Value of ETF
— Investment Value of Index S&P 500

| | 1996 | 1997 | 1998 | 1999 | 2000 | 2001 | 2002 | 2003 | 2004 | 2005 | History |
|---|---|---|---|---|---|---|---|---|---|---|---|
| | — | — | — | — | 38.36 | 42.88 | 36.28 | 50.24 | 61.04 | 63.99 | NAV $ |
| | — | — | — | — | 38.50 | 42.67 | 36.38 | 50.27 | 60.90 | 63.88 | Market Price $ |
| | — | — | — | — | 13.39* | 12.61 | -14.65 | 39.75 | 22.96 | 5.93 | NAV Return% |
| | — | — | — | — | 13.36* | 11.68 | -14.04 | 39.48 | 22.60 | 5.99 | Market Price Return% |
| | — | — | — | — | -0.04 | -0.01 | 0.03 | 0.11 | -0.01 | -0.20 | Avg Premium/Discount% |
| | — | — | — | — | 13.39 | 24.49 | 7.44 | 11.08 | 12.09 | 1.02 | NAV Rtrn% +/-S&P 500 |
| | — | — | — | — | 13.39 | -1.41 | -3.22 | -6.28 | 0.71 | 1.22 | NAV Rtrn% +/-Russ 2000 VL |
| | — | — | — | — | — | 3 | 3 | 3 | 3 | 5 | NAV Return% Rank in Cat |
| | — | — | — | — | 0.00 | 0.77 | 0.81 | 1.05 | 1.35 | 1.07 | Income Return % |
| | — | — | — | — | — | 11.84 | -15.46 | 38.70 | 21.61 | 4.86 | Capital Return % |
| | — | — | — | — | 0.13 | 0.29 | 0.35 | 0.38 | 0.68 | 0.65 | Income $ |
| | — | — | — | — | 0.17 | 0.00 | 0.00 | 0.00 | 0.00 | 0.00 | Capital Gains $ |
| | — | — | — | — | 0.25 | 0.25 | 0.25 | 0.25 | 0.25 | 0.25 | Expense Ratio % |
| | — | — | — | — | 0.98 | 0.92 | 0.99 | 0.95 | 1.36 | | Income Ratio % |
| | — | — | — | — | 17 | 14 | 14 | 14 | 13 | | Turnover Rate % |
| | — | — | — | — | — | 704 | 864 | 1,618 | 1,606 | | Net Assets $mil |

## Risk Profile

| | Standard Index S&P 500 | Best Fit Index Russ 2000 VL |
|---|---|---|
| Alpha | 2.5 | -0.9 |
| Beta | 1.39 | 1.00 |
| R-Squared | 77 | 97 |
| Standard Deviation | 14.60 | |
| Mean | 22.10 | |
| Sharpe Ratio | 1.31 | |

## Morningstar Fair Value

| Price/Fair Value Ratio | Fair Value Estimate ($) | Hit Rate % |
|---|---|---|
| — | — | — |

## Portfolio Analysis 12-31-05

| Share change since 11-05 Total Stocks:456 | Sector | PE | Tot Ret% | % Assets |
|---|---|---|---|---|
| ✪ Energen | Energy | 18.2 | 24.70 | 0.98 |
| ⊖ Shurgard Storage Centers | Financial | | 35.00 | 0.98 |
| ⊖ Standard Pacific | Consumer | 6.0 | 15.20 | 0.93 |
| ⊖ Hughes Supply | Business | 17.2 | 12.06 | 0.88 |
| ⊖ Commercial Metals | Ind Mtrls | 8.1 | 49.76 | 0.81 |
| ✪ UGI | Utilities | 11.6 | 3.51 | 0.80 |
| ⊖ Atmos Energy | Utilities | 15.2 | 0.05 | 0.78 |
| ⊖ South Financial Group | Financial | 18.6 | -13.43 | 0.76 |
| ⊖ Briggs & Stratton | Ind Mtrls | 16.4 | -4.67 | 0.74 |
| ✪ Vintage Petroleum | Energy | 18.3 | 136.37 | 0.71 |
| ⊖ Colonial Properties Trus | Financial | | 14.28 | 0.69 |
| ⊖ Piedmont Natural Gas | Utilities | 20.3 | 8.02 | 0.68 |
| ✪ Roper Industries | Ind Mtrls | 27.9 | 30.86 | 0.68 |
| ✪ Massey Energy Company | Energy | 28.5 | 8.77 | 0.67 |
| ⊖ Kansas City Southern | Business | 23.7 | 37.79 | 0.66 |
| ⊖ Corn Products Internatio | Goods | 22.8 | -9.70 | 0.65 |
| ⊖ Whitney Holding | Financial | 18.4 | -5.04 | 0.64 |
| ✪ Reliance Steel and Alumi | Ind Mtrls | 10.7 | 58.14 | 0.62 |
| ✪ Lennox International | Business | 15.8 | 41.01 | 0.59 |
| ⊖ United Stationers | Ind Mtrls | 17.6 | 4.98 | 0.58 |

## Morningstar's Take by Dan Culloton

This exchange-traded fund is adopting a better benchmark.

Standard & Poor's, which publishes the benchmark for the iShares S&P SmallCap 600/Barra Value Index, will drop the style index methodology developed by risk-management firm Barra, which relied on a stock's price/book value to determine if it was growth or value. Instead, it will adopt bogies derived from a multifactor model created by Citigroup.

The switch will rearrange the guts of this fund. Barclays Global Investors, this fund's advisor, planned to make the switch to the new index on or about Dec. 16, 2005. The fund will change its name to iShares S&P SmallCap 600 Value Index Fund at that time. Barclays, however, doesn't expect the changeover to require much more turnover than a normal rebalancing of the old Barra index. It also said it would try to minimize transaction costs and capital gains, though there's no guarantee transition won't have an impact on either of those

fronts.

More importantly this ETF's new index could help the fund keep turnover low on an ongoing basis and offer more realistic exposure to the small-cap value universe. The new S&P SmallCap 600/Citigroup Value Index will still draw its constituents from the S&P SmallCap 600, but it will look at seven valuation and growth factors instead of one to figure out if a stock belongs. Unlike the Barra index, it also will allow some stocks that have both value and growth characteristics to live in both value and growth indexes. This addresses a few knocks against the old Barra index: that its refusal to allow style overlap and its reliance on one factor made it an unrealistic measure of the small-value universe; and that turnover was increased as stocks migrated based on their price/book values.

Much of the indexing world has adopted multifactor style indexes. It's about time S&P joined the party.

### Current Investment Style

Value Blnd Growth — Large/Mid/Small

| Market Cap | % |
|---|---|
| Giant | 0.0 |
| Large | 0.0 |
| Mid | 26.2 |
| Small | 64.8 |
| Micro | 9.0 |

Avg $mil: 1,025

| Value Measures | | Rel Category |
|---|---|---|
| Price/Earnings | 16.33 | 1.10 |
| Price/Book | 1.79 | 1.02 |
| Price/Sales | 0.76 | 0.94 |
| Price/Cash Flow | 7.94 | 1.20 |
| Dividend Yield % | 1.31 | 0.69 |

| Growth Measures | % | Rel Category |
|---|---|---|
| Long-Term Erngs | 11.91 | 1.12 |
| Book Value | 6.43 | 1.15 |
| Sales | 7.17 | 1.58 |
| Cash Flow | 0.48 | 1.37 |
| Historical Erngs | 11.84 | 1.19 |

| Profitability | % | Rel Category |
|---|---|---|
| Return on Equity | 10.97 | 0.95 |
| Return on Assets | 6.25 | 0.89 |
| Net Margin | 7.73 | 0.74 |

| Sector Weightings | % of Stocks | Rel S&P 500 | 3 Year High Low |
|---|---|---|---|
| ⟳ Info | 13.20 | 0.65 | |
| Software | 3.10 | 0.87 | 3  1 |
| Hardware | 9.00 | 0.90 | 9  6 |
| Media | 0.10 | 0.03 | 0  0 |
| Telecom | 1.00 | 0.33 | 1  0 |
| Service | 42.53 | 0.92 | |
| Health | 3.88 | 0.29 | 8  4 |
| Consumer | 10.28 | 1.26 | 14  10 |
| Business | 10.02 | 2.59 | 12  9 |
| Financial | 18.35 | 0.87 | 23  16 |
| Mfg | 44.29 | 1.33 | |
| Goods | 7.29 | 0.85 | 9  5 |
| Ind Mtrls | 25.52 | 2.10 | 26  19 |
| Energy | 4.88 | 0.52 | 9  4 |
| Utilities | 6.60 | 1.96 | 8  4 |

### Composition

| | | |
|---|---|---|
| ● Cash | | 0.4 |
| ● Stocks | | 99.6 |
| ○ Bonds | | 0.0 |
| ○ Other | | 0.0 |
| | Foreign (% of Stock) | 0.0 |

| Address: | 45 Fremont Street San Francisco CA 94105 800-474-2737 | Management Fee: | 0.25% |
|---|---|---|---|
| | | Expense Projections: | 3Yr:$80   5Yr:$141   10Yr:$318 |
| | | Income Distrib: | Quarterly |
| Web Address: | www.ishares.com | Exchange: | NYSE |
| Inception: | 07-24-00* | | |
| Advisor: | Barclays Global Fund Advisers | | |

MØRNINGSTAR® ETFs 100

# iShares SP Glb Hlth

| | Ticker | NAV | Market Price | 52 wk High/Low | Yield | Mstar Category |
|---|---|---|---|---|---|---|
| | IXJ | $52.20 | $53.85 | $54.26 - $47.01 | 0.7% | Specialty-Health |

## Management

### Portfolio Manager(s)

The fund's advisor, Barclays Global Fund Advisors, is one of the world's largest and most experienced managers of index-tracking portfolios. Senior international portfolio manager J. Lisa Chen, who has been with Barclays since 1999, leads a team of four managers who run this and more than 30 other international ETFs. Before joining Barclays Chen managed money for a Canadian public pension plan.

### Strategy

This fund tracks the S&P Global Healthcare Sector Index. The index is a subset of the S&P Global 1200 Index, which is a composite of seven blue-chip indexes from around the world. The S&P 500 and S&P Europe 350 make up more than 80% of the S&P Global 1200, so the sector indexes carved out of it lean heavily on the U.S. and European market. There is a qualitative element to this fund's bogey and its parent index because the S&P's index committees use criterion such as profitability when assembling the underlying regional benchmarks. The Index is float-adjusted and market-capitalization weighted.

## Performance

### Historic Quarterly NAV Returns

| | 1st Qtr | 2nd Qtr | 3rd Qtr | 4th Qtr | Total |
|---|---|---|---|---|---|
| 2001 | — | — | — | — | —* |
| 2002 | -0.57 | -12.49 | -9.32 | 4.07 | -17.89 |
| 2003 | -1.14 | 10.98 | -2.81 | 10.41 | 17.73 |
| 2004 | -0.93 | 2.31 | -2.74 | 5.81 | 4.31 |
| 2005 | -1.29 | 3.95 | 3.38 | 1.63 | 7.80 |

| Trailing | NAV Return% | Market Return% | NAV Rtrn% +/-S&P 500 | %Rank Cat.(NAV) |
|---|---|---|---|---|
| 3 Mo | 1.63 | 1.35 | -0.45 | 7 |
| 6 Mo | 5.06 | 5.27 | -0.70 | 7 |
| 1 Yr | 7.80 | 6.81 | 2.89 | 5 |
| 3 Yr Avg | 9.80 | 9.70 | -4.58 | 4 |
| 5 Yr Avg | — | — | — | 0 |
| 10 Yr Avg | — | — | — | 0 |

| Tax Analysis | Tax-Adj Return% | Tax-Cost Ratio |
|---|---|---|
| 3 Yr (estimated) | 9.53 | 0.25 |
| 5 Yr (estimated) | — | — |
| 10 Yr (estimated) | — | — |

### Growth of $10,000

— Investment Value of ETF
— Investment Value of Index S&P 500

| | 1996 | 1997 | 1998 | 1999 | 2000 | 2001 | 2002 | 2003 | 2004 | 2005 | History |
|---|---|---|---|---|---|---|---|---|---|---|---|
| | — | — | — | — | — | 49.34 | 40.27 | 47.10 | 48.76 | 52.20 | NAV $ |
| | — | — | — | — | — | 49.50 | 40.38 | 47.68 | 49.21 | 52.20 | Market Price $ |
| | — | — | — | — | — | 1.95* | -17.89 | 17.73 | 4.31 | 7.80 | NAV Return% |
| | — | — | — | — | — | 1.95* | -17.93 | 18.85 | 3.99 | 6.81 | Market Price Return% |
| | — | — | — | — | — | 0.34 | 0.19 | 0.69 | 0.78 | 0.23 | Avg Premium/Discount% |
| | — | — | — | — | — | 1.95 | 4.20 | -10.94 | -6.56 | 2.89 | NAV Rtrn% +/-S&P 500 |
| | — | — | — | — | — | 1.95 | 2.92 | -1.70 | -0.24 | -0.52 | NAV Rtrn% +/-DJ Hlthcare |
| | — | — | — | — | — | — | 4 | 5 | 5 | 5 | NAV Return% Rank in Cat |
| | — | — | — | — | — | 0.00 | 0.50 | 0.75 | 0.77 | 0.75 | Income Return % |
| | — | — | — | — | — | — | -18.39 | 16.98 | 3.54 | 7.05 | Capital Return % |
| | — | — | — | — | — | 0.01 | 0.25 | 0.30 | 0.36 | 0.37 | Income $ |
| | — | — | — | — | — | 0.00 | 0.00 | 0.00 | 0.00 | 0.00 | Capital Gains $ |
| | — | — | — | — | — | — | 0.65 | 0.65 | 0.65 | 0.65 | Expense Ratio % |
| | — | — | — | — | — | — | 0.62 | 0.96 | 1.25 | 1.12 | Income Ratio % |
| | — | — | — | — | — | — | 1 | 4 | 6 | 10 | Turnover Rate % |
| | — | — | — | — | — | — | 26 | 52 | 190 | 457 | Net Assets $mil |

## Risk Profile

| | Standard Index S&P 500 | Best Fit Index DJ Hlthcare |
|---|---|---|
| Alpha | 1.4 | -0.1 |
| Beta | 0.54 | 0.93 |
| R-Squared | 30 | 89 |
| Standard Deviation | 9.04 | |
| Mean | 9.80 | |
| Sharpe Ratio | 0.87 | |

## Morningstar Fair Value

| Price/Fair Value Ratio | Fair Value Estimate ($) | Hit Rate % |
|---|---|---|
| 1.0 Fairly valued | 43.65 | 67 Fair |

## Portfolio Analysis 12-31-05

| Share change since 11-05 Total Stocks:80 | Sector | PE | Tot Ret% | % Assets |
|---|---|---|---|---|
| ⊕ Johnson & Johnson | Health | 19.1 | -3.36 | 7.97 |
| ⊕ Pfizer | Health | 21.2 | -10.62 | 7.66 |
| ⊕ GlaxoSmithKline | Health | — | — | 6.58 |
| ⊕ Novartis | Health | — | — | 6.47 |
| ⊕ Roche Holding | Health | — | — | 4.70 |
| ⊕ Amgen | Health | 28.3 | 22.93 | 4.35 |
| ⊕ Sanofi-Synthelabo | Health | — | — | 3.90 |
| ⊕ UnitedHealth Group | Health | 26.2 | 41.22 | 3.78 |
| ⊕ AstraZeneca | Health | — | — | 3.45 |
| ⊕ Medtronic | Health | 37.4 | 16.72 | 3.14 |
| ⊕ Merck | Health | 15.2 | 4.04 | 3.10 |
| ⊕ Eli Lilly & Company | Health | 48.4 | 2.52 | 2.91 |
| ⊕ Wyeth | Health | 54.2 | 10.54 | 2.77 |
| ⊕ Abbott Laboratories | Health | 18.3 | -13.47 | 2.76 |
| ⊕ WellPoint | Health | 24.7 | 38.77 | 2.35 |
| ⊕ Bristol-Myers Squibb | Health | 17.1 | -6.16 | 2.02 |
| ⊕ Takeda Chemical Industri | Health | — | — | 1.86 |
| ⊕ Schering-Plough | Health | — | 0.95 | 1.39 |
| ⊕ Cardinal Health | Health | 28.3 | 18.63 | 1.32 |
| ⊕ Aetna | Health | 18.9 | 51.27 | 1.21 |

### Current Investment Style

Value Blnd Growth — Large Mid Small

| Market Cap | % |
|---|---|
| Giant | 69.3 |
| Large | 23.9 |
| Mid | 6.7 |
| Small | 0.0 |
| Micro | 0.0 |

Avg $mil: 56,891

| Value Measures | | Rel Category |
|---|---|---|
| Price/Earnings | 19.47 | 0.84 |
| Price/Book | 2.89 | 0.88 |
| Price/Sales | 2.09 | 0.57 |
| Price/Cash Flow | 13.25 | 0.86 |
| Dividend Yield % | 1.62 | 1.59 |

| Growth Measures | % | Rel Category |
|---|---|---|
| Long-Term Erngs | 11.91 | 0.82 |
| Book Value | 17.31 | 1.41 |
| Sales | 11.74 | 0.81 |
| Cash Flow | 14.37 | 0.94 |
| Historical Erngs | 11.01 | 0.94 |

| Profitability | % | Rel Category |
|---|---|---|
| Return on Equity | 19.94 | 1.56 |
| Return on Assets | 9.72 | 1.75 |
| Net Margin | 13.24 | 1.10 |

| Industry Weightings | % of Stocks | Rel Cat |
|---|---|---|
| Biotech | 11.7 | 0.3 |
| Drugs | 48.9 | 1.8 |
| Mgd Care | 11.3 | 1.5 |
| Hospitals | 2.0 | 0.9 |
| Other HC Srv | 0.2 | 0.1 |
| Diagnostics | 1.1 | 0.9 |
| Equipment | 15.0 | 1.0 |
| Good/Srv | 9.2 | 1.0 |
| Other | 0.6 | 0.3 |

### Composition

| | | |
|---|---|---|
| ● Cash | 0.2 |
| ● Stocks | 99.8 |
| ● Bonds | 0.0 |
| ○ Other | 0.0 |
| Foreign (% of Stock) | 33.0 |

## Morningstar's Take by Dan Culloton

iShares S&P Global Healthcare Sector is less diversified and more expensive than it looks.

This exchange-traded fund owns more foreign stocks than the typical fund that focuses on this sector. Its 0.65% expense ratio also is less than half that of the typical traditional health-care fund. The fund offers more regional diversification for less money than others do in this category.

That's good but not perfect. This ETF tracks an index of health-care stocks carved out of the S&P Global 1200 Index. Because that broader benchmark focuses on large-cap stocks from developed markets around the globe and pharmaceutical stocks compose most of the world's health-care market capitalization, this portfolio leans heavily on large-cap drugmakers. It has the highest average market cap among its ETF rivals and keeps more than a third of its assets in its top five holdings: Pfizer, Johnson & Johnson, GlaxoSmithKline, Novartis, and Sanofi-Aventis.

This could be beneficial if you believe large-cap drug stocks are undervalued. Big pharma, especially U.S.-based firms, have been under pressure in recent years amid concerns about generic competition, patent expirations, government regulation, and drug safety. After years of sluggish performance a lot of bad news may be factored into their stock prices.

A sustained rebound is not a cinch, though. If large-cap drug stocks run into more problems, this fund will, too, because it has virtually no small-cap holdings and fewer biotech stocks.

Indeed this ETF has shown some downside. It has lost money in more than half of the 15 quarters from its inception through Sept. 30, 2005, while the average health-care fund has fallen in five quarters over that time span.

Furthermore, its expense ratio is still the highest among health-care ETFs. Due to cost and concentration, we'd encourage investors to shop around before settling for this fund.

| Address: | 45 Fremont Street | Management Fee: | 0.65% | | |
|---|---|---|---|---|---|
| | San Francisco CA 94105 | Expense Projections: | 3Yr:$208 | 5Yr:$362 | 10Yr:$810 |
| | 800-474-2737 | Income Distrib: | Annually | | |
| Web Address: | www.ishares.com | Exchange: | AMEX | | |
| Inception: | 11-13-01* | | | | |
| Advisor: | Barclays Global Fund Advisers | | | | |

MᴏRNINGSTAR® ETFs 100

# iShares SP MidCap400

| | Ticker | NAV | Market Price | 52 wk High/Low | Yield | Mstar Category |
|---|---|---|---|---|---|---|
| | IJH | $73.76 | $77.08 | $77.08 - $62.68 | 1.1% | Mid-Cap Blend |

## Management

### Portfolio Manager(s)

Barclays Global Fund Advisors serves as advisor here. The firm is the world's largest manager of indexed portfolios.Barclays Global Fund Advisors is the advisor. The firm is the world's largest manager of indexed portfolios. Patrick O'Connor, the head of Barclay's U.S. shares portfolio management group leads a team of a half dozen managers in running this and about 60 other ETFs. IShares' domestic portfolio-management group is responsible for billions of dollars in assets. Most of the managers have at least five years of experience with Barclays as well as prior industry experience.

### Strategy

This index-based offering mirrors the holdings and performance of the Standard & Poor's MidCap 400 index, which represents the universe of midsize U.S. companies. The resulting portfolio is a broadly diverse mix of mid-caps. The benchmark is compiled and maintained by S&P index committee. The bogy includes domestic stocks with market capitalizations between $1 billion and $4 billion. Constituents must have a record of at least four profitable quarters and good liquidity to be included. Stocks can move in or out of the index if they get too large or small or if they are acquired. That could result in more turnover.

## Performance

### Historic Quarterly NAV Returns

| | 1st Qtr | 2nd Qtr | 3rd Qtr | 4th Qtr | Total |
|---|---|---|---|---|---|
| 2001 | -10.81 | 13.14 | -16.59 | 18.00 | -0.68 |
| 2002 | 6.64 | -9.36 | -16.57 | 5.77 | -14.70 |
| 2003 | -4.47 | 17.58 | 6.52 | 13.14 | 35.36 |
| 2004 | 5.01 | 0.93 | -2.13 | 12.11 | 16.29 |
| 2005 | -0.44 | 4.34 | 4.84 | 3.28 | 12.48 |

| Trailing | NAV Return% | Market Return% | NAV Rtrn% +/-S&P 500 | %Rank Cat.(NAV) |
|---|---|---|---|---|
| 3 Mo | 3.28 | 3.12 | 1.20 | 7 |
| 6 Mo | 8.28 | 8.40 | 2.52 | 7 |
| 1 Yr | 12.48 | 12.88 | 7.57 | 7 |
| 3 Yr Avg | 20.98 | 21.05 | 6.60 | 4 |
| 5 Yr Avg | 8.45 | 8.43 | 7.91 | 2 |
| 10 Yr Avg | — | — | — | 0 |

| Tax Analysis | Tax-Adj Return% | Tax-Cost Ratio |
|---|---|---|
| 3 Yr (estimated) | 20.53 | 0.37 |
| 5 Yr (estimated) | 8.07 | 0.35 |
| 10 Yr (estimated) | — | — |

### Growth of $10,000

— Investment Value of ETF
— Investment Value of Index S&P 500

| | 1996 | 1997 | 1998 | 1999 | 2000 | 2001 | 2002 | 2003 | 2004 | 2005 | History |
|---|---|---|---|---|---|---|---|---|---|---|---|
| | — | — | — | — | 51.56 | 50.78 | 42.99 | 57.60 | 66.36 | 73.76 | NAV $ |
| | — | — | — | — | 51.64 | 50.58 | 42.93 | 57.53 | 66.16 | 73.80 | Market Price $ |
| | — | — | — | — | 9.72* | -0.68 | -14.70 | 35.36 | 16.29 | 12.48 | NAV Return% |
| | — | — | — | — | 9.73* | -1.24 | -14.47 | 35.37 | 16.09 | 12.88 | Market Price Return% |
| | — | — | — | — | 0.05 | -0.07 | -0.00 | -0.03 | -0.02 | -0.01 | Avg Premium/Discount% |
| | — | — | — | — | 9.72 | 11.20 | 7.39 | 6.69 | 5.42 | 7.57 | NAV Rtrn% +/-S&P 500 |
| | — | — | — | — | 9.72 | -0.08 | -0.17 | -0.23 | -0.18 | -0.07 | NAV Rtrn% +/-S&P Mid 400 |
| | — | — | — | — | — | 2 | 4 | 4 | 5 | 7 | NAV Return% Rank in Cat |
| | — | — | — | — | 0.00 | 0.78 | 0.71 | 1.17 | 1.00 | 1.26 | Income Return % |
| | — | — | — | — | — | -1.46 | -15.41 | 34.19 | 15.29 | 11.22 | Capital Return % |
| | — | — | — | — | 0.24 | 0.40 | 0.36 | 0.50 | 0.57 | 0.83 | Income $ |
| | — | — | — | — | 0.15 | 0.00 | 0.00 | 0.00 | 0.00 | 0.00 | Capital Gains $ |
| | — | — | — | — | 0.20 | 0.20 | 0.20 | 0.20 | 0.20 | 0.20 | Expense Ratio % |
| | — | — | — | — | 0.86 | 0.87 | 0.98 | 1.02 | 1.21 | Income Ratio % |
| | — | — | — | — | — | 32 | 14 | 12 | 11 | 10 | Turnover Rate % |
| | — | — | — | — | — | 1,221 | 1,411 | 2,323 | 3,389 | | Net Assets $mil |

## Risk Profile

| | Standard Index S&P 500 | Best Fit Index S&P Mid 400 |
|---|---|---|
| Alpha | 4.1 | -0.1 |
| Beta | 1.15 | 1.00 |
| R-Squared | 82 | 100 |
| Standard Deviation | 11.66 | |
| Mean | 20.98 | |
| Sharpe Ratio | 1.53 | |

## Morningstar Fair Value

| Price/Fair Value Ratio | Fair Value Estimate ($) | Hit Rate % |
|---|---|---|
| 1.1 Overvalued | 34.30 | 79 Fair |

## Portfolio Analysis  12-31-05

Share change since 11-05   Total Stocks:400

| | Sector | PE | Tot Ret% | % Assets |
|---|---|---|---|---|
| ⊕ Legg Mason | Financial | 30.9 | 64.48 | 1.33 |
| ⊕ SanDisk | Hardware | 36.1 | 151.58 | 1.05 |
| ⊕ Peabody Energy | Energy | 33.1 | 104.95 | 0.99 |
| ⊕ Whole Foods Market | Consumer | 78.2 | 63.73 | 0.97 |
| ⊕ Chico's FAS | Consumer | 43.9 | 92.97 | 0.72 |
| ⊖ Smith International | Energy | 27.9 | 37.41 | 0.68 |
| ⊕ Expeditors International | Business | 41.4 | 21.41 | 0.65 |
| ⊕ Noble Energy | Energy | 11.3 | 31.24 | 0.64 |
| ⊕ Cognizant Technology Sol | Business | 52.9 | 18.76 | 0.63 |
| ⊕ Precision Castparts | Ind Mtrls | 26.0 | 58.08 | 0.63 |
| ⊕ Omnicare | Health | 26.1 | 65.62 | 0.62 |
| ⊕ Ensco International | Energy | 30.8 | 40.08 | 0.62 |
| ⊕ Microchip Technology | Hardware | 29.0 | 22.80 | 0.61 |
| ⊕ Ivax | Health | 42.9 | 98.04 | 0.61 |
| ⊕ Barr Pharmaceuticals | Health | 26.9 | 36.78 | 0.61 |
| ⊕ Varian Medical Systems | Health | 33.6 | 16.42 | 0.60 |
| ⊖ Pioneer Natural Resource | Energy | 18.6 | 46.75 | 0.60 |
| ⊕ Questar | Energy | 22.3 | 50.64 | 0.59 |
| ⊕ Harman International Ind | Goods | 27.0 | -22.91 | 0.59 |
| ⊕ Fidelity National Financ | Financial | 6.4 | 23.52 | 0.58 |

### Current Investment Style

Value  Blnd  Growth

Large / Mid / Small

| | Market Cap | % |
|---|---|---|
| | Giant | 0.0 |
| | Large | 4.3 |
| | Mid | 85.8 |
| | Small | 9.8 |
| | Micro | 0.0 |

Avg $mil: 3,457

| Value Measures | | Rel Category |
|---|---|---|
| Price/Earnings | 18.61 | 1.06 |
| Price/Book | 2.39 | 1.00 |
| Price/Sales | 1.25 | 1.09 |
| Price/Cash Flow | 7.38 | 0.98 |
| Dividend Yield % | 1.18 | 1.02 |

| Growth Measures | % | Rel Category |
|---|---|---|
| Long-Term Erngs | 12.71 | 1.01 |
| Book Value | 9.91 | 1.14 |
| Sales | 9.41 | 1.16 |
| Cash Flow | 8.46 | 0.84 |
| Historical Erngs | 13.70 | 0.85 |

| Profitability | % | Rel Category |
|---|---|---|
| Return on Equity | 14.23 | 0.94 |
| Return on Assets | 7.98 | 1.02 |
| Net Margin | 10.33 | 0.97 |

### Sector Weightings

| | % of Stocks | Rel S&P 500 | 3 Year High Low | |
|---|---|---|---|---|
| ↻ Info | 14.04 | 0.70 | | |
| 🖥 Software | 2.88 | 0.81 | 4 | 3 |
| 🖫 Hardware | 8.91 | 0.89 | 10 | 7 |
| 🎙 Media | 1.75 | 0.49 | 4 | 2 |
| 📶 Telecom | 0.50 | 0.17 | 1 | 1 |
| ☞ Service | 53.56 | 1.15 | | |
| ⚕ Health | 11.47 | 0.86 | 15 | 10 |
| 🛒 Consumer | 13.16 | 1.62 | 17 | 11 |
| 💼 Business | 11.24 | 2.90 | 11 | 10 |
| $ Financial | 17.69 | 0.84 | 20 | 16 |
| ⏎ Mfg | 32.40 | 0.97 | | |
| 🏭 Goods | 5.50 | 0.64 | 9 | 6 |
| ⚙ Ind Mtrls | 9.29 | 0.76 | 9 | 7 |
| ⛽ Energy | 11.20 | 1.20 | 11 | 7 |
| ⚡ Utilities | 6.41 | 1.91 | 7 | 6 |

### Composition

| | |
|---|---|
| ● Cash | 0.1 |
| ● Stocks | 99.9 |
| ● Bonds | 0.0 |
| ● Other | 0.0 |
| Foreign | 0.0 |
| (% of Stock) | |

## Morningstar's Take  by Dan Culloton

Ishares S&P MidCap 400 Index may be smaller, but it has advantages over its biggest rival.

The fund offers everything the MidCap SPDR does at a lower expense ratio (0.2%). Like the SPDR the fund tracks the S&P MidCap 400 Index, which is made up of U.S. stocks in the $1 billion to $4 billion capitalization range. The fund can't match the assets or volume of the MidCap SPDR, but it should have little problem trading since demand is usually healthy for the stocks of the S&P 400, which must meet profitability and trading volume standards set by Standard & Poor's index committee. Indeed, this ETF's shares have traded very close to their net asset value since the fund's inception.

This ETF also has the added advantage of being organized as an open-end investment company. That allows it to reinvest dividends. The MidCap SPDR, which is structured as a unit investment trust, must hold its dividends as cash until they can be distributed. That can soften declines but also brake rises. Plus this fund is cheaper than the

SPDR, which has made a difference. From June 2000 through Oct. 31, 2005, this ETF's 8.5% gain edges the MidCap SPDR's 8.3% advance.

That said, the ETF has its risks. Because mid-cap stocks have enjoyed such a strong run in recent years, they could be due for a breather. The ETF's large stake of financial stocks also could hamper performance should interest rates rise. Competition also is heating up. Vanguard's Mid Cap Viper covers similar ground for less and may be more tax-efficient, too. This fund must sell stocks that get too big--as it did when apparel maker Coach graduated to the S&P 500 in August--which raises the possibility of capital gains. To reduce turnover, the MSCI index used by the Vanguard ETF uses buffer zones between market cap bands. Despite those caveats, though, this is still a solid choice for investors seeking exposure to the S&P MidCap 400.

| Address: | 45 Fremont Street San Francisco CA 94105 800-474-2737 |
|---|---|
| Web Address: | www.ishares.com |
| Inception: | 05-22-00* |
| Advisor: | Barclays Global Fund Advisers |

| Management Fee: | 0.20% | | |
|---|---|---|---|
| Expense Projections: | 3Yr:$64 | 5Yr:$113 | 10Yr:$255 |
| Income Distrib: | Quarterly | | |
| Exchange: | NYSE | | |

MORNINGSTAR® ETFs 100

# iShares SP Small 600

| Ticker | NAV | Market Price | 52 wk High/Low | Yield | Mstar Category |
|---|---|---|---|---|---|
| IJR | $57.89 | $60.98 | $60.98 - $49.60 | 0.9% | Small Blend |

## Management

### Portfolio Manager(s)

Barclays Global Fund Advisors is the advisor. The firm is the world's largest manager of indexed portfolios. Patrick O'Connor, the head of Barclay's U.S. shares portfolio management group leads a team of a half dozen managers in running this and about 60 other ETFs. IShares' domestic portfolio-management group is responsible for about $75 billion in assets. Most of the managers have at least five years of experience with Barclays as well as prior industry experience.

### Strategy

The fund tracks the S&P SmallCap 600 Index. To join the bogy, stocks have to be U.S. companies with market caps between $300 million and $1 billion, good liquidity, and at least four profitable quarters. S&P defines profits as GAAP net income excluding discontinued operations and extraordinary items.

### Growth of $10,000

— Investment Value of ETF
— Investment Value of Index S&P 500

| 1996 | 1997 | 1998 | 1999 | 2000 | 2001 | 2002 | 2003 | 2004 | 2005 | History |
|---|---|---|---|---|---|---|---|---|---|---|
| — | — | — | — | 36.27 | 38.35 | 32.51 | 44.73 | 54.34 | 57.89 | NAV $ |
| — | — | — | — | 36.03 | 38.13 | 32.48 | 44.67 | 54.24 | 57.80 | Market Price $ |
| — | — | — | — | 11.71* | 6.34 | -14.73 | 38.59 | 22.45 | 7.50 | NAV Return% |
| — | — | — | — | 11.68* | 6.43 | -14.31 | 38.50 | 22.41 | 7.53 | Market Price Return% |
| — | — | — | — | -0.13 | -0.11 | -0.15 | 0.05 | -0.05 | -0.12 | Avg Premium/Discount% |
| — | — | — | — | 11.71 | 18.22 | 7.36 | 9.92 | 11.58 | 2.59 | NAV Rtrn% +/-S&P 500 |
| — | — | — | — | 11.71 | 3.85 | 5.75 | -8.66 | 4.12 | 2.95 | NAV Rtrn% +/-Russ 2000 |
| — | — | — | — | — | 2 | 2 | 2 | 2 | 4 | NAV Return% Rank in Cat |
| — | — | — | — | 0.00 | 0.53 | 0.55 | 0.84 | 0.89 | 0.93 | Income Return % |
| — | — | — | — | — | 5.81 | -15.28 | 37.75 | 21.56 | 6.57 | Capital Return % |
| — | — | — | — | 0.07 | 0.19 | 0.21 | 0.27 | 0.40 | 0.50 | Income $ |
| — | — | — | — | 0.37 | 0.00 | 0.00 | 0.00 | 0.00 | 0.00 | Capital Gains $ |
| — | — | — | — | — | 0.20 | 0.20 | 0.20 | 0.20 | 0.20 | Expense Ratio % |
| — | — | — | — | — | 0.61 | 0.60 | 0.70 | 0.73 | 0.95 | Income Ratio % |
| — | — | — | — | — | 28 | 16 | 17 | 11 | 14 | Turnover Rate % |
| — | — | — | — | — | 1,341 | 1,986 | 4,198 | 3,862 | | Net Assets $mil |

## Performance

### Historic Quarterly NAV Returns

| | 1st Qtr | 2nd Qtr | 3rd Qtr | 4th Qtr | Total |
|---|---|---|---|---|---|
| 2001 | -6.59 | 13.53 | -16.86 | 20.62 | 6.34 |
| 2002 | 6.94 | -6.56 | -18.62 | 4.86 | -14.73 |
| 2003 | -5.83 | 19.80 | 7.05 | 14.76 | 38.59 |
| 2004 | 6.18 | 3.56 | -1.41 | 12.95 | 22.45 |
| 2005 | -2.10 | 3.89 | 5.34 | 0.34 | 7.50 |

| Trailing | NAV Return% | Market Return% | NAV Rtrn% +/-S&P 500 | %Rank Cat.(NAV) |
|---|---|---|---|---|
| 3 Mo | 0.34 | 0.29 | -1.74 | 7 |
| 6 Mo | 5.70 | 5.47 | -0.06 | 4 |
| 1 Yr | 7.50 | 7.53 | 2.59 | 4 |
| 3 Yr Avg | 22.19 | 22.16 | 7.81 | 2 |
| 5 Yr Avg | 10.59 | 10.70 | 10.05 | 2 |
| 10 Yr Avg | — | — | — | 0 |

| Tax Analysis | Tax-Adj Return% | Tax-Cost Ratio |
|---|---|---|
| 3 Yr (estimated) | 21.85 | 0.28 |
| 5 Yr (estimated) | 10.31 | 0.25 |
| 10 Yr (estimated) | — | — |

## Risk Profile

| | Standard Index S&P 500 | Best Fit Index Mstar Small Core |
|---|---|---|
| Alpha | 3.4 | -0.4 |
| Beta | 1.32 | 0.97 |
| R-Squared | 75 | 98 |
| Standard Deviation | 14.01 | |
| Mean | 22.19 | |
| Sharpe Ratio | 1.37 | |

## Morningstar Fair Value

| Price/Fair Value Ratio | Fair Value Estimate ($) | Hit Rate % |
|---|---|---|
| — | — | — |

## Portfolio Analysis 12-31-05

Share change since 11-05 Total Stocks:600

| | | Sector | PE | Tot Ret% | % Assets |
|---|---|---|---|---|---|
| ⊖ | NVR | Consumer | 8.8 | -8.76 | 0.70 |
| ⊖ | Cimarex Energy | Energy | 11.5 | 13.48 | 0.67 |
| ⊖ | Roper Industries | Ind Mtrls | 27.9 | 30.86 | 0.64 |
| ⊖ | Oshkosh Truck | Ind Mtrls | 20.4 | 31.21 | 0.62 |
| ⊖ | Pharmaceutical Product D | Health | 29.1 | 52.84 | 0.59 |
| ⊖ | Global Payments | Business | 37.7 | 59.62 | 0.58 |
| ⊖ | Vintage Petroleum | Energy | 18.3 | 136.37 | 0.55 |
| ⊖ | Massey Energy Company | Energy | 28.5 | 8.77 | 0.55 |
| ⊖ | Cerner | Software | 43.7 | 70.98 | 0.53 |
| ⊕ | Cal Dive International | Energy | 24.0 | 76.15 | 0.53 |
| ⊖ | ResMed | Health | 40.8 | 49.94 | 0.51 |
| ⊖ | Respironics | Health | 61.3 | 36.39 | 0.50 |
| ⊖ | Energen | Energy | 18.2 | 24.70 | 0.50 |
| ⊖ | Shurgard Storage Centers | Financial | — | 35.00 | 0.50 |
| ⊖ | Unit | Energy | 16.0 | 44.02 | 0.48 |
| ⊖ | Standard Pacific | Consumer | 6.0 | 15.20 | 0.48 |
| ⊖ | Landstar System | Business | 25.1 | 13.52 | 0.46 |
| ⊖ | Hughes Supply | Business | 17.2 | 12.06 | 0.45 |
| ⊖ | JLG Industries | Ind Mtrls | 23.7 | 132.76 | 0.44 |
| ⊖ | Southern Union | Utilities | 25.1 | 3.47 | 0.44 |

### Current Investment Style

Value Blnd Growth / Large Mid Small

| Market Cap | % |
|---|---|
| Giant | 0.0 |
| Large | 0.0 |
| Mid | 34.2 |
| Small | 59.6 |
| Micro | 6.2 |
| Avg $mil: | |
| 1,189 | |

| Value Measures | | Rel Category |
|---|---|---|
| Price/Earnings | 16.67 | 0.97 |
| Price/Book | 2.18 | 1.13 |
| Price/Sales | 0.99 | 1.09 |
| Price/Cash Flow | 8.60 | 1.31 |
| Dividend Yield % | 0.87 | 0.97 |

| Growth Measures | % | Rel Category |
|---|---|---|
| Long-Term Erngs | 13.50 | 0.97 |
| Book Value | 9.30 | 2.58 |
| Sales | 9.58 | 1.82 |
| Cash Flow | 8.50 | 94.44 |
| Historical Erngs | 16.02 | 1.30 |

| Profitability | % | Rel Category |
|---|---|---|
| Return on Equity | 14.37 | 1.48 |
| Return on Assets | 8.46 | 1.65 |
| Net Margin | 9.66 | 1.19 |

### Sector Weightings

| | % of Stocks | Rel S&P 500 | 3 Year High Low | |
|---|---|---|---|---|
| ☎ Info | 12.84 | 0.64 | | |
| Software | 5.17 | 1.45 | 5 | 4 |
| Hardware | 6.59 | 0.66 | 9 | 6 |
| Media | 0.05 | 0.01 | 0 | 0 |
| Telecom | 1.03 | 0.34 | 1 | 0 |
| Service | 48.78 | 1.05 | | |
| Health | 11.01 | 0.83 | 14 | 11 |
| Consumer | 11.38 | 1.40 | 15 | 11 |
| Business | 11.18 | 2.89 | 12 | 9 |
| Financial | 15.21 | 0.72 | 16 | 14 |
| Mfg | 38.39 | 1.15 | | |
| Goods | 6.68 | 0.78 | 8 | 6 |
| Ind Mtrls | 20.09 | 1.65 | 20 | 17 |
| Energy | 7.90 | 0.84 | 10 | 6 |
| Utilities | 3.72 | 1.11 | 4 | 3 |

### Composition

| | | |
|---|---|---|
| ● Cash | | 0.2 |
| ● Stocks | | 99.8 |
| ● Bonds | | 0.0 |
| ● Other | | 0.0 |
| Foreign | | 0.0 |
| (% of Stock) | | |

## Morningstar's Take by Dan Culloton

IShares S&P SmallCap 600 Index offers investors an attractive combination, but it has competition.

The exchange-traded fund offers broad exposure to small-cap stocks at an attractive expense ratio. It also has done a good job of tracking its index since its inception. It has trailed is bogy, the Standard & Poor's SmallCap 600 Index, by less than its expense ratio in each of the last five calendar years, which shows the ETF's advisor is reducing tracking error. However, the fund has some attractive rivals.

This ETF's 0.20% expense ratio is a fraction of the category average and much lower than the vast majority of small-cap index funds. That gives the fund a big head start. The fund also is diversified in terms of the number of individual stocks it owns and in terms of sector exposure. Since the fund's benchmark requires its constituents to meet profitability and liquidity standards, it won't always behave like funds that track other more inclusive indexes in every market environment. Over the long term, though, the offering correlates closely with

the small-cap blend fund universe, which means as long as it tracks its benchmark closely the fund's low costs stand a good chance of pushing it in front of most of its peers.

Investors, however, can squander that low-cost advantage if they aren't careful. Trading frequently or making small, regular investments can rack up return-sapping transaction costs because, like all ETFs, you have to buy this fund through a broker and pay a commission. This ETF also isn't the cheapest index fund in the category. Vanguard's Tax-Managed Small Cap and Small Cap VIPERs ETF are both a few basis points, or hundredths of a percent, cheaper. The former offering has the added advantages of being managed to reduce taxable distributions and sold without a commission.

This fund can get the job done, but there are other able options. Investors should shop around before committing.

| Address: | 45 Fremont Street San Francisco CA 94105 800-474-2737 | Management Fee: | 0.20% | | |
|---|---|---|---|---|---|
| | | Expense Projections: | 3Yr:$64 | 5Yr:$113 | 10Yr:$255 |
| | | Income Distrib: | Quarterly | | |
| Web Address: | www.ishares.com | Exchange: | NYSE | | |
| Inception: | 05-22-00 * | | | | |
| Advisor: | Barclays Global Fund Advisers | | | | |

# iShares SP TOPIX 150

| | Ticker | NAV | Market Price | 52 wk High/Low | Yield | Mstar Category |
|---|---|---|---|---|---|---|
| | ITF | $115.79 | $119.99 | $122.53 - $85.55 | 0.3% | Japan Stock |

## Management

### Portfolio Manager(s)

The fund's advisor, Barclays Global Fund Advisors, is one of the world's largest and most experienced managers of index-tracking portfolios. Lisa Chen and Carl Gilchrist are the primary portfolio managers of this and Barclays other international and global iShares. Chen has been a portfolio manager with Barclays for six years. Gilchrist has been on board for a decade.

### Strategy

This fund tracks the Standard & Poor's Topix 150, an index of leading companies from every major sector in the Tokyo Stock Price Index. S&P's index committee selects the shares of large, frequently traded, profitable companies that are representative of their industries and sectors for the index. The bogy represents about 70% of the Japanese market. Fund manager Barclays Global Fund Advisors passively tracks the benchmark.

**Growth of $10,000**

— Investment Value of ETF
— Investment Value of Index MSCI EAFE

| 1996 | 1997 | 1998 | 1999 | 2000 | 2001 | 2002 | 2003 | 2004 | 2005 | History |
|---|---|---|---|---|---|---|---|---|---|---|
| — | — | — | — | — | 70.41 | 62.42 | 82.66 | 93.49 | 115.79 | NAV $ |
| — | — | — | — | — | 69.70 | 62.02 | 83.63 | 93.89 | 116.00 | Market Price $ |
| — | — | — | — | — | 10.66* | -10.32 | 32.82 | 13.52 | 24.25 | NAV Return% |
| — | — | — | — | — | 10.71* | -9.99 | 35.24 | 12.69 | 23.95 | Market Price Return% |
| — | — | — | — | — | 0.20 | -0.40 | 0.64 | 0.28 | 0.15 | Avg Premium/Discount% |
| — | — | — | — | — | 10.66 | 5.62 | -5.77 | -6.73 | 10.71 | NAV Rtrn% +/-MSCI EAFE |
| — | — | — | — | — | 10.66 | -0.04 | -3.09 | -2.34 | -1.27 | NAV Rtrn% +/-MSCI JP NDT |
| — | — | — | — | — | — | 2 | 2 | 2 | 2 | NAV Return% Rank in Cat |
| — | — | — | — | — | 0.00 | 0.99 | 0.38 | 0.41 | 0.41 | Income Return % |
| — | — | — | — | — | — | -11.31 | 32.44 | 13.11 | 23.84 | Capital Return % |
| — | — | — | — | — | 0.00 | 0.70 | 0.24 | 0.34 | 0.38 | Income $ |
| — | — | — | — | — | 0.00 | 0.00 | 0.00 | 0.00 | 0.00 | Capital Gains $ |
| — | — | — | — | — | — | 0.50 | 0.50 | 0.50 | 0.50 | Expense Ratio % |
| — | — | — | — | — | — | 0.32 | 0.26 | 1.00 | 0.67 | Income Ratio % |
| — | — | — | — | — | — | 5 | 4 | 4 | 4 | Turnover Rate % |
| — | — | — | — | — | — | 9 | 25 | 98 | 208 | Net Assets $mil |

## Performance

**Historic Quarterly NAV Returns**

| | 1st Qtr | 2nd Qtr | 3rd Qtr | 4th Qtr | Total |
|---|---|---|---|---|---|
| 2001 | — | — | — | — | —* |
| 2002 | 4.52 | 3.37 | -12.86 | -4.75 | -10.32 |
| 2003 | -8.35 | 11.29 | 20.61 | 7.96 | 32.82 |
| 2004 | 14.41 | -4.61 | -7.47 | 12.42 | 13.52 |
| 2005 | -2.96 | -3.66 | 19.90 | 10.86 | 24.25 |

| Trailing | NAV Return% | Market Return%+/-MSCI EAFE | NAV Rtrn% +/-MSCI EAFE | %Rank Cat.(NAV) |
|---|---|---|---|---|
| 3 Mo | 10.86 | 10.29 | 6.78 | 3 |
| 6 Mo | 32.91 | 33.63 | 18.03 | 3 |
| 1 Yr | 24.25 | 23.95 | 10.71 | 2 |
| 3 Yr Avg | 23.28 | 23.62 | -0.40 | 2 |
| 5 Yr Avg | — | — | — | 0 |
| 10 Yr Avg | — | — | — | 0 |

| Tax Analysis | Tax-Adj Return% | Tax-Cost Ratio |
|---|---|---|
| 3 Yr (estimated) | 23.14 | 0.11 |
| 5 Yr (estimated) | — | — |
| 10 Yr (estimated) | — | — |

## Risk Profile

| | Standard Index S&P 500 | Best Fit Index MSCI JP NDT |
|---|---|---|
| Alpha | 4.5 | -1.4 |
| Beta | 0.80 | 0.98 |
| R-Squared | 31 | 99 |
| Standard Deviation | 16.62 | |
| Mean | 23.28 | |
| Sharpe Ratio | 1.24 | |

## Morningstar Fair Value

| Price/Fair Value Ratio | Fair Value Estimate ($) | Hit Rate % |
|---|---|---|
| — | — | — |

## Portfolio Analysis 12-31-05

| Share change since 11-05 Total Stocks:147 | Sector | Country | % Assets |
|---|---|---|---|
| ⊕ Toyota Motor | Goods | Japan | 6.57 |
| ⊕ Mitsubishi Tokyo Fin. Gr | Financial | Japan | 6.24 |
| ⊕ Mizuho Financial Grp | Financial | Japan | 3.93 |
| ⊕ Sumitomo Mitsui Financia | Financial | Japan | 3.17 |
| ⊕ Canon | Goods | Japan | 2.19 |
| ⊕ Honda Motor | Goods | Japan | 2.13 |
| ⊕ Nippon Telegraph & Telep | Telecom | Japan | 2.12 |
| ⊕ Takeda Chemical Industri | Health | Japan | 2.05 |
| ⊕ Matsushita Electric Indu | Ind Mtrls | Japan | 1.89 |
| ⊕ Sony | Goods | Japan | 1.88 |
| ⊕ Nomura Hldgs | Financial | Japan | 1.76 |
| ⊕ Seven & I Hldgs | — | Japan | 1.58 |
| ⊕ SOFTBANK CORP. | Financial | Japan | 1.46 |
| ⊕ Mitsubishi | Ind Mtrls | Japan | 1.35 |
| ⊕ Millea Hldgs | Financial | Japan | 1.29 |
| ⊕ The Tokyo Electric Power | Utilities | Japan | 1.29 |
| ⊕ NTT DoCoMo | Telecom | Japan | 1.24 |
| ⊕ East Japan Railway | Business | Japan | 1.15 |
| ⊕ Mitsubishi Estate | Financial | Japan | 1.08 |
| ⊕ Nippon Steel | Ind Mtrls | Japan | 1.07 |

**Current Investment Style**

| Value Blnd Growth | | |
|---|---|---|
| ■ (Large) | | |

| Market Cap | % |
|---|---|
| Giant | 68.4 |
| Large | 30.6 |
| Mid | 1.1 |
| Small | 0.0 |
| Micro | 0.0 |
| Avg $mil: | 26,337 |

| Value Measures | | Rel Category |
|---|---|---|
| Price/Earnings | 19.86 | 1.03 |
| Price/Book | 1.89 | 1.03 |
| Price/Sales | 1.04 | 1.04 |
| Price/Cash Flow | 7.36 | 1.01 |
| Dividend Yield % | 1.04 | 0.72 |

| Growth Measures | % | Rel Category |
|---|---|---|
| Long-Term Erngs | 9.29 | 0.98 |
| Book Value | 6.42 | 1.03 |
| Sales | -0.81 | NMF |
| Cash Flow | 3.60 | 1.08 |
| Historical Erngs | 19.03 | 0.96 |

**Composition**

| Cash | 0.2 | Bonds | 0.0 |
|---|---|---|---|
| Stocks | 99.8 | Other | 0.0 |
| Foreign (% of Stock) | | | 100.0 |

| Sector Weightings | % of Stocks | Rel MSCI EAFE | 3 Year High | Low |
|---|---|---|---|---|
| ☁ Info | 10.82 | 0.77 | | |
| 🔲 Software | 0.52 | 0.49 | 1 | 0 |
| 🖥 Hardware | 5.84 | 1.62 | 10 | 5 |
| 🎙 Media | 1.01 | 0.48 | 2 | 1 |
| 📶 Telecom | 3.45 | 0.48 | 9 | 3 |
| ☞ Service | 40.69 | 0.89 | | |
| 🏥 Health | 3.91 | 0.55 | 7 | 3 |
| 🛒 Consumer | 2.11 | 0.48 | 4 | 2 |
| 📋 Business | 6.93 | 1.15 | 7 | 7 |
| 💲 Financial | 27.74 | 0.99 | 28 | 7 |
| 🏭 Mfg | 48.50 | 1.20 | | |
| 🏠 Goods | 23.11 | 1.69 | 32 | 23 |
| ⚙ Ind Mtrls | 20.80 | 1.47 | 22 | 17 |
| 🔋 Energy | 0.59 | 0.07 | 1 | 1 |
| 💡 Utilities | 4.00 | 0.87 | 8 | 4 |

**Regional Exposure** % Stock

| UK/W. Europe | 0 | N. America | 0 |
|---|---|---|---|
| Japan | 100 | Latn America | 0 |
| Asia X Japan | 0 | Other | 0 |

**Country Exposure** % Stock

| Japan | 100 |
|---|---|

## Morningstar's Take by Dan Culloton

IShares S&P Topix 150 Index offers the cheapest pure exposure to Japanese stocks, but it has its drawbacks.

This fund tracks a benchmark of leading companies from every sector in the Tokyo Stock Exchange. That provides exposure to leading Japanese stocks, such as Toyota Motor, Nippon Telegraph & Telephone, and Takeda Pharmaceuticals. Its bogy represents 70% of Japanese market. The offering's 0.50% expense ratio also is 75% less expensive than the average Japan fund and also lower than all other index funds and ETFs in the group save Vanguard Pacific Stock Index. The Vanguard fund, however, does not provide unadulterated exposure to Nippon. It includes the shares of companies from Australia, Hong Kong, and Singapore.

The low cost make this ETF attractive to investors who want to own the largest Japanese stocks, especially when you consider the scarcity of traditional Japan funds with long-tenured managers, attractive risk/reward profiles, and affordable expense ratios. This ETF, however, wouldn't be our first choice. It has a shorter track record and is a bit less diversified than its sibling iShares MSCI Japan. In head-to-head competition over the last three years, the MSCI Japan fund has a slight edge, turning in a 21.7% market return for the period ending Nov. 17, 2005, while this ETF's shares have risen 20.7%.

Investors also should note that the fund is capable of both big gains--as its more than 35% gain in 2003 shows and significant losses. The offering's index has fallen in six of the last nine years. There is hope that Japan's economy has finally turned a corner and improved many of the political and structural problems that have held its stock market back over the last decade. However, the country's export-fueled economy is notoriously hard to predict. That said, this offers acceptable, but not exceptional, access to Japanese stocks.

| Address: | 45 Fremont Street San Francisco CA 94105 800-474-2737 | Management Fee: | 0.50% |
|---|---|---|---|
| | | Expense Projections: | 3Yr:$160  5Yr:$280  10Yr:$628 |
| Web Address: | www.ishares.com | Income Distrib: | Annually |
| Inception: | 10-23-01 * | Exchange: | AMEX |
| Advisor: | Barclays Global Fund Advisers | | |

**MORNINGSTAR® ETFs 100**

# MidCap SPDR Trust

| | Ticker | NAV | Market Price | 52 wk High/Low | Yield | Mstar Category |
|---|---|---|---|---|---|---|
| | MDY | $134.72 | $140.89 | $140.89 - $114.79 | 1.0% | Mid-Cap Blend |

## Management

### Portfolio Manager(s)

A management team at the Bank of New York, the fund's trustee, is in charge here.

### Strategy

This fund seeks to duplicate as closely as possible the holdings and returns of the S&P MidCap 400 Index. The result is a broadly diversified portfolio of mid-cap stocks. The fund is structured as a unit investment trust, which inhibits it from reinvesting dividends immediately. That can lead to a cash drag on this fund relative to its rivals that have an open-end structure.

**Growth of $10,000**

— Investment Value of ETF
— Investment Value of Index S&P 500

| 1996 | 1997 | 1998 | 1999 | 2000 | 2001 | 2002 | 2003 | 2004 | 2005 | History |
|---|---|---|---|---|---|---|---|---|---|---|
| 49.78 | 64.32 | 73.98 | 81.62 | 94.76 | 94.32 | 78.78 | 105.51 | 121.38 | 134.72 | NAV $ |
| 49.50 | 64.08 | 72.75 | 81.12 | 94.38 | 92.80 | 78.65 | 105.40 | 121.00 | 134.69 | Market Price $ |
| 18.62 | 31.64 | 18.62 | 14.28 | 17.08 | 0.37 | -15.77 | 35.20 | 15.84 | 12.17 | NAV Return% |
| 17.52 | 31.89 | 17.08 | 15.50 | 17.33 | -0.85 | -14.53 | 35.28 | 15.60 | 12.50 | Market Price Return% |
| -0.02 | 0.03 | -0.32 | -0.11 | -0.04 | 0.05 | -0.17 | -0.13 | -0.07 | -0.06 | Avg Premium/Discount% |
| -4.33 | -1.71 | -9.96 | -6.76 | 26.18 | 12.25 | 6.32 | 6.53 | 4.97 | 7.26 | NAV Rtrn% +/-S&P 500 |
| -0.56 | -0.61 | -0.49 | -0.44 | -0.41 | 0.97 | -1.24 | -0.39 | -0.63 | -0.38 | NAV Rtrn% +/-S&P Mid 400 |
| 1 | 1 | 1 | 1 | 1 | 2 | 4 | 4 | 5 | 7 | NAV Return% Rank in Cat |
| 1.49 | 1.23 | 0.93 | 0.96 | 0.95 | 0.76 | 0.76 | 1.09 | 0.71 | 1.13 | Income Return % |
| 17.13 | 30.41 | 17.69 | 13.32 | 16.13 | -0.39 | -16.53 | 34.11 | 15.13 | 11.04 | Capital Return % |
| 0.64 | 0.61 | 0.60 | 0.71 | 0.78 | 0.71 | 0.72 | 0.86 | 0.75 | 1.37 | Income $ |
| 0.88 | 0.50 | 1.50 | 2.00 | 0.00 | 0.00 | 0.00 | 0.00 | 0.00 | 0.00 | Capital Gains $ |
| 0.63 | 0.39 | 0.30 | 0.26 | 0.28 | 0.26 | 0.25 | 0.25 | 0.25 | — | Expense Ratio % |
| 1.42 | 0.98 | 0.92 | 0.97 | 0.85 | 0.75 | 0.81 | 0.96 | 0.96 | — | Income Ratio % |
| 20 | 20 | 30 | 43 | 30 | 33 | 21 | 13 | 16 | — | Turnover Rate % |
| — | — | — | — | — | — | 5,050 | 6,427 | 7,895 | 8,942 | Net Assets $mil |

## Performance

### Historic Quarterly NAV Returns

| | 1st Qtr | 2nd Qtr | 3rd Qtr | 4th Qtr | Total |
|---|---|---|---|---|---|
| 2001 | -10.82 | 11.68 | -17.62 | 22.33 | 0.37 |
| 2002 | 5.35 | -9.36 | -16.59 | 5.76 | -15.77 |
| 2003 | -4.51 | 17.53 | 6.52 | 13.10 | 35.20 |
| 2004 | 5.00 | 0.89 | -2.17 | 11.78 | 15.84 |
| 2005 | -0.47 | 4.19 | 4.78 | 3.23 | 12.17 |

| Trailing | NAV Return% | Market Return% | NAV Rtrn% +/-S&P 500 | %Rank Cat.(NAV) |
|---|---|---|---|---|
| 3 Mo | 3.23 | 3.13 | 1.15 | 7 |
| 6 Mo | 8.17 | 8.06 | 2.41 | 7 |
| 1 Yr | 12.17 | 12.50 | 7.26 | 7 |
| 3 Yr Avg | 20.66 | 20.72 | 6.28 | 4 |
| 5 Yr Avg | 8.23 | 8.31 | 7.69 | 2 |
| 10 Yr Avg | 13.92 | 13.87 | 4.85 | 1 |

| Tax Analysis | Tax-Adj Return% | Tax-Cost Ratio |
|---|---|---|
| 3 Yr (estimated) | 20.28 | 0.31 |
| 5 Yr (estimated) | 7.89 | 0.31 |
| 10 Yr (estimated) | 13.23 | 0.61 |

## Risk Profile

| | Standard Index S&P 500 | Best Fit Index S&P Mid 400 |
|---|---|---|
| Alpha | 3.9 | -0.3 |
| Beta | 1.15 | 1.00 |
| R-Squared | 82 | 100 |
| Standard Deviation | 11.63 | |
| Mean | 20.66 | |
| Sharpe Ratio | 1.51 | |

## Morningstar Fair Value

| Price/Fair Value Ratio | Fair Value Estimate ($) | Hit Rate % |
|---|---|---|
| 1.1 Overvalued | 34.07 | 78 Fair |

## Portfolio Analysis 10-31-05

Share change since 09-04 Total Stocks:399

| | Sector | PE | Tot Ret% | % Assets |
|---|---|---|---|---|
| ⊕ Legg Mason | Financial | 30.9 | 64.48 | 1.15 |
| ⊕ SanDisk | Hardware | 36.1 | 151.58 | 1.02 |
| ⊕ Peabody Energy | Energy | 33.1 | 104.95 | 0.98 |
| ⊕ Whole Foods Market | Consumer | 78.2 | 63.73 | 0.93 |
| ⊕ PacifiCare Health System | Health | — | — | 0.69 |
| ⊕ Chico's FAS | Consumer | 43.9 | 92.97 | 0.68 |
| ⊕ Pioneer Natural Resource | Energy | 18.6 | 46.75 | 0.68 |
| ⊕ Noble Energy | Energy | 11.3 | 31.24 | 0.67 |
| ⊕ Ensco International | Energy | 30.8 | 40.08 | 0.66 |
| ⊕ Smith International | Energy | 27.9 | 37.41 | 0.66 |
| ⊕ Questar | Energy | 22.3 | 50.64 | 0.64 |
| ⊕ Harman International Ind | Goods | 27.0 | -22.91 | 0.63 |
| ⊕ Fidelity National Financ | Financial | 6.4 | 23.52 | 0.62 |
| ⊕ Expeditors International | Business | 41.4 | 21.41 | 0.62 |
| ⊕ Microchip Technology | Hardware | 29.0 | 22.80 | 0.60 |
| ⊕ Precision Castparts | Ind Mtrls | 26.0 | 58.08 | 0.60 |
| ⊖ Ivax | Health | 42.9 | 98.04 | 0.59 |
| ⊕ Everest Re Group | Financial | — | 12.58 | 0.59 |
| ⊕ Barr Pharmaceuticals | Health | 26.9 | 36.78 | 0.58 |
| ☼ C H Robinson Worldwide | Business | — | — | 0.58 |

### Current Investment Style

Value Blnd Growth — Large Mid Small

| Market Cap | % |
|---|---|
| Giant | 0.0 |
| Large | 4.1 |
| Mid | 85.5 |
| Small | 10.4 |
| Micro | 0.0 |
| Avg $mil: | 3,250 |

| Value Measures | | Rel Category |
|---|---|---|
| Price/Earnings | 17.84 | 1.02 |
| Price/Book | 2.25 | 0.95 |
| Price/Sales | 1.18 | 1.03 |
| Price/Cash Flow | 6.97 | 0.93 |
| Dividend Yield % | 1.23 | 1.06 |

| Growth Measures | % | Rel Category |
|---|---|---|
| Long-Term Erngs | 12.56 | 0.99 |
| Book Value | 9.85 | 1.13 |
| Sales | 8.63 | 1.06 |
| Cash Flow | 7.68 | 0.77 |
| Historical Erngs | 13.73 | 0.85 |

| Profitability | % | Rel Category |
|---|---|---|
| Return on Equity | 13.30 | 0.88 |
| Return on Assets | 7.90 | 1.01 |
| Net Margin | 9.89 | 0.93 |

### Sector Weightings

| | % of Stocks | Rel S&P 500 | 3 Year High | Low |
|---|---|---|---|---|
| ↻ Info | 14.32 | 0.71 | | |
| 🄽 Software | 3.30 | 0.93 | 3 | 3 |
| 🄷 Hardware | 8.56 | 0.85 | 10 | 7 |
| 🄼 Media | 1.92 | 0.54 | 4 | 2 |
| 🄵 Telecom | 0.54 | 0.18 | 1 | 1 |
| ⬡ Service | 53.52 | 1.15 | | |
| 🄷 Health | 11.84 | 0.89 | 14 | 10 |
| 🄲 Consumer | 12.93 | 1.59 | 15 | 11 |
| 🄱 Business | 10.80 | 2.79 | 11 | 9 |
| 🄵 Financial | 17.95 | 0.85 | 20 | 17 |
| ⬡ Mfg | 32.16 | 0.96 | | |
| 🄶 Goods | 5.71 | 0.67 | 8 | 6 |
| 🄸 Ind Mtrls | 9.16 | 0.75 | 9 | 7 |
| 🄴 Energy | 10.62 | 1.14 | 11 | 8 |
| 🄾 Utilities | 6.67 | 1.99 | 7 | 6 |

### Composition

| | |
|---|---|
| ● Cash | 0.0 |
| ● Stocks | 99.6 |
| ● Bonds | 0.4 |
| ○ Other | 0.0 |
| Foreign | 0.0 |
| (% of Stock) | |

## Morningstar's Take by Dan Culloton

This exchange-traded fund has strengths but also a lot of competition.

MidCap SPDR is large and liquid. The fund, which tracks the S&P MidCap 400 Index, has amassed more than $8 billion in assets and boasts a healthy average daily trading volume. The fund's low costs, as well as the liquidity of its underlying stocks--which must meet S&P's profitability and trading volume standards--help explain the fund's popularity.

Recent years also have shown this fund's value as a portfolio diversifier. This fund has enjoyed a strong run of relative performance in recent years as larger cap stocks have languished. Its 8.3% annualized gain for the trailing five-year period ending Nov. 17, 2005 could have bolstered any portfolio focused the S&P 500, which lost 0.3% over the same period.

The fund's recent successes, however, accentuate some of its risks. Because mid-cap stocks have enjoyed such a strong run, they could be due for a breather. Its large stake of financial stocks also could hamper performance should interest rates rise.

Cheaper rivals have emerged, too. The iShares S&P MidCap 400 covers the same territory and charges less. The iShares have the added advantage of being organized as an open-end investment company. That allows the iShares to reinvest dividends instead of hold them as cash as this fund, which is structured as a unit investment trust, must.

Furthermore newer indexes, such as the MSCI bogy used by the Vanguard Mid Cap VIPERs, may be more tax-efficient. This fund must sell stocks that graduate to the S&P 500--as it did with home builder Lennar in October 2005--and incur capital gains. To reduce turnover, the MSCI indexes use buffer zones between market cap bands to slow stocks' comings and goings.

This fund offers cheap mid-cap exposure. It may pay to shop around, though.

| Address: | PDR Services, 86 Trinity Place New York NY 10006 800-843-2639 | Management Fee: | 0.10% |
|---|---|---|---|
| | | Expense Projections: | 3Yr: — 5Yr: — 10Yr: — |
| Web Address: | www.amex.com | Income Distrib: | Quarterly |
| Inception: | 05-04-95 | Exchange: | AMEX |
| Advisor: | PDR Services | | |

# Nasdaq 100 Trust

| | Ticker | NAV | Market Price | 52 wk High/Low | Yield | Mstar Category |
|---|---|---|---|---|---|---|
| | QQQQ | $40.46 | $42.88 | $42.88 - $34.70 | 0.3% | Large Growth |

## Management

### Portfolio Manager(s)

The fund began trading publicly in 1999. A management team with Bank of New York, the fund's trustee, executes trades.

**Growth of $10,000**

— Investment Value of ETF
— Investment Value of Index S&P 500

| | 1996 | 1997 | 1998 | 1999 | 2000 | 2001 | 2002 | 2003 | 2004 | 2005 | History |
|---|---|---|---|---|---|---|---|---|---|---|---|
| | — | — | — | 92.61 | 58.40 | 40.36 | 24.47 | 36.49 | 39.94 | 40.46 | NAV $ |
| | — | — | — | 91.38 | 58.38 | 38.91 | 24.37 | 36.46 | 39.91 | 40.41 | Market Price $ |
| | — | — | — | -3.15* | -36.94 | -30.89 | -39.37 | 49.18 | 10.51 | 1.55 | NAV Return% |
| | — | — | — | -3.20* | -36.11 | -33.35 | -37.37 | 49.67 | 10.53 | 1.49 | Market Price Return% |
| | — | — | — | -0.20 | 0.08 | -0.05 | -0.08 | 0.00 | 0.03 | -0.03 | Avg Premium/Discount% |
| | — | — | — | -3.15 | -27.84 | -19.01 | -17.28 | 20.51 | -0.36 | -3.36 | NAV Rtrn% +/-S&P 500 |
| | — | — | — | -3.15 | -14.52 | -10.47 | -11.49 | 19.43 | 4.21 | -3.71 | NAV Rtrn% +/-Russ 1000Gr |
| | — | — | — | — | 1 | 5 | 5 | 5 | 6 | 9 | NAV Return% Rank in Cat |
| | — | — | — | 0.00 | 0.00 | 0.00 | 0.00 | 0.06 | 1.04 | 0.25 | Income Return % |
| | — | — | — | — | -36.94 | -30.89 | -39.37 | 49.12 | 9.47 | 1.30 | Capital Return % |
| | — | — | — | 0.00 | 0.00 | 0.00 | 0.00 | 0.01 | 0.38 | 0.10 | Income $ |
| | — | — | — | 0.00 | 0.00 | 0.00 | 0.00 | 0.00 | 0.00 | 0.00 | Capital Gains $ |
| | — | — | — | 0.18 | 0.18 | 0.18 | 0.18 | 0.20 | 0.20 | — | Expense Ratio % |
| | — | — | — | -0.16 | -0.13 | -0.13 | -0.13 | -0.03 | 0.70 | — | Income Ratio % |
| | — | — | — | 23 | 22 | 13 | 13 | 7 | — | | Turnover Rate % |
| | — | — | — | — | — | — | 17,034 | 25,632 | 22,196 | 20,311 | Net Assets $mil |

## Strategy

The fund, known popularly as Cubes or Qubes, tracks the Nasdaq 100 Index. The index was created in 1985 to represent the 100 largest (in terms of market cap) nonfinancial stocks in the Nasdaq Composite Index. Each company in the fund is reviewed in the fall of every year and must meet two market-capitalization criteria: It must be among the top 150 companies in the larger index, and it must have been among the top 100 in the index during the last annual review. Companies failing one or both of these criteria are replaced. Unlike the S&P 500, the index has no profitability requirement.

## Performance

**Historic Quarterly NAV Returns**

| | 1st Qtr | 2nd Qtr | 3rd Qtr | 4th Qtr | Total |
|---|---|---|---|---|---|
| 2001 | -32.84 | 14.94 | -36.76 | 41.56 | -30.89 |
| 2002 | -10.41 | -27.68 | -20.84 | 18.21 | -39.37 |
| 2003 | 3.51 | 17.96 | 8.47 | 12.63 | 49.18 |
| 2004 | -2.00 | 5.43 | -6.82 | 14.79 | 10.51 |
| 2005 | -8.51 | 0.68 | 7.28 | 2.76 | 1.55 |

| Trailing | NAV Return% | Market Return% | NAV Rtrn% +/-S&P 500 | %Rank Cat.(NAV) |
|---|---|---|---|---|
| 3 Mo | 2.76 | 2.66 | 0.68 | 10 |
| 6 Mo | 10.24 | 10.14 | 4.48 | 10 |
| 1 Yr | 1.55 | 1.49 | -3.36 | 9 |
| 3 Yr Avg | 18.74 | 18.85 | 4.36 | 5 |
| 5 Yr Avg | -6.85 | -6.86 | -7.39 | 5 |
| 10 Yr Avg | — | — | — | 0 |

| Tax Analysis | Tax-Adj Return% | Tax-Cost Ratio |
|---|---|---|
| 3 Yr (estimated) | 18.57 | 0.14 |
| 5 Yr (estimated) | -6.93 | 0.09 |
| 10 Yr (estimated) | — | — |

## Risk Profile

| | Standard Index S&P 500 | Best Fit Index ArcaEx Tech 100 |
|---|---|---|
| Alpha | 0.0 | -1.4 |
| Beta | 1.37 | 0.92 |
| R-Squared | 70 | 92 |
| Standard Deviation | 15.09 | |
| Mean | 18.74 | |
| Sharpe Ratio | 1.09 | |

## Morningstar Fair Value

| Price/Fair Value Ratio | Fair Value Estimate ($) | Hit Rate % |
|---|---|---|
| 1.0 Fairly valued | 30.37 | 96 Good |

## Portfolio Analysis 10-31-05

| Share change since 09-04 Total Stocks:100 | Sector | PE | Tot Ret% | % Assets |
|---|---|---|---|---|
| ⊖ Microsoft | Software | 22.2 | -0.95 | 7.31 |
| ⊖ Qualcomm | Hardware | 34.2 | 2.50 | 6.81 |
| ⊕ Apple Computer | Hardware | 46.1 | 123.26 | 4.78 |
| ⊖ Intel | Hardware | 18.6 | 8.12 | 4.05 |
| ⊖ Amgen | Health | 28.3 | 22.93 | 3.53 |
| ⊕ eBay | Consumer | 59.2 | -25.70 | 3.21 |
| ⊖ Cisco Systems | Hardware | 19.9 | -11.39 | 3.16 |
| ⊖ Dell | Hardware | 23.2 | -28.93 | 2.33 |
| ⊕ Symantec | Software | 53.0 | -32.07 | 2.19 |
| ⊖ Comcast A | Media | 47.1 | -22.12 | 2.16 |
| ⊖ Starbucks | Consumer | 49.2 | -3.75 | 2.06 |
| ⊖ Oracle | Software | 22.2 | -11.01 | 2.06 |
| ⊖ Genzyme | Health | NMF | 21.89 | 1.78 |
| ⊖ Yahoo | Media | 36.3 | 3.98 | 1.77 |
| ⊖ Gilead Sciences | Health | 38.1 | 50.24 | 1.69 |
| ⊕ Sears Holdings | Consumer | 22.7 | 16.76 | 1.65 |
| ⊖ Maxim Integrated Product | Hardware | 24.6 | -13.57 | 1.51 |
| ⊖ Electronic Arts | Software | 44.0 | -15.19 | 1.34 |
| ⊖ Teva Pharmaceutical Indu | Health | 86.0 | 45.03 | 1.24 |
| ⊖ Bed Bath & Beyond | Consumer | 20.2 | -9.24 | 1.23 |

**Current Investment Style**

Value Blnd Growth — Large Mid Small

| Market Cap | % |
|---|---|
| Giant | 41.5 |
| Large | 35.4 |
| Mid | 23.2 |
| Small | 0.0 |
| Micro | 0.0 |

Avg $mil: 25,431

| Value Measures | | Rel Category |
|---|---|---|
| Price/Earnings | 25.21 | 1.20 |
| Price/Book | 3.93 | 1.17 |
| Price/Sales | 2.69 | 1.38 |
| Price/Cash Flow | 12.70 | 1.21 |
| Dividend Yield % | 0.45 | 0.51 |

| Growth Measures | % | Rel Category |
|---|---|---|
| Long-Term Erngs | 16.26 | 1.15 |
| Book Value | 5.44 | 0.67 |
| Sales | 11.05 | 0.99 |
| Cash Flow | 17.93 | 1.10 |
| Historical Erngs | 23.35 | 1.22 |

| Profitability | % | Rel Category |
|---|---|---|
| Return on Equity | 16.98 | 0.84 |
| Return on Assets | 10.90 | 1.01 |
| Net Margin | 17.66 | 1.27 |

| Sector Weightings | % of Stocks | Rel S&P 500 | 3 Year High Low | |
|---|---|---|---|---|
| ↻ Info | 63.62 | 3.15 | | |
| Software | 18.12 | 5.09 | 23 | 18 |
| Hardware | 37.50 | 3.74 | 38 | 32 |
| Media | 6.70 | 1.87 | 7 | 5 |
| Telecom | 1.30 | 0.43 | 3 | 1 |
| ⊆ Service | 34.47 | 0.74 | | |
| Health | 15.18 | 1.14 | 16 | 13 |
| Consumer | 14.79 | 1.82 | 15 | 13 |
| Business | 4.50 | 1.16 | 5 | 4 |
| Financial | 0.00 | 0.00 | 0 | 0 |
| ⊔ Mfg | 1.91 | 0.06 | | |
| Goods | 0.00 | 0.00 | 0 | 0 |
| Ind Mtrls | 1.91 | 0.16 | 2 | 2 |
| Energy | 0.00 | 0.00 | 0 | 0 |
| Utilities | 0.00 | 0.00 | 0 | 0 |

**Composition**

| | |
|---|---|
| Cash | 0.0 |
| Stocks | 100.0 |
| Bonds | 0.0 |
| Other | 0.0 |
| Foreign | 3.4 |
| (% of Stock) | |

## Morningstar's Take by Dan Culloton

Nasdaq 100 Trust Shares just got Googled.

From its August 2004 initial public offering through mid-December 2005, Google has been the hottest stock on the Nasdaq. The Internet search firm's shares could have been trading on the moon for all the good it did this ETF. Google was not "seasoned" enough for this fund's target index, the Nasdaq 100, which requires constituents to be listed on the Nasdaq for at least two years or one year if the stock is bigger than three fourths of the other securities in the index.

That has changed, but our view of this ETF remains the same. When the Nasdaq 100 rebalanced in December, Google, which already met the benchmark's other eligibility criteria, was finally large and seasoned enough to join the bogy. That will make the index and this fund more representative of the Nasdaq Composite's largest nonfinancial stocks. Even before Google's share price hit $400 in November, the stock was one of the 10 largest in the composite.

It's not like this portfolio needs another richly valued stock, though. Google may dominate Web searching and advertising, but analysts have to make heroic growth assumptions to justify its current price. This portfolio already keeps more than half of its money in software and hardware stocks and has large helpings of other high-growth industries, such as biotech. Its biggest holdings include high-priced stocks such as online auctioneer eBay and Apple Computer.

So the addition of Google does nothing for this ETF's risk profile. Neither do the other 11 stocks the index added to its ranks with Google. Most of them are either speculative stocks such as software firm CheckFree or telecom service provider NII Holdings, or companies whose shares are trading above Morningstar stock analysts' estimates of their fair values, such as oil driller Patterson-UTI Energy or Linux software distributor Red Hat.

With or without Google, this is a dicey fund.

| | | | |
|---|---|---|---|
| Address: | Nasdaq Global Fds, 9513 Key West Ave Rockville MD 20850 800-843-2639 | Management Fee: | 0.06% |
| | | Expense Projections: | 3Yr:$6  5Yr:$11  10Yr:$26 |
| Web Address: | www.nasdaq.com | Income Distrib: | Annually |
| Inception: | 03-10-99 * | Exchange: | NASDAQ |
| Advisor: | Nasdaq Global Funds Inc | | |

**MORNINGSTAR® ETFs 100**

# PowerShares Dynam OTC

| Ticker | NAV | Market Price | 52 wk High/Low | Yield | Mstar Category |
|---|---|---|---|---|---|
| PWO | $49.20 | $51.78 | $51.78 - $41.51 | 0.1% | Mid-Cap Growth |

## Management

### Portfolio Manager(s)

The fund is managed by PowerShares Capital Management, which was founded in 2002. John W. Southard Jr. is the lead portfolio manager. He is a former senior analyst of Chicago Investment Analytics, a quantitative research firm bought by Charles Schwab in 2000. He also worked as an analyst and portfolio manager at a unit investment trust firm, First Trust Portfolios of Lisle, Ill. But he has a short track record as a retail mutual fund or ETF manager.

### Strategy

This ETF tracks the AMEX Dynamic OTC Intellidex, which uses a 25-factor quantitative model to select 100 stocks from the 1,000 largest U.S. companies listed on the Nasdaq Stock Market. The factors employed include both technical (i.e., price and volume trends) and fundamental (P/E ratios and growth rates) data points. The bogy follows rules to make sure its sector weightings stay close to those of its selection universe. It also caps position sizes and employs a stratified weighting scheme to keep large stocks from dominating the portfolio. The Intellidex reconstitutes quarterly.

## Performance

### Historic Quarterly NAV Returns

| | 1st Qtr | 2nd Qtr | 3rd Qtr | 4th Qtr | Total |
|---|---|---|---|---|---|
| 2001 | — | — | — | — | — |
| 2002 | — | — | — | — | — |
| 2003 | — | — | 11.82 | 13.24 | —* |
| 2004 | 1.21 | 0.30 | -6.29 | 18.67 | 12.88 |
| 2005 | -1.34 | 3.86 | 3.38 | 3.60 | 9.76 |

| Trailing | NAV Return% | Market Return% | NAV Rtrn% +/-S&P 500 | %Rank Cat.(NAV) |
|---|---|---|---|---|
| 3 Mo | 3.60 | 3.64 | 1.52 | 5 |
| 6 Mo | 7.11 | 7.20 | 1.35 | 5 |
| 1 Yr | 9.76 | 9.56 | 4.85 | 4 |
| 3 Yr Avg | — | — | — | 0 |
| 5 Yr Avg | — | — | — | 0 |
| 10 Yr Avg | — | — | — | 0 |

| Tax Analysis | Tax-Adj Return% | Tax-Cost Ratio |
|---|---|---|
| 3 Yr (estimated) | — | — |
| 5 Yr (estimated) | — | — |
| 10 Yr (estimated) | — | — |

### Growth of $10,000

— Investment Value of ETF
— Investment Value of Index S&P 500

| | 1996 | 1997 | 1998 | 1999 | 2000 | 2001 | 2002 | 2003 | 2004 | 2005 | History |
|---|---|---|---|---|---|---|---|---|---|---|---|
| | — | — | — | — | — | — | — | 39.76 | 44.88 | 49.20 | NAV $ |
| | — | — | — | — | — | — | — | 39.75 | 44.96 | 49.20 | Market Price $ |
| | — | — | — | — | — | — | — | 22.54* | 12.88 | 9.76 | NAV Return% |
| | — | — | — | — | — | — | — | 22.65* | 13.11 | 9.56 | Market Price Return% |
| | — | — | — | — | — | — | — | -0.24 | 0.26 | -0.01 | Avg Premium/Discount% |
| | — | — | — | — | — | — | — | 22.54 | 2.01 | 4.85 | NAV Rtrn% +/-S&P 500 |
| | — | — | — | — | — | — | — | 22.54 | -2.60 | -2.34 | NAV Rtrn% +/-Russ MG |
| | — | — | — | — | — | — | — | — | 3 | 4 | NAV Return% Rank in Cat |
| | — | — | — | — | — | — | — | 0.00 | 0.00 | 0.13 | Income Return % |
| | — | — | — | — | — | — | — | — | 12.88 | 9.63 | Capital Return % |
| | — | — | — | — | — | — | — | 0.00 | 0.00 | 0.06 | Income $ |
| | — | — | — | — | — | — | — | 0.00 | 0.00 | 0.00 | Capital Gains $ |
| | — | — | — | — | — | — | — | — | 0.60 | 0.60 | Expense Ratio % |
| | — | — | — | — | — | — | — | — | -0.10 | -0.06 | Income Ratio % |
| | — | — | — | — | — | — | — | — | 79 | 112 | Turnover Rate % |
| | — | — | — | — | — | — | — | 22 | 58 | 187 | Net Assets $mil |

## Risk Profile

| | Standard Index S&P 500 | Best Fit Index |
|---|---|---|
| Alpha | — | — |
| Beta | — | — |
| R-Squared | — | — |
| Standard Deviation | — | |
| Mean | — | |
| Sharpe Ratio | — | |

## Morningstar Fair Value

| Price/Fair Value Ratio | Fair Value Estimate ($) | Hit Rate % |
|---|---|---|
| 1.2 Overvalued | 32.35 | 64 Poor |

## Portfolio Analysis 11-30-05

| Share change since 09-05 Total Stocks:100 | Sector | PE | Tot Ret% | % Assets |
|---|---|---|---|---|
| ⊕ Compuware | Software | 28.9 | 39.94 | 3.13 |
| ⊕ Autodesk | Software | 34.1 | 13.18 | 3.08 |
| ✵ SanDisk | Hardware | 36.1 | 151.58 | 3.07 |
| ✵ Cadence Design Systems | Software | 60.4 | 22.52 | 3.03 |
| ⊕ Cisco Systems | Hardware | 19.9 | -11.39 | 3.01 |
| ⊕ Microsoft | Software | 22.2 | -0.95 | 3.01 |
| ⊕ Intel | Hardware | 18.6 | 8.12 | 3.00 |
| ⊕ Fiserv | Business | 18.2 | 7.66 | 2.98 |
| ✵ Apple Computer | Hardware | 46.1 | 123.26 | 2.95 |
| ✵ Macromedia | Software | — | — | 2.92 |
| ✵ Broadcom | Hardware | 58.9 | 46.07 | 2.92 |
| ✵ Adtran | Hardware | 27.5 | 57.52 | 2.86 |
| ⊕ Staples | Consumer | 21.4 | 1.87 | 2.60 |
| ✵ Apollo Group A | Consumer | 25.3 | -25.09 | 2.59 |
| ⊕ O'Reilly Automotive | Consumer | 24.7 | 42.11 | 2.58 |
| ⊕ Express Scripts | Health | 34.0 | 119.26 | 2.51 |
| ✵ American Eagle Outfitter | Consumer | 12.7 | -1.30 | 2.47 |
| ✵ Dade Behring Holdings | Health | 32.7 | 46.27 | 2.46 |
| ✵ Cerner | Software | 43.7 | 70.98 | 2.38 |
| ⊕ Idexx Laboratories | Health | 32.9 | 31.86 | 2.34 |

### Current Investment Style

Value Blnd Growth — Large Mid Small

| Market Cap | % |
|---|---|
| Giant | 12.0 |
| Large | 18.5 |
| Mid | 40.8 |
| Small | 23.5 |
| Micro | 5.1 |

Avg $mil: 4,361

| Value Measures | | Rel Category |
|---|---|---|
| Price/Earnings | 21.24 | 0.95 |
| Price/Book | 3.70 | 1.02 |
| Price/Sales | 1.79 | 0.92 |
| Price/Cash Flow | 9.13 | 0.80 |
| Dividend Yield % | 0.35 | 0.78 |

| Growth Measures | % | Rel Category |
|---|---|---|
| Long-Term Erngs | 14.71 | 0.94 |
| Book Value | 5.50 | 0.55 |
| Sales | 7.56 | 0.67 |
| Cash Flow | 15.51 | 1.02 |
| Historical Erngs | 21.79 | 1.05 |

| Profitability | % | Rel Category |
|---|---|---|
| Return on Equity | 20.61 | 1.05 |
| Return on Assets | 12.03 | 1.16 |
| Net Margin | 12.40 | 1.05 |

| Sector Weightings | % of Stocks | Rel S&P 500 | 3 Year High | Low |
|---|---|---|---|---|
| ↻ Info | 48.19 | 2.39 | | |
| Software | 23.15 | 6.50 | 33 | 16 |
| Hardware | 21.51 | 2.14 | 34 | 9 |
| Media | 0.59 | 0.16 | 5 | 0 |
| Telecom | 2.94 | 0.98 | 4 | 2 |
| ⊂ Service | 44.20 | 0.95 | | |
| Health | 11.01 | 0.83 | 14 | 10 |
| Consumer | 12.85 | 1.58 | 16 | 11 |
| Business | 10.39 | 2.68 | 15 | 6 |
| Financial | 9.95 | 0.47 | 10 | 8 |
| Mfg | 7.61 | 0.23 | | |
| Goods | 3.77 | 0.44 | 6 | 1 |
| Ind Mtrls | 2.89 | 0.24 | 5 | 1 |
| Energy | 0.95 | 0.10 | 1 | 0 |
| Utilities | 0.00 | 0.00 | 0 | 0 |

### Composition

| | |
|---|---|
| ● Cash | 0.0 |
| ● Stocks | 100.0 |
| ● Bonds | 0.0 |
| ● Other | 0.0 |
| Foreign | 0.0 |
| (% of Stock) | |

## Morningstar's Take by Dan Culloton

This fund pushes indexing to the edge.

PowerShares Dynamic OTC tries to match the returns of an index: The Amex Dynamic OTC Intellidex. Similarities to conventional indexing end there. Instead of matching the return of a market segment (in this case the Nasdaq stock market) with a market-cap-weighted portfolio, the OTC Intellidex uses computers to build a portfolio of Nasdaq Composite stocks that tries to do better than the broader benchmark. Rather than holding onto the same holdings year after year, the OTC Intellidex reshuffles components quarterly.

This ETF's distinctions are both intriguing and intimidating. Those disenchanted with conventional indexing might like the bogy's construction methods. A quantitative model employs 25 measures of valuation, financial strength, momentum, and risk to build a 100-stock portfolio. Sector weightings stay close to the Nasdaq's, and the bogy follows strict rules for sizing positions to mute the influence of giant stocks, such as

Microsoft and Qualcomm. Indeed, the latter stock is so muted, it's missing.

The ETF has put up outstanding returns so far, but it's not perfect. In recent years the market has favored small-cap stocks, an area where this ETF has more than one quarter of its assets. The portfolio may suffer when large-cap stocks take their turn. A big stake in technology stocks is also sure to increase volatility.

Then there is the fund's turnover rate. It hasn't resulted in capital gains distributions yet because its advisor has exploited the advantages of the ETF structure (i.e., using in-kind redemptions to get rid of shares with large unrealized gains). Controlling tax and transaction costs with a 100% turnover rate will always be a challenge, though.

The future success of the OTC Intellidex isn't a sure thing. The market often catches up to quantitative models, and it's not clear this bogy will stay ahead of the curve. This ETF needs to build a longer track record.

| Address: | 227 E Prairie Ave |
|---|---|
| | Wheaton IL 60187 |
| | 800-843-2639 |
| Web Address: | www.powershares.com |
| Inception: | 05-01-03 * |
| Advisor: | Powershares Capital Management LLC |

| Management Fee: | 0.50% | | |
|---|---|---|---|
| Expense Projections: | 3Yr:$307 | 5Yr:$555 | 10Yr:$1266 |
| Income Distrib: | Quarterly | | |
| Exchange: | | | |

# PowerShares Dynam Mkt

| | Ticker | NAV | Market Price | 52 wk High/Low | Yield | Mstar Category |
|---|---|---|---|---|---|---|
| | PWC | $45.31 | $47.24 | $47.24 - $38.70 | 0.7% | Large Blend |

## Management

### Portfolio Manager(s)

The fund is managed by PowerShares Capital Management, which was founded in 2002. John W. Southard Jr. is the lead portfolio manager. He is a former senior analyst of Chicago Investment Analytics, a quantitative research firm bought by Charles Schwab in 2000. He also worked as an analyst and portfolio manager at a unit investment trust firm, First Trust Portfolios of Lisle, Ill. But he has a short track record as a retail mutual fund or ETF manager.

### Strategy

This ETF tracks the AMEX Dynamic Market Intellidex, which uses a 25 factor quantitative model to select 100 stocks from the 2000 largest U.S. companies listed on major U.S. exchanges. The factors employed include both technical (i.e. price and volume trends) and fundamental (P/E ratios and growth rates) data points. The bogy follows rules to make sure its sector weights stay close to those of its selection universe. It also caps position sizes and employs a stratified weighting scheme to keep large stocks from dominating the portfolio. The Intellidex reconstitutes quarterly.

**Growth of $10,000**

— Investment Value of ETF
— Investment Value of Index S&P 500

| | 1996 | 1997 | 1998 | 1999 | 2000 | 2001 | 2002 | 2003 | 2004 | 2005 | History |
|---|---|---|---|---|---|---|---|---|---|---|---|
| | — | — | — | — | — | — | — | 34.10 | 40.34 | 45.31 | NAV $ |
| | — | — | — | — | — | — | — | 34.02 | 40.48 | 45.32 | Market Price $ |
| | — | — | — | — | — | — | — | 22.40* | 19.08 | 13.12 | NAV Return% |
| | — | — | — | — | — | — | — | 22.44* | 19.77 | 12.76 | Market Price Return% |
| | — | — | — | — | — | — | — | -0.01 | 0.22 | 0.12 | Avg Premium/Discount% |
| | — | — | — | — | — | — | — | 22.40 | 8.21 | 8.21 | NAV Rtrn% +/-S&P 500 |
| | — | — | — | — | — | — | — | 22.40 | 7.68 | 6.85 | NAV Rtrn% +/-Russ 1000 |
| | — | — | — | — | — | — | — | — | 17 | 23 | NAV Return% Rank in Cat |
| | — | — | — | — | — | — | — | 0.00 | 0.72 | 0.78 | Income Return % |
| | — | — | — | — | — | — | — | — | 18.36 | 12.34 | Capital Return % |
| | — | — | — | — | — | — | — | 0.25 | 0.24 | 0.31 | Income $ |
| | — | — | — | — | — | — | — | 0.00 | 0.00 | 0.00 | Capital Gains $ |
| | — | — | — | — | — | — | — | — | 0.60 | 0.60 | Expense Ratio % |
| | — | — | — | — | — | — | — | — | 0.46 | 0.68 | Income Ratio % |
| | — | — | — | — | — | — | — | — | 58 | 94 | Turnover Rate % |
| | — | — | — | — | — | — | — | 36 | 230 | 691 | Net Assets $mil |

## Performance

**Historic Quarterly NAV Returns**

| | 1st Qtr | 2nd Qtr | 3rd Qtr | 4th Qtr | Total |
|---|---|---|---|---|---|
| 2001 | — | — | — | — | — |
| 2002 | — | — | — | — | — |
| 2003 | — | — | 3.73 | 11.56 | — * |
| 2004 | 6.46 | 2.13 | -1.08 | 10.70 | 19.08 |
| 2005 | 0.47 | 4.86 | 6.34 | 0.98 | 13.12 |

| Trailing | NAV Return% | Market Return% | NAV Rtrn% +/-S&P 500 | %Rank Cat.(NAV) |
|---|---|---|---|---|
| 3 Mo | 0.98 | 0.91 | -1.10 | 27 |
| 6 Mo | 7.38 | 7.36 | 1.62 | 27 |
| 1 Yr | 13.12 | 12.76 | 8.21 | 23 |
| 3 Yr Avg | — | — | — | 0 |
| 5 Yr Avg | — | — | — | 0 |
| 10 Yr Avg | — | — | — | 0 |

| Tax Analysis | Tax-Adj Return% | Tax-Cost Ratio |
|---|---|---|
| 3 Yr (estimated) | — | — |
| 5 Yr (estimated) | — | — |
| 10 Yr (estimated) | — | — |

## Risk Profile

| | Standard Index S&P 500 | Best Fit Index |
|---|---|---|
| Alpha | — | — |
| Beta | — | — |
| R-Squared | — | — |
| Standard Deviation | — | |
| Mean | — | |
| Sharpe Ratio | — | |

## Morningstar Fair Value

| Price/Fair Value Ratio | Fair Value Estimate ($) | Hit Rate % |
|---|---|---|
| 1.1 Overvalued | 45.09 | 87 Good |

## Portfolio Analysis 11-30-05

Share change since 09-05 Total Stocks:100

| | Sector | PE | Tot Ret% | % Assets |
|---|---|---|---|---|
| ☼ Devon Energy | Energy | 11.4 | 61.57 | 3.19 |
| ☼ Procter & Gamble | Goods | 21.2 | 7.18 | 3.18 |
| ⊕ Coca-Cola | Goods | 18.6 | -0.66 | 3.18 |
| ☼ Sunoco | Energy | 12.6 | 94.37 | 3.12 |
| ☼ Precision Castparts | Ind Mtrls | 26.0 | 58.08 | 2.52 |
| ☼ Equifax | Business | 21.0 | 35.90 | 2.45 |
| ⊕ Lockheed Martin | Ind Mtrls | 17.5 | 16.50 | 2.44 |
| ☼ Moody's | Business | 35.4 | 41.96 | 2.42 |
| ☼ Principal Financial Grou | Financial | 16.5 | 17.36 | 2.40 |
| ⊕ Prudential Financial | Financial | 11.7 | 34.54 | 2.40 |
| ☼ PG & E | Utilities | 16.3 | 15.32 | 2.39 |
| ⊖ Express Scripts | Health | 34.0 | 119.26 | 2.39 |
| ☼ Lincoln National | Financial | 11.7 | 17.15 | 2.38 |
| ☼ UnionBanCal | Financial | 13.3 | 9.20 | 2.38 |
| ⊕ Loews | Financial | 13.1 | 35.92 | 2.36 |
| ☼ AmerisourceBergen | Health | 30.3 | 41.35 | 2.31 |
| ☼ McGraw-Hill Companies | Media | 23.5 | 14.38 | 2.30 |
| ☼ Genuine Parts | Consumer | 18.2 | 2.57 | 2.29 |
| ⊕ Yum Brands | Consumer | 17.8 | 0.23 | 2.29 |
| ☼ NCR | Hardware | 12.8 | -1.95 | 2.27 |

### Current Investment Style

Value Blnd Growth — Large Mid Small

| Market Cap | % |
|---|---|
| Giant | 12.5 |
| Large | 40.4 |
| Mid | 35.9 |
| Small | 11.2 |
| Micro | 0.0 |

Avg $mil: 9,721

| Value Measures | | Rel Category |
|---|---|---|
| Price/Earnings | 15.72 | 0.93 |
| Price/Book | 2.77 | 1.03 |
| Price/Sales | 0.98 | 0.77 |
| Price/Cash Flow | 7.66 | 1.06 |
| Dividend Yield % | 1.01 | 0.57 |

| Growth Measures | % | Rel Category |
|---|---|---|
| Long-Term Erngs | 10.41 | 0.94 |
| Book Value | 7.68 | 0.82 |
| Sales | 8.62 | 1.07 |
| Cash Flow | 15.13 | 1.47 |
| Historical Erngs | 26.17 | 1.85 |

| Profitability | % | Rel Category |
|---|---|---|
| Return on Equity | 25.67 | 1.26 |
| Return on Assets | 11.82 | 1.27 |
| Net Margin | 11.89 | 1.09 |

| Sector Weightings | % of Stocks | Rel S&P 500 | 3 Year High | Low |
|---|---|---|---|---|
| ☊ Info | 17.85 | 0.88 | | |
| 🖥 Software | 2.51 | 0.71 | 7 | 2 |
| 💻 Hardware | 9.12 | 0.91 | 12 | 1 |
| 📺 Media | 2.72 | 0.76 | 3 | 0 |
| 📱 Telecom | 3.50 | 1.16 | 4 | 3 |
| ⊂ Service | 52.11 | 1.12 | | |
| ❤ Health | 11.99 | 0.90 | 14 | 8 |
| 🛒 Consumer | 9.95 | 1.22 | 16 | 6 |
| 💼 Business | 12.09 | 3.12 | 14 | 4 |
| 💲 Financial | 18.08 | 0.86 | 24 | 18 |
| 🏭 Mfg | 30.04 | 0.90 | | |
| 🚗 Goods | 8.60 | 1.00 | 13 | 9 |
| ⚙ Ind Mtrls | 8.94 | 0.74 | 16 | 6 |
| 🔋 Energy | 9.08 | 0.97 | 10 | 6 |
| 💡 Utilities | 3.42 | 1.02 | 3 | 1 |

### Composition

| | | |
|---|---|---|
| ● Cash | 0.1 | |
| ● Stocks | 99.9 | |
| ● Bonds | 0.0 | |
| Other | 0.0 | |
| Foreign | 0.0 | |
| | (% of Stock) | |

## Morningstar's Take  by Dan Culloton

This is not your father's index fund.

PowerShares Dynamic Market Portfolio tries to match the returns of an index, but it's a bogy that blurs the line between active and passive investing. Instead of matching the equity market's return with an array of stocks weighted by market capitalization, the Amex Dynamic Market Intellidex uses computers in an attempt to build a market-beating portfolio. Rather than keeping the same holdings year after year, the Intellidex remakes itself quarterly.

This ETF's distinctions are both intriguing and intimidating. Those disenchanted with conventional indexing might like the bogy's construction methods. A quantitative model employs 25 measures of valuation, financial strength, momentum, and risk to select 100 stocks from the largest 2,000 listed on major exchanges. Sector weightings stay close to the market's, and the bogy follows strict rules for sizing positions to keep giant stocks, such as Microsoft, ExxonMobil, and

Citigroup, from dominating. Sure enough, those stocks are notably absent.

Despite putting up outstanding returns since its inception, however, the fund is still spooky. A strong market for small-value stocks, which play a bigger role here than in most other core stock funds, has helped the ETF in recent years, and it could be hard for the fund to maintain its torrid pace when large-cap stocks take their turn. The ETF's high turnover also is worrisome. Controlling tax and transaction costs will be a challenge, even though the ETF has done a good job avoiding capital gains so far.

An objectively built, broadly diversified, low-priced fund like this one probably won't bomb over the long term. That doesn't make this ETF a sure winner, though. It's not clear how well it will do in less favorable market environments or if trading-induced costs will sap returns over the long run. In short, this ETF is worth watching, but needs more seasoning.

| Address: | 227 E Prairie Ave |
|---|---|
| | Wheaton IL 60187 |
| | 800-843-2639 |
| Web Address: | www.powershares.com |
| Inception: | 05-01-03 * |
| Advisor: | Powershares Capital Management LLC |

| Management Fee: | 0.50% | | |
|---|---|---|---|
| Expense Projections: | 3Yr:$217 | 5Yr:$383 | 10Yr:$864 |
| Income Distrib: | Quarterly | | |
| Exchange: | AMEX | | |

**Morningstar® ETFs 100**

# PowerShares Halter USX

| | Ticker | NAV | Market Price | 52 wk High/Low | Yield | Mstar Category |
|---|---|---|---|---|---|---|
| | PGJ | $13.85 | $15.06 | $15.13 - $12.68 | 1.2% | Pacific/Asia ex-Japan Stk |

## Management

**Portfolio Manager(s)**

The fund is managed by PowerShares Capital Management LLC, which provides about 20 separate exchange-traded funds.

**Strategy**

This fund tracks the Halter USX China index. The bogy may include any U.S.-listed stocks of companies that derive a majority of their revenues from China. It considers stocks of all sizes. The index is rebalanced quarterly.

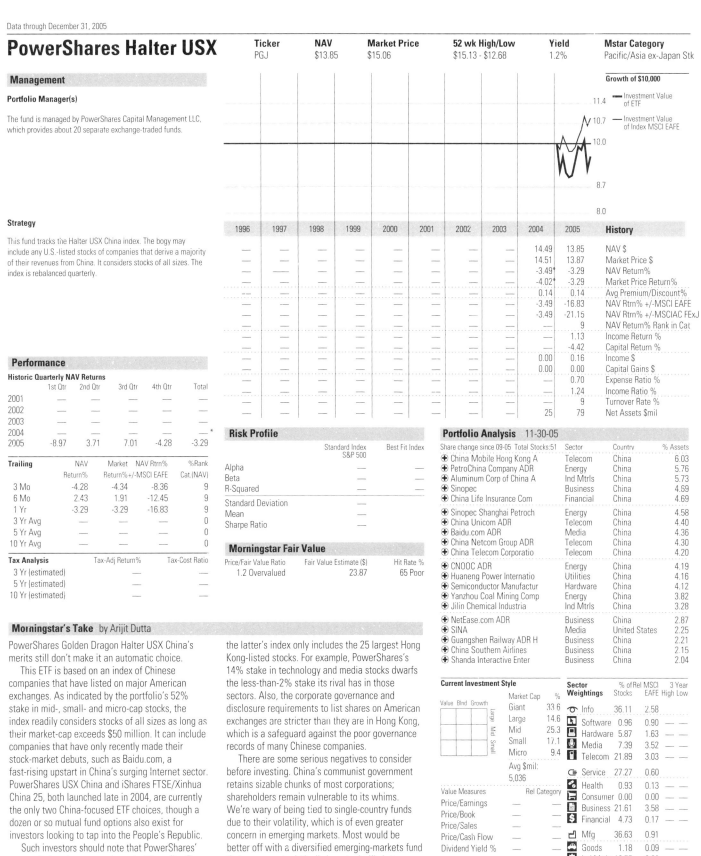

| | | | | | | | | | Growth of $10,000 |
|---|---|---|---|---|---|---|---|---|---|
| | | | | | | | | | ▬ Investment Value of ETF |
| | | | | | | | | | ▬ Investment Value of Index MSCI EAFE |

| 1996 | 1997 | 1998 | 1999 | 2000 | 2001 | 2002 | 2003 | 2004 | 2005 | History |
|---|---|---|---|---|---|---|---|---|---|---|
| — | — | — | — | — | — | — | — | 14.49 | 13.85 | NAV $ |
| — | — | — | — | — | — | — | — | 14.51 | 13.87 | Market Price $ |
| — | — | — | — | — | — | — | — | -3.49* | -3.29 | NAV Return% |
| — | — | — | — | — | — | — | — | -4.02* | -3.29 | Market Price Return% |
| — | — | — | — | — | — | — | — | 0.14 | 0.14 | Avg Premium/Discount% |
| — | — | — | — | — | — | — | — | -3.49 | -16.83 | NAV Rtrn% +/-MSCI EAFE |
| — | — | — | — | — | — | — | — | -3.49 | -21.15 | NAV Rtrn% +/-MSCIAC FExJ |
| — | — | — | — | — | — | — | — | — | 9 | NAV Return% Rank in Cat |
| — | — | — | — | — | — | — | — | — | 1.13 | Income Return % |
| — | — | — | — | — | — | — | — | — | -4.42 | Capital Return % |
| — | — | — | — | — | — | — | — | 0.00 | 0.16 | Income $ |
| — | — | — | — | — | — | — | — | 0.00 | 0.00 | Capital Gains $ |
| — | — | — | — | — | — | — | — | — | 0.70 | Expense Ratio % |
| — | — | — | — | — | — | — | — | — | 1.24 | Income Ratio % |
| — | — | — | — | — | — | — | — | — | 9 | Turnover Rate % |
| — | — | — | — | — | — | — | — | 25 | 79 | Net Assets $mil |

## Performance

**Historic Quarterly NAV Returns**

| | 1st Qtr | 2nd Qtr | 3rd Qtr | 4th Qtr | Total |
|---|---|---|---|---|---|
| 2001 | — | — | — | — | — |
| 2002 | — | — | — | — | — |
| 2003 | — | — | — | — | — |
| 2004 | — | — | — | — | —* |
| 2005 | -8.97 | 3.71 | 7.01 | -4.28 | -3.29 |

| Trailing | NAV Return% | Market Return%+/-MSCI EAFE | NAV Rtrn% | %Rank Cat.(NAV) |
|---|---|---|---|---|
| 3 Mo | -4.28 | -4.34 | -8.36 | 9 |
| 6 Mo | 2.43 | 1.91 | -12.45 | 9 |
| 1 Yr | -3.29 | -3.29 | -16.83 | 9 |
| 3 Yr Avg | — | — | — | 0 |
| 5 Yr Avg | — | — | — | 0 |
| 10 Yr Avg | — | — | — | 0 |

| Tax Analysis | Tax-Adj Return% | Tax-Cost Ratio |
|---|---|---|
| 3 Yr (estimated) | — | — |
| 5 Yr (estimated) | — | — |
| 10 Yr (estimated) | — | — |

## Risk Profile

| | Standard Index S&P 500 | Best Fit Index |
|---|---|---|
| Alpha | — | — |
| Beta | — | — |
| R-Squared | — | — |
| Standard Deviation | — | |
| Mean | — | |
| Sharpe Ratio | — | |

## Morningstar Fair Value

| Price/Fair Value Ratio | Fair Value Estimate ($) | Hit Rate % |
|---|---|---|
| 1.2 Overvalued | 23.87 | 65 Poor |

## Portfolio Analysis 11-30-05

| Share change since 09-05 Total Stocks:51 | Sector | Country | % Assets |
|---|---|---|---|
| ⊕ China Mobile Hong Kong A | Telecom | China | 6.03 |
| ⊕ PetroChina Company ADR | Energy | China | 5.76 |
| ⊕ Aluminum Corp of China A | Ind Mtrls | China | 5.73 |
| ⊕ Sinopec | Business | China | 4.69 |
| ⊕ China Life Insurance Com | Financial | China | 4.69 |
| ⊕ Sinopec Shanghai Petroch | Energy | China | 4.58 |
| ⊕ China Unicom ADR | Telecom | China | 4.40 |
| ⊕ Baidu.com ADR | Media | China | 4.36 |
| ⊕ China Netcom Group ADR | Telecom | China | 4.30 |
| ⊕ China Telecom Corporatio | Telecom | China | 4.20 |
| ⊕ CNOOC ADR | Energy | China | 4.19 |
| ⊕ Huaneng Power Internatio | Utilities | China | 4.16 |
| ⊕ Semiconductor Manufactur | Hardware | China | 4.12 |
| ⊕ Yanzhou Coal Mining Comp | Energy | China | 3.82 |
| ⊕ Jilin Chemical Industria | Ind Mtrls | China | 3.28 |
| ⊕ NetEase.com ADR | Business | China | 2.87 |
| ⊕ SINA | Media | United States | 2.25 |
| ⊕ Guangshen Railway ADR H | Business | China | 2.21 |
| ⊕ China Southern Airlines | Business | China | 2.15 |
| ⊕ Shanda Interactive Enter | Business | China | 2.04 |

**Current Investment Style**

Value Blnd Growth — Large/Mid/Small

| Market Cap | % |
|---|---|
| Giant | 33.6 |
| Large | 14.6 |
| Mid | 25.3 |
| Small | 17.1 |
| Micro | 9.4 |

Avg $mil: 5,036

| Value Measures | Rel Category |
|---|---|
| Price/Earnings | — |
| Price/Book | — |
| Price/Sales | — |
| Price/Cash Flow | — |
| Dividend Yield % | — |

| Growth Measures | % Rel Category |
|---|---|
| Long-Term Erngs | — |
| Book Value | — |
| Sales | — |
| Cash Flow | — |
| Historical Erngs | — |

| Sector Weightings | % of Stocks | Rel MSCI EAFE | 3 Year High Low | |
|---|---|---|---|---|
| ↻ Info | 36.11 | 2.58 | | |
| ⬙ Software | 0.96 | 0.90 | — | — |
| ⬙ Hardware | 5.87 | 1.63 | — | — |
| ⬙ Media | 7.39 | 3.52 | — | — |
| ⬙ Telecom | 21.89 | 3.03 | — | — |
| ⬙ Service | 27.27 | 0.60 | | |
| ⬙ Health | 0.93 | 0.13 | — | — |
| ⬙ Consumer | 0.00 | 0.00 | — | — |
| ⬙ Business | 21.61 | 3.58 | — | — |
| ⬙ Financial | 4.73 | 0.17 | — | — |
| ⬙ Mfg | 36.63 | 0.91 | | |
| ⬙ Goods | 1.18 | 0.09 | — | — |
| ⬙ Ind Mtrls | 12.75 | 0.90 | — | — |
| ⬙ Energy | 18.50 | 2.34 | — | — |
| ⬙ Utilities | 4.20 | 0.91 | — | — |

**Regional Exposure** % Stock

| | | | |
|---|---|---|---|
| UK/W. Europe | 0 | N. America | 5 |
| Japan | 0 | Latn America | 0 |
| Asia X Japan | 95 | Other | 0 |

**Composition**

| Cash | 0.2 | Bonds | 0.0 |
|---|---|---|---|
| Stocks | 99.8 | Other | 0.0 |
| Foreign (% of Stock) | | | 95.0 |

**Country Exposure** % Stock

| | | | |
|---|---|---|---|
| China | 92 | South Korea | 1 |
| United States | 5 | | |
| Hong Kong | 3 | | |

## Morningstar's Take by Arijit Dutta

PowerShares Golden Dragon Halter USX China's merits still don't make it an automatic choice.

This ETF is based on an index of Chinese companies that have listed on major American exchanges. As indicated by the portfolio's 52% stake in mid-, small- and micro-cap stocks, the index readily considers stocks of all sizes as long as their market-cap exceeds $50 million. It can include companies that have only recently made their stock-market debuts, such as Baidu.com, a fast-rising upstart in China's surging Internet sector. PowerShares USX China and iShares FTSE/Xinhua China 25, both launched late in 2004, are currently the only two China-focused ETF choices, though a dozen or so mutual fund options also exist for investors looking to tap into the People's Republic.

Such investors should note that PowerShares' approach does have some important benefits. Due to its all-cap mandate, the fund is able to provide more diversified access to more areas of the Chinese market than does the iShares ETF because

the latter's index only includes the 25 largest Hong Kong-listed stocks. For example, PowerShares's 14% stake in technology and media stocks dwarfs the less-than-2% stake its rival has in those sectors. Also, the corporate governance and disclosure requirements to list shares on American exchanges are stricter than they are in Hong Kong, which is a safeguard against the poor governance records of many Chinese companies.

There are some serious negatives to consider before investing. China's communist government retains sizable chunks of most corporations; shareholders remain vulnerable to its whims. We're wary of being tied to single-country funds due to their volatility, which is of even greater concern in emerging markets. Most would be better off with a diversified emerging-markets fund that can opportunistically buy stocks likely to benefit from China's robust growth.

This is a low-cost option for those bullish on China's long-term prospects, but we'd tread lightly.

| Address: | 227 E Prairie Ave Wheaton IL 60187 800-843-2639 | Management Fee: | 0.50% |
|---|---|---|---|
| | | Expense Projections: | 3Yr:$240  5Yr: —  10Yr: — |
| Web Address: | www.powershares.com | Income Distrib: | Annually |
| Inception: | 12-09-04 * | Exchange: | AMEX |
| Advisor: | Powershares Capital Management LLC | | |

# PowerShares HY Div Achiev

| Ticker | NAV | Market Price | 52 wk High/Low | Yield | Mstar Category |
|---|---|---|---|---|---|
| PEY | $14.95 | $15.28 | $15.64 - $14.19 | 3.3% | Mid-Cap Value |

## Management

### Portfolio Manager(s)

The fund is managed by PowerShares Capital management, which was founded in 2002. It is the ETF industry upstart with just a handful of employees and one portfolio manager, but big plans. The firm manages 11 other ETFs and hopes to roll out at least a dozen more.

### Strategy

This ETF tracks the Mergent Dividend Achievers 50. The benchmark includes the 50 highest-yielding members of the Dividend Achievers, a list of stocks (compiled by equity data and research firm Mergent) that have increased their dividends in each of the last 10 years. The benchmark has been published and calculated since 2004, but Mergent has been assembling its Dividend Achievers list for more than 20 years. The index selects the 50 highest-yielding stocks from the Dividend Achiever universe of more than 300 stocks and weights them by the size of their yields. The index rebalances quarterly.

**Growth of $10,000**

— Investment Value of ETF
— Investment Value of Index S&P 500

| | 1996 | 1997 | 1998 | 1999 | 2000 | 2001 | 2002 | 2003 | 2004 | 2005 | History |
|---|---|---|---|---|---|---|---|---|---|---|---|
| | — | — | — | — | — | — | — | — | 15.27 | 14.95 | NAV $ |
| | — | — | — | — | — | — | — | — | 15.27 | 14.93 | Market Price $ |
| | — | — | — | — | — | — | — | — | 4.16* | 1.13 | NAV Return% |
| | — | — | — | — | — | — | — | — | 4.27* | 0.99 | Market Price Return% |
| | — | — | — | — | — | — | — | — | 0.00 | 0.05 | Avg Premium/Discount% |
| | — | — | — | — | — | — | — | — | 4.16 | -3.78 | NAV Rtrn% +/-S&P 500 |
| | — | — | — | — | — | — | — | — | 4.16 | -11.52 | NAV Rtrn% +/-Russ MV |
| | — | — | — | — | — | — | — | — | — | 5 | NAV Return% Rank in Cat |
| | — | — | — | — | — | — | — | — | — | 3.25 | Income Return % |
| | — | — | — | — | — | — | — | — | — | -2.12 | Capital Return % |
| | — | — | — | — | — | — | — | — | 0.00 | 0.49 | Income $ |
| | — | — | — | — | — | — | — | — | 0.00 | 0.00 | Capital Gains $ |
| | — | — | — | — | — | — | — | — | — | 0.60 | Expense Ratio % |
| | — | — | — | — | — | — | — | — | — | 3.57 | Income Ratio % |
| | — | — | — | — | — | — | — | — | — | 21 | Turnover Rate % |
| | — | — | — | — | — | — | — | — | 102 | 492 | Net Assets $mil |

## Performance

### Historic Quarterly NAV Returns

| | 1st Qtr | 2nd Qtr | 3rd Qtr | 4th Qtr | Total |
|---|---|---|---|---|---|
| 2001 | — | — | — | — | — |
| 2002 | — | — | — | — | — |
| 2003 | — | — | — | — | — |
| 2004 | — | — | — | — | —* |
| 2005 | -4.02 | 4.30 | 1.08 | -0.06 | 1.13 |

| Trailing | NAV Return% | Market Return% | NAV Rtrn% +/-S&P 500 | %Rank Cat.(NAV) |
|---|---|---|---|---|
| 3 Mo | -0.06 | -0.26 | -2.14 | 6 |
| 6 Mo | 1.02 | 0.95 | -4.74 | 6 |
| 1 Yr | 1.13 | 0.99 | -3.78 | 5 |
| 3 Yr Avg | — | — | — | 0 |
| 5 Yr Avg | — | — | — | 0 |
| 10 Yr Avg | — | — | — | 0 |

| Tax Analysis | Tax-Adj Return% | Tax-Cost Ratio |
|---|---|---|
| 3 Yr (estimated) | — | — |
| 5 Yr (estimated) | — | — |
| 10 Yr (estimated) | — | — |

## Risk Profile

| | Standard Index S&P 500 | Best Fit Index |
|---|---|---|
| Alpha | — | — |
| Beta | — | — |
| R-Squared | — | — |
| Standard Deviation | — | |
| Mean | — | |
| Sharpe Ratio | — | |

## Morningstar Fair Value

| Price/Fair Value Ratio | Fair Value Estimate ($) | Hit Rate % |
|---|---|---|
| 1.0 Fairly valued | 31.31 | 75 Fair |

## Portfolio Analysis 11-30-05

| Share change since 09-05 Total Stocks:50 | Sector | PE | Tot Ret% | % Assets |
|---|---|---|---|---|
| ⊕ Merck | Health | 15.2 | 4.04 | 2.95 |
| ⊕ F.N.B. | Financial | 14.4 | -10.39 | 2.78 |
| ⊖ AT&T | Telecom | 21.1 | 0.25 | 2.73 |
| ⊕ Progress Energy | Utilities | 13.8 | 2.47 | 2.70 |
| ⊕ Peoples Energy | Utilities | 17.1 | -15.86 | 2.69 |
| ⊕ Washington Mutual | Financial | 11.9 | 7.79 | 2.58 |
| ⊕ First Commonwealth Finan | Financial | 14.4 | -11.73 | 2.54 |
| ⊕ Bank of America | Financial | 11.1 | 2.39 | 2.44 |
| ⊕ Consolidated Edison | Utilities | 17.8 | 11.32 | 2.33 |
| ⊕ National City | Financial | 8.6 | -6.77 | 2.29 |
| ⊕ Universal | Goods | 11.2 | -5.82 | 2.23 |
| ⊕ Nicor | Utilities | 14.3 | 11.50 | 2.22 |
| ⊕ Regions Financial | Financial | 16.4 | 0.03 | 2.21 |
| ⊕ Atmos Energy | Utilities | 15.2 | 0.05 | 2.18 |
| ⊕ Pinnacle West Capital | Utilities | 17.4 | -2.58 | 2.13 |
| ⊕ Vectren | Utilities | 16.4 | 5.87 | 2.12 |
| ⊕ Wesbanco | Financial | 16.4 | -1.48 | 2.10 |
| ⊕ FirstMerit | Financial | 16.7 | -5.23 | 2.09 |
| ⊕ AmSouth Bancorporation | Financial | 13.0 | 5.18 | 2.07 |
| ⊕ Sara Lee | Goods | 23.3 | -18.56 | 2.05 |

### Current Investment Style

Value Blnd Growth — Large Mid Small

| Market Cap | % |
|---|---|
| Giant | 13.8 |
| Large | 23.1 |
| Mid | 35.5 |
| Small | 27.6 |
| Micro | 0.0 |

Avg $mil: 5,013

| Value Measures | | Rel Category |
|---|---|---|
| Price/Earnings | 14.79 | 1.02 |
| Price/Book | 1.82 | 0.99 |
| Price/Sales | 1.31 | 1.27 |
| Price/Cash Flow | 6.02 | 1.03 |
| Dividend Yield % | 4.10 | 1.52 |

| Growth Measures | % | Rel Category |
|---|---|---|
| Long-Term Erngs | 6.85 | 0.79 |
| Book Value | 7.59 | 0.99 |
| Sales | 6.51 | 1.03 |
| Cash Flow | 2.57 | 0.66 |
| Historical Erngs | 0.22 | 0.02 |

| Profitability | % | Rel Category |
|---|---|---|
| Return on Equity | 13.80 | 0.99 |
| Return on Assets | 9.31 | 1.09 |
| Net Margin | 16.43 | 1.30 |

| Sector Weightings | % of Stocks | Rel S&P 500 | 3 Year High Low |
|---|---|---|---|
| ⚡ Info | 2.74 | 0.14 | |
| 📷 Software | 0.00 | 0.00 | — — |
| 💻 Hardware | 0.00 | 0.00 | — — |
| 📺 Media | 0.00 | 0.00 | — — |
| ☎ Telecom | 2.74 | 0.91 | — — |
| ⊂ Service | 57.71 | 1.24 | |
| ⚕ Health | 2.95 | 0.22 | — — |
| 🏠 Consumer | 1.49 | 0.18 | — — |
| 📋 Business | 0.00 | 0.00 | — — |
| 💲 Financial | 53.27 | 2.53 | — — |
| ⬜ Mfg | 39.55 | 1.18 | |
| 🏭 Goods | 8.15 | 0.95 | — — |
| ⚙ Ind Mtrls | 0.00 | 0.00 | — — |
| 🛢 Energy | 0.00 | 0.00 | — — |
| 💡 Utilities | 31.40 | 9.35 | — — |

### Composition

| | | |
|---|---|---|
| ● Cash | | 0.1 |
| ● Stocks | | 99.9 |
| ● Bonds | | 0.0 |
| Other | | 0.0 |
| Foreign | | 0.0 |
| (% of Stock) | | |

## Morningstar's Take by Dan Culloton

PowerShares HighYield Dividend Achievers has got yield, as well as some risks.

This ETF is one of a spate of new funds trying to take advantage of investor interest in dividend-paying stocks. It tracks the Mergent Dividend Achievers 50 Index, which consist of the 50 highest yielding stocks among U.S. equities that have increased their dividends in each of the previous 10 years. The bogey is not that old but draws its constituents from the Dividend Achievers list, which has been compiled by equity data and research firm Mergent for more than two decades.

The ETF's benchmark takes the 50 highest-yielding stocks from the broader Dividend Achievers universe and weights them by their yields instead of market capitalization. That means high-yield stocks with histories of increasing their dividends, such as Altria Group, take up bigger positions than mega-cap companies, such as Citigroup. That also gives the portfolio a yield that ranks high among diversified domestic stock offerings. The extra income could serve as both a cushion in rough periods and a source of extra total return. The bogey's back-tested results--15.9% for the 10-year period ending in February--beat broad market indexes, such as the S&P 500 and Wilshire 5000, which each gained about 11% during that time.

Be on your guard, though. This fund has risks. It concentrates its money in 50 stocks and a couple of sectors. More than 80% of the ETF's assets are clustered in financial or utilities stocks. So its yield could come with more volatility than more diversified rivals among ETFs and traditional funds. The ETF's track record is too short to definitively judge, but it did trail the iShares Dow Jones Select Dividend Index and more established traditional yield-centric funds, such as Vanguard Equity-Income in 2005.

So, be sure to look beyond this fund's yield.

| | | | | |
|---|---|---|---|---|
| Address: | 227 E Prairie Ave Wheaton IL 60187 800-843-2639 | Management Fee: | 0.40% | |
| | | Expense Projections: | 3Yr:$208 | 5Yr: — 10Yr:— |
| Web Address: | www.powershares.com | Income Distrib: | Quarterly | |
| Inception: | 12-09-04* | Exchange: | AMEX | |
| Advisor: | Powershares Capital Management LLC | | | |

MORNINGSTAR® ETFs 100

# PowerShares Zacks MicroCp

| | Ticker | NAV | Market Price | 52 wk High/Low | Yield | Mstar Category |
|---|---|---|---|---|---|---|
| | PZI | $15.16 | $15.80 | $15.80 - $13.93 | 0.0% | Small Blend |

## Management

### Portfolio Manager(s)

The fund is managed by PowerShares Capital Management, which was founded in 2002. John W. Southard Jr. is the lead portfolio manager. He is a former senior analyst of Chicago Investment Analytics, a quantitative research firm bought by Charles Schwab in 2000. He also worked as an analyst and portfolio manager at a unit investment trust firm, First Trust Portfolios of Lisle, IL. But he has a short track record as a retail mutual fund or ETF manager.

### Strategy

This ETF tracks the Zacks Micro Cap Index, which is a quasi-actively managed benchmark. The benchmark includes the 300 to 500 stocks with market capitalizations between $58 million and $575 million. Zacks uses a computer model to select the index's constitutes based on several valuation and momentum factors. The index is equal weighted and rebalanced once per quarter, but Zacks will kick out benchmark members on weekly basis if the stocks stop meeting the model's screens. The index omits stocks that trade over the counter or on the pink sheets. The advisor uses representative sampling.

## Performance

### Historic Quarterly NAV Returns

| | 1st Qtr | 2nd Qtr | 3rd Qtr | 4th Qtr | Total |
|---|---|---|---|---|---|
| 2001 | — | — | — | — | — |
| 2002 | — | — | — | — | — |
| 2003 | — | — | — | — | — |
| 2004 | — | — | — | — | — |
| 2005 | — | — | — | 0.93 | —* |

| Trailing | NAV Return% | Market Return% | NAV Rtrn% +/-S&P 500 | %Rank Cat.(NAV) |
|---|---|---|---|---|
| 3 Mo | 0.93 | 0.86 | -1.15 | 7 |
| 6 Mo | — | — | — | 0 |
| 1 Yr | — | — | — | 0 |
| 3 Yr Avg | — | — | — | 0 |
| 5 Yr Avg | — | — | — | 0 |
| 10 Yr Avg | — | — | — | 0 |

| Tax Analysis | Tax-Adj Return% | Tax-Cost Ratio |
|---|---|---|
| 3 Yr (estimated) | — | — |
| 5 Yr (estimated) | — | — |
| 10 Yr (estimated) | — | — |

### Growth of $10,000

- Investment Value of ETF
- Investment Value of Index S&P 500

| | 1996 | 1997 | 1998 | 1999 | 2000 | 2001 | 2002 | 2003 | 2004 | 2005 | History |
|---|---|---|---|---|---|---|---|---|---|---|---|
| | — | — | — | — | — | — | — | — | — | 15.16 | NAV $ |
| | — | — | — | — | — | — | — | — | — | 15.15 | Market Price $ |
| | — | — | — | — | — | — | — | — | — | 2.57* | NAV Return% |
| | — | — | — | — | — | — | — | — | — | 2.36* | Market Price Return% |
| | — | — | — | — | — | — | — | — | — | -0.01 | Avg Premium/Discount% |
| | — | — | — | — | — | — | — | — | — | 2.57 | NAV Rtrn% +/-S&P 500 |
| | — | — | — | — | — | — | — | — | — | 2.57 | NAV Rtrn% +/-Russ 2000 |
| | — | — | — | — | — | — | — | — | — | — | NAV Return% Rank in Cat |
| | — | — | — | — | — | — | — | — | — | — | Income Return % |
| | — | — | — | — | — | — | — | — | — | — | Capital Return % |
| | — | — | — | — | — | — | — | — | — | 0.01 | Income $ |
| | — | — | — | — | — | — | — | — | — | 0.00 | Capital Gains $ |
| | — | — | — | — | — | — | — | — | — | — | Expense Ratio % |
| | — | — | — | — | — | — | — | — | — | — | Income Ratio % |
| | — | — | — | — | — | — | — | — | — | — | Turnover Rate % |
| | — | — | — | — | — | — | — | — | — | 103 | Net Assets $mil |

## Risk Profile

| | Standard Index S&P 500 | Best Fit Index |
|---|---|---|
| Alpha | — | — |
| Beta | — | — |
| R-Squared | — | — |
| Standard Deviation | — | |
| Mean | — | |
| Sharpe Ratio | — | |

## Morningstar Fair Value

| Price/Fair Value Ratio | Fair Value Estimate ($) | Hit Rate % |
|---|---|---|
| — | — | — |

## Portfolio Analysis 11-30-05

| Share change since 09-05 Total Stocks:392 | Sector | PE | Tot Ret% | % Assets |
|---|---|---|---|---|
| ✿ Merge Technologies | Health | — | 12.54 | 0.42 |
| ⊖ Cutera | Health | — | 110.88 | 0.38 |
| ✿ Quidel | Health | — | 111.81 | 0.37 |
| ⊖ Brightpoint | Telecom | 26.6 | 112.86 | 0.37 |
| ✿ Encore Wire | Ind Mtrls | 25.0 | 70.74 | 0.36 |
| ✿ SCPIE Holdings | Financial | — | 109.26 | 0.36 |
| ✿ CalAmp | Hardware | 22.8 | 17.34 | 0.36 |
| ✿ Marchex | Business | — | 7.10 | 0.35 |
| ✿ Supertex | Hardware | 60.6 | 103.92 | 0.35 |
| ✿ Andersons | Ind Mtrls | 17.2 | 70.63 | 0.35 |
| ⊕ PAR Technology | Business | 33.0 | 145.22 | 0.35 |
| ⊖ Hurco Companies | Ind Mtrls | 16.8 | 86.79 | 0.35 |
| ✿ Nu Horizons Electronics | Ind Mtrls | 91.8 | 26.57 | 0.34 |
| ⊖ Natus Medical | Health | 55.7 | 101.75 | 0.34 |
| ⊖ Redback Networks | Hardware | — | 162.31 | 0.34 |
| ⊕ United Retail Group | Consumer | 22.7 | 203.70 | 0.34 |
| ⊖ LoJack | Business | 27.1 | 99.59 | 0.33 |
| ✿ Air Methods | Health | 24.4 | 101.16 | 0.33 |
| ✿ Lamson & Sessions | Ind Mtrls | 26.6 | 174.95 | 0.33 |
| ✿ Neoware Systems | Hardware | 48.5 | 150.27 | 0.33 |

### Current Investment Style

Value Blend Growth — Large Mid Small

| Market Cap | % |
|---|---|
| Giant | 0.0 |
| Large | 0.0 |
| Mid | 0.0 |
| Small | 26.3 |
| Micro | 73.7 |

Avg $mil: 290

| Value Measures | | Rel Category |
|---|---|---|
| Price/Earnings | 16.98 | 0.99 |
| Price/Book | 1.52 | 0.79 |
| Price/Sales | 0.43 | 0.47 |
| Price/Cash Flow | 4.37 | 0.66 |
| Dividend Yield % | 0.58 | 0.64 |

| Growth Measures | % | Rel Category |
|---|---|---|
| Long-Term Erngs | 15.14 | 1.09 |
| Book Value | -6.09 | NMF |
| Sales | -5.21 | NMF |
| Cash Flow | -16.30 | NMF |
| Historical Erngs | 18.63 | 1.51 |

| Profitability | % | Rel Category |
|---|---|---|
| Return on Equity | 5.93 | 0.61 |
| Return on Assets | 3.76 | 0.73 |
| Net Margin | 5.65 | 0.69 |

### Sector Weightings

| | % of Stocks | Rel S&P 500 | 3 Year High Low |
|---|---|---|---|
| ↻ Info | 17.87 | 0.89 | |
| 🖥 Software | 5.12 | 1.44 | — — |
| 💾 Hardware | 10.57 | 1.05 | — — |
| 🎤 Media | 0.25 | 0.07 | — — |
| 📶 Telecom | 1.93 | 0.64 | — — |
| ⊕ Service | 55.86 | 1.20 | |
| 🏥 Health | 9.51 | 0.72 | — — |
| 🛒 Consumer | 11.72 | 1.44 | — — |
| 📋 Business | 15.88 | 4.10 | — — |
| 💲 Financial | 18.75 | 0.89 | — — |
| 🔧 Mfg | 26.26 | 0.79 | |
| 🏭 Goods | 5.16 | 0.60 | — — |
| ⚙ Ind Mtrls | 15.95 | 1.31 | — — |
| 🔋 Energy | 4.47 | 0.48 | — — |
| 💡 Utilities | 0.68 | 0.20 | — — |

### Composition

| | | |
|---|---|---|
| ● Cash | 0.0 |
| ● Stocks | 100.0 |
| ● Bonds | 0.0 |
| ● Other | 0.0 |
| Foreign | 2.4 |
| (% of Stock) | |

## Morningstar's Take by Dan Culloton

This new exchange-traded fund might be fun to watch, but it's not clear it's worth using.

Powershares Zacks Micro Cap Portfolio offers cheap exposure to the smallest of small caps. The ETF's 0.6% expense ratio, while high for an ETF, is less than half that of the typical micro-cap fund (those with average market caps under $500 million).

The ETF also is innovative. It tracks a more actively managed bogy: the Zacks Micro Cap Index, which uses a quantitative model to pick stocks.

The back-tested results of the index provided by Zacks look strong, but the ETF and its benchmark have qualities that give us pause. Because it's equal weighted and employs valuation screens, the portfolio could lean toward the value side of the style box. Such a predilection would have worked well over the past five years when small-cap value stocks rallied but could hamper the portfolio when the market favors larger and more growth-oriented fare. The fund's active construction methods (it rebalances quarterly and drops stocks that stop meeting the index's screens weekly) also entails a lot of turnover, which could increase tax and transaction costs.

There are other issues. The methodology behind the ETF's bogy is a mystery. Indeed, even the ETF's advisor knows little more than this: Zacks' model uses value and momentum factors to select securities. It's not usual for quantitative funds to closely guard their computer models. One oft touted advantage of ETFs, however, has been being able to know all a fund's holdings and why they're there. This fund sacrifices some of that transparency by using an index with opaque construction rules. Furthermore, the shares of ETFs that track less liquid stocks could trade at premiums or discounts to the net asset values of their underlying holdings.

This fund pushes the envelope in interesting directions, but it's best to let it build a track record.

| | |
|---|---|
| Address: | 227 E Prairie Ave Wheaton IL 60187 800-843-2639 |
| Web Address: | www.powershares.com |
| Inception: | 08-18-05 * |
| Advisor: | Powershares Capital Management LLC |

| | |
|---|---|
| Management Fee: | 0.50% |
| Expense Projections: | 3Yr:$240  5Yr: —  10Yr: — |
| Income Distrib: | Quarterly |
| Exchange: | AMEX |

MORNINGSTAR® ETFs 100

# Rydex S&P Equal Weight

| | Ticker | NAV | Market Price | 52 wk High/Low | Yield | Mstar Category |
|---|---|---|---|---|---|---|
| | RSP | $166.21 | $172.59 | $172.59 - $145.60 | 1.1% | Large Blend |

## Management

### Portfolio Manager(s)

Rydex Investments offers a suite of mutual funds and exchange traded funds that employ unique investment strategies. They emphasize efficient trading in many of these portfolios, but often have high expenses attached to the funds they manage.

### Strategy

This fund allocates an equal amount of assets to each of the individual components of the S&P 500 Index rather than using a market weighting. That means that companies such as General Electric get a weighting of just 0.2% of assets as opposed to the much larger position the stock gets in more common index offerings. Management rebalances the portfolio on a quarterly basis.

Growth of $10,000
— Investment Value of ETF
— Investment Value of Index S&P 500

| 1996 | 1997 | 1998 | 1999 | 2000 | 2001 | 2002 | 2003 | 2004 | 2005 | History |
|---|---|---|---|---|---|---|---|---|---|---|
| — | — | — | — | — | — | — | 135.35 | 156.07 | 166.21 | NAV $ |
| — | — | — | — | — | — | — | 135.45 | 156.16 | 165.93 | Market Price $ |
| — | — | — | — | — | — | — | 21.64* | 16.50 | 7.65 | NAV Return% |
| — | — | — | — | — | — | — | — | 16.48 | 7.41 | Market Price Return% |
| — | — | — | — | — | — | — | 0.03 | 0.02 | -0.03 | Avg Premium/Discount% |
| — | — | — | — | — | — | — | 21.64 | 5.63 | 2.74 | NAV Rtrn% +/-S&P 500 |
| — | — | — | — | — | — | — | 21.64 | 5.10 | 1.38 | NAV Rtrn% +/-Russ 1000 |
| — | — | — | — | — | — | — | — | 17 | 23 | NAV Return% Rank in Cat |
| — | — | — | — | — | — | — | 0.00 | 1.09 | 1.12 | Income Return % |
| — | — | — | — | — | — | — | — | 15.41 | 6.53 | Capital Return % |
| — | — | — | — | — | — | — | 1.00 | 1.47 | 1.74 | Income $ |
| — | — | — | — | — | — | — | 0.00 | 0.00 | 0.00 | Capital Gains $ |
| — | — | — | — | — | — | — | 0.40 | 0.40 | — | Expense Ratio % |
| — | — | — | — | — | — | — | 1.13 | 1.09 | — | Income Ratio % |
| — | — | — | — | — | — | — | 42 | 55 | — | Turnover Rate % |
| — | — | — | — | — | — | — | 223 | 765 | 1,313 | Net Assets $mil |

## Performance

### Historic Quarterly NAV Returns

| | 1st Qtr | 2nd Qtr | 3rd Qtr | 4th Qtr | Total |
|---|---|---|---|---|---|
| 2001 | — | — | — | — | — |
| 2002 | — | — | — | — | — |
| 2003 | — | — | 5.14 | 14.91 | —* |
| 2004 | 3.71 | 2.26 | -2.09 | 12.19 | 16.50 |
| 2005 | -2.27 | 2.68 | 4.73 | 2.43 | 7.65 |

| Trailing | NAV Return% | Market Return% | NAV Rtrn% +/-S&P 500 | %Rank Cat.(NAV) |
|---|---|---|---|---|
| 3 Mo | 2.43 | 2.29 | 0.35 | 27 |
| 6 Mo | 7.28 | 7.11 | 1.52 | 27 |
| 1 Yr | 7.65 | 7.41 | 2.74 | 23 |
| 3 Yr Avg | — | — | — | 0 |
| 5 Yr Avg | — | — | — | 0 |
| 10 Yr Avg | — | — | — | 0 |

| Tax Analysis | Tax-Adj Return% | Tax-Cost Ratio |
|---|---|---|
| 3 Yr (estimated) | — | — |
| 5 Yr (estimated) | — | — |
| 10 Yr (estimated) | — | — |

## Risk Profile

| | Standard Index S&P 500 | Best Fit Index |
|---|---|---|
| Alpha | — | — |
| Beta | — | — |
| R-Squared | — | — |
| Standard Deviation | — | |
| Mean | — | |
| Sharpe Ratio | — | |

## Morningstar Fair Value

| Price/Fair Value Ratio | Fair Value Estimate ($) | Hit Rate % |
|---|---|---|
| 1.1 Overvalued | 28.17 | 93 Good |

## Portfolio Analysis 06-30-05

| Share change since 03-04  Total Stocks:500 | Sector | PE | Tot Ret% | % Assets |
|---|---|---|---|---|
| ⊕ MBNA | Financial | — | — | 0.25 |
| ⊕ Bausch & Lomb | Health | 21.4 | 6.06 | 0.23 |
| ⊕ Calpine | Utilities | — | -94.72 | 0.22 |
| ⊕ Kroger | Consumer | — | 7.64 | 0.22 |
| ⊕ St. Jude Medical | Health | 36.9 | 19.72 | 0.22 |
| ⊕ King Pharmaceuticals | Health | 18.2 | 36.45 | 0.22 |
| ⊕ Franklin Resources | Financial | 23.2 | 39.74 | 0.22 |
| ⊕ LSI Logic | Hardware | — | 45.99 | 0.22 |
| ⊕ Oracle | Software | 22.2 | -11.01 | 0.22 |
| ⊕ Capital One Financial | Financial | 13.1 | 2.74 | 0.22 |
| ⊕ E*Trade Financial | Financial | 19.3 | 39.53 | 0.22 |
| ⊕ Paychex | Business | 36.6 | 13.71 | 0.22 |
| ⊕ Jabil Circuit | Hardware | 33.1 | 45.00 | 0.22 |
| ⊕ Convergys | Business | 19.1 | 5.74 | 0.22 |
| ⊕ Public Service Enterpris | Utilities | 22.2 | 30.22 | 0.22 |
| ⊕ Exelon | Utilities | 17.0 | 24.58 | 0.21 |
| ⊕ Edison International | Utilities | 13.5 | 39.63 | 0.21 |
| ⊕ Molson Coors Brewing Com | Goods | 23.2 | -9.68 | 0.21 |
| ⊕ PMC-Sierra | Hardware | 64.3 | -31.47 | 0.21 |
| ⊕ Millipore | Health | 32.4 | 32.58 | 0.21 |

### Current Investment Style

Value Blnd Growth — Large / Mid / Small

| Market Cap | % |
|---|---|
| Giant | 12.0 |
| Large | 47.3 |
| Mid | 39.2 |
| Small | 1.6 |
| Micro | 0.0 |

Avg $mil: 11,528

| Value Measures | | Rel Category |
|---|---|---|
| Price/Earnings | 16.32 | 0.96 |
| Price/Book | 2.19 | 0.81 |
| Price/Sales | 0.93 | 0.73 |
| Price/Cash Flow | 7.68 | 1.06 |
| Dividend Yield % | 1.60 | 0.90 |

| Growth Measures | % | Rel Category |
|---|---|---|
| Long-Term Erngs | 11.13 | 1.00 |
| Book Value | 5.36 | 0.57 |
| Sales | 4.47 | 0.55 |
| Cash Flow | 0.84 | 0.08 |
| Historical Erngs | 12.20 | 0.86 |

| Profitability | % | Rel Category |
|---|---|---|
| Return on Equity | 15.46 | 0.76 |
| Return on Assets | 7.89 | 0.85 |
| Net Margin | 10.23 | 0.94 |

| Sector Weightings | % of Stocks | Rel S&P 500 | 3 Year High Low | |
|---|---|---|---|---|
| ↻ Info | 18.65 | 0.92 | | |
| Software | 3.21 | 0.90 | 3 | 3 |
| Hardware | 10.42 | 1.04 | 11 | 10 |
| Media | 2.99 | 0.84 | 3 | 3 |
| Telecom | 2.03 | 0.67 | 2 | 2 |
| ☞ Service | 44.04 | 0.95 | | |
| Health | 10.84 | 0.82 | 11 | 9 |
| Consumer | 10.56 | 1.30 | 11 | 10 |
| Business | 6.43 | 1.66 | 7 | 7 |
| Financial | 16.21 | 0.77 | 17 | 16 |
| ⬒ Mfg | 37.31 | 1.12 | | |
| Goods | 10.16 | 1.19 | 10 | 10 |
| Ind Mtrls | 14.50 | 1.19 | 16 | 15 |
| Energy | 5.81 | 0.62 | 6 | 5 |
| Utilities | 6.84 | 2.04 | 7 | 7 |

### Composition

| | | % |
|---|---|---|
| ● Cash | | 0.0 |
| ● Stocks | | 100.0 |
| ● Bonds | | 0.0 |
| Other | | 0.0 |
| Foreign | | 0.0 |
| (% of Stock) | | |

## Morningstar's Take  by Terence Geenty

Rydex S&P Equal Weight isn't as cheap as it could be, but it remains a good index option nonetheless.

When investors are evaluating the merits of an index offering it's important to take a close look at the expense ratio. Typically the fees being charged explain the margin of difference between a portfolio and its benchmark. In this case, the fund charges 0.40%. That looks like a bargain next to most actively managed large-blend mutual funds, but it appears expensive when compared with other ETFs that are tied to the same benchmark. The iShares S&P 500 Index, for example, costs just 0.09%.

But to say that these two funds do the same thing would be incorrect. As the name suggests, this ETF allocates an equal amount of assets to each of the individual components of the bogy. That means that giants such as General Electric and ExxonMobil--each firm soaks up more than 3% of the weighting in the market-cap portfolio--don't get any more of the attention than the other companies do.

As a result, this strategy has a much lower median market capitalization than the typical S&P 500 Index offering. In addition, management is forced to take assets away from the winners in the portfolio and add to the losers when they rebalance each quarter. That tends to keep things from getting too frothy and gives the fund a slight value tilt relative to a market-cap weighted offering.

Those characteristics have suited this fund just fine in recent times. A year-to-date gain of 5.3% puts it nearly 1.4 percentage points ahead of the more common approach. The most significant contributor has been the portfolio's natural bias toward smaller companies. We wouldn't count on that run continuing, but this can still be a nice addition to a portfolio. Investors who want to avoid loading up on mega-cap stocks should consider this fund.

| Address: | 9601 Blackwell Rd United States 800-820-0888 | Management Fee: | 0.40% |
|---|---|---|---|
| | | Expense Projections: | 3Yr:$132  5Yr:$230  10Yr:$518 |
| Web Address: | www.rydex.com | Income Distrib: | Quarterly |
| Inception: | 04-24-03* | Exchange: | AMEX |
| Advisor: | Rydex Global Advisors, Inc. | | |

 MORNINGSTAR® ETFs 100

# SPDR Trust Series 1

| Ticker | NAV | Market Price | 52 wk High/Low | Yield | Mstar Category |
|---|---|---|---|---|---|
| SPY | $124.70 | $128.90 | $128.90 - $113.80 | 1.7% | Large Blend |

## Management

### Portfolio Manager(s)

State Street Global Advisors has managed this fund since its inception in 1993. State Street is one of the world's largest money managers and runs 22 ETFs with a more than $58 billion in net assets. The organization has a lot of experience running index ETF portfolios.

### Strategy

This fund owns and passively tracks the stocks in the S&P 500 Index in proportion to their weight in the benchmark. The offering is organized as a unit investment trust, so unlike open-ended mutual funds, it cannot use futures contracts or lend securities for a fee to close the expense gap between it and its bogy. It also cannot reinvest the dividends it receives until it pays them out to investors. It has to hold the payouts in a non-interest bearing account until they are distributed once a quarter.

### Growth of $10,000

— Investment Value of ETF
— Investment Value of Index S&P 500

| 1996 | 1997 | 1998 | 1999 | 2000 | 2001 | 2002 | 2003 | 2004 | 2005 | History |
|---|---|---|---|---|---|---|---|---|---|---|
| 74.08 | 97.07 | 123.00 | 147.08 | 132.21 | 115.05 | 88.21 | 111.45 | 121.10 | 124.70 | NAV $ |
| 73.84 | 97.06 | 123.31 | 146.88 | 131.19 | 114.23 | 88.23 | 111.28 | 120.87 | 124.51 | Market Price $ |
| 22.74 | 33.06 | 28.35 | 20.86 | -9.15 | -11.86 | -22.12 | 28.39 | 10.75 | 4.79 | NAV Return% |
| 22.58 | 33.48 | 28.69 | 20.39 | -9.73 | -11.81 | -21.54 | 28.17 | 10.70 | 4.82 | Market Price Return% |
| -0.16 | -0.13 | -0.12 | -0.17 | -0.08 | -0.09 | -0.21 | -0.00 | 0.02 | -0.01 | Avg Premium/Discount% |
| -0.21 | -0.29 | -0.23 | -0.18 | -0.05 | 0.02 | -0.03 | -0.28 | -0.12 | -0.12 | NAV Rtrn% +/-S&P 500 |
| 0.29 | 0.21 | 1.33 | -0.05 | -1.36 | 0.59 | -0.47 | -1.50 | -0.65 | -1.48 | NAV Rtrn% +/-Russ 1000 |
| 1 | 1 | 1 | 4 | 4 | 13 | 15 | 15 | 17 | 23 | NAV Return% Rank in Cat |
| 2.08 | 1.87 | 1.47 | 1.18 | 1.03 | 1.08 | 1.31 | 1.86 | 1.99 | 1.79 | Income Return % |
| 20.66 | 31.19 | 26.88 | 19.68 | -10.18 | -12.94 | -23.43 | 26.53 | 8.76 | 3.00 | Capital Return % |
| 1.28 | 1.38 | 1.42 | 1.44 | 1.51 | 1.42 | 1.50 | 1.63 | 2.20 | 2.15 | Income $ |
| 0.13 | 0.00 | 0.00 | 0.00 | 0.00 | 0.00 | 0.00 | 0.00 | 0.00 | 0.00 | Capital Gains $ |
| 0.18 | 0.18 | 0.18 | 0.17 | 0.13 | 0.11 | 0.11 | 0.12 | 0.11 | — | Expense Ratio % |
| 2.03 | 1.63 | 1.35 | 1.18 | 1.01 | 1.14 | 1.40 | 1.67 | 1.63 | — | Income Ratio % |
| 4 | 3 | 6 | 6 | 8 | 5 | 4 | 2 | 2 | — | Turnover Rate % |
| — | — | — | — | — | — | 39,273 | 43,815 | 55,944 | 58,539 | Net Assets $mil |

## Performance

### Historic Quarterly NAV Returns

| | 1st Qtr | 2nd Qtr | 3rd Qtr | 4th Qtr | Total |
|---|---|---|---|---|---|
| 2001 | -11.84 | 5.83 | -14.63 | 10.65 | -11.86 |
| 2002 | 0.24 | -13.38 | -17.24 | 8.39 | -22.12 |
| 2003 | -3.20 | 15.31 | 2.60 | 12.11 | 28.39 |
| 2004 | 1.67 | 1.69 | -1.89 | 9.18 | 10.75 |
| 2005 | -2.16 | 1.33 | 3.58 | 2.05 | 4.79 |

| Trailing | NAV Return% | Market Return% | NAV Rtrn% +/- S&P 500 | %Rank Cat.(NAV) |
|---|---|---|---|---|
| 3 Mo | 2.05 | 1.73 | -0.03 | 27 |
| 6 Mo | 5.70 | 5.47 | -0.06 | 27 |
| 1 Yr | 4.79 | 4.82 | -0.12 | 23 |
| 3 Yr Avg | 14.22 | 14.15 | -0.16 | 14 |
| 5 Yr Avg | 0.45 | 0.58 | -0.09 | 13 |
| 10 Yr Avg | 8.94 | 8.94 | -0.13 | 1 |

| Tax Analysis | Tax-Adj Return% | Tax-Cost Ratio |
|---|---|---|
| 3 Yr (estimated) | 13.52 | 0.61 |
| 5 Yr (estimated) | -0.14 | 0.59 |
| 10 Yr (estimated) | 8.32 | 0.57 |

## Risk Profile

| | Standard Index S&P 500 | Best Fit Index S&P 500 |
|---|---|---|
| Alpha | -0.1 | -0.1 |
| Beta | 1.00 | 1.00 |
| R-Squared | 100 | 100 |
| Standard Deviation | 9.14 | |
| Mean | 14.22 | |
| Sharpe Ratio | 1.29 | |

## Morningstar Fair Value

| Price/Fair Value Ratio | Fair Value Estimate ($) | Hit Rate % |
|---|---|---|
| 1.0 Fairly valued | 38.86 | 97 Good |

## Portfolio Analysis 12-31-05

| Share change since 11-05 Total Stocks:500 | Sector | PE | Tot Ret% | % Assets |
|---|---|---|---|---|
| ⊖ General Electric | Ind Mtrls | 19.9 | -1.43 | 3.27 |
| ⊖ ExxonMobil | Energy | 10.6 | 11.76 | 3.09 |
| ⊖ Citigroup | Financial | 12.1 | 4.63 | 2.17 |
| ⊖ Microsoft | Software | 22.2 | -0.95 | 2.11 |
| ⊖ Procter & Gamble | Goods | 21.2 | 7.18 | 1.71 |
| ⊖ Bank of America | Financial | 11.1 | 2.39 | 1.64 |
| ⊖ Johnson & Johnson | Health | 19.1 | -3.36 | 1.58 |
| ⊖ American International G | Financial | 15.6 | 4.83 | 1.56 |
| ⊖ Pfizer | Health | 21.2 | -10.62 | 1.52 |
| ⊖ Altria Group | Goods | 15.0 | 27.72 | 1.37 |
| ⊖ Intel | Hardware | 18.6 | 8.12 | 1.33 |
| ⊖ J.P. Morgan Chase & Co. | Financial | 18.8 | 5.74 | 1.23 |
| ⊖ IBM | Hardware | 16.0 | -15.83 | 1.15 |
| ⊖ Chevron | Energy | 9.0 | 11.51 | 1.13 |
| ⊖ Wal-Mart Stores | Consumer | 18.2 | -10.30 | 1.03 |
| ⊖ Wells Fargo | Financial | 14.3 | 4.47 | 0.93 |
| ⊖ Cisco Systems | Hardware | 19.9 | -11.39 | 0.93 |
| ⊖ PepsiCo | Goods | 25.8 | 15.24 | 0.87 |
| ⊖ Amgen | Health | 28.3 | 22.93 | 0.86 |
| ⊖ AT&T | Telecom | 21.1 | 0.25 | 0.84 |

### Current Investment Style

Value Blnd Growth — Large Mid Small

| Market Cap | % |
|---|---|
| Giant | 54.0 |
| Large | 37.4 |
| Mid | 8.5 |
| Small | 0.1 |
| Micro | 0.0 |

Avg $mil: 46,951

| Value Measures | | Rel Category |
|---|---|---|
| Price/Earnings | 15.98 | 0.94 |
| Price/Book | 2.50 | 0.93 |
| Price/Sales | 1.48 | 1.16 |
| Price/Cash Flow | 6.09 | 0.84 |
| Dividend Yield % | 1.92 | 1.08 |

| Growth Measures | % | Rel Category |
|---|---|---|
| Long-Term Erngs | 10.51 | 0.95 |
| Book Value | 10.68 | 1.14 |
| Sales | 8.94 | 1.11 |
| Cash Flow | 12.26 | 1.18 |
| Historical Erngs | 15.34 | 1.08 |

| Profitability | % | Rel Category |
|---|---|---|
| Return on Equity | 19.61 | 0.96 |
| Return on Assets | 10.42 | 1.12 |
| Net Margin | 13.33 | 1.22 |

### Sector Weightings

| Sector Weightings | % of Stocks | Rel S&P 500 | 3 Year High | Low |
|---|---|---|---|---|
| Info | 20.16 | 1.00 | | |
| Software | 3.55 | 1.00 | 5 | 4 |
| Hardware | 10.02 | 1.00 | 12 | 9 |
| Media | 3.58 | 1.00 | 4 | 3 |
| Telecom | 3.01 | 1.00 | 4 | 3 |
| Service | 46.44 | 1.00 | | |
| Health | 13.27 | 1.00 | 16 | 12 |
| Consumer | 8.23 | 1.01 | 10 | 8 |
| Business | 3.86 | 1.00 | 4 | 4 |
| Financial | 21.08 | 1.00 | 21 | 20 |
| Mfg | 33.41 | 1.00 | | |
| Goods | 8.56 | 1.00 | 10 | 9 |
| Ind Mtrls | 12.16 | 1.00 | 13 | 11 |
| Energy | 9.34 | 1.00 | 10 | 5 |
| Utilities | 3.35 | 1.00 | 4 | 3 |

### Composition

| | | % |
|---|---|---|
| ● | Cash | 0.5 |
| ● | Stocks | 99.5 |
| ○ | Bonds | 0.0 |
| | Other | 0.0 |
| | Foreign | 0.0 |
| | (% of Stock) | |

## Morningstar's Take by Dan Culloton

It's harder to make a case for the SPDR.

The exchange-traded fund is not the cheapest large-blend index fund available. Its 0.11% expense ratio is low, but other ETFs and conventional index funds that cover the same territory charge less. Indeed, price competition for core index funds has heated up in 2005, with Fidelity Investments further cutting the levies on certain share classes of its traditional broad market index funds, and Vanguard lowering expenses for its large-cap and total market ETFs.

The fund has been tax efficient. Its 10-year tax cost ratio is lower than about 90% of the ETFs and regular funds in the large-blend category, which means its long-term shareholders lost less money to taxes over the time period than its rivals' investors did. Yet, there are conventional funds that can be bought without brokerage fees that have been more tax friendly, including Vanguard 500, Domini Social Equity and Schwab 1000. So, this ETF is not a slam-dunk from a tax perspective either.

And then there is this fund's structure. This offering is a unit-investment trust (UIT), not an open-end mutual fund. So, it can't reinvest dividends it receives and must hold them as cash until they're distributed quarterly. That provides a cushion in down markets, but also can hold the fund back when stocks rise. UITs also can't use options or securities lending to help reduce tracking error, while open-end funds such as Vanguard 500 can. This is part of the reason this ETF's long-term returns have lagged those of the Vanguard 500 even though the ETF has lower expenses.

Flexibility and diversification will keep this ETF popular among traders. It's not a bad option for buy-and-hold investors who want to sock away a lump sum for several years, either. It's not the cheapest or best built option, though, and wouldn't be our first choice.

| | |
|---|---|
| Address: | PDR Services, 86 Trinity Place New York NY 10006 800-843-2639 |
| Web Address: | www.amex.com |
| Inception: | 01-29-93 |
| Advisor: | PDR Services |

| | |
|---|---|
| Management Fee: | 0.06% |
| Expense Projections: | 3Yr: — 5Yr: — 10Yr: — |
| Income Distrib: | Quarterly |
| Exchange: | AMEX |

MORNINGSTAR® ETFs 100

# streetTRACKS DJ STOXX 50

| | Ticker | NAV | Market Price | 52 wk High/Low | Yield | Mstar Category |
|---|---|---|---|---|---|---|
| | FEU | $39.34 | $41.54 | $41.72 - $36.20 | 3.0% | Europe Stock |

## Management

### Portfolio Manager(s)

The advisor is SSgA Funds Management, which is a subsidiary of State Street Global Advisors and of State Street Corp. SSgA manages more than $1 trillion in institutional, mutual fund, and separate accounts, including $70 billion in domestically available ETF assets.

### Strategy

The fund tracks the Dow Jones Stoxx 50, which is an index of the largest stocks from each sector in 17 European countries with developed economies. As a result, this index and fund cover 57% of the market capitalization of the total market capitalization of the stocks traded on major European bourses. It's a free-float market-capitalization-weighted index that rebalances annually in September.

**Growth of $10,000**

— Investment Value of ETF
— Investment Value of Index S&P 500

| 1996 | 1997 | 1998 | 1999 | 2000 | 2001 | 2002 | 2003 | 2004 | 2005 | History |
|---|---|---|---|---|---|---|---|---|---|---|
| — | — | — | — | — | — | 25.49 | 33.62 | 37.80 | 39.34 | NAV $ |
| — | — | — | — | — | — | 24.80 | 33.98 | 37.72 | 39.47 | Market Price $ |
| — | — | — | — | — | — | 17.78* | 35.50 | 15.26 | 7.38 | NAV Return% |
| — | — | — | — | — | — | 16.93* | 40.76 | 13.80 | 7.97 | Market Price Return% |
| — | — | — | — | — | — | -1.21 | 0.02 | 0.67 | 0.21 | Avg Premium/Discount% |
| — | — | — | — | — | — | 17.78 | 6.83 | 4.39 | 2.47 | NAV Rtrn% +/-S&P 500 |
| — | — | — | — | — | — | 17.78 | 5.61 | 3.86 | 1.11 | NAV Rtrn% +/-Russ 1000 |
| — | — | — | — | — | — | — | 15 | 15 | 15 | NAV Return% Rank in Cat |
| — | — | — | — | — | — | 0.00 | 2.98 | 2.49 | 3.21 | Income Return % |
| — | — | — | — | — | — | — | 32.52 | 12.77 | 4.17 | Capital Return % |
| — | — | — | — | — | — | 0.00 | 0.75 | 0.83 | 1.20 | Income $ |
| — | — | — | — | — | — | 0.00 | 0.00 | 0.00 | 0.00 | Capital Gains $ |
| — | — | — | — | — | — | — | 0.35 | 0.33 | 0.32 | Expense Ratio % |
| — | — | — | — | — | — | — | 2.96 | 2.98 | 2.75 | Income Ratio % |
| — | — | — | — | — | — | — | 6 | 7 | 9 | Turnover Rate % |
| — | — | — | — | — | — | 31 | 9 | 28 | 31 | Net Assets $mil |

## Performance

**Historic Quarterly NAV Returns**

| | 1st Qtr | 2nd Qtr | 3rd Qtr | 4th Qtr | Total |
|---|---|---|---|---|---|
| 2001 | — | — | — | — | — |
| 2002 | — | — | — | — | —* |
| 2003 | -9.25 | 21.53 | 1.65 | 20.87 | 35.50 |
| 2004 | -1.80 | 1.01 | 1.88 | 14.05 | 15.26 |
| 2005 | -0.55 | -0.09 | 7.30 | 0.73 | 7.38 |

| Trailing | NAV Return% | Market Return% | NAV Rtrn% +/-S&P 500 | %Rank Cat (NAV) |
|---|---|---|---|---|
| 3 Mo | 0.73 | 1.20 | -1.35 | 16 |
| 6 Mo | 8.08 | 7.94 | 2.32 | 16 |
| 1 Yr | 7.38 | 7.97 | 2.47 | 15 |
| 3 Yr Avg | 18.81 | 20.03 | 4.43 | 15 |
| 5 Yr Avg | — | — | — | 0 |
| 10 Yr Avg | — | — | — | 0 |

| Tax Analysis | Tax-Adj Return% | Tax-Cost Ratio |
|---|---|---|
| 3 Yr (estimated) | 17.67 | 0.96 |
| 5 Yr (estimated) | — | — |
| 10 Yr (estimated) | — | — |

## Risk Profile

| | Standard Index S&P 500 | Best Fit Index MSCI Eur |
|---|---|---|
| Alpha | -4.7 | -2.7 |
| Beta | 1.04 | 0.99 |
| R-Squared | 82 | 97 |
| Standard Deviation | 13.22 | |
| Mean | 18.81 | |
| Sharpe Ratio | 1.23 | |

## Morningstar Fair Value

| Price/Fair Value Ratio | Fair Value Estimate ($) | Hit Rate % |
|---|---|---|
| — | — | — |

## Portfolio Analysis 12-31-05

Share change since 11-05 Total Stocks:50

| | | Sector | Country | % Assets |
|---|---|---|---|---|
| ☼ | Bp | Energy | U.K. | 6.48 |
| ⊕ | HSBC Hldgs | Financial | U.K. | 5.11 |
| ⊖ | GlaxoSmithKline | Health | U.K. | 4.14 |
| ⊖ | TOTAL | Energy | France | 4.05 |
| ⊖ | Vodafone Grp | Telecom | U.K. | 3.74 |
| ⊖ | Novartis | Health | Switzerland | 3.66 |
| ⊖ | Royal Dutch Shell | Energy | U.K. | 3.42 |
| ⊖ | Nestle | Goods | Switzerland | 3.39 |
| ⊖ | Roche Holding | Health | Switzerland | 2.96 |
| ⊖ | Royal Bank Of Scotland G | Financial | U.K. | 2.70 |
| ⊕ | UBS | Financial | Switzerland | 2.66 |
| ⊖ | Banco Santander Central | | Spain | 2.32 |
| ⊖ | Nokia | Hardware | Finland | 2.28 |
| ⊖ | AstraZeneca | Health | U.K. | 2.18 |
| | E. On Ag Npv | Utilities | Germany | 2.03 |
| ⊖ | Siemens | Hardware | Germany | 2.01 |
| ⊖ | Eni | Energy | Italy | 1.97 |
| ⊖ | ING Groep | Financial | Netherlands | 1.93 |
| | Barclays | Financial | U.K. | 1.92 |
| | Telefonica | Telecom | Spain | 1.86 |

### Current Investment Style

| Value | Blnd | Growth | | Market Cap | % |
|---|---|---|---|---|---|
| | | | Large | Giant | 96.5 |
| | | | | Large | 3.5 |
| | | | Mid | Mid | 0.0 |
| | | | | Small | 0.0 |
| | | | Small | Micro | 0.0 |

Avg $mil: 86,571

| Value Measures | | Rel Category |
|---|---|---|
| Price/Earnings | 12.87 | 0.95 |
| Price/Book | 2.51 | 1.05 |
| Price/Sales | 1.33 | 1.12 |
| Price/Cash Flow | 8.30 | 1.14 |
| Dividend Yield % | 3.11 | 1.07 |

| Growth Measures | % | Rel Category |
|---|---|---|
| Long-Term Erngs | 10.99 | 0.97 |
| Book Value | 0.90 | 0.41 |
| Sales | 2.46 | 0.95 |
| Cash Flow | 5.78 | 1.68 |
| Historical Erngs | 18.22 | 1.14 |

### Composition

| Cash | 1.2 | Bonds | 0.0 |
|---|---|---|---|
| Stocks | 98.8 | Other | 0.0 |
| Foreign (% of Stock) | | | 100.0 |

### Sector Weightings

| | | % of Stocks | Rel S&P 500 | 3 Year High Low |
|---|---|---|---|---|
| ↻ | Info | 17.26 | 0.85 | |
| | Software | 1.15 | 0.32 | — — |
| | Hardware | 5.60 | 0.56 | — — |
| | Media | 0.00 | 0.00 | — — |
| | Telecom | 10.51 | 3.49 | — — |
| ☖ | Service | 49.47 | 1.07 | |
| | Health | 13.67 | 1.03 | — — |
| | Consumer | 1.99 | 0.24 | — — |
| | Business | 0.00 | 0.00 | — — |
| | Financial | 33.81 | 1.60 | — — |
| ⊟ | Mfg | 33.28 | 1.00 | |
| | Goods | 9.06 | 1.06 | — — |
| | Ind Mtrls | 3.87 | 0.32 | — — |
| | Energy | 17.39 | 1.86 | — — |
| | Utilities | 2.96 | 0.88 | — — |

### Regional Exposure

| | % Stock | | % Stock |
|---|---|---|---|
| UK/W. Europe | 100 | N. America | 0 |
| Japan | 0 | Latn America | 0 |
| Asia X Japan | 0 | Other | 0 |

### Country Exposure

| | % Stock | | % Stock |
|---|---|---|---|
| U.K. | 40 | Germany | 12 |
| Switzerland | 15 | Netherlands | 7 |
| France | 12 | | |

## Morningstar's Take by Dan Culloton

There is little appeal in this exchange-traded fund's focus on big European stocks.

The StreetTracks Dow Jones Stoxx 50 offers a straight shot of European blue chips for a decent price. Its 0.33% expense ratio is one of the lowest in a group that has many expensive funds run by short-tenured managers.

On the surface, it would seem this fund could serve as a no-muss, no-fuss way to get exposure to corporate titans from Europe's developed economies. The offering tracks the Dow Jones Stoxx 50, an index of the largest European equities from each major sector. It has one of the highest average market capitalizations among international ETFs and keeps more than 95% of its assets in giant-cap stocks.

You probably want broader exposure than this, though. The fund is concentrated, with just 50 holdings and about 40% of its assets in its top 10. Funds with similar characteristics tend to be volatile. In its short life, this offering has shown symptoms of risk. It has finished more of the 28 rolling three-month periods from its October 2002 inception through the end of April 2005 in the red than the typical fund in the European stock category, as well as its largest index fund alternative, Vanguard European Stock Index.

Furthermore, it's not clear there's any advantage in focusing on the largest 50 stocks in any one region. The approach smacks of the Nifty Fifty, a batch of U.S. stocks that became market darlings in the 1960s and early 1970s because they were supposed to be big and successful enough to be worth owning at any price. Those issues tanked in the bear market of 1973-74. What happened to the Nifty Fifty in the U.S. three decades ago doesn't presage a similar fate for European mega-caps, but it does illustrate that size is no guarantee. Many more-diversified foreign funds with longer track records already offer exposure to this area of the global market and, for long-term investors, probably make better sense.

| | | | | |
|---|---|---|---|---|
| Address: | State Street Bank & Tr, 225 Franklin St Boston MA 02210 866-787-2257 | Management Fee: | 0.29% | |
| Web Address: | www.advisors.ssga.com | Expense Projections: | 3Yr:$106 | 5Yr:$186 10Yr:$421 |
| Inception: | 10-21-02* | Income Distrib: | Quarterly | |
| Advisor: | SSGA Funds Management, Inc. | Exchange: | NYSE | |

**MORNINGSTAR® ETFs 100**

# streetTRACK Global T

| | Ticker | NAV | Market Price | 52 wk High/Low | Yield | Mstar Category |
|---|---|---|---|---|---|---|
| | DGT | $64.89 | $67.26 | $67.28 - $62.13 | 2.0% | World Stock |

## Management

### Portfolio Manager(s)

SSgA Funds Management is this ETF's advisor. Karl Schneider and John Tucker are the principal members of the fund's management team. Schneider has been with SSgA since 1996 and manages more than $400 billion in funds and accounts, including some tracking the Wilshire 5000, Russell 2000, and Wilshire 4500. Tucker is the head of the portfolio management team for the firm's ETFs. He's the former head of SSgA's structured-products group in the firm's London office. Tucker also is responsible for new-product research and development.

### Strategy

This fund tracks the Dow Jones Global Titans 50, which includes the some of biggest multinational companies in the world. Down Jones screens 5000 stocks across the globe, ranking them by a mixture of free-float market capitalization, sales and net income (weighted 60%, 20%, and 20%, respectively) and takes the highest-ranking stocks for the Global Titans Index. Constituents additionally have to be established companies that derive at least some revenue from outside their home country. The float-adjusted, market-cap-weighted index checks the weightings of its holdings quarterly and reconstitutes in April.

## Performance

### Historic Quarterly NAV Returns

| | 1st Qtr | 2nd Qtr | 3rd Qtr | 4th Qtr | Total |
|---|---|---|---|---|---|
| 2001 | -11.37 | 4.17 | -12.63 | 7.99 | -12.88 |
| 2002 | -2.26 | -13.14 | -18.00 | 10.08 | -23.37 |
| 2003 | -4.66 | 14.79 | 1.53 | 12.43 | 24.92 |
| 2004 | -0.32 | 1.48 | -1.64 | 7.88 | 7.34 |
| 2005 | -1.28 | -0.06 | 4.00 | 0.21 | 2.82 |

| Trailing | NAV Return% | Market Return%+/-MSCI EAFE | NAV Rtrn% +/-MSCI EAFE | %Rank Cat.(NAV) |
|---|---|---|---|---|
| 3 Mo | 0.21 | 0.62 | -3.87 | 2 |
| 6 Mo | 4.21 | 3.68 | -10.67 | 2 |
| 1 Yr | 2.82 | 2.97 | -10.72 | 2 |
| 3 Yr Avg | 11.30 | 11.38 | -12.38 | 2 |
| 5 Yr Avg | -1.64 | -1.61 | -6.20 | 2 |
| 10 Yr Avg | — | — | — | 0 |

| Tax Analysis | Tax-Adj Return% | Tax-Cost Ratio |
|---|---|---|
| 3 Yr (estimated) | 10.51 | 0.71 |
| 5 Yr (estimated) | -2.27 | 0.64 |
| 10 Yr (estimated) | — | — |

### Growth of $10,000

— Investment Value of ETF
— Investment Value of Index MSCI EAFE

| History | 1996 | 1997 | 1998 | 1999 | 2000 | 2001 | 2002 | 2003 | 2004 | 2005 |
|---|---|---|---|---|---|---|---|---|---|---|
| NAV $ | — | — | — | — | 76.96 | 66.32 | 50.02 | 61.22 | 64.40 | 64.89 |
| Market Price $ | — | — | — | — | 76.97 | 66.94 | 50.00 | 61.22 | 64.43 | 65.01 |
| NAV Return% | — | — | — | — | -3.22* | -12.88 | -23.37 | 24.92 | 7.34 | 2.82 |
| Market Price Return% | — | — | — | — | -3.18* | -12.08 | -24.11 | 24.97 | 7.39 | 2.97 |
| Avg Premium/Discount% | — | — | — | — | -0.60 | 0.34 | 0.06 | 0.05 | 0.08 | 0.17 |
| NAV Rtrn% +/-MSCI EAFE | — | — | — | — | -3.22 | 8.54 | -7.43 | -13.67 | -12.91 | -10.72 |
| NAV Rtrn% +/-MSCI World | — | — | — | — | -3.22 | 3.92 | -3.48 | -8.19 | -7.38 | -6.67 |
| NAV Return% Rank in Cat | — | — | — | — | — | 2 | 2 | 2 | 2 | 2 |
| Income Return % | — | — | — | — | 0.00 | 0.93 | 1.25 | 2.28 | 2.06 | 2.06 |
| Capital Return % | — | — | — | — | — | -13.81 | -24.62 | 22.64 | 5.28 | 0.76 |
| Income $ | — | — | — | — | 0.13 | 0.71 | 0.83 | 1.13 | 1.25 | 1.32 |
| Capital Gains $ | — | — | — | — | 0.00 | 0.00 | 0.00 | 0.00 | 0.00 | 0.00 |
| Expense Ratio % | — | — | — | — | — | 0.52 | 0.55 | 0.54 | 0.51 | 0.51 |
| Income Ratio % | — | — | — | — | — | 0.87 | 1.07 | 1.77 | 1.84 | 2.47 |
| Turnover Rate % | — | — | — | — | — | 16 | 12 | 13 | 15 | 36 |
| Net Assets $mil | — | — | — | — | — | 15 | 24 | 93 | 91 | |

## Risk Profile

| | Standard Index S&P 500 | Best Fit Index MSCI World |
|---|---|---|
| Alpha | -4.3 | -3.9 |
| Beta | 0.67 | 0.83 |
| R-Squared | 78 | 87 |
| Standard Deviation | 8.71 | |
| Mean | 11.30 | |
| Sharpe Ratio | 1.05 | |

## Morningstar Fair Value

| Price/Fair Value Ratio | Fair Value Estimate ($) | Hit Rate % |
|---|---|---|
| 0.9 Undervalued | 42.76 | 93 Good |

## Portfolio Analysis 12-31-05

| Share change since 11-05 Total Stocks:50 | Sector | Country | % Assets |
|---|---|---|---|
| ⊖ General Electric | Ind Mtrls | United States | 5.83 |
| ⊖ ExxonMobil | Energy | United States | 5.60 |
| Citigroup | Financial | United States | 3.96 |
| ⊖ Microsoft | Software | United States | 3.89 |
| ⊖ BP PLC ADR | Energy | U.K. | 3.63 |
| ⊕ Bank of America | Financial | United States | 3.37 |
| ⊖ Procter & Gamble | Goods | United States | 3.10 |
| ⊖ HSBC Holdings PLC ADR | Financial | U.K. | 2.86 |
| ⊖ Johnson & Johnson | Health | United States | 2.80 |
| ⊖ Pfizer | Health | United States | 2.72 |
| ⊖ Toyota Motor ADR | Goods | Japan | 2.52 |
| American International G | Financial | United States | 2.44 |
| ⊖ Altria Group | Goods | United States | 2.42 |
| ⊖ Intel | Hardware | United States | 2.38 |
| ⊖ GlaxoSmithKline PLC ADR | Health | U.K. | 2.30 |
| ⊖ Total SA ADR | Energy | France | 2.27 |
| ⊖ J.P. Morgan Chase & Co. | Financial | United States | 2.19 |
| ⊖ Vodafone Group PLC ADR | Telecom | U.K. | 2.07 |
| ⊖ IBM | Hardware | United States | 2.06 |
| ⊖ Novartis AG ADR | Health | Switzerland | 2.04 |

### Current Investment Style

| Value Blnd Growth | | Market Cap | % |
|---|---|---|---|
| | Large | Giant | 100.0 |
| | Mid | Large | 0.0 |
| | Small | Mid | 0.0 |
| | | Small | 0.0 |
| | | Micro | 0.0 |

Avg $mil: 150,174

| Value Measures | | Rel Category |
|---|---|---|
| Price/Earnings | 14.52 | 1.00 |
| Price/Book | 2.63 | 1.03 |
| Price/Sales | 1.84 | 1.16 |
| Price/Cash Flow | 9.25 | 1.06 |
| Dividend Yield % | 2.52 | 0.99 |

| Growth Measures | % | Rel Category |
|---|---|---|
| Long-Term Erngs | 9.67 | 0.96 |
| Book Value | 12.82 | 1.33 |
| Sales | 10.91 | 1.32 |
| Cash Flow | 11.94 | 1.04 |
| Historical Erngs | 17.60 | 1.07 |

### Composition

| | | | |
|---|---|---|---|
| Cash | 0.5 | Bonds | 0.0 |
| Stocks | 99.5 | Other | 0.0 |
| Foreign | (% of Stock) | | 36.7 |

### Sector Weightings

| | % of Stocks | Rel MSCI EAFE | 3 Year High | Low |
|---|---|---|---|---|
| ↻ Info | 23.13 | 1.65 | | |
| 🖥 Software | 4.21 | 3.93 | 5 | 4 |
| 💻 Hardware | 9.95 | 2.76 | 14 | 10 |
| 📶 Media | 2.06 | 0.98 | 2 | 2 |
| ☎ Telecom | 6.91 | 0.96 | 9 | 6 |
| ☞ Service | 38.50 | 0.84 | | |
| ⚕ Health | 15.47 | 2.16 | 22 | 15 |
| 🛒 Consumer | 1.99 | 0.45 | 3 | 2 |
| 📋 Business | 0.00 | 0.00 | 0 | 0 |
| 💲 Financial | 21.04 | 0.75 | 22 | 18 |
| 🔧 Mfg | 38.37 | 0.95 | | |
| ⚙ Goods | 14.09 | 1.03 | 14 | 10 |
| ⚙ Ind Mtrls | 5.99 | 0.42 | 7 | 5 |
| 🔋 Energy | 18.29 | 2.31 | 20 | 13 |
| 💡 Utilities | 0.00 | 0.00 | 0 | 0 |

### Regional Exposure

| | % Stock | | % Stock |
|---|---|---|---|
| UK/W. Europe 33 | | N. America | 63 |
| Japan | 3 | Latn America | 0 |
| Asia X Japan | 1 | Other | 0 |

### Country Exposure

| | % Stock | | % Stock |
|---|---|---|---|
| United States | 63 | Netherlands | 3 |
| U.K. | 16 | Japan | 3 |
| Switzerland | 7 | | |

## Morningstar's Take by Dan Culloton

You can't get any larger-cap than this.

StreetTracks Dow Jones Global Titans' benchmark, the Dow Jones Global Titans 50, includes the biggest multinational stocks in the world. As a result the portfolio has the highest average market capitalization of any fund, exchange traded or otherwise, in Morningstar's database.

This could be a good thing if you think large-cap stocks, after years of playing second fiddle to the shares of smaller companies, are due for their day in the sun. The ETF's bogy includes financially solid, market-leading firms that get some of their revenue from outside of their home country. Because the United States is home to many global conglomerates, such as General Electric and American International Group, domestic companies account for nearly two thirds of the fund's assets. Dow Jones, however, contends that when you consider the revenue sources of the Global Titans' constituents, the index's domestic exposure is lower. For example, 47% of GE's 2004 revenue came from overseas.

It's true that many of this ETF's holdings move more in tandem with the fortunes of the sectors in which they do business than with their home economies. Yet, this fund has some traits that could cause it to diverge from other globe-spanning portfolios. The ETF is concentrated. The portfolio has about 50 stocks and keeps close to 40% of its assets in its top 10 holdings. The fund also is less diversified by sector than the iShares S&P Global 100 Index and other large-blend and world-stock funds. The ETF is light on utility, industrial, and consumer stocks and heavier on telecom, financial, and energy equities.

That doesn't disqualify it, but its 0.51% expense ratio makes it hard to recommend over iShares S&P Global 100, which is relatively cheaper at 0.4%. It's the cheaper and more diversified option.

| Address: | State Street Bank & Tr, 225 Franklin St Boston MA 02210 866-787-2257 | Management Fee: | 0.50% |
|---|---|---|---|
| | | Expense Projections: | 3Yr:$161  5Yr:$281  10Yr:$628 |
| Web Address: | www.advisors.ssga.com | Income Distrib: | Quarterly |
| Inception: | 09-25-00 * | Exchange: | AMEX |
| Advisor: | SSGA Funds Management, Inc. | | |

# streetTRACKS DJ Lg Growth

| | Ticker | NAV | Market Price | 52 wk High/Low | Yield | Mstar Category |
|---|---|---|---|---|---|---|
| | ELG | $49.44 | $51.23 | $51.23 - $44.10 | 0.7% | Large Growth |

## Management

### Portfolio Manager(s)

SSgA Funds Management is this ETF's advisor. Karl Schneider and John Tucker are the principal members of the fund's management team. Schneider has been with SSgA since 1996 and manages more than $400 billion in funds and accounts, including some tracking the Wilshire 5000, Russell 2000, and Wilshire 4500. Tucker is the head of the portfolio management team for the firm's ETFs. He's the former head of SSgA's structured products group in the firm's London office. Tucker also is responsible for new-product research and development.

### Strategy

This fund tracks the Dow Jones Wilshire Large Cap Growth Index. The bogy uses six factors to sort the biggest 750 stocks in the Dow Jones Wilshire 5000 into value or growth buckets. Stocks' style scores are based on their projected price/earnings, projected earnings growth, and price/book ratios; dividend yield, trailing revenue growth, and trailing earnings growth. Half the universe's float-adjusted market cap ends up in value and half in growth. Buffer zones keep constituents from jumping in and out of the index due to market cap or style score changes. It rebalances in March and December.

### Growth of $10,000

— Investment Value of ETF
— Investment Value of Index S&P 500

| | 1996 | 1997 | 1998 | 1999 | 2000 | 2001 | 2002 | 2003 | 2004 | 2005 | History |
|---|---|---|---|---|---|---|---|---|---|---|---|
| | — | — | — | — | 71.97 | 53.39 | 36.33 | 46.68 | 48.32 | 49.44 | NAV $ |
| | — | — | — | — | 73.12 | 54.09 | 36.55 | 46.65 | 48.45 | 49.42 | Market Price $ |
| | — | — | — | — | -11.53* | -25.65 | -31.66 | 29.19 | 4.94 | 3.00 | NAV Return% |
| | — | — | — | — | -11.54* | -25.86 | -32.14 | 28.34 | 5.28 | 2.69 | Market Price Return% |
| | — | — | — | — | -0.18 | 0.81 | 0.14 | 0.28 | 0.12 | 0.01 | Avg Premium/Discount% |
| | — | — | — | — | -11.53 | -13.77 | -9.57 | 0.52 | -5.93 | -1.91 | NAV Rtrn% +/-S&P 500 |
| | — | — | — | — | -11.53 | -5.23 | -3.78 | -0.56 | -1.36 | -2.26 | NAV Rtrn% +/-Russ 1000Gr |
| | — | — | — | — | — | 5 | 5 | 5 | 6 | 9 | NAV Return% Rank in Cat |
| | — | — | — | — | 0.00 | 0.16 | 0.32 | 0.65 | 1.38 | 0.67 | Income Return % |
| | — | — | — | — | — | -25.81 | -31.98 | 28.54 | 3.56 | 2.33 | Capital Return % |
| | — | — | — | — | 0.02 | 0.12 | 0.17 | 0.23 | 0.64 | 0.32 | Income $ |
| | — | — | — | — | 0.00 | 0.00 | 0.00 | 0.00 | 0.00 | 0.00 | Capital Gains $ |
| | — | — | — | — | | 0.22 | 0.25 | 0.23 | 0.21 | 0.21 | Expense Ratio % |
| | — | — | — | — | | 0.10 | 0.32 | 0.64 | 0.59 | 1.57 | Income Ratio % |
| | — | — | — | — | | 16 | 18 | 37 | 20 | 21 | Turnover Rate % |
| | — | — | — | — | | 15 | 35 | 82 | 143 | | Net Assets $mil |

## Performance

### Historic Quarterly NAV Returns

| | 1st Qtr | 2nd Qtr | 3rd Qtr | 4th Qtr | Total |
|---|---|---|---|---|---|
| 2001 | -22.88 | 9.63 | -24.88 | 17.07 | -25.65 |
| 2002 | -4.61 | -19.28 | -17.18 | 7.15 | -31.66 |
| 2003 | 0.62 | 12.40 | 3.02 | 10.88 | 29.19 |
| 2004 | 0.37 | 1.79 | -5.28 | 8.43 | 4.94 |
| 2005 | -4.96 | 1.08 | 3.47 | 3.62 | 3.00 |

| Trailing | NAV Return% | Market Return% | NAV Rtrn% +/-S&P 500 | %Rank Cat.(NAV) |
|---|---|---|---|---|
| 3 Mo | 3.62 | 3.59 | 1.54 | 10 |
| 6 Mo | 7.22 | 7.07 | 1.46 | 10 |
| 1 Yr | 3.00 | 2.69 | -1.91 | 9 |
| 3 Yr Avg | 11.77 | 11.53 | -2.61 | 5 |
| 5 Yr Avg | -6.63 | -6.94 | -7.17 | 5 |
| 10 Yr Avg | — | — | — | 0 |

| Tax Analysis | Tax-Adj Return% | Tax-Cost Ratio |
|---|---|---|
| 3 Yr (estimated) | 11.43 | 0.30 |
| 5 Yr (estimated) | -6.85 | 0.24 |
| 10 Yr (estimated) | — | — |

## Risk Profile

| | Standard Index S&P 500 | Best Fit Index Russ 1000Gr |
|---|---|---|
| Alpha | -1.9 | -0.9 |
| Beta | 0.96 | 0.97 |
| R-Squared | 86 | 96 |
| Standard Deviation | 9.53 | |
| Mean | 11.77 | |
| Sharpe Ratio | 1.01 | |

## Morningstar Fair Value

| Price/Fair Value Ratio | Fair Value Estimate ($) | Hit Rate % |
|---|---|---|
| 1.0 Fairly valued | 41.32 | 95 Good |

## Portfolio Analysis 12-31-05

| Share change since 11-05 | Total Stocks:385 | Sector | PE | Tot Ret% | % Assets |
|---|---|---|---|---|---|
| ⊕ Microsoft | | Software | 22.2 | -0.95 | 4.19 |
| ⊕ Procter & Gamble | | Goods | 21.2 | 7.18 | 3.34 |
| ⊕ Johnson & Johnson | | Health | 19.1 | -3.36 | 3.02 |
| ⊕ IBM | | Hardware | 16.0 | -15.83 | 2.22 |
| ⊕ Wal-Mart Stores | | Consumer | 18.2 | -10.30 | 2.04 |
| ⊕ Cisco Systems | | Hardware | 19.9 | -11.39 | 1.91 |
| ⊕ PepsiCo | | Goods | 25.8 | 15.24 | 1.66 |
| ⊕ Amgen | | Health | 28.3 | 22.93 | 1.65 |
| ⊕ Berkshire Hathaway A | | Financial | — | | 1.55 |
| ⊕ Home Depot | | Consumer | 15.6 | -4.35 | 1.47 |
| ⊕ UnitedHealth Group | | Health | 26.2 | 41.22 | 1.43 |
| ⊕ Google | | Business | — | 115.19 | 1.41 |
| ⊕ Time Warner | | Media | 30.6 | -9.83 | 1.29 |
| ⊕ Qualcomm | | Hardware | 34.2 | 2.50 | 1.19 |
| ⊕ Medtronic | | Health | 37.4 | 16.72 | 1.17 |
| ⊕ Dell | | Hardware | 23.2 | -28.93 | 1.10 |
| ⊕ Apple Computer | | Hardware | 46.1 | 123.26 | 1.02 |
| ⊕ Schlumberger | | Energy | 31.1 | 46.62 | 0.96 |
| ⊕ American Express | | Financial | 16.4 | 5.31 | 0.96 |
| ⊕ 3M Company | | Ind Mtrls | 19.2 | -3.51 | 0.92 |

### Current Investment Style

Value Blnd Growth — Large Mid Small

| Market Cap | % |
|---|---|
| Giant | 43.4 |
| Large | 39.5 |
| Mid | 17.1 |
| Small | 0.0 |
| Micro | 0.0 |

Avg $mil: 32,276

| Value Measures | | Rel Category |
|---|---|---|
| Price/Earnings | 20.26 | 0.96 |
| Price/Book | 3.32 | 0.99 |
| Price/Sales | 1.74 | 0.89 |
| Price/Cash Flow | 10.98 | 1.05 |
| Dividend Yield % | 1.00 | 1.12 |

| Growth Measures | % | Rel Category |
|---|---|---|
| Long-Term Erngs | 13.66 | 0.97 |
| Book Value | 8.74 | 1.07 |
| Sales | 12.30 | 1.11 |
| Cash Flow | 15.71 | 0.96 |
| Historical Erngs | 19.92 | 1.04 |

| Profitability | % | Rel Category |
|---|---|---|
| Return on Equity | 21.88 | 1.09 |
| Return on Assets | 11.28 | 1.05 |
| Net Margin | 13.83 | 0.99 |

| Sector Weightings | % of Stocks | Rel S&P 500 | 3 Year High Low | |
|---|---|---|---|---|
| ↻ Info | 26.18 | 1.30 | | |
| Software | 6.14 | 1.72 | 12 | 6 |
| Hardware | 13.57 | 1.35 | 22 | 13 |
| Media | 6.00 | 1.68 | 9 | 6 |
| Telecom | 0.47 | 0.16 | 2 | 0 |
| ☞ Service | 51.13 | 1.10 | | |
| Health | 19.06 | 1.43 | 23 | 17 |
| Consumer | 14.96 | 1.84 | 16 | 11 |
| Business | 7.53 | 1.95 | 8 | 2 |
| Financial | 9.58 | 0.45 | 10 | 4 |
| Mfg | 22.68 | 0.68 | | |
| Goods | 8.76 | 1.02 | 14 | 9 |
| Ind Mtrls | 5.55 | 0.46 | 12 | 3 |
| Energy | 8.20 | 0.88 | 9 | 0 |
| Utilities | 0.17 | 0.05 | 1 | 0 |

### Composition

| | |
|---|---|
| ● Cash | 0.0 |
| ● Stocks | 100.0 |
| ● Bonds | 0.0 |
| ● Other | 0.0 |
| Foreign | 0.0 |
| (% of Stock) | |

## Morningstar's Take by Dan Culloton

Internal changes make this fund more competitive, but it's still a runner up.

StreetTracks Dow Jones Wilshire Large Cap Growth ETF has a lot to offer long-term investors. The fund tracks a benchmark that relies on up-to-date, multivariate index-construction methods, so it should do a good job of capturing the return of the large-cap growth market without too much turnover. The most recent expense ratio of 0.21% also is lower than the vast majority of exchange-traded and conventional options.

The offering is actually switching its benchmark, but this shouldn't result in dramatic changes. The ETF, which used to draw its constituents from the large-cap portion of the Dow Jones U.S. Total Market Index, is switching to a bogy that uses the biggest 750 members of Dow Jones Wilshire 5000 as a starting point. The actual contents of the fund should not change much, though, because the new benchmark uses the same six valuation and growth factors to sort stocks into the growth or value camp.

The new index, however, does have clear rules that will keep it from automatically kicking out stocks on the benchmark's size and style borders, which should control turnover.

Because the benchmark trolls a universe of 750 companies, the ETF could end up holding more stocks, particularly in the mid-cap area. Its holdings and sector allocations should remain familiar, though. Microsoft, Johnson & Johnson, and Google aren't going anywhere. Hardware, health-care, and consumer services also should remain its favorite sectors

So, the offering should correlate closely with other index funds that cover this area. That's why investors should still opt for other choices, though. Expenses play a huge role in differentiating index funds that cover the same territory, and this ETF's expense ratio, while low, is not the lowest available. This offering is a decent option, but, all other things being equal, go with the cheaper ETF or mutual fund.

| Address: | State Street Bank & Tr, 225 Franklin St Boston MA 02210 866-787-2257 |
|---|---|
| Web Address: | www.advisors.ssga.com |
| Inception: | 09-25-00* |
| Advisor: | SSGA Funds Management, Inc. |

| Management Fee: | 0.20% | | |
|---|---|---|---|
| Expense Projections: | 3Yr:$65 | 5Yr:$113 | 10Yr:$257 |
| Income Distrib: | Quarterly | | |
| Exchange: | AMEX | | |

 **MORNINGSTAR® ETFs 100**

# streetTracks DJ Lg Value

| Ticker | NAV | Market Price | 52 wk High/Low | Yield | Mstar Category |
|---|---|---|---|---|---|
| ELV | $70.13 | $72.42 | $72.42 - $65.44 | 2.6% | Large Value |

## Management

### Portfolio Manager(s)

SSgA Funds Management is this ETF's advisor. Karl Schneider and John Tucker are the principal members of the fund's management team. Schneider has been with SSgA since 1996 and manages more than $400 billion in funds and accounts, including some tracking the Wilshire 5000, Russell 2000, and Wilshire 4500. Tucker is the head of the portfolio management team for the firm's ETFs. He's the former head of SSgA's structured products group in the firm's London office. Tucker also is responsible for new-product research and development.

### Strategy

This fund tracks the Dow Jones Wilshire Large Cap Value Index. The bogy uses six factors to sort the biggest 750 stocks in the Dow Jones Wilshire 5000 into value or growth buckets. Stocks' style scores are based on their projected price/earnings, projected earnings growth, and price/book ratios; dividend yield, trailing revenue growth, and trailing earnings growth. Half the universe's float-adjusted market cap ends up in value and half in growth. Buffer zones keep constituents from jumping in and out of the index due to market cap or style score changes. It rebalances in March and December.

## Performance

### Historic Quarterly NAV Returns

| | 1st Qtr | 2nd Qtr | 3rd Qtr | 4th Qtr | Total |
|---|---|---|---|---|---|
| 2001 | -7.35 | 3.22 | -6.93 | 5.33 | -6.25 |
| 2002 | 1.55 | -11.89 | -16.48 | 10.23 | -17.63 |
| 2003 | -5.52 | 18.25 | 0.16 | 12.15 | 25.52 |
| 2004 | 1.62 | 1.23 | 1.27 | 8.60 | 13.13 |
| 2005 | -0.78 | 1.16 | 3.21 | 1.76 | 5.43 |

| Trailing | NAV Return% | Market Return% | NAV Rtrn% +/-S&P 500 | %Rank Cat.(NAV) |
|---|---|---|---|---|
| 3 Mo | 1.76 | 1.84 | -0.32 | 13 |
| 6 Mo | 5.03 | 4.95 | -0.73 | 11 |
| 1 Yr | 5.43 | 5.32 | 3.52 | 10 |
| 3 Yr Avg | 14.40 | 14.29 | 0.02 | 7 |
| 5 Yr Avg | 2.94 | 2.95 | 2.40 | 7 |
| 10 Yr Avg | — | — | — | 0 |

| Tax Analysis | Tax-Adj Return% | Tax-Cost Ratio |
|---|---|---|
| 3 Yr (estimated) | 13.43 | 0.85 |
| 5 Yr (estimated) | 2.06 | 0.85 |
| 10 Yr (estimated) | — | — |

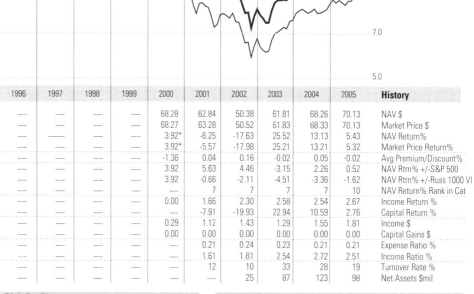

Growth of $10,000

— Investment Value of ETF
— Investment Value of Index S&P 500

| | 1996 | 1997 | 1998 | 1999 | 2000 | 2001 | 2002 | 2003 | 2004 | 2005 | History |
|---|---|---|---|---|---|---|---|---|---|---|---|
| | — | — | — | — | 68.28 | 62.84 | 50.38 | 61.81 | 68.26 | 70.13 | NAV $ |
| | — | — | — | — | 68.27 | 63.28 | 50.52 | 61.83 | 68.33 | 70.13 | Market Price $ |
| | — | — | — | — | 3.92* | -6.25 | -17.63 | 25.52 | 13.13 | 5.43 | NAV Return% |
| | — | — | — | — | 3.92* | -5.57 | -17.98 | 25.21 | 13.21 | 5.32 | Market Price Return% |
| | — | — | — | — | -1.36 | 0.04 | 0.16 | -0.02 | 0.05 | -0.02 | Avg Premium/Discount% |
| | — | — | — | — | 3.92 | 5.63 | 4.46 | -3.15 | 2.26 | 0.52 | NAV Rtrn% +/-S&P 500 |
| | — | — | — | — | 3.92 | -0.66 | -2.11 | -4.51 | -3.36 | -1.62 | NAV Rtrn% +/-Russ 1000 VI |
| | — | — | — | — | — | 7 | 7 | 7 | 7 | 10 | NAV Return% Rank in Cat |
| | — | — | — | — | 0.00 | 1.66 | 2.30 | 2.58 | 2.54 | 2.67 | Income Return % |
| | — | — | — | — | — | -7.91 | -19.93 | 22.94 | 10.59 | 2.76 | Capital Return % |
| | — | — | — | — | 0.29 | 1.12 | 1.43 | 1.29 | 1.55 | 1.81 | Income $ |
| | — | — | — | — | 0.00 | 0.00 | 0.00 | 0.00 | 0.00 | 0.00 | Capital Gains $ |
| | — | — | — | — | 0.21 | 0.24 | 0.23 | 0.21 | 0.21 | 0.21 | Expense Ratio % |
| | — | — | — | — | 1.61 | 1.81 | 2.54 | 2.72 | 2.51 | | Income Ratio % |
| | — | — | — | — | 12 | 10 | 33 | 28 | 19 | | Turnover Rate % |
| | — | — | — | — | — | 25 | 87 | 123 | 98 | | Net Assets $mil |

## Risk Profile

| | Standard Index S&P 500 | Best Fit Index Mstar Large Value |
|---|---|---|
| Alpha | 0.6 | 0.0 |
| Beta | 0.96 | 0.92 |
| R-Squared | 86 | 94 |
| Standard Deviation | 9.44 | |
| Mean | 14.40 | |
| Sharpe Ratio | 1.27 | |

## Morningstar Fair Value

| Price/Fair Value Ratio | Fair Value Estimate ($) | Hit Rate % |
|---|---|---|
| 1.0 Fairly valued | 37.05 | 96 Good |

## Portfolio Analysis 12-31-05

Share change since 11-05 Total Stocks:359

| | Sector | PE | Tot Ret% | % Assets |
|---|---|---|---|---|
| ⊖ General Electric | Ind Mtrls | 19.9 | -1.43 | 5.66 |
| ⊖ ExxonMobil | Energy | 10.6 | 11.76 | 5.45 |
| ⊖ Citigroup | Financial | 12.1 | 4.63 | 3.84 |
| ⊕ Bank of America | Financial | 11.1 | 2.39 | 3.28 |
| ⊖ Pfizer | Health | 21.2 | -10.62 | 2.64 |
| ⊖ American International G | Financial | 15.6 | 4.83 | 2.36 |
| ⊖ Altria Group | Goods | 15.0 | 27.72 | 2.36 |
| ⊖ Intel | Hardware | 18.6 | 8.12 | 2.31 |
| ⊖ J.P. Morgan Chase & Co. | Financial | 18.8 | 5.74 | 2.12 |
| ⊖ Chevron | Energy | 9.0 | 11.51 | 1.94 |
| ⊖ Wells Fargo | Financial | 14.3 | 4.47 | 1.59 |
| ⊖ AT&T | Telecom | 21.1 | 0.25 | 1.46 |
| ⊖ Coca-Cola | Goods | 18.6 | -0.66 | 1.36 |
| ⊖ Verizon Communications | Telecom | 10.2 | -22.18 | 1.27 |
| ⊖ Wachovia | Financial | 13.0 | 4.29 | 1.25 |
| ⊖ Hewlett-Packard | Hardware | 27.3 | 38.29 | 1.25 |
| ⊖ ConocoPhillips | Energy | 6.7 | 36.89 | 1.13 |
| ⊖ Merck | Health | 15.2 | 4.04 | 1.06 |
| ⊖ Sprint Nextel | Telecom | 19.1 | -4.81 | 1.04 |
| ⊖ Wyeth | Health | 54.2 | 10.54 | 0.93 |

### Current Investment Style

Value Blnd Growth — Large Mid Small

| Market Cap | % |
|---|---|
| Giant | 54.6 |
| Large | 31.8 |
| Mid | 13.7 |
| Small | 0.0 |
| Micro | 0.0 |

Avg $mil: 48,172

| Value Measures | | Rel Category |
|---|---|---|
| Price/Earnings | 13.96 | 0.97 |
| Price/Book | 2.10 | 0.94 |
| Price/Sales | 1.37 | 1.04 |
| Price/Cash Flow | 4.43 | 0.86 |
| Dividend Yield % | 2.53 | 1.04 |

| Growth Measures | % | Rel Category |
|---|---|---|
| Long-Term Erngs | 9.08 | 0.95 |
| Book Value | 11.67 | 0.97 |
| Sales | 6.89 | 0.86 |
| Cash Flow | 9.80 | 0.80 |
| Historical Erngs | 12.92 | 0.79 |

| Profitability | % | Rel Category |
|---|---|---|
| Return on Equity | 16.99 | 0.92 |
| Return on Assets | 9.56 | 0.96 |
| Net Margin | 13.24 | 1.03 |

### Sector Weightings

| | % of Stocks | Rel S&P 500 | 3 Year High Low | |
|---|---|---|---|---|
| ↻ Info | 15.52 | 0.77 | | |
| 📋 Software | 1.28 | 0.36 | 1 | 0 |
| 💻 Hardware | 6.60 | 0.66 | 7 | 2 |
| 🎤 Media | 2.13 | 0.59 | 3 | 0 |
| 📶 Telecom | 5.51 | 1.83 | 9 | 5 |
| ⊂ Service | 43.48 | 0.94 | | |
| 🏥 Health | 7.02 | 0.53 | 18 | 7 |
| 🛒 Consumer | 2.58 | 0.32 | 3 | 2 |
| 💼 Business | 1.67 | 0.43 | 2 | 1 |
| $ Financial | 32.21 | 1.53 | 41 | 31 |
| ⊓ Mfg | 40.99 | 1.23 | | |
| 🏭 Goods | 7.81 | 0.91 | 10 | 5 |
| ⚙ Ind Mtrls | 16.43 | 1.35 | 17 | 9 |
| 🔥 Energy | 10.82 | 1.16 | 17 | 10 |
| 💡 Utilities | 5.93 | 1.76 | 6 | 3 |

### Composition

| | |
|---|---|
| ● Cash | 0.3 |
| ● Stocks | 99.7 |
| ● Bonds | 0.0 |
| ● Other | 0.0 |
| Foreign | 0.0 |

(% of Stock)

## Morningstar's Take by Dan Culloton

This fund has a new and improved benchmark, but it's still an also-ran.

StreetTracks Dow Jones Wilshire Large Cap Value ETF has a lot to offer long-term investors. The fund tracks a benchmark that relies on up-to-date, multivariate index-construction methods, so it should do a good job of capturing the return of the large-cap value market without too much turnover. The most recent expense ratio of 0.21% also is lower than the vast majority of exchange-traded and conventional options.

The offering is actually switching its benchmark, but this shouldn't result in dramatic changes. The ETF, which used to draw its constituents from the large-cap portion of the Dow Jones U.S. Total Market Index, is switching to a bogy that uses the biggest 750 members of Dow Jones Wilshire 5000 as a starting point. The actual contents of the fund should not change much, though, because the new benchmark uses the same six valuation and growth factors to sort stocks into the growth or value camp.

The new index, however, does have clear rules that will keep it from automatically kicking out stocks on the benchmark's size and style borders, which should control turnover.

Because the benchmark trolls a universe of 750 companies, the ETF could end up holding more stocks, particularly in the mid-cap area. Its holdings and sector allocations should remain familiar, though. ExxonMobil, American International Group, and Altria aren't going anywhere. Financial services, industrial, and energy should remain the ETF's favorite sectors

So, the offering should correlate closely with other index funds that cover this area. But investors should still opt for other choices. Expenses play a huge role in differentiating index funds that cover the same territory, and this ETF's expense ratio, while low, is not the lowest available. All things being equal, go with the cheaper ETF.

| Address: | State Street Bank & Tr, 225 Franklin St Boston MA 02210 866-787-2257 | Management Fee: | 0.20% |
|---|---|---|---|
| | | Expense Projections: | 3Yr:$65  5Yr:$113  10Yr:$257 |
| Web Address: | www.advisors.ssga.com | Income Distrib: | Quarterly |
| Inception: | 09-25-00* | Exchange: | AMEX |
| Advisor: | SSGA Funds Management, Inc. | | |

# streetTRACK DJ Small Gr

| | Ticker | NAV | Market Price | 52 wk High/Low | Yield | Mstar Category |
|---|---|---|---|---|---|---|
| | DSG | $82.01 | $86.46 | $86.46 - $69.94 | 0.4% | Small Growth |

## Management

### Portfolio Manager(s)

SSgA Funds Management is this ETF's advisor. Karl Schneider and John Tucker are the principal members of the fund's management team. Schneider has been with SSgA since 1996 and manages more than $400 billion in funds and accounts, including some tracking the Wilshire 5000, Russell 2000, and Wilshire 4500. Tucker is the head of the portfolio management team for the firm's ETFs. He's the former head of SSgA's structured products group in the firm's London office. Tucker also is responsible for new-product research and development.

### Strategy

This fund tracks the Dow Jones Wilshire Small Cap Growth Index. The bogy uses six factors to sort the biggest small cap stocks in the Dow Jones Wilshire 5000 into value or growth buckets. Stocks' style scores are based on their projected price/earnings, projected earnings growth, and price/book ratios; dividend yield, trailing revenue growth, and trailing earnings growth. Half the universe's float-adjusted market cap ends up in value and half in growth. Buffer zones keep constituents from jumping in and out of the index due to market cap or style score changes. It rebalances in March and December.

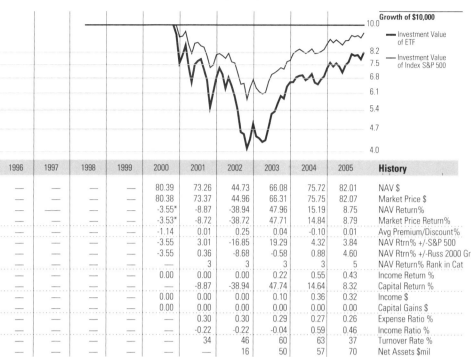

Growth of $10,000
— Investment Value of ETF
— Investment Value of Index S&P 500

| | 1996 | 1997 | 1998 | 1999 | 2000 | 2001 | 2002 | 2003 | 2004 | 2005 | History |
|---|---|---|---|---|---|---|---|---|---|---|---|
| | — | — | — | — | 80.39 | 73.26 | 44.73 | 66.08 | 75.72 | 82.01 | NAV $ |
| | — | — | — | — | 80.38 | 73.37 | 44.96 | 66.31 | 75.75 | 82.07 | Market Price $ |
| | — | — | — | — | -3.55* | -8.87 | -38.94 | 47.96 | 15.19 | 8.75 | NAV Return% |
| | — | — | — | — | -3.53* | -8.72 | -38.72 | 47.71 | 14.84 | 8.79 | Market Price Return% |
| | — | — | — | — | -1.14 | 0.01 | 0.25 | 0.04 | -0.10 | 0.01 | Avg Premium/Discount% |
| | — | — | — | — | -3.55 | 3.01 | -16.85 | 19.29 | 4.32 | 3.84 | NAV Rtrn% +/-S&P 500 |
| | — | — | — | — | -3.55 | 0.36 | -8.68 | -0.58 | 0.88 | 4.60 | NAV Rtrn% +/-Russ 2000 Gr |
| | — | — | — | — | — | 3 | 3 | 3 | 3 | 5 | NAV Return% Rank in Cat |
| | — | — | — | — | 0.00 | 0.00 | 0.00 | 0.22 | 0.55 | 0.43 | Income Return % |
| | — | — | — | — | — | -8.87 | -38.94 | 47.74 | 14.64 | 8.32 | Capital Return % |
| | — | — | — | — | 0.00 | 0.00 | 0.00 | 0.10 | 0.36 | 0.32 | Income $ |
| | — | — | — | — | 0.00 | 0.00 | 0.00 | 0.00 | 0.00 | 0.00 | Capital Gains $ |
| | — | — | — | — | — | 0.30 | 0.30 | 0.29 | 0.27 | 0.26 | Expense Ratio % |
| | — | — | — | — | — | -0.22 | -0.22 | -0.04 | 0.59 | 0.46 | Income Ratio % |
| | — | — | — | — | — | 34 | 46 | 60 | 63 | 37 | Turnover Rate % |
| | — | — | — | — | — | 16 | 50 | 57 | 70 | Net Assets $mil |

## Performance

### Historic Quarterly NAV Returns

| | 1st Qtr | 2nd Qtr | 3rd Qtr | 4th Qtr | Total |
|---|---|---|---|---|---|
| 2001 | -17.88 | 18.36 | -29.45 | 32.89 | -8.87 |
| 2002 | -6.61 | -20.93 | -24.20 | 9.07 | -38.94 |
| 2003 | -2.77 | 23.13 | 9.80 | 12.56 | 47.96 |
| 2004 | 5.12 | 0.92 | -3.87 | 12.95 | 15.19 |
| 2005 | -2.82 | 3.44 | 5.34 | 2.69 | 8.75 |

| Trailing | NAV Return% | Market Return% | NAV Rtrn% +/-S&P 500 | %Rank Cat.(NAV) |
|---|---|---|---|---|
| 3 Mo | 2.69 | 2.72 | 0.61 | 6 |
| 6 Mo | 8.18 | 7.52 | 2.42 | 6 |
| 1 Yr | 8.75 | 8.79 | 3.84 | 5 |
| 3 Yr Avg | 22.84 | 22.66 | 8.46 | 3 |
| 5 Yr Avg | 0.62 | 0.64 | 0.08 | 3 |
| 10 Yr Avg | — | — | — | 0 |

| Tax Analysis | Tax-Adj Return% | Tax-Cost Ratio |
|---|---|---|
| 3 Yr (estimated) | 22.68 | 0.13 |
| 5 Yr (estimated) | 0.54 | 0.08 |
| 10 Yr (estimated) | — | — |

## Risk Profile

| | Standard Index S&P 500 | Best Fit Index Russ 2000 Gr |
|---|---|---|
| Alpha | 3.9 | 4.7 |
| Beta | 1.32 | 0.81 |
| R-Squared | 77 | 97 |
| Standard Deviation | 13.80 | |
| Mean | 22.84 | |
| Sharpe Ratio | 1.43 | |

## Morningstar Fair Value

| Price/Fair Value Ratio | Fair Value Estimate ($) | Hit Rate % |
|---|---|---|
| — | — | — |

## Portfolio Analysis 12-31-05

| Share change since 11-05 Total Stocks:870 | Sector | PE | Tot Ret% | % Assets |
|---|---|---|---|---|
| ⊖ Red Hat | Software | NMF | 104.19 | 0.54 |
| ⊕ Intuitive Surgical | Health | 77.2 | 193.03 | 0.49 |
| Amylin Pharmaceuticals | Health | — | 70.89 | 0.48 |
| ⊕ Western Digital | Hardware | 17.2 | 71.68 | 0.48 |
| Axis Capital Holdings | Financial | — | 16.76 | 0.46 |
| Intersil | Hardware | 50.8 | 50.19 | 0.45 |
| ⊕ JDS Uniphase | Hardware | — | -25.55 | 0.45 |
| ⊖ Corporate Executive Boar | Business | 51.9 | 34.71 | 0.44 |
| Glamis Gold Ltd | Ind Mtrls | — | 60.14 | 0.44 |
| ⊖ CB Richard Ellis Group | Financial | — | 75.41 | 0.43 |
| Global Payments | Business | 37.7 | 59.62 | 0.43 |
| Cimarex Energy | Energy | 11.5 | 13.48 | 0.42 |
| ⊕ Range Resources | Energy | 40.8 | 93.68 | 0.40 |
| MEMC Electronic Material | Hardware | 18.6 | 67.32 | 0.40 |
| ⊕ HCC Insurance Holdings | Financial | 17.4 | 35.84 | 0.39 |
| ⊖ Oshkosh Truck | Ind Mtrls | 20.4 | 31.21 | 0.39 |
| Renal Care Group | Health | 25.9 | 31.45 | 0.38 |
| ⊕ Protein Design Labs | Health | — | 37.56 | 0.38 |
| Inamed | Health | 47.1 | 38.62 | 0.38 |
| ⊕ Affymetrix | Health | 53.1 | 30.64 | 0.38 |

### Current Investment Style

Value Blnd Growth — Large / Mid / Small

| | Market Cap | % |
|---|---|---|
| | Giant | 0.0 |
| | Large | 0.0 |
| | Mid | 46.7 |
| | Small | 48.5 |
| | Micro | 4.8 |
| | Avg $mil: 1,443 | |

| Value Measures | | Rel Category |
|---|---|---|
| Price/Earnings | 21.59 | 0.98 |
| Price/Book | 2.73 | 0.92 |
| Price/Sales | 1.41 | 0.95 |
| Price/Cash Flow | 7.84 | 0.92 |
| Dividend Yield % | 0.32 | 1.10 |

| Growth Measures | % | Rel Category |
|---|---|---|
| Long-Term Erngs | 16.32 | 0.94 |
| Book Value | 8.08 | 0.87 |
| Sales | 10.88 | 0.89 |
| Cash Flow | 10.08 | 0.62 |
| Historical Erngs | 16.77 | 0.83 |

| Profitability | % | Rel Category |
|---|---|---|
| Return on Equity | 13.04 | 0.95 |
| Return on Assets | 6.49 | 0.92 |
| Net Margin | 9.27 | 1.06 |

| Sector Weightings | % of Stocks | Rel S&P 500 | 3 Year High Low | |
|---|---|---|---|---|
| ⊙ Info | 23.44 | 1.16 | | |
| Software | 7.89 | 2.22 | 9 | 4 |
| Hardware | 10.48 | 1.04 | 18 | 6 |
| Media | 2.37 | 0.66 | 4 | 2 |
| Telecom | 2.70 | 0.90 | 3 | 0 |
| ⊆ Service | 52.85 | 1.14 | | |
| Health | 17.64 | 1.33 | 23 | 18 |
| Consumer | 11.47 | 1.41 | 17 | 11 |
| Business | 14.01 | 3.62 | 14 | 7 |
| Financial | 9.73 | 0.46 | 17 | 8 |
| ⊟ Mfg | 23.73 | 0.71 | | |
| Goods | 5.15 | 0.60 | 8 | 4 |
| Ind Mtrls | 9.17 | 0.75 | 17 | 7 |
| Energy | 9.32 | 1.00 | 10 | 2 |
| Utilities | 0.09 | 0.03 | 0 | 0 |

### Composition

| | | % |
|---|---|---|
| ● | Cash | 0.0 |
| ● | Stocks | 100.0 |
| ● | Bonds | 0.0 |
| | Other | 0.0 |
| | Foreign | 0.8 |
| | (% of Stock) | |

## Morningstar's Take by Dan Culloton

This exchange-traded fund has a better new benchmark, but it's still not the best.

StreetTracks Dow Jones Wilshire Small Cap Growth ETF has a lot to offer long-term investors. The fund tracks a benchmark that relies on up-to-date, multivariate index-construction methods, so it should do a good job of capturing the return of the small-cap growth market without too much turnover. The most recent expense ratio of 0.26% also is lower than the vast majority of rival exchange-traded and traditional funds.

The offering is actually switching its benchmark, but this shouldn't result in dramatic changes. The ETF, which used to draw its constituents from the Dow Jones U.S. Small Cap Growth Index, is switching to a bogy that uses Dow Jones Wilshire 5000 stocks ranking from 751 to 2,500 in size as a starting point. The switch will scramble the fund's holdings a bit, but its exposures should not change much. The benchmark uses the same six valuation and growth factors as the ETF's previous bogy to

sort stocks into the growth or value camp. The new index, however, does have clear rules that will keep it from automatically kicking out stocks on the benchmark's size and style borders, which should control turnover.

Because the benchmark trolls a universe of 1,750 companies, the ETF could end up holding more individual stocks and keeping less money in the mid-cap area. A healthy dose of industrial stocks, such as electric instrument and motor manufacturer Ametek, should be expected, as should big stakes in tech and consumer stocks.

As a result, the offering should correlate closely with other index funds that cover this area. But investors should still opt for other choices. Expenses play a huge role in differentiating index funds covering the same ground, and this ETF's expense ratio, while low, is not the lowest available. All things being equal, go with the cheaper fund.

| Address: | State Street Bank & Tr, 225 Franklin St Boston MA 02210 866-787-2257 |
|---|---|
| Web Address: | www.advisors.ssga.com |
| Inception: | 09-25-00* |
| Advisor: | SSGA Funds Management, Inc. |

| Management Fee: | 0.25% | | |
|---|---|---|---|
| Expense Projections: | 3Yr:$81 | 5Yr:$141 | 10Yr:$320 |
| Income Distrib: | Quarterly | | |
| Exchange: | AMEX | | |

MORNINGSTAR® ETFs 100

# streetTRACKS DJ Small Val

| | Ticker | NAV | Market Price | 52 wk High/Low | Yield | Mstar Category |
|---|---|---|---|---|---|---|
| | DSV | $60.58 | $63.11 | $64.26 - $53.58 | 1.8% | Small Value |

## Management

### Portfolio Manager(s)

SSgA Funds Management is this ETF's advisor. Karl Schneider and John Tucker are the principal members of the fund's management team. Schneider has been with SSgA since 1996 and manages more than $400 billion in funds and accounts, including some tracking the Wilshire 5000, Russell 2000, and Wilshire 4500. Tucker is the head of the portfolio management team for the firm's ETFs. He's the former head of SSgA's structured products group in the firm's London office. Tucker also is responsible for new-product research and development.

### Strategy

This fund tracks the Dow Jones Wilshire Small Cap Value Index. The bogy uses six factors to sort the small cap stocks in the Dow Jones Wilshire 5000 into value or growth buckets. Stocks' style scores are based on their projected price/earnings, projected earnings growth, and price/book ratios; dividend yield, trailing revenue growth, and trailing earnings growth. Half the universe's float-adjusted market cap ends up in value and half in growth. Buffer zones keep constituents from jumping in and out of the index due to market cap or style score changes. It rebalances in March and December.

**Growth of $10,000**

— Investment Value of ETF
— Investment Value of Index S&P 500

| | 1996 | 1997 | 1998 | 1999 | 2000 | 2001 | 2002 | 2003 | 2004 | 2005 | History |
|---|---|---|---|---|---|---|---|---|---|---|---|
| | — | — | — | — | 39.70 | 42.16 | 39.66 | 54.16 | 60.27 | 60.58 | NAV $ |
| | — | — | — | — | 39.25 | 42.38 | 39.70 | 54.20 | 60.40 | 60.50 | Market Price $ |
| | — | — | — | — | 16.04* | 12.51 | -2.74 | 43.00 | 18.06 | 2.29 | NAV Return% |
| | — | — | — | — | 16.01* | 14.41 | -3.15 | 42.96 | 18.22 | 1.93 | Market Price Return% |
| | — | — | — | — | -1.29 | 0.22 | 0.03 | 0.04 | -0.14 | -0.13 | Avg Premium/Discount% |
| | — | — | — | — | 16.04 | 24.39 | 19.35 | 14.33 | 7.19 | -2.62 | NAV Rtrn% +/-S&P 500 |
| | — | — | — | — | 16.04 | -1.51 | 8.69 | -3.03 | -4.19 | -2.42 | NAV Rtrn% +/-Russ 2000 VL |
| | — | — | — | — | — | 3 | 3 | 3 | 3 | 5 | NAV Return% Rank in Cat |
| | — | — | — | — | 0.00 | 2.07 | 2.66 | 2.61 | 1.94 | 1.81 | Income Return % |
| | — | — | — | — | — | 10.44 | -5.40 | 40.39 | 16.12 | 0.48 | Capital Return % |
| | — | — | — | — | 0.31 | 0.82 | 1.11 | 1.03 | 1.04 | 1.08 | Income $ |
| | — | — | — | — | 0.00 | 1.58 | 0.30 | 1.18 | 2.49 | 0.00 | Capital Gains $ |
| | — | — | — | — | — | 0.28 | 0.28 | 0.29 | 0.27 | 0.26 | Expense Ratio % |
| | — | — | — | — | — | 2.70 | 2.31 | 2.76 | 1.88 | 2.00 | Income Ratio % |
| | — | — | — | — | — | 47 | 29 | 43 | 54 | 33 | Turnover Rate % |
| | — | — | — | — | — | 42 | 57 | 99 | 97 | Net Assets $mil |

## Performance

### Historic Quarterly NAV Returns

| | 1st Qtr | 2nd Qtr | 3rd Qtr | 4th Qtr | Total |
|---|---|---|---|---|---|
| 2001 | -1.09 | 10.65 | -9.14 | 13.14 | 12.51 |
| 2002 | 11.35 | -2.42 | -13.92 | 3.99 | -2.74 |
| 2003 | -5.69 | 22.69 | 5.16 | 17.52 | 43.00 |
| 2004 | 7.11 | -1.01 | -0.93 | 12.39 | 18.06 |
| 2005 | -5.00 | 3.83 | 5.81 | -1.99 | 2.29 |

| Trailing | NAV Return% | Market Return% | NAV Rtrn% +/-S&P 500 | %Rank Cat.(NAV) |
|---|---|---|---|---|
| 3 Mo | -1.99 | -1.91 | -4.07 | 6 |
| 6 Mo | 3.70 | 3.27 | -2.06 | 6 |
| 1 Yr | 2.29 | 1.93 | -2.62 | 5 |
| 3 Yr Avg | 19.97 | 19.88 | 5.59 | 3 |
| 5 Yr Avg | 13.57 | 13.80 | 13.03 | 3 |
| 10 Yr Avg | — | — | — | 0 |

| Tax Analysis | Tax-Adj Return% | Tax-Cost Ratio |
|---|---|---|
| 3 Yr (estimated) | 18.43 | 1.28 |
| 5 Yr (estimated) | 11.93 | 1.44 |
| 10 Yr (estimated) | — | — |

## Risk Profile

| | Standard Index S&P 500 | Best Fit Index Russ 2000 VL |
|---|---|---|
| Alpha | 0.0 | -2.8 |
| Beta | 1.46 | 1.01 |
| R-Squared | 83 | 96 |
| Standard Deviation | 14.71 | |
| Mean | 19.97 | |
| Sharpe Ratio | 1.18 | |

## Morningstar Fair Value

| Price/Fair Value Ratio | Fair Value Estimate ($) | Hit Rate % |
|---|---|---|
| | | |

## Portfolio Analysis 12-31-05

| Share change since 11-05 Total Stocks:871 | Sector | PE | Tot Ret% | % Assets |
|---|---|---|---|---|
| ⊕ AMR | Business | — | 103.01 | 0.42 |
| ⊖ PartnerRe | Financial | 37.5 | 8.57 | 0.41 |
| ⊕ Aqua America | Utilities | 38.3 | 50.76 | 0.40 |
| ⊖ Carolina Group | Financial | — | 60.13 | 0.39 |
| ⊖ Ventas | Financial | 26.5 | 22.74 | 0.37 |
| ⊖ CMS Energy | Utilities | — | 38.85 | 0.36 |
| ⊖ Federal Realty Investmen | Financial | 46.0 | 22.33 | 0.36 |
| ⊖ Renaissance Re Holdings | Financial | 26.3 | -13.80 | 0.36 |
| ⊖ LSI Logic | Hardware | — | 45.99 | 0.35 |
| ⊖ Compuware | Software | 28.9 | 39.94 | 0.35 |
| ⊖ SL Green Realty | Financial | 35.2 | 30.54 | 0.35 |
| ⊖ Goodyear Tire & Rubber | Ind Mtrls | 8.3 | 18.55 | 0.34 |
| ⊖ Rayonier | Ind Mtrls | 18.9 | 28.10 | 0.34 |
| ⊖ Camden Property Trust | Financial | 19.8 | 19.14 | 0.34 |
| ⊖ Arden Realty | Financial | 95.4 | 25.34 | 0.34 |
| ⊖ Vintage Petroleum | Energy | 18.3 | 136.37 | 0.34 |
| ⊖ Allegheny Technologies | Ind Mtrls | 12.9 | 68.22 | 0.34 |
| ⊖ CNF | Business | 15.0 | 12.48 | 0.34 |
| ⊖ Terex | Ind Mtrls | — | 24.66 | 0.33 |
| ⊖ Reckson Associates Realt | Financial | 19.1 | 15.38 | 0.33 |

### Current Investment Style

Value Blnd Growth — Large Mid Small

| | Market Cap | % |
|---|---|---|
| | Giant | 0.0 |
| | Large | 0.0 |
| | Mid | 47.5 |
| | Small | 48.1 |
| | Micro | 4.4 |
| | Avg $mil: | 1,420 |

| Value Measures | | Rel Category |
|---|---|---|
| Price/Earnings | 15.27 | 1.03 |
| Price/Book | 1.76 | 1.01 |
| Price/Sales | 0.86 | 1.06 |
| Price/Cash Flow | 6.75 | 1.02 |
| Dividend Yield % | 2.18 | 1.14 |

| Growth Measures | % | Rel Category |
|---|---|---|
| Long-Term Erngs | 10.22 | 0.96 |
| Book Value | 4.33 | 0.77 |
| Sales | 2.74 | 0.60 |
| Cash Flow | -0.84 | NMF |
| Historical Erngs | 9.97 | 1.01 |

| Profitability | % | Rel Category |
|---|---|---|
| Return on Equity | 11.11 | 0.97 |
| Return on Assets | 6.70 | 0.96 |
| Net Margin | 11.09 | 1.06 |

### Sector Weightings

| | % of Stocks | Rel S&P 500 | 3 Year High Low | |
|---|---|---|---|---|
| ⟳ Info | 9.90 | 0.49 | | |
| 🖥 Software | 1.18 | 0.33 | 5 | 0 |
| 💾 Hardware | 6.27 | 0.62 | 12 | 3 |
| 🔊 Media | 1.66 | 0.46 | 2 | 1 |
| 📶 Telecom | 0.79 | 0.26 | 2 | 0 |
| Ⓢ Service | 54.39 | 1.17 | | |
| 🩺 Health | 2.32 | 0.17 | 4 | 2 |
| Consumer | 7.50 | 0.92 | 10 | 7 |
| 🏢 Business | 8.13 | 2.10 | 8 | 5 |
| $ Financial | 36.44 | 1.73 | 43 | 29 |
| ⟱ Mfg | 35.69 | 1.07 | | |
| 🏭 Goods | 5.25 | 0.61 | 6 | 4 |
| ⚙ Ind Mtrls | 18.65 | 1.53 | 19 | 14 |
| 🔆 Energy | 4.36 | 0.47 | 6 | 2 |
| 💡 Utilities | 7.43 | 2.21 | 14 | 7 |

### Composition

| | |
|---|---|
| ● Cash | 0.3 |
| ● Stocks | 99.7 |
| ● Bonds | 0.0 |
| ○ Other | 0.0 |
| Foreign | 0.8 |
| (% of Stock) | |

## Morningstar's Take by Dan Culloton

A new benchmark improves this fund, but there are still better options.

StreetTracks Dow Jones Wilshire Small Cap Value ETF has a lot to offer long-term investors. The fund tracks a benchmark that relies on up-to-date, multivariate index-construction methods, so it should do a good job of capturing the return of the small-cap growth market without too much turnover. The most recent expense ratio of 0.26% also is lower than the vast majority of rival exchange-traded and traditional funds.

The offering is actually switching its benchmark, but this shouldn't result in dramatic changes. The ETF, which used to draw its constituents from the Dow Jones U.S. Small Cap Value Index, is switching to a bogy that uses Dow Jones Wilshire 5000 stocks ranking from 751 to 2,500 in size as a starting point. The switch will scramble the fund's holdings a bit, but its exposures should not change much. The benchmark uses the same six valuation and growth factors as the ETF's previous bogy to

sort stocks into the growth or value camp. The new index, however, does have clear rules that will keep it from automatically kicking out stocks on the benchmark's size and style borders, which should control turnover.

Because the benchmark trolls a universe of 1,750 companies, the ETF could end up holding more individual stocks and keeping less money in the mid-cap area. A very large helping of financial stocks (about a third of assets) should be expected. That includes a healthy stake of REITs such as Camden Property Trust and Reckson Associates Realty, which, given the way REIT yields have fallen in the last five years, adds some risk.

Nevertheless, this offering should correlate closely with other index funds that cover this area. But investors should still opt for other choices. This ETF's expense ratio, while low, is not the lowest available. All things being equal, go with the cheaper fund.

| Address: | State Street Bank & Tr, 225 Franklin St Boston MA 02210 866-787-2257 | Management Fee: | 0.25% |
|---|---|---|---|
| | | Expense Projections: | 3Yr:$81  5Yr:$141  10Yr:$320 |
| Web Address: | www.advisors.ssga.com | Income Distrib: | Quarterly |
| Inception: | 09-25-00 * | Exchange: | AMEX |
| Advisor: | SSGA Funds Management, Inc. | | |

MORNINGSTAR® ETFs 100

# streetTRACKS Total Market

| Ticker | NAV | Market Price | 52 wk High/Low | Yield | Mstar Category |
|---|---|---|---|---|---|
| TMW | $90.02 | $93.24 | $93.24 - $81.33 | 1.5% | Large Blend |

## Management

### Portfolio Manager(s)

SSgA Funds Management is this ETF's advisor. Karl Schneider and John Tucker are the principal members of the fund's management team. Schneider has been with SSgA since 1996 and manages more than $400 billion in funds and accounts, including some tracking the Wilshire 5000, Russell 2000, and Wilshire 4500. Tucker is the head of the portfolio management team for the firm's ETFs. He's the former head of SSgA's structured products group in the firm's London office. Tucker also is responsible for new-product research and development.

### Strategy

This fund used to track the Fortune 500, an index of the largest U.S. companies as determined by revenues. Fortune, however, has said it no longer will calculate and publish the index for investment purposes (though it will still run it in its magazine), so this fund has switched to the Dow Jones Wilshire 5000 Index. The latter bogy includes virtually every U.S.-based stock. This fund is now the only ETF tracking the Dow Jones Wilshire 5000. Vanguard Total Stock Market Vipers, which had been tracking the Wilshire 5000, recently switched its benchmark to the MSCI U.S. Broad Market Index.

## Performance

### Historic Quarterly NAV Returns

|  | 1st Qtr | 2nd Qtr | 3rd Qtr | 4th Qtr | Total |
|---|---|---|---|---|---|
| 2001 | -10.05 | 5.43 | -13.48 | 9.47 | -10.18 |
| 2002 | 0.75 | -12.65 | -16.73 | 7.52 | -21.22 |
| 2003 | -3.43 | 14.77 | 2.30 | 11.68 | 26.62 |
| 2004 | 1.35 | 1.32 | -1.68 | 8.98 | 10.03 |
| 2005 | -1.32 | 1.61 | 4.21 | 2.20 | 6.78 |

| Trailing | NAV Return% | Market Return% | NAV Rtrn% +/-S&P 500 | %Rank Cat.(NAV) |
|---|---|---|---|---|
| 3 Mo | 2.20 | 2.52 | 0.12 | 27 |
| 6 Mo | 6.49 | 6.04 | 0.73 | 27 |
| 1 Yr | 6.78 | 6.54 | 1.87 | 23 |
| 3 Yr Avg | 14.16 | 14.36 | -0.22 | 14 |
| 5 Yr Avg | 1.03 | 1.06 | 0.49 | 13 |
| 10 Yr Avg | — | — | — | 0 |

| Tax Analysis | Tax-Adj Return% | Tax-Cost Ratio |
|---|---|---|
| 3 Yr (estimated) | 13.50 | 0.58 |
| 5 Yr (estimated) | 0.46 | 0.56 |
| 10 Yr (estimated) | — | — |

Growth of $10,000
— Investment Value of ETF
— Investment Value of Index S&P 500

| | 1996 | 1997 | 1998 | 1999 | 2000 | 2001 | 2002 | 2003 | 2004 | 2005 | History |
|---|---|---|---|---|---|---|---|---|---|---|---|
| | — | — | — | — | 92.42 | 81.86 | 63.61 | 79.30 | 85.62 | 90.02 | NAV $ |
| | — | — | — | — | 92.42 | 81.93 | 63.36 | 79.20 | 85.94 | 90.16 | Market Price $ |
| | — | — | — | — | -0.06* | -10.18 | -21.22 | 26.62 | 10.03 | 6.78 | NAV Return% |
| | — | — | — | — | -0.04* | -10.11 | -21.60 | 26.97 | 10.57 | 6.54 | Market Price Return% |
| | — | — | — | — | -0.49 | 0.11 | -0.05 | -0.05 | 0.04 | -0.01 | Avg Premium/Discount% |
| | — | — | — | — | -0.06 | 1.70 | 0.87 | -2.05 | -0.84 | 1.87 | NAV Rtrn% +/-S&P 500 |
| | — | — | — | — | -0.06 | 2.27 | 0.43 | -3.27 | -1.37 | 0.51 | NAV Rtrn% +/-Russ 1000 |
| | — | — | — | — | — | 13 | 15 | 15 | 17 | 23 | NAV Return% Rank in Cat |
| | — | — | — | — | 0.00 | 1.19 | 1.15 | 1.78 | 1.96 | 1.60 | Income Return % |
| | — | — | — | — | — | -11.37 | -22.37 | 24.84 | 8.07 | 5.18 | Capital Return % |
| | — | — | — | — | 0.22 | 1.09 | 0.94 | 1.13 | 1.55 | 1.36 | Income $ |
| | — | — | — | — | 0.00 | 0.00 | 0.00 | 0.00 | 0.00 | 0.00 | Capital Gains $ |
| | — | — | — | — | — | 0.21 | 0.23 | 0.24 | 0.22 | 0.21 | Expense Ratio % |
| | — | — | — | — | — | 1.06 | 1.25 | 1.65 | 1.59 | 2.05 | Income Ratio % |
| | — | — | — | — | — | 6 | 6 | 6 | 5 | 32 | Turnover Rate % |
| | — | — | — | — | — | 83 | 103 | 120 | 104 | Net Assets $mil |

## Risk Profile

| | Standard Index S&P 500 | Best Fit Index S&P 500 |
|---|---|---|
| Alpha | 0.1 | 0.1 |
| Beta | 0.97 | 0.97 |
| R-Squared | 99 | 99 |
| Standard Deviation | 8.92 | |
| Mean | 14.16 | |
| Sharpe Ratio | 1.31 | |

## Morningstar Fair Value

| Price/Fair Value Ratio | Fair Value Estimate ($) | Hit Rate % |
|---|---|---|
| 1.0 Fairly valued | 36.50 | 90 Good |

## Portfolio Analysis 12-31-05

Share change since 11-05 Total Stocks:819

| | Sector | PE | Tot Ret% | % Assets |
|---|---|---|---|---|
| ⊖ General Electric | Ind Mtrls | 19.9 | -1.43 | 2.54 |
| ⊖ ExxonMobil | Energy | 10.6 | 11.76 | 2.47 |
| ⊖ Microsoft | Software | 22.2 | -0.95 | 1.76 |
| ⊖ Citigroup | Financial | 12.1 | 4.63 | 1.70 |
| ⊖ Procter & Gamble | Goods | 21.2 | 7.18 | 1.32 |
| ⊖ Pfizer | Health | 21.2 | -10.62 | 1.23 |
| ⊖ Bank of America | Financial | 11.1 | 2.39 | 1.23 |
| ⊖ Johnson & Johnson | Health | 19.1 | -3.36 | 1.21 |
| ⊖ Intel | Hardware | 18.6 | 8.12 | 1.09 |
| ⊖ American International G | Financial | 15.6 | 4.83 | 1.09 |
| ⊖ Altria Group | Goods | 15.0 | 27.72 | 1.05 |
| ⊖ IBM | Hardware | 16.0 | -15.83 | 0.95 |
| ⊖ J.P. Morgan Chase & Co. | Financial | 18.8 | 5.74 | 0.95 |
| ⊖ Chevron | Energy | 9.0 | 11.51 | 0.85 |
| ⊖ Wal-Mart Stores | Consumer | 18.2 | -10.30 | 0.80 |
| ⊖ Cisco Systems | Hardware | 19.9 | -11.39 | 0.80 |
| ⊖ Amgen | Health | 28.3 | 22.93 | 0.71 |
| Berkshire Hathaway A | Financial | — | — | 0.69 |
| ⊖ Wells Fargo | Financial | 14.3 | 4.47 | 0.68 |
| ⊖ PepsiCo | Goods | 25.8 | 15.24 | 0.66 |

### Current Investment Style

Value Blnd Growth — Large Mid Small

| Market Cap | % |
|---|---|
| Giant | 42.2 |
| Large | 33.6 |
| Mid | 18.6 |
| Small | 3.0 |
| Micro | 2.5 |

Avg $mil: 26,615

| Value Measures | | Rel Category |
|---|---|---|
| Price/Earnings | 16.66 | 0.98 |
| Price/Book | 2.48 | 0.92 |
| Price/Sales | 1.46 | 1.14 |
| Price/Cash Flow | 6.68 | 0.92 |
| Dividend Yield % | 1.75 | 0.99 |

| Growth Measures | % | Rel Category |
|---|---|---|
| Long-Term Erngs | 11.05 | 0.99 |
| Book Value | 9.77 | 1.04 |
| Sales | 8.29 | 1.03 |
| Cash Flow | 11.32 | 1.10 |
| Historical Erngs | 14.77 | 1.04 |

| Profitability | % | Rel Category |
|---|---|---|
| Return on Equity | 18.35 | 0.90 |
| Return on Assets | 9.89 | 1.06 |
| Net Margin | 12.99 | 1.19 |

### Sector Weightings

| | % of Stocks | Rel S&P 500 | 3 Year High | Low |
|---|---|---|---|---|
| ☎ Info | 20.28 | 1.00 | | |
| Software | 3.82 | 1.07 | 5 | 3 |
| Hardware | 10.01 | 1.00 | 11 | 8 |
| Media | 3.63 | 1.01 | 5 | 4 |
| Telecom | 2.82 | 0.94 | 4 | 3 |
| ☞ Service | 48.22 | 1.04 | | |
| Health | 12.59 | 0.95 | 15 | 12 |
| Consumer | 8.86 | 1.09 | 11 | 9 |
| Business | 5.23 | 1.35 | 5 | 4 |
| Financial | 21.54 | 1.02 | 22 | 19 |
| Mfg | 31.51 | 0.94 | | |
| Goods | 7.64 | 0.89 | 10 | 8 |
| Ind Mtrls | 11.37 | 0.94 | 13 | 11 |
| Energy | 9.25 | 0.99 | 10 | 5 |
| Utilities | 3.25 | 0.97 | 4 | 3 |

### Composition

| | |
|---|---|
| ● Cash | 0.3 |
| ● Stocks | 99.7 |
| ● Bonds | 0.0 |
| ● Other | 0.0 |
| Foreign | 0.0 |
| (% of Stock) | |

## Morningstar's Take by Dan Culloton

This exchange traded fund has dumped the Fortune 500 for the whole market.

This ETF used to be called StreetTracks Fortune 500 Index, but in 2005 it switched its benchmark from the Fortune 500 to the Dow Jones Wilshire 5000 Index and its name to StreetTracks Total Market ETF. Fortune Inc. is no longer publishing its 500 index for investment purposes.

Not many people should miss the Fortune 500 ETF. Despite using a household name for a benchmark, the Fortune 500 fund attracted little interest over its five-year life span. Even now the fund has little more than $100 million in assets and a low trading volume.

The Wilshire 5000 is a better choice for a benchmark. The old offering was a gimmick. It was the only way to invest in Fortune's list of the largest U.S. companies, but it was not the only way to get exposure to those types of stocks. Rival large blend index funds offered similar exposure for lower expense ratios.

That said, it's hard to see why an investor who signed on here would want to swap the Fortune 500 for a Wilshire 5000 fund. True, you can find virtually everything in the Fortune 500 in the Wilshire 5000. But there's more, too. The Wilshire 5000 has more than three times the exposure to small-cap stocks than the Fortune 500. The Wilshire 5000 also owns more software, hardware, media, and business- and financial-services stocks than the Fortune 500.

There is nothing wrong with the Wilshire 5000, which tracks every U.S. stock. It ably served as the bogy for Vanguard Total Stock Market Index for more than 12 years until that fund switched its benchmark this year to MSCI's all-market index. However, a total-market fund may not have been what investors wanted when they bought this ETF. Even if investors don't mind trading a mega-cap stock fund for a total-market offering, other funds cover the territory for less.

| Address: | State Street Bank & Tr, 225 Franklin St Boston MA 02210 866-787-2257 |
|---|---|
| Web Address: | www.advisors.ssga.com |
| Inception: | 10-04-00 * |
| Advisor: | SSGA Funds Management, Inc. |

| Management Fee: | 0.20% | | |
|---|---|---|---|
| Expense Projections: | 3Yr:$65 | 5Yr:$113 | 10Yr:$257 |
| Income Distrib: | Quarterly | | |
| Exchange: | AMEX | | |

M⊃RNINGSTAR® ETFs 100

# streetTRACKS WR REIT

| | Ticker | NAV | Market Price | 52 wk High/Low | Yield | Mstar Category |
|---|---|---|---|---|---|---|
| | RWR | $67.52 | $71.91 | $71.91 - $56.83 | 5.9% | Specialty-Real Estate |

## Management

### Portfolio Manager(s)

The Tuckerman Group, a subsidiary of SSgA that manages $2 billion in real estate investments, runs this fund. The Purchase, N.Y.-based firm uses a replication approach to run the fund. That means it tries to own all of the securities in the index.

### Strategy

This exchange-traded fund tracks the Wilshire REIT Index. It's a benchmark of about 90 stocks that derive at least three fourths of their revenue from the equity ownership or operation of real estate. The bogey rebalances monthly but makes additions quarterly and deletions at year-end.

**Growth of $10,000**

— Investment Value of ETF
— Investment Value of Index S&P 500

| 1996 | 1997 | 1998 | 1999 | 2000 | 2001 | 2002 | 2003 | 2004 | 2005 | History |
|---|---|---|---|---|---|---|---|---|---|---|
| — | — | — | — | — | 39.38 | 38.67 | 49.83 | 62.54 | 67.52 | NAV $ |
| — | — | — | — | — | 39.56 | 38.76 | 49.93 | 62.53 | 67.50 | Market Price $ |
| — | — | — | — | — | 20.66* | 2.88 | 35.58 | 32.75 | 14.51 | NAV Return% |
| — | — | — | — | — | 20.65* | 2.66 | 35.51 | 32.46 | 14.50 | Market Price Return% |
| — | — | — | — | — | 0.07 | 0.23 | 0.06 | -0.05 | 0.09 | Avg Premium/Discount% |
| — | — | — | — | — | 20.66 | 24.97 | 6.91 | 21.88 | 9.60 | NAV Rtrn% +/-S&P 500 |
| — | — | — | — | — | 20.66 | -0.72 | -0.48 | -0.39 | 0.51 | NAV Rtrn% +/-DJ Wilshire REIT |
| — | — | — | — | — | — | 3 | 3 | 3 | 4 | NAV Return% Rank in Cat |
| — | — | — | — | — | 0.00 | 4.93 | 5.43 | 6.41 | 6.47 | Income Return % |
| — | — | — | — | — | — | -2.05 | 30.15 | 26.34 | 8.04 | Capital Return % |
| — | — | — | — | — | 1.71 | 1.91 | 2.06 | 3.12 | 3.98 | Income $ |
| — | — | — | — | — | 0.23 | 0.00 | 0.16 | 0.00 | 0.00 | Capital Gains $ |
| — | — | — | — | — | 0.32 | 0.30 | 0.28 | 0.26 | 0.26 | Expense Ratio % |
| — | — | — | — | — | 6.88 | 6.74 | 6.95 | 5.23 | 5.06 | Income Ratio % |
| — | — | — | — | — | 2 | 15 | 10 | 15 | 12 | Turnover Rate % |
| — | — | — | — | — | — | 87 | 284 | 535 | 604 | Net Assets $mil |

## Performance

### Historic Quarterly NAV Returns

| | 1st Qtr | 2nd Qtr | 3rd Qtr | 4th Qtr | Total |
|---|---|---|---|---|---|
| 2001 | — | — | -2.38 | 4.79 | —* |
| 2002 | 8.26 | 4.43 | -9.11 | 0.11 | 2.88 |
| 2003 | 1.20 | 11.96 | 9.77 | 9.02 | 35.58 |
| 2004 | 11.99 | -5.38 | 8.17 | 15.82 | 32.75 |
| 2005 | -7.23 | 14.50 | 3.88 | 3.77 | 14.51 |

| Trailing | NAV Return% | Market Return% | NAV Rtrn% +/-S&P 500 | %Rank Cat.(NAV) |
|---|---|---|---|---|
| 3 Mo | 3.77 | 3.88 | 1.69 | 4 |
| 6 Mo | 7.80 | 7.70 | 2.04 | 4 |
| 1 Yr | 14.51 | 14.50 | 9.60 | 4 |
| 3 Yr Avg | 27.26 | 27.14 | 12.88 | 3 |
| 5 Yr Avg | — | — | — | 0 |
| 10 Yr Avg | — | — | — | 0 |

| Tax Analysis | Tax-Adj Return% | Tax-Cost Ratio |
|---|---|---|
| 3 Yr (estimated) | 24.86 | 1.89 |
| 5 Yr (estimated) | — | — |
| 10 Yr (estimated) | — | — |

## Risk Profile

| | Standard Index S&P 500 | Best Fit Index DJ Wilshire REIT |
|---|---|---|
| Alpha | 14.6 | 0.1 |
| Beta | 0.75 | 0.99 |
| R-Squared | 20 | 100 |
| Standard Deviation | 15.58 | |
| Mean | 27.26 | |
| Sharpe Ratio | 1.52 | |

## Morningstar Fair Value

| Price/Fair Value Ratio | Fair Value Estimate ($) | Hit Rate % |
|---|---|---|
| 1.2 Overvalued | 42.87 | 86 Good |

## Portfolio Analysis  12-31-05

Share change since 11-05  Total Stocks:93

| | Sector | PE | Tot Ret% | % Assets |
|---|---|---|---|---|
| ⊖ Simon Property Group | Financial | 57.2 | 23.30 | 6.83 |
| ⊖ Equity Office Properties | Financial | — | 10.93 | 4.97 |
| ⊖ ProLogis Trust | Financial | 32.0 | 11.73 | 4.57 |
| ⊖ Equity Residential | Financial | 75.2 | 13.37 | 4.53 |
| ⊖ Vornado Realty Trust | Financial | 19.4 | 15.15 | 4.43 |
| ⊖ General Growth Propertie | Financial | NMF | 35.15 | 4.23 |
| ⊖ Archstone-Smith Trust | Financial | 55.1 | 14.47 | 3.58 |
| ⊖ Boston Properties | Financial | 24.8 | 23.57 | 3.36 |
| ⊖ Kimco Realty | Financial | 24.5 | 15.41 | 2.76 |
| ⊖ AvalonBay Communities | Financial | 60.7 | 22.84 | 2.62 |
| ⊖ Host Marriott | Financial | 94.8 | 12.16 | 2.49 |
| ⊖ Public Storage | Financial | 36.2 | 25.10 | 2.42 |
| ⊖ Developers Diversified R | Financial | 20.4 | 11.07 | 2.06 |
| ⊖ Duke Realty | Financial | 41.8 | 6.98 | 1.93 |
| ⊖ AMB Property | Financial | 47.7 | 26.78 | 1.69 |
| ⊖ Macerich | Financial | 79.9 | 11.47 | 1.60 |
| ⊖ Liberty Property Trust | Financial | 25.4 | 5.19 | 1.53 |
| ⊖ Regency Centers | Financial | 33.1 | 10.80 | 1.45 |
| ⊖ Apartment Investment & M | Financial | — | 4.57 | 1.45 |
| ⊖ United Dominion Realty | Financial | — | -0.30 | 1.30 |

### Current Investment Style

Value Blnd Growth — Large Mid Small

| Market Cap | % |
|---|---|
| Giant | 0.0 |
| Large | 29.9 |
| Mid | 56.8 |
| Small | 12.1 |
| Micro | 1.1 |
| Avg $mil: | 4,608 |

| Value Measures | | Rel Category |
|---|---|---|
| Price/Earnings | 16.24 | 1.02 |
| Price/Book | 2.56 | 1.00 |
| Price/Sales | 4.82 | 1.01 |
| Price/Cash Flow | 13.44 | 1.01 |
| Dividend Yield % | 4.19 | 0.97 |

| Growth Measures | % | Rel Category |
|---|---|---|
| Long-Term Erngs | 6.82 | 1.02 |
| Book Value | -1.86 | NMF |
| Sales | 3.30 | 0.73 |
| Cash Flow | -67.57 | NMF |
| Historical Erngs | -3.46 | NMF |

| Profitability | % | Rel Category |
|---|---|---|
| Return on Equity | 9.68 | 0.94 |
| Return on Assets | 8.59 | 0.95 |
| Net Margin | 23.49 | 0.94 |

| Sector Weightings | % of Stocks | Rel S&P 500 | 3 Year High | Low |
|---|---|---|---|---|
| ↻ Info | 0.00 | 0.00 | | |
| 🖥 Software | 0.00 | 0.00 | 0 | 0 |
| 💻 Hardware | 0.00 | 0.00 | 0 | 0 |
| 📶 Media | 0.00 | 0.00 | 0 | 0 |
| ☎ Telecom | 0.00 | 0.00 | 0 | 0 |
| ⊑ Service | 100.00 | 2.16 | | |
| 🏥 Health | 0.00 | 0.00 | 0 | 0 |
| 🛒 Consumer | 0.35 | 0.04 | 0 | 0 |
| 📋 Business | 0.00 | 0.00 | 0 | 0 |
| 💲 Financial | 99.65 | 4.72 | 100 | 100 |
| ⊏ Mfg | 0.00 | 0.00 | | |
| 🏭 Goods | 0.00 | 0.00 | 0 | 0 |
| ⚙ Ind Mtrls | 0.00 | 0.00 | 0 | 0 |
| ⛽ Energy | 0.00 | 0.00 | 0 | 0 |
| 💧 Utilities | 0.00 | 0.00 | 0 | 0 |

### Composition

| | | |
|---|---|---|
| ● Cash | 0.2 | |
| ● Stocks | 99.8 | |
| ● Bonds | 0.0 | |
| Other | 0.0 | |
| Foreign | 0.0 | |
| (% of Stock) | | |

## Morningstar's Take  by Dan Culloton

StreetTRACKS Wilshire REIT Fund has some but not all of the advantages.

This fund has a low expense ratio and is more diversified than some of its passively managed peers in the real estate category. Those are positive traits, but there are options out there that cover much of the same territory for lower fees.

The ETF's subadvisor, SSgA subsidiary The Tuckerman Group, has done a good job tracking this fund's benchmark index. The Wilshire REIT Index tracks a substantial part of the US REIT market. It typically owns about 90 or so stocks and spreads its money across more small-cap issues than rivals such as iShares Cohen & Steers Realty Majors and iShares Dow Jones US Real Estate. The added diversification could afford this fund a smoother ride. To date, however, these funds' volatility measures, such as standard deviation, have tended to stick close together.

This fund offers cheap, convenient, and pure access to the real estate asset class. Like other index funds in this category, though, it doesn't have an impressive relative record. Traditional actively managed funds in this group often have beat the average index offering through extra detective work or by betting on securities outside of the benchmarks. This ETF has been no exception. It has posted strong absolute returns since its April 2001 inception but has lagged the typical traditional real estate fund.

The fund also suffers by not being the cheapest of the lot. The results of all of the competing ETFs and index funds in this category have correlated closely in recent years. If the pattern holds, the biggest difference among the offerings in the future may be expenses. This fund's 0.26% expense ratio is a fraction of the average levy in the traditional real estate fund category, but it's still more expensive than both the investor and exchange-traded share classes of Vanguard's REIT index fund. You won't veer too far from the mark with this fund, but there are other options.

| | | | | |
|---|---|---|---|---|
| Address: | State Street Bank & Tr, 225 Franklin St Boston MA 02210 866-787-2257 | Management Fee: | 0.25% | |
| | | Expense Projections: | 3Yr:$81   5Yr:$141   10Yr:$320 | |
| Web Address: | www.advisors.ssga.com | Income Distrib: | Quarterly | |
| Inception: | 04-23-01* | Exchange: | AMEX | |
| Advisor: | SSGA Funds Management, Inc. | | | |

# Technology SPDR

| | Ticker | NAV | Market Price | 52 wk High/Low | Yield | Mstar Category |
|---|---|---|---|---|---|---|
| | XLK | $20.92 | $22.05 | $22.07 - $18.47 | 0.7% | Specialty-Technology |

## Management

### Portfolio Manager(s)

State Street Global Advisors serves as advisor to the trust, but the creation of the index tracked by the portfolio falls to Merrill Lynch Pierce Fenner & Smith. They allocate stocks in the S&P 500 to the sector they think is appropriate. The American Stock Exchange Index Services Group rebalances holdings based on periodic index adjustments and diversification requirements.

### Strategy

This fund contains all the technology companies in the S&P 500 Index, which screens its components for profitability, industry leadership, and certain trading criteria. The index is limited to U.S. companies, which eliminates some big international technology players, including Nokia. The fund holds 90 stocks, giving it some diversification, but it keeps more than one third of its assets are in its top five stocks. S&P's index committee controls which stocks are included in the broader S&P 500, but Merrill Lynch Pierce Fenner & Smith decides what stocks belong here.

### Growth of $10,000

— Investment Value of ETF
— Investment Value of Index S&P 500

| | 1996 | 1997 | 1998 | 1999 | 2000 | 2001 | 2002 | 2003 | 2004 | 2005 | History |
|---|---|---|---|---|---|---|---|---|---|---|---|
| | — | — | 32.64 | 54.19 | 31.32 | 24.13 | 14.82 | 20.47 | 21.12 | 20.92 | NAV $ |
| | — | — | 32.62 | 53.88 | 31.31 | 24.00 | 14.80 | 20.38 | 21.11 | 20.90 | Market Price $ |
| | — | — | -5.39* | 66.03 | -42.20 | -22.96 | -38.42 | 39.08 | 5.26 | -0.26 | NAV Return% |
| | — | — | -5.42* | 65.18 | -41.89 | -23.35 | -38.17 | 38.68 | 5.66 | -0.31 | Market Price Return% |
| | — | — | -0.06 | -0.05 | 0.02 | 0.09 | -0.13 | -0.07 | 0.00 | -0.06 | Avg Premium/Discount% |
| | — | — | -5.39 | 44.99 | -33.10 | -11.08 | -16.33 | 10.41 | -5.61 | -5.17 | NAV Rtrn% +/-S&P 500 |
| | — | — | -5.39 | -50.37 | -25.98 | -7.37 | -5.09 | -13.06 | -6.47 | -7.62 | NAV Rtrn% +/-ArcaEx Tech 100 |
| | — | — | — | 1 | 1 | 3 | 8 | 8 | 8 | 9 | NAV Return% Rank in Cat |
| | — | — | — | 0.00 | 0.00 | 0.00 | 0.17 | 0.95 | 2.04 | 0.70 | Income Return % |
| | — | — | — | 66.03 | -42.20 | -22.96 | -38.59 | 38.13 | 3.22 | -0.96 | Capital Return % |
| | — | — | 0.00 | 0.00 | 0.00 | 0.00 | 0.04 | 0.14 | 0.42 | 0.15 | Income $ |
| | — | — | 0.00 | 0.00 | 0.00 | 0.00 | 0.00 | 0.00 | 0.00 | 0.00 | Capital Gains $ |
| | — | — | — | 0.56 | 0.42 | 0.28 | 0.27 | 0.28 | 0.26 | 0.26 | Expense Ratio % |
| | — | — | — | -0.15 | -0.16 | -0.05 | 0.12 | 0.65 | 0.68 | 2.33 | Income Ratio % |
| | — | — | — | 21 | 24 | 11 | 18 | 10 | 3 | 8 | Turnover Rate % |
| | — | — | — | — | — | — | 972 | 1,101 | 1,236 | 1,541 | Net Assets $mil |

## Performance

### Historic Quarterly NAV Returns

| | 1st Qtr | 2nd Qtr | 3rd Qtr | 4th Qtr | Total |
|---|---|---|---|---|---|
| 2001 | -20.69 | 12.08 | -31.11 | 25.81 | -22.96 |
| 2002 | -9.90 | -26.95 | -25.44 | 25.50 | -38.42 |
| 2003 | -3.24 | 18.76 | 7.18 | 12.92 | 39.08 |
| 2004 | -1.22 | 2.12 | -7.46 | 12.76 | 5.26 |
| 2005 | -7.52 | 2.01 | 4.86 | 0.82 | -0.26 |

| Trailing | NAV Return% | Market Return% | NAV Rtrn% +/-S&P 500 | %Rank Cat.(NAV) |
|---|---|---|---|---|
| 3 Mo | 0.82 | 0.69 | -1.26 | 12 |
| 6 Mo | 5.71 | 5.64 | -0.05 | 12 |
| 1 Yr | -0.26 | -0.31 | -5.17 | 9 |
| 3 Yr Avg | 13.45 | 13.46 | -0.93 | 8 |
| 5 Yr Avg | -7.08 | -7.09 | -7.62 | 3 |
| 10 Yr Avg | — | — | — | 0 |

| Tax Analysis | Tax-Adj Return% | Tax-Cost Ratio |
|---|---|---|
| 3 Yr (estimated) | 13.00 | 0.40 |
| 5 Yr (estimated) | -7.32 | 0.26 |
| 10 Yr (estimated) | — | — |

## Risk Profile

| | Standard Index S&P 500 | Best Fit Index ArcaEx Tech 100 |
|---|---|---|
| Alpha | -4.5 | -5.2 |
| Beta | 1.35 | 0.87 |
| R-Squared | 78 | 95 |
| Standard Deviation | 14.04 | |
| Mean | 13.45 | |
| Sharpe Ratio | 0.83 | |

## Morningstar Fair Value

| Price/Fair Value Ratio | Fair Value Estimate ($) | Hit Rate % |
|---|---|---|
| 1.0 Fairly valued | 23.99 | 99 Good |

## Portfolio Analysis 12-31-05

| Share change since 11-05 Total Stocks:86 | Sector | PE | Tot Ret% | % Assets |
|---|---|---|---|---|
| ⊖ Microsoft | Software | 22.2 | -0.95 | 11.55 |
| ⊖ Intel | Hardware | 18.6 | 8.12 | 7.26 |
| ⊖ IBM | Hardware | 16.0 | -15.83 | 6.27 |
| ⊖ Cisco Systems | Hardware | 19.9 | -11.39 | 5.08 |
| ⊖ Verizon Communications | Telecom | 10.2 | -22.18 | 4.02 |
| ⊖ Hewlett-Packard | Hardware | 27.3 | 38.29 | 3.98 |
| ⊖ AT&T | Telecom | 21.1 | 0.25 | 3.52 |
| ⊖ Qualcomm | Hardware | 34.2 | 2.50 | 3.45 |
| ⊖ Dell | Hardware | 23.2 | -28.93 | 3.42 |
| ⊖ Sprint Nextel | Telecom | 19.1 | -4.81 | 3.40 |
| ⊖ Apple Computer | Hardware | 46.1 | 123.26 | 3.08 |
| ⊖ Motorola | Hardware | 13.9 | 32.43 | 2.75 |
| ⊖ Texas Instruments | Hardware | 25.3 | 30.78 | 2.53 |
| ⊖ Yahoo | Media | 36.3 | 3.98 | 2.45 |
| ⊖ BellSouth | Telecom | 18.1 | 1.77 | 2.41 |
| ⊖ Oracle | Software | 22.2 | -11.01 | 2.23 |
| ⊖ EMC | Hardware | 25.7 | -8.41 | 1.60 |
| ⊖ First Data | Business | 20.8 | 1.70 | 1.59 |
| ⊕ Corning | Hardware | 36.4 | 67.03 | 1.56 |
| ⊖ Applied Materials | Hardware | 24.6 | 5.46 | 1.42 |

### Current Investment Style

Value Blnd Growth — Large/Mid/Small

| Market Cap | % |
|---|---|
| Giant | 69.2 |
| Large | 21.8 |
| Mid | 8.8 |
| Small | 0.3 |
| Micro | 0.0 |

Avg $mil: 55,669

| Value Measures | | Rel Category |
|---|---|---|
| Price/Earnings | 20.15 | 0.85 |
| Price/Book | 3.62 | 1.09 |
| Price/Sales | 2.33 | 0.77 |
| Price/Cash Flow | 10.21 | 0.93 |
| Dividend Yield % | 1.18 | 2.11 |

| Growth Measures | % | Rel Category |
|---|---|---|
| Long-Term Erngs | 11.53 | 0.77 |
| Book Value | 3.91 | 1.22 |
| Sales | 4.85 | 0.84 |
| Cash Flow | 5.38 | 0.27 |
| Historical Erngs | 19.09 | 0.74 |

| Profitability | % | Rel Category |
|---|---|---|
| Return on Equity | 19.83 | 1.28 |
| Return on Assets | 10.92 | 1.16 |
| Net Margin | 16.77 | 1.19 |

| Industry Weightings | % of Stocks | Rel Cat |
|---|---|---|
| Software | 19.8 | 1.0 |
| Hardware | 21.1 | 1.8 |
| Networking Eq | 8.1 | 1.2 |
| Semis | 15.7 | 0.8 |
| Semi Equip | 2.2 | 0.5 |
| Comp/Data Sv | 3.9 | 0.5 |
| Telecom | 15.7 | 5.1 |
| Health Care | 0.0 | 0.0 |
| Other | 13.5 | 0.6 |

### Composition

| | | % |
|---|---|---|
| ● Cash | | 0.7 |
| ● Stocks | | 99.3 |
| ● Bonds | | 0.0 |
| Other | | 0.0 |
| Foreign (% of Stock) | | 0.0 |

## Morningstar's Take by Dan Culloton

This fund is a little too top-heavy.

Technology Select Sector SPDR has its good points. For one thing, this exchange-traded fund is cheap. Its 0.26% expense ratio is one of the lowest among ETFs in the technology category and is a fraction of the levy of the typical conventional mutual fund in this area.

The portfolio is also simple to understand. The ETF tracks an index of the S&P 500 tech stocks. It is full of sector bellwethers such as Microsoft and Intel. The offering has one of the highest average market caps in the category, and its bias toward established stocks gives it stability when the sector's more speculative fare tanks.

The ETF is still risky, though. Not only is it focused on one volatile sector, but it is also concentrated. Though it owns nearly 90 stocks, it packs more than one third of its money in its top five holdings. And there are other peculiarities. The portfolio includes a huge shot of telecommunications stocks, such as SBC

Communications. Phone companies provide high-tech services and are voracious technology users. Few tech offerings match this one's telecom stake, though. The portfolio also lacks small-cap and foreign-stock exposure.

These quirks can cause the ETF to act differently than peers that offer purer, more global tech exposure. Indeed, the portfolio is capable of some extreme swings. It lost money in nearly half of the 78 rolling three-month periods from the fund's inception through August 2005; it fell by double digits in most of those down periods.

It's not clear the ETF has compensated investors for its risks. Returns versus the category average are mixed, and its Sharpe ratio, a gauge of risk-adjusted returns, is lower than the typical tech fund's. This ETF might work if all you want is a low-cost play on giant tech stocks, but there are other options that do a better job of capturing the return of the broad tech sector.

| Address: | c/o State Street Bk&Tr, 225 Franklin St Boston MA 02210 800-843-2639 |
|---|---|
| Web Address: | www.spdrindex.com |
| Inception: | 12-22-98 * |
| Advisor: | SSGA Funds Management, Inc. |

| Management Fee: | 0.05% | | |
|---|---|---|---|
| Expense Projections: | 3Yr:$84 | 5Yr:$147 | 10Yr:$333 |
| Income Distrib: | Quarterly | | |
| Exchange: | AMEX | | |

MORNINGSTAR® ETFs 100

# Utilities SPDR

| | Ticker | NAV | Market Price | 52 wk High/Low | Yield | Mstar Category |
|---|---|---|---|---|---|---|
| | XLU | $31.44 | $32.03 | $33.98 - $27.11 | 3.2% | Specialty-Utilities |

## Management

### Portfolio Manager(s)

State Street Global Advisors has managed this fund since its inception in December 1998. State Street is one of the world's largest money managers and runs 23 ETFs. The organization has a lot of experience running index ETF portfolios.

### Strategy

This mutual fund owns and passively tracks the utilities-sector stocks in the S&P 500 in proportion to their weight in the utilities sector. The fund includes companies providing water, electric, and natural-gas service.

**Growth of $10,000**

— Investment Value of ETF
— Investment Value of Index S&P 500

| | 1996 | 1997 | 1998 | 1999 | 2000 | 2001 | 2002 | 2003 | 2004 | 2005 | History |
|---|---|---|---|---|---|---|---|---|---|---|---|
| | — | — | 30.13 | 28.18 | 33.11 | 27.94 | 19.21 | 23.29 | 27.86 | 31.44 | NAV $ |
| | — | — | 30.23 | 28.14 | 33.19 | 28.03 | 19.15 | 23.33 | 27.85 | 31.39 | Market Price $ |
| | — | — | 4.42* | -3.33 | 22.02 | -13.05 | -28.31 | 25.80 | 23.86 | 16.53 | NAV Return% |
| | — | — | 4.32* | -3.79 | 22.49 | -12.98 | -28.77 | 26.44 | 23.58 | 16.37 | Market Price Return% |
| | — | — | 0.33 | -0.04 | 0.07 | -0.11 | 0.02 | 0.11 | -0.01 | -0.02 | Avg Premium/Discount% |
| | — | — | 4.42 | -24.37 | 31.12 | -1.17 | -6.22 | -2.87 | 12.99 | 11.62 | NAV Rtrn% +/-S&P 500 |
| | — | — | 4.42 | 2.69 | -28.74 | 13.22 | -4.93 | -3.59 | -6.38 | -8.61 | NAV Rtrn% +/-DOWJNS UTIL |
| | — | — | — | 1 | 1 | 2 | 2 | 2 | 2 | 3 | NAV Return% Rank in Cat |
| | — | — | — | 2.62 | 3.26 | 2.69 | 3.34 | 4.21 | 3.81 | 3.67 | Income Return % |
| | — | — | — | -5.95 | 18.76 | -15.74 | -31.65 | 21.59 | 20.05 | 12.86 | Capital Return % |
| | — | — | 0.00 | 0.78 | 0.91 | 0.88 | 0.92 | 0.80 | 0.87 | 1.01 | Income $ |
| | — | — | 0.00 | 0.18 | 0.25 | 0.00 | 0.00 | 0.00 | 0.00 | 0.00 | Capital Gains $ |
| | — | — | — | 0.57 | 0.40 | 0.29 | 0.27 | 0.27 | 0.27 | 0.26 | Expense Ratio % |
| | — | — | — | 2.62 | 3.45 | 2.87 | 3.60 | 4.02 | 3.64 | 3.33 | Income Ratio % |
| | — | — | — | 39 | 45 | 12 | 57 | 6 | 10 | 4 | Turnover Rate % |
| | — | — | — | — | — | — | 534 | 1,284 | 1,686 | 1,752 | Net Assets $mil |

## Performance

### Historic Quarterly NAV Returns

| | 1st Qtr | 2nd Qtr | 3rd Qtr | 4th Qtr | Total |
|---|---|---|---|---|---|
| 2001 | -4.21 | -0.67 | -4.75 | -4.06 | -13.05 |
| 2002 | 1.13 | -12.65 | -22.51 | 4.73 | -28.31 |
| 2003 | -3.26 | 21.20 | -0.54 | 7.87 | 25.80 |
| 2004 | 5.07 | -1.36 | 6.64 | 12.08 | 23.86 |
| 2005 | 5.36 | 9.22 | 7.17 | -5.52 | 16.53 |

| Trailing | NAV Return% | Market Return% | NAV Rtrn% +/-S&P 500 | %Rank Cat.(NAV) |
|---|---|---|---|---|
| 3 Mo | -5.52 | -5.74 | -7.60 | 3 |
| 6 Mo | 1.26 | 1.10 | -4.50 | 3 |
| 1 Yr | 16.53 | 16.37 | 11.62 | 3 |
| 3 Yr Avg | 22.00 | 22.06 | 7.62 | 2 |
| 5 Yr Avg | 2.51 | 2.42 | 1.97 | 2 |
| 10 Yr Avg | — | — | — | 0 |

| Tax Analysis | Tax-Adj Return% | Tax-Cost Ratio |
|---|---|---|
| 3 Yr (estimated) | 20.53 | 1.20 |
| 5 Yr (estimated) | 1.20 | 1.28 |
| 10 Yr (estimated) | — | — |

## Risk Profile

| | Standard Index S&P 500 | Best Fit Index DOWJNS UTIL |
|---|---|---|
| Alpha | 10.9 | -4.1 |
| Beta | 0.66 | 0.96 |
| R-Squared | 24 | 96 |
| Standard Deviation | 12.42 | |
| Mean | 22.00 | |
| Sharpe Ratio | 1.52 | |

## Morningstar Fair Value

| Price/Fair Value Ratio | Fair Value Estimate ($) | Hit Rate % |
|---|---|---|
| 1.1 Fairly valued | 37.82 | 100 Good |

## Portfolio Analysis 12-31-05

| Share change since 11-05 Total Stocks:32 | Sector | PE | Tot Ret% | % Assets |
|---|---|---|---|---|
| ⊖ Exelon | Utilities | 17.0 | 24.58 | 9.29 |
| ⊖ Dominion Resources | Utilities | 26.5 | 18.19 | 7.01 |
| ⊖ Southern | Utilities | 15.8 | 7.57 | 6.71 |
| ⊖ Duke Energy | Utilities | 11.2 | 13.11 | 6.67 |
| ⊕ TXU | Utilities | — | 59.98 | 6.35 |
| ⊖ FPL Group | Utilities | 18.5 | 15.05 | 4.30 |
| ⊖ Public Service Enterpris | Utilities | 22.2 | 30.22 | 4.25 |
| ⊖ FirstEnergy | Utilities | 18.8 | 28.72 | 4.23 |
| ⊖ American Electric Power | Utilities | 12.0 | 12.33 | 3.82 |
| ⊖ Entergy | Utilities | 15.5 | 4.67 | 3.73 |
| ⊖ Edison International | Utilities | 13.5 | 39.63 | 3.72 |
| ⊖ PG & E | Utilities | 16.3 | 15.32 | 3.34 |
| ⊖ Sempra Energy | Utilities | 12.1 | 25.62 | 3.02 |
| ⊖ Consolidated Edison | Utilities | 17.8 | 11.32 | 2.97 |
| ⊖ PPL | Utilities | 15.8 | 14.03 | 2.93 |
| ⊖ Progress Energy | Utilities | 13.8 | 2.47 | 2.90 |
| ⊖ Ameren | Utilities | 15.3 | 7.18 | 2.74 |
| ⊕ AES | Utilities | 24.4 | 15.80 | 2.71 |
| ⊖ Constellation Energy Gro | Utilities | 18.1 | 35.05 | 2.69 |
| ⊖ Cinergy | Utilities | 18.5 | 6.90 | 2.22 |

### Current Investment Style

Value Blnd Growth — Large/Mid/Small

| Market Cap | % |
|---|---|
| Giant | 0.0 |
| Large | 84.2 |
| Mid | 15.4 |
| Small | 0.4 |
| Micro | 0.1 |

Avg $mil: 14,825

| Value Measures | | Rel Category |
|---|---|---|
| Price/Earnings | 15.93 | 0.97 |
| Price/Book | 1.95 | 0.97 |
| Price/Sales | 1.24 | 0.98 |
| Price/Cash Flow | 7.68 | 1.13 |
| Dividend Yield % | 3.13 | 1.04 |

| Growth Measures | % | Rel Category |
|---|---|---|
| Long-Term Erngs | 5.85 | 1.02 |
| Book Value | 1.41 | 2.76 |
| Sales | 1.78 | 1.24 |
| Cash Flow | -4.12 | NMF |
| Historical Erngs | 7.61 | 0.94 |

| Profitability | % | Rel Category |
|---|---|---|
| Return on Equity | 16.71 | 1.20 |
| Return on Assets | 3.00 | 0.99 |
| Net Margin | 8.10 | 1.01 |

| Industry Weightings | % of Stocks | Rel Cat |
|---|---|---|
| Telecom Srv | 0.0 | 0.0 |
| Electric Utls | 94.2 | 1.6 |
| Nat Gas Utls | 5.8 | 0.6 |
| Wireless Srv | 0.0 | 0.0 |
| Energy | 0.0 | 0.0 |
| Media | 0.0 | 0.0 |
| Network Eq | 0.0 | 0.0 |
| Water | 0.0 | 0.0 |
| Other | 0.0 | 0.0 |

### Composition

| | % |
|---|---|
| ● Cash | 0.9 |
| ● Stocks | 99.1 |
| ● Bonds | 0.0 |
| Other | 0.0 |
| Foreign | 0.0 |
| (% of Stock) | |

## Morningstar's Take by Dan Culloton

Utilities Select Sector SPDR offers cheap exposure to utilities stocks, but mind its risks.

This fund keeps it simple. This exchange-traded fund tracks an index of all the utilities stocks in the S&P 500 and charges a low fee for it. The fund's 0.27% expense ratio is a fraction of the levy for the typical traditional utilities-sector mutual fund and is cheaper than all the fund's ETF and index-fund rivals.

Unlike a lot of traditional utilities-sector funds, this ETF also maintains its focus. It doesn't stray into other industries such as wireless telecommunications. Many traditional utilities funds have done that in recent years and have become more volatile as a result. This ETF merely passively apes its benchmark of firms that are in the business of supplying water, electrical power, and natural gas. That focus on slow-growing companies also gives the fund a generous yield.

That doesn't mean this is a tame offering, though. The ETF's annualized 2.3% gain over the five years ending Nov. 21, 2005, is competitive with 2.4% advance of the typical domestic stock fund over that time. Yet that return trails the 4.8% gain of the average large-value fund (the other hunting ground for dividend strategies), and it was came with more volatility. This ETF has lost money in nearly half of the 27 quarters since its inception.

The rough ride should not come as a surprise. Not only is this a narrowly focused sector fund, but it is a concentrated one that owns 33 stocks and keeps more than half of its assets packed into its top 10 holdings. Utilities stocks also are not as staid as they used to be. Many have grown more risky as they have expanded into deregulated businesses, such as merchant energy provider AES. Furthermore, government regulation and fuel cost fluctuations can still adversely affect utilities' businesses and stock prices.

If you are looking for diversified exposure to dividend paying stocks, there are better options.

| Address: | c/o State Street Bk&Tr, 225 Franklin St Boston MA 02210 800-843-2639 | Management Fee: | 0.05% | | |
|---|---|---|---|---|---|
| | | Expense Projections: | 3Yr:$87 | 5Yr:$152 | 10Yr:$345 |
| Web Address: | www.spdrindex.com | Income Distrib: | Quarterly | | |
| Inception: | 12-22-98 * | Exchange: | AMEX | | |
| Advisor: | SSGA Funds Management, Inc. | | | | |

**MORNINGSTAR® ETFs 100**

# Vanguard Cons Disc VIPERs

| | Ticker | NAV | Market Price | 52 wk High/Low | Yield | Mstar Category |
|---|---|---|---|---|---|---|
| | VCR | $52.49 | $53.92 | $56.27 - $49.01 | 0.6% | Large Growth |

## Management

### Portfolio Manager(s)

Gus Sauter, Vanguard's chief investment officer and indexing pro, is in charge here. He and his team of quantitative analysts have a strong record of closely tracking benchmarks.

### Strategy

This ETF tracks the MSCI U.S. Investable Consumer Discretionary Index, a subset of the market-cap-weighted MSCI U.S. Investable Market 2500 Index. The MSCI Consumer Discretionary Index holds a little more than 440 stocks in mostly the giant-, large-, and mid-cap ranges. Companies held in the index are those traditionally sensitive to consumer spending and economic cycles, such as those in the automotive, household-durable, leisure, media, and retail industries. This fund in particular is heavily weighted towards media and retail stocks.

### Growth of $10,000

— Investment Value of ETF
— Investment Value of Index S&P 500

| | 1996 | 1997 | 1998 | 1999 | 2000 | 2001 | 2002 | 2003 | 2004 | 2005 | History |
|---|---|---|---|---|---|---|---|---|---|---|---|
| | — | — | — | — | — | — | — | — | 55.12 | 52.49 | NAV $ |
| | — | — | — | — | — | — | — | — | 55.16 | 52.59 | Market Price $ |
| | — | — | — | — | — | — | — | — | 3.10* | -4.22 | NAV Return% |
| | — | — | — | — | — | — | — | — | 3.21* | -4.10 | Market Price Return% |
| | — | — | — | — | — | — | — | — | 0.00 | -0.11 | Avg Premium/Discount% |
| | — | — | — | — | — | — | — | — | 3.10 | -9.13 | NAV Rtrn% +/-S&P 500 |
| | — | — | — | — | — | — | — | — | 3.10 | -9.48 | NAV Rtrn% +/-Russ 1000Gr |
| | — | — | — | — | — | — | — | — | — | 9 | NAV Return% Rank in Cat |
| | — | — | — | — | — | — | — | — | 0.00 | 0.56 | Income Return % |
| | — | — | — | — | — | — | — | — | — | -4.78 | Capital Return % |
| | — | — | — | — | — | — | — | — | 0.35 | 0.31 | Income $ |
| | — | — | — | — | — | — | — | — | 0.00 | 0.00 | Capital Gains $ |
| | — | — | — | — | — | — | — | — | 0.28 | 0.26 | Expense Ratio % |
| | — | — | — | — | — | — | — | — | 0.68 | 0.69 | Income Ratio % |
| | — | — | — | — | — | — | — | — | — | 13 | Turnover Rate % |
| | — | — | — | — | — | — | — | — | 17 | 37 | Net Assets $mil |

## Performance

### Historic Quarterly NAV Returns

| | 1st Qtr | 2nd Qtr | 3rd Qtr | 4th Qtr | Total |
|---|---|---|---|---|---|
| 2001 | — | — | — | — | — |
| 2002 | — | — | — | — | — |
| 2003 | — | — | — | — | — |
| 2004 | — | -0.98 | -1.62 | 14.43 | —* |
| 2005 | -4.54 | 0.76 | -1.57 | 1.16 | -4.22 |

| Trailing | NAV Return% | Market Return% | NAV Rtrn% +/-S&P 500 | %Rank Cat.(NAV) |
|---|---|---|---|---|
| 3 Mo | 1.16 | 1.33 | -0.92 | 10 |
| 6 Mo | -0.42 | -0.20 | -6.18 | 10 |
| 1 Yr | -4.22 | -4.10 | -9.13 | 9 |
| 3 Yr Avg | — | — | — | 0 |
| 5 Yr Avg | — | — | — | 0 |
| 10 Yr Avg | — | — | — | 0 |

| Tax Analysis | Tax-Adj Return% | Tax-Cost Ratio |
|---|---|---|
| 3 Yr (estimated) | — | — |
| 5 Yr (estimated) | — | — |
| 10 Yr (estimated) | — | — |

## Risk Profile

| | Standard Index S&P 500 | Best Fit Index |
|---|---|---|
| Alpha | — | — |
| Beta | — | — |
| R-Squared | — | — |
| Standard Deviation | — | |
| Mean | — | |
| Sharpe Ratio | — | |

## Morningstar Fair Value

| Price/Fair Value Ratio | Fair Value Estimate ($) | Hit Rate % |
|---|---|---|
| 0.9 Undervalued | 28.39 | 83 Fair |

## Portfolio Analysis 09-30-05

Share change since 06-05   Total Stocks:437

| | Sector | PE | Tot Ret% | % Assets |
|---|---|---|---|---|
| ⊕ Time Warner | Media | 30.6 | -9.83 | 4.97 |
| ⊕ Home Depot | Consumer | 15.6 | -4.35 | 4.89 |
| ⊕ Walt Disney | Media | 19.3 | -12.85 | 2.94 |
| ⊕ Lowe's Companies | Consumer | 20.7 | 16.14 | 2.83 |
| ⊕ Viacom B | Media | — | -8.42 | 2.77 |
| ⊕ Target | Consumer | 21.6 | 6.57 | 2.60 |
| ⊕ McDonald's | Consumer | 18.0 | 7.30 | 2.54 |
| ⊕ eBay | Consumer | 59.2 | -25.70 | 2.49 |
| ⊕ Comcast A | Media | 47.1 | -22.12 | 2.27 |
| ⊕ News Cl A | Media | — | — | 1.78 |
| ⊕ Comcast | Media | — | — | 1.44 |
| ⊕ Carnival | Goods | 20.3 | -5.80 | 1.33 |
| ⊕ Liberty Media | Media | — | -15.71 | 1.22 |
| ⊕ Starbucks | Consumer | 49.2 | -3.75 | 1.18 |
| ⊕ McGraw-Hill Companies | Media | 23.5 | 14.38 | 1.09 |
| ⊕ Best Buy Co. | Consumer | 21.4 | 10.79 | 1.09 |
| ⊕ Federated Department Sto | Consumer | 11.0 | 15.68 | 1.07 |
| ⊕ Ford Motor | Goods | 7.9 | -45.12 | 1.04 |
| ⊕ Gannett | Media | 12.1 | -24.68 | 1.04 |
| ⊕ Staples | Consumer | 21.4 | 1.87 | 0.94 |

### Current Investment Style

Value Blnd Growth — Large/Mid/Small

| Market Cap | % |
|---|---|
| Giant | 28.4 |
| Large | 35.1 |
| Mid | 27.3 |
| Small | 8.3 |
| Micro | 0.8 |

Avg $mil: 12,796

| Value Measures | | Rel Category |
|---|---|---|
| Price/Earnings | 18.01 | 0.86 |
| Price/Book | 2.21 | 0.66 |
| Price/Sales | 0.91 | 0.47 |
| Price/Cash Flow | 7.12 | 0.68 |
| Dividend Yield % | 0.95 | 1.07 |

| Growth Measures | % | Rel Category |
|---|---|---|
| Long-Term Erngs | 12.99 | 0.92 |
| Book Value | 4.12 | 0.50 |
| Sales | 6.88 | 0.62 |
| Cash Flow | 14.26 | 0.87 |
| Historical Erngs | 16.22 | 0.85 |

| Profitability | % | Rel Category |
|---|---|---|
| Return on Equity | 14.04 | 0.70 |
| Return on Assets | 6.65 | 0.62 |
| Net Margin | 4.83 | 0.35 |

### Sector Weightings

| | % of Stocks | Rel S&P 500 | 3 Year High Low |
|---|---|---|---|
| ⊙ Info | 29.24 | 1.45 | |
| ▢ Software | 0.00 | 0.00 | — — |
| ▣ Hardware | 0.36 | 0.04 | — — |
| ◐ Media | 28.33 | 7.91 | — — |
| ▦ Telecom | 0.55 | 0.18 | — — |
| ⊑ Service | 53.65 | 1.16 | |
| ◪ Health | 0.04 | 0.00 | — — |
| ▤ Consumer | 51.18 | 6.29 | — — |
| ▥ Business | 2.24 | 0.58 | — — |
| $ Financial | 0.19 | 0.01 | — — |
| ⊟ Mfg | 17.12 | 0.51 | |
| ⊞ Goods | 13.54 | 1.58 | — — |
| ✦ Ind Mtrls | 3.58 | 0.29 | — — |
| ◔ Energy | 0.00 | 0.00 | — — |
| ▾ Utilities | 0.00 | 0.00 | — — |

### Composition

| | | % |
|---|---|---|
| ● Cash | | 0.0 |
| ● Stocks | | 99.0 |
| ● Bonds | | 0.1 |
| ○ Other | | 0.9 |
| Foreign | | 0.3 |
| (% of Stock) | | |

## Morningstar's Take by Emiko Kurotsu

Within its sector, this fund gives you the most bang for your buck.

With 442 holdings, it may not seem like Vanguard Consumer Discretionary VIPERs excludes much. But it differentiates itself from conventional rivals by what it doesn't own. Like other Vanguard sector ETFs, the fund is a subset of the MSCI U.S. Investable Market 2500 Index and focuses on businesses sensitive to consumer spending. Unlike some consumer-oriented funds, such as Fidelity Advisor Consumer Industries, however, this fund refrains from mixing online-services stocks such as Google with more traditional consumer-goods companies like Coca-Cola and Procter & Gamble. This ETF includes its share of consumer-goods stocks, notably troubled car makers Ford and General Motors, but its bogy focuses on those stocks that are most sensitive to economic cycles, or the providers of goods and services that people can do without in a pitch. As a result, the fund keeps nearly half its assets in retail and media

stocks, such as Home Depot and Time Warner.

This ETF is also less concentrated than its competitors. It has more than four times the number of holdings than Consumer Discretionary SPDR and the actively managed ICON Consumer Discretionary Fund, while offering more breadth of holdings. With no more than 5% of its assets in any one stock, the fund is relatively cushioned against the travails of any one company, and isn't overly concentrated in its top10 holdings.

The fund is also attractive for its competitive expenses. While its 0.28% expense ratio matches that of the Consumer Discretionary SPDR, we'd pick this fund over that and other offerings in its sector on the merit of its diversification alone. Like all sector funds, this one is narrowly focused and probably unnecessary if you already have broad domestic-stock exposure, but it does provide cheap and fairly diverse exposure to consumer discretionary stocks.

| | |
|---|---|
| Address: | PO Box 2600 |
| | Valley Forge PA 19482 |
| | 866-499-8473 |
| Web Address: | www.vanguard.com |
| Inception: | 01-26-04 * |
| Advisor: | Vanguard Advisers, Inc. |

| | | | |
|---|---|---|---|
| Management Fee: | 0.26% | | |
| Expense Projections: | 3Yr:$90 | 5Yr: — | 10Yr: — |
| Income Distrib: | Annually | | |
| Exchange: | AMEX | | |

MORNINGSTAR® ETFs 100

# Vanguard Cons Stap VIPERs

| | Ticker | NAV | Market Price | 52 wk High/Low | Yield | Mstar Category |
|---|---|---|---|---|---|---|
| | VDC | $55.94 | $56.69 | $57.80 - $53.83 | 1.3% | Large Blend |

## Management

### Portfolio Manager(s)

Gus Sauter, Vanguard's chief investment officer and indexing pro, is in charge here. He and his team of quantitative analysts have a strong record of closely tracking benchmarks.

### Strategy

This ETF tracks the MSCI U.S. Investable Consumer Staples Index, a subset of the market-cap weighted MSCI U.S. Investable Market 2500 Index. The MSCI Consumer Staples index holds roughly 100 stocks, including manufacturers and distributors of food, beverages, and tobacco; producers of nondurable household goods and personal products; drug retailers; and consumer supercenters. It doesn't include consumer-goods stocks in the automotive or leisure industries.

## Performance

### Historic Quarterly NAV Returns

| | 1st Qtr | 2nd Qtr | 3rd Qtr | 4th Qtr | Total |
|---|---|---|---|---|---|
| 2001 | — | — | — | — | — |
| 2002 | — | — | — | — | — |
| 2003 | — | — | — | — | — |
| 2004 | — | 2.03 | -6.05 | 9.17 | — * |
| 2005 | 1.21 | 0.05 | 2.66 | -0.01 | 3.95 |

| Trailing | NAV Return% | Market Return% | NAV Rtrn% +/-S&P 500 | %Rank Cat.(NAV) |
|---|---|---|---|---|
| 3 Mo | -0.01 | 0.09 | -2.09 | 27 |
| 6 Mo | 2.65 | 2.67 | -3.11 | 27 |
| 1 Yr | 3.95 | 3.76 | -0.96 | 23 |
| 3 Yr Avg | — | — | — | 0 |
| 5 Yr Avg | — | — | — | 0 |
| 10 Yr Avg | — | — | — | 0 |

| Tax Analysis | Tax-Adj Return% | Tax-Cost Ratio |
|---|---|---|
| 3 Yr (estimated) | — | — |
| 5 Yr (estimated) | — | — |
| 10 Yr (estimated) | — | — |

### Growth of $10,000

— Investment Value of ETF
— Investment Value of Index S&P 500

| | 1996 | 1997 | 1998 | 1999 | 2000 | 2001 | 2002 | 2003 | 2004 | 2005 | History |
|---|---|---|---|---|---|---|---|---|---|---|---|
| | — | — | — | — | — | — | — | — | 54.48 | 55.94 | NAV $ |
| | — | — | — | — | — | — | — | — | 54.57 | 55.93 | Market Price $ |
| | — | — | — | — | — | — | — | — | 6.85* | 3.95 | NAV Return% |
| | — | — | — | — | — | — | — | — | 6.84* | 3.76 | Market Price Return% |
| | — | — | — | — | — | — | — | — | 0.08 | 0.01 | Avg Premium/Discount% |
| | — | — | — | — | — | — | — | — | 6.85 | -0.96 | NAV Rtrn% +/-S&P 500 |
| | — | — | — | — | — | — | — | — | 6.85 | -2.32 | NAV Rtrn% +/-Russ 1000 |
| | — | — | — | — | — | — | — | — | — | 23 | NAV Return% Rank in Cat |
| | — | — | — | — | — | — | — | — | 0.00 | 1.29 | Income Return % |
| | — | — | — | — | — | — | — | — | — | 2.66 | Capital Return % |
| | — | — | — | — | — | — | — | — | 0.85 | 0.70 | Income $ |
| | — | — | — | — | — | — | — | — | 0.24 | 0.00 | Capital Gains $ |
| | — | — | — | — | — | — | — | — | 0.28 | 0.26 | Expense Ratio % |
| | — | — | — | — | — | — | — | — | 1.51 | 1.71 | Income Ratio % |
| | — | — | — | — | — | — | — | — | 20 | 7 | Turnover Rate % |
| | — | — | — | — | — | — | — | — | 22 | 90 | Net Assets $mil |

## Risk Profile

| | Standard Index S&P 500 | Best Fit Index |
|---|---|---|
| Alpha | — | — |
| Beta | — | — |
| R-Squared | — | — |
| Standard Deviation | — | |
| Mean | — | |
| Sharpe Ratio | — | |

## Morningstar Fair Value

| Price/Fair Value Ratio | Fair Value Estimate ($) | Hit Rate % |
|---|---|---|
| 0.9 Undervalued | 40.13 | 91 Good |

## Morningstar's Take by Emiko Kurotsu

This exchange-traded fund offers cheap exposure to established consumer-staples stocks, but its biggest holdings may be redundant in your portfolio.

Vanguard Consumer Staples VIPERs tracks the MSCI U.S. Investable Market Consumer Staples Index. The definition of "consumer-staple stock" can differ, but this ETF's benchmark considers manufacturers or distributors of food, beverages, tobacco, and household and personal products fair game. That excludes some big names that appear in competing ETFs. For example, iShares Dow Jones US Consumer Goods includes auto manufacturers Ford and Harley Davidson, and the luxury retailer Coach. The index used for this ETF includes about 100 mostly domestic large-cap stocks and a smattering of mid-, small-, and micro-cap companies, ranging from Coca-Cola to Boston Beer Group.

Because the fund is market-cap weighted, it is extremely top-heavy, with a third of its assets stuffed in its top three holdings: Altria Group, Procter & Gamble, and Wal-Mart. Nevertheless, this ETF is still more diversified than some of its rivals. It owns, for instance, more stocks and invests in more mid-, small-, and micro-cap companies than the Consumer Staples Select Sector SPDR. As a result, this offering may be less volatile and more representative of the broad consumer goods sector than the more concentrated SPDR.

Overall, this ETF looks good relative to other funds that track this sector. It is cheap, with an annual expense ratio of 0.28%, and while cheaper ETFs in similar sectors are out there, (the SPDR's expense ratio is one basis point lower), this offering is more diversified than most. At the same time, however, if you already have a diversified portfolio, you probably don't need this fund because its name-brand holdings are already widely held. Think twice before using this one.

| Address: | PO Box 2600 Valley Forge PA 19482 866-499-8473 | Management Fee: | 0.26% |
|---|---|---|---|
| | | Expense Projections: | 3Yr:$90   5Yr:$157   10Yr:$356 |
| Web Address: | www.vanguard.com | Income Distrib: | Annually |
| Inception: | 01-26-04* | Exchange: | AMEX |
| Advisor: | Vanguard Advisers, Inc. | | |

## Portfolio Analysis 09-30-05

| Share change since 06-05 Total Stocks:105 | Sector | PE | Tot Ret% | % Assets |
|---|---|---|---|---|
| ⊕ Altria Group | Goods | 15.0 | 27.72 | 10.96 |
| ⊕ Procter & Gamble | Goods | 21.2 | 7.18 | 10.28 |
| ⊕ Wal-Mart Stores | Consumer | 18.2 | -10.30 | 7.36 |
| ⊕ PepsiCo | Goods | 25.8 | 15.24 | 5.97 |
| ⊕ Coca-Cola | Goods | 18.6 | -0.66 | 5.86 |
| ⊕ Gillette | Goods | — | — | 4.86 |
| ⊕ Walgreen | Consumer | 29.1 | 15.94 | 4.16 |
| ⊕ Anheuser-Busch Companies | Goods | 17.1 | -13.38 | 3.16 |
| ⊕ Kimberly-Clark | Goods | 17.5 | -6.73 | 2.71 |
| ⊕ Colgate-Palmolive | Goods | 24.1 | 9.55 | 2.64 |
| ⊕ CVS | Consumer | 20.8 | 17.89 | 2.23 |
| ⊕ Costco Wholesale | Consumer | 22.7 | 3.19 | 1.99 |
| ⊕ Sysco | Consumer | 21.7 | -17.25 | 1.93 |
| ⊕ General Mills | Goods | 15.1 | 1.88 | 1.58 |
| ⊕ Sara Lee | Goods | 23.3 | -18.56 | 1.48 |
| ⊕ Archer Daniels Midland | Ind Mtrls | 16.8 | 12.25 | 1.45 |
| ⊕ Kroger | Consumer | — | 7.64 | 1.41 |
| ⊕ ConAgra Foods | Goods | 12.1 | -28.12 | 1.29 |
| ⊕ H.J. Heinz | Goods | 17.6 | -10.55 | 1.28 |
| ⊕ Avon Products | Goods | 14.3 | -24.77 | 1.28 |

### Current Investment Style

Value Blnd Growth — Large Mid Small

| Market Cap | % |
|---|---|
| Giant | 50.3 |
| Large | 32.7 |
| Mid | 11.5 |
| Small | 4.5 |
| Micro | 1.1 |

Avg $mil: 32,754

| Value Measures | | Rel Category |
|---|---|---|
| Price/Earnings | 18.17 | 1.07 |
| Price/Book | 3.90 | 1.44 |
| Price/Sales | 0.93 | 0.73 |
| Price/Cash Flow | 6.99 | 0.97 |
| Dividend Yield % | 2.06 | 1.16 |

| Growth Measures | % | Rel Category |
|---|---|---|
| Long-Term Erngs | 10.08 | 0.91 |
| Book Value | 11.74 | 1.25 |
| Sales | 8.31 | 1.03 |
| Cash Flow | 7.07 | 0.69 |
| Historical Erngs | 10.02 | 0.71 |

| Profitability | % | Rel Category |
|---|---|---|
| Return on Equity | 30.12 | 1.48 |
| Return on Assets | 10.47 | 1.12 |
| Net Margin | 9.44 | 0.87 |

| Sector Weightings | % of Stocks | Rel S&P 500 | 3 Year High | Low |
|---|---|---|---|---|
| ↗ Info | 0.00 | 0.00 | | |
| 🖥 Software | 0.00 | 0.00 | — | — |
| 💻 Hardware | 0.00 | 0.00 | — | — |
| 📡 Media | 0.00 | 0.00 | — | — |
| 📶 Telecom | 0.00 | 0.00 | — | — |
| ☞ Service | 25.70 | 0.55 | | |
| ⚕ Health | 0.64 | 0.05 | — | — |
| 🏢 Consumer | 24.76 | 3.04 | — | — |
| 📊 Business | 0.00 | 0.00 | — | — |
| 💲 Financial | 0.30 | 0.01 | — | — |
| ⬆ Mfg | 74.30 | 2.22 | | |
| 🏭 Goods | 72.05 | 8.42 | — | — |
| ⚙ Ind Mtrls | 2.09 | 0.17 | — | — |
| ⛽ Energy | 0.16 | 0.02 | — | — |
| 💡 Utilities | 0.00 | 0.00 | — | — |

### Composition

| | | |
|---|---|---|
| ● Cash | 0.0 | |
| ● Stocks | 100.0 | |
| ○ Bonds | 0.0 | |
| | Other | 0.0 |
| | Foreign | 0.2 |
| | (% of Stock) | |

MᴏRNINGSTAR® ETFs 100

# Vanguard EmergMkts VIPERs

| | Ticker | NAV | Market Price | 52 wk High/Low | Yield | Mstar Category |
|---|---|---|---|---|---|---|
| | VWO | $60.40 | $64.80 | $65.38 - $45.25 | 0.0% | Diversified Emerging Mkts |

## Management

### Portfolio Manager(s)

This fund is run by Vanguard's index-tracking quantitative-equity group, which has extensive experience running a multitude of index funds. The individual running this fund is currently Gus Sauter, who has led Vanguard's index-tracking effort for years and is also the company's chief investment officer. However, as a result of his increased range of duties, Vanguard is in the process of taking Sauter off the individual index funds, so it's likely other individuals will be appointed to handle the day-to-day management responsibilities at this fund in the near future. However, the investment process here will remain the same.

### Strategy

This exchange-traded fund tries to mirror the performance of a customized version of an MSCI emerging-markets index. One difference between this index and the standard MSCI Emerging Markets Index is that this fund's benchmark excludes Russia. The fund does not engage in currency hedging. Vanguard uses fair-value pricing on occasion when it deems it necessary.

### Growth of $10,000

— Investment Value of ETF
— Investment Value of Index MSCI EAFE

| | 1996 | 1997 | 1998 | 1999 | 2000 | 2001 | 2002 | 2003 | 2004 | 2005 | History |
|---|---|---|---|---|---|---|---|---|---|---|---|
| | — | — | — | — | — | — | — | — | — | 60.40 | NAV $ |
| | — | — | — | — | — | — | — | — | — | 60.88 | Market Price $ |
| | — | — | — | — | — | — | — | — | — | 22.72* | NAV Return% |
| | — | — | — | — | — | — | — | — | — | 23.54* | Market Price Return% |
| | — | — | — | — | — | — | — | — | — | 0.53 | Avg Premium/Discount% |
| | — | — | — | — | — | — | — | — | — | 22.72 | NAV Rtrn% +/-MSCI EAFE |
| | — | — | — | — | — | — | — | — | — | 22.72 | NAV Rtrn% +/-MSCI EmrMkt |
| | — | — | — | — | — | — | — | — | — | — | NAV Return% Rank in Cat |
| | — | — | — | — | — | — | — | — | — | — | Income Return % |
| | — | — | — | — | — | — | — | — | — | — | Capital Return % |
| | — | — | — | — | — | — | — | — | — | 1.08 | Income $ |
| | — | — | — | — | — | — | — | — | — | 0.00 | Capital Gains $ |
| | — | — | — | — | — | — | — | — | — | 0.30 | Expense Ratio % |
| | — | — | — | — | — | — | — | — | — | 2.59 | Income Ratio % |
| | — | — | — | — | — | — | — | — | — | 15 | Turnover Rate % |
| | — | — | — | — | — | — | — | — | — | 553 | Net Assets $mil |

## Performance

### Historic Quarterly NAV Returns

| | 1st Qtr | 2nd Qtr | 3rd Qtr | 4th Qtr | Total |
|---|---|---|---|---|---|
| 2001 | — | — | — | — | — |
| 2002 | — | — | — | — | — |
| 2003 | — | — | — | — | — |
| 2004 | — | — | — | — | — |
| 2005 | — | 3.73 | 17.22 | 7.15 | —* |

| Trailing | NAV Return% | Market Return% | NAV Rtrn% +/-MSCI EAFE | %Rank Cat.(NAV) |
|---|---|---|---|---|
| 3 Mo | 7.15 | 7.53 | 3.07 | 4 |
| 6 Mo | 25.60 | 26.26 | 10.72 | 4 |
| 1 Yr | — | — | — | 0 |
| 3 Yr Avg | — | — | — | 0 |
| 5 Yr Avg | — | — | — | 0 |
| 10 Yr Avg | — | — | — | 0 |

| Tax Analysis | Tax-Adj Return% | Tax-Cost Ratio |
|---|---|---|
| 3 Yr (estimated) | — | — |
| 5 Yr (estimated) | — | — |
| 10 Yr (estimated) | — | — |

## Risk Profile

| | Standard Index S&P 500 | Best Fit Index |
|---|---|---|
| Alpha | — | — |
| Beta | — | — |
| R-Squared | — | — |
| Standard Deviation | — | |
| Mean | — | |
| Sharpe Ratio | — | |

## Morningstar Fair Value

| Price/Fair Value Ratio | Fair Value Estimate ($) | Hit Rate % |
|---|---|---|
| | — | — |

## Portfolio Analysis 06-30-05

Share change since 03-05  Total Stocks:710

| | Sector | Country | % Assets |
|---|---|---|---|
| ⊖ Samsung Electronics | Goods | Korea | 4.58 |
| ⊕ Taiwan Semiconductor Mfg | Hardware | Taiwan | 2.69 |
| ⊕ Teva Pharmaceutical Indu | Health | Israel | 1.59 |
| ⊕ China Mobile | Telecom | Hong Kong | 1.58 |
| ⊖ Petroleo Brasileiro Sa P | Energy | Brazil | 1.51 |
| ⊕ Sasol Ltd | Ind Mtrls | South Africa | 1.34 |
| ⊖ America Movil S.A. de C. | Telecom | Mexico | 1.25 |
| ⊖ Petroleo Brasileiro | Energy | Brazil | 1.24 |
| ⊕ Hon Hai Precision Indust | Hardware | Taiwan | 1.16 |
| ⊕ Kookmin Bank | Financial | Korea | 1.15 |
| ⊕ CEMEX | Ind Mtrls | Mexico | 1.09 |
| ⊕ Standard Bank Investment | Financial | South Africa | 1.02 |
| ⊕ PetroChina | Energy | Hong Kong | 1.01 |
| ⊕ Infosys Technologies Ltd | Software | India | 0.95 |
| ⊕ United Microelect | Hardware | Taiwan | 0.93 |
| ⊖ Cia Vale Rio Doce | | Brazil | 0.88 |
| ⊕ Cathay Finl Hldg | Financial | Taiwan | 0.87 |
| ⊖ Cia Vale Rio Doce | Ind Mtrls | Brazil | 0.83 |
| ⊖ Banco Itau Hldg Financei | Financial | Brazil | 0.82 |
| ⊕ POSCO | | Korea | 0.82 |

### Current Investment Style

Value  Blnd  Growth — Large Mid Small

| | Market Cap | % |
|---|---|---|
| | Giant | 38.7 |
| | Large | 38.1 |
| | Mid | 19.6 |
| | Small | 3.2 |
| | Micro | 0.5 |
| | Avg $mil: | 7,862 |

| Value Measures | | Rel Category |
|---|---|---|
| Price/Earnings | 10.67 | 0.89 |
| Price/Book | 1.65 | 0.78 |
| Price/Sales | 0.11 | 0.13 |
| Price/Cash Flow | 4.29 | 0.72 |
| Dividend Yield % | 5.72 | 1.43 |

| Growth Measures | % | Rel Category |
|---|---|---|
| Long-Term Erngs | 16.86 | 1.09 |
| Book Value | 9.69 | 1.27 |
| Sales | 14.25 | 1.51 |
| Cash Flow | 17.76 | 1.58 |
| Historical Erngs | 17.20 | 0.73 |

### Composition

| Cash | 0.0 | Bonds | 0.0 |
|---|---|---|---|
| Stocks | 95.1 | Other | 4.9 |
| Foreign (% of Stock) | | | 99.4 |

### Sector Weightings

| | % of Stocks | Rel MSCI EAFE | 3 Year High | Low |
|---|---|---|---|---|
| ⚙ Info | 25.38 | 1.81 | | |
| 🖥 Software | 1.91 | 1.79 | 2 | 2 |
| 🖥 Hardware | 10.43 | 2.89 | 10 | 5 |
| 🎙 Media | 1.27 | 0.60 | 1 | 1 |
| 📶 Telecom | 11.77 | 1.63 | 13 | 12 |
| ☞ Service | 31.11 | 0.68 | | |
| 🩺 Health | 2.86 | 0.40 | 4 | 3 |
| 🛒 Consumer | 3.75 | 0.86 | 4 | 3 |
| 💼 Business | 5.53 | 0.92 | 6 | 4 |
| 💲 Financial | 18.97 | 0.67 | 20 | 15 |
| 🏭 Mfg | 43.51 | 1.08 | | |
| Goods | 14.32 | 1.05 | 18 | 14 |
| ⚙ Ind Mtrls | 17.81 | 1.26 | 25 | 18 |
| Energy | 8.75 | 1.11 | 9 | 5 |
| 💡 Utilities | 2.63 | 0.57 | 3 | 2 |

### Regional Exposure % Stock

| UK/W. Europe | 1 | N. America | 1 |
|---|---|---|---|
| Japan | 0 | Latn America | 18 |
| Asia X Japan | 60 | Other | 20 |

### Country Exposure % Stock

| Taiwan | 21 | Hong Kong | 9 |
|---|---|---|---|
| South Korea | 18 | Brazil | 7 |
| South Africa | 11 | | |

## Morningstar's Take  by Gregg Wolper

Vanguard Emerging Markets Stock VIPERs has essentially the same portfolio as its mutual-fund sibling, so the same cautions apply to both.

This exchange-traded vehicle has only existed for about seven months, but Vanguard's similar mutual fund, Vanguard Emerging Markets Stock Index, has a much longer record. And through Dec. 15, 2005, that fund, which attempts to match the return of a customized version of an MSCI emerging-markets index, has an astounding trailing three-year average annual return of 35.9%. That includes a year-to-date showing of 28.8% in 2005. Such returns can tempt anyone to invest either in that fund or this one.

Of course, the likelihood that either offering will keep up that torrid pace for many more years is next to zero. True, the sibling's trailing three-year return is no fluke or gimmick. It does a reasonably sound job tracking its benchmark--as this one probably will--and many companies in the portfolios are impressive global leaders in their fields. The reason for the high return is that most emerging markets have been on fire for several years, outperforming even the rallying markets in Western Europe and Japan. And Vanguard Emerging Markets Stock Index has done at least as well as its rivals in the diversified emerging-markets category. It lands around the middle of that group for the year to date, and is in the top half for the three- and five-year periods.

However, not only are 30%-plus returns unlikely to continue indefinitely, there's also a decent chance--given the history of emerging markets--that these funds could suffer sharp losses. When evaluating this fund, also keep in mind that investors who own broad-based international funds probably already own emerging-markets stocks to some degree.

In short, this is a sound option; just be sure to keep expectations in check.

| Address: | PO Box 2600 Valley Forge PA 19482 866-499-8473 | Management Fee: | 0.15% |
|---|---|---|---|
| | | Expense Projections: | 3Yr:$97  5Yr:$169  10Yr:$381 |
| Web Address: | www.vanguard.com | Income Distrib: | Annually |
| Inception: | 03-10-05* | Exchange: | AMEX |
| Advisor: | Vanguard Advisers, Inc. | | |

MORNINGSTAR® ETFs 100

Data through December 31, 2005

# Vanguard Energy VIPERs

| Ticker | NAV | Market Price | 52 wk High/Low | Yield | Mstar Category |
|---|---|---|---|---|---|
| VDE | $72.16 | $77.30 | $78.65 - $50.79 | 1.0% | Specialty-Natural Res |

## Management

### Portfolio Manager(s)

Gus Sauter, Vanguard's chief investment officer and index pro, is in charge here. He and his team of quantitative analysts have a strong record of closely tracking benchmarks.

### Strategy

This ETF is tethered to the MSCI US Investable Market Energy Index, a market-cap-weighted index that focuses on firms involved in the U.S. energy sector, including those in exploration and production, oil service, natural gas, and coal. The fund invests across the market-cap spectrum, but it is dominated by major U.S. oil firms. It does not have exposure to energy firms headquartered overseas.

**Growth of $10,000**

— Investment Value of ETF
— Investment Value of Index S&P 500

| | 1996 | 1997 | 1998 | 1999 | 2000 | 2001 | 2002 | 2003 | 2004 | 2005 | History |
|---|---|---|---|---|---|---|---|---|---|---|---|
| | — | — | — | — | — | — | — | — | 52.39 | 72.16 | NAV $ |
| | — | — | — | — | — | — | — | — | 52.41 | 72.19 | Market Price $ |
| | — | — | — | — | — | — | — | — | 35.45* | 39.05 | NAV Return% |
| | — | — | — | — | — | — | — | — | 35.55* | 39.05 | Market Price Return% |
| | — | — | — | — | — | — | — | — | 0.02 | 0.01 | Avg Premium/Discount% |
| | — | — | — | — | — | — | — | — | 35.45 | 34.14 | NAV Rtrn% +/-S&P 500 |
| | — | — | — | — | — | — | — | — | 35.45 | 2.57 | NAV Rtrn% +/-GS NATR RES |
| | — | — | — | — | — | — | — | — | — | 6 | NAV Return% Rank in Cat |
| | — | — | — | — | — | — | — | — | 0.00 | 1.34 | Income Return % |
| | — | — | — | — | — | — | — | — | — | 37.71 | Capital Return % |
| | — | — | — | — | — | — | — | — | 0.22 | 0.70 | Income $ |
| | — | — | — | — | — | — | — | — | 0.00 | 0.00 | Capital Gains $ |
| | — | — | — | — | — | — | — | — | — | 0.26 | Expense Ratio % |
| | — | — | — | — | — | — | — | — | — | 1.97 | Income Ratio % |
| | — | — | — | — | — | — | — | — | — | 32 | Turnover Rate % |
| | — | — | — | — | — | — | — | — | 31 | 209 | Net Assets $mil |

## Performance

**Historic Quarterly NAV Returns**

| | 1st Qtr | 2nd Qtr | 3rd Qtr | 4th Qtr | Total |
|---|---|---|---|---|---|
| 2001 | — | — | — | — | — |
| 2002 | — | — | — | — | — |
| 2003 | — | — | — | — | — |
| 2004 | — | — | — | 4.34 | —* |
| 2005 | 17.43 | 3.61 | 21.57 | -5.99 | 39.05 |

| Trailing | NAV Return% | Market Return% | NAV Rtrn% +/-S&P 500 | %Rank Cat.(NAV) |
|---|---|---|---|---|
| 3 Mo | -5.99 | -5.99 | -8.07 | 7 |
| 6 Mo | 14.29 | 14.30 | 8.53 | 7 |
| 1 Yr | 39.05 | 39.05 | 34.14 | 6 |
| 3 Yr Avg | — | — | — | 0 |
| 5 Yr Avg | — | — | — | 0 |
| 10 Yr Avg | — | — | — | 0 |

| Tax Analysis | Tax-Adj Return% | Tax-Cost Ratio |
|---|---|---|
| 3 Yr (estimated) | — | — |
| 5 Yr (estimated) | — | — |
| 10 Yr (estimated) | — | — |

## Risk Profile

| | Standard Index S&P 500 | Best Fit Index |
|---|---|---|
| Alpha | — | — |
| Beta | — | — |
| R Squared | — | — |
| Standard Deviation | — | |
| Mean | — | |
| Sharpe Ratio | — | |

## Morningstar Fair Value

| Price/Fair Value Ratio | Fair Value Estimate ($) | Hit Rate % |
|---|---|---|
| 1.2 Overvalued | 59.36 | 94 Good |

## Portfolio Analysis 09-30-05

Share change since 06-05  Total Stocks:128

| | Sector | PE | Tot Ret% | % Assets |
|---|---|---|---|---|
| ⊕ ExxonMobil | Energy | 10.6 | 11.76 | 19.33 |
| ⊕ Chevron | Energy | 9.0 | 11.51 | 14.46 |
| ⊕ ConocoPhillips | Energy | 6.7 | 36.89 | 10.37 |
| ⊕ Schlumberger | Energy | 31.1 | 46.62 | 3.61 |
| ⊕ Halliburton | Energy | 21.7 | 59.46 | 2.52 |
| ⊕ Occidental Petroleum | Energy | 6.7 | 39.15 | 2.48 |
| ⊕ Valero Energy | Energy | 10.7 | 128.46 | 2.35 |
| ⊕ Burlington Resources | Energy | 15.4 | 99.35 | 2.29 |
| ⊕ Devon Energy | Energy | 11.4 | 61.57 | 2.25 |
| ⊕ Marathon Oil | Energy | 9.8 | 66.01 | 1.83 |
| ⊕ Apache | Energy | 9.8 | 36.28 | 1.80 |
| ⊕ Anadarko Petroleum | Energy | 11.4 | 47.42 | 1.64 |
| ⊕ Baker Hughes | Energy | 25.9 | 43.78 | 1.48 |
| ⊕ Transocean | Energy | 48.1 | 64.40 | 1.46 |
| ⊕ EOG Resources | Energy | 17.9 | 106.26 | 1.32 |
| ⊕ XTO Energy | Energy | 22.7 | 66.57 | 1.14 |
| ⊕ Williams Companies | Energy | 38.0 | 43.97 | 1.05 |
| ⊕ Chesapeake Energy | Energy | 17.0 | 93.70 | 0.91 |
| ⊕ BJ Services | Energy | 26.6 | 58.54 | 0.87 |
| ⊕ Amerada Hess | Energy | 12.9 | 55.55 | 0.85 |

**Current Investment Style**

Value Blnd Growth — Large Mid Small

| Market Cap | % |
|---|---|
| Giant | 47.8 |
| Large | 34.6 |
| Mid | 13.8 |
| Small | 3.6 |
| Micro | 0.2 |
| Avg $mil: | 40,838 |

| Value Measures | | Rel Category |
|---|---|---|
| Price/Earnings | 12.44 | 0.82 |
| Price/Book | 2.98 | 1.09 |
| Price/Sales | 1.14 | 0.82 |
| Price/Cash Flow | 7.70 | 0.82 |
| Dividend Yield % | 1.17 | 0.97 |

| Growth Measures | % | Rel Category |
|---|---|---|
| Long-Term Erngs | 7.52 | 0.72 |
| Book Value | 11.96 | 1.71 |
| Sales | 18.01 | 1.29 |
| Cash Flow | 26.26 | 1.38 |
| Historical Erngs | 46.00 | 1.39 |

| Profitability | % | Rel Category |
|---|---|---|
| Return on Equity | 21.30 | 1.34 |
| Return on Assets | 10.14 | 1.45 |
| Net Margin | 12.08 | 1.29 |

| Industry Weightings | % of Stocks | Rel Cat |
|---|---|---|
| Oil & Gas | 70.5 | 1.8 |
| Oil/Gas Products | 3.9 | 1.0 |
| Oil & Gas Srv | 19.6 | 0.7 |
| Pipelines | 2.9 | 1.9 |
| Utilities | 0.0 | 0.0 |
| Hard Commd | 0.3 | 0.0 |
| Soft Commd | 0.0 | 0.0 |
| Misc. Indstrl | 0.2 | 0.0 |
| Other | 2.6 | 0.3 |

**Composition**

| | % |
|---|---|
| ● Cash | 0.0 |
| ● Stocks | 100.0 |
| ● Bonds | 0.0 |
| ○ Other | 0.0 |
| Foreign | 0.0 |
| (% of Stock) | |

## Morningstar's Take by Sonya Morris

Investors can do without Vanguard Energy VIPERs.

Vanguard introduced this exchange-traded fund (ETF) in late-September 2004. In the midst of the ongoing energy rally, it has gotten off to a strong start, with a total return of 54% in its first year of operation. Such high-octane performance has lured scads of investors to energy funds, including this one. It has become one of Vanguard's most popular ETFs (though its average daily volume looks practically puny compared to that of Energy Select Spiders). But investors shouldn't let this strong recent showing blind them to its risks: The energy sector is extremely volatile, and its lows can be as harrowing as its highs are exhilarating.

What's more, because of the structure of this ETF's benchmark, it takes on more risk than many of its rivals in the natural-resources category. Specifically, the MSCI US Investable Market Energy Index ranks stocks by market capitalization, which has the effect of making this offering quite top-heavy. Over 60% of the portfolio is dedicated to its top 10 stocks. And because major U.S. oil firms have grown so large over the past several months, the funds' top three holdings--ExxonMobil, Chevron, and ConocoPhillips--now consume over 44% of assets. So not only does this ETF take on sector risk, but it courts considerable stock-specific risk as well.

Extremely volatile funds like this one can be difficult for investors to use, and particularly challenging for those who try to play them for short-term gains. It's important to remember that this ETF's recent robust returns won't continue indefinitely. That risk was highlighted in late August, when Vanguard took the unusual step of warnings its investors about the perils of performance-chasing, particularly in volatile sectors like energy.

And when it comes right down to it, the vast majority of investors don't need this ETF; they already have exposure to the energy sector through their other diversified holdings.

| | | |
|---|---|---|
| Address: | PO Box 2600 Valley Forge PA 19482 866-499-8473 | |
| Web Address: | www.vanguard.com | |
| Inception: | 09-29-04* | |
| Advisor: | Vanguard Advisers, Inc. | |

| Management Fee: | 0.26% | | |
|---|---|---|---|
| Expense Projections: | 3Yr:$90 | 5Yr: — | 10Yr: — |
| Income Distrib: | Annually | | |
| Exchange: | AMEX | | |

**MORNINGSTAR ETFs 100**

147

# Vanguard Euro Stk VIPERs

| Ticker | NAV | Market Price | 52 wk High/Low | Yield | Mstar Category |
|--------|-----|--------------|----------------|-------|----------------|
| VGK | $52.05 | $54.80 | $55.47 - $47.68 | 0.0% | Europe Stock |

## Management

### Portfolio Manager(s)

Vanguard's index-tracking quantitative-equity group, which has extensive experience running a multitude of index funds, manages this offering. Gus Sauter, who heads up that effort, has become the company's chief investment officer. As a result of his increased range of duties, Vanguard is in the process of taking Sauter off individual index funds. So Vanguard is likely to appoint another manager to handle day-to-day management responsibilities in the near future. However, the investment process here will remain the same and Sauter will still be involved in an oversight capacity.

### Strategy

This exchange-traded fund is designed to mirror the performance of the MSCI Europe Index, a capitalization-weighted benchmark of the region's largest markets and stocks. The portfolio is dominated by familiar global leaders such as BP, Nestle, and Novartis, but the large number of holdings dilutes exposure to individual names. The fund has a fair amount of mid-cap exposure but does not own stocks from Central or Eastern Europe. Vanguard does not hedge foreign currency exposure.

**Growth of $10,000**

— Investment Value of ETF
— Investment Value of Index MSCI EAFE

| | 1996 | 1997 | 1998 | 1999 | 2000 | 2001 | 2002 | 2003 | 2004 | 2005 | History |
|---|------|------|------|------|------|------|------|------|------|------|---------|
| | — | — | — | — | — | — | — | — | — | 52.05 | NAV $ |
| | — | — | — | — | — | — | — | — | — | 52.60 | Market Price $ |
| | — | — | — | — | — | — | — | — | — | 5.50* | NAV Return% |
| | — | — | — | — | — | — | — | — | — | 6.07* | Market Price Return% |
| | — | — | — | — | — | — | — | — | — | 0.54 | Avg Premium/Discount% |
| | — | — | — | — | — | — | — | — | — | 5.50 | NAV Rtrn% +/-MSCI EAFE |
| | — | — | — | — | — | — | — | — | — | 5.50 | NAV Rtrn% +/-MSCI Eur |
| | — | — | — | — | — | — | — | — | — | — | NAV Return% Rank in Cat |
| | — | — | — | — | — | — | — | — | — | — | Income Return % |
| | — | — | — | — | — | — | — | — | — | — | Capital Return % |
| | — | — | — | — | — | — | — | — | — | 1.38 | Income $ |
| | — | — | — | — | — | — | — | — | — | 0.00 | Capital Gains $ |
| | — | — | — | — | — | — | — | — | — | 0.18 | Expense Ratio % |
| | — | — | — | — | — | — | — | — | — | 2.93 | Income Ratio % |
| | — | — | — | — | — | — | — | — | — | 5 | Turnover Rate % |
| | — | — | — | — | — | — | — | — | — | 178 | Net Assets $mil |

## Performance

**Historic Quarterly NAV Returns**

| | 1st Qtr | 2nd Qtr | 3rd Qtr | 4th Qtr | Total |
|---|---------|---------|---------|---------|-------|
| 2001 | — | — | — | — | — |
| 2002 | — | — | — | — | — |
| 2003 | — | — | — | — | — |
| 2004 | — | — | — | — | — |
| 2005 | — | -1.10 | 8.18 | 1.78 | —* |

| Trailing | NAV Return% | Market Return%+/-MSCI EAFE | NAV Rtrn% +/-MSCI EAFE | %Rank Cat.(NAV) |
|----------|-------------|---------------------------|------------------------|-----------------|
| 3 Mo | 1.78 | 2.97 | -2.30 | 16 |
| 6 Mo | 10.11 | 10.25 | -4.77 | 16 |
| 1 Yr | — | — | — | 0 |
| 3 Yr Avg | — | — | — | 0 |
| 5 Yr Avg | — | — | — | 0 |
| 10 Yr Avg | — | — | — | 0 |

| Tax Analysis | Tax-Adj Return% | Tax-Cost Ratio |
|--------------|-----------------|----------------|
| 3 Yr (estimated) | — | — |
| 5 Yr (estimated) | — | — |
| 10 Yr (estimated) | — | — |

## Risk Profile

| | Standard Index S&P 500 | Best Fit Index |
|---|------------------------|----------------|
| Alpha | — | — |
| Beta | — | — |
| R-Squared | — | — |
| Standard Deviation | — | |
| Mean | — | |
| Sharpe Ratio | — | |

## Morningstar Fair Value

| Price/Fair Value Ratio | Fair Value Estimate ($) | Hit Rate % |
|------------------------|-------------------------|------------|
| — | — | — |

## Portfolio Analysis 09-30-05

| Share change since 06-05 Total Stocks:573 | Sector | Country | % Assets |
|-------------------------------------------|--------|---------|----------|
| ⊕ BP Plc ADR | Energy | U.K. | 3.72 |
| ⊕ HSBC Hldgs | Financial | U.K. | 2.70 |
| ⊕ TOTAL | Energy | France | 2.32 |
| ⊕ Vodafone Grp | Telecom | U.K. | 2.25 |
| ⊕ GlaxoSmithKline | Health | U.K. | 2.22 |
| ☼ Royal Dutch Shell | Energy | U.K. | 2.03 |
| ⊕ Novartis | Health | Switzerland | 1.79 |
| ⊕ Nestle | Goods | Switzerland | 1.77 |
| ⊕ Roche Holding | Health | Switzerland | 1.45 |
| ☼ Royal Dutch Shell | Energy | U.K. | 1.42 |
| ⊕ UBS | Financial | Switzerland | 1.36 |
| ⊕ Royal Bank Of Scotland G | Financial | U.K. | 1.35 |
| ⊕ Sanofi-Synthelabo | Health | France | 1.31 |
| ⊕ Banco Santander Central | Financial | Spain | 1.16 |
| ⊕ ENI | Energy | Italy | 1.15 |
| ⊕ AstraZeneca | Health | U.K. | 1.13 |
| ⊕ Nokia | Hardware | Finland | 1.11 |
| ⊕ Telefonica | Telecom | Spain | 1.06 |
| ⊕ Barclays | Financial | U.K. | 0.97 |
| ⊕ Siemens | Hardware | Germany | 0.92 |

**Current Investment Style**

Value Blnd Growth — Large / Mid / Small

| Market Cap | % |
|------------|---|
| Giant | 58.7 |
| Large | 27.9 |
| Mid | 12.7 |
| Small | 0.7 |
| Micro | 0.0 |
| Avg $mil: | 37,217 |

| Value Measures | | Rel Category |
|----------------|---|--------------|
| Price/Earnings | 13.75 | 1.02 |
| Price/Book | 2.29 | 0.96 |
| Price/Sales | 1.13 | 0.95 |
| Price/Cash Flow | 7.75 | 1.06 |
| Dividend Yield % | 3.37 | 1.16 |

| Growth Measures | % | Rel Category |
|-----------------|---|--------------|
| Long-Term Erngs | 10.58 | 0.93 |
| Book Value | 1.55 | 0.70 |
| Sales | 0.89 | 0.34 |
| Cash Flow | 4.03 | 1.17 |
| Historical Erngs | 17.50 | 1.10 |

**Composition**

| Cash | 0.4 | Bonds | 0.0 |
|------|-----|-------|-----|
| Stocks | 96.9 | Other | 2.8 |
| Foreign (% of Stock) | | | 100.0 |

| Sector Weightings | % of Stocks | Rel MSCI EAFE | 3 Year High | Low |
|-------------------|-------------|---------------|-------------|-----|
| ↻ Info | 15.18 | 1.08 | | |
| Software | 0.70 | 0.65 | 1 | 0 |
| Hardware | 3.82 | 1.06 | 5 | 4 |
| Media | 2.60 | 1.24 | 3 | 2 |
| Telecom | 8.06 | 1.12 | 11 | 8 |
| ☞ Service | 45.14 | 0.99 | | |
| Health | 9.77 | 1.36 | 13 | 9 |
| Consumer | 4.07 | 0.93 | 5 | 4 |
| Business | 3.87 | 0.64 | 4 | 3 |
| Financial | 27.43 | 0.98 | 28 | 21 |
| Mfg | 39.68 | 0.98 | | |
| Goods | 11.27 | 0.82 | 13 | 11 |
| Ind Mtrls | 10.44 | 0.74 | 10 | 8 |
| Energy | 13.20 | 1.67 | 13 | 11 |
| Utilities | 4.77 | 1.04 | 5 | 4 |

**Regional Exposure** % Stock

| UK/W. Europe | 100 | N. America | 0 |
|--------------|-----|------------|---|
| Japan | 0 | Latn America | 0 |
| Asia X Japan | 0 | Other | 0 |

**Country Exposure** % Stock

| U.K. | 37 | Germany | 10 |
|------|-----|---------|----|
| France | 14 | Italy | 6 |
| Switzerland | 10 | | |

## Morningstar's Take by Dan Lefkovitz

Unexciting performance is not a reason to avoid Vanguard European Stock VIPERs, but there are other issues to consider.

When compared with the Europe-stock mutual fund category, this exchange-traded fund, which is a share class of Vanguard European Stock Index, has lagged badly. Two factors have held it back. First of all, the ETF, which tracks the MSCI Europe Index, only invests in Western European stocks, and Central and Eastern European markets have been white hot. Second, the fund's focus on large caps has hurt during a period of smaller-cap outperformance.

Of course, Western European large caps have been no slouches themselves, which is why this ETF's performance has been strong on an absolute basis. Energy firms like BP, Total, and Royal Dutch Shell are benefiting from the same high energy prices as their U.S. cousins. And other global players, such as Roche and Nestle, are soaring as well. European stock gains have even overcome the headwind of a rising dollar, which diminishes the value of foreign-currency-denominated shares.

We think it makes sense for U.S. investors to have exposure to Europe, and we consider this fund's portfolio more well-rounded than other Europe ETFs on the market. The folks at Vanguard also do an excellent job of tracking the MSCI Europe--the traditional mutual fund has been around 15 years--and we won't change that view when manager Gus Sauter cedes management duties to an experienced lieutenant, as Vanguard has indicated he will do in February 2006. The price is right here, too. This is by far the cheapest Europe ETF on the market.

Investors should keep a couple things in mind, though. First, if you own a diversified foreign fund, this fund's Western European large-cap exposure will be redundant. Second, brokerage commissions can easily erode this fund's price advantage over its traditional mutual fund clone.

| Address: | PO Box 2600 Valley Forge PA 19482 866-499-8473 |
|----------|------------------------------------------------|
| Web Address: | www.vanguard.com |
| Inception: | 03-10-05* |
| Advisor: | Vanguard Advisers, Inc. |

| Management Fee: | 0.14% |
|-----------------|-------|
| Expense Projections: | 3Yr:$58   5Yr:$101   10Yr:$230 |
| Income Distrib: | Annually |
| Exchange: | AMEX |

**MORNINGSTAR® ETFs 100**

# Vanguard ExMkt VIPERs

| Ticker | NAV | Market Price | 52 wk High/Low | Yield | Mstar Category |
|---|---|---|---|---|---|
| VXF | $90.40 | $94.80 | $94.80 - $76.93 | 1.1% | Mid-Cap Blend |

## Management

### Portfolio Manager(s)

Vanguard's indexing guru, Gus Sauter, will take on a supportive role at this offering. He recently handed over day-to-day managerial responsibilities to Donald Butler, who has been with Vanguard since 1992 and has worked with Sauter on this offering since 1997.

### Strategy

This ETF is in the process of switching its benchmark from the Dow Jones Wilshire 4500 Index to the newly created S&P Completion Index. That shouldn't bring about dramatic changes. But unlike the Wilshire index, the new bogy is free-float-weighted, and it also screens out profit-challenged firms and companies with limited operating histories.

**Growth of $10,000**

— Investment Value of ETF
— Investment Value of Index S&P 500

| 1996 | 1997 | 1998 | 1999 | 2000 | 2001 | 2002 | 2003 | 2004 | 2005 | History |
|---|---|---|---|---|---|---|---|---|---|---|
| — | — | — | — | — | 60.94 | 49.47 | 70.37 | 82.74 | 90.40 | NAV $ |
| — | — | — | — | — | 60.94 | 49.61 | 70.70 | 82.82 | 90.47 | Market Price $ |
| — | — | — | — | — | 11.45* | -17.95 | 43.52 | 18.75 | 10.48 | NAV Return% |
| — | — | — | — | — | 11.48* | — | 43.79 | 18.31 | 10.46 | Market Price Return% |
| — | — | — | — | — | — | 0.21 | 0.07 | -0.03 | 0.01 | Avg Premium/Discount% |
| — | — | — | — | — | 11.45 | 4.14 | 14.85 | 7.88 | 5.57 | NAV Rtrn% +/-S&P 500 |
| — | — | — | — | — | 11.45 | -3.42 | 7.93 | 2.28 | -2.07 | NAV Rtrn% +/-S&P Mid 400 |
| — | — | — | — | — | — | 4 | 4 | 5 | 7 | NAV Return% Rank in Cat |
| — | — | — | — | — | — | 0.88 | 1.24 | 1.16 | 1.23 | Income Return % |
| — | — | — | — | — | — | -18.83 | 42.28 | 17.59 | 9.25 | Capital Return % |
| — | — | — | — | — | 0.00 | 0.54 | 0.61 | 0.81 | 1.02 | Income $ |
| — | — | — | — | — | 0.00 | 0.00 | 0.00 | 0.00 | 0.00 | Capital Gains $ |
| — | — | — | — | — | — | 0.20 | 0.20 | 0.20 | — | Expense Ratio % |
| — | — | — | — | — | — | 1.04 | 1.07 | 1.12 | — | Income Ratio % |
| — | — | — | — | — | 20 | 17 | 8 | 17 | — | Turnover Rate % |
| — | — | — | — | — | — | — | 107 | 231 | 368 | Net Assets $mil |

## Performance

**Historic Quarterly NAV Returns**

| | 1st Qtr | 2nd Qtr | 3rd Qtr | 4th Qtr | Total |
|---|---|---|---|---|---|
| 2001 | — | — | — | — | —* |
| 2002 | 1.94 | -10.00 | -15.51 | 5.84 | -17.95 |
| 2003 | -3.32 | 21.33 | 7.55 | 13.76 | 43.52 |
| 2004 | 5.93 | 0.12 | -1.82 | 14.05 | 18.75 |
| 2005 | -3.28 | 5.52 | 5.47 | 2.63 | 10.48 |

| Trailing | NAV Return% | Market Return% | NAV Rtrn% +/-S&P 500 | %Rank Cat.(NAV) |
|---|---|---|---|---|
| 3 Mo | 2.63 | 2.72 | 0.55 | 7 |
| 6 Mo | 8.25 | 8.19 | 2.49 | 7 |
| 1 Yr | 10.48 | 10.46 | 5.57 | 7 |
| 3 Yr Avg | 23.49 | 23.40 | 9.11 | 4 |
| 5 Yr Avg | — | — | — | 0 |
| 10 Yr Avg | — | — | — | 0 |

| Tax Analysis | Tax-Adj Return% | Tax-Cost Ratio |
|---|---|---|
| 3 Yr (estimated) | 23.24 | 0.20 |
| 5 Yr (estimated) | — | — |
| 10 Yr (estimated) | — | — |

## Risk Profile

| | Standard Index S&P 500 | Best Fit Index DJ Wilshire 4500 |
|---|---|---|
| Alpha | 5.0 | -0.1 |
| Beta | 1.26 | 1.01 |
| R-Squared | 82 | 100 |
| Standard Deviation | 12.72 | |
| Mean | 23.49 | |
| Sharpe Ratio | 1.58 | |

## Morningstar Fair Value

| Price/Fair Value Ratio | Fair Value Estimate ($) | Hit Rate % |
|---|---|---|
| 1.1 Overvalued | 30.63 | 60 Poor |

## Portfolio Analysis 09-30-05

Share change since 06-05 Total Stocks:3561

| | Sector | PE | Tot Ret% | % Assets |
|---|---|---|---|---|
| ⊕ Google | Business | — | 115.19 | 1.88 |
| ⊕ Genentech | Health | 86.5 | 69.91 | 1.21 |
| ⊕ Liberty Media | Media | — | -15.71 | 0.67 |
| ⊕ Genworth Financial | Financial | — | 29.27 | 0.49 |
| ⊕ Accenture | Business | 18.5 | 8.21 | 0.46 |
| ⊕ Legg Mason | Financial | 30.9 | 64.48 | 0.40 |
| ⊕ Juniper Networks | Hardware | 41.3 | -17.98 | 0.37 |
| ⊕ Chicago Mercantile Excha | Financial | 44.4 | 61.83 | 0.37 |
| ⊕ Amazon.com | Consumer | 41.4 | 6.46 | 0.36 |
| ⊕ Peabody Energy | Energy | 33.1 | 104.95 | 0.36 |
| ⊕ General Growth Propertie | Financial | NMF | 35.15 | 0.34 |
| ⊕ Chesapeake Energy | Energy | 17.0 | 93.70 | 0.34 |
| ⊕ DirecTV | Media | — | -15.65 | 0.31 |
| ⊕ Marvell Technology | Hardware | 60.3 | 58.13 | 0.31 |
| ⊕ Celgene | Health | NMF | 144.34 | 0.29 |
| ⊕ Whole Foods Market | Consumer | 78.2 | 63.73 | 0.29 |
| ⊕ GlobalSantaFe | Energy | 50.2 | 47.43 | 0.28 |
| ⊕ SanDisk | Hardware | 36.1 | 151.58 | 0.28 |
| ⊕ Ultra Petroleum | Energy | 47.9 | 131.87 | 0.28 |
| ⊕ Sirius Satellite Radio | Media | — | -12.07 | 0.28 |

### Current Investment Style

Value Blnd Growth — Large Mid Small

| Market Cap | % |
|---|---|
| Giant | 3.4 |
| Large | 7.1 |
| Mid | 53.6 |
| Small | 26.3 |
| Micro | 9.6 |

Avg $mil: 2,321

| Value Measures | | Rel Category |
|---|---|---|
| Price/Earnings | 18.46 | 1.05 |
| Price/Book | 2.23 | 0.94 |
| Price/Sales | 1.21 | 1.05 |
| Price/Cash Flow | 7.55 | 1.01 |
| Dividend Yield % | 1.10 | 0.95 |

| Growth Measures | % | Rel Category |
|---|---|---|
| Long-Term Erngs | 12.77 | 1.01 |
| Book Value | 6.14 | 0.71 |
| Sales | 7.52 | 0.92 |
| Cash Flow | 6.32 | 0.63 |
| Historical Erngs | 12.63 | 0.78 |

| Profitability | % | Rel Category |
|---|---|---|
| Return on Equity | 12.16 | 0.81 |
| Return on Assets | 6.75 | 0.87 |
| Net Margin | 10.96 | 1.03 |

### Sector Weightings

| | % of Stocks | Rel S&P 500 | 3 Year High | Low |
|---|---|---|---|---|
| ↻ Info | 16.63 | 0.82 | | |
| 🖩 Software | 3.62 | 1.02 | 4 | 3 |
| 🖥 Hardware | 6.99 | 0.70 | 8 | 6 |
| 🎤 Media | 4.02 | 1.12 | 6 | 4 |
| 📞 Telecom | 2.00 | 0.66 | 2 | 1 |
| ☞ Service | 56.42 | 1.22 | | |
| ⚕ Health | 12.16 | 0.91 | 13 | 11 |
| 🛒 Consumer | 10.37 | 1.27 | 12 | 10 |
| 🏦 Business | 10.82 | 2.80 | 11 | 8 |
| $ Financial | 23.07 | 1.09 | 29 | 23 |
| ⏋ Mfg | 26.96 | 0.81 | | |
| 🏭 Goods | 4.97 | 0.58 | 7 | 5 |
| ⚙ Ind Mtrls | 9.65 | 0.79 | 10 | 8 |
| 🔋 Energy | 8.72 | 0.93 | 9 | 5 |
| 💡 Utilities | 3.62 | 1.08 | 4 | 3 |

### Composition

| | % |
|---|---|
| ● Cash | 0.7 |
| ● Stocks | 98.7 |
| ● Bonds | 0.0 |
| ● Other | 0.6 |
| Foreign | 0.1 |
| (% of Stock) | |

## Morningstar's Take by Sonya Morris

Change is in the air for Vanguard Extended Market Index VIPERs, but the mission remains the same.

This exchange-traded fund is in the process of switching benchmarks from the Dow Jones Wilshire 4500 Index to the S&P Completion Index. It moved a step closer to its new bogy in June 2005 when it began tracking the S&P Transitional Completion Index. That was the first step in a two-phase process designed to minimize the market impact of the switch. The transition is expected to be completed by the end of 2005.

The fund will probably change some around the edges, but this isn't a major transformation. We can't compare the two indexes directly because S&P has not yet released the index's constituents or methodology. However, we can make some observations based on the information that has been provided thus far. First of all, unlike the old benchmark, the S&P index is float-weighted, meaning its stock weightings are adjusted for shares that are not freely available for trading. In

addition, S&P has a more subjective way of identifying U.S. firms, relying on where the firm does the bulk of its business rather than where its headquarters is located. Finally, like the S&P 500, the new index will likely screen out profit-challenged firms with limited operating histories. Because the Wilshire 4500 has no such screens, it includes a handful of large-cap names excluded from the S&P 500, such as Amazon.com and Whole Foods Markets. This passel of more speculative stocks has contributed to this fund's streaky track record.

Whether the new benchmark will deliver more consistent results remains to be seen. In any case, to view this ETF's performance in isolation is to miss the point. The fund is intended to serve as a cheap and convenient diversifier that, in combination with an S&P 500 Index fund, will provide investors exposure to virtually the entire U.S. stock market. And it will serve the same useful purpose under its new benchmark.

| | | | | |
|---|---|---|---|---|
| Address: | PO Box 2600 Valley Forge PA 19482 866-499-8473 | Management Fee: | 0.05% | |
| Web Address: | www.vanguard.com | Expense Projections: | 3Yr:$26 | 5Yr:$45 | 10Yr:$103 |
| Inception: | 12-27-01* | Income Distrib: | Annually | |
| Advisor: | Vanguard Advisers, Inc. | Exchange: | AMEX | |

Ⓜ MORNINGSTAR® ETFs 100

# Vanguard Financial VIPERs

| | Ticker | NAV | Market Price | 52 wk High/Low | Yield | Mstar Category |
|---|---|---|---|---|---|---|
| | VFH | $55.95 | $57.66 | $57.66 - $48.75 | 1.3% | Specialty-Financial |

## Management

### Portfolio Manager(s)

Vanguard chief investment officer George Sauter and a team of quantitative analysts have managed this offering since its 2003 inception. Sauter and his team manage many of Vanguard's index funds, including other sector-specific VIPERs and the widely held Vanguard 500 Index. They are experienced indexers who closely follow each fund's designated benchmark. This ETF's shares are traded on the American Stock Exchange.

### Strategy

This portfolio includes all of the financials stocks included in the MSCI US Investable Market 2500 Index, which represents 98% of the capitalization of the U.S. equity market. That turns out to be more than 540 financial companies, ranging from global financial-services firms to tiny community banks. The fund is market-cap-weighted, so the market's biggest players have larger positions in the portfolio. About one quarter of the fund's assets are in mid- and small-cap stocks.

**Growth of $10,000**

— Investment Value of ETF
— Investment Value of Index S&P 500

| | 1996 | 1997 | 1998 | 1999 | 2000 | 2001 | 2002 | 2003 | 2004 | 2005 | History |
|---|---|---|---|---|---|---|---|---|---|---|---|
| | — | — | — | — | — | — | — | — | 53.75 | 55.95 | NAV $ |
| | — | — | — | — | — | — | — | — | 53.81 | 56.01 | Market Price $ |
| | — | — | — | — | — | — | — | — | 7.37* | 5.53 | NAV Return% |
| | — | — | — | — | — | — | — | — | 7.43† | 5.53 | Market Price Return% |
| | — | — | — | — | — | — | — | — | 0.03 | -0.02 | Avg Premium/Discount% |
| | — | — | — | — | — | — | — | — | 7.37 | 0.62 | NAV Rtrn% +/-S&P 500 |
| | — | — | — | — | — | — | — | — | 7.37 | -0.92 | NAV Rtrn% +/-DJ Finance |
| | — | — | — | — | — | — | — | — | — | 5 | NAV Return% Rank in Cat |
| | — | — | — | — | — | — | — | — | 0.00 | 1.40 | Income Return % |
| | — | — | — | — | — | — | — | — | — | 4.13 | Capital Return % |
| | — | — | — | — | — | — | — | — | 1.15 | 0.75 | Income $ |
| | — | — | — | — | — | — | — | — | 0.00 | 0.00 | Capital Gains $ |
| | — | — | — | — | — | — | — | — | 0.28 | 0.26 | Expense Ratio % |
| | — | — | — | — | — | — | — | — | 2.38 | 2.61 | Income Ratio % |
| | — | — | — | — | — | — | — | — | 9 | 6 | Turnover Rate % |
| | — | — | — | — | — | — | — | — | 27 | 62 | Net Assets $mil |

## Performance

### Historic Quarterly NAV Returns

| | 1st Qtr | 2nd Qtr | 3rd Qtr | 4th Qtr | Total |
|---|---|---|---|---|---|
| 2001 | — | — | — | — | — |
| 2002 | — | — | — | — | — |
| 2003 | — | — | — | — | — |
| 2004 | — | -2.53 | 1.37 | 8.95 | —* |
| 2005 | -6.60 | 5.33 | 0.23 | 7.04 | 5.53 |

| Trailing | NAV Return% | Market Return% | NAV Rtrn% +/-S&P 500 | %Rank Cat.(NAV) |
|---|---|---|---|---|
| 3 Mo | 7.04 | 7.15 | 4.96 | 5 |
| 6 Mo | 7.28 | 6.63 | 1.52 | 5 |
| 1 Yr | 5.53 | 5.53 | 0.62 | 5 |
| 3 Yr Avg | — | — | — | 0 |
| 5 Yr Avg | — | — | — | 0 |
| 10 Yr Avg | — | — | — | 0 |

| Tax Analysis | Tax-Adj Return% | Tax-Cost Ratio |
|---|---|---|
| 3 Yr (estimated) | — | — |
| 5 Yr (estimated) | — | — |
| 10 Yr (estimated) | — | — |

## Risk Profile

| | Standard Index S&P 500 | Best Fit Index |
|---|---|---|
| Alpha | — | — |
| Beta | — | — |
| R-Squared | — | — |
| Standard Deviation | — | |
| Mean | — | |
| Sharpe Ratio | — | |

## Morningstar Fair Value

| Price/Fair Value Ratio | Fair Value Estimate ($) | Hit Rate % |
|---|---|---|
| 1.0 Fairly valued | 48.29 | 88 Good |

## Portfolio Analysis 09-30-05

| Share change since 06-05 Total Stocks:528 | Sector | PE | Tot Ret% | % Assets |
|---|---|---|---|---|
| ⊕ Citigroup | Financial | 12.1 | 4.63 | 8.24 |
| ⊕ Bank of America | Financial | 11.1 | 2.39 | 5.91 |
| ⊕ American International G | Financial | 15.6 | 4.83 | 4.77 |
| ⊕ J.P. Morgan Chase & Co. | Financial | 18.8 | 5.74 | 4.19 |
| ⊕ Wells Fargo | Financial | 14.3 | 4.47 | 3.48 |
| ⊕ Wachovia | Financial | 13.0 | 4.29 | 2.67 |
| ⊕ American Express | Financial | 16.4 | 5.31 | 2.27 |
| ⊕ Merrill Lynch & Company | Financial | 13.7 | 14.77 | 1.94 |
| ⊕ Morgan Stanley | Financial | 13.3 | 4.28 | 1.88 |
| ⊕ US Bancorp | Financial | 12.7 | -0.46 | 1.84 |
| ⊕ Goldman Sachs Group | Financial | 12.4 | 23.89 | 1.74 |
| ⊕ Fannie Mae | Financial | — | -30.14 | 1.51 |
| ⊕ Freddie Mac | Financial | 16.6 | -9.16 | 1.37 |
| ⊕ Metropolitan Life Insura | Financial | 11.8 | 22.22 | 1.29 |
| ⊕ Allstate | Financial | 18.2 | 6.93 | 1.25 |
| ⊕ Prudential Financial | Financial | 11.7 | 34.54 | 1.24 |
| ⊕ Washington Mutual | Financial | 11.9 | 7.79 | 1.20 |
| ⊕ St. Paul Travelers Compa | Financial | 13.9 | 23.20 | 1.06 |
| ⊕ MBNA | Financial | — | — | 1.05 |
| ⊕ Lehman Brothers Holdings | Financial | 12.7 | 47.67 | 0.96 |

### Current Investment Style

Value Blnd Growth — Large Mid Small

| Market Cap | % |
|---|---|
| Giant | 40.2 |
| Large | 32.9 |
| Mid | 20.7 |
| Small | 5.5 |
| Micro | 0.7 |

Avg $mil: 24,758

| Value Measures | | Rel Category |
|---|---|---|
| Price/Earnings | 12.40 | 0.95 |
| Price/Book | 1.65 | 0.98 |
| Price/Sales | 2.23 | 0.88 |
| Price/Cash Flow | 2.58 | 0.68 |
| Dividend Yield % | 2.86 | 0.98 |

| Growth Measures | % | Rel Category |
|---|---|---|
| Long-Term Erngs | 10.52 | 1.02 |
| Book Value | 13.83 | 0.92 |
| Sales | 7.20 | 1.23 |
| Cash Flow | 5.06 | 0.40 |
| Historical Erngs | 11.76 | 0.98 |

| Profitability | % | Rel Category |
|---|---|---|
| Return on Equity | 15.17 | 0.95 |
| Return on Assets | 14.41 | 1.02 |
| Net Margin | 21.51 | 1.00 |

| Industry Weightings | % of Stocks | Rel Cat |
|---|---|---|
| Intl Banks | 20.6 | 1.3 |
| Banks | 19.8 | 0.9 |
| Real Estate | 10.0 | 2.9 |
| Sec Mgmt | 10.9 | 0.9 |
| S & Ls | 4.9 | 0.6 |
| Prop & Reins | 13.9 | 0.9 |
| Life Ins | 6.2 | 1.2 |
| Misc. Ins | 3.6 | 1.2 |
| Other | 10.1 | 0.7 |

### Composition

| | | % |
|---|---|---|
| ● | Cash | 0.1 |
| ● | Stocks | 98.9 |
| ● | Bonds | 0.0 |
| ● | Other | 1.0 |
| | Foreign | 0.1 |
| | (% of Stock) | |

## Morningstar's Take by Laura Pavlenko Lutton

Vanguard Financials VIPERs is a sensible way to get exposure to financials stocks.

This exchanged-traded fund takes a diversified approach to investing in financials. Its portfolio includes all of the financials stocks included in the MSCI US Investable Market 2500 Index, which represents 98% of the capitalization of the U.S. equity market. Thus, investors get exposure to more than 540 financials stocks that reside throughout the market-cap spectrum.

This broad approach has some plusses. While many actively managed financials funds make sizable industry bets, this offering maintains exposure to all industries in this broad sector, and it won't miss out should one or more areas suddenly take off. In addition, the fund isn't as skewed to giant- and large-cap names as some of its ETF and actively managed competitors, including Financial Select Sector SPDR. This offering keeps about one quarter of its assets in small- and mid-cap stocks, which in recent years have outperformed their larger-cap peers.

Overall, this fund is well diversified, but it's worth noting that a handful of mega-cap stocks--including Citigroup, Bank of American, and American International Group--dominates the fund's portfolio. In fact, the offering has more than one third of its assets parked in its top 10 holdings, so the industry's big hitters will have an outsized impact on performance.

In the end, however, we think this fund's biggest challenge will be distinguishing itself within the financials category. The offering's wide scope makes it unlikely that the fund will turn in category-killing returns. On the other hand, it shouldn't dramatically underperform, either, and the fund certainly is helped by its 0.25% expense ratio, which is attractive even by ETF standards. We think this fund's middle-of-the-road approach holds appeal for investors seeking no-nonsense financials exposure, particularly those out to diversify an otherwise growth-heavy portfolio.

| | |
|---|---|
| Address: | PO Box 2600 |
| | Valley Forge PA 19482 |
| | 866-499-8473 |
| Web Address: | www.vanguard.com |
| Inception: | 01-26-04* |
| Advisor: | Vanguard Advisers, Inc. |

| | |
|---|---|
| Management Fee: | 0.26% |
| Expense Projections: | 3Yr:$90    5Yr:$157    10Yr:$356 |
| Income Distrib: | Quarterly |
| Exchange: | AMEX |

**MORNINGSTAR® ETFs 100**

# Vanguard Growth VIPERs

| | Ticker | NAV | Market Price | 52 wk High/Low | Yield | Mstar Category |
|---|---|---|---|---|---|---|
| | VUG | $53.52 | $55.53 | $55.53 - $47.64 | 0.9% | Large Growth |

## Management

### Portfolio Manager(s)

Gus Sauter, Vanguard's index guru, has stepped down as the day-to-day manager of this fund so he can concentrate on his responsibilities as the firm's chief investment officer. Although he will retain a supervisory role here, Gerard O'Reilly will handle the daily managerial chores. O'Reilly has been with Vanguard since 1992 and has assisted here since 1992.

### Strategy

This exchange-traded fund, or ETF, is tethered to the MSCI U.S. Prime Market Growth Index, which contains the 750 largest companies--in terms of free-float market capitalization--in the U.S. MSCI defines style (growth versus value) using an eight-factor model that includes measures ranging from dividend yield to long-term historical sales per share. MSCI employs buffer zones to limit the migration of stocks between the growth and value camps. This should serve to limit turnover.

**Growth of $10,000**

— Investment Value of ETF
— Investment Value of Index S&P 500

| | 1996 | 1997 | 1998 | 1999 | 2000 | 2001 | 2002 | 2003 | 2004 | 2005 | History |
|---|---|---|---|---|---|---|---|---|---|---|---|
| | — | — | — | — | — | — | — | — | 51.33 | 53.52 | NAV $ |
| | — | — | — | — | — | — | — | — | 51.40 | 53.50 | Market Price $ |
| | — | — | — | — | — | — | — | — | 4.05* | 5.20 | NAV Return% |
| | — | — | — | — | — | — | — | — | 4.03* | 5.02 | Market Price Return% |
| | — | — | — | — | — | — | — | — | 0.14 | 0.14 | Avg Premium/Discount% |
| | — | — | — | — | — | — | — | — | 4.05 | 0.29 | NAV Rtrn% +/-S&P 500 |
| | — | — | — | — | — | — | — | — | 4.05 | -0.06 | NAV Rtrn% +/-Russ 1000Gr |
| | — | — | — | — | — | — | — | — | — | 9 | NAV Return% Rank in Cat |
| | — | — | — | — | — | — | — | — | 0.00 | 0.90 | Income Return % |
| | — | — | — | — | — | — | — | — | — | 4.30 | Capital Return % |
| | — | — | — | — | — | — | — | — | 0.61 | 0.46 | Income $ |
| | — | — | — | — | — | — | — | — | 0.00 | 0.00 | Capital Gains $ |
| | — | — | — | — | — | — | — | — | 0.15 | — | Expense Ratio % |
| | — | — | — | — | — | — | — | — | 1.22 | — | Income Ratio % |
| | — | — | — | — | — | — | — | — | 24 | — | Turnover Rate % |
| | — | — | — | — | — | — | — | — | 104 | 324 | Net Assets $mil |

## Performance

**Historic Quarterly NAV Returns**

| | 1st Qtr | 2nd Qtr | 3rd Qtr | 4th Qtr | Total |
|---|---|---|---|---|---|
| 2001 | — | — | — | — | — |
| 2002 | — | — | — | — | — |
| 2003 | — | — | — | — | — |
| 2004 | — | 1.51 | -4.84 | 9.41 | —* |
| 2005 | -3.53 | 2.17 | 3.58 | 3.05 | 5.20 |

| Trailing | NAV Return% | Market Return% | NAV Rtrn% +/-S&P 500 | %Rank Cat.(NAV) |
|---|---|---|---|---|
| 3 Mo | 3.05 | 2.79 | 0.97 | 10 |
| 6 Mo | 6.73 | 6.31 | 0.97 | 10 |
| 1 Yr | 5.20 | 5.02 | 0.29 | 9 |
| 3 Yr Avg | — | — | — | 0 |
| 5 Yr Avg | — | — | — | 0 |
| 10 Yr Avg | — | — | — | 0 |

| Tax Analysis | Tax-Adj Return% | Tax-Cost Ratio |
|---|---|---|
| 3 Yr (estimated) | — | — |
| 5 Yr (estimated) | — | — |
| 10 Yr (estimated) | — | — |

## Risk Profile

| | Standard Index S&P 500 | Best Fit Index |
|---|---|---|
| Alpha | — | — |
| Beta | — | — |
| R-Squared | — | — |
| Standard Deviation | — | |
| Mean | — | |
| Sharpe Ratio | — | |

## Morningstar Fair Value

| Price/Fair Value Ratio | Fair Value Estimate ($) | Hit Rate % |
|---|---|---|
| 1.0 Fairly valued | 38.04 | 96 Good |

## Portfolio Analysis 09-30-05

Share change since 06-05  Total Stocks:423

| | | Sector | PE | Tot Ret% | % Assets |
|---|---|---|---|---|---|
| ⊖ | Microsoft | Software | 22.2 | -0.95 | 4.10 |
| ⊖ | Johnson & Johnson | Health | 19.1 | -3.36 | 3.08 |
| ⊖ | General Electric | Ind Mtrls | 19.9 | -1.43 | 2.92 |
| ⊖ | Intel | Hardware | 18.6 | 8.12 | 2.49 |
| ⊖ | Procter & Gamble | Goods | 21.2 | 7.18 | 2.34 |
| ⊖ | IBM | Hardware | 16.0 | -15.83 | 2.12 |
| ⊖ | Cisco Systems | Hardware | 19.9 | -11.39 | 1.88 |
| ⊖ | Wal-Mart Stores | Consumer | 18.2 | -10.30 | 1.82 |
| ⊖ | Amgen | Health | 28.3 | 22.93 | 1.61 |
| ⊖ | PepsiCo | Goods | 25.8 | 15.24 | 1.56 |
| ⊖ | Home Depot | Consumer | 15.6 | -4.35 | 1.34 |
| ⊕ | Dell | Hardware | 23.2 | -28.93 | 1.29 |
| ⊖ | UnitedHealth Group | Health | 26.2 | 41.22 | 1.20 |
| ⊖ | Qualcomm | Hardware | 34.2 | 2.50 | 1.20 |
| ⊕ | Sprint Nextel | Telecom | 19.1 | -4.81 | 1.09 |
| ⊖ | Abbott Laboratories | Health | 18.3 | -13.47 | 1.08 |
| ⊖ | Medtronic | Health | 37.4 | 16.72 | 1.06 |
| ⊖ | American Express | Financial | 16.4 | 5.31 | 1.05 |
| ⊕ | Google | Business | — | 115.19 | 0.99 |
| ⊕ | Gillette | Goods | — | — | 0.94 |

## Morningstar's Take  by Sonya Morris

Vanguard Growth VIPERs stays true to its mission.

This fund does what it's supposed to do: provide investors with broad exposure to large-growth stocks. Because its benchmark, the MSCI U.S. Prime Market Growth Index, uses a multifactor model to identify growth stocks, it does a good job of accurately reflecting its selected universe.

However, that's been a tough place to be in recent years as the market has preferred small caps and value stocks to large-growth fare. And because this fund must remain fully invested, it has had no place to hide. Consequently, this offering's twin mutual fund, Vanguard Growth Index has produced five-year annualized returns that are more than 6 percentage points lower than those of its value-oriented sibling, Vanguard Value Index.

But lately there have been signs of life from this beleaguered market segment. Large-growth stocks have struggled for so long that their valuations have become more reasonable. Indeed, some well-respected value managers have recently been scooping up beaten-down growth stocks.

We're certainly not suggesting that shareholders try to time a comeback in the segment. But given value stocks' prolonged dominance, now may be an appropriate time for investors to check their asset allocations to make sure their portfolios haven't taken on an unintended value bias. Those in need of growth exposure could do worse than this ETF, as it can be relied upon to provide pure exposure to large-growth stocks at a bargain-basement price.

Finally, it's worth noting that a new manager has taken the controls at this fund. In April 2005, Gerard O'Reilly assumed the daily managerial chores from Gus Sauter, Vanguard's index pro and chief investment officer. O'Reilly has assisted in the management of the fund since 1994, so we don't expect this fund to miss a beat. It remains a fine choice.

### Current Investment Style

Value Blnd Growth — Large / Mid / Small

| | Market Cap | % |
|---|---|---|
| | Giant | 49.6 |
| | Large | 35.2 |
| | Mid | 15.2 |
| | Small | 0.0 |
| | Micro | 0.0 |

Avg $mil: 36,686

| Value Measures | | Rel Category |
|---|---|---|
| Price/Earnings | 20.26 | 0.96 |
| Price/Book | 3.44 | 1.02 |
| Price/Sales | 1.79 | 0.92 |
| Price/Cash Flow | 11.26 | 1.07 |
| Dividend Yield % | 1.03 | 1.16 |

| Growth Measures | % | Rel Category |
|---|---|---|
| Long-Term Erngs | 13.61 | 0.97 |
| Book Value | 10.04 | 1.23 |
| Sales | 11.26 | 1.01 |
| Cash Flow | 13.19 | 0.81 |
| Historical Erngs | 17.36 | 0.91 |

| Profitability | % | Rel Category |
|---|---|---|
| Return on Equity | 21.38 | 1.06 |
| Return on Assets | 10.60 | 0.99 |
| Net Margin | 13.07 | 0.94 |

| Sector Weightings | % of Stocks | Rel S&P 500 | 3 Year High | Low |
|---|---|---|---|---|
| ↻ Info | 28.86 | 1.43 | | |
| Software | 6.90 | 1.94 | 9 | 6 |
| Hardware | 15.77 | 1.57 | 21 | 13 |
| Media | 4.48 | 1.25 | 6 | 1 |
| Telecom | 1.71 | 0.57 | 3 | 1 |
| ⊂ Service | 45.65 | 0.98 | | |
| Health | 19.42 | 1.46 | 27 | 19 |
| Consumer | 13.24 | 1.63 | 14 | 12 |
| Business | 6.41 | 1.66 | 6 | 4 |
| Financial | 6.58 | 0.31 | 10 | 5 |
| Mfg | 25.47 | 0.76 | | |
| Goods | 9.86 | 1.15 | 16 | 9 |
| Ind Mtrls | 10.03 | 0.83 | 10 | 3 |
| Energy | 4.99 | 0.53 | 5 | 0 |
| Utilities | 0.59 | 0.18 | 1 | 0 |

**Composition**

| | | |
|---|---|---|
| ● Cash | | 0.0 |
| ● Stocks | | 100.0 |
| ● Bonds | | 0.0 |
| ● Other | | 0.0 |
| Foreign | | 0.1 |
| (% of Stock) | | |

| Address: | PO Box 2600 Valley Forge PA 19482 866-499-8473 | Management Fee: | 0.07% | | |
|---|---|---|---|---|---|
| | | Expense Projections: | 3Yr:$35 | 5Yr:$62 | 10Yr:$141 |
| | | Income Distrib: | Quarterly | | |
| Web Address: | www.vanguard.com | Exchange: | AMEX | | |
| Inception: | 01-26-04* | | | | |
| Advisor: | Vanguard Advisers, Inc. | | | | |

MORNINGSTAR® ETFs 100

# Vanguard HealthCar VIPERs

| | Ticker | NAV | Market Price | 52 wk High/Low | Yield | Mstar Category |
|---|---|---|---|---|---|---|
| | VHT | $54.00 | $55.59 | $55.86 - $48.38 | 0.7% | Specialty-Health |

## Management

### Portfolio Manager(s)

Gus Sauter has been at the helm of this offering since its January 2004 inception. Sauter is an highly capable, experienced index fund manager who also runs Vanguard 500 Index among other index funds.

### Strategy

This exchange-traded fund tracks the MSCI U.S. Investable Market Health Care Index. Large-cap drug names dominate the benchmark, though biotechnology, medical-equipment, and health-care services stocks play supporting roles. The ETF is concentrated in its largest holdings, with more than half of its assets in its top 10. Given the MSCI index's domestic focus, the fund has no international exposure.

**Growth of $10,000**

— Investment Value of ETF
— Investment Value of Index S&P 500

| 1996 | 1997 | 1998 | 1999 | 2000 | 2001 | 2002 | 2003 | 2004 | 2005 | History |
|---|---|---|---|---|---|---|---|---|---|---|
| — | — | — | — | — | — | — | — | 50.24 | 54.00 | NAV $ |
| — | — | — | — | — | — | — | — | 50.28 | 54.02 | Market Price $ |
| — | — | — | — | — | — | — | — | 4.00* | 8.24 | NAV Return% |
| — | — | — | — | — | — | — | — | 4.02* | 8.20 | Market Price Return% |
| — | — | — | — | — | — | — | — | 0.07 | 0.06 | Avg Premium/Discount% |
| — | — | — | — | — | — | — | — | 4.00 | 3.33 | NAV Rtrn% +/-S&P 500 |
| — | — | — | — | — | — | — | — | 4.00 | -0.08 | NAV Rtrn% +/-DJ Hlthcare |
| — | — | — | — | — | — | — | — | — | 5 | NAV Return% Rank in Cat |
| — | — | — | — | — | — | — | — | 0.00 | 0.77 | Income Return % |
| — | — | — | — | — | — | — | — | — | 7.47 | Capital Return % |
| — | — | — | — | — | — | — | — | 0.13 | 0.39 | Income $ |
| — | — | — | — | — | — | — | — | 0.00 | 0.00 | Capital Gains $ |
| — | — | — | — | — | — | — | — | 0.28 | 0.26 | Expense Ratio % |
| — | — | — | — | — | — | — | — | 1.09 | 1.13 | Income Ratio % |
| — | — | — | — | — | — | — | — | 8 | 9 | Turnover Rate % |
| — | — | — | — | — | — | — | — | 55 | 238 | Net Assets $mil |

## Performance

### Historic Quarterly NAV Returns

| | 1st Qtr | 2nd Qtr | 3rd Qtr | 4th Qtr | Total |
|---|---|---|---|---|---|
| 2001 | — | — | — | — | — |
| 2002 | — | — | — | — | — |
| 2003 | — | — | — | — | — |
| 2004 | — | 2.62 | -5.60 | 6.30 | —* |
| 2005 | -0.86 | 5.14 | 2.21 | 1.59 | 8.24 |

| Trailing | NAV Return% | Market Return% | NAV Rtrn% +/-S&P 500 | %Rank Cat.(NAV) |
|---|---|---|---|---|
| 3 Mo | 1.59 | 1.76 | -0.49 | 7 |
| 6 Mo | 3.84 | 3.86 | -1.92 | 7 |
| 1 Yr | 8.24 | 8.20 | 3.33 | 5 |
| 3 Yr Avg | — | — | — | 0 |
| 5 Yr Avg | — | — | — | 0 |
| 10 Yr Avg | — | — | — | 0 |

| Tax Analysis | Tax-Adj Return% | Tax-Cost Ratio |
|---|---|---|
| 3 Yr (estimated) | — | — |
| 5 Yr (estimated) | — | — |
| 10 Yr (estimated) | — | — |

## Risk Profile

| | Standard Index S&P 500 | Best Fit Index |
|---|---|---|
| Alpha | — | — |
| Beta | — | — |
| R-Squared | — | — |
| Standard Deviation | — | |
| Mean | — | |
| Sharpe Ratio | — | |

## Morningstar Fair Value

| Price/Fair Value Ratio | Fair Value Estimate ($) | Hit Rate % |
|---|---|---|
| 1.0 Fairly valued | 42.74 | 91 Good |

## Morningstar's Take  by Christopher Davis

Vanguard Health Care VIPERs is no substitute for its recently shuttered sibling--or for many of its actively managed rivals.

With the Vanguard Health Care now closed to new investments, some folks may consider this exchange-traded fund as an alternative. But it is less diversified by industry subsector, individual stock, and region than its mutual fund sibling.

The differences stem from the VIPER's benchmark, the MSCI U.S. Investable Market Health Care Index, which features a heavy large-cap pharmaceuticals weighting. Such names account for roughly 55% of assets, versus just 35% for Vanguard Health Care. The index is also more concentrated in its largest holdings--the VIPER's top 10 holdings soak up 55% of assets, with bellwethers Pfizer and Johnson & Johnson each accounting for 11% (Vanguard Health Care's top 10 accounts for just under a third of assets). And in contrast to Vanguard Health Care's sizable foreign stake, the VIPER has no overseas exposure.

The VIPER's portfolio poses some potential drawbacks. Thanks to its reliance on big pharma, it is relatively light on smaller drug names and biotechnology stocks, which are growing more quickly and generally have better drug pipelines. And the fund's concentration exposes it to plenty of stock-specific risk. When holdings like Pfizer take a hit, it will likely feel the sting. Moreover, with many health-care managers (including Vanguard Health's Owens) arguing that foreign drug stocks have better prospects than their domestic counterparts, the fund's all-U.S. portfolio could be a liability.

To be sure, the fund has a huge edge in its 0.28% expense ratio over the typical health-care mutual fund and other health-care ETFs (though as with any ETF, a lot of trading will dull its expense advantage). This wouldn't be a terrible choice, but we think a more-diversified actively managed fund such as Analyst Pick T. Rowe Price Health Sciences is a better option.

| Address: | PO Box 2600 Valley Forge PA 19482 866-499-8473 |
|---|---|
| Web Address: | www.vanguard.com |
| Inception: | 01-26-04 * |
| Advisor: | Vanguard Advisers, Inc. |

| Management Fee: | 0.26% | | |
|---|---|---|---|
| Expense Projections: | 3Yr:$90 | 5Yr:$157 | 10Yr:$356 |
| Income Distrib: | Annually | | |
| Exchange: | AMEX | | |

## Portfolio Analysis  09-30-05

Share change since 06-05   Total Stocks:281

| | Sector | PE | Tot Ret% | % Assets |
|---|---|---|---|---|
| ⊕ Johnson & Johnson | Health | 19.1 | -3.36 | 10.43 |
| ⊕ Pfizer | Health | 21.2 | -10.62 | 10.29 |
| ⊕ Amgen | Health | 28.3 | 22.93 | 5.46 |
| ⊕ UnitedHealth Group | Health | 26.2 | 41.22 | 4.07 |
| ⊕ Abbott Laboratories | Health | 18.3 | -13.47 | 3.64 |
| ⊕ Medtronic | Health | 37.4 | 16.72 | 3.59 |
| ⊕ Wyeth | Health | 54.2 | 10.54 | 3.43 |
| ⊕ Merck | Health | 15.2 | 4.04 | 3.32 |
| ⊕ Eli Lilly & Company | Health | 48.4 | 2.52 | 3.02 |
| ⊕ Bristol-Myers Squibb | Health | 17.1 | -6.16 | 2.61 |
| ⊕ WellPoint | Health | 24.7 | 38.77 | 2.52 |
| ⊕ Genentech | Health | 86.5 | 69.91 | 2.22 |
| ⊕ Schering-Plough | Health | — | 0.95 | 1.72 |
| ⊕ Cardinal Health | Health | 28.3 | 18.63 | 1.51 |
| ⊕ Aetna | Health | 18.9 | 51.27 | 1.39 |
| ⊕ Baxter International | Health | 30.6 | 10.63 | 1.37 |
| ⊕ Guidant | Health | 44.4 | -9.68 | 1.24 |
| ⊕ Caremark RX | Health | 27.7 | 31.35 | 1.24 |
| ⊕ Gilead Sciences | Health | 38.1 | 50.24 | 1.22 |
| ⊕ HCA | Health | 16.0 | 27.87 | 1.06 |

### Current Investment Style

Value Blnd Growth — Large Mid Small

| Market Cap | % |
|---|---|
| Giant | 55.0 |
| Large | 22.7 |
| Mid | 16.6 |
| Small | 5.1 |
| Micro | 0.6 |

Avg $mil: 30,626

| Value Measures | | Rel Category |
|---|---|---|
| Price/Earnings | 19.44 | 0.84 |
| Price/Book | 2.77 | 0.85 |
| Price/Sales | 1.87 | 0.51 |
| Price/Cash Flow | 12.42 | 0.81 |
| Dividend Yield % | 1.22 | 1.20 |

| Growth Measures | % | Rel Category |
|---|---|---|
| Long-Term Erngs | 12.87 | 0.88 |
| Book Value | 17.64 | 1.44 |
| Sales | 12.77 | 0.88 |
| Cash Flow | 16.08 | 1.06 |
| Historical Erngs | 11.93 | 1.01 |

| Profitability | % | Rel Category |
|---|---|---|
| Return on Equity | 16.53 | 1.29 |
| Return on Assets | 8.41 | 1.51 |
| Net Margin | 12.19 | 1.01 |

### Industry Weightings

| | % of Stocks | Rel Cat |
|---|---|---|
| Biotech | 15.5 | 0.5 |
| Drugs | 43.7 | 1.6 |
| Mgd Care | 9.1 | 1.2 |
| Hospitals | 2.5 | 1.1 |
| Other HC Srv | 1.6 | 1.0 |
| Diagnostics | 1.4 | 1.1 |
| Equipment | 16.7 | 1.1 |
| Good/Srv | 8.1 | 0.9 |
| Other | 1.5 | 0.6 |

### Composition

| | | |
|---|---|---|
| ● | Cash | 0.2 |
| ● | Stocks | 99.3 |
| ● | Bonds | 0.0 |
| ● | Other | 0.5 |
| | Foreign | 0.0 |
| | (% of Stock) | |

**Morningstar® ETFs 100**

# Vanguard InfoTech VIPERs

| Ticker | NAV | Market Price | 52 wk High/Low | Yield | Mstar Category |
|---|---|---|---|---|---|
| VGT | $48.31 | $51.51 | $51.51 - $40.61 | 0.2% | Specialty-Technology |

## Management

### Portfolio Manager(s)

Vanguard Quantitative Equity Group runs this fund. Gus Sauter, Vanguard's chief investment officer and indexing pro, oversees the group. He and his team of quantitative analysts have a strong record of closely tracking benchmarks.

### Strategy

This ETF tracks the MSCI U.S. Investable Information Technology Index, a subset of the market-cap weighted MSCI U.S. Investable Market 2500 Index. The MSCI IT index holds more than 400 stocks in the software, hardware, semiconductor, IT consulting, Internet, data processing, and outsourcing industries. The fund takes a more diversified approach than many tech portfolios, but it's still pretty concentrated.

**Growth of $10,000**

— Investment Value of ETF
— Investment Value of Index S&P 500

| | 1996 | 1997 | 1998 | 1999 | 2000 | 2001 | 2002 | 2003 | 2004 | 2005 | History |
|---|---|---|---|---|---|---|---|---|---|---|---|
| | — | — | — | — | — | — | — | — | 47.04 | 48.31 | NAV $ |
| | — | — | — | — | — | — | — | — | 47.06 | 48.38 | Market Price $ |
| | — | — | — | — | — | — | — | — | -1.91† | 2.89 | NAV Return% |
| | — | — | — | — | — | — | — | — | -1.84† | 2.99 | Market Price Return% |
| | — | — | — | — | — | — | — | — | 0.11 | -0.00 | Avg Premium/Discount% |
| | — | — | — | — | — | — | — | — | -1.91 | -2.02 | NAV Rtrn% +/-S&P 500 |
| | — | — | — | — | — | — | — | — | -1.91 | -4.47 | NAV Rtrn% +/-ArcaEx Tech 100 |
| | — | — | — | — | — | — | — | — | — | 9 | NAV Return% Rank in Cat |
| | — | — | — | — | — | — | — | — | 0.00 | 0.19 | Income Return % |
| | — | — | — | — | — | — | — | — | — | 2.70 | Capital Return % |
| | — | — | — | — | — | — | — | — | 0.61 | 0.09 | Income $ |
| | — | — | — | — | — | — | — | — | 0.00 | 0.00 | Capital Gains $ |
| | — | — | — | — | — | — | — | — | 0.28 | 0.26 | Expense Ratio % |
| | — | — | — | — | — | — | — | — | 0.12 | 1.28 | Income Ratio % |
| | — | — | — | — | — | — | — | — | 9 | 7 | Turnover Rate % |
| | — | — | — | — | — | — | — | — | 19 | 65 | Net Assets $mil |

## Performance

### Historic Quarterly NAV Returns

| | 1st Qtr | 2nd Qtr | 3rd Qtr | 4th Qtr | Total |
|---|---|---|---|---|---|
| 2001 | — | — | — | — | — |
| 2002 | — | — | — | — | — |
| 2003 | — | — | — | — | — |
| 2004 | — | 1.41 | -10.56 | 14.08 | — * |
| 2005 | -7.63 | 1.96 | 6.34 | 2.74 | 2.89 |

| Trailing | NAV Return% | Market Return% | NAV Rtrn% +/-S&P 500 | %Rank Cat.(NAV) |
|---|---|---|---|---|
| 3 Mo | 2.74 | 2.93 | 0.66 | 12 |
| 6 Mo | 9.25 | 9.17 | 3.49 | 12 |
| 1 Yr | 2.89 | 2.99 | -2.02 | 9 |
| 3 Yr Avg | — | — | — | 0 |
| 5 Yr Avg | — | — | — | 0 |
| 10 Yr Avg | — | — | — | 0 |

| Tax Analysis | Tax-Adj Return% | Tax-Cost Ratio |
|---|---|---|
| 3 Yr (estimated) | — | — |
| 5 Yr (estimated) | — | — |
| 10 Yr (estimated) | — | — |

## Risk Profile

| | Standard Index S&P 500 | Best Fit Index |
|---|---|---|
| Alpha | — | — |
| Beta | — | — |
| R-Squared | — | — |
| Standard Deviation | — | |
| Mean | — | |
| Sharpe Ratio | — | |

## Morningstar Fair Value

| Price/Fair Value Ratio | Fair Value Estimate ($) | Hit Rate % |
|---|---|---|
| 1.1 Fairly valued | 24.72 | 93 Good |

## Portfolio Analysis 09-30-05

| Share change since 06-05 Total Stocks:424 | Sector | PE | Tot Ret% | % Assets |
|---|---|---|---|---|
| ⊕ Microsoft | Software | 22.2 | -0.95 | 11.56 |
| ⊕ Intel | Hardware | 18.6 | 8.12 | 7.03 |
| ⊕ IBM | Hardware | 16.0 | -15.83 | 5.98 |
| ⊕ Cisco Systems | Hardware | 19.9 | -11.39 | 5.30 |
| ⊕ Hewlett-Packard | Hardware | 27.3 | 38.29 | 3.91 |
| ⊕ Dell | Hardware | 23.2 | -28.93 | 3.64 |
| ⊕ Qualcomm | Hardware | 34.2 | 2.50 | 3.38 |
| ⊕ Google | Business | — | 115.19 | 2.79 |
| ⊕ Texas Instruments | Hardware | 25.3 | 30.78 | 2.60 |
| ⊕ Motorola | Hardware | 13.9 | 32.43 | 2.50 |
| ⊕ Oracle | Software | 22.2 | -11.01 | 2.21 |
| ⊕ Apple Computer | Hardware | 46.1 | 123.26 | 2.04 |
| ⊕ Yahoo | Media | 36.3 | 3.98 | 1.97 |
| ⊕ First Data | Business | 20.8 | 1.70 | 1.45 |
| ⊕ EMC | Hardware | 25.7 | -8.41 | 1.44 |
| ⊕ Corning | Hardware | 36.4 | 67.03 | 1.29 |
| ⊕ Applied Materials | Hardware | 24.6 | 5.46 | 1.29 |
| ⊕ Symantec | Software | 53.0 | -32.07 | 1.25 |
| ⊕ Automatic Data Processin | Business | 25.2 | 5.03 | 1.16 |
| ⊕ Electronic Arts | Software | 44.0 | -15.19 | 0.81 |

### Current Investment Style

Value Blnd Growth — Large/Mid/Small

| Market Cap | % |
|---|---|
| Giant | 55.2 |
| Large | 20.1 |
| Mid | 17.1 |
| Small | 6.5 |
| Micro | 1.1 |

Avg $mil: 30,662

| Value Measures | | Rel Category |
|---|---|---|
| Price/Earnings | 22.11 | 0.93 |
| Price/Book | 3.52 | 1.06 |
| Price/Sales | 2.28 | 0.76 |
| Price/Cash Flow | 11.41 | 1.04 |
| Dividend Yield % | 0.62 | 1.11 |

| Growth Measures | % | Rel Category |
|---|---|---|
| Long-Term Erngs | 14.17 | 0.95 |
| Book Value | 3.26 | 1.02 |
| Sales | 6.09 | 1.06 |
| Cash Flow | 14.59 | 0.73 |
| Historical Erngs | 24.22 | 0.94 |

| Profitability | % | Rel Category |
|---|---|---|
| Return on Equity | 18.73 | 1.21 |
| Return on Assets | 11.03 | 1.17 |
| Net Margin | 15.66 | 1.11 |

| Industry Weightings | % of Stocks | Rel Cat |
|---|---|---|
| Software | 23.2 | 1.1 |
| Hardware | 21.1 | 1.8 |
| Networking Eq | 8.8 | 1.3 |
| Semis | 18.5 | 0.9 |
| Semi Equip | 3.1 | 0.7 |
| Comp/Data Sv | 8.5 | 1.1 |
| Telecom | 0.3 | 0.1 |
| Health Care | 0.1 | 0.0 |
| Other | 16.5 | 0.8 |

**Composition**

| | | |
|---|---|---|
| ● Cash | 0.0 | |
| ● Stocks | 99.9 | |
| ● Bonds | 0.0 | |
| ○ Other | 0.1 | |
| Foreign | 0.3 | |
| (% of Stock) | | |

## Morningstar's Take by Dan Culloton

If you must have a technology fund, you could do worse than Vanguard Information Technology VIPERs.

This fund comes with all the perils of a sector fund in a high-growth area. Yet it has redeeming characteristics, namely, strong management, low costs, and broad diversification. That should make it competitive with most conventional technology funds.

This being a Vanguard fund, you'd expect it to track its benchmark like a shadow. Sure enough, firm's quantitative equity team, whose work on investments such as Vanguard 500 Index has earned it a sterling reputation for indexing expertise, has done a quality job here. The fund's 4.47% loss from January 2004 through the end of October 2005 trails that of its index by less than the fund's expense ratio.

This being a Vanguard fund, you'd also expect very low costs. The ETF does not disappoint. Its 0.26% expense ratio makes it one of the cheapest

ETFs in the technology category. It also is one of the cheapest tech funds, exchange-traded or otherwise, that retail investors can buy.

Remain cognizant of this fund's risks, though. It is less concentrated than a lot of its rivals, such as the Technology Select Sector SPDR. It owns more stocks than the SPDR and spreads more money around mid- and small-cap stocks. Yet it still keeps close to half of its assets in its top-10 holdings, including nearly 20% in Microsoft and Intel alone. Those are two of the sector's elder statesmen and are no longer as volatile as more speculative tech companies, but the concentration still courts volatility. Indeed, when concerns about slower information technology spending battered tech stocks in 2004's third quarter, this fund shed more than 10% of its value.

This fund is worth considering for tech exposure because it's cheap, diversified, and well-run. Due to its risks, however, it should be used only in carefully controlled doses.

| Address: | PO Box 2600<br>Valley Forge PA 19482<br>866-499-8473 | Management Fee: | 0.26% |
|---|---|---|---|
| | | Expense Projections: | 3Yr:$90  5Yr:$157  10Yr:$356 |
| Web Address: | www.vanguard.com | Income Distrib: | Annually |
| Inception: | 01-26-04 * | Exchange: | AMEX |
| Advisor: | Vanguard Advisers, Inc. | | |

MORNINGSTAR® ETFs 100

# Vanguard Large Cap VIPERs

| | Ticker | NAV | Market Price | 52 wk High/Low | Yield | Mstar Category |
|---|---|---|---|---|---|---|
| | VV | $55.40 | $57.30 | $57.35 - $50.00 | 1.6% | Large Blend |

## Management

### Portfolio Manager(s)

Ryan Ludt, who has been with Vanguard since 1997, handles the day-to-day operations of this fund. Vanguard's indexing pro, Gus Sauter, serves a supervisory role.

### Strategy

This index fund tracks the MSCI U.S. Prime Market 750 Index, which gives investors exposure to the 750 largest U.S. stocks. Unlike the S&P 500 Index, the ubiquitous large-cap bogy, its methodology is purely quantitative and transparent. It also dips down a bit further on the market cap ladder, pulling in a passel of mid-cap stocks.

**Growth of $10,000**

— Investment Value of ETF
— Investment Value of Index S&P 500

| | 1996 | 1997 | 1998 | 1999 | 2000 | 2001 | 2002 | 2003 | 2004 | 2005 | History |
|---|---|---|---|---|---|---|---|---|---|---|---|
| | — | — | — | — | — | — | — | — | 52.99 | 55.40 | NAV $ |
| | — | — | — | — | — | — | — | — | 53.19 | 55.49 | Market Price $ |
| | — | — | — | — | — | — | — | — | 7.40* | 6.26 | NAV Return% |
| | — | — | — | — | — | — | — | — | 7.49* | 6.03 | Market Price Return% |
| | — | — | — | — | — | — | — | — | -0.14 | 0.02 | Avg Premium/Discount% |
| | — | — | — | — | — | — | — | — | 7.40 | 1.35 | NAV Rtrn% +/-S&P 500 |
| | — | — | — | — | — | — | — | — | 7.40 | -0.01 | NAV Rtrn% +/-Russ 1000 |
| | — | — | — | — | — | — | — | — | — | 23 | NAV Return% Rank in Cat |
| | — | — | — | — | — | — | — | — | 0.00 | 1.66 | Income Return % |
| | — | — | — | — | — | — | — | — | — | 4.60 | Capital Return % |
| | — | — | — | — | — | — | — | — | 0.96 | 0.87 | Income $ |
| | — | — | — | — | — | — | — | — | 0.00 | 0.00 | Capital Gains $ |
| | — | — | — | — | — | — | — | — | 0.12 | — | Expense Ratio % |
| | — | — | — | — | — | — | — | — | 2.00 | — | Income Ratio % |
| | — | — | — | — | — | — | — | — | 5 | — | Turnover Rate % |
| | — | — | — | — | — | — | — | — | 48 | 178 | Net Assets $mil |

## Performance

### Historic Quarterly NAV Returns

| | 1st Qtr | 2nd Qtr | 3rd Qtr | 4th Qtr | Total |
|---|---|---|---|---|---|
| 2001 | — | — | — | — | — |
| 2002 | — | — | — | — | — |
| 2003 | — | — | — | — | — |
| 2004 | — | 1.53 | -1.78 | 9.59 | — * |
| 2005 | -1.93 | 1.93 | 3.86 | 2.35 | 6.26 |

| Trailing | NAV Return% | Market Return% | NAV Rtrn% +/-S&P 500 | %Rank Cat.(NAV) |
|---|---|---|---|---|
| 3 Mo | 2.35 | 2.55 | 0.27 | 27 |
| 6 Mo | 6.30 | 6.13 | 0.54 | 27 |
| 1 Yr | 6.26 | 6.03 | 1.35 | 23 |
| 3 Yr Avg | — | — | — | 0 |
| 5 Yr Avg | — | — | — | 0 |
| 10 Yr Avg | — | — | — | 0 |

| Tax Analysis | Tax-Adj Return% | Tax-Cost Ratio |
|---|---|---|
| 3 Yr (estimated) | — | — |
| 5 Yr (estimated) | — | — |
| 10 Yr (estimated) | — | — |

## Risk Profile

| | Standard Index S&P 500 | Best Fit Index |
|---|---|---|
| Alpha | — | — |
| Beta | — | — |
| R-Squared | — | — |
| Standard Deviation | — | |
| Mean | — | |
| Sharpe Ratio | — | |

## Morningstar Fair Value

| Price/Fair Value Ratio | Fair Value Estimate ($) | Hit Rate % |
|---|---|---|
| 1.0 Fairly valued | 39.05 | 95 Good |

## Portfolio Analysis 09-30-05

| Share change since 06-05 Total Stocks:741 | Sector | PE | Tot Ret% | % Assets |
|---|---|---|---|---|
| ⊕ ExxonMobil | Energy | 10.6 | 11.76 | 3.33 |
| ⊕ General Electric | Ind Mtrls | 19.9 | -1.43 | 2.94 |
| ⊕ Microsoft | Software | 22.2 | -0.95 | 2.06 |
| ⊕ Citigroup | Financial | 12.1 | 4.63 | 1.95 |
| ⊕ Johnson & Johnson | Health | 19.1 | -3.36 | 1.55 |
| ⊕ Pfizer | Health | 21.2 | -10.62 | 1.53 |
| ⊕ Bank of America | Financial | 11.1 | 2.39 | 1.39 |
| ⊕ Altria Group | Goods | 15.0 | 27.72 | 1.26 |
| ⊕ Intel | Hardware | 18.6 | 8.12 | 1.25 |
| ⊕ Chevron | Energy | 9.0 | 11.51 | 1.21 |
| ⊕ Procter & Gamble | Goods | 21.2 | 7.18 | 1.18 |
| ⊕ American International G | Financial | 15.6 | 4.83 | 1.12 |
| ⊕ IBM | Hardware | 16.0 | -15.83 | 1.06 |
| ⊕ J.P. Morgan Chase & Co. | Financial | 18.8 | 5.74 | 0.98 |
| ⊕ Cisco Systems | Hardware | 19.9 | -11.39 | 0.94 |
| ⊕ Wal-Mart Stores | Consumer | 18.2 | -10.30 | 0.91 |
| ⊕ Wells Fargo | Financial | 14.3 | 4.47 | 0.81 |
| ⊕ Amgen | Health | 28.3 | 22.93 | 0.81 |
| ⊕ PepsiCo | Goods | 25.8 | 15.24 | 0.78 |
| ⊕ Coca-Cola | Goods | 18.6 | -0.66 | 0.77 |

### Current Investment Style

Value Blnd Growth — Large/Mid/Small

| | Market Cap | % |
|---|---|---|
| | Giant | 49.6 |
| | Large | 35.5 |
| | Mid | 14.8 |
| | Small | 0.0 |
| | Micro | 0.0 |

Avg $mil: 39,401

| Value Measures | | Rel Category |
|---|---|---|
| Price/Earnings | 16.04 | 0.94 |
| Price/Book | 2.49 | 0.92 |
| Price/Sales | 1.50 | 1.17 |
| Price/Cash Flow | 6.32 | 0.87 |
| Dividend Yield % | 1.84 | 1.04 |

| Growth Measures | % | Rel Category |
|---|---|---|
| Long-Term Erngs | 10.83 | 0.97 |
| Book Value | 10.39 | 1.11 |
| Sales | 8.50 | 1.05 |
| Cash Flow | 11.42 | 1.11 |
| Historical Erngs | 15.29 | 1.08 |

| Profitability | % | Rel Category |
|---|---|---|
| Return on Equity | 18.63 | 0.91 |
| Return on Assets | 9.99 | 1.07 |
| Net Margin | 13.10 | 1.20 |

| Sector Weightings | % of Stocks | Rel S&P 500 | 3 Year High Low |
|---|---|---|---|
| ↻ Info | 20.66 | 1.02 | |
| Software | 3.66 | 1.03 | — — |
| Hardware | 10.05 | 1.00 | — — |
| Media | 3.78 | 1.06 | — — |
| Telecom | 3.17 | 1.05 | — — |
| ☞ Service | 45.81 | 0.99 | |
| Health | 13.19 | 0.99 | — — |
| Consumer | 8.26 | 1.01 | — — |
| Business | 4.28 | 1.11 | — — |
| Financial | 20.08 | 0.95 | — — |
| ⊣ Mfg | 33.54 | 1.00 | |
| Goods | 8.55 | 1.00 | — — |
| Ind Mtrls | 11.01 | 0.91 | — — |
| Energy | 10.51 | 1.12 | — — |
| Utilities | 3.47 | 1.03 | — — |

### Composition

| | | |
|---|---|---|
| ● Cash | | 0.1 |
| ● Stocks | | 99.3 |
| ● Bonds | | 0.0 |
| Other | | 0.6 |
| Foreign | | 0.1 |
| (% of Stock) | | |

## Morningstar's Take by Sonya Morris

Is Vanguard Large Cap VIPERs throwing stones at a giant?

This ETF, rolled out in February 2004, competes with other large-cap index funds including sibling Vanguard 500 Index and the popular SPDRs. But even though these offerings cover the same territory, there are some noteworthy differences that can impact their behavior.

Vanguard 500 and SPDRs, of course, track the S&P 500 Index, which essentially includes the top 500 stocks ranked by free-float market capitalization. (Free float means that market caps are adjusted for restricted shares such as those held by insiders). However, the S&P is not purely a quantitative index. Instead, it's controlled by a committee that makes some subjective decisions about which stocks to include. For instance, the committee won't immediately include IPOs in the index until they've been "seasoned" for six to 12 months. The committee also screens out firms with limited operating histories and companies that

don't have a record of four straight quarters of positive earnings.

Unlike the S&P index, this ETF's benchmark, the MSCI (Morgan Stanley Capital International) U.S. Prime Market 750 Index, employs a transparent and purely quantitative methodology. It includes the top 750 stocks by free-float market capitalization (including the stocks that don't pass S&P's financial viability screens). As such, this fund holds more mid-cap stocks than S&P 500 Index funds.

Because MSCI includes these smaller stocks as well as a handful of more speculative names, this ETF courts a bit more volatility than its rivals. But over the long haul, it shouldn't produce dramatically different returns. Moreover, this fund is easy to combine with Vanguard's other index offerings, most of which now also track MSCI indexes. All told, we think this ETF is a worthy choice to anchor a portfolio.

| | | | | |
|---|---|---|---|---|
| Address: | PO Box 2600 | Management Fee: | 0.02% | |
| | Valley Forge PA 19482 | Expense Projections: | 3Yr:$23 | 5Yr:$40 | 10Yr:$90 |
| | 866-499-8473 | Income Distrib: | Quarterly | |
| Web Address: | www.vanguard.com | Exchange: | AMEX | |
| Inception: | 01-27-04 * | | | |
| Advisor: | Vanguard Advisers, Inc. | | | |

**MORNINGSTAR®** ETFs 100

# Vanguard Mid Cap VIPERs

| Ticker | NAV | Market Price | 52 wk High/Low | Yield | Mstar Category |
|---|---|---|---|---|---|
| VO | $64.61 | $67.56 | $67.56 - $54.46 | 1.2% | Mid-Cap Blend |

## Management

### Portfolio Manager(s)

Vanguard index maven Gus Sauter handed off the daily managerial chores here to Donald Butler, who has been with Vanguard since 1992 and has worked with Sauter on this fund since its inception. Butler also handles the day-to-day management of Vanguard Extended Market Index and Vanguard Institutional Index. As Vanguard's chief investment officer, Sauter still serves a supervisory role here.

### Strategy

The ETF tracks the MSCI U.S. Mid-Cap 450 Index, which spans the 301st to 750th largest stocks by market capitalization. The index's quantitative methodology should limit turnover and provide a close approximation of the mid-cap universe.

### Growth of $10,000

- Investment Value of ETF
- Investment Value of Index S&P 500

| | 1996 | 1997 | 1998 | 1999 | 2000 | 2001 | 2002 | 2003 | 2004 | 2005 | History |
|---|---|---|---|---|---|---|---|---|---|---|---|
| | — | — | — | — | — | — | — | — | 57.32 | 64.61 | NAV $ |
| | — | — | — | — | — | — | — | — | 57.35 | 64.61 | Market Price $ |
| | — | — | — | — | — | — | — | — | 15.16* | 14.03 | NAV Return% |
| | — | — | — | — | — | — | — | — | 15.16* | 13.97 | Market Price Return% |
| | — | — | — | — | — | — | — | — | 0.11 | 0.04 | Avg Premium/Discount% |
| | — | — | — | — | — | — | — | — | 15.16 | 9.12 | NAV Rtrn% +/-S&P 500 |
| | — | — | — | — | — | — | — | — | 15.16 | 1.48 | NAV Rtrn% +/-S&P Mid 400 |
| | — | — | — | — | — | — | — | — | — | 7 | NAV Return% Rank in Cat |
| | — | — | — | — | — | — | — | — | 0.00 | 1.31 | Income Return % |
| | — | — | — | — | — | — | — | — | — | 12.72 | Capital Return % |
| | — | — | — | — | — | — | — | — | 0.64 | 0.75 | Income $ |
| | — | — | — | — | — | — | — | — | 0.00 | 0.00 | Capital Gains $ |
| | — | — | — | — | — | — | — | — | 0.18 | — | Expense Ratio % |
| | — | — | — | — | — | — | — | — | 1.30 | — | Income Ratio % |
| | — | — | — | — | — | — | — | — | 16 | — | Turnover Rate % |
| | — | — | — | — | — | — | — | — | 58 | 1,044 | Net Assets $mil |

## Performance

### Historic Quarterly NAV Returns

| | 1st Qtr | 2nd Qtr | 3rd Qtr | 4th Qtr | Total |
|---|---|---|---|---|---|
| 2001 | — | — | — | — | — |
| 2002 | — | — | — | — | — |
| 2003 | — | — | — | — | — * |
| 2004 | — | 1.05 | -0.86 | 14.79 | — * |
| 2005 | -0.38 | 4.41 | 6.41 | 3.03 | 14.03 |

| Trailing | NAV Return% | Market Return% | NAV Rtrn% +/-S&P 500 | %Rank Cat.(NAV) |
|---|---|---|---|---|
| 3 Mo | 3.03 | 2.85 | 0.95 | 7 |
| 6 Mo | 9.63 | 9.43 | 3.87 | 7 |
| 1 Yr | 14.03 | 13.97 | 9.12 | 7 |
| 3 Yr Avg | — | — | — | 0 |
| 5 Yr Avg | — | — | — | 0 |
| 10 Yr Avg | — | — | — | 0 |

| Tax Analysis | Tax-Adj Return% | Tax-Cost Ratio |
|---|---|---|
| 3 Yr (estimated) | — | — |
| 5 Yr (estimated) | — | — |
| 10 Yr (estimated) | — | — |

## Risk Profile

| | Standard Index S&P 500 | Best Fit Index |
|---|---|---|
| Alpha | — | — |
| Beta | — | — |
| R-Squared | — | — |
| Standard Deviation | — | |
| Mean | — | |
| Sharpe Ratio | — | |

## Morningstar Fair Value

| Price/Fair Value Ratio | Fair Value Estimate ($) | Hit Rate % |
|---|---|---|
| 1.1 Overvalued | 33.26 | 90 Good |

## Portfolio Analysis 09-30-05

| Share change since 06-05 Total Stocks:447 | Sector | PE | Tot Ret% | % Assets |
|---|---|---|---|---|
| ⊕ XTO Energy | Energy | 22.7 | 66.57 | 0.71 |
| ⊕ Williams Companies | Energy | 38.0 | 43.97 | 0.66 |
| ⊕ Phelps Dodge | Ind Mtrls | 8.2 | 53.13 | 0.58 |
| ⊕ Starwood Hotels & Resort | Consumer | 37.8 | 10.80 | 0.57 |
| ⊕ PPL | Utilities | 15.8 | 14.03 | 0.56 |
| ⊕ Chesapeake Energy | Energy | 17.0 | 93.70 | 0.56 |
| ⊕ Coach | Goods | 30.9 | 18.23 | 0.54 |
| ⊕ BJ Services | Energy | 26.6 | 58.54 | 0.54 |
| ⊕ Chicago Mercantile Excha | Financial | 44.4 | 61.83 | 0.53 |
| ⊕ Amerada Hess | Energy | 12.9 | 55.55 | 0.52 |
| ⊕ Nabors Industries | Energy | 22.2 | 47.69 | 0.52 |
| ⊕ National Oilwell Varco | Energy | 35.0 | 77.67 | 0.52 |
| ⊕ Legg Mason | Financial | 30.9 | 64.48 | 0.51 |
| ⊕ Peabody Energy | Energy | 33.1 | 104.95 | 0.51 |
| ⊕ Constellation Energy Gro | Utilities | 18.1 | 35.05 | 0.50 |
| ⊕ Vornado Realty Trust | Financial | 19.4 | 15.15 | 0.50 |
| ⊕ ProLogis Trust | Financial | 32.0 | 11.73 | 0.50 |
| ⊕ Sunoco | Energy | 12.6 | 94.37 | 0.49 |
| ⊕ Autodesk | Software | 34.1 | 13.18 | 0.49 |
| ⊕ GlobalSantaFe | Energy | 50.2 | 47.43 | 0.48 |

### Current Investment Style

Value Blnd Growth — Large Mid Small

| Market Cap | % |
|---|---|
| Giant | 0.0 |
| Large | 24.0 |
| Mid | 75.8 |
| Small | 0.2 |
| Micro | 0.0 |

Avg $mil: 6,130

| Value Measures | | Rel Category |
|---|---|---|
| Price/Earnings | 17.60 | 1.01 |
| Price/Book | 2.47 | 1.04 |
| Price/Sales | 1.28 | 1.11 |
| Price/Cash Flow | 8.65 | 1.15 |
| Dividend Yield % | 1.25 | 1.08 |

| Growth Measures | % | Rel Category |
|---|---|---|
| Long-Term Erngs | 12.17 | 0.96 |
| Book Value | 7.85 | 0.90 |
| Sales | 7.20 | 0.88 |
| Cash Flow | 6.99 | 0.70 |
| Historical Erngs | 15.37 | 0.95 |

| Profitability | % | Rel Category |
|---|---|---|
| Return on Equity | 14.95 | 0.99 |
| Return on Assets | 7.99 | 1.02 |
| Net Margin | 11.47 | 1.08 |

### Sector Weightings

| | % of Stocks | Rel S&P 500 | 3 Year High | Low |
|---|---|---|---|---|
| ☎ Info | 17.74 | 0.88 | | |
| 🖳 Software | 2.96 | 0.83 | 3 | 3 |
| 💾 Hardware | 9.21 | 0.92 | 13 | 7 |
| 📺 Media | 2.83 | 0.79 | 4 | 2 |
| 📞 Telecom | 2.74 | 0.91 | 3 | 1 |
| ☞ Service | 47.16 | 1.02 | | |
| 🏥 Health | 9.83 | 0.74 | 14 | 10 |
| 🛒 Consumer | 11.29 | 1.39 | 12 | 11 |
| 📋 Business | 7.20 | 1.86 | 11 | 7 |
| 💲 Financial | 18.84 | 0.89 | 20 | 18 |
| 🔧 Mfg | 35.09 | 1.05 | | |
| 🏭 Goods | 7.02 | 0.82 | 8 | 7 |
| ⚙ Ind Mtrls | 9.55 | 0.79 | 12 | 7 |
| 🔥 Energy | 12.47 | 1.33 | 12 | 7 |
| 💡 Utilities | 6.05 | 1.80 | 7 | 6 |

### Composition

| | | |
|---|---|---|
| ● Cash | 0.2 | |
| ● Stocks | 99.2 | |
| ● Bonds | 0.0 | |
| ● Other | 0.6 | |
| Foreign | 0.5 | |
| (% of Stock) | | |

## Morningstar's Take by Sonya Morris

Vanguard Mid Cap VIPERs may not always look this good, but it's still a perennial low-cost favorite.

This exchange-traded fund has gotten off to a strong start. Since its inception in January 2004, it has generated average annual returns that surpass 80% of its mid-cap rivals. This strong showing is partly due to its benchmark, the MSCI U.S. MidCap 450 Index, which uses a methodology that allows it to hold its winners longer than other indexes. Specifically, the index employs buffer zones to manage the migration of stocks between market-cap boundaries. That means the fund can hold on to strongly performing stocks for several months before they move up to the large-cap realm. Presently, many top-performing energy and utility stocks have climbed to the top of the portfolio and have contributed to the fund's strong recent returns. However, MSCI recently announced that a handful of these names, including Valero Energy and EOG Resources, have graduated to the MSCI U.S. Large-Cap 300 Index.

We don't expect this ETF to consistently benefit from such strong tailwinds. The real benefit of buffer zones is low turnover, which should help the fund keep a lid on trading costs and boost its already-powerful cost advantage. Although it may not always sit at the top of the category, the odds are favorable that, over time, it will edge past its typical actively managed rival.

Finally, it's worth noting that Gus Sauter is no longer listed as the fund's manager. Recently tightened SEC rules now require disclosure of the individual responsible for the day-to-day management of the fund. Because Sauter now serves a supervisory role, he no longer meets that standard. The daily managerial chores here fall to Donald Butler, a 13-year Vanguard veteran who has worked with Sauter on this ETF since its inception and on Vanguard Mid-Cap Index since it was rolled out in May 1998. As such, it's hard to view this as much of a change, and the case for this ETF remains as strong as ever.

| Address: | PO Box 2600 Valley Forge PA 19482 866-499-8473 |
|---|---|
| Web Address: | www.vanguard.com |
| Inception: | 01-26-04 * |
| Advisor: | Vanguard Advisers, Inc. |

| Management Fee: | 0.11% | | |
|---|---|---|---|
| Expense Projections: | 3Yr:$42 | 5Yr:$73 | 10Yr:$166 |
| Income Distrib: | Annually | | |
| Exchange: | AMEX | | |

# Vanguard Pacif Stk VIPERs

| Ticker | NAV | Market Price | 52 wk High/Low | Yield | Mstar Category |
|---|---|---|---|---|---|
| VPL | $60.03 | $62.70 | $63.37 - $46.74 | 0.0% | Japan Stock |

## Management

### Portfolio Manager(s)

This ETF is run by Vanguard's quantitative equity group, which has exceptional indexing experience and expertise. Gus Sauter, who has a long and successful history managing index offerings and is Vanguard's chief investment officer, is currently the lead manager. But Vanguard is in the process of taking Sauter off individual index funds due to his increased responsibilities, so it's likely other individuals will take over day-to-day management responsibilities of this offering and its mutual fund twin before too long.

### Strategy

This ETF tracks the MSCI Pacific Index, a capitalization-weighted benchmark of the region's largest stocks in developed markets, as defined by MSCI. Although its 70%-80% Japan stake lands it in the Japan-stock category, it puts the remainder of its assets in Australia, Hong Kong, Singapore, and New Zealand. It does not have any exposure to other popular Asian markets such as Taiwan, Korea, India, or Thailand. Its bogy gives it hefty exposure to its markets' biggest stocks. It does not hedge its currency exposure.

### Growth of $10,000

— Investment Value of ETF
— Investment Value of Index MSCI EAFE

| | 1996 | 1997 | 1998 | 1999 | 2000 | 2001 | 2002 | 2003 | 2004 | 2005 | History |
|---|---|---|---|---|---|---|---|---|---|---|---|
| | — | — | — | — | — | — | — | — | — | 60.03 | NAV $ |
| | — | — | — | — | — | — | — | — | — | 60.89 | Market Price $ |
| | — | — | — | — | — | — | — | — | — | 20.11* | NAV Return% |
| | — | — | — | — | — | — | — | — | — | 21.14* | Market Price Return% |
| | — | — | — | — | — | — | — | — | — | 0.81 | Avg Premium/Discount% |
| | — | — | — | — | — | — | — | — | — | 20.11 | NAV Rtrn% +/-MSCI EAFE |
| | — | — | — | — | — | — | — | — | — | 20.11 | NAV Rtrn% +/-MSCI JP NDT |
| | — | — | — | — | — | — | — | — | — | — | NAV Return% Rank in Cat |
| | — | — | — | — | — | — | — | — | — | — | Income Return % |
| | — | — | — | — | — | — | — | — | — | — | Capital Return % |
| | — | — | — | — | — | — | — | — | — | 0.93 | Income $ |
| | — | — | — | — | — | — | — | — | — | 0.00 | Capital Gains $ |
| | — | — | — | — | — | — | — | — | — | 0.18 | Expense Ratio % |
| | — | — | — | — | — | — | — | — | — | 1.89 | Income Ratio % |
| | — | — | — | — | — | — | — | — | — | 7 | Turnover Rate % |
| | — | — | — | — | — | — | — | — | — | 203 | Net Assets $mil |

## Performance

### Historic Quarterly NAV Returns

| | 1st Qtr | 2nd Qtr | 3rd Qtr | 4th Qtr | Total |
|---|---|---|---|---|---|
| 2001 | — | — | — | — | — |
| 2002 | — | — | — | — | — |
| 2003 | — | — | — | — | — |
| 2004 | — | — | — | — | — |
| 2005 | — | -1.58 | 17.33 | 8.21 | —* |

| Trailing | NAV Return% | Market Return% | NAV Rtrn% +/-MSCI EAFE | %Rank Cat.(NAV) |
|---|---|---|---|---|
| 3 Mo | 8.21 | 8.28 | 4.13 | 3 |
| 6 Mo | 26.96 | 27.35 | 12.08 | 3 |
| 1 Yr | — | — | — | 0 |
| 3 Yr Avg | — | — | — | 0 |
| 5 Yr Avg | — | — | — | 0 |
| 10 Yr Avg | — | — | — | 0 |

| Tax Analysis | Tax-Adj Return% | Tax-Cost Ratio |
|---|---|---|
| 3 Yr (estimated) | — | — |
| 5 Yr (estimated) | — | — |
| 10 Yr (estimated) | — | — |

## Risk Profile

| | Standard Index S&P 500 | Best Fit Index |
|---|---|---|
| Alpha | — | — |
| Beta | — | — |
| R-Squared | — | — |
| Standard Deviation | — | |
| Mean | — | |
| Sharpe Ratio | — | |

## Morningstar Fair Value

| Price/Fair Value Ratio | Fair Value Estimate ($) | Hit Rate % |
|---|---|---|
| — | — | — |

## Portfolio Analysis 09-30-05

Share change since 06-05 Total Stocks:544

| | Sector | Country | % Assets |
|---|---|---|---|
| ⊕ Toyota Motor | Goods | Japan | 4.23 |
| ⊕ Mitsubishi Tokyo Fin. Gr | Financial | Japan | 2.05 |
| ⊕ BHP Billiton Ltd | Ind Mtrls | Australia | 1.94 |
| ⊕ Mizuho Financial Grp | Financial | Japan | 1.71 |
| ⊕ Takeda Chemical Industri | Health | Japan | 1.69 |
| ⊕ Honda Motor | Goods | Japan | 1.42 |
| ⊕ Sumitomo Mitsui Financia | Financial | Japan | 1.36 |
| ⊕ Canon | Goods | Japan | 1.30 |
| ⊕ National Australia Bank | Financial | Australia | 1.25 |
| ⊕ Commonwealth Bank of Aus | Financial | Australia | 1.19 |
| ⊕ Matsushita Electric Indu | Ind Mtrls | Japan | 1.13 |
| ⊕ Australia & New Zealand | Financial | Australia | 1.06 |
| ⊕ Sony | Goods | Japan | 1.05 |
| ⊕ UFJ Hldgs | Financial | Japan | 1.01 |
| ⊕ NTT DoCoMo | Telecom | Japan | 0.97 |
| ⊕ Tokyo Elec Pwr | Utilities | Japan | 0.92 |
| ⊕ Westpac Banking | Financial | Australia | 0.92 |
| ⊕ Nomura Hldgs | Financial | Japan | 0.87 |
| ✵ Seven & I Hldgs | — | Japan | 0.85 |
| ⊕ Nissan Motor | Goods | Japan | 0.83 |

### Current Investment Style

Value Blnd Growth — Large Mid Small

| Market Cap | % |
|---|---|
| Giant | 51.9 |
| Large | 36.3 |
| Mid | 11.7 |
| Small | 0.1 |
| Micro | 0.0 |

Avg $mil: 14,761

| Value Measures | | Rel Category |
|---|---|---|
| Price/Earnings | 17.25 | 0.90 |
| Price/Book | 1.67 | 0.91 |
| Price/Sales | 0.96 | 0.96 |
| Price/Cash Flow | 7.00 | 0.96 |
| Dividend Yield % | 2.28 | 1.57 |

| Growth Measures | % | Rel Category |
|---|---|---|
| Long-Term Erngs | 9.36 | 0.99 |
| Book Value | 5.91 | 0.95 |
| Sales | 1.57 | 6.04 |
| Cash Flow | 3.81 | 1.14 |
| Historical Erngs | 19.37 | 0.98 |

### Composition

| Cash | 0.1 | Bonds | 0.0 |
|---|---|---|---|
| Stocks | 98.9 | Other | 0.9 |
| Foreign (% of Stock) | | | 100.0 |

### Sector Weightings

| | % of Stocks | Rel MSCI EAFE | 3 Year High | Low |
|---|---|---|---|---|
| ☁ Info | 10.13 | 0.72 | | |
| 🖩 Software | 0.57 | 0.53 | 1 | 0 |
| 💻 Hardware | 4.37 | 1.21 | 6 | 4 |
| 🎬 Media | 1.15 | 0.55 | 3 | 1 |
| 📶 Telecom | 4.04 | 0.56 | 6 | 4 |
| ⊜ Service | 43.71 | 0.96 | | |
| 🏥 Health | 4.15 | 0.58 | 5 | 4 |
| 🛒 Consumer | 4.54 | 1.04 | 6 | 5 |
| 📋 Business | 7.03 | 1.16 | 7 | 7 |
| 💲 Financial | 27.99 | 1.00 | 28 | 19 |
| 🏭 Mfg | 46.16 | 1.14 | | |
| 🏠 Goods | 17.62 | 1.29 | 24 | 18 |
| ⚙ Ind Mtrls | 22.54 | 1.59 | 23 | 18 |
| ⛽ Energy | 1.53 | 0.19 | 2 | 1 |
| 💡 Utilities | 4.47 | 0.97 | 6 | 4 |

### Regional Exposure

| | % Stock | | |
|---|---|---|---|
| UK/W. Europe | 0 | N. America | 0 |
| Japan | 74 | Latn America | 0 |
| Asia X Japan | 26 | Other | 0 |

### Country Exposure

| | % Stock | | |
|---|---|---|---|
| Japan | 74 | Singapore | 3 |
| Australia | 17 | New Zealand | 1 |
| Hong Kong | 5 | | |

## Morningstar's Take by William Samuel Rocco

Vanguard Pacific Stock VIPERs' pros and cons are clear.

This ETF's positive attributes begin with its costs. Its 0.18% expense ratio gives it a substantial cost advantage over all the actively run mutual offerings in the Japan-stock category and a significant expense edge over all the other passive offerings in the group (except this fund's own high-minimum version). And due to its low expenses and Vanguard's indexing expertise, this young ETF should replicate the performance of its bogy, the MSCI Pacific Index, quite closely over time. In fact, the mutual fund clone of this ETF boasts 10-year returns that are within four basis points of the index's.

But performance here is likely to be more mixed relative to other Japan funds. While the vast majority of this fund's category peers focus exclusively on Japan, it--like its bogy--devotes roughly 17% of its assets to Australia, 5% to Hong Kong, 2% to Singapore, and 1% to New Zealand,

while investing approximately 75% of its assets in Japan. That extra exposure has hurt this ETF's mutual fund twin whenever Japan has led the way and helped it whenever that nation has lagged. That fund has gained a less than the Japan-stock group average in 10-years.

This ETF's 25% stake outside Japan means it also makes sense to compare it with diversified Pacific/Asia offerings. Unfortunately, its mutual fund clone has lagged the typical diversified Pacific/Asia fund by a significant margin over the past 10 years, largely because India and several other emerging-Asia markets outside the MSCI Pacific Index have thrived.

This ETF is also hard to use. Its Australia, Hong Kong, and Singapore stakes keep it from being a pure-Japan vehicle, while the limited size and scope of its non-Japan positions mean that it's not really a pan-Asia vehicle, either.

For all these reasons, we're not very excited about this ETF.

| Address: | PO Box 2600 Valley Forge PA 19482 866-499-8473 | Management Fee: | 0.14% |
|---|---|---|---|
| | | Expense Projections: | 3Yr:$58 5Yr:$101 10Yr:$230 |
| Web Address: | www.vanguard.com | Income Distrib: | Annually |
| Inception: | 03-10-05* | Exchange: | AMEX |
| Advisor: | Vanguard Advisers, Inc. | | |

**MORNINGSTAR® ETFs 100**

# Vanguard REIT Index VIPER

| | Ticker | NAV | Market Price | 52 wk High/Low | Yield | Mstar Category |
|---|---|---|---|---|---|---|
| | VNQ | $59.59 | $63.17 | $63.30 - $51.24 | 4.8% | Specialty-Real Estate |

## Management

### Portfolio Manager(s)

Gerard O'Reilly is the day-to-day manager of this fund, although Gus Sauter oversees Vanguard's Quantitative Equity Group. O'Reilly has been with Vanguard since 1992, and he runs several of Vanguard's other index funds.

### Strategy

This fund attempts to track the MCSI U.S. REIT Index, a broad benchmark that includes REITs of all property types. Investing exclusively in REITs and lows costs help drive a fairly high dividend yield relative to other real estate funds, but that restriction can be a limitation when non-REITs shine. The REIT universe is fairly stable, so the fund has few challenges on the trading front. Mortgage REITs are excluded from the index.

**Growth of $10,000**

— Investment Value of ETF
— Investment Value of Index S&P 500

13.5
12.8
12.1
11.4
10.7
10.0

| 1996 | 1997 | 1998 | 1999 | 2000 | 2001 | 2002 | 2003 | 2004 | 2005 | History |
|---|---|---|---|---|---|---|---|---|---|---|
| — | — | — | — | — | — | — | — | 56.55 | 59.59 | NAV $ |
| — | — | — | — | — | — | — | — | 56.55 | 59.56 | Market Price $ |
| — | — | — | — | — | — | — | — | 23.73* | 12.00 | NAV Return% |
| — | — | — | — | — | — | — | — | — | 11.94 | Market Price Return% |
| — | — | — | — | — | — | — | — | 0.06 | 0.02 | Avg Premium/Discount% |
| — | — | — | — | — | — | — | — | 23.73 | 7.09 | NAV Rtrn% +/-S&P 500 |
| — | — | — | — | — | — | — | — | 23.73 | -2.00 | NAV Rtrn% +/-DJ Wilshire REIT |
| — | — | — | — | — | — | — | — | — | 4 | NAV Return% Rank in Cat |
| — | — | — | — | — | — | — | — | 0.00 | 5.22 | Income Return % |
| — | — | — | — | — | — | — | — | — | 6.78 | Capital Return % |
| — | — | — | — | — | — | — | — | 0.68 | 2.89 | Income $ |
| — | — | — | — | — | — | — | — | 0.59 | 0.68 | Capital Gains $ |
| — | — | — | — | — | — | — | — | — | — | Expense Ratio % |
| — | — | — | — | — | — | — | — | — | — | Income Ratio % |
| — | — | — | — | — | — | — | — | 7 | — | Turnover Rate % |
| — | — | — | — | — | — | — | — | 171 | 410 | Net Assets $mil |

## Performance

### Historic Quarterly NAV Returns

| | 1st Qtr | 2nd Qtr | 3rd Qtr | 4th Qtr | Total |
|---|---|---|---|---|---|
| 2001 | — | — | — | — | — |
| 2002 | — | — | — | — | — |
| 2003 | — | — | — | — | — |
| 2004 | — | — | — | 15.00 | —* |
| 2005 | -7.31 | 14.65 | 3.59 | 1.73 | 12.00 |

| Trailing | NAV Return% | Market Return% | NAV Rtrn% +/-S&P 500 | %Rank Cat.(NAV) |
|---|---|---|---|---|
| 3 Mo | 1.73 | 1.19 | -0.35 | 4 |
| 6 Mo | 5.38 | 5.40 | -0.38 | 4 |
| 1 Yr | 12.00 | 11.94 | 7.09 | 4 |
| 3 Yr Avg | — | — | — | 0 |
| 5 Yr Avg | — | — | — | 0 |
| 10 Yr Avg | — | — | — | 0 |

| Tax Analysis | Tax-Adj Return% | Tax-Cost Ratio |
|---|---|---|
| 3 Yr (estimated) | — | — |
| 5 Yr (estimated) | — | — |
| 10 Yr (estimated) | — | — |

## Risk Profile

| | Standard Index S&P 500 | Best Fit Index |
|---|---|---|
| Alpha | — | — |
| Beta | — | — |
| R-Squared | — | — |
| Standard Deviation | — | |
| Mean | — | |
| Sharpe Ratio | — | |

## Morningstar Fair Value

| Price/Fair Value Ratio | Fair Value Estimate ($) | Hit Rate % |
|---|---|---|
| 1.2 Overvalued | 41.62 | 83 |

## Portfolio Analysis   09-30-05

Share change since 06-05  Total Stocks:105

| | Sector | PE | Tot Ret% | % Assets |
|---|---|---|---|---|
| ⊕ Simon Property Group | Financial | 57.2 | 23.30 | 5.69 |
| ⊕ Equity Office Properties | Financial | — | 10.93 | 4.91 |
| ⊕ Vornado Realty Trust | Financial | 19.4 | 15.15 | 4.01 |
| ⊕ Equity Residential | Financial | 75.2 | 13.37 | 3.99 |
| ⊕ ProLogis Trust | Financial | 32.0 | 11.73 | 3.98 |
| ⊕ General Growth Propertie | Financial | NMF | 35.15 | 3.74 |
| ⊕ Archstone-Smith Trust | Financial | 55.1 | 14.47 | 3.11 |
| ⊕ Boston Properties | Financial | 24.8 | 23.57 | 2.89 |
| ⊕ AvalonBay Communities | Financial | 60.7 | 22.84 | 2.30 |
| ⊕ Kimco Realty | Financial | 24.5 | 15.41 | 2.22 |
| ⊕ Host Marriott | Financial | 94.8 | 12.16 | 2.08 |
| ⊕ Public Storage | Financial | 36.2 | 25.10 | 2.07 |
| ⊕ Duke Realty | Financial | 41.8 | 6.98 | 1.79 |
| ⊕ Developers Diversified R | Financial | 20.4 | 11.07 | 1.77 |
| ⊕ Macerich | Financial | 79.9 | 11.47 | 1.43 |
| ⊕ Regency Centers | Financial | 33.1 | 10.80 | 1.41 |
| ⊕ AMB Property | Financial | 47.7 | 26.78 | 1.39 |
| ⊕ Liberty Property Trust | Financial | 25.4 | 5.19 | 1.36 |
| ⊕ Apartment Investment & M | Financial | — | 4.57 | 1.36 |
| ⊕ Health Care Property | Financial | 24.1 | -1.57 | 1.33 |

### Current Investment Style

Value Blnd Growth — Large/Mid/Small

| Market Cap | % |
|---|---|
| Giant | 0.0 |
| Large | 22.9 |
| Mid | 61.2 |
| Small | 14.9 |
| Micro | 0.9 |

Avg $mil: 4,073

| Value Measures | | Rel Category |
|---|---|---|
| Price/Earnings | 15.51 | 0.97 |
| Price/Book | 2.47 | 0.97 |
| Price/Sales | 4.24 | 0.89 |
| Price/Cash Flow | 12.92 | 0.97 |
| Dividend Yield % | 4.44 | 1.03 |

| Growth Measures | % | Rel Category |
|---|---|---|
| Long-Term Erngs | 6.34 | 0.95 |
| Book Value | -1.66 | NMF |
| Sales | 4.25 | 0.94 |
| Cash Flow | 0.02 | 0.00 |
| Historical Erngs | -1.97 | NMF |

| Profitability | % | Rel Category |
|---|---|---|
| Return on Equity | 9.56 | 0.93 |
| Return on Assets | 8.42 | 0.93 |
| Net Margin | 22.75 | 0.91 |

### Sector Weightings

| | % of Stocks | Rel S&P 500 | 3 Year High Low |
|---|---|---|---|
| ↻ Info | 0.00 | 0.00 | |
| 🄺 Software | 0.00 | 0.00 | 0 0 |
| 🄷 Hardware | 0.00 | 0.00 | 0 0 |
| 🄼 Media | 0.00 | 0.00 | 0 0 |
| 🄵 Telecom | 0.00 | 0.00 | 0 0 |
| ☞ Service | 100.00 | 2.16 | |
| 🄷 Health | 0.00 | 0.00 | 0 0 |
| 🄴 Consumer | 0.29 | 0.04 | 0 0 |
| 🄱 Business | 0.00 | 0.00 | 0 0 |
| 🄵 Financial | 99.71 | 4.73 | 100 100 |
| 🄼 Mfg | 0.00 | 0.00 | |
| 🄶 Goods | 0.00 | 0.00 | 0 0 |
| 🄸 Ind Mtrls | 0.00 | 0.00 | 0 0 |
| 🄴 Energy | 0.00 | 0.00 | 0 0 |
| 🄾 Utilities | 0.00 | 0.00 | 0 0 |

### Composition

| | % |
|---|---|
| ● Cash | 1.7 |
| ● Stocks | 97.4 |
| ● Bonds | 0.0 |
| ● Other | 1.0 |
| Foreign | 0.0 |
| (% of Stock) | |

## Morningstar's Take   by Dan McNeela

Vanguard REIT Index VIPERs is solid enough to overcome some drawbacks.

This fund shares many of the benefits of other exchange-traded funds. Its 0.12% expense ratio is much lower than actively managed real estate funds. That cost represents a nice savings over both the Investor shares and Admiral shares of the Vanguard REIT Index Fund, which charge 0.21% and 0.16%, respectively. The fund is also the low cost leader among its real estate ETF peers, which charge from 0.26% to 0.60% annually.

In tracking the MSCI U.S. REIT Index, the fund owns stakes in equity REITs of all property types, as determined by their market cap. Investors get exposure to office REITs, apartment REITs, regional mall REITs and other subsectors, allowing for broad geographic diversification too.

The combination of ultralow costs and an exclusive focus on REITs gives the fund one of the highest yields in the category. The fund's benchmark historically has had low turnover, so trading costs aren't an issue either.

All that said, investors should be aware of a few caveats. Investors must pay brokerage costs to buy and sell ETFs. Those costs may eat up any benefit for those that are regularly buying and selling shares, especially when the amount invested is low. Furthermore, owning only REITs means the fund is more limited than most of its peers, which can invest in some hotels and other real estate operating companies that aren't organized as REITs. Finally, investors who are buying in now need to realize that the huge gains of the past five years are unlikely to be repeated and this sector may be due for a cooling-off period.

Long-term investors have good reason to ride out any sluggishness, though. This offering is stable enough to meet expectations despite its limitations.

| | | | | |
|---|---|---|---|---|
| Address: | PO Box 2600 United States 866-499-8473 | Management Fee: | 0.16% | |
| | | Expense Projections: | 3Yr:$58 | 5Yr:$101   10Yr:$230 |
| Web Address: | www.vanguard.com | Income Distrib: | Quarterly | |
| Inception: | 09-23-04 * | Exchange: | AMEX | |
| Advisor: | Vanguard Advisers, Inc. | | | |

Mᴏʀɴɪɴɢsᴛᴀʀ® **ETFs 100**

# Vanguard Small Cap VIPERs

| Ticker | NAV | Market Price | 52 wk High/Low | Yield | Mstar Category |
|--------|-----|--------------|----------------|-------|----------------|
| VB | $59.59 | $62.34 | $62.34 - $51.23 | 1.1% | Small Blend |

## Management

### Portfolio Manager(s)

In 2005, Vanguard announced that Gus Sauter, the firm's index guru, is no longer the day-to-day manager of this ETF. Since assuming the role of Vanguard's chief investment officer in March 2003, he has gradually scaled back his involvement with individual funds. Sauter will still have oversight responsibilities here, but the daily management of this ETF is now handled by Michael Buek, who has been with Vanguard for 18 years and has worked closely with Sauter for the past 14 years.

### Strategy

This exchange-traded fund tracks the MSCI U.S. Small Cap 1750 Index, which contains the smallest 1,750 of the top 2,500 publicly traded companies in the United States that are ranked by market capitalization. Because it pulls in a passel of mid-cap names (those that rank from 750th- to 999th-largest by market cap), its median market cap is a tad higher than that of the Russell 2000 Index, a common small-cap bogy.

### Growth of $10,000

— Investment Value of ETF
— Investment Value of Index S&P 500

| | 1996 | 1997 | 1998 | 1999 | 2000 | 2001 | 2002 | 2003 | 2004 | 2005 | History |
|---|------|------|------|------|------|------|------|------|------|------|---------|
| | — | — | — | — | — | — | — | — | 56.05 | 59.59 | NAV $ |
| | — | — | — | — | — | — | — | — | 56.16 | 59.55 | Market Price $ |
| | — | — | — | — | — | — | — | — | 10.06* | 7.53 | NAV Return% |
| | — | — | — | — | — | — | — | — | 10.03* | 7.25 | Market Price Return% |
| | — | — | — | — | — | — | — | — | -0.10 | -0.08 | Avg Premium/Discount% |
| | — | — | — | — | — | — | — | — | 10.06 | 2.62 | NAV Rtrn% +/-S&P 500 |
| | — | — | — | — | — | — | — | — | 10.06 | 2.98 | NAV Rtrn% +/-Russ 2000 |
| | — | — | — | — | — | — | — | — | — | 4 | NAV Return% Rank in Cat |
| | — | — | — | — | — | — | — | — | 0.00 | 1.22 | Income Return % |
| | — | — | — | — | — | — | — | — | — | 6.31 | Capital Return % |
| | — | — | — | — | — | — | — | — | 0.62 | 0.68 | Income $ |
| | — | — | — | — | — | — | — | — | 0.00 | 0.00 | Capital Gains $ |
| | — | — | — | — | — | — | — | — | 0.18 | — | Expense Ratio % |
| | — | — | — | — | — | — | — | — | 1.19 | — | Income Ratio % |
| | — | — | — | — | — | — | — | — | 19 | — | Turnover Rate % |
| | — | — | — | — | — | — | — | — | 186 | 265 | Net Assets $mil |

## Performance

### Historic Quarterly NAV Returns

| | 1st Qtr | 2nd Qtr | 3rd Qtr | 4th Qtr | Total |
|---|---------|---------|---------|---------|-------|
| 2001 | — | — | — | — | — |
| 2002 | — | — | — | — | — |
| 2003 | — | — | — | — | — |
| 2004 | — | 1.01 | -2.26 | 13.93 | —* |
| 2005 | -3.74 | 4.86 | 5.25 | 1.22 | 7.53 |

| Trailing | NAV Return% | Market Return% | NAV Rtrn% +/-S&P 500 | %Rank Cat.(NAV) |
|----------|-------------|----------------|----------------------|-----------------|
| 3 Mo | 1.22 | 1.24 | -0.86 | 7 |
| 6 Mo | 6.53 | 6.63 | 0.77 | 4 |
| 1 Yr | 7.53 | 7.25 | 2.62 | 4 |
| 3 Yr Avg | — | — | — | 0 |
| 5 Yr Avg | — | — | — | 0 |
| 10 Yr Avg | — | — | — | 0 |

| Tax Analysis | Tax-Adj Return% | Tax-Cost Ratio |
|--------------|-----------------|----------------|
| 3 Yr (estimated) | — | — |
| 5 Yr (estimated) | — | — |
| 10 Yr (estimated) | — | — |

## Risk Profile

| | Standard Index S&P 500 | Best Fit Index |
|---|------------------------|----------------|
| Alpha | — | — |
| Beta | — | — |
| R-Squared | — | — |
| Standard Deviation | — | |
| Mean | — | |
| Sharpe Ratio | — | |

## Morningstar Fair Value

| Price/Fair Value Ratio | Fair Value Estimate ($) | Hit Rate % |
|------------------------|-------------------------|------------|
| — | — | — |

## Portfolio Analysis    09-30-05

Share change since 06-05  Total Stocks:1711

| Sector | | PE | Tot Ret% | % Assets |
|--------|---|----|----------|----------|
| ⊕ Southwestern Energy | Energy | 41.1 | 183.60 | 0.36 |
| ⊕ Grant Prideco | Energy | 41.2 | 120.05 | 0.30 |
| ⊕ Allegheny Energy | Utilities | 29.9 | 60.58 | 0.30 |
| ⊕ Reliant Energy | Utilities | — | -24.40 | 0.28 |
| ⊕ Tesoro | Energy | 9.9 | 93.93 | 0.27 |
| ⊕ Arch Coal | Energy | NMF | 124.97 | 0.26 |
| ⊕ Activision | Software | 46.6 | 21.05 | 0.25 |
| ⊕ Joy Global | Ind Mtrls | 44.2 | 109.41 | 0.24 |
| ⊕ MEMC Electronic Material | Hardware | 18.6 | 67.32 | 0.24 |
| ⊕ Massey Energy Company | Energy | 28.5 | 8.77 | 0.23 |
| ⊕ American Capital Strateg | Financial | 8.9 | 18.27 | 0.23 |
| ⊕ Arrow Electronics | Hardware | 17.1 | 31.81 | 0.22 |
| ⊕ Cummins | Ind Mtrls | 8.8 | 8.79 | 0.22 |
| ⊕ First American | Financial | 10.0 | 31.26 | 0.22 |
| ⊕ Martin Marietta Material | Ind Mtrls | 20.3 | 44.88 | 0.22 |
| ⊕ Aqua America | Utilities | 38.3 | 50.76 | 0.22 |
| ⊕ CMS Energy | Utilities | — | 38.85 | 0.22 |
| ⊕ AmeriCredit | Financial | 15.4 | 4.83 | 0.21 |
| ⊕ Roper Industries | Ind Mtrls | 27.9 | 30.86 | 0.20 |
| ⊕ Range Resources | Energy | 40.8 | 93.68 | 0.20 |

### Current Investment Style

Value Blnd Growth — Large Mid Small

| Market Cap | % |
|------------|---|
| Giant | 0.0 |
| Large | 0.0 |
| Mid | 48.7 |
| Small | 46.0 |
| Micro | 5.4 |

Avg $mil: 1,453

| Value Measures | | Rel Category |
|----------------|---|--------------|
| Price/Earnings | 17.47 | 1.01 |
| Price/Book | 2.11 | 1.09 |
| Price/Sales | 1.05 | 1.15 |
| Price/Cash Flow | 6.87 | 1.04 |
| Dividend Yield % | 1.20 | 1.33 |

| Growth Measures | % | Rel Category |
|-----------------|---|--------------|
| Long-Term Erngs | 12.44 | 0.90 |
| Book Value | 5.94 | 1.65 |
| Sales | 6.69 | 1.27 |
| Cash Flow | 4.30 | 47.78 |
| Historical Erngs | 12.18 | 0.99 |

| Profitability | % | Rel Category |
|---------------|---|--------------|
| Return on Equity | 11.56 | 1.19 |
| Return on Assets | 6.29 | 1.22 |
| Net Margin | 9.78 | 1.20 |

### Sector Weightings

| | % of Stocks | Rel S&P 500 | 3 Year High Low |
|---|-------------|-------------|-----------------|
| ↻ Info | 14.63 | 0.72 | |
| 🖳 Software | 4.24 | 1.19 | 5  4 |
| 🖥 Hardware | 7.38 | 0.74 | 10  7 |
| 🔊 Media | 1.75 | 0.49 | 2  1 |
| 📶 Telecom | 1.26 | 0.42 | 2  1 |
| ☞ Service | 52.92 | 1.14 | |
| ♥ Health | 10.97 | 0.83 | 13  11 |
| 🛒 Consumer | 9.91 | 1.22 | 12  9 |
| 🏢 Business | 9.90 | 2.56 | 11  10 |
| 💲 Financial | 22.14 | 1.05 | 23  22 |
| ⊐ Mfg | 32.44 | 0.97 | |
| 🛢 Goods | 4.94 | 0.58 | 5  4 |
| ⚙ Ind Mtrls | 14.82 | 1.22 | 15  12 |
| 🔋 Energy | 7.66 | 0.82 | 8  5 |
| 🔌 Utilities | 5.02 | 1.49 | 5  4 |

### Composition

| | % |
|---|---|
| ● Cash | 0.3 |
| ● Stocks | 98.9 |
| ● Bonds | 0.1 |
| ○ Other | 0.7 |
| | |
| Foreign | 0.3 |
| (% of Stock) | |

## Morningstar's Take  by Sonya Morris

Competition is tough for Vanguard Small-Cap VIPERs, particularly from within.

Exchange-traded funds (ETFs) often compare favorably to open-ended funds in terms of cost and tax efficiency. However, Vanguard's open-ended funds compete strongly on both counts. For instance, this fund's internal rival, Vanguard Tax-Managed Small-Cap, charges just 0.14% in expenses, compared with this fund's 0.18%. And its tax-management mandate means it's likely to give this ETF a run for its money in terms of tax-adjusted returns.

Still, these funds have important differences that may influence an investor's choice. This fund tracks the MSCI (Morgan Stanley Capital International) U.S. Small Cap 1750 Index, while its internal rival is tethered to the S&P SmallCap 600. The MSCI index includes a passel of mid-cap stocks, which give this fund a higher average market cap. Furthermore, MSCI's methodology is entirely quantitative and transparent. In contrast, the S&P index is constructed by a committee that uses more subjective factors. For example, the committee won't immediately include IPOs in the index until they've been "seasoned" for six to 12 months. They also screen out firms that don't have a record of four straight quarters of positive earnings. Because this fund's benchmark includes these racier stocks, it may be more volatile.

Investors shopping for a small-cap fund at Vanguard face a tough choice. This fund's internal rival is most suited for those who plan to dollar-cost average as well as those seeking a slightly smoother ride. But investors who prefer the ETF format have a decent pick here. Granted, indexing hasn't fared all that well in the small-cap space, but we think there's logical reasons to own this fund. It's cheap and broadly diversified. And because many of the best small-cap funds are closed, superior alternatives are hard to find.

| Address: | PO Box 2600 Valley Forge PA 19482 866-499-8473 | Management Fee: | 0.08% |
|----------|-------------|-----------------|-------|
| | | Expense Projections: | 3Yr:$32   5Yr:$56   10Yr:$128 |
| Web Address: | www.vanguard.com | Income Distrib: | Annually |
| Inception: | 01-26-04* | Exchange: | AMEX |
| Advisor: | Vanguard Advisers, Inc. | | |

MⓄRNINGSTAR® ETFs 100

# Vanguard Sm Cp Val VIPER

| Ticker | NAV | Market Price | 52 wk High/Low | Yield | Mstar Category |
|---|---|---|---|---|---|
| VBR | $60.76 | $63.80 | $63.80 - $53.44 | 1.9% | Small Value |

## Management

### Portfolio Manager(s)

Earlier in 2005, Vanguard revealed that index guru Gus Sauter is no longer responsible for this ETF's daily management. Although Sauter will still provide oversight, the daily managerial tasks now fall to Michael Buek, who has been with the firm since 1987. Buek has worked closely with Sauter on this offering since its inception. He's also in charge of day-to-day operations at Vanguard Small Cap VIPERs.

### Strategy

This exchange-traded fund is tethered to the MSCI U.S. Small Cap Value Index, which consists of the cheapest stocks (as determined by its eight-pronged classification scheme) in the small-cap universe. The index uses bands to limit the migration of stocks between market-cap and style boundaries, thus limiting turnover.

**Growth of $10,000**

— Investment Value of ETF
— Investment Value of Index S&P 500

| | 1996 | 1997 | 1998 | 1999 | 2000 | 2001 | 2002 | 2003 | 2004 | 2005 | History |
|---|---|---|---|---|---|---|---|---|---|---|---|
| | — | — | — | — | — | — | — | — | 58.31 | 60.76 | NAV $ |
| | — | — | — | — | — | — | — | — | 58.30 | 60.69 | Market Price $ |
| | — | — | — | — | — | — | — | — | 12.07* | 6.20 | NAV Return% |
| | — | — | — | — | — | — | — | — | 12.01* | 6.09 | Market Price Return% |
| | — | — | — | — | — | — | — | — | -0.03 | -0.14 | Avg Premium/Discount% |
| | — | — | — | — | — | — | — | — | 12.07 | 1.29 | NAV Rtrn% +/-S&P 500 |
| | — | — | — | — | — | — | — | — | 12.07 | 1.49 | NAV Rtrn% +/-Russ 2000 VL |
| | — | — | — | — | — | — | — | — | — | 5 | NAV Return% Rank in Cat |
| | — | — | — | — | — | — | — | — | 0.00 | 2.00 | Income Return % |
| | — | — | — | — | — | — | — | — | — | 4.20 | Capital Return % |
| | — | — | — | — | — | — | — | — | 0.97 | 1.17 | Income $ |
| | — | — | — | — | — | — | — | — | 0.00 | 0.00 | Capital Gains $ |
| | — | — | — | — | — | — | — | — | 0.22 | — | Expense Ratio % |
| | — | — | — | — | — | — | — | — | 2.16 | — | Income Ratio % |
| | — | — | — | — | — | — | — | — | 30 | — | Turnover Rate % |
| | — | — | — | — | — | — | — | — | 47 | 188 | Net Assets $mil |

## Performance

### Historic Quarterly NAV Returns

| | 1st Qtr | 2nd Qtr | 3rd Qtr | 4th Qtr | Total |
|---|---|---|---|---|---|
| 2001 | — | — | — | — | — |
| 2002 | — | — | — | — | — |
| 2003 | — | — | — | — | — |
| 2004 | — | 0.93 | 1.06 | 13.04 | — * |
| 2005 | -3.28 | 5.23 | 4.06 | 0.27 | 6.20 |

| Trailing | NAV Return% | Market Return% | NAV Rtrn% +/-S&P 500 | %Rank Cat.(NAV) |
|---|---|---|---|---|
| 3 Mo | 0.27 | 0.04 | -1.81 | 6 |
| 6 Mo | 4.34 | 4.17 | -1.42 | 6 |
| 1 Yr | 6.20 | 6.09 | 1.29 | 5 |
| 3 Yr Avg | — | — | — | 0 |
| 5 Yr Avg | — | — | — | 0 |
| 10 Yr Avg | — | — | — | 0 |

| Tax Analysis | Tax-Adj Return% | Tax-Cost Ratio |
|---|---|---|
| 3 Yr (estimated) | — | — |
| 5 Yr (estimated) | — | — |
| 10 Yr (estimated) | — | — |

## Risk Profile

| | Standard Index S&P 500 | Best Fit Index |
|---|---|---|
| Alpha | — | — |
| Beta | — | — |
| R-Squared | — | — |
| Standard Deviation | — | |
| Mean | — | |
| Sharpe Ratio | — | |

## Morningstar Fair Value

| Price/Fair Value Ratio | Fair Value Estimate ($) | Hit Rate % |
|---|---|---|
| | | |

## Portfolio Analysis 09-30-05

| Share change since 06-05 Total Stocks:948 | Sector | PE | Tot Ret% | % Assets |
|---|---|---|---|---|
| ⊕ Reliant Energy | Utilities | — | -24.40 | 0.55 |
| ⊕ Tesoro | Energy | 9.9 | 93.93 | 0.54 |
| ⊕ Arch Coal | Energy | NMF | 124.97 | 0.51 |
| ⊕ American Capital Strateg | Financial | 8.9 | 18.27 | 0.46 |
| ⊕ Arrow Electronics | Hardware | 17.1 | 31.81 | 0.44 |
| ⊕ First American | Financial | 10.0 | 31.26 | 0.44 |
| ⊕ Martin Marietta Material | Ind Mtrls | 20.3 | 44.88 | 0.44 |
| ⊕ CMS Energy | Utilities | — | 38.85 | 0.43 |
| ⊕ AmeriCredit | Financial | 15.4 | 4.83 | 0.42 |
| ⊕ Oneok | Utilities | 10.7 | -2.78 | 0.39 |
| ⊕ Allegheny Energy | Utilities | 29.9 | 60.58 | 0.39 |
| ⊕ United Dominion Realty | Financial | — | -0.30 | 0.39 |
| ⊕ Federal Realty Investmen | Financial | 46.0 | 22.33 | 0.38 |
| ⊕ BorgWarner | Ind Mtrls | 14.3 | 13.12 | 0.38 |
| ⊕ Conseco | Financial | 12.8 | 16.14 | 0.38 |
| ⊕ Mills | Financial | — | -31.30 | 0.37 |
| ⊕ Colonial BancGroup A | Financial | 15.9 | 15.34 | 0.37 |
| ⊕ Energen | Energy | 18.2 | 24.70 | 0.36 |
| ⊕ Avnet | Business | 19.0 | 31.25 | 0.36 |
| ⊕ Ventas | Financial | 26.5 | 22.74 | 0.35 |

### Current Investment Style

Value Blnd Growth — Large/Mid/Small

| Market Cap | % |
|---|---|
| Giant | 0.0 |
| Large | 0.0 |
| Mid | 48.4 |
| Small | 46.0 |
| Micro | 5.6 |

Avg $mil: 1,441

| Value Measures | | Rel Category |
|---|---|---|
| Price/Earnings | 15.03 | 1.02 |
| Price/Book | 1.70 | 0.97 |
| Price/Sales | 0.90 | 1.11 |
| Price/Cash Flow | 5.89 | 0.89 |
| Dividend Yield % | 2.16 | 1.13 |

| Growth Measures | % | Rel Category |
|---|---|---|
| Long-Term Erngs | 9.82 | 0.92 |
| Book Value | 5.28 | 0.94 |
| Sales | 5.29 | 1.17 |
| Cash Flow | -0.94 | NMF |
| Historical Erngs | 10.14 | 1.02 |

| Profitability | % | Rel Category |
|---|---|---|
| Return on Equity | 10.30 | 0.90 |
| Return on Assets | 6.56 | 0.94 |
| Net Margin | 12.04 | 1.15 |

| Sector Weightings | % of Stocks | Rel S&P 500 | 3 Year High | Low |
|---|---|---|---|---|
| ☎ Info | 9.00 | 0.45 | | |
| 🖥 Software | 1.15 | 0.32 | 2 | 1 |
| 💻 Hardware | 5.64 | 0.56 | 8 | 3 |
| 📷 Media | 1.65 | 0.46 | 2 | 0 |
| 📶 Telecom | 0.56 | 0.19 | 1 | 0 |
| ⚙ Service | 53.72 | 1.16 | | |
| 🏥 Health | 1.89 | 0.14 | 6 | 2 |
| 🛒 Consumer | 7.58 | 0.93 | 12 | 7 |
| 💼 Business | 6.70 | 1.73 | 9 | 6 |
| 💲 Financial | 37.55 | 1.78 | 39 | 18 |
| 🏭 Mfg | 37.27 | 1.12 | | |
| 🏬 Goods | 4.55 | 0.53 | 9 | 5 |
| ⚗ Ind Mtrls | 18.64 | 1.53 | 20 | 18 |
| 🔋 Energy | 4.72 | 0.50 | 8 | 4 |
| 💡 Utilities | 9.36 | 2.79 | 10 | 6 |

### Composition

| | | |
|---|---|---|
| ● Cash | 0.3 | |
| ● Stocks | 99.0 | |
| ● Bonds | 0.0 | |
| ○ Other | 0.7 | |
| Foreign | 0.3 (% of Stock) | |

## Morningstar's Take by Sonya Morris

There's justification for owning Vanguard Small-Cap Value VIPERs.

In the less efficient small-cap world, active managers have had an easier time trumping indexes than in other areas of the market. But for the past couple of years, investors have flooded small-value funds with cash, and it's getting harder to find good active managers who aren't overburdened with assets. Because investors' choices are limited, index funds like this one can be decent alternatives. And the menu for index funds keeps growing as the market for exchange-traded funds (ETFs) heats up. This ETF's rivals include iShares Russell 2000 Value, iShares S&P SmallCap 600, and StreetTracks DJ US SmallCap Value.

We think this fund stands up to its ETF rivals. First and foremost, this fund has the lowest expense ratio of the bunch. That's key in the competitive world of indexing where every percentage point counts. Furthermore, this fund's benchmark, the MSCI U.S. Small Cap Index, has some methodological advantages. For example, unlike both the S&P and Russell indexes, the MSCI bogy uses buffer zones to limit the migration of stocks between style and market-cap zones. That should help keep turnover and trading costs low.

Although this ETF has some appealing traits, it also has a few foibles. For example, it includes more mid-caps than both iShares ETFs, and that could be a liability when that market segment lags. Similarly, this fund also holds an outsized financials stake, leaving it vulnerable to a downturn in that sector. But despite those risks, we still think it's a decent way to get exposure to small-cap value stocks.

It's worth noting that investors incur brokerage commissions each time they trade ETF shares, making them inappropriate for investors who dollar-cost average. Those investors should give this fund's open-ended twin, Vanguard Small-Cap Value, a closer look.

| Address: | PO Box 2600 | Management Fee: | 0.09% | | |
|---|---|---|---|---|---|
| | Valley Forge PA 19482 | Expense Projections: | 3Yr:$39 | 5Yr:$68 | 10Yr:$154 |
| | 866-499-8473 | Income Distrib: | Annually | | |
| Web Address: | www.vanguard.com | Exchange: | AMEX | | |
| Inception: | 01-26-04 * | | | | |
| Advisor: | Vanguard Advisers, Inc. | | | | |

**Morningstar® ETFs 100**

# Vanguard Sm Cap Gr VIPERs

| | Ticker | NAV | Market Price | 52 wk High/Low | Yield | Mstar Category |
|---|---|---|---|---|---|---|
| | VBK | $58.47 | $61.67 | $61.67 - $48.79 | 0.4% | Small Growth |

## Management

### Portfolio Manager(s)

Gus Sauter is one of the most seasoned hands in the indexing business. He has been very successful guiding Vanguard's index lineup over a number of years.

### Strategy

This ETF tracks the MSCI U.S. Small Cap Growth Index, which uses an eight-pronged classification system to identify small-growth stocks. Vanguard chose this index because its sophisticated methodology should provide purer exposure to the small-growth universe than indexes that use a more simplistic approach such as the S&P Small Cap 600/Barra Growth Index.

### Growth of $10,000

— Investment Value of ETF
— Investment Value of Index S&P 500

| | 1996 | 1997 | 1998 | 1999 | 2000 | 2001 | 2002 | 2003 | 2004 | 2005 | History |
|---|---|---|---|---|---|---|---|---|---|---|---|
| | — | — | — | — | — | — | — | — | 53.95 | 58.47 | NAV $ |
| | — | — | — | — | — | — | — | — | 53.94 | 58.40 | Market Price $ |
| | — | — | — | — | — | — | — | — | 7.89* | 8.77 | NAV Return% |
| | — | — | — | — | — | — | — | — | 7.82* | 8.66 | Market Price Return% |
| | — | — | — | — | — | — | — | — | -0.21 | -0.06 | Avg Premium/Discount% |
| | — | — | — | — | — | — | — | — | 7.89 | 3.86 | NAV Rtrn% +/-S&P 500 |
| | — | — | — | — | — | — | — | — | 7.89 | 4.62 | NAV Rtrn% +/-Russ 2000 Gr |
| | — | — | — | — | — | — | — | — | — | 5 | NAV Return% Rank in Cat |
| | — | — | — | — | — | — | — | — | 0.00 | 0.40 | Income Return % |
| | — | — | — | — | — | — | — | — | — | 8.37 | Capital Return % |
| | — | — | — | — | — | — | — | — | 0.09 | 0.21 | Income $ |
| | — | — | — | — | — | — | — | — | 0.00 | 0.00 | Capital Gains $ |
| | — | — | — | — | — | — | — | — | 0.22 | — | Expense Ratio % |
| | — | — | — | — | — | — | — | — | 0.15 | — | Income Ratio % |
| | — | — | — | — | — | — | — | — | 41 | — | Turnover Rate % |
| | — | — | — | — | — | — | — | — | 92 | 206 | Net Assets $mil |

## Performance

### Historic Quarterly NAV Returns

| | 1st Qtr | 2nd Qtr | 3rd Qtr | 4th Qtr | Total |
|---|---|---|---|---|---|
| 2001 | — | — | — | — | — |
| 2002 | — | — | — | — | — |
| 2003 | — | — | — | — | — |
| 2004 | — | 1.11 | -5.73 | 14.85 | —* |
| 2005 | -4.19 | 4.43 | 6.45 | 2.13 | 8.77 |

| Trailing | NAV Return% | Market Return% | NAV Rtrn% +/-S&P 500 | %Rank Cat.(NAV) |
|---|---|---|---|---|
| 3 Mo | 2.13 | 2.01 | 0.05 | 6 |
| 6 Mo | 8.71 | 8.54 | 2.95 | 6 |
| 1 Yr | 8.77 | 8.66 | 3.86 | 5 |
| 3 Yr Avg | — | — | — | 0 |
| 5 Yr Avg | — | — | — | 0 |
| 10 Yr Avg | — | — | — | 0 |

| Tax Analysis | Tax-Adj Return% | Tax-Cost Ratio |
|---|---|---|
| 3 Yr (estimated) | — | — |
| 5 Yr (estimated) | — | — |
| 10 Yr (estimated) | — | — |

## Risk Profile

| | Standard Index S&P 500 | Best Fit Index |
|---|---|---|
| Alpha | — | — |
| Beta | — | — |
| R-Squared | — | — |
| Standard Deviation | — | |
| Mean | — | |
| Sharpe Ratio | — | |

## Morningstar Fair Value

| Price/Fair Value Ratio | Fair Value Estimate ($) | Hit Rate % |
|---|---|---|
| | | |

## Portfolio Analysis 09-30-05

Share change since 06-05  Total Stocks:969

| | Sector | PE | Tot Ret% | % Assets |
|---|---|---|---|---|
| ⊕ Southwestern Energy | Energy | 41.1 | 183.60 | 0.72 |
| ⊕ Grant Prideco | Energy | 41.2 | 120.05 | 0.61 |
| ⊕ Activision | Software | 46.6 | 21.05 | 0.50 |
| ⊕ Joy Global | Ind Mtrls | 44.2 | 109.41 | 0.49 |
| ⊕ MEMC Electronic Material | Hardware | 18.6 | 67.32 | 0.48 |
| ⊕ Massey Energy Company | Energy | 28.5 | 8.77 | 0.47 |
| ⊕ Roper Industries | Ind Mtrls | 27.9 | 30.86 | 0.40 |
| ⊕ Range Resources | Energy | 40.8 | 93.68 | 0.40 |
| ⊕ Amylin Pharmaceuticals | Health | — | 70.89 | 0.39 |
| ⊕ Corporate Executive Boar | Business | 51.9 | 34.71 | 0.39 |
| ⊕ Renal Care Group | Health | 25.9 | 31.45 | 0.39 |
| ⊕ Cooper Companies | Health | 18.9 | -27.25 | 0.39 |
| ⊕ Plains Exploration & Pro | Energy | — | 52.81 | 0.38 |
| ⊕ Oshkosh Truck | Ind Mtrls | 20.4 | 31.21 | 0.38 |
| ⊕ Macromedia | Software | — | — | 0.38 |
| ⊕ Helmerich & Payne | Energy | 25.3 | 83.15 | 0.37 |
| ⊕ Cytyc | Health | 32.1 | 2.39 | 0.37 |
| ⊕ Covance | Health | 26.4 | 25.29 | 0.36 |
| ⊕ Respironics | Health | 61.3 | 36.39 | 0.36 |
| ⊕ Ametek | Ind Mtrls | 22.4 | 19.96 | 0.36 |

### Current Investment Style

Value Blnd Growth — Large / Mid / Small

| Market Cap | % |
|---|---|
| Giant | 0.0 |
| Large | 0.0 |
| Mid | 49.0 |
| Small | 45.9 |
| Micro | 5.1 |

Avg $mil: 1,466

| Value Measures | | Rel Category |
|---|---|---|
| Price/Earnings | 21.13 | 0.96 |
| Price/Book | 2.85 | 0.96 |
| Price/Sales | 1.26 | 0.85 |
| Price/Cash Flow | 8.32 | 0.98 |
| Dividend Yield % | 0.23 | 0.79 |

| Growth Measures | % | Rel Category |
|---|---|---|
| Long-Term Erngs | 16.51 | 0.95 |
| Book Value | 7.53 | 0.81 |
| Sales | 8.93 | 0.73 |
| Cash Flow | 11.90 | 0.73 |
| Historical Erngs | 16.60 | 0.82 |

| Profitability | % | Rel Category |
|---|---|---|
| Return on Equity | 12.88 | 0.94 |
| Return on Assets | 6.02 | 0.85 |
| Net Margin | 7.47 | 0.85 |

### Sector Weightings

| | % of Stocks | Rel S&P 500 | 3 Year High | Low |
|---|---|---|---|---|
| ⌖ Info | 20.34 | 1.01 | | |
| Software | 7.36 | 2.07 | 9 | 6 |
| Hardware | 9.16 | 0.91 | 17 | 6 |
| Media | 1.85 | 0.52 | 3 | 0 |
| Telecom | 1.97 | 0.65 | 3 | 1 |
| ⌦ Service | 52.11 | 1.12 | | |
| Health | 20.19 | 1.52 | 21 | 19 |
| Consumer | 12.27 | 1.51 | 14 | 12 |
| Business | 13.15 | 3.40 | 15 | 12 |
| Financial | 6.50 | 0.31 | 11 | 6 |
| Mfg | 27.56 | 0.82 | | |
| Goods | 5.34 | 0.62 | 7 | 4 |
| Ind Mtrls | 10.94 | 0.90 | 16 | 7 |
| Energy | 10.65 | 1.14 | 11 | 5 |
| Utilities | 0.63 | 0.19 | 1 | 0 |

### Composition

| | % |
|---|---|
| ● Cash | 0.1 |
| ● Stocks | 99.0 |
| ● Bonds | 0.1 |
| Other | 0.8 |
| Foreign | 0.3 |
| (% of Stock) | |

## Morningstar's Take  by Sonya Morris

Vanguard Small-Cap Growth VIPERs are a respectable, if uninspiring, option.

This ETF has its charms. Yes, it offers the broad diversification that one would expect in an index-tracking offering, as assets are spread across 980 holdings and the full panoply of market sectors. But a few traits set it apart from rivals. For starters, its 0.22% price tag makes it the cheapest small-growth ETF around. Moreover, it's run by Gus Sauter, Vanguard's vaunted index-fund manager, who has proven particularly adept at keeping up with a benchmark. In addition, because the fund's bogy, the MSCI U.S. Small Cap Growth Index, employs multiple variables to classify stocks, it should provide consistently pure exposure to small, fast-growing stocks. Finally, the MSCI Index should circumvent the technical reconstitution problems that have dogged the Russell 2000 Growth Index.

Still, these strengths may not be enough to lift this fund past its actively managed rivals. Indeed, active managers have had an easier time edging past indexes in the less efficient small-cap space. Also, given that small-cap stocks have been on an extended run, a cold streak could be in the offing. A tepid environment of this sort typically doesn't favor index funds, which must remain fully invested and can't take refuge in more stable parts of the market when trouble hits, as an active manager can.

That said, because many successful actively managed small-cap offerings have been flooded with assets in recent years, asset bloat is a persistent concern and some of our favorite small-growth funds have closed to try to head off that problem. As a result, there are now fewer small-growth funds to choose from. Of course, with a bit of work, investors can identify actively managed small-growth funds that still have some headroom. But, for those without the time or inclination to exercise such due diligence, this fund stands as a cheap, no-fuss alternative.

| Address: | PO Box 2600 |
|---|---|
| | Valley Forge PA 19482 |
| | 866-499-8473 |
| Web Address: | www.vanguard.com |
| Inception: | 01-26-04* |
| Advisor: | Vanguard Advisers, Inc. |

| Management Fee: | 0.06% | | |
|---|---|---|---|
| Expense Projections: | 3Yr:$39 | 5Yr:$68 | 10Yr:$154 |
| Income Distrib: | Annually | | |
| Exchange: | AMEX | | |

Morningstar® ETFs 100

# Vanguard TelcomSrv VIPERs

| | Ticker | NAV | Market Price | 52 wk High/Low | Yield | Mstar Category |
|---|---|---|---|---|---|---|
| | VOX | $54.45 | $56.06 | $58.14 - $49.83 | 2.9% | Specialty-Communications |

## Management

### Portfolio Manager(s)

Vanguard Quantitative Equity Group runs this fund. Gus Sauter, Vanguard's chief investment officer and indexing pro, oversees the group. He and his team of quantitative analysts have a strong record of closely tracking benchmarks.

### Strategy

This ETF tracks the MSCI U.S. Investable Telecommunications Services Index, a subset of the market-cap weighted MSCI U.S. Investable Market 2500 Index. The MSCI Telecom index holds fewer than 50 stocks that offer communications services through fixed-line, cellular, wireless, high bandwidth, or fiber-optic cable networks. The index and ETF doesn't include equipment makers, such as Qualcomm. The index is so concentrated, the ETF has to modify the weightings of its largest holdings to comply with IRS diversification rules. So, the fund won't exactly mimic its bogy.

### Growth of $10,000

— Investment Value of ETF
— Investment Value of Index S&P 500

| | 1996 | 1997 | 1998 | 1999 | 2000 | 2001 | 2002 | 2003 | 2004 | 2005 | History |
|---|---|---|---|---|---|---|---|---|---|---|---|
| | — | — | — | — | — | — | — | — | 54.93 | 54.45 | NAV $ |
| | — | — | — | — | — | — | — | — | 54.90 | 54.46 | Market Price $ |
| | — | — | — | — | — | — | — | — | 10.09* | 1.92 | NAV Return% |
| | — | — | — | — | — | — | — | — | 11.26† | 2.00 | Market Price Return% |
| | — | — | — | — | — | — | — | — | 0.02 | -0.07 | Avg Premium/Discount% |
| | — | — | — | — | — | — | — | — | 10.09 | 2.99 | NAV Rtrn% +/-S&P 500 |
| | — | — | — | — | — | — | — | — | 10.09 | 5.92 | NAV Rtrn% +/-DJ Telecom |
| | — | — | — | — | — | — | — | — | — | 3 | NAV Return% Rank in Cat |
| | — | — | — | — | — | — | — | — | 0.00 | 2.83 | Income Return % |
| | — | — | — | — | — | — | — | — | — | -0.91 | Capital Return % |
| | — | — | — | — | — | — | — | — | 0.41 | 1.56 | Income $ |
| | — | — | — | — | — | — | — | — | 0.00 | 0.00 | Capital Gains $ |
| | — | — | — | — | — | — | — | — | — | 0.26 | Expense Ratio % |
| | — | — | — | — | — | — | — | — | — | 2.72 | Income Ratio % |
| | — | — | — | — | — | — | — | — | — | 41 | Turnover Rate % |
| | — | — | — | — | — | — | — | — | 16 | 22 | Net Assets $mil |

## Performance

### Historic Quarterly NAV Returns

| | 1st Qtr | 2nd Qtr | 3rd Qtr | 4th Qtr | Total |
|---|---|---|---|---|---|
| 2001 | — | — | — | — | — |
| 2002 | — | — | — | — | — |
| 2003 | — | — | — | — | — |
| 2004 | — | — | — | 11.91 | —* |
| 2005 | -6.55 | 4.75 | 2.57 | 1.52 | 1.92 |

| Trailing | NAV Return% | Market Return% | NAV Rtrn% +/-S&P 500 | %Rank Cat.(NAV) |
|---|---|---|---|---|
| 3 Mo | 1.52 | 1.55 | -0.56 | 4 |
| 6 Mo | 4.12 | 4.01 | -1.64 | 4 |
| 1 Yr | 1.92 | 2.00 | -2.99 | 3 |
| 3 Yr Avg | — | — | — | 0 |
| 5 Yr Avg | — | — | — | 0 |
| 10 Yr Avg | — | — | — | 0 |

| Tax Analysis | Tax-Adj Return% | Tax-Cost Ratio |
|---|---|---|
| 3 Yr (estimated) | — | — |
| 5 Yr (estimated) | — | — |
| 10 Yr (estimated) | — | — |

## Risk Profile

| | Standard Index S&P 500 | Best Fit Index |
|---|---|---|
| Alpha | — | — |
| Beta | — | — |
| R-Squared | — | — |
| Standard Deviation | — | |
| Mean | — | |
| Sharpe Ratio | — | |

## Morningstar Fair Value

| Price/Fair Value Ratio | Fair Value Estimate ($) | Hit Rate % |
|---|---|---|
| 0.9 Undervalued | 17.96 | 59 Poor |

## Morningstar's Take by Dan Culloton

You're better off hanging up on Vanguard Telecom Services VIPERs.

There is no denying this fund offers cheap exposure to communication service providers. Its 0.26% expense ratio is the cheapest among exchange-traded or conventional funds in its category.

This fund has problems, though. It's supposed to track an index of all the telecom services firms the MSCI U.S. Investable 2500 Index. From the ETF's September 2004 inception through the end of October 2005, its annualized gain of 9.83% has more than doubled the return of its target index. That's great news for an actively managed fund, but troubling for an index fund. You may not be able to count on this fund to faithfully track its benchmark.

The large tracking error is the index's fault. If Vanguard exactly replicated MSCI's telecom bogy it would run afoul of IRS diversification rules for regulated investment companies, particularly a 25% cap on any single position and a requirement that

individual positions in half of the portfolio not exceed 5%. So Vanguard has to modify the portfolio by owning less of the index's biggest denizens, such as Verizon Communications and AT&T, and spreading the money around more evenly. That means there could always be a big divergence between this ETFs returns and those of its index. And there is no guarantee the ETF's results will always be better, even though they have been higher so far.

It also makes it hard to assess the fund. Its management team has acquitted itself well at other index funds, but this fund's lopsided bogy makes it hard to gauge how well the squad is tracking telecom services stocks.

Even with its efforts to comply with the IRS, the fund remains concentrated. Nearly two thirds of its assets are in its top 10 holdings. If that wasn't asking for volatility, its focus on a sector fraught with intense competition and rapid technological change would. Don't answer this call.

## Portfolio Analysis 09-30-05

| Share change since 06-05 Total Stocks:42 | Sector | PE | Tot Ret% | % Assets |
|---|---|---|---|---|
| ⊖ Verizon Communications | Telecom | 10.2 | -22.18 | 16.37 |
| ⊕ SBC Communications | Telecom | 21.1 | 0.25 | 13.68 |
| ⊖ Sprint Nextel | Telecom | 19.1 | -4.81 | 10.37 |
| ⊖ BellSouth | Telecom | 18.1 | 1.77 | 5.51 |
| ⊖ Alltel | Telecom | 15.5 | 10.12 | 4.62 |
| ⊕ AT&T | Telecom | — | — | 4.43 |
| ⊕ American Tower A | Telecom | — | 47.28 | 3.40 |
| ⊕ Qwest Communications Int | Telecom | — | 27.25 | 2.46 |
| ⊕ MCI | Telecom | 37.2 | 27.68 | 2.38 |
| ⊕ NII Holdings | Telecom | 37.8 | 84.11 | 2.37 |
| ⊖ Crown Castle Internation | Telecom | — | 61.72 | 2.23 |
| ⊕ Citizens Communications | Telecom | 29.1 | -4.31 | 1.99 |
| ⊕ Centurytel | Telecom | 13.1 | -5.85 | 1.84 |
| ⊕ Nextel Partners A | Telecom | 14.3 | 42.99 | 1.56 |
| ⊕ Alamosa Holdings | Telecom | — | 49.24 | 1.39 |
| ⊕ Level 3 Communications | Telecom | — | -15.34 | 1.22 |
| ⊕ Cincinnati Bell | Telecom | — | -15.42 | 1.09 |
| ⊖ SBA Communications | Telecom | — | 92.89 | 1.08 |
| ⊖ Dobson Communications A | Telecom | — | 336.05 | 1.08 |
| ⊕ Price Communications | Telecom | 41.3 | -20.01 | 1.05 |

### Current Investment Style

Value Blnd Growth — Large Mid Small

| | Market Cap | % |
|---|---|---|
| | Giant | 36.6 |
| | Large | 20.0 |
| | Mid | 23.5 |
| | Small | 14.0 |
| | Micro | 5.9 |
| | Avg $mil: 12,619 | |

| Value Measures | | Rel Category |
|---|---|---|
| Price/Earnings | 16.09 | 0.87 |
| Price/Book | 2.35 | 0.98 |
| Price/Sales | 0.34 | 0.22 |
| Price/Cash Flow | 6.56 | 1.20 |
| Dividend Yield % | 2.51 | 1.03 |

| Growth Measures | % | Rel Category |
|---|---|---|
| Long-Term Erngs | 5.62 | 0.61 |
| Book Value | -3.56 | NMF |
| Sales | 6.59 | 3.11 |
| Cash Flow | -11.59 | NMF |
| Historical Erngs | -7.43 | NMF |

| Profitability | % | Rel Category |
|---|---|---|
| Return on Equity | 3.97 | 0.34 |
| Return on Assets | 0.82 | 0.17 |
| Net Margin | 3.55 | 0.36 |

| Industry Weightings | % of Stocks | Rel Cat |
|---|---|---|
| Telecom Srv | 61.6 | 2.4 |
| Wireless Srv | 34.8 | 1.1 |
| Network Eq | 0.9 | 0.1 |
| Semis | 0.0 | 0.0 |
| Big Media | 0.0 | 0.0 |
| Cable TV | 0.0 | 0.0 |
| Other Media | 0.0 | 0.0 |
| Soft/Hardwr | 0.0 | 0.0 |
| Other | 2.8 | 0.3 |

### Composition

| | | |
|---|---|---|
| ● Cash | 0.4 | |
| ● Stocks | 98.7 | |
| ● Bonds | 0.0 | |
| ● Other | 0.9 | |
| ● Foreign | 0.0 | |
| (% of Stock) | | |

| Address: | PO Box 2600 Valley Forge PA 19482 866-499-8473 | Management Fee: | 0.26% |
|---|---|---|---|
| | | Expense Projections: | 3Yr:$90  5Yr: —  10Yr: — |
| Web Address: | www.vanguard.com | Income Distrib: | Annually |
| Inception: | 09-29-04 * | Exchange: | AMEX |
| Advisor: | Vanguard Advisers, Inc. | | |

# Vanguard TSM VIPERs

| | Ticker | NAV | Market Price | 52 wk High/Low | Yield | Mstar Category |
|---|---|---|---|---|---|---|
| | VTI | $123.25 | $127.69 | $127.69 - $110.84 | 1.7% | Large Blend |

## Management

### Portfolio Manager(s)

Vanguard recently revealed that Gus Sauter, the firm's index maven, no longer handles this fund's day-to-day management. Since assuming CIO responsibilities at the firm early in 2003, Sauter has gradually handed off daily managerial chores to Gerard O'Reilly. O'Reilly is a 13-year Vanguard veteran and has worked closely with Sauter on this ETF since its inception.

### Strategy

The fund now shadows the Wilshire 5000 Index, which includes nearly all publicly traded stocks. But soon it will switch its benchmark to the MSCI U.S. Broad Market Index. It would be impractical to own each smaller company in the index, so, among the tiniest firms, manager Gerard O'Reilly selects a representative sample. In an effort to boost returns by a few basis points, O'Reilly uses various techniques, including securities lending.

**Growth of $10,000**

— Investment Value of ETF
— Investment Value of Index S&P 500

| 1996 | 1997 | 1998 | 1999 | 2000 | 2001 | 2002 | 2003 | 2004 | 2005 | History |
|---|---|---|---|---|---|---|---|---|---|---|
| — | — | — | — | — | 105.80 | 82.47 | 106.81 | 118.21 | 123.25 | NAV $ |
| — | — | — | — | — | 105.39 | 82.52 | 106.46 | 118.05 | 123.33 | Market Price $ |
| — | — | — | — | — | 3.16* | -20.94 | 31.43 | 12.56 | 6.10 | NAV Return% |
| — | — | — | — | — | 3.20* | -20.58 | 30.92 | 12.78 | 6.31 | Market Price Return% |
| — | — | — | — | — | 0.32 | -0.09 | -0.01 | 0.01 | 0.04 | Avg Premium/Discount% |
| — | — | — | — | — | 3.16 | 1.15 | 2.76 | 1.69 | 1.19 | NAV Rtrn% +/-S&P 500 |
| — | — | — | — | — | 3.16 | 0.71 | 1.54 | 1.16 | -0.17 | NAV Rtrn% +/-Russ 1000 |
| — | — | — | — | — | — | 15 | 15 | 17 | 23 | NAV Return% Rank in Cat |
| — | — | — | — | — | 0.00 | 1.19 | 1.69 | 1.79 | 1.77 | Income Return % |
| — | — | — | — | — | — | -22.13 | 29.74 | 10.77 | 4.33 | Capital Return % |
| — | — | — | — | — | 0.99 | 1.25 | 1.38 | 1.90 | 2.08 | Income $ |
| — | — | — | — | — | 0.00 | 0.00 | 0.00 | 0.00 | 0.00 | Capital Gains $ |
| — | — | — | — | — | 0.15 | 0.15 | 0.15 | 0.13 | — | Expense Ratio % |
| — | — | — | — | — | 1.26 | 1.38 | 1.54 | 1.79 | — | Income Ratio % |
| — | — | — | — | — | 7 | 4 | 11 | 4 | — | Turnover Rate % |
| — | — | — | — | — | — | 1,452 | 2,517 | 4,259 | 5,612 | Net Assets $mil |

## Performance

### Historic Quarterly NAV Returns

| | 1st Qtr | 2nd Qtr | 3rd Qtr | 4th Qtr | Total |
|---|---|---|---|---|---|
| 2001 | — | — | -17.78 | 14.91 | —* |
| 2002 | 0.95 | -12.67 | -16.82 | 7.81 | -20.94 |
| 2003 | -3.13 | 16.46 | 3.62 | 12.43 | 31.43 |
| 2004 | 2.59 | 1.29 | -1.82 | 10.33 | 12.56 |
| 2005 | -2.38 | 2.20 | 4.05 | 2.19 | 6.10 |

| Trailing | NAV Return% | Market Return% | NAV Rtrn% +/-S&P 500 | %Rank Cat.(NAV) |
|---|---|---|---|---|
| 3 Mo | 2.19 | 2.18 | 0.11 | 27 |
| 6 Mo | 6.34 | 6.33 | 0.58 | 27 |
| 1 Yr | 6.10 | 6.31 | 1.19 | 23 |
| 3 Yr Avg | 16.22 | 16.22 | 1.84 | 14 |
| 5 Yr Avg | — | — | — | 0 |
| 10 Yr Avg | — | — | — | 0 |

| Tax Analysis | Tax-Adj Return% | Tax-Cost Ratio |
|---|---|---|
| 3 Yr (estimated) | 15.88 | 0.29 |
| 5 Yr (estimated) | — | — |
| 10 Yr (estimated) | — | — |

## Risk Profile

| | Standard Index S&P 500 | Best Fit Index Russ 1000 |
|---|---|---|
| Alpha | 1.0 | 0.1 |
| Beta | 1.05 | 1.05 |
| R-Squared | 99 | 99 |
| Standard Deviation | 9.73 | |
| Mean | 16.22 | |
| Sharpe Ratio | 1.40 | |

## Morningstar Fair Value

| Price/Fair Value Ratio | Fair Value Estimate ($) | Hit Rate % |
|---|---|---|
| 1.0 Fairly valued | 37.25 | 89 Good |

## Morningstar's Take by Sonya Morris

Vanguard Total Stock Market VIPER's new benchmark doesn't squelch its appeal.

On Feb. 1, 2005, Vanguard announced its plan to replace this ETF's current bogy, the Wilshire 5000 Index, with the MSCI U.S. Broad Market Index. The firm is expected to gradually phase in the new index between March 31 and Dec. 31, 2005.

There are some noteworthy differences between the two indexes. Whereas the Wilshire bogy covers all U.S. stocks, the MSCI index stops just shy of that mark, excluding a raft of tiny firms that account for 0.5% of the U.S. market's capitalization. Unlike Wilshire, MSCI also adjusts weightings to remove the effect of shares that aren't investable, meaning that stocks with heavy insider ownership, such as Microsoft, will see their influence wane. Finally, the MSCI index includes the stocks of firms that are headquartered abroad but do most of their business in the U.S., while omitting limited partnerships.

Nevertheless, these differences shouldn't give the ETF a markedly different risk/reward profile. In fact, while back-tested long-term returns aren't available for the new MSCI index, available data suggests that returns won't deviate far from the Wilshire index's.

To be sure, transaction costs are likely to tick up slightly in the near term. But judging from the relative ease with which other Vanguard index funds have made similar transitions in recent years, we don't expect the drag on returns to be onerous. In addition, we don't anticipate the fund will incur heavy capital gains as a result of the change since the fund's top holdings--where selling is likely to be heaviest--teem with shares that are under water. (The fund added many shares at the tail end of the bull market, meaning that it bought near stocks' historic peaks.) As such, selling should be confined primarily to high-cost share lots, allowing management to harvest additional losses.

All told, the thesis for this ETF remains intact: It's a fine choice to anchor a portfolio.

## Portfolio Analysis 09-30-05

Share change since 06-05 Total Stocks:3719

| | Sector | PE | Tot Ret% | % Assets |
|---|---|---|---|---|
| ⊕ ExxonMobil | Energy | 10.6 | 11.76 | 2.87 |
| ⊕ General Electric | Ind Mtrls | 19.9 | -1.43 | 2.53 |
| ⊕ Microsoft | Software | 22.2 | -0.95 | 1.77 |
| ⊕ Citigroup | Financial | 12.1 | 4.63 | 1.68 |
| ⊕ Johnson & Johnson | Health | 19.1 | -3.36 | 1.33 |
| ⊕ Pfizer | Health | 21.2 | -10.62 | 1.32 |
| ⊕ Bank of America | Financial | 11.1 | 2.39 | 1.20 |
| ⊕ Altria Group | Goods | 15.0 | 27.72 | 1.08 |
| ⊕ Intel | Hardware | 18.6 | 8.12 | 1.08 |
| ⊕ Chevron | Energy | 9.0 | 11.51 | 1.04 |
| ⊕ Procter & Gamble | Goods | 21.2 | 7.18 | 1.01 |
| ⊕ American International G | Financial | 15.6 | 4.83 | 0.97 |
| ⊕ IBM | Hardware | 16.0 | -15.83 | 0.92 |
| ⊕ J.P. Morgan Chase & Co. | Financial | 18.8 | 5.74 | 0.85 |
| ⊕ Cisco Systems | Hardware | 19.9 | -11.39 | 0.81 |
| ⊕ Wal-Mart Stores | Consumer | 18.2 | -10.30 | 0.79 |
| ⊕ Wells Fargo | Financial | 14.3 | 4.47 | 0.70 |
| ⊕ Amgen | Health | 28.3 | 22.93 | 0.70 |
| ⊕ PepsiCo | Goods | 25.8 | 15.24 | 0.67 |
| ⊕ Coca-Cola | Goods | 18.6 | -0.66 | 0.66 |

### Current Investment Style

Value Blend Growth — Large / Mid / Small

| | Market Cap | % |
|---|---|---|
| | Giant | 43.0 |
| | Large | 30.8 |
| | Mid | 18.8 |
| | Small | 5.7 |
| | Micro | 1.7 |
| | Avg $mil: 24,826 | |

| Value Measures | | Rel Category |
|---|---|---|
| Price/Earnings | 16.23 | 0.96 |
| Price/Book | 2.43 | 0.90 |
| Price/Sales | 1.41 | 1.10 |
| Price/Cash Flow | 6.38 | 0.88 |
| Dividend Yield % | 1.75 | 0.99 |

| Growth Measures | % | Rel Category |
|---|---|---|
| Long-Term Erngs | 11.00 | 0.99 |
| Book Value | 9.45 | 1.01 |
| Sales | 8.04 | 1.00 |
| Cash Flow | 10.45 | 1.01 |
| Historical Erngs | 14.86 | 1.05 |

| Profitability | % | Rel Category |
|---|---|---|
| Return on Equity | 17.60 | 0.86 |
| Return on Assets | 9.41 | 1.01 |
| Net Margin | 12.62 | 1.16 |

| Sector Weightings | % of Stocks | Rel S&P 500 | 3 Year High Low | |
|---|---|---|---|---|
| ☉ Info | 19.92 | 0.99 | | |
| Software | 3.76 | 1.06 | 5 | 4 |
| Hardware | 9.74 | 0.97 | 11 | 9 |
| Media | 3.50 | 0.98 | 5 | 4 |
| Telecom | 2.92 | 0.97 | 3 | 3 |
| Service | 46.84 | 1.01 | | |
| Health | 13.01 | 0.98 | 14 | 12 |
| Consumer | 8.46 | 1.04 | 10 | 8 |
| Business | 5.01 | 1.29 | 5 | 5 |
| Financial | 20.36 | 0.97 | 23 | 20 |
| Mfg | 33.25 | 0.99 | | |
| Goods | 8.07 | 0.94 | 9 | 8 |
| Ind Mtrls | 11.46 | 0.94 | 12 | 10 |
| Energy | 10.10 | 1.08 | 10 | 6 |
| Utilities | 3.62 | 1.08 | 4 | 3 |

### Composition

| | | |
|---|---|---|
| ● Cash | 0.7 | |
| ● Stocks | 98.6 | |
| ● Bonds | 0.0 | |
| ● Other | 0.6 | |
| Foreign | 0.1 | |
| (% of Stock) | | |

---

| Address: | PO Box 2600 | Management Fee: | 0.05% | | |
|---|---|---|---|---|---|
| | Valley Forge PA 19482 | Expense Projections: | 3Yr:$23 | 5Yr:$40 | 10Yr:$90 |
| | 866-499-8473 | Income Distrib: | Quarterly | | |
| Web Address: | www.vanguard.com | Exchange: | AMEX | | |
| Inception: | 05-31-01 * | | | | |
| Advisor: | Vanguard Advisers, Inc. | | | | |

**MORNINGSTAR® ETFs 100**

# Vanguard Utilities VIPERs

| | Ticker | NAV | Market Price | 52 wk High/Low | Yield | Mstar Category |
|---|---|---|---|---|---|---|
| | VPU | $65.15 | $66.63 | $70.70 - $56.85 | 2.3% | Specialty-Utilities |

## Management

### Portfolio Manager(s)

Gus Sauter has managed this fund since its January 2004 inception. He also manages many other Vanguard index funds, including the other sector VIPERs, though his name is no longer on the flagship Vanguard 500 Index.

### Strategy

This exchange-traded fund tracks the MSCI U.S. Investable Market Utilities Index, an index of 91 domestic utility stocks. This index consists almost entirely of electric and natural gas utilities, and thus doesn't contain the telecom and energy stocks found in the portfolios of most actively managed utilities sector funds.

### Growth of $10,000

— Investment Value of ETF
— Investment Value of Index S&P 500

| 1996 | 1997 | 1998 | 1999 | 2000 | 2001 | 2002 | 2003 | 2004 | 2005 | History |
|---|---|---|---|---|---|---|---|---|---|---|
| — | — | — | — | — | — | — | — | 58.46 | 65.15 | NAV $ |
| — | — | — | — | — | — | — | — | 58.56 | 65.14 | Market Price $ |
| — | — | — | — | — | — | — | — | 18.11* | 14.08 | NAV Return% |
| — | — | — | — | — | — | — | — | 18.10* | 13.87 | Market Price Return% |
| — | — | — | — | — | — | — | — | -0.02 | -0.01 | Avg Premium/Discount% |
| — | — | — | — | — | — | — | — | 18.11 | 9.17 | NAV Rtrn% +/-S&P 500 |
| — | — | — | — | — | — | — | — | 18.11 | -11.06 | NAV Rtrn% +/-DOWJNS UTIL |
| — | — | — | — | — | — | — | — | — | 3 | NAV Return% Rank in Cat |
| — | — | — | — | — | — | — | — | 0.00 | 2.59 | Income Return % |
| — | — | — | — | — | — | — | — | — | 11.49 | Capital Return % |
| — | — | — | — | — | — | — | — | 1.55 | 1.50 | Income $ |
| — | — | — | — | — | — | — | — | 0.00 | 0.00 | Capital Gains $ |
| — | — | — | — | — | — | — | — | 0.28 | 0.26 | Expense Ratio % |
| — | — | — | — | — | — | — | — | 3.82 | 3.36 | Income Ratio % |
| — | — | — | — | — | — | — | — | 7 | 7 | Turnover Rate % |
| — | — | — | — | — | — | — | — | 53 | 105 | Net Assets $mil |

## Performance

### Historic Quarterly NAV Returns

| | 1st Qtr | 2nd Qtr | 3rd Qtr | 4th Qtr | Total |
|---|---|---|---|---|---|
| 2001 | — | — | — | — | — |
| 2002 | — | — | — | — | — |
| 2003 | — | — | — | — | — |
| 2004 | — | -0.86 | 6.00 | 11.79 | —* |
| 2005 | 4.41 | 9.41 | 6.26 | -6.02 | 14.08 |

| Trailing | NAV Return% | Market Return% | NAV Rtrn% +/-S&P 500 | %Rank Cat.(NAV) |
|---|---|---|---|---|
| 3 Mo | -6.02 | -6.04 | -8.10 | 3 |
| 6 Mo | -0.14 | -0.23 | -5.90 | 3 |
| 1 Yr | 14.08 | 13.87 | 9.17 | 3 |
| 3 Yr Avg | — | — | — | 0 |
| 5 Yr Avg | — | — | — | 0 |
| 10 Yr Avg | — | — | — | 0 |

| Tax Analysis | Tax-Adj Return% | Tax-Cost Ratio |
|---|---|---|
| 3 Yr (estimated) | — | — |
| 5 Yr (estimated) | — | — |
| 10 Yr (estimated) | — | — |

## Risk Profile

| | Standard Index S&P 500 | Best Fit Index |
|---|---|---|
| Alpha | — | — |
| Beta | — | — |
| R-Squared | — | — |
| Standard Deviation | — | |
| Mean | — | |
| Sharpe Ratio | — | |

## Morningstar Fair Value

| Price/Fair Value Ratio | Fair Value Estimate ($) | Hit Rate % |
|---|---|---|
| 1.0 Fairly valued | 33.69 | 94 Good |

## Portfolio Analysis 09-30-05

| Share change since 06-05 Total Stocks:90 | Sector | PE | Tot Ret% | % Assets |
|---|---|---|---|---|
| ⊕ Exelon | Utilities | 17.0 | 24.58 | 6.87 |
| ⊕ Dominion Resources | Utilities | 26.5 | 18.19 | 5.64 |
| ⊕ Duke Energy | Utilities | 11.2 | 13.11 | 5.19 |
| ⊕ Southern | Utilities | 15.8 | 7.57 | 5.12 |
| ⊕ TXU | Utilities | — | 59.98 | 4.94 |
| ⊕ FPL Group | Utilities | 18.5 | 15.05 | 3.41 |
| ⊕ FirstEnergy | Utilities | 18.8 | 28.72 | 3.30 |
| ⊕ Entergy | Utilities | 15.5 | 4.67 | 3.03 |
| ⊕ Public Service Enterpris | Utilities | 22.2 | 30.22 | 2.95 |
| ⊕ American Electric Power | Utilities | 12.0 | 12.33 | 2.93 |
| ⊕ PG & E | Utilities | 16.3 | 15.32 | 2.83 |
| ⊕ Edison International | Utilities | 13.5 | 39.63 | 2.81 |
| ⊕ PPL | Utilities | 15.8 | 14.03 | 2.36 |
| ⊕ Consolidated Edison | Utilities | 17.8 | 11.32 | 2.27 |
| ⊕ Constellation Energy Gro | Utilities | 18.1 | 35.05 | 2.10 |
| ⊕ Progress Energy | Utilities | 13.8 | 2.47 | 2.03 |
| ⊕ Ameren | Utilities | 15.3 | 7.18 | 2.01 |
| ⊕ AES | Utilities | 24.4 | 15.80 | 1.96 |
| ⊕ Sempra Energy | Utilities | 12.1 | 25.62 | 1.95 |
| ⊕ Cinergy | Utilities | 18.5 | 6.90 | 1.61 |

## Morningstar's Take by David Kathman

Vanguard Utilities VIPERs offers nearly pure exposure to utilities, but investors should keep their expectations in check.

This is the newest, and by far the smallest, of the three exchange-traded funds (ETFs) offering exposure to the utilities sector. It tracks the MSCI U.S. Investable Market Utilities Index, which consists of 91 utility stocks drawn from the broader MSCI 2500 Index. It has done great in absolute terms, gaining more than 40% from its January 2004 launch through mid-August 2005, but that has been a stellar period for all utilities funds. Thus, it's important to look past the gaudy numbers and focus on this fund's pluses and minuses compared with similar offerings.

Unlike most actively managed utilities-sector funds, this one does not hold stocks in other areas, such as energy or telecom, making for purer utilities exposure. That has been a mixed blessing lately; while this fund has mostly missed out on the big energy gains that have boosted some actively

managed utilities funds, it has also not been dragged down by tepid telecom stocks.

This fund's two ETF rivals also offer pure-play utilities exposure, but not in exactly the same way. The Utilities Select SPDR tracks the 33 utility stocks in the S&P 500, so it's significantly more concentrated and large-cap-oriented than this fund. The iShares Dow Jones Utilities fund has a portfolio that is much more similar, but it has a significantly lower yield--2.6%, versus 3.7% for this fund.

A key factor for any index fund is price, and this ETF looks pretty good in that regard. Its 0.28% expense ratio is comparable to the 0.27% of the Utilities SPDR, and is less than half the 0.60% charged by the iShares fund. That price tag gives this fund a significant advantage right off the bat. As with any ETF, though, investors should only buy this fund if they don't plan to trade much. Otherwise, brokerage commissions can add up fast.

### Current Investment Style

Value Blnd Growth — Large Mid Small

| | Market Cap | % |
|---|---|---|
| | Giant | 0.0 |
| | Large | 62.0 |
| | Mid | 32.9 |
| | Small | 5.0 |
| | Micro | 0.1 |
| | Avg $mil: | 9,990 |

| Value Measures | | Rel Category |
|---|---|---|
| Price/Earnings | 17.50 | 1.07 |
| Price/Book | 2.05 | 1.01 |
| Price/Sales | 1.25 | 0.98 |
| Price/Cash Flow | 6.35 | 0.94 |
| Dividend Yield % | 2.87 | 0.96 |

| Growth Measures | % | Rel Category |
|---|---|---|
| Long-Term Erngs | 5.80 | 1.01 |
| Book Value | 1.97 | 3.86 |
| Sales | 2.07 | 1.44 |
| Cash Flow | -3.84 | NMF |
| Historical Erngs | 6.78 | 0.83 |

| Profitability | % | Rel Category |
|---|---|---|
| Return on Equity | 14.58 | 1.04 |
| Return on Assets | 3.16 | 1.04 |
| Net Margin | 8.07 | 1.01 |

| Industry Weightings | % of Stocks | Rel Cat |
|---|---|---|
| Telecom Srv | 0.0 | 0.0 |
| Electric Utls | 85.8 | 1.4 |
| Nat Gas Utls | 10.1 | 1.1 |
| Wireless Srv | 0.0 | 0.0 |
| Energy | 3.1 | 0.3 |
| Media | 0.0 | 0.0 |
| Network Eq | 0.0 | 0.0 |
| Water | 1.0 | 1.5 |
| Other | 0.0 | 0.0 |

### Composition

| | % |
|---|---|
| ● Cash | 0.6 |
| ● Stocks | 99.4 |
| ● Bonds | 0.0 |
| ● Other | 0.0 |
| Foreign | 0.0 |
| (% of Stock) | |

| Address: | PO Box 2600 Valley Forge PA 19482 866-499-8473 |
|---|---|
| Web Address: | www.vanguard.com |
| Inception: | 01-26-04* |
| Advisor: | Vanguard Advisers, Inc. |

| Management Fee: | 0.26% | | |
|---|---|---|---|
| Expense Projections: | 3Yr:$90 | 5Yr:$157 | 10Yr:$356 |
| Income Distrib: | Quarterly | | |
| Exchange: | AMEX | | |

# Vanguard Value VIPERs

| | Ticker | NAV | Market Price | 52 wk High/Low | Yield | Mstar Category |
|---|---|---|---|---|---|---|
| | VTV | $57.14 | $59.06 | $59.07 - $52.49 | 2.6% | Large Value |

## Management

### Portfolio Manager(s)

Gerard O'Reilly is now listed as the fund's day-to-day manager. Vanguard's index pro, Gus Sauter, has scaled back his managerial responsibilities since becoming the firm's chief investment officer in 2003. O'Reilly has been with Vanguard since 1992, and he has worked closely with Sauter on Vanguard Value Index since 1994. He also runs Vanguard Total Stock Market Index, Vanguard Growth Index, and Vanguard Small-Cap Growth Index.

### Strategy

This ETF tracks the MSCI U.S. Prime Market Value Index, which consists of the value stocks within a universe of the 750 largest U.S. companies. MSCI classifies stocks as growth or value using an eight-factor model and also employs "buffer zones" to limit the migration of stocks between the growth and value camps and, thus, turnover.

**Growth of $10,000**

— Investment Value of ETF
— Investment Value of Index S&P 500

| 1996 | 1997 | 1998 | 1999 | 2000 | 2001 | 2002 | 2003 | 2004 | 2005 | History |
|---|---|---|---|---|---|---|---|---|---|---|
| — | — | — | — | — | — | — | — | 54.74 | 57.14 | NAV $ |
| — | — | — | — | — | — | — | — | 54.75 | 57.17 | Market Price $ |
| — | — | — | — | — | — | — | — | 9.61* | 7.19 | NAV Return% |
| — | — | — | — | — | — | — | — | 9.64* | 7.22 | Market Price Return% |
| — | — | — | — | — | — | — | — | 0.02 | 0.08 | Avg Premium/Discount% |
| — | — | — | — | — | — | — | — | 9.61 | 2.28 | NAV Rtrn% +/-S&P 500 |
| — | — | — | — | — | — | — | — | 9.61 | 0.14 | NAV Rtrn% +/-Russ 1000 VI |
| — | — | — | — | — | — | — | — | — | 10 | NAV Return% Rank in Cat |
| — | — | — | — | — | — | — | — | 0.00 | 2.73 | Income Return % |
| — | — | — | — | — | — | — | — | — | 4.46 | Capital Return % |
| — | — | — | — | — | — | — | — | 1.22 | 1.48 | Income $ |
| — | — | — | — | — | — | — | — | 0.00 | 0.00 | Capital Gains $ |
| — | — | — | — | — | — | — | — | 0.15 | — | Expense Ratio % |
| — | — | — | — | — | — | — | — | 2.46 | — | Income Ratio % |
| — | — | — | — | — | — | — | — | 18 | — | Turnover Rate % |
| — | — | — | — | — | — | — | — | 406 | 600 | Net Assets $mil |

## Performance

### Historic Quarterly NAV Returns

| | 1st Qtr | 2nd Qtr | 3rd Qtr | 4th Qtr | Total |
|---|---|---|---|---|---|
| 2001 | — | — | — | — | — |
| 2002 | — | — | — | — | — |
| 2003 | — | — | — | — | — |
| 2004 | — | 1.55 | 1.26 | 9.79 | —* |
| 2005 | -0.37 | 1.73 | 4.08 | 1.60 | 7.19 |

| Trailing | NAV Return% | Market Return% | NAV Rtrn% +/-S&P 500 | %Rank Cat.(NAV) |
|---|---|---|---|---|
| 3 Mo | 1.60 | 1.49 | -0.48 | 13 |
| 6 Mo | 5.75 | 5.24 | -0.01 | 11 |
| 1 Yr | 7.19 | 7.22 | 2.28 | 10 |
| 3 Yr Avg | — | — | — | 0 |
| 5 Yr Avg | — | — | — | 0 |
| 10 Yr Avg | — | — | — | 0 |

| Tax Analysis | Tax-Adj Return% | Tax-Cost Ratio |
|---|---|---|
| 3 Yr (estimated) | — | — |
| 5 Yr (estimated) | — | — |
| 10 Yr (estimated) | — | — |

## Risk Profile

| | Standard Index S&P 500 | Best Fit Index |
|---|---|---|
| Alpha | — | — |
| Beta | — | — |
| R-Squared | — | — |
| Standard Deviation | — | |
| Mean | — | |
| Sharpe Ratio | — | |

## Morningstar Fair Value

| Price/Fair Value Ratio | Fair Value Estimate ($) | Hit Rate % |
|---|---|---|
| 1.0 Fairly valued | 39.38 | 94 Good |

## Portfolio Analysis 09-30-05

Share change since 06-05 Total Stocks:397

| | Sector | PE | Tot Ret% | % Assets |
|---|---|---|---|---|
| ⊕ ExxonMobil | Energy | 10.6 | 11.76 | 6.70 |
| ⊕ Citigroup | Financial | 12.1 | 4.63 | 3.92 |
| ⊕ Pfizer | Health | 21.2 | -10.62 | 3.08 |
| ⊕ General Electric | Ind Mtrls | 19.9 | -1.43 | 2.96 |
| ⊕ Bank of America | Financial | 11.1 | 2.39 | 2.81 |
| ⊕ Altria Group | Goods | 15.0 | 27.72 | 2.53 |
| ⊕ Chevron | Energy | 9.0 | 11.51 | 2.43 |
| ⊕ J.P. Morgan Chase & Co. | Financial | 18.8 | 5.74 | 1.98 |
| ⊕ Wells Fargo | Financial | 14.3 | 4.47 | 1.64 |
| ⊕ ConocoPhillips | Energy | 6.7 | 36.89 | 1.53 |
| ⊕ Verizon Communications | Telecom | 10.2 | -22.18 | 1.50 |
| ⊕ American International G | Financial | 15.6 | 4.83 | 1.47 |
| ⊕ Hewlett-Packard | Hardware | 27.3 | 38.29 | 1.40 |
| ⊕ Time Warner | Media | 30.6 | -9.83 | 1.38 |
| ⊕ SBC Communications | Telecom | 21.1 | 0.25 | 1.32 |
| ⊕ Wachovia | Financial | 13.0 | 4.29 | 1.24 |
| ⊕ Coca-Cola | Goods | 18.6 | -0.66 | 1.01 |
| ⊕ Merck | Health | 15.2 | 4.04 | 0.99 |
| ⊕ Merrill Lynch & Company | Financial | 13.7 | 14.77 | 0.91 |
| ⊕ Motorola | Hardware | 13.9 | 32.43 | 0.90 |

### Current Investment Style

Value Blnd Growth — Large Mid Small

| Market Cap | % |
|---|---|
| Giant | 49.6 |
| Large | 35.8 |
| Mid | 14.6 |
| Small | 0.1 |
| Micro | 0.0 |

Avg $mil: 42,053

| Value Measures | | Rel Category |
|---|---|---|
| Price/Earnings | 13.28 | 0.92 |
| Price/Book | 1.96 | 0.88 |
| Price/Sales | 1.29 | 0.98 |
| Price/Cash Flow | 4.21 | 0.82 |
| Dividend Yield % | 2.66 | 1.09 |

| Growth Measures | % | Rel Category |
|---|---|---|
| Long-Term Erngs | 9.08 | 0.95 |
| Book Value | 10.69 | 0.88 |
| Sales | 6.72 | 0.84 |
| Cash Flow | 10.10 | 0.82 |
| Historical Erngs | 14.11 | 0.86 |

| Profitability | % | Rel Category |
|---|---|---|
| Return on Equity | 15.85 | 0.86 |
| Return on Assets | 9.40 | 0.95 |
| Net Margin | 13.15 | 1.02 |

### Sector Weightings

| | % of Stocks | Rel S&P 500 | 3 Year High | Low |
|---|---|---|---|---|
| ⟳ Info | 12.78 | 0.63 | | |
| 🖳 Software | 0.34 | 0.10 | 2 | 0 |
| 🖥 Hardware | 4.14 | 0.41 | 5 | 2 |
| 🎬 Media | 3.70 | 1.03 | 7 | 3 |
| 📶 Telecom | 4.60 | 1.53 | 6 | 5 |
| ⟳ Service | 45.99 | 0.99 | | |
| ⚕ Health | 6.85 | 0.52 | 8 | 3 |
| 🛒 Consumer | 3.15 | 0.39 | 6 | 3 |
| 📋 Business | 2.14 | 0.55 | 3 | 2 |
| 💲 Financial | 33.85 | 1.61 | 35 | 33 |
| ⬜ Mfg | 41.23 | 1.23 | | |
| 🚗 Goods | 7.11 | 0.83 | 9 | 3 |
| ⚙ Ind Mtrls | 11.84 | 0.97 | 20 | 12 |
| ⛽ Energy | 15.94 | 1.70 | 16 | 10 |
| 💡 Utilities | 6.34 | 1.89 | 6 | 5 |

### Composition

| | | |
|---|---|---|
| ● Cash | | 0.0 |
| ● Stocks | | 100.0 |
| ● Bonds | | 0.0 |
| ● Other | | 0.0 |
| Foreign | | 0.1 |
| (% of Stock) | | |

## Morningstar's Take by Sonya Morris

Vanguard Value VIPERs are a solid option, but they face strong competition from within.

ETFs are only as good as the benchmarks they track. But we think this fund's bogy is up to the challenge. The MSCI U.S. Prime Market Value Index uses a sophisticated multivariate methodology that should help it closely reflect the universe of large-cap value stocks. Plus, the index employs buffer zones to limit the migration of stocks between market-cap and style bands, thus limiting turnover. Our confidence is further bolstered by the index's performance record. Since this ETF's sibling Vanguard Value Index Fund began tracking the MSCI index in June 2003, the fund has outpaced almost three fourths of its rivals.

Given its bargain-basement price tag, we think the odds are good that this ETF will edge out most active managers burdened with much higher expense hurdles. But it faces a tougher challenge at home because Vanguard boasts a strong lineup of cheap actively managed large-value funds in its

stable. Consider the likes of Vanguard Windsor II and Vanguard U.S. Value. Both have veteran managers who practice disciplined, low turnover strategies, and they have delivered superior returns and below-average volatility over the long haul.

Even though we'd give the edge to these actively managed options, we think there's justification for owning this ETF. It provides cheap, reliable exposure to large-value stocks, and it's less subject to manager risk than its actively managed rivals.

And we're not disturbed at all by a change at the top here. Gus Sauter has gradually relinquished his daily managerial duties since becoming Vanguard's CIO in 2003 and is no longer listed as this ETF's day-to-day manager. However, Sauter will stay on board in a supervisory capacity. His replacement, Gerard O'Reilly, has worked closely with Sauter for several years and oversees a number of other Vanguard offerings, including Vanguard Total Stock Market Index.

| Address: | PO Box 2600 | Management Fee: | 0.08% | | |
|---|---|---|---|---|---|
| | Valley Forge PA 19482 | Expense Projections: | 3Yr:$35 | 5Yr:$62 | 10Yr:$141 |
| | 866-499-8473 | Income Distrib: | Quarterly | | |
| Web Address: | www.vanguard.com | Exchange: | AMEX | | |
| Inception: | 01-26-04* | | | | |
| Advisor: | Vanguard Advisers, Inc. | | | | |

M⟋RNINGSTAR® ETFs 100

# Tables and Charts

This section breaks down the performance of all exchange-traded funds and lists the best and worst ETFs in a variety of categories.

| Page | Name | Cat | Style Box | NAV ($) | Market Price ($) | 2005 Avg. Prem. Discount% | NAV Return% through 12-30-05 1Yr | Annualized 3Yr | 5Yr | Mkt Price Rtn% through 12-30-05 1Yr | Annualized 3Yr | 5Yr | Risk Statistics Standard Deviation | Sharpe Ratio |
|---|---|---|---|---|---|---|---|---|---|---|---|---|---|---|
| — | BLDRS Asia 50 ADR Index | DP | | 82.05 | 82.01 | 0.03 | 18.29 | 21.99 | — | 18.08 | 21.90 | — | 13.84 | 1.38 |
| — | BLDRS Dev Mkts 100 ADR | FB | | 72.04 | 72.02 | 0.01 | 9.24 | 19.40 | — | 9.18 | 19.62 | — | 11.76 | 1.41 |
| — | BLDRS Emerg Mkts 50 ADR | EM | | 115.23 | 115.33 | 0.07 | 40.81 | 35.22 | — | 40.80 | 34.81 | — | 17.73 | 1.70 |
| — | BLDRS Europe 100 ADR | ES | | 71.78 | 71.85 | 0.11 | 7.61 | 19.35 | — | 7.58 | 19.60 | — | 12.92 | 1.29 |
| — | Consumer Discr SPDR | LB | | 32.65 | 32.65 | −0.01 | −6.56 | 13.06 | 5.85 | −6.57 | 13.11 | 5.82 | 13.64 | 0.83 |
| 65 | Consumer Staple SPDR | LB | | 23.30 | 23.29 | 0.01 | 2.84 | 7.14 | −2.39 | 2.84 | 7.16 | −2.39 | 8.03 | 0.66 |
| 66 | DIAMONDS Trust | LV | | 107.08 | 106.95 | 0.02 | 2.40 | 11.28 | 2.02 | 2.47 | 11.23 | 2.19 | 9.60 | 0.96 |
| 67 | Energy SPDR | SN | | 50.28 | 50.31 | 0.01 | 40.20 | 33.21 | 10.46 | 40.17 | 33.18 | 10.53 | 18.39 | 1.56 |
| 68 | Fidelity Nasdaq Comp Trac | LG | | 86.62 | 86.62 | −0.07 | 1.92 | — | — | 1.89 | — | — | — | — |
| 69 | Financial SPDR | SF | | 31.69 | 31.67 | 0.00 | 6.20 | 15.32 | 3.49 | 6.20 | 15.39 | 3.48 | 11.40 | 1.14 |
| — | First Trust DJ S MicroCap | SB | | 20.73 | 20.72 | −0.24 | — | — | — | — | — | — | — | — |
| 70 | Health Care Sel SPDR | SH | | 31.72 | 31.72 | 0.01 | 6.44 | 7.40 | 3.99 | 6.41 | 7.39 | 4.04 | 9.39 | 0.60 |
| 71 | Industrial SPDR | LB | | 31.43 | 31.42 | 0.03 | 2.75 | 16.93 | 1.54 | 2.74 | 16.84 | 1.56 | 11.83 | 1.22 |
| — | iShares Australia | PJ | | 18.83 | 18.81 | −0.07 | 16.66 | 31.75 | 18.47 | 16.68 | 31.95 | 18.27 | 13.02 | 2.05 |
| — | iShares Austria Index | ES | | 27.41 | 27.59 | 0.05 | 21.50 | 48.74 | 30.33 | 21.13 | 48.78 | 31.01 | 14.39 | 2.73 |
| — | iShares Belgium Indx | ES | | 19.10 | 19.21 | −0.08 | 7.75 | 29.81 | 11.52 | 7.90 | 30.54 | 12.32 | 17.46 | 1.48 |
| — | iShares Brazil Index | LS | | 33.16 | 33.37 | −0.11 | 52.46 | 63.33 | 18.02 | 52.66 | 64.08 | 18.00 | 27.28 | 1.89 |
| 72 | iShares C&S Realty | SR | | 74.72 | 74.84 | 0.10 | 14.13 | 28.28 | — | 14.57 | 28.26 | — | 16.14 | 1.52 |
| — | iShares Canada Index | FV | | 21.80 | 21.90 | 0.19 | 27.84 | 33.89 | 11.35 | 27.53 | 33.86 | 11.33 | 13.96 | 2.05 |
| — | iShares COMEX Gold Trust | SP | | 51.52 | 51.73 | 0.09 | — | — | — | — | — | — | — | — |
| — | iShares DJ BMaterial | LV | | 51.58 | 51.54 | −0.07 | 4.32 | 16.47 | 7.81 | 4.13 | 16.36 | 7.41 | 16.40 | 0.90 |
| — | iShares DJ Cons Services | LB | | 59.59 | 59.61 | −0.06 | −2.32 | 12.79 | 1.67 | −2.33 | 12.89 | 1.56 | 12.73 | 0.86 |
| — | iShares DJ Consumer Goods | LB | | 53.24 | 53.26 | 0.07 | 1.44 | 10.94 | 5.81 | 1.52 | 11.10 | 5.67 | 10.42 | 0.86 |
| — | iShares DJ Fin Sectr | SF | | 101.16 | 101.09 | −0.01 | 5.82 | 16.15 | 4.89 | 5.72 | 16.26 | 4.88 | 11.19 | 1.22 |
| — | iShares DJ Fin Svcs | SF | | 114.38 | 114.45 | 0.06 | 3.45 | 15.78 | 4.94 | 3.35 | 15.79 | 4.88 | 11.28 | 1.19 |
| 73 | iShares DJ Health | SH | | 62.96 | 63.04 | −0.02 | 7.65 | 9.91 | −1.94 | 7.66 | 9.91 | −1.95 | 9.13 | 0.87 |
| — | iShares DJ Industry | LB | | 58.25 | 58.24 | −0.03 | 4.18 | 17.10 | 1.54 | 4.06 | 17.02 | 1.51 | 11.83 | 1.23 |
| 74 | iShares DJ RE Index | SR | | 64.36 | 64.15 | −0.21 | 9.19 | 24.55 | 17.16 | 8.94 | 24.27 | 17.03 | 15.60 | 1.37 |
| 75 | iShares DJ Sel Dividend | MV | | 61.30 | 61.26 | 0.03 | 2.98 | — | — | 2.81 | — | — | — | — |
| 76 | iShares DJ Tech | ST | | 49.76 | 49.72 | −0.06 | 2.72 | 15.98 | −7.48 | 2.77 | 15.84 | −7.49 | 16.71 | 0.86 |
| 77 | iShares DJ Telecom | SC | | 22.87 | 22.86 | −0.03 | −2.42 | 9.16 | −8.12 | −2.58 | 9.20 | −8.13 | 12.58 | 0.61 |
| 78 | iShares DJ Total Mkt | LB | | 60.53 | 60.51 | 0.01 | 6.14 | 15.67 | 1.14 | 6.00 | 15.63 | 1.09 | 9.53 | 1.37 |
| 79 | iShares DJ US Energy | SN | | 85.52 | 85.76 | 0.07 | 34.29 | 31.01 | 10.88 | 34.67 | 31.31 | 10.80 | 18.25 | 1.48 |
| 80 | iShares DJ Utilities | SU | | 76.47 | 76.46 | −0.04 | 14.63 | 20.59 | 0.23 | 14.54 | 20.49 | 0.25 | 11.72 | 1.50 |
| — | iShares Dow Jones TransAv | MB | | 75.44 | 75.42 | −0.07 | 11.03 | — | — | 10.88 | — | — | — | — |
| 81 | iShares EMU Index | ES | | 77.23 | 77.65 | 0.12 | 8.61 | 23.25 | 2.49 | 8.77 | 23.27 | 2.59 | 15.29 | 1.32 |
| — | iShares France Index | ES | | 25.87 | 25.98 | 0.09 | 9.52 | 21.90 | 1.96 | 10.13 | 22.21 | 2.11 | 14.89 | 1.28 |
| 82 | iShares FTSE/Xinhua China | PJ | | 61.44 | 61.62 | 0.44 | 14.15 | — | — | 13.33 | — | — | — | — |
| — | iShares Germany Indx | ES | | 20.22 | 20.31 | 0.01 | 9.86 | 27.55 | 1.70 | 9.64 | 28.52 | 1.89 | 20.31 | 1.21 |
| — | iShares GS Nat Res | SN | | 88.20 | 88.33 | 0.08 | 35.79 | 31.12 | — | 35.98 | 31.16 | — | 17.06 | 1.57 |
| — | iShares GS Network | ST | | 31.04 | 31.00 | −0.03 | 2.31 | 32.08 | — | 2.34 | 31.64 | — | 30.44 | 1.00 |
| — | iShares GS Software | ST | | 40.27 | 40.25 | 0.00 | −5.49 | 16.91 | — | −5.53 | 16.97 | — | 18.49 | 0.83 |
| 84 | iShares GS Tech | ST | | 47.39 | 47.35 | −0.10 | 1.54 | 16.84 | — | 1.52 | 16.71 | — | 17.68 | 0.86 |
| 83 | iShares GS$ InvesTop | CL | | 107.50 | 107.69 | 0.09 | 1.00 | 4.74 | — | 1.18 | 4.26 | — | 6.58 | 0.44 |
| — | iShares Hong Kong | PJ | | 12.63 | 12.62 | 0.20 | 7.84 | 22.31 | 3.72 | 7.31 | 21.95 | 4.14 | 15.55 | 1.25 |
| — | iShares Italy Index | ES | | 25.48 | 25.58 | 0.04 | 1.49 | 23.04 | 4.95 | 1.88 | 23.61 | 4.93 | 15.88 | 1.27 |
| 85 | iShares Japan Index | JS | | 13.48 | 13.52 | 0.00 | 24.65 | 24.71 | 4.01 | 24.34 | 25.19 | 4.28 | 16.78 | 1.29 |
| 86 | iShares KLD Sel Soc Idx | LB | | 53.14 | 53.17 | −0.09 | — | — | — | — | — | — | — | — |
| 87 | iShares Lehman 1-3 T | GS | | 80.16 | 80.21 | −0.09 | 1.48 | 1.35 | — | 1.53 | 1.35 | — | 1.37 | −0.4 |
| — | iShares Lehman 20+ | GL | | 91.78 | 91.90 | −0.18 | 8.44 | 6.30 | — | 8.61 | 6.26 | — | 11.41 | 0.43 |

# Performance Summary
## Morningstar's ETF Universe

| Portfolio | | | | Costs | | Trading Information | | | | | Contact |
|---|---|---|---|---|---|---|---|---|---|---|---|
| Top 3 Sectors | Avg. Mkt. Cap. ($mil) | P/E Ratio | P/B Ratio | Expense Ratio % | Tax-Cost Ratio | 52-week High/Low | Total Assets ($) | Exchange | Ticker | Phone | Web Address |
| [icons] | 39952.72 | 15.81 | 1.86 | 0.30 | 0.43 | 84.67–64.97 | 51,000,000 | NASDAQ | ADRA | 888-627-3837 | www.bldrsfunds.com |
| [icons] | 67625.68 | 16.32 | 2.01 | 0.30 | 0.63 | 75.06–64.37 | 43,000,000 | NASDAQ | ADRD | 888-627-3837 | www.bldrsfunds.com |
| [icons] | 22646.57 | 13.86 | 2.49 | 0.30 | 0.92 | 120.62–78.56 | 282,000,000 | NASDAQ | ADRE | 888-627-3837 | www.bldrsfunds.com |
| [icons] | 65704.45 | 16.04 | 2.05 | 0.30 | 0.67 | 74.91–65.28 | 29,000,000 | NASDAQ | ADRU | 888-627-3837 | www.bldrsfunds.com |
| [icons] | 23967.29 | 19.94 | 2.39 | 0.26 | 0.27 | 34.99–30.75 | 611,000,000 | AMEX | XLY | 800-843-2639 | www.spdrindex.com |
| [icons] | 57285.43 | 19.17 | 4.80 | 0.26 | 0.61 | 23.93–22.48 | 785,000,000 | AMEX | XLP | 800-843-2639 | www.spdrindex.com |
| [icons] | 98554.14 | 17.22 | 3.12 | 0.18 | 0.84 | 109.59–100.07 | 7,634,000,000 | AMEX | DIA | 800-843-2639 | www.amex.com |
| [icons] | 45938.16 | 11.91 | 2.74 | 0.26 | 0.55 | 54.48–35.00 | 3,526,000,000 | AMEX | XLE | 800-843-2639 | www.spdrindex.com |
| [icons] | 9598.04 | 24.20 | 3.45 | 0.30 | — | 90.59–75.09 | 121,000,000 | AMEX | ONEQ | 800-544-6666 | www.fidelity.com |
| [icons] | 51984.54 | 13.97 | 2.01 | 0.26 | 0.75 | 32.46–27.65 | 1,872,000,000 | AMEX | XLF | 800-843-2639 | www.spdrindex.com |
| — | — | — | — | — | — | 21.28–18.99 | 35,000,000 | AMEX | FDM | 800-621-1675 | www.ftportfolios.com |
| [icons] | 46240.04 | 22.99 | 3.80 | 0.26 | 0.42 | 32.59–29.11 | 1,787,000,000 | AMEX | XLV | 800-843-2639 | www.spdrindex.com |
| [icons] | 43946.63 | 19.09 | 3.00 | 0.25 | 0.51 | 31.83–28.86 | 886,000,000 | AMEX | XLI | 800-843-2639 | www.spdrindex.com |
| [icons] | 13710.93 | 15.51 | 3.03 | 0.57 | 1.18 | 19.63–16.14 | 463,000,000 | AMEX | EWA | 800-474-2737 | www.ishares.com |
| [icons] | 5535.74 | 19.06 | 3.30 | 0.57 | 0.32 | 28.94–21.39 | 222,000,000 | AMEX | EWO | 800-474-2737 | www.ishares.com |
| [icons] | 13476.09 | 12.31 | 2.39 | 0.57 | 1.52 | 20.13–17.71 | 65,000,000 | NYSE | EWK | 800-474-2737 | www.ishares.com |
| [icons] | 13248.14 | 11.40 | 2.40 | 0.74 | 0.64 | 36.56–20.19 | 1,224,000,000 | NYSE | EWZ | 800-474-2737 | www.ishares.com |
| [icons] | 7125.43 | 33.33 | 2.74 | 0.35 | 1.61 | 78.37–61.62 | 1,666,000,000 | AMEX | ICF | 800-474-2737 | www.ishares.com |
| [icons] | 15442.00 | 18.58 | 3.33 | 0.57 | 0.39 | 22.59–16.23 | 621,000,000 | AMEX | EWC | 800-474-2737 | www.ishares.com |
| — | — | — | — | — | — | 53.19–41.25 | 368,000,000 | AMEX | IAU | 800-474-2737 | www.ishares.com |
| [icons] | 11796.30 | 15.35 | 2.64 | 0.60 | 0.59 | 54.28–45.52 | 382,000,000 | NYSE | IYM | 800-474-2737 | www.ishares.com |
| [icons] | 19532.81 | 21.48 | 2.64 | 0.60 | 0.07 | 62.32–55.68 | 253,000,000 | NYSE | IYC | 800-474-2737 | www.ishares.com |
| [icons] | 29012.18 | 17.06 | 3.76 | 0.60 | 0.53 | 54.65–50.75 | 484,000,000 | NYSE | IYK | 800-474-2737 | www.ishares.com |
| [icons] | 31102.02 | 14.48 | 2.02 | 0.60 | 0.67 | 103.68–88.38 | 389,000,000 | NYSE | IYF | 800-474-2737 | www.ishares.com |
| [icons] | 44305.21 | 13.97 | 2.10 | 0.60 | 0.71 | 117.08–102.19 | 177,000,000 | NYSE | IYG | 800-474-2737 | www.ishares.com |
| [icons] | 35313.16 | 24.66 | 4.05 | 0.60 | 0.25 | 64.68–56.73 | 1,300,000,000 | NYSE | IYH | 800-474-2737 | www.ishares.com |
| [icons] | 27624.40 | 19.34 | 2.97 | 0.60 | 0.34 | 59.31–52.56 | 236,000,000 | NYSE | IYJ | 800-474-2737 | www.ishares.com |
| [icons] | 4802.67 | 25.38 | 2.45 | 0.60 | 1.44 | 68.40–55.56 | 1,046,000,000 | NYSE | IYR | 800-474-2737 | www.ishares.com |
| [icons] | 11836.90 | 14.42 | 2.03 | 0.40 | — | 64.47–58.10 | 7,252,000,000 | NYSE | DVY | 800-474-2737 | www.ishares.com |
| [icons] | 39261.51 | 23.00 | 3.95 | 0.60 | 0.19 | 52.86–41.90 | 513,000,000 | NYSE | IYW | 800-474-2737 | www.ishares.com |
| [icons] | 31587.80 | 15.47 | 1.85 | 0.60 | 0.95 | 24.36–22.04 | 497,000,000 | NYSE | IYZ | 800-474-2737 | www.ishares.com |
| [icons] | 29878.90 | 17.62 | 2.79 | 0.20 | 0.55 | 62.44–54.50 | 472,000,000 | NYSE | IYY | 800-474-2737 | www.ishares.com |
| [icons] | 51379.82 | 11.92 | 2.80 | 0.60 | 0.46 | 92.66–62.06 | 812,000,000 | NYSE | IYE | 800-474-2737 | www.ishares.com |
| [icons] | 10592.01 | 16.58 | 2.04 | 0.60 | 1.10 | 83.03–66.52 | 704,000,000 | NYSE | IDU | 800-474-2737 | www.ishares.com |
| [icons] | 8056.37 | 16.06 | 2.42 | 0.60 | — | 76.65–60.90 | 223,000,000 | NYSE | IYT | 800-474-2737 | www.ishares.com |
| [icons] | 28698.08 | 15.01 | 3.24 | 0.58 | 0.55 | 81.49–69.18 | 552,000,000 | AMEX | EZU | 800-474-2737 | www.ishares.com |
| [icons] | 36033.40 | 14.15 | 3.69 | 0.57 | 0.45 | 27.50–22.91 | 88,000,000 | NYSE | EWQ | 800-474-2737 | www.ishares.com |
| [icons] | 19961.44 | 13.37 | 2.26 | 0.74 | — | 65.56–51.65 | 1,352,000,000 | NYSE | FXI | 800-474-2737 | www.ishares.com |
| [icons] | 31501.77 | 17.77 | 2.82 | 0.57 | 0.34 | 21.33–17.20 | 479,000,000 | AMEX | EWG | 800-474-2737 | www.ishares.com |
| [icons] | 28531.04 | 14.52 | 2.91 | 0.50 | 0.45 | 93.29–63.03 | 1,094,000,000 | AMEX | IGE | 800-474-2737 | www.ishares.com |
| [icons] | 13707.82 | 24.02 | 3.72 | 0.50 | 0.00 | 33.47–23.40 | 228,000,000 | AMEX | IGN | 800-474-2737 | www.ishares.com |
| [icons] | 11051.75 | 30.43 | 3.57 | 0.50 | 0.07 | 42.36–35.88 | 248,000,000 | AMEX | IGV | 800-474-2737 | www.ishares.com |
| [icons] | 31915.17 | 24.13 | 3.90 | 0.50 | 0.10 | 50.29–39.66 | 280,000,000 | AMEX | IGM | 800-474-2737 | www.ishares.com |
| — | — | — | — | 0.15 | 1.65 | 113.44–105.74 | 2,419,000,000 | AMEX | LQD | 800-474-2737 | www.ishares.com |
| [icons] | 12243.16 | 16.03 | 1.85 | 0.57 | 0.76 | 13.45–11.24 | 639,000,000 | NYSE | EWH | 800-474-2737 | www.ishares.com |
| [icons] | 26292.11 | 14.28 | 2.76 | 0.57 | 0.87 | 26.82–24.15 | 53,000,000 | NYSE | EWI | 800-474-2737 | www.ishares.com |
| [icons] | 16932.39 | 20.66 | 2.18 | 0.57 | 0.10 | 14.15–9.93 | 13,040,000,000 | NYSE | EWJ | 800-474-2737 | www.ishares.com |
| [icons] | 33448.52 | 17.68 | 3.15 | 0.50 | — | 54.88–48.15 | 117,000,000 | AMEX | KLD | 800-474-2737 | www.ishares.com |
| — | — | — | — | 0.15 | 0.76 | 81.43–80.01 | 4,401,000,000 | AMEX | SHY | 800-474-2737 | www.ishares.com |
| — | — | — | — | 0.15 | 1.67 | 96.74–87.84 | 1,053,000,000 | AMEX | TLT | 800-474-2737 | www.ishares.com |

# Performance Summary
**Morningstar's ETF Universe**

| Page | Name | Cat | Style Box | NAV ($) | Market Price ($) | 2005 Avg. Prem. Discount% | NAV Return% through 12-30-05 | | | Mkt Price Rtn% through 12-30-05 | | | Risk Statistics | |
|---|---|---|---|---|---|---|---|---|---|---|---|---|---|---|
| | | | | | | | 1Yr | Annualized 3Yr | 5Yr | 1Yr | Annualized 3Yr | 5Yr | Standard Deviation | Sharpe Ratio |
| — | iShares Lehman 7-10 | GI | | 83.71 | 83.91 | −0.13 | 2.27 | 2.91 | — | 2.64 | 2.95 | — | 7.04 | 0.17 |
| 88 | iShares Lehman Aggregate | CI | | 100.13 | 100.59 | 0.12 | 2.16 | — | — | 2.28 | — | — | — | — |
| 89 | iShares Lehman TIPS Bond | GL | | 102.80 | 102.82 | 0.06 | 2.65 | — | — | 2.50 | — | — | — | — |
| — | iShares Malaysia | PJ | | 6.88 | 6.82 | 0.09 | 1.57 | 13.26 | 8.86 | −0.58 | 13.75 | 8.59 | 14.07 | 0.82 |
| — | iShares Mexico Index | LS | | 35.78 | 35.71 | 0.25 | 45.61 | 43.29 | 23.73 | 43.82 | 43.84 | 23.98 | 18.60 | 1.95 |
| 90 | iShares MSCI EAFE | FB | | 59.12 | 59.43 | 0.24 | 13.39 | 23.42 | — | 13.34 | 23.52 | — | 11.51 | 1.73 |
| 91 | iShares MSCI EAFE Growth | FG | | 56.31 | 56.60 | 0.36 | — | — | — | — | — | — | — | — |
| 92 | iShares MSCI EAFE Value I | FV | | 56.00 | 56.32 | 0.48 | — | — | — | — | — | — | — | — |
| 93 | iShares MSCI Emerg Mkts | EM | | 88.52 | 88.25 | 0.07 | 33.78 | — | — | 32.62 | — | — | — | — |
| 94 | iShares MSCI ex-Japn | PJ | | 98.55 | 98.67 | 0.19 | 14.03 | 28.83 | — | 13.57 | 28.68 | — | 11.25 | 2.15 |
| — | iShares MSCI South Africa | EM | | 97.97 | 98.23 | 0.09 | 26.50 | — | — | 25.88 | — | — | — | — |
| — | iShares MstarLargeCore | LB | | 66.50 | 66.51 | −0.01 | 3.60 | — | — | 3.49 | — | — | — | — |
| — | iShares MstarLargeGrowth | LG | | 61.11 | 61.16 | 0.04 | 3.17 | — | — | 3.15 | — | — | — | — |
| — | iShares MstarLargeValue | LV | | 68.59 | 68.56 | 0.08 | 6.79 | — | — | 6.71 | — | — | — | — |
| — | iShares MstarMidCore | MB | | 72.88 | 72.97 | 0.06 | 9.91 | — | — | 9.56 | — | — | — | — |
| — | iShares MstarMidGrowth | MG | | 77.30 | 77.33 | −0.04 | 15.92 | — | — | 15.94 | — | — | — | — |
| — | iShares MstarMidValue | MV | | 73.91 | 73.91 | 0.00 | 11.56 | — | — | 11.30 | — | — | — | — |
| — | iShares MstarSmallCore | SB | | 71.96 | 71.90 | −0.11 | 6.01 | — | — | 6.09 | — | — | — | — |
| — | iShares MstarSmallGrowth | SG | | 67.43 | 67.33 | −0.08 | 5.49 | — | — | 5.28 | — | — | — | — |
| — | iShares MstarSmallValue | SV | | 70.62 | 70.55 | −0.09 | 4.79 | — | — | 4.52 | — | — | — | — |
| 95 | iShares NASD Biotech | SH | | 77.46 | 77.24 | 0.03 | 2.73 | 16.00 | — | 2.44 | 16.11 | — | 19.57 | 0.76 |
| — | iShares Netherlands | ES | | 20.23 | 20.32 | 0.16 | 12.79 | 17.18 | −0.55 | 12.98 | 17.80 | −0.28 | 16.49 | 0.93 |
| — | iShares NYSE 100 Index | LV | | 65.14 | 65.23 | 0.05 | 3.52 | — | — | 3.45 | — | — | — | — |
| 96 | iShares NYSE Composite | LB | | 70.88 | 70.84 | 0.41 | 9.05 | — | — | 8.64 | — | — | — | — |
| 97 | iShares R. Midcap | MB | | 88.08 | 87.93 | 0.03 | 12.60 | 23.58 | — | 12.48 | 23.44 | — | 11.35 | 1.76 |
| 98 | iShares R. Midcap Gr | MG | | 94.06 | 93.96 | 0.01 | 11.82 | 22.39 | — | 11.74 | 22.44 | — | 12.36 | 1.55 |
| 99 | iShares R. Midcap Vl | MV | | 124.59 | 124.42 | 0.00 | 12.68 | 24.12 | — | 12.54 | 24.26 | — | 11.04 | 1.85 |
| 100 | iShares R1000 Growth | LG | | 51.11 | 51.01 | 0.02 | 5.08 | 13.01 | −3.78 | 4.75 | 12.83 | −3.85 | 9.66 | 1.12 |
| 101 | iShares R1000 Index | LB | | 67.78 | 67.70 | 0.02 | 6.15 | 15.26 | 0.94 | 6.34 | 15.22 | 0.87 | 9.24 | 1.38 |
| 102 | iShares R1000 Value | LV | | 69.22 | 69.03 | −0.05 | 6.92 | 17.26 | 5.09 | 6.64 | 17.06 | 4.98 | 9.57 | 1.51 |
| 103 | iShares R2000 Growth | SG | | 69.86 | 69.66 | −0.11 | 4.04 | 20.73 | 2.04 | 4.02 | 20.92 | 2.01 | 16.74 | 1.10 |
| 104 | iShares R2000 Index | SB | | 66.86 | 66.72 | −0.06 | 4.46 | 21.95 | 8.01 | 4.46 | 22.09 | 8.08 | 15.27 | 1.25 |
| 105 | iShares R2000 Value | SV | | 66.10 | 65.93 | −0.13 | 4.49 | 22.90 | 13.25 | 4.36 | 22.98 | 13.23 | 14.26 | 1.39 |
| 106 | iShares R3000 Growth | LG | | 41.48 | 41.45 | 0.00 | 4.92 | 13.50 | −3.41 | 5.06 | 13.37 | −3.63 | 10.08 | 1.12 |
| 107 | iShares R3000 Index | LB | | 72.01 | 72.02 | 0.02 | 5.97 | 15.70 | 1.38 | 6.08 | 15.68 | 1.44 | 9.60 | 1.37 |
| 108 | iShares R3000 Value | LV | | 90.21 | 90.28 | 0.06 | 6.63 | 17.60 | 5.60 | 6.59 | 17.70 | 5.43 | 9.82 | 1.51 |
| 109 | iShares Russell Microcap | SB | | 51.31 | 51.15 | −0.23 | — | — | — | — | — | — | — | — |
| 110 | iShares S&P 100 Ind. | LB | | 56.86 | 56.90 | 0.09 | 1.00 | 10.56 | −2.12 | 1.03 | 10.67 | −2.15 | 8.84 | 0.96 |
| — | iShares S&P 1500 Index | LB | | 111.02 | 110.98 | −0.03 | 5.47 | — | — | 5.32 | — | — | — | — |
| 111 | iShares S&P 500 | LB | | 124.87 | 124.67 | −0.01 | 4.83 | 14.28 | 0.45 | 4.87 | 14.15 | 0.54 | 9.15 | 1.29 |
| 112 | iShares S&P Euro-350 | ES | | 80.15 | 80.77 | 0.29 | 9.17 | 21.54 | 3.28 | 9.84 | 21.73 | 3.01 | 13.20 | 1.40 |
| 113 | iShares S&P Glob 100 | WS | | 62.92 | 62.95 | 0.09 | 4.66 | 14.38 | −0.64 | 4.29 | 14.20 | −0.64 | 9.71 | 1.23 |
| — | iShares S.Korea Indx | PJ | | 44.67 | 44.75 | 0.41 | 55.00 | 34.82 | 30.70 | 53.90 | 35.46 | 30.27 | 24.40 | 1.28 |
| — | iShares Semiconductor | ST | | 61.01 | 60.97 | −0.03 | 13.35 | 20.88 | — | 13.38 | 20.72 | — | 28.93 | 0.73 |
| — | iShares Singapore | PJ | | 7.90 | 7.90 | 0.40 | 15.57 | 25.56 | 5.98 | 14.28 | 26.73 | 6.66 | 11.56 | 1.87 |
| 115 | iShares SP 400 Growth | MG | | 75.73 | 75.62 | −0.03 | 13.31 | 18.96 | 4.48 | 13.23 | 18.88 | 4.45 | 11.08 | 1.46 |
| 116 | iShares SP 400 Value | MV | | 70.60 | 70.49 | −0.01 | 11.47 | 22.74 | 12.15 | 11.59 | 22.61 | 12.08 | 12.64 | 1.54 |
| 117 | iShares SP 500 Growth | LG | | 59.33 | 59.28 | 0.08 | 3.81 | 11.30 | −1.73 | 3.99 | 11.26 | −1.62 | 8.51 | 1.08 |
| 118 | iShares SP 500 Value | LV | | 65.11 | 65.05 | 0.02 | 5.67 | 17.09 | 2.26 | 5.63 | 17.08 | 2.32 | 10.47 | 1.38 |
| 119 | iShares SP 600 Growth | SG | | 116.41 | 116.07 | −0.08 | 8.99 | 22.02 | 8.63 | 9.00 | 21.81 | 8.52 | 13.73 | 1.38 |

**Tables and Charts**

# Performance Summary

**Morningstar's ETF Universe**

| Portfolio — Top 3 Sectors | Avg. Mkt. Cap. ($mil) | P/E Ratio | P/B Ratio | Costs — Expense Ratio % | Tax-Cost Ratio | Trading Information — 52-week High/Low | Total Assets ($) | Exchange | Ticker | Phone | Web Address |
|---|---|---|---|---|---|---|---|---|---|---|---|
| — | — | — | — | 0.15 | 1.31 | 87.10–82.23 | 1,164,000,000 | AMEX | IEF | 800-474-2737 | www.ishares.com |
| — | — | — | — | 0.20 | — | 103.07–99.07 | 2,894,000,000 | AMEX | AGG | 800-474-2737 | www.ishares.com |
| — | — | — | — | 0.20 | — | 107.41–101.65 | 3,310,000,000 | NYSE | TIP | 800-474-2737 | www.ishares.com |
| (icons) | 2555.81 | 15.19 | 1.89 | 0.57 | 0.92 | 7.54–6.70 | 329,000,000 | NYSE | EWM | 800-474-2737 | www.ishares.com |
| (icons) | 15328.08 | 16.91 | 3.50 | 0.57 | 0.43 | 37.76–22.70 | 479,000,000 | AMEX | EWW | 800-474-2737 | www.ishares.com |
| (icons) | 27645.94 | 16.87 | 3.04 | 0.36 | 0.53 | 62.13–51.07 | 22,730,000,000 | AMEX | EFA | 800-474-2737 | www.ishares.com |
| (icons) | 24037.38 | 19.98 | 3.95 | — | — | 59.16–50.88 | 45,000,000 | NYSE | EFG | 800-474-2737 | www.ishares.com |
| (icons) | 31436.23 | 14.72 | 2.52 | — | — | 58.87–51.00 | 65,000,000 | NYSE | EFV | 800-474-2737 | www.ishares.com |
| (icons) | 11259.37 | 14.21 | 2.41 | 0.77 | — | 93.85–63.60 | 10,260,000,000 | AMEX | EEM | 800-474-2737 | www.ishares.com |
| (icons) | 12075.29 | 15.65 | 2.67 | 0.50 | 1.06 | 103.06–86.85 | 1,675,000,000 | AMEX | EPP | 800-474-2737 | www.ishares.com |
| (icons) | 7424.77 | 13.39 | 3.61 | 0.74 | — | 104.52–67.92 | 171,000,000 | AMEX | EZA | 800-474-2737 | www.ishares.com |
| (icons) | 59242.23 | 18.26 | 2.95 | — | — | 67.81–61.42 | 90,000,000 | NYSE | JKD | 800-474-2737 | www.ishares.com |
| (icons) | 51373.66 | 25.91 | 4.54 | — | — | 63.69–54.22 | 150,000,000 | NYSE | JKE | 800-474-2737 | www.ishares.com |
| (icons) | 69420.68 | 13.05 | 2.17 | — | — | 70.87–63.71 | 123,000,000 | NYSE | JKF | 800-474-2737 | www.ishares.com |
| (icons) | 4955.62 | 18.11 | 2.70 | — | — | 75.22–62.37 | 102,000,000 | NYSE | JKG | 800-474-2737 | www.ishares.com |
| (icons) | 5123.77 | 27.18 | 3.93 | — | — | 80.17–62.32 | 131,000,000 | NYSE | JKH | 800-474-2737 | www.ishares.com |
| (icons) | 4804.76 | 14.13 | 1.85 | — | — | 75.96–65.18 | 78,000,000 | NYSE | JKI | 800-474-2737 | www.ishares.com |
| (icons) | 1103.44 | 17.91 | 2.21 | — | — | 74.50–61.88 | 50,000,000 | NYSE | JKJ | 800-474-2737 | www.ishares.com |
| (icons) | 1136.31 | 27.98 | 3.36 | — | — | 70.55–55.93 | 47,000,000 | NYSE | JKK | 800-474-2737 | www.ishares.com |
| (icons) | 1139.99 | 12.78 | 1.68 | — | — | 73.65–61.87 | 53,000,000 | NYSE | JKL | 800-474-2737 | www.ishares.com |
| (icons) | 4474.99 | 32.93 | 4.46 | 0.50 | 0.00 | 80.34–62.97 | 1,607,000,000 | AMEX | IBB | 800-474-2737 | www.ishares.com |
| (icons) | 22828.57 | 13.38 | 2.96 | 0.57 | 0.70 | 21.20–17.63 | 68,000,000 | NYSE | EWN | 800-474-2737 | www.ishares.com |
| (icons) | 90952.62 | 16.07 | 2.79 | 0.20 | — | 66.79–61.12 | 29,000,000 | NYSE | NY | 800-474-2737 | www.ishares.com |
| (icons) | 35433.91 | 16.73 | 2.52 | 0.25 | — | 73.43–63.31 | 32,000,000 | NYSE | NYC | 800-474-2737 | www.ishares.com |
| (icons) | 6381.90 | 18.44 | 2.64 | 0.20 | 0.46 | 90.89–75.53 | 1,696,000,000 | AMEX | IWR | 800-474-2737 | www.ishares.com |
| (icons) | 6403.12 | 22.23 | 3.91 | 0.25 | 0.11 | 97.32–79.15 | 1,312,000,000 | AMEX | IWP | 800-474-2737 | www.ishares.com |
| (icons) | 6361.39 | 15.82 | 2.01 | 0.25 | 0.64 | 128.24–108.07 | 2,012,000,000 | AMEX | IWS | 800-474-2737 | www.ishares.com |
| (icons) | 35857.73 | 21.78 | 4.25 | 0.20 | 0.34 | 52.64–45.38 | 5,399,000,000 | AMEX | IWF | 800-474-2737 | www.ishares.com |
| (icons) | 35376.37 | 17.49 | 2.82 | 0.15 | 0.62 | 69.82–61.22 | 2,413,000,000 | AMEX | IWB | 800-474-2737 | www.ishares.com |
| (icons) | 34913.82 | 14.51 | 2.09 | 0.20 | 0.78 | 71.31–63.52 | 6,185,000,000 | AMEX | IWD | 800-474-2737 | www.ishares.com |
| (icons) | 970.09 | 21.65 | 3.34 | 0.25 | 0.13 | 72.87–58.39 | 2,620,000,000 | AMEX | IWO | 800-474-2737 | www.ishares.com |
| (icons) | 936.30 | 18.58 | 2.26 | 0.20 | 0.39 | 69.47–57.20 | 7,432,000,000 | AMEX | IWM | 800-474-2737 | www.ishares.com |
| (icons) | 902.49 | 16.33 | 1.70 | 0.25 | 0.48 | 68.84–57.81 | 3,014,000,000 | AMEX | IWN | 800-474-2737 | www.ishares.com |
| (icons) | 26208.65 | 21.77 | 4.15 | 0.25 | 0.31 | 42.77–36.70 | 214,000,000 | AMEX | IWZ | 800-474-2737 | www.ishares.com |
| (icons) | 25792.97 | 17.57 | 2.76 | 0.20 | 0.60 | 74.23–64.85 | 1,955,000,000 | AMEX | IWV | 800-474-2737 | www.ishares.com |
| (icons) | 25321.55 | 14.63 | 2.05 | 0.25 | 0.75 | 92.96–82.48 | 433,000,000 | AMEX | IWW | 800-474-2737 | www.ishares.com |
| (icons) | 332.33 | 18.67 | 2.08 | — | — | 53.19–47.47 | 103,000,000 | NYSE | IWC | 800-474-2737 | www.ishares.com |
| (icons) | 99370.51 | 16.73 | 2.90 | 0.20 | 0.66 | 58.48–54.23 | 685,000,000 | CBOE | OEF | 800-474-2737 | www.ishares.com |
| (icons) | 32216.39 | 17.51 | 2.77 | 0.20 | — | 114.43–100.29 | 133,000,000 | NYSE | ISI | 800-474-2737 | www.ishares.com |
| (icons) | 46962.20 | 17.27 | 2.81 | 0.09 | 0.61 | 128.66–113.66 | 14,220,000,000 | NYSE | IVV | 800-474-2737 | www.ishares.com |
| (icons) | 41774.37 | 15.47 | 3.57 | 0.60 | 0.67 | 84.43–72.22 | 1,270,000,000 | NYSE | IEV | 800-474-2737 | www.ishares.com |
| (icons) | 110750.75 | 16.34 | 3.26 | 0.40 | 0.54 | 65.62–58.99 | 374,000,000 | NYSE | IOO | 800-474-2737 | www.ishares.com |
| (icons) | 12315.20 | 9.51 | 1.86 | 0.74 | 0.22 | 46.49–27.80 | 1,077,000,000 | NYSE | EWY | 800-474-2737 | www.ishares.com |
| (icons) | 15021.79 | 25.52 | 3.36 | 0.50 | 0.01 | 66.32–46.79 | 415,000,000 | AMEX | IGW | 800-747-2737 | www.ishares.com |
| (icons) | 6072.52 | 13.14 | 2.30 | 0.57 | 1.09 | 8.24–7.08 | 393,000,000 | NYSE | EWS | 800-474-2737 | www.ishares.com |
| (icons) | 4149.54 | 22.33 | 3.66 | 0.25 | 0.18 | 78.22–63.67 | 1,787,000,000 | NYSE | IJK | 800-474-2737 | www.ishares.com |
| (icons) | 2872.29 | 17.92 | 2.02 | 0.25 | 0.52 | 73.02–60.69 | 2,513,000,000 | NYSE | IJJ | 800-474-2737 | www.ishares.com |
| (icons) | 53583.50 | 19.40 | 3.82 | 0.18 | 0.49 | 61.21–54.64 | 3,242,000,000 | NYSE | IVW | 800-474-2737 | www.ishares.com |
| (icons) | 41012.26 | 15.48 | 2.21 | 0.18 | 0.66 | 66.98–58.59 | 3,015,000,000 | NYSE | IVE | 800-474-2737 | www.ishares.com |
| (icons) | 1387.79 | 19.31 | 3.02 | 0.25 | 0.16 | 120.37–98.73 | 1,280,000,000 | NYSE | IJT | 800-474-2737 | www.ishares.com |

# Performance Summary
**Morningstar's ETF Universe**

| Page | Name | Cat | Style Box | NAV ($) | Market Price ($) | 2005 Avg. Prem. Discount % | NAV Return% through 12-30-05 1Yr | Annualized 3Yr | 5Yr | Mkt Price Rtn% through 12-30-05 1Yr | Annualized 3Yr | 5Yr | Risk Statistics Standard Deviation | Sharpe Ratio |
|---|---|---|---|---|---|---|---|---|---|---|---|---|---|---|
| 120 | iShares SP 600 Value | SV | | 63.99 | 63.88 | −0.20 | 5.93 | 22.10 | 11.84 | 5.99 | 21.93 | 11.72 | 14.60 | 1.31 |
| — | iShares SP Glb Enrgy | SN | | 93.23 | 93.62 | 0.28 | 28.79 | 28.36 | — | 29.47 | 28.69 | — | 16.85 | 1.46 |
| — | iShares SP Glb Fincl | SF | | 73.13 | 73.53 | 0.21 | 11.65 | 21.44 | — | 11.60 | 21.82 | — | 12.17 | 1.51 |
| 121 | iShares SP Glb Hlth | SH | | 52.20 | 52.20 | 0.23 | 7.80 | 9.80 | — | 6.81 | 9.70 | — | 9.04 | 0.87 |
| — | iShares SP Glb Tech | ST | | 53.09 | 53.23 | 0.16 | 3.90 | 16.23 | — | 3.43 | 16.11 | — | 15.57 | 0.92 |
| — | iShares SP Glb Tele | SC | | 48.32 | 48.66 | 0.33 | −6.27 | 11.74 | — | −6.72 | 11.75 | — | 12.44 | 0.80 |
| 114 | iShares SP Latin 40 | LS | | 123.00 | 122.85 | 0.37 | 56.00 | 52.06 | — | 54.59 | 51.67 | — | 19.72 | 2.16 |
| 122 | iShares SP MidCap400 | MB | | 73.76 | 73.80 | −0.01 | 12.48 | 20.98 | 8.45 | 12.88 | 21.05 | 8.43 | 11.66 | 1.53 |
| 123 | iShares SP Small 600 | SB | | 57.89 | 57.80 | −0.12 | 7.50 | 22.19 | 10.59 | 7.53 | 22.16 | 10.70 | 14.01 | 1.37 |
| 124 | iShares SP TOPIX 150 | JS | | 115.79 | 116.00 | 0.15 | 24.25 | 23.28 | — | 23.95 | 23.62 | — | 16.62 | 1.24 |
| — | iShares Spain Index | ES | | 36.02 | 36.17 | 0.05 | 4.45 | 28.46 | 10.44 | 4.56 | 28.90 | 10.94 | 14.44 | 1.68 |
| — | iShares Sweden Index | ES | | 22.61 | 22.70 | −0.01 | 10.20 | 34.92 | 5.61 | 10.32 | 35.34 | 6.11 | 17.88 | 1.67 |
| — | iShares Switzerland | ES | | 19.26 | 19.31 | 0.31 | 14.34 | 20.77 | 3.20 | 12.97 | 20.84 | 3.33 | 12.08 | 1.47 |
| — | iShares Taiwan Index | PJ | | 12.45 | 12.48 | 0.43 | 4.89 | 16.80 | 4.46 | 4.62 | 16.02 | 3.81 | 21.68 | 0.74 |
| — | iShares U.K. Index | ES | | 18.49 | 18.58 | −0.03 | 6.63 | 18.24 | 3.33 | 5.91 | 18.37 | 3.86 | 11.75 | 1.32 |
| — | Materials Sel SPDR | LV | | 30.29 | 30.28 | −0.01 | 4.10 | 17.48 | 9.42 | 4.08 | 17.51 | 9.44 | 16.31 | 0.95 |
| 125 | MidCap SPDR Trust | MB | | 134.72 | 134.69 | −0.06 | 12.17 | 20.66 | 8.23 | 12.50 | 20.72 | 8.31 | 11.63 | 1.51 |
| 126 | Nasdaq 100 Trust | LG | | 40.46 | 40.41 | −0.03 | 1.55 | 18.74 | −6.85 | 1.49 | 18.85 | −6.86 | 15.09 | 1.09 |
| — | PowerShares Aero&Defense | ST | | 15.54 | 15.52 | 0.07 | — | — | — | — | — | — | — | — |
| — | PowerShares Biotech & Gen | SH | | 17.33 | 17.30 | 0.02 | — | — | — | — | — | — | — | — |
| — | PowerShares Div Achievers | LV | | 15.38 | 15.04 | −0.66 | — | — | — | — | — | — | — | — |
| — | PowerShares Dyn Building | LB | | 16.22 | 16.23 | 0.23 | — | — | — | — | — | — | — | — |
| — | PowerShares Dyn Energy | SN | | 16.76 | 16.76 | 0.12 | — | — | — | — | — | — | — | — |
| — | PowerShares Dyn Insurance | SF | | 16.35 | 16.35 | −0.76 | — | — | — | — | — | — | — | — |
| — | PowerShares Dyn Lg Growth | LG | | 15.86 | 15.86 | 0.04 | — | — | — | — | — | — | — | — |
| — | PowerShares Dyn Lg Value | LV | | 16.11 | 16.12 | 0.12 | — | — | — | — | — | — | — | — |
| — | PowerShares Dyn Mid Value | MV | | 16.46 | 16.45 | −0.01 | — | — | — | — | — | — | — | — |
| — | PowerShares Dyn MidGrowth | MG | | 17.49 | 17.50 | 0.01 | — | — | — | — | — | — | — | — |
| — | PowerShares Dyn Oil & Gas | SN | | 18.06 | 18.10 | 0.27 | — | — | — | — | — | — | — | — |
| — | PowerShares Dyn Retail | LB | | 16.13 | 16.13 | −0.02 | — | — | — | — | — | — | — | — |
| — | PowerShares Dyn Sm Growth | SG | | 16.75 | 16.77 | −0.01 | — | — | — | — | — | — | — | — |
| — | PowerShares Dyn Sm Value | SV | | 15.50 | 15.51 | 0.03 | — | — | — | — | — | — | — | — |
| — | PowerShares Dyn Utilities | SU | | 15.62 | 15.61 | 0.21 | — | — | — | — | — | — | — | — |
| 128 | PowerShares Dynam Mkt | LB | | 45.31 | 45.32 | 0.12 | 13.12 | — | — | 12.76 | — | — | — | — |
| 127 | PowerShares Dynam OTC | MG | | 49.20 | 49.20 | −0.01 | 9.76 | — | — | 9.56 | — | — | — | — |
| — | PowerShares Food & Bevera | LB | | 14.38 | 14.37 | 0.13 | — | — | — | — | — | — | — | — |
| 129 | PowerShares Halter USX | PJ | | 13.85 | 13.87 | 0.14 | −3.29 | — | — | −3.29 | — | — | — | — |
| — | PowerShares High Gr Div | LV | | 15.25 | 15.25 | 0.08 | — | — | — | — | — | — | — | — |
| 130 | PowerShares HY Div Achiev | MV | | 14.95 | 14.93 | 0.05 | 1.13 | — | — | 0.99 | — | — | — | — |
| — | PowerShares Intl Div Ach | FV | | 15.04 | 15.38 | 0.87 | — | — | — | — | — | — | — | — |
| — | PowerShares Leisure & Ent | LB | | 15.21 | 15.21 | −0.09 | — | — | — | — | — | — | — | — |
| — | PowerShares Lux Nanotech | ST | | 16.32 | 16.40 | 0.24 | — | — | — | — | — | — | — | — |
| — | PowerShares Media | SC | | 14.33 | 14.33 | −0.04 | — | — | — | — | — | — | — | — |
| — | PowerShares Networking | ST | | 15.60 | 15.63 | 0.06 | — | — | — | — | — | — | — | — |
| — | PowerShares Pharma | SH | | 16.49 | 16.49 | 0.04 | — | — | — | — | — | — | — | — |
| — | PowerShares Semiconductor | ST | | 16.43 | 16.43 | 0.19 | — | — | — | — | — | — | — | — |
| — | PowerShares Software | ST | | 17.36 | 17.41 | 0.04 | — | — | — | — | — | — | — | — |
| — | PowerShares WilderHill | SN | | 16.17 | 16.19 | 0.00 | — | — | — | — | — | — | — | — |
| 131 | PowerShares Zacks MicroCp | SB | | 15.16 | 15.15 | −0.01 | — | — | — | — | — | — | — | — |
| — | Rydex Russell Top 50 | LB | | 93.18 | 93.13 | 0.01 | — | — | — | — | — | — | — | — |

| Top 3 Sectors | Avg. Mkt. Cap. ($mil) | P/E Ratio | P/B Ratio | Expense Ratio % | Tax-Cost Ratio | 52-week High/Low | Total Assets ($) | Exchange | Ticker | Phone | Web Address |
|---|---|---|---|---|---|---|---|---|---|---|---|
| | 1025.10 | 17.45 | 1.92 | 0.25 | 0.37 | 66.29–55.69 | 1,606,000,000 | NYSE | IJS | 800-474-2737 | www.ishares.com |
| | 84854.35 | 12.98 | 3.03 | 0.65 | 0.46 | 102.67–70.61 | 601,000,000 | AMEX | IXC | 800-474-2737 | www.ishares.com |
| | 43340.10 | 14.61 | 2.36 | 0.65 | 0.60 | 75.68–62.64 | 110,000,000 | AMEX | IXG | 800-474-2737 | www.ishares.com |
| | 56890.64 | 23.72 | 4.38 | 0.65 | 0.25 | 54.01–46.80 | 457,000,000 | AMEX | IXJ | 800-474-2737 | www.ishares.com |
| | 43627.39 | 23.25 | 3.87 | 0.66 | 0.15 | 56.30–44.86 | 61,000,000 | AMEX | IXN | 800-474-2737 | www.ishares.com |
| | 53178.28 | 14.90 | 2.69 | 0.65 | 0.60 | 52.66–48.32 | 56,000,000 | AMEX | IXP | 800-474-2737 | www.ishares.com |
| | 21382.35 | 16.19 | 4.01 | 0.50 | 0.44 | 131.91–74.32 | 1,230,000,000 | AMEX | ILF | 800-474-2737 | www.ishares.com |
| | 3457.27 | 19.99 | 2.61 | 0.20 | 0.37 | 76.24–62.72 | 3,389,000,000 | NYSE | IJH | 800-474-2737 | www.ishares.com |
| | 1189.22 | 18.35 | 2.34 | 0.20 | 0.28 | 59.82–49.73 | 3,862,000,000 | NYSE | IJR | 800-474-2737 | www.ishares.com |
| | 26337.42 | 21.80 | 2.30 | 0.50 | 0.11 | 121.28–85.26 | 208,000,000 | AMEX | ITF | 800-474-2737 | www.ishares.com |
| | 27172.87 | 16.08 | 4.42 | 0.57 | 0.55 | 37.78–33.43 | 78,000,000 | NYSE | EWP | 800-474-2737 | www.ishares.com |
| | 13374.88 | 17.68 | 3.48 | 0.58 | 0.48 | 23.72–19.70 | 66,000,000 | NYSE | EWD | 800-474-2737 | www.ishares.com |
| | 37508.59 | 17.61 | 4.19 | 0.57 | 0.17 | 20.32–16.34 | 125,000,000 | NYSE | EWL | 800-474-2737 | www.ishares.com |
| | 6678.60 | 13.60 | 1.93 | 1.03 | 0.23 | 13.11–10.55 | 1,054,000,000 | NYSE | EWT | 800-474-2737 | www.ishares.com |
| | 46249.51 | 14.29 | 3.62 | 0.57 | 0.93 | 19.45–17.41 | 514,000,000 | NYSE | EWU | 800-474-2737 | www.ishares.com |
| | 15244.33 | 14.88 | 2.56 | 0.26 | 0.72 | 31.93–26.22 | 953,000,000 | AMEX | XLB | 800-843-2639 | www.spdrindex.com |
| | 3249.83 | 19.26 | 2.48 | 0.25 | 0.31 | 137.70–114.87 | 8,942,000,000 | AMEX | MDY | 800-843-2639 | www.amex.com |
| | 25431.49 | 27.34 | 4.03 | 0.20 | 0.14 | 42.12–34.68 | 20,310,000,000 | NASDAQ | QQQQ | 800-843-2639 | www.nasdaq.com |
| | — | — | — | — | — | 15.76–14.54 | 61,000,000 | AMEX | PPA | 888-983-0903 | www.powershares.com |
| | 3358.02 | 28.29 | 4.17 | — | — | 17.87–14.66 | 165,000,000 | AMEX | PBE | 800-843-2639 | www.powershares.com |
| | 58237.87 | 16.34 | 2.96 | — | — | 15.89–14.19 | 56,000,000 | AMEX | PFM | 800-843-2639 | www.powershares.com |
| | — | — | — | — | — | 16.83–14.77 | 50,000,000 | AMEX | PKB | 800-843-2639 | www.powershares.com |
| | — | — | — | — | — | 17.65–15.23 | 50,000,000 | AMEX | PXE | 800-843-2639 | www.powershares.com |
| | — | — | — | — | — | 16.83–15.42 | 41,000,000 | AMEX | PIC | 800-843-2639 | www.powershares.com |
| | 43112.88 | 25.30 | 4.34 | 0.63 | — | 16.33–13.80 | 97,000,000 | AMEX | PWB | 800-843-2639 | www.powershares.com |
| | 44040.03 | 13.32 | 2.23 | 0.63 | — | 16.46–14.21 | 50,000,000 | AMEX | PWV | 800-843-2639 | www.powershares.com |
| | 6879.23 | 12.93 | 1.94 | 0.63 | — | 17.15–14.34 | 41,000,000 | AMEX | PWP | 800-843-2639 | www.powershares.com |
| | 6339.43 | 25.16 | 4.44 | 0.63 | — | 17.94–13.80 | 68,000,000 | AMEX | PWJ | 800-843-2639 | www.powershares.com |
| | — | — | — | — | — | 19.41–15.95 | 49,000,000 | AMEX | PXJ | 800-843-2639 | www.powershares.com |
| | — | — | — | — | — | 16.57–14.77 | 21,000,000 | AMEX | PMR | 800-843-2639 | www.powershares.com |
| | 1360.30 | 26.31 | 3.80 | 0.63 | — | 17.08–13.71 | 59,000,000 | AMEX | PWT | 800-843-2639 | www.powershares.com |
| | 1362.20 | 14.72 | 2.14 | 0.63 | — | 16.11–13.63 | 40,000,000 | AMEX | PWY | 800-843-2639 | www.powershares.com |
| | — | — | — | — | — | 16.12–15.11 | 36,000,000 | AMEX | PUI | 800-843-2639 | www.powershares.com |
| | 9720.74 | 15.86 | 2.85 | 0.60 | — | 46.44–38.67 | 691,000,000 | AMEX | PWC | 800-843-2639 | www.powershares.com |
| | 4360.98 | 23.41 | 3.76 | 0.60 | — | 50.57–41.84 | 187,000,000 | NASDAQ | PWO | 800-843-2639 | www.powershares.com |
| | 7922.90 | 14.95 | 2.74 | — | — | 15.23–13.94 | 23,000,000 | AMEX | PBJ | 800-843-2639 | www.powershares.com |
| | 5035.90 | 11.20 | 1.75 | 0.70 | — | 14.99–12.66 | 79,000,000 | AMEX | PGJ | 800-843-2639 | www.powershares.com |
| | 29818.35 | 17.16 | 2.91 | — | — | 15.61–14.29 | 32,000,000 | AMEX | PHJ | 800-843-2639 | www.powershares.com |
| | 5012.85 | 15.07 | 1.96 | 0.60 | — | 15.65–14.16 | 492,000,000 | AMEX | PEY | 800-843-2639 | www.powershares.com |
| | 19670.64 | 15.24 | 2.21 | — | — | 15.35–14.38 | 27,000,000 | AMEX | PID | 800-843-2639 | www.powershares.com |
| | 3629.44 | 20.33 | 2.43 | — | — | 15.45–13.47 | 26,000,000 | AMEX | PEJ | 800-843-2639 | www.powershares.com |
| | — | — | — | — | — | 17.55–14.80 | 36,000,000 | AMEX | PXN | 800-843-2639 | www.powershares.com |
| | 5120.92 | 19.53 | 2.75 | — | — | 15.11–13.61 | 24,000,000 | AMEX | PBS | 800-843-2639 | www.powershares.com |
| | 4195.84 | 23.58 | 3.08 | — | — | 16.17–14.40 | 25,000,000 | AMEX | PXQ | 800-843-2639 | www.powershares.com |
| | 15693.05 | 24.84 | 3.57 | — | — | 16.87–14.70 | 35,000,000 | AMEX | PJP | 800-843-2639 | www.powershares.com |
| | 4922.86 | 29.32 | 3.08 | — | — | 17.66–14.35 | 66,000,000 | AMEX | PSI | 800-843-2639 | www.powershares.com |
| | 3962.83 | 28.11 | 4.65 | — | — | 17.88–14.75 | 35,000,000 | AMEX | PSJ | 800-843-2639 | www.powershares.com |
| | 672.30 | — | 2.57 | 0.70 | — | 18.27–12.81 | 188,000,000 | AMEX | PBW | 800-843-2639 | www.powershares.com |
| | 289.88 | 15.72 | 1.64 | — | — | 15.50–13.93 | 103,000,000 | AMEX | PZI | 800-843-2639 | www.powershares.com |
| | — | — | — | — | — | 95.94–89.39 | 140,000,000 | AMEX | XLG | 800-820-0888 | www.rydex.com |

# Performance Summary
## Morningstar's ETF Universe

| Page | Name | Cat | Style Box | NAV ($) | Market Price ($) | 2005 Avg. Prem. Discount% | NAV Return% through 12-30-05 1Yr | Annualized 3Yr | 5Yr | Mkt Price Rtn% through 12-30-05 1Yr | Annualized 3Yr | 5Yr | Risk Statistics Standard Deviation | Sharpe Ratio |
|---|---|---|---|---|---|---|---|---|---|---|---|---|---|---|
| 132 | Rydex S&P Equal Weight | LB | ▦ | 166.21 | 165.93 | −0.03 | 7.65 | — | — | 7.41 | — | — | — | — |
| — | SPDR Dividend ETF | LV | — | 54.09 | 54.15 | 0.07 | — | — | — | — | — | — | — | — |
| — | SPDR O-Strip | LB | — | 52.45 | 52.46 | 0.15 | −1.85 | — | — | −2.16 | — | — | — | — |
| 133 | SPDR Trust Series 1 | LB | ▦ | 124.70 | 124.51 | −0.01 | 4.79 | 14.22 | 0.45 | 4.82 | 14.15 | 0.58 | 9.14 | 1.29 |
| 138 | streetTRACK DJ Small Gr | SG | ▦ | 82.01 | 82.07 | 0.01 | 8.75 | 22.84 | 0.62 | 8.79 | 22.66 | 0.64 | 13.80 | 1.43 |
| 135 | streetTRACK Global T | WS | ▦ | 64.89 | 65.01 | 0.17 | 2.82 | 11.30 | −1.64 | 2.97 | 11.38 | −1.61 | 8.71 | 1.05 |
| — | streetTRACKS DJ Euro 50 | ES | ▦ | 42.20 | 42.38 | 0.00 | 7.66 | 21.65 | — | 8.45 | 22.03 | — | 16.40 | 1.16 |
| — | streetTRACKS DJ Large Cap | LB | — | 57.47 | 57.93 | 0.86 | — | — | — | — | — | — | — | — |
| 136 | streetTRACKS DJ Lg Growth | LG | ▦ | 49.44 | 49.42 | 0.01 | 3.00 | 11.77 | −6.63 | 2.69 | 11.53 | −6.94 | 9.53 | 1.01 |
| 137 | streetTracks DJ Lg Value | LV | ▦ | 70.13 | 70.13 | −0.02 | 5.43 | 14.40 | 2.94 | 5.32 | 14.29 | 2.95 | 9.44 | 1.27 |
| — | streetTRACKS DJ Mid Cap | MB | — | 51.23 | 51.50 | 0.28 | — | — | — | — | — | — | — | — |
| — | streetTRACKS DJ Mid Value | MV | — | 52.47 | 52.37 | 0.10 | — | — | — | — | — | — | — | — |
| — | streetTRACKS DJ MidGrowth | MG | — | 56.28 | 56.31 | 0.09 | — | — | — | — | — | — | — | — |
| 139 | streetTRACKS DJ Small Val | SV | ▦ | 60.58 | 60.50 | −0.13 | 2.29 | 19.97 | 13.57 | 1.93 | 19.88 | 13.80 | 14.71 | 1.18 |
| 134 | streetTRACKS DJ STOXX 50 | ES | ▦ | 39.34 | 39.47 | 0.21 | 7.38 | 18.81 | — | 7.97 | 20.03 | — | 13.22 | 1.23 |
| — | streetTRACKS Gold Shares | SP | — | 51.07 | 51.58 | −0.04 | 16.65 | — | — | 17.76 | — | — | — | — |
| — | streetTRACKS MS Tech | ST | ▦ | 51.95 | 51.90 | −0.06 | 2.86 | 21.85 | −4.99 | 2.76 | 21.99 | −5.01 | 19.08 | 1.03 |
| 140 | streetTRACKS Total Market | LB | ▦ | 90.02 | 90.16 | −0.01 | 6.78 | 14.16 | 1.03 | 6.54 | 14.36 | 1.06 | 8.92 | 1.31 |
| 141 | streetTRACKS WR REIT | SR | ▦ | 67.52 | 67.50 | 0.09 | 14.51 | 27.26 | — | 14.50 | 27.14 | — | 15.58 | 1.52 |
| 142 | Technology SPDR | ST | ▦ | 20.92 | 20.90 | −0.06 | −0.26 | 13.45 | −7.08 | −0.31 | 13.46 | −7.09 | 14.04 | 0.83 |
| 143 | Utilities SPDR | SU | ▦ | 31.44 | 31.39 | −0.02 | 16.53 | 22.00 | 2.51 | 16.37 | 22.06 | 2.42 | 12.42 | 1.52 |
| 144 | Vanguard Cons Disc VIPERs | LG | ▦ | 52.49 | 52.59 | −0.11 | −4.22 | — | — | −4.10 | — | — | — | — |
| 145 | Vanguard Cons Stap VIPERs | LB | ▦ | 55.94 | 55.93 | 0.01 | 3.95 | — | — | 3.76 | — | — | — | — |
| 146 | Vanguard EmergMkts VIPERs | EM | ▦ | 60.40 | 60.88 | 0.53 | — | — | — | — | — | — | — | — |
| 147 | Vanguard Energy VIPERs | SN | ▦ | 72.16 | 72.19 | 0.01 | 39.05 | — | — | 39.05 | — | — | — | — |
| 148 | Vanguard Euro Stk VIPERs | ES | ▦ | 52.05 | 52.60 | 0.54 | — | — | — | — | — | — | — | — |
| 149 | Vanguard ExMkt VIPERs | MB | ▦ | 90.40 | 90.47 | 0.01 | 10.48 | 23.49 | — | 10.46 | 23.40 | — | 12.72 | 1.58 |
| 150 | Vanguard Financial VIPERs | SF | ▦ | 55.95 | 56.01 | −0.02 | 5.53 | — | — | 5.53 | — | — | — | — |
| 151 | Vanguard Growth VIPERs | LG | ▦ | 53.52 | 53.50 | 0.14 | 5.20 | — | — | 5.02 | — | — | — | — |
| 152 | Vanguard HealthCar VIPERs | SH | ▦ | 54.00 | 54.02 | 0.06 | 8.24 | — | — | 8.20 | — | — | — | — |
| — | Vanguard Indstrls VIPERs | LB | ▦ | 57.39 | 57.46 | −0.06 | 5.31 | — | — | 5.48 | — | — | — | — |
| 153 | Vanguard InfoTech VIPERs | ST | ▦ | 48.31 | 48.38 | 0.00 | 2.89 | — | — | 2.99 | — | — | — | — |
| 154 | Vanguard Large Cap VIPERs | LB | ▦ | 55.40 | 55.49 | 0.02 | 6.26 | — | — | 6.03 | — | — | — | — |
| — | Vanguard Materials VIPERs | SN | ▦ | 60.03 | 59.94 | 0.03 | 3.71 | — | — | 3.42 | — | — | — | — |
| 155 | Vanguard Mid Cap VIPERs | MB | ▦ | 64.61 | 64.61 | 0.04 | 14.03 | — | — | 13.97 | — | — | — | — |
| 156 | Vanguard Pacif Stk VIPERs | JS | ▦ | 60.03 | 60.89 | 0.81 | — | — | — | — | — | — | — | — |
| 157 | Vanguard REIT Index VIPER | SR | ▦ | 59.59 | 59.56 | 0.02 | 12.00 | — | — | 11.94 | — | — | — | — |
| 160 | Vanguard Sm Cap Gr VIPERs | SG | ▦ | 58.47 | 58.40 | −0.06 | 8.77 | — | — | 8.66 | — | — | — | — |
| 159 | Vanguard Sm Cp Val VIPER | SV | ▦ | 60.76 | 60.69 | −0.14 | 6.20 | — | — | 6.09 | — | — | — | — |
| 158 | Vanguard Small Cap VIPERs | SB | ▦ | 59.59 | 59.55 | −0.08 | 7.53 | — | — | 7.25 | — | — | — | — |
| 161 | Vanguard TelcomSrv VIPERs | SC | ▦ | 54.45 | 54.46 | −0.07 | 1.92 | — | — | 2.00 | — | — | — | — |
| 162 | Vanguard TSM VIPERs | LB | ▦ | 123.25 | 123.33 | 0.04 | 6.10 | 16.22 | — | 6.31 | 16.22 | — | 9.73 | 1.40 |
| 163 | Vanguard Utilities VIPERs | SU | ▦ | 65.15 | 65.14 | −0.01 | 14.08 | — | — | 13.87 | — | — | — | — |
| 164 | Vanguard Value VIPERs | LV | ▦ | 57.14 | 57.17 | 0.08 | 7.19 | — | — | 7.22 | — | — | — | — |

## Fund Categories

| | | | | | |
|---|---|---|---|---|---|
| CI | Intermediate-Term Bond | GI | Intermediate-Term Government Bond | LV | Large-Cap Value |
| CL | Long-Term Bond | GL | Long-Term Government Bond | MB | Mid-Cap Blend |
| CS | Short-Term Bond | GS | Short-Term Government Bond | MG | Mid-Cap Growth |
| CV | Convertible Bond | HY | High-Yield Bond | MU | Multisector Bond |
| DH | Domestic Hybrid | IB | International Bond | MV | Mid-Cap Value |
| DP | Diversified Pacific Stock | IH | International Hybrid | PJ | Pacific ex-Japan Stock |
| EB | Emerging Markets Bond | JS | Japan Stock | SB | Small-Cap Blend |
| EM | Diversified Emerging Markets | LB | Large-Cap Blend | SC | Specialty–Communications |
| ES | Europe Stock | LG | Large-Cap Growth | SF | Specialty–Financials |
| FS | Foreign Stock | LS | Latin America Stock | SG | Small-Cap Growth |

| | |
|---|---|
| SH | Specialty–Health |
| SP | Specialty–Precious Metals |
| SN | Specialty–Natural Resources |
| SR | Specialty–Real Estate |
| SS | Specialty–Unaligned |
| ST | Specialty–Technology |
| SU | Specialty–Utilities |
| SV | Small-Cap Value |
| UB | Ultrashort Bond |
| WS | World Stock |

# Performance Summary
## Morningstar's ETF Universe

| Portfolio Top 3 Sectors | Avg. Mkt. Cap. ($mil) | P/E Ratio | P/B Ratio | Expense Ratio % | Tax-Cost Ratio | 52-week High/Low | Total Assets ($) | Exchange | Ticker | Phone | Web Address |
|---|---|---|---|---|---|---|---|---|---|---|---|
| ■■■ | 11528.47 | 17.85 | 2.48 | 0.40 | — | 169.22–145.69 | 1,313,000,000 | AMEX | RSP | 800-820-0888 | www.rydex.com |
| — | — | — | — | — | — | 55.49–53.49 | 32,000,000 | AMEX | SDY | 866-787-2257 | www.advisors.ssga.com |
|  | — | — | — | — | — | 55.16–46.78 | 39,000,000 | AMEX | OOO | 877-521-4083 | www.advisors.ssga.com |
| ■■■ | 47703.46 | 17.28 | 2.81 | 0.11 | 0.61 | 128.48–113.78 | 58,530,000,000 | AMEX | SPY | 800-843-2639 | www.amex.com |
| ■■■ | 1443.03 | 22.05 | 3.15 | 0.26 | 0.13 | 85.27–69.95 | 70,000,000 | AMEX | DSG | 866-787-2257 | www.advisors.ssga.com |
| ■■■ | 150173.59 | 15.63 | 2.83 | 0.51 | 0.71 | 67.37–61.99 | 91,000,000 | AMEX | DGT | 866-787-2257 | www.advisors.ssga.com |
| ■■■ | 52779.91 | 14.13 | 2.99 | 0.32 | 0.83 | 42.81–38.03 | 120,000,000 | NYSE | FEZ | 866-787-2257 | www.advisors.ssga.com |
|  | — | — | — | — | — | 59.24–56.03 | 14,000,000 | AMEX | ELR | 866-787-2257 | www.advisors.ssga.com |
| ■■■ | 32275.78 | 21.86 | 3.79 | 0.21 | 0.30 | 50.98–44.06 | 143,000,000 | AMEX | ELG | 866-787-2257 | www.advisors.ssga.com |
| ■■■ | 48172.44 | 15.00 | 2.31 | 0.21 | 0.85 | 72.26–65.39 | 98,000,000 | AMEX | ELV | 866-787-2257 | www.advisors.ssga.com |
| — | — | — | — | — | — | 52.93–49.18 | 26,000,000 | AMEX | EMM | 866-787-2257 | www.advisors.ssga.com |
| — | — | — | — | — | — | 54.15–50.42 | 26,000,000 | AMEX | EMV | 866-787-2257 | www.advisors.ssga.com |
|  | — | — | — | — | — | 58.21–53.95 | 25,000,000 | AMEX | EMG | 866-787-2257 | www.advisors.ssga.com |
| ■■■ | 1419.60 | 15.77 | 1.87 | 0.26 | 1.28 | 64.24–53.63 | 97,000,000 | AMEX | DSV | 866-787-2257 | www.advisors.ssga.com |
| ■■■ | 86570.75 | 14.88 | 3.59 | 0.32 | 0.96 | 40.24–36.12 | 31,000,000 | NYSE | FEU | 866-787-2257 | www.advisors.ssga.com |
|  | — | — | — | — | — | 53.42–41.07 | 4,341,000,000 | NYSE | GLD | 866-320-4053 | www.streettracksgoldshare |
| ■■■ | 32841.49 | 25.39 | 4.03 | 0.51 | 0.02 | 55.03–42.30 | 161,000,000 | AMEX | MTK | 866-787-2257 | www.advisors.ssga.com |
| ■■■ | 26615.09 | 18.00 | 2.75 | 0.21 | 0.58 | 92.83–81.25 | 104,000,000 | AMEX | TMW | 866-787-2257 | www.advisors.ssga.com |
| ■■ | 4608.16 | 32.84 | 2.53 | 0.26 | 1.89 | 71.11–56.86 | 604,000,000 | AMEX | RWR | 866-787-2257 | www.advisors.ssga.com |
| ■■■ | 55669.04 | 21.98 | 3.49 | 0.26 | 0.40 | 22.05–18.47 | 1,541,000,000 | AMEX | XLK | 800-843-2639 | www.spdrindex.com |
| ■ | 14825.12 | 16.07 | 2.07 | 0.26 | 1.20 | 33.92–27.03 | 1,752,000,000 | AMEX | XLU | 800-843-2639 | www.spdrindex.com |
| ■■■ | 12796.29 | 18.98 | 2.37 | 0.26 | — | 56.25–49.17 | 37,000,000 | AMEX | VCR | 866-499-8473 | www.vanguard.com |
| ■■■ | 32754.34 | 19.26 | 4.21 | 0.26 | — | 57.77–53.86 | 90,000,000 | AMEX | VDC | 866-499-8473 | www.vanguard.com |
| ■■■ | 7862.14 | 11.39 | 2.07 | 0.30 | — | 63.39–45.34 | 553,000,000 | AMEX | VWO | 866-499-8473 | www.vanguard.com |
| ■■■ | 40838.33 | 14.86 | 3.19 | 0.26 | — | 78.59–50.33 | 209,000,000 | AMEX | VDE | 866-499-8473 | www.vanguard.com |
| ■■■ | 37216.52 | 15.14 | 3.42 | 0.18 | — | 54.44–47.58 | 178,000,000 | AMEX | VGK | 866-499-8473 | www.vanguard.com |
| ■■■ | 2321.07 | 19.80 | 2.50 | 0.20 | 0.20 | 92.86–76.93 | 368,000,000 | AMEX | VXF | 866-499-8473 | www.vanguard.com |
| ■■■ | 24758.17 | 13.82 | 1.89 | 0.26 | — | 57.35–48.79 | 62,000,000 | AMEX | VFH | 866-499-8473 | www.vanguard.com |
| ■■■ | 36686.37 | 22.32 | 4.06 | 0.15 | — | 54.85–47.02 | 324,000,000 | AMEX | VUG | 866-499-8473 | www.vanguard.com |
| ■■■ | 30625.98 | 24.08 | 4.01 | 0.26 | — | 55.13–48.28 | 238,000,000 | AMEX | VHT | 866-499-8473 | www.vanguard.com |
| ■■■ | 21068.30 | 19.43 | 2.82 | 0.26 | — | 58.22–51.34 | 29,000,000 | AMEX | VIS | 866-499-8473 | www.vanguard.com |
| ■■■ | 30662.09 | 23.15 | 3.86 | 0.26 | — | 50.33–40.62 | 65,000,000 | AMEX | VGT | 866-499-8473 | www.vanguard.com |
| ■■■ | 39401.12 | 17.80 | 2.85 | 0.12 | — | 56.67–49.96 | 178,000,000 | AMEX | VV | 866-499-8473 | www.vanguard.com |
| ■■■ | 8694.06 | 14.39 | 2.43 | 0.26 | — | 63.40–53.03 | 54,000,000 | AMEX | VAW | 866-499-8473 | www.vanguard.com |
| ■■■ | 6129.60 | 19.12 | 2.67 | 0.18 | — | 66.18–54.39 | 1,044,000,000 | AMEX | VO | 866-499-8473 | www.vanguard.com |
| ■■■ | 14761.07 | 17.83 | 2.14 | 0.18 | — | 62.13–46.40 | 203,000,000 | AMEX | VPL | 866-499-8473 | www.vanguard.com |
| ■ | 4073.14 | 32.45 | 2.50 | — | — | 63.39–49.29 | 410,000,000 | AMEX | VNQ | 866-499-8473 | www.vanguard.com |
| ■■■ | 1466.14 | 22.75 | 3.33 | 0.22 | — | 60.08–48.65 | 206,000,000 | AMEX | VBK | 866-499-8473 | www.vanguard.com |
| ■■■ | 1441.18 | 15.88 | 1.81 | 0.22 | — | 63.43–53.74 | 188,000,000 | AMEX | VBR | 866-499-8473 | www.vanguard.com |
| ■■■ | 1453.35 | 18.58 | 2.34 | 0.18 | — | 61.49–51.33 | 265,000,000 | AMEX | VB | 866-499-8473 | www.vanguard.com |
| ■■■ | 12618.67 | 16.78 | 2.33 | 0.26 | — | 58.15–49.85 | 22,000,000 | AMEX | VOX | 866-499-8473 | www.vanguard.com |
| ■■■ | 24825.55 | 17.90 | 2.77 | 0.13 | 0.29 | 126.19–110.86 | 5,612,000,000 | AMEX | VTI | 866-499-8473 | www.vanguard.com |
| ■■ | 9989.51 | 18.91 | 2.15 | 0.26 | — | 70.70–56.62 | 105,000,000 | AMEX | VPU | 866-499-8473 | www.vanguard.com |
| ■■■ | 42052.56 | 14.83 | 2.20 | 0.15 | — | 58.42–52.45 | 600,000,000 | AMEX | VTV | 866-499-8473 | www.vanguard.com |

**Equity Style Box**

Val Blnd Grth / Lrg Mid Sm

**Sectors**

- Information
- Software
- Hardware
- Media
- Telecom
- Service
- Healthcare
- Consumer Svs
- Business Svs
- Financial
- Manufacturing
- Consumer Goods
- Industrial Materials
- Energy
- Utilities

# Performance Summary

Indexes

| Index | 2005 Total Return % | | | | | Annualized Total Return% | | | Annual Total Return % | | | | | | | | |
|---|---|---|---|---|---|---|---|---|---|---|---|---|---|---|---|---|---|
| | 1st Qrt | 2nd Qrt | 3rd Qrt | 4th Qrt | 2005 | 3 Yr | 5 Yr | 10 Yr | 2004 | 2003 | 2002 | 2001 | 2000 | 1999 | 1998 | 1997 | 1996 |
| **Domestic Stock** | | | | | | | | | | | | | | | | | |
| Barra Large Cap Growth | 0.02 | 2.69 | −4.78 | 8.51 | 7.94 | 9.12 | −2.38 | 8.46 | 25.66 | −23.59 | −12.72 | −22.08 | 28.25 | 42.16 | 36.53 | 23.97 | 38.13 |
| Barra Large Cap Value | 3.35 | 0.79 | 1.04 | 9.93 | 8.97 | 15.12 | 3.41 | 9.65 | 31.79 | −20.86 | −11.71 | 6.09 | 12.72 | 14.67 | 29.99 | 21.99 | 37.00 |
| Barra MidCap Growth | 4.56 | 0.77 | −3.42 | 12.04 | 17.54 | 17.07 | 5.60 | 13.64 | 30.95 | −19.17 | −7.97 | 9.14 | 28.73 | 34.86 | 30.27 | 18.41 | 27.30 |
| Barra MidCap Value | 5.53 | 1.20 | −0.78 | 12.24 | 15.31 | 21.22 | 14.45 | 14.72 | 40.18 | −10.11 | 7.15 | 27.84 | 2.32 | 4.67 | 34.39 | 19.40 | 34.04 |
| Barra SmallCap Growth | 5.72 | 4.42 | −3.04 | 13.99 | 12.82 | 20.92 | 10.97 | 9.92 | 37.32 | −15.36 | −1.19 | 0.57 | 19.57 | 2.29 | 15.67 | 16.09 | 29.07 |
| Barra SmallCap Value | 6.65 | 2.87 | 0.26 | 12.04 | 9.38 | 21.75 | 15.40 | 14.11 | 40.03 | −14.47 | 13.10 | 20.88 | 3.05 | −5.06 | 36.46 | 26.10 | 30.69 |
| DJ Wilshire 4500 | −3.27 | 5.65 | 4.90 | 2.87 | 10.27 | 23.40 | 6.97 | 9.85 | 18.57 | 43.72 | −17.81 | −9.30 | −15.77 | 35.49 | 8.63 | 25.69 | 17.25 |
| DJ Wilshire 5000 | −2.39 | 2.47 | 3.89 | 2.32 | 6.32 | 16.37 | 2.14 | 9.16 | 12.63 | 31.63 | −20.85 | −10.89 | −10.93 | 23.56 | 23.43 | 31.29 | 21.20 |
| Dow Jones Financials Sector | −6.46 | 5.16 | 0.74 | 7.43 | 6.45 | 16.87 | 5.54 | 13.72 | 13.39 | 32.23 | −12.35 | −6.38 | 26.94 | 1.52 | 7.51 | 48.94 | 33.84 |
| Dow Jones Health Care Sector | −0.48 | 5.02 | 2.00 | 1.61 | 8.32 | 10.59 | −1.31 | 10.79 | 4.55 | 19.43 | −20.81 | −12.61 | 37.47 | −4.03 | 39.09 | 36.88 | 18.55 |
| Dow Jones Industrial Average TR | −2.06 | −1.62 | 3.44 | 2.06 | 1.72 | 11.18 | 2.01 | 9.76 | 5.31 | 28.28 | −15.01 | −5.44 | −4.85 | 27.21 | 18.13 | 24.87 | 28.71 |
| Dow Jones Large Growth | −4.94 | 1.22 | 3.52 | 2.97 | 2.56 | 11.80 | −6.55 | 4.94 | 5.20 | 29.54 | −31.58 | −25.46 | −32.40 | 36.38 | 45.78 | 34.15 | 26.06 |
| Dow Jones Large Value | −0.77 | 1.24 | 3.26 | 1.34 | 5.13 | 14.49 | 3.07 | 9.06 | 13.39 | 25.89 | −17.42 | −6.11 | 10.34 | 1.35 | 15.40 | 33.04 | 19.20 |
| Dow Jones Small Growth | −2.77 | 3.48 | 5.39 | 2.58 | 8.78 | 23.09 | 0.84 | 8.23 | 15.47 | 48.48 | −38.89 | −8.50 | −14.91 | 61.48 | 6.44 | 21.27 | 19.26 |
| Dow Jones Small Value | −4.90 | 4.12 | 5.87 | 1.76 | 6.68 | 21.96 | 14.84 | 14.06 | 18.37 | 43.67 | −2.39 | 12.79 | 23.98 | −5.06 | −6.51 | 32.60 | 27.89 |
| Dow Jones Telecommunications Sector | −7.04 | 3.62 | −0.45 | 0.12 | −4.00 | 6.94 | −6.93 | 0.54 | 18.70 | 7.33 | −34.55 | −12.77 | −40.27 | 18.41 | 51.82 | 40.64 | 0.11 |
| Dow Jones Transportation Average TR | −1.91 | −5.88 | 7.52 | 12.47 | 11.65 | 23.43 | 8.59 | 9.15 | 27.73 | 31.84 | −11.48 | −9.30 | 0.40 | −4.52 | −2.45 | 48.07 | 14.84 |
| Dow Jones Utilities Sector | 4.77 | 9.43 | 7.04 | −6.01 | 15.35 | 21.36 | 0.78 | 7.89 | 24.04 | 24.91 | −21.19 | −26.18 | 56.07 | −13.19 | 13.32 | 28.76 | 3.95 |
| Goldman Sachs Natural Resources | 12.24 | 3.71 | 20.75 | −2.90 | 36.48 | 31.58 | 10.77 | — | 24.57 | 34.01 | −13.26 | −15.59 | 15.81 | 27.22 | −24.67 | 16.94 | — |
| MSCI US Mid Cap 450 Index | −0.36 | 4.29 | 6.41 | 3.05 | 13.94 | 24.06 | 8.35 | 12.79 | 20.52 | 39.05 | −16.46 | −6.38 | −1.85 | 34.32 | 9.26 | 28.58 | 20.47 |
| MSCI US Prime Market 750 Index | −1.92 | 1.92 | 3.85 | 2.35 | 6.26 | 15.29 | 0.84 | 9.21 | 11.41 | 29.45 | −21.93 | −12.84 | −11.89 | 24.56 | 28.90 | 33.38 | 22.64 |
| MSCI US Prime Market Value Index | −0.35 | 1.74 | 4.11 | 1.62 | 7.26 | 17.11 | 5.22 | 10.83 | 15.44 | 29.72 | −16.95 | −3.33 | 9.02 | 6.25 | 14.63 | 33.25 | 22.51 |
| MSCI US Prime Market Growth Index | −3.48 | 2.12 | 3.60 | 3.06 | 5.25 | 13.45 | −3.74 | 7.30 | 7.38 | 29.20 | −27.30 | −22.14 | −27.79 | 43.96 | 43.62 | 33.57 | 22.74 |
| MSCI US Small Cap Growth Index | −4.20 | 4.38 | 6.46 | 2.11 | 8.71 | 23.82 | 4.69 | 9.15 | 16.13 | 50.37 | −29.31 | −6.29 | −8.25 | 49.55 | 6.63 | 14.56 | 13.88 |
| MSCI US Small Cap Value Index | −3.25 | 5.25 | 4.05 | 0.30 | 6.28 | 23.81 | 14.89 | 14.13 | 23.72 | 44.34 | −6.63 | 12.95 | 21.22 | −2.17 | −5.12 | 34.73 | 23.52 |
| MSCI US Small Cap 1750 Index | −3.73 | 4.82 | 5.25 | 1.21 | 7.48 | 23.88 | 9.88 | 12.19 | 20.01 | 47.38 | −18.37 | 3.22 | 8.67 | 21.94 | 0.58 | 24.34 | 19.02 |
| Morningstar Large Cap TR | −2.08 | 1.38 | 3.40 | 2.16 | 4.87 | 13.43 | −1.06 | 8.29 | 9.54 | 27.04 | −23.47 | −15.10 | −11.38 | 21.05 | 30.74 | 34.78 | 23.71 |
| Morningstar Large Core TR | −1.93 | −0.10 | 2.91 | 2.97 | 3.82 | 13.86 | −0.75 | — | 13.99 | 24.71 | −23.82 | −14.35 | 4.24 | 17.81 | 23.18 | — | — |
| Morningstar Large Growth TR | −5.44 | 2.77 | 3.46 | 2.87 | 3.43 | 10.63 | −8.48 | — | 0.19 | 30.65 | −33.15 | −29.07 | −33.51 | 42.59 | 51.23 | — | — |
| Morningstar Large Value TR | 0.43 | 1.87 | 3.85 | 0.75 | 7.05 | 15.52 | 4.82 | — | 14.05 | 26.26 | −15.05 | −3.38 | 5.66 | 0.57 | 17.85 | — | — |
| Morningstar Mid Cap TR | −1.14 | 4.57 | 6.04 | 2.80 | 12.70 | 23.11 | 7.84 | 10.81 | 19.66 | 38.38 | −18.06 | −4.63 | 6.94 | 15.55 | 6.01 | 23.65 | 18.15 |
| Morningstar Mid Core TR | −2.38 | 3.79 | 6.13 | 2.35 | 10.05 | 22.03 | 11.03 | — | 19.05 | 38.68 | −12.42 | 6.05 | 14.77 | 1.89 | 2.87 | — | — |
| Morningstar Mid Growth TR | −1.51 | 4.25 | 8.34 | 4.52 | 16.27 | 23.41 | −0.11 | — | 15.45 | 40.02 | −32.54 | −21.59 | −11.10 | 52.46 | 9.49 | — | — |
| Morningstar Mid Value TR | 0.44 | 5.66 | 3.62 | 1.43 | 11.54 | 23.52 | 12.25 | — | 24.30 | 35.94 | −10.00 | 5.06 | 24.59 | −6.83 | 5.85 | — | — |
| Morningstar Small Growth TR | −6.44 | 4.48 | 5.99 | 2.08 | 5.77 | 22.36 | 0.14 | — | 13.48 | 52.65 | −36.87 | −12.92 | −12.10 | 46.80 | −6.55 | — | — |
| Morningstar Small Value TR | −4.18 | 5.12 | 3.77 | 0.56 | 5.12 | 24.74 | 16.13 | — | 24.03 | 48.87 | −8.24 | 18.58 | 18.65 | −5.19 | −3.67 | — | — |
| Morningstar Small Cap TR | −4.50 | 4.45 | 4.47 | 1.50 | 5.76 | 23.45 | 9.54 | 10.36 | 20.44 | 47.70 | −20.36 | 5.26 | 7.66 | 17.78 | −6.01 | 20.58 | 18.20 |
| Morningstar Small Core TR | −3.13 | 3.75 | 3.83 | 1.87 | 6.30 | 23.28 | 13.01 | — | 23.61 | 42.59 | −14.16 | 14.60 | 23.21 | 16.74 | −7.55 | — | — |
| Morningstar U.S. Core TR | −2.10 | 0.91 | 3.60 | 2.78 | 5.19 | 16.09 | 2.26 | — | 15.62 | 28.63 | −21.18 | −9.31 | 7.10 | 14.67 | 17.75 | — | — |
| Morningstar U.S. Growth TR | −4.58 | 3.22 | 4.74 | 3.15 | 6.41 | 14.21 | −6.02 | — | 4.37 | 34.12 | −33.20 | −26.32 | −28.45 | 44.51 | 39.76 | — | — |
| Morningstar U.S. Market TR | −2.06 | 2.26 | 4.02 | 2.24 | 6.52 | 16.09 | 1.42 | 9.08 | 12.35 | 30.73 | −22.17 | −11.88 | −7.02 | 19.79 | 23.86 | 31.78 | 22.23 |
| Morningstar U.S. Value TR | 0.12 | 2.85 | 3.80 | 0.87 | 7.82 | 17.80 | 6.99 | — | 16.85 | 29.75 | −13.68 | −0.68 | 10.06 | −1.27 | 14.13 | — | — |
| NASDAQ Composite | −8.10 | 2.89 | 4.61 | 2.49 | 1.37 | 18.20 | −2.25 | 7.68 | 8.59 | 50.01 | −31.53 | −21.05 | −39.29 | 85.59 | 39.63 | 21.64 | 22.71 |
| NYSE Composite | −1.14 | 0.70 | 5.75 | 1.58 | 6.95 | 15.75 | 2.23 | 8.33 | 12.16 | 29.28 | −19.83 | −10.21 | 1.01 | 9.15 | 16.55 | 30.31 | 19.06 |
| Russell 1000 | −1.91 | 2.05 | 3.95 | 2.12 | 6.27 | 15.42 | 1.07 | 9.29 | 11.40 | 29.89 | −21.65 | −12.45 | −7.79 | 20.91 | 27.02 | 32.85 | 22.45 |
| Russell 1000 Growth | −4.09 | 2.46 | 4.01 | 2.98 | 5.26 | 13.23 | −3.58 | 6.73 | 6.30 | 29.75 | −27.88 | −20.42 | −22.42 | 33.16 | 38.71 | 30.49 | 23.12 |
| Russell 1000 Value | 0.09 | 1.67 | 3.88 | 1.27 | 7.05 | 17.49 | 5.28 | 10.94 | 16.49 | 30.03 | −15.52 | −5.59 | 7.01 | 7.35 | 15.63 | 35.18 | 21.64 |
| Russell 2000 | −5.34 | 4.32 | 4.69 | 1.13 | 4.55 | 22.13 | 8.22 | 9.26 | 18.33 | 47.25 | −20.48 | 2.49 | −3.02 | 21.26 | −2.55 | 22.36 | 16.49 |
| Russell 2000 Growth | −6.83 | 3.48 | 6.32 | 1.61 | 4.15 | 20.93 | 2.28 | 4.69 | 14.31 | 48.54 | −30.26 | −9.23 | −22.43 | 43.09 | 1.23 | 12.95 | 11.26 |
| Russell 2000 Value | −3.98 | 5.08 | 3.09 | 0.66 | 4.71 | 23.18 | 13.55 | 13.08 | 22.25 | 46.03 | −11.43 | 14.02 | 22.83 | −1.49 | −6.45 | 31.78 | 21.37 |

# Performance Summary

**Indexes**

| Index | 2005 Total Return % | | | | | Annualized Total Return% | | | Annual Total Return % | | | | | | | | |
|---|---|---|---|---|---|---|---|---|---|---|---|---|---|---|---|---|---|
| | 1st Qrt | 2nd Qrt | 3rd Qrt | 4th Qrt | 2005 | 3 Yr | 5 Yr | 10 Yr | 2004 | 2003 | 2002 | 2001 | 2000 | 1999 | 1998 | 1997 | 1996 |
| Russell 3000 | −2.20 | 2.24 | 4.01 | 2.04 | 6.12 | 15.90 | 1.58 | 9.20 | 11.95 | 31.06 | −21.54 | −11.46 | −7.46 | 20.90 | 24.14 | 31.78 | 21.82 |
| Russell Midcap | −0.25 | 4.18 | 5.92 | 2.35 | 12.65 | 23.79 | 8.45 | 12.49 | 20.22 | 40.06 | −16.19 | −5.62 | 8.25 | 18.23 | 10.09 | 29.01 | 19.00 |
| Russell Midcap Growth | −1.67 | 3.43 | 6.55 | 3.44 | 12.10 | 22.70 | 1.38 | 9.27 | 15.48 | 42.71 | −27.41 | −20.15 | −11.75 | 51.29 | 17.86 | 22.54 | 17.48 |
| Russell Midcap Value | 0.78 | 4.70 | 5.35 | 1.34 | 12.65 | 24.38 | 12.21 | 13.65 | 23.71 | 38.07 | −9.64 | 2.33 | 19.18 | −0.11 | 5.08 | 34.37 | 20.26 |
| Standard & Poor's 100 | −1.84 | 0.02 | 2.07 | 1.13 | 1.35 | 10.84 | −1.89 | 8.66 | 6.43 | 26.24 | −22.58 | −13.80 | −12.55 | 32.78 | 33.21 | 30.01 | 25.53 |
| Standard & Poor's 500 | −2.15 | 1.37 | 3.60 | 2.08 | 4.91 | 14.38 | 0.54 | 9.07 | 10.87 | 28.67 | −22.09 | −11.88 | −9.10 | 21.04 | 28.58 | 33.35 | 22.95 |
| Standard & Poor's Midcap 400 | −0.40 | 4.26 | 4.88 | 3.34 | 12.55 | 21.13 | 8.59 | 14.35 | 16.47 | 35.59 | −14.53 | −0.60 | 17.49 | 14.72 | 19.11 | 32.25 | 19.18 |
| Standard & Poor's Smallcap 600 | −2.07 | 3.94 | 5.37 | 0.38 | 7.67 | 22.37 | 10.76 | 12.15 | 22.64 | 38.77 | −14.63 | 6.54 | 11.79 | 12.40 | −1.31 | 25.58 | 21.31 |
| **Bond** | | | | | | | | | | | | | | | | | |
| Lehman Brothers 1-3 Year Government | −0.25 | 1.20 | 0.09 | 0.69 | 1.73 | 1.60 | 3.83 | 4.89 | 1.07 | 2.01 | 6.01 | 8.53 | 8.17 | 2.97 | 6.97 | 6.65 | 5.08 |
| Lehman Brothers Aggregate Bond | −0.48 | 3.01 | −0.67 | 0.59 | 2.43 | 3.62 | 5.87 | 6.16 | 4.34 | 4.10 | 10.25 | 8.44 | 11.63 | −0.82 | 8.69 | 9.65 | 3.63 |
| Lehman Brothers Intermediate Gove Bond | −0.68 | 2.31 | −0.52 | 0.59 | 1.68 | 2.10 | 4.82 | 5.50 | 2.33 | 2.29 | 9.64 | 8.42 | 10.47 | 0.49 | 8.49 | 7.72 | 4.06 |
| Lehman Brothers Intermediate Treasury | −0.75 | 2.32 | −0.61 | 0.63 | 1.56 | 1.89 | 4.57 | 5.35 | 2.02 | 2.10 | 9.28 | 8.16 | 10.26 | 0.41 | 8.62 | 7.69 | 3.98 |
| Lehman Brothers Long Term Govt Bond | 0.59 | 7.75 | −2.63 | 1.01 | 6.61 | 5.70 | 7.59 | 7.44 | 7.94 | 2.61 | 16.99 | 4.34 | 20.29 | −8.73 | 13.41 | 15.12 | −0.84 |
| Lehman Brothers Long Term Treasury Bond | 0.52 | 7.70 | −2.67 | 1.07 | 6.50 | 5.54 | 7.43 | 7.36 | 7.70 | 2.48 | 16.79 | 4.21 | 20.27 | −8.74 | 13.52 | 15.08 | −0.87 |
| **International** | | | | | | | | | | | | | | | | | |
| MSCI Argentina ID | 13.19 | 9.43 | 49.36 | −13.69 | 59.68 | 58.06 | 8.55 | 4.14 | 24.57 | 98.53 | −50.99 | −22.11 | −26.09 | 30.03 | −27.28 | 21.84 | 16.88 |
| MSCI Australia Ndtr_D | 1.81 | 3.72 | 10.62 | −0.69 | 16.02 | 31.23 | 17.81 | 10.27 | 30.34 | 49.46 | −1.34 | 1.76 | −10.05 | 17.66 | 6.05 | −10.44 | 16.49 |
| MSCI Austria Ndtr_D | 1.53 | 6.02 | 12.34 | 3.08 | 24.64 | 49.71 | 29.84 | 12.14 | 71.52 | 56.96 | 16.55 | −5.65 | −11.93 | −9.13 | 0.34 | 1.57 | 4.51 |
| MSCI BRAZIL ID | 4.20 | 5.08 | 36.19 | 0.56 | 49.96 | 58.34 | 15.52 | 10.50 | 30.49 | 102.85 | −33.78 | −21.75 | −14.17 | 61.64 | −44.11 | 23.46 | 37.89 |
| MSCI Belgium Ndtr_D | 2.12 | −4.22 | 7.01 | 4.19 | 9.05 | 28.42 | 9.93 | 9.34 | 43.53 | 35.33 | −14.97 | −10.88 | −16.81 | −14.26 | 67.66 | 13.55 | 12.03 |
| MSCI Canada Ndtr_D | 3.59 | 2.48 | 18.39 | 2.09 | 28.31 | 34.33 | 10.87 | 13.95 | 22.20 | 54.60 | −13.19 | −20.40 | 5.30 | 53.82 | −6.19 | 12.80 | 28.54 |
| MSCI EAFE NDTR_D | −0.17 | −1.01 | 10.38 | 4.08 | 13.54 | 23.68 | 4.56 | 5.84 | 20.25 | 38.59 | −15.94 | −21.42 | −14.19 | 27.03 | 19.93 | 1.78 | 6.05 |
| MSCI EM ID | 1.20 | 3.00 | 17.01 | 6.83 | 30.31 | 34.23 | 16.23 | 4.43 | 22.45 | 51.59 | −7.97 | −4.68 | −31.90 | 64.09 | −27.67 | −13.45 | 3.93 |
| MSCI EMU ID | −0.30 | −2.98 | 7.69 | 1.97 | 6.22 | 20.81 | 0.69 | 7.93 | 18.68 | 39.88 | −23.34 | −23.42 | −9.84 | 17.68 | 37.82 | 19.00 | 19.05 |
| MSCI France Ndtr_D | 1.84 | −1.38 | 8.70 | 0.65 | 9.88 | 22.22 | 2.25 | 10.25 | 18.48 | 40.22 | −21.18 | −22.34 | −4.32 | 29.31 | 41.48 | 11.94 | 21.20 |
| MSCI Germany Ndtr_D | −2.27 | −1.87 | 9.74 | 4.44 | 9.92 | 27.89 | 1.64 | 7.25 | 16.17 | 63.80 | −33.18 | −22.38 | −15.61 | 20.08 | 29.41 | 24.57 | 13.58 |
| MSCI Hong Kong Ndtr_D | −4.22 | 8.08 | 7.93 | −2.99 | 8.40 | 23.22 | 4.60 | 5.37 | 24.98 | 38.10 | −17.79 | −18.61 | −14.43 | 59.44 | −3.23 | −23.29 | 33.08 |
| MSCI Italy Ndtr_D | 0.51 | −4.84 | 6.80 | −0.25 | 1.90 | 23.00 | 4.84 | 11.23 | 32.49 | 37.83 | −7.33 | −26.53 | −1.27 | −0.13 | 52.11 | 35.48 | 12.59 |
| MSCI Japan NDTR_D | −2.37 | −3.56 | 19.18 | 11.85 | 25.52 | 25.50 | 4.60 | −0.16 | 15.86 | 35.91 | −10.28 | −29.39 | −28.17 | 61.53 | 5.05 | −23.67 | −15.50 |
| MSCI KOREA ID | 9.72 | 0.07 | 21.88 | 15.28 | 54.28 | 34.88 | 31.16 | 5.76 | 19.96 | 32.60 | 7.43 | 47.23 | −50.63 | 90.36 | 137.14 | −67.29 | −38.15 |
| MSCI MALYSI ID | −4.05 | 0.71 | 5.64 | −3.53 | −1.52 | 10.67 | 6.27 | −4.56 | 11.81 | 23.12 | −2.66 | 2.71 | −17.53 | 113.19 | −32.59 | −68.75 | 24.86 |
| MSCI MEXICO ID | −2.66 | 11.23 | 21.79 | 10.13 | 45.22 | 39.82 | 21.92 | 15.91 | 44.98 | 29.82 | −15.04 | 16.00 | −21.54 | 78.56 | −34.52 | 51.71 | 16.76 |
| MSCI Netherlands Ndtr_D | 2.43 | −0.06 | 2.88 | 8.10 | 13.85 | 17.85 | 0.19 | 7.24 | 12.24 | 28.09 | −20.83 | −22.09 | −4.08 | 6.91 | 23.17 | 23.77 | 27.51 |
| MSCI Pacific ex Japan ID | −0.33 | 3.59 | 8.23 | −1.35 | 10.23 | 24.73 | 9.19 | 2.50 | 24.63 | 41.26 | −9.00 | −12.13 | −17.42 | 39.33 | −9.56 | −32.74 | 17.81 |
| MSCI Singapore Ndtr_D | 1.94 | 3.10 | 4.36 | 4.27 | 14.37 | 24.38 | 5.56 | 0.70 | 22.27 | 37.60 | −11.05 | −23.41 | −27.46 | 99.58 | −13.28 | −30.05 | −6.86 |
| MSCI South Africa ID | −7.94 | −1.48 | 26.10 | 8.45 | 24.03 | 34.63 | 19.21 | 4.05 | 40.67 | 39.88 | 23.26 | −19.98 | −19.90 | 54.33 | −30.22 | −10.34 | −20.08 |
| MSCI Spain Ndtr_D | −2.41 | −1.08 | 11.01 | −2.57 | 4.41 | 28.73 | 9.89 | 14.04 | 28.93 | 58.46 | −15.29 | −11.33 | −15.80 | 4.77 | 49.83 | 25.41 | 40.05 |
| MSCI Sweden Ndtr D | −2.14 | −0.81 | 10.91 | 2.46 | 10.31 | 35.23 | 4.60 | 12.08 | 36.28 | 64.53 | −30.49 | −27.17 | −21.40 | 79.94 | 13.99 | 12.92 | 37.21 |
| MSCI Switzerland Ndtr_D | −0.25 | −1.04 | 9.85 | 7.29 | 16.33 | 21.49 | 4.81 | 8.53 | 14.96 | 34.08 | −10.31 | −21.37 | 6.04 | −7.04 | 23.33 | 44.25 | 2.28 |
| MSCI Taiwan ID | −3.39 | 5.01 | −6.34 | 8.69 | 3.28 | 15.50 | 4.65 | 0.55 | 6.54 | 40.01 | −25.38 | 9.19 | −45.43 | 51.52 | −21.43 | −6.96 | 39.21 |
| MSCI United Kingd Ndtr_D | 1.35 | −0.43 | 6.18 | 0.19 | 7.35 | 19.23 | 4.31 | 8.50 | 19.57 | 32.06 | −15.23 | −14.04 | −11.66 | 12.44 | 17.97 | 22.62 | 27.42 |

NDTR_D=the index is listed in US dollars, with net dividends reinvested.    ID=the index is listed in dollars, without net dividends reinvested.

# Largest & Smallest ETFs

**Morningstar's ETF Universe**

## Largest ETFs

| Page | Name | Assets ($mil) |
|---|---|---|
| | **Domestic Stocks** | |
| 133 | SPDR Trust Series 1 | 58539.00 |
| 126 | Nasdaq 100 Trust | 20311.00 |
| 111 | iShares S&P 500 | 14229.00 |
| 125 | MidCap SPDR Trust | 8942.00 |
| 66 | DIAMONDS Trust | 7634.00 |
| 104 | iShares R2000 Index | 7432.00 |
| 75 | iShares DJ Sel Dividend | 7252.00 |
| 102 | iShares R1000 Value | 6185.00 |
| 162 | Vanguard TSM VIPERs | 5612.00 |
| 100 | iShares R1000 Growth | 5399.00 |
| 87 | iShares Lehman 1-3 T | 4401.00 |
| 123 | iShares SP Small 600 | 3862.00 |
| 67 | Energy SPDR | 3526.00 |
| 122 | iShares SP MidCap400 | 3389.00 |
| 89 | iShares Lehman TIPS Bond | 3310.00 |
| 117 | iShares SP 500 Growth | 3242.00 |
| 118 | iShares SP 500 Value | 3015.00 |
| 105 | iShares R2000 Value | 3014.00 |
| 88 | iShares Lehman Aggregate | 2894.00 |
| 103 | iShares R2000 Growth | 2620.00 |
| | **International Stocks** | |
| 90 | iShares MSCI EAFE | 22739.00 |
| 85 | iShares Japan Index | 13042.00 |
| 93 | iShares MSCI Emerg Mkts | 10264.00 |
| — | streetTRACKS Gold Shares | 4341.00 |
| 94 | iShares MSCI ex-Japn | 1675.00 |
| 82 | iShares FTSE/Xinhua China | 1352.00 |
| 112 | iShares S&P Euro-350 | 1270.00 |
| 114 | iShares SP Latin 40 | 1230.00 |
| — | iShares Brazil Index | 1224.00 |
| — | iShares S.Korea Indx | 1077.00 |
| — | iShares Taiwan Index | 1054.00 |
| — | iShares Hong Kong | 639.00 |
| — | iShares Canada Index | 621.00 |
| 146 | Vanguard EmergMkts VIPERs | 553.00 |
| 81 | iShares EMU Index | 552.00 |
| — | iShares U.K. Index | 514.00 |
| — | iShares Mexico Index | 479.00 |
| — | iShares Germany Indx | 479.00 |
| — | iShares Australia | 463.00 |
| — | iShares Singapore | 393.00 |

## Smallest ETFs

| Page | Name | Assets ($mil) |
|---|---|---|
| | **Domestic Stocks** | |
| — | streetTRACKS DJ Large Cap | 14.00 |
| — | PowerShares Dyn Retail | 21.00 |
| 161 | Vanguard TelcomSrv VIPERs | 22.00 |
| — | PowerShares Food & Bevera | 23.00 |
| — | PowerShares Media | 24.00 |
| — | PowerShares Networking | 25.00 |
| — | streetTRACKS DJ MidGrowth | 25.00 |
| — | PowerShares Leisure & Ent | 26.00 |
| — | streetTRACKS DJ Mid Cap | 26.00 |
| — | streetTRACKS DJ Mid Value | 26.00 |
| — | Vanguard Indstrls VIPERs | 29.00 |
| — | iShares NYSE 100 Index | 29.00 |
| 96 | iShares NYSE Composite | 32.00 |
| — | PowerShares High Gr Div | 32.00 |
| — | SPDR Dividend ETF | 32.00 |
| — | PowerShares Pharma | 35.00 |
| — | PowerShares Software | 35.00 |
| — | First Trust DJ S MicroCap | 35.00 |
| — | PowerShares Lux Nanotech | 36.00 |
| — | PowerShares Dyn Utilities | 36.00 |
| | **International Stocks** | |
| — | PowerShares Intl Div Ach | 27.00 |
| — | BLDRS Europe 100 ADR | 29.00 |
| 134 | streetTRACKS DJ STOXX 50 | 31.00 |
| — | BLDRS Dev Mkts 100 ADR | 43.00 |
| 91 | iShares MSCI EAFE Growth | 45.00 |
| — | BLDRS Asia 50 ADR Index | 51.00 |
| — | iShares Italy Index | 53.00 |
| — | iShares Belgium Indx | 65.00 |
| 92 | iShares MSCI EAFE Value I | 65.00 |
| — | iShares Sweden Index | 66.00 |
| — | iShares Netherlands | 68.00 |
| — | iShares Spain Index | 78.00 |
| 129 | PowerShares Halter USX | 79.00 |
| — | iShares France Index | 88.00 |
| 135 | streetTRACK Global T | 91.00 |
| — | streetTRACKS DJ Euro 50 | 120.00 |
| — | iShares Switzerland | 125.00 |
| — | iShares MSCI South Africa | 171.00 |
| 148 | Vanguard Euro Stk VIPERs | 178.00 |
| 156 | Vanguard Pacif Stk VIPERs | 203.00 |

# Best & Worst Performing ETFs

Morningstar's ETF 100 Universe

## Best Performing

| Page | Name | Market Return %* |
|------|------|------------------|
| | **One Year (12-30-2005)** | |
| 114 | iShares SP Latin 40 | 54.59 |
| 67 | Energy SPDR | 40.17 |
| 147 | Vanguard Energy VIPERs | 39.05 |
| 79 | iShares DJ US Energy | 34.67 |
| 93 | iShares MSCI Emerg Mkts | 32.62 |
| 85 | iShares Japan Index | 24.34 |
| 124 | iShares SP TOPIX 150 | 23.95 |
| 143 | Utilities SPDR | 16.37 |
| 72 | iShares C&S Realty | 14.57 |
| 80 | iShares DJ Utilities | 14.54 |
| 141 | streetTRACKS WR REIT | 14.50 |
| 155 | Vanguard Mid Cap VIPERs | 13.97 |
| 163 | Vanguard Utilities VIPERs | 13.87 |
| 94 | iShares MSCI ex-Japn | 13.57 |
| 90 | iShares MSCI EAFE | 13.34 |
| | **Three Year (12-30-2005)** | |
| 114 | iShares SP Latin 40 | 51.67 |
| 67 | Energy SPDR | 33.18 |
| 79 | iShares DJ US Energy | 31.31 |
| 94 | iShares MSCI ex-Japn | 28.68 |
| 72 | iShares C&S Realty | 28.26 |
| 141 | streetTRACKS WR REIT | 27.14 |
| 85 | iShares Japan Index | 25.19 |
| 74 | iShares DJ RE Index | 24.27 |
| 99 | iShares R. Midcap VI | 24.26 |
| 124 | iShares SP TOPIX 150 | 23.62 |
| 90 | iShares MSCI EAFE | 23.52 |
| 97 | iShares R. Midcap | 23.44 |
| 149 | Vanguard ExMkt VIPERs | 23.40 |
| 81 | iShares EMU Index | 23.27 |
| 105 | iShares R2000 Value | 22.98 |
| | **Five Year (12-30-2005)** | |
| 74 | iShares DJ RE Index | 17.03 |
| 139 | streetTRACKS DJ Small Val | 13.80 |
| 105 | iShares R2000 Value | 13.23 |
| 116 | iShares SP 400 Value | 12.08 |
| 120 | iShares SP 600 Value | 11.72 |
| 79 | iShares DJ US Energy | 10.80 |
| 123 | iShares SP Small 600 | 10.70 |
| 67 | Energy SPDR | 10.53 |
| 119 | iShares SP 600 Growth | 8.52 |
| 122 | iShares SP MidCap400 | 8.43 |
| 125 | MidCap SPDR Trust | 8.31 |
| 104 | iShares R2000 Index | 8.08 |
| 108 | iShares R3000 Value | 5.43 |
| 102 | iShares R1000 Value | 4.98 |
| 115 | iShares SP 400 Growth | 4.45 |

## Worst Performing

| Page | Name | Market Return %* |
|------|------|------------------|
| | **One Year (12-30-2005)** | |
| 144 | Vanguard Cons Disc VIPERs | −4.10 |
| 129 | PowerShares Halter USX | −3.29 |
| 77 | iShares DJ Telecom | −2.58 |
| 142 | Technology SPDR | −0.31 |
| 130 | PowerShares HY Div Achiev | 0.99 |
| 110 | iShares S&P 100 Ind. | 1.03 |
| 83 | iShares GS$ InvesTop | 1.18 |
| 126 | Nasdaq 100 Trust | 1.49 |
| 84 | iShares GS Tech | 1.52 |
| 87 | iShares Lehman 1-3 T | 1.53 |
| 68 | Fidelity Nasdaq Comp Trac | 1.89 |
| 139 | streetTRACKS DJ Small Val | 1.93 |
| 161 | Vanguard TelcomSrv VIPERs | 2.00 |
| 88 | iShares Lehman Aggregate | 2.28 |
| 95 | iShares NASD Biotech | 2.44 |
| | **Three Year (12-30-2005)** | |
| 87 | iShares Lehman 1-3 T | 1.35 |
| 83 | iShares GS$ InvesTop | 4.26 |
| 65 | Consumer Staple SPDR | 7.16 |
| 70 | Health Care Sel SPDR | 7.39 |
| 77 | iShares DJ Telecom | 9.20 |
| 121 | iShares SP Glb Hlth | 9.70 |
| 73 | iShares DJ Health | 9.91 |
| 110 | iShares S&P 100 Ind. | 10.67 |
| 66 | DIAMONDS Trust | 11.23 |
| 117 | iShares SP 500 Growth | 11.26 |
| 135 | streetTRACK Global T | 11.38 |
| 136 | streetTRACKS DJ Lg Growth | 11.53 |
| 100 | iShares R1000 Growth | 12.83 |
| 106 | iShares R3000 Growth | 13.37 |
| 142 | Technology SPDR | 13.46 |
| | **Five Year (12-30-2005)** | |
| 77 | iShares DJ Telecom | −8.13 |
| 76 | iShares DJ Tech | −7.49 |
| 142 | Technology SPDR | −7.09 |
| 136 | streetTRACKS DJ Lg Growth | −6.94 |
| 126 | Nasdaq 100 Trust | −6.86 |
| 100 | iShares R1000 Growth | −3.85 |
| 106 | iShares R3000 Growth | −3.63 |
| 65 | Consumer Staple SPDR | −2.39 |
| 110 | iShares S&P 100 Ind. | −2.15 |
| 73 | iShares DJ Health | −1.95 |
| 117 | iShares SP 500 Growth | −1.62 |
| 135 | streetTRACK Global T | −1.61 |
| 113 | iShares S&P Glob 100 | −0.64 |
| 80 | iShares DJ Utilities | 0.25 |
| 111 | iShares S&P 500 | 0.54 |

* Three- and five-year returns are annualized.

# Most & Least Costly ETFs

**Morningstar's ETF 100 Universe**

## Highest Expense Ratio

| Page | Name | Expense Ratio % |
|---|---|---|
| 93 | iShares MSCI Emerg Mkts | 0.77 |
| 82 | iShares FTSE/Xinhua China | 0.74 |
| 129 | PowerShares Halter USX | 0.70 |
| 121 | iShares SP Glb Hlth | 0.65 |
| 80 | iShares DJ Utilities | 0.60 |
| 112 | iShares S&P Euro-350 | 0.60 |
| 79 | iShares DJ US Energy | 0.60 |
| 73 | iShares DJ Health | 0.60 |
| 74 | iShares DJ RE Index | 0.60 |
| 76 | iShares DJ Tech | 0.60 |
| 77 | iShares DJ Telecom | 0.60 |
| 130 | PowerShares HY Div Achiev | 0.60 |
| 128 | PowerShares Dynam Mkt | 0.60 |
| 127 | PowerShares Dynam OTC | 0.60 |
| 81 | iShares EMU Index | 0.58 |
| 85 | iShares Japan Index | 0.57 |
| 135 | streetTRACK Global T | 0.51 |
| 94 | iShares MSCI ex-Japn | 0.50 |
| 95 | iShares NASD Biotech | 0.50 |
| 84 | iShares GS Tech | 0.50 |

## Lowest Expense Ratio

| Page | Name | Expense Ratio % |
|---|---|---|
| 111 | iShares S&P 500 | 0.09 |
| 133 | SPDR Trust Series 1 | 0.11 |
| 154 | Vanguard Large Cap VIPERs | 0.12 |
| 162 | Vanguard TSM VIPERs | 0.13 |
| 101 | iShares R1000 Index | 0.15 |
| 83 | iShares GS$ InvesTop | 0.15 |
| 87 | iShares Lehman 1-3 T | 0.15 |
| 164 | Vanguard Value VIPERs | 0.15 |
| 151 | Vanguard Growth VIPERs | 0.15 |
| 66 | DIAMONDS Trust | 0.18 |
| 118 | iShares SP 500 Value | 0.18 |
| 117 | iShares SP 500 Growth | 0.18 |
| 158 | Vanguard Small Cap VIPERs | 0.18 |
| 148 | Vanguard Euro Stk VIPERs | 0.18 |
| 155 | Vanguard Mid Cap VIPERs | 0.18 |
| 156 | Vanguard Pacif Stk VIPERs | 0.18 |
| 88 | iShares Lehman Aggregate | 0.20 |
| 122 | iShares SP MidCap400 | 0.20 |
| 123 | iShares SP Small 600 | 0.20 |
| 102 | iShares R1000 Value | 0.20 |

## Highest Tax Cost Ratio

| Page | Name | Tax Cost Ratio % |
|---|---|---|
| 141 | streetTRACKS WR REIT | 1.89 |
| 83 | iShares GS$ InvesTop | 1.65 |
| 72 | iShares C&S Realty | 1.61 |
| 74 | iShares DJ RE Index | 1.44 |
| 139 | streetTRACKS DJ Small Val | 1.28 |
| 143 | Utilities SPDR | 1.20 |
| 80 | iShares DJ Utilities | 1.10 |
| 94 | iShares MSCI ex-Japn | 1.06 |
| 134 | streetTRACKS DJ STOXX 50 | 0.96 |
| 77 | iShares DJ Telecom | 0.95 |
| 137 | streetTracks DJ Lg Value | 0.85 |
| 66 | DIAMONDS Trust | 0.84 |
| 102 | iShares R1000 Value | 0.78 |
| 87 | iShares Lehman 1-3 T | 0.76 |
| 108 | iShares R3000 Value | 0.75 |
| 69 | Financial SPDR | 0.75 |
| 135 | streetTRACK Global T | 0.71 |
| 112 | iShares S&P Euro-350 | 0.67 |
| 118 | iShares SP 500 Value | 0.66 |
| 110 | iShares S&P 100 Ind. | 0.66 |

## Lowest Tax Cost Ratio

| Page | Name | Tax Cost Ratio % |
|---|---|---|
| 95 | iShares NASD Biotech | 0.00 |
| 85 | iShares Japan Index | 0.10 |
| 84 | iShares GS Tech | 0.10 |
| 124 | iShares SP TOPIX 150 | 0.11 |
| 98 | iShares R. Midcap Gr | 0.11 |
| 138 | streetTRACK DJ Small Gr | 0.13 |
| 103 | iShares R2000 Growth | 0.13 |
| 126 | Nasdaq 100 Trust | 0.14 |
| 119 | iShares SP 600 Growth | 0.16 |
| 115 | iShares SP 400 Growth | 0.18 |
| 76 | iShares DJ Tech | 0.19 |
| 149 | Vanguard ExMkt VIPERs | 0.20 |
| 121 | iShares SP Glb Hlth | 0.25 |
| 73 | iShares DJ Health | 0.25 |
| 123 | iShares SP Small 600 | 0.28 |
| 162 | Vanguard TSM VIPERs | 0.29 |
| 136 | streetTRACKS DJ Lg Growth | 0.30 |
| 106 | iShares R3000 Growth | 0.31 |
| 125 | MidCap SPDR Trust | 0.31 |
| 100 | iShares R1000 Growth | 0.34 |

**Tables and Charts**

# Most & Least Concentrated ETFs

**Morningstar's ETF 100 Universe**

| **Highest % of Assets in Top 10 Holdings** | | |
|---|---|---|
| Page | Name | % |
| 77 | iShares DJ Telecom | 79.34 |
| 65 | Consumer Staple SPDR | 72.77 |
| 79 | iShares DJ US Energy | 68.12 |
| 114 | iShares SP Latin 40 | 66.03 |
| 161 | Vanguard TelcomSrv VIPERs | 65.59 |
| 67 | Energy SPDR | 64.97 |
| 147 | Vanguard Energy VIPERs | 61.49 |
| 82 | iShares FTSE/Xinhua China | 60.28 |
| 70 | Health Care Sel SPDR | 59.29 |
| 72 | iShares C&S Realty | 59.21 |
| 145 | Vanguard Cons Stap VIPERs | 57.96 |
| 71 | Industrial SPDR | 57.89 |
| 143 | Utilities SPDR | 56.75 |
| 76 | iShares DJ Tech | 54.04 |
| 142 | Technology SPDR | 53.63 |
| 73 | iShares DJ Health | 52.84 |
| 121 | iShares SP Glb Hlth | 52.00 |
| 152 | Vanguard HealthCar VIPERs | 49.86 |
| 69 | Financial SPDR | 49.29 |
| 66 | DIAMONDS Trust | 49.10 |

| **Lowest % of Assets in Top 10 Holdings** | | |
|---|---|---|
| Page | Name | % |
| 132 | Rydex S&P Equal Weight | 2.24 |
| 104 | iShares R2000 Index | 2.43 |
| 109 | iShares Russell Microcap | 2.49 |
| 158 | Vanguard Small Cap VIPERs | 2.73 |
| 131 | PowerShares Zacks MicroCp | 3.67 |
| 139 | streetTRACKS DJ Small Val | 3.73 |
| 105 | iShares R2000 Value | 3.92 |
| 103 | iShares R2000 Growth | 4.33 |
| 138 | streetTRACK DJ Small Gr | 4.41 |
| 97 | iShares R. Midcap | 4.43 |
| 159 | Vanguard Sm Cp Val VIPER | 4.62 |
| 160 | Vanguard Sm Cap Gr VIPERs | 4.85 |
| 155 | Vanguard Mid Cap VIPERs | 5.77 |
| 123 | iShares SP Small 600 | 5.96 |
| 149 | Vanguard ExMkt VIPERs | 6.57 |
| 99 | iShares R. Midcap VI | 7.89 |
| 98 | iShares R. Midcap Gr | 8.04 |
| 125 | MidCap SPDR Trust | 8.12 |
| 122 | iShares SP MidCap400 | 8.29 |
| 120 | iShares SP 600 Value | 8.37 |

# Most & Least Volatile ETFs
**Morningstar's ETF 100 Universe**

## Highest Standard Deviation

| Page | Name | Standard Deviation |
|---|---|---|
| 114 | iShares SP Latin 40 | 19.72 |
| 95 | iShares NASD Biotech | 19.57 |
| 67 | Energy SPDR | 18.39 |
| 79 | iShares DJ US Energy | 18.25 |
| 84 | iShares GS Tech | 17.68 |
| 85 | iShares Japan Index | 16.78 |
| 103 | iShares R2000 Growth | 16.74 |
| 76 | iShares DJ Tech | 16.71 |
| 124 | iShares SP TOPIX 150 | 16.62 |
| 72 | iShares C&S Realty | 16.14 |
| 74 | iShares DJ RE Index | 15.60 |
| 141 | streetTRACKS WR REIT | 15.58 |
| 81 | iShares EMU Index | 15.29 |
| 104 | iShares R2000 Index | 15.27 |
| 126 | Nasdaq 100 Trust | 15.09 |
| 139 | streetTRACKS DJ Small Val | 14.71 |
| 120 | iShares SP 600 Value | 14.60 |
| 105 | iShares R2000 Value | 14.26 |
| 142 | Technology SPDR | 14.04 |
| 123 | iShares SP Small 600 | 14.01 |

## Lowest Standard Deviation

| Page | Name | Standard Deviation |
|---|---|---|
| 87 | iShares Lehman 1-3 T | 1.37 |
| 83 | iShares GS$ InvesTop | 6.58 |
| 65 | Consumer Staple SPDR | 8.03 |
| 117 | iShares SP 500 Growth | 8.51 |
| 135 | streetTRACK Global T | 8.71 |
| 110 | iShares S&P 100 Ind. | 8.84 |
| 140 | streetTRACKS Total Market | 8.92 |
| 121 | iShares SP Glb Hlth | 9.04 |
| 73 | iShares DJ Health | 9.13 |
| 133 | SPDR Trust Series 1 | 9.14 |
| 111 | iShares S&P 500 | 9.15 |
| 101 | iShares R1000 Index | 9.24 |
| 70 | Health Care Sel SPDR | 9.39 |
| 137 | streetTracks DJ Lg Value | 9.44 |
| 136 | streetTRACKS DJ Lg Growth | 9.53 |
| 78 | iShares DJ Total Mkt | 9.53 |
| 102 | iShares R1000 Value | 9.57 |
| 66 | DIAMONDS Trust | 9.60 |
| 107 | iShares R3000 Index | 9.60 |
| 100 | iShares R1000 Growth | 9.66 |

## Highest Beta

| Page | Name | Beta |
|---|---|---|
| 84 | iShares GS Tech | 1.60 |
| 83 | iShares GS$ InvesTop | 1.58 |
| 103 | iShares R2000 Growth | 1.56 |
| 95 | iShares NASD Biotech | 1.48 |
| 104 | iShares R2000 Index | 1.47 |
| 76 | iShares DJ Tech | 1.47 |
| 139 | streetTRACKS DJ Small Val | 1.46 |
| 120 | iShares SP 600 Value | 1.39 |
| 105 | iShares R2000 Value | 1.39 |
| 126 | Nasdaq 100 Trust | 1.37 |
| 142 | Technology SPDR | 1.35 |
| 138 | streetTRACK DJ Small Gr | 1.32 |
| 123 | iShares SP Small 600 | 1.32 |
| 114 | iShares SP Latin 40 | 1.27 |
| 116 | iShares SP 400 Value | 1.26 |
| 149 | Vanguard ExMkt VIPERs | 1.26 |
| 119 | iShares SP 600 Growth | 1.25 |
| 81 | iShares EMU Index | 1.22 |
| 98 | iShares R. Midcap Gr | 1.18 |
| 71 | Industrial SPDR | 1.17 |

## Lowest Beta

| Page | Name | Beta |
|---|---|---|
| 87 | iShares Lehman 1-3 T | 0.30 |
| 70 | Health Care Sel SPDR | 0.52 |
| 121 | iShares SP Glb Hlth | 0.54 |
| 73 | iShares DJ Health | 0.56 |
| 65 | Consumer Staple SPDR | 0.62 |
| 143 | Utilities SPDR | 0.66 |
| 135 | streetTRACK Global T | 0.67 |
| 80 | iShares DJ Utilities | 0.67 |
| 67 | Energy SPDR | 0.68 |
| 79 | iShares DJ US Energy | 0.71 |
| 72 | iShares C&S Realty | 0.75 |
| 141 | streetTRACKS WR REIT | 0.75 |
| 94 | iShares MSCI ex-Japn | 0.77 |
| 113 | iShares S&P Glob 100 | 0.78 |
| 85 | iShares Japan Index | 0.80 |
| 124 | iShares SP TOPIX 150 | 0.80 |
| 74 | iShares DJ RE Index | 0.83 |
| 117 | iShares SP 500 Growth | 0.89 |
| 110 | iShares S&P 100 Ind. | 0.94 |
| 136 | streetTRACKS DJ Lg Growth | 0.96 |

**Tables and Charts**

# New ETFs in 2005

**Morningstar's ETF Universe**

| Page | Name | Category | Inception Date | Ticker | Family | Phone | Web Address |
|---|---|---|---|---|---|---|---|
| — | First Trust DJ S MicroCap | SB | 09-30-2005 | FDM | First Trust | 800-621-1675 | www.ftportfolios.com |
| — | iShares COMEX Gold Trust | SP | 01-21-2005 | IAU | Barclays | 800-474-2737 | www.ishares.com |
| 86 | iShares KLD Sel Soc Idx | LB | 01-24-2005 | KLD | Barclays | 800-474-2737 | www.ishares.com |
| 91 | iShares MSCI EAFE Growth | FG | 08-01-2005 | EFG | Barclays | 800-474-2737 | www.ishares.com |
| 92 | iShares MSCI EAFE Value I | FV | 08-01-2005 | EFV | Barclays | 800-474-2737 | www.ishares.com |
| 109 | iShares Russell Microcap | SB | 08-12-2005 | IWC | Barclays | 800-474-2737 | www.ishares.com |
| — | PowerShares Aero&Defense | ST | 10-26-2005 | PPA | Powershares | 888-983-0903 | www.powershares.com |
| — | PowerShares Biotech & Gen | SH | 06-23-2005 | PBE | Powershares | 800-843-2639 | www.powershares.com |
| — | PowerShares Div Achievers | LV | 09-15-2005 | PFM | Powershares | 800-843-2639 | www.powershares.com |
| — | PowerShares Dyn Building | LB | 10-26-2005 | PKB | Powershares | 800-843-2639 | www.powershares.com |
| — | PowerShares Dyn Energy | SN | 10-26-2005 | PXE | Powershares | 800-843-2639 | www.powershares.com |
| — | PowerShares Dyn Insurance | SF | 10-26-2005 | PIC | Powershares | 800-843-2639 | www.powershares.com |
| — | PowerShares Dyn Lg Growth | LG | 03-04-2005 | PWB | Powershares | 800-843-2639 | www.powershares.com |
| — | PowerShares Dyn Lg Value | LV | 03-04-2005 | PWV | Powershares | 800-843-2639 | www.powershares.com |
| — | PowerShares Dyn Mid Value | MV | 03-04-2005 | PWP | Powershares | 800-843-2639 | www.powershares.com |
| — | PowerShares Dyn MidGrowth | MG | 03-04-2005 | PWJ | Powershares | 800-843-2639 | www.powershares.com |
| — | PowerShares Dyn Oil & Gas | SN | 10-26-2005 | PXJ | Powershares | 800-843-2639 | www.powershares.com |
| — | PowerShares Dyn Retail | LB | 10-26-2005 | PMR | Powershares | 800-843-2639 | www.powershares.com |
| — | PowerShares Dyn Sm Growth | SG | 03-04-2005 | PWT | Powershares | 800-843-2639 | www.powershares.com |
| — | PowerShares Dyn Sm Value | SV | 03-04-2005 | PWY | Powershares | 800-843-2639 | www.powershares.com |
| — | PowerShares Dyn Utilities | SU | 10-26-2005 | PUI | Powershares | 800-843-2639 | www.powershares.com |
| — | PowerShares Food & Bevera | LB | 06-23-2005 | PBJ | Powershares | 800-843-2639 | www.powershares.com |
| — | PowerShares FTSE RAFI1000 | LB | 12-19-2005 | PRF | Powershares | 888-983-0903 | www.powershares.com |
| — | PowerShares Hardware&Elec | ST | 12-06-2005 | PHW | Powershares | 888 983-0903 | www.powershares.com |
| — | PowerSharcs High Gr Div | LV | 09-15-2005 | PHJ | Powershares | 800-843-2639 | www.powershares.com |
| — | PowerShares Intl Div Ach | FV | 09-15-2005 | PID | Powershares | 800-843-2639 | www.powershares.com |
| — | PowerShares Leisure & Ent | LB | 06-23-2005 | PEJ | Powershares | 800-843-2639 | www.powershares.com |
| — | PowerShares Lux Nanotech | ST | 10-26-2005 | PXN | Powershares | 800-843-2639 | www.powershares.com |
| — | PowerShares Media | SC | 06-23-2005 | PBS | Powershares | 800-843-2639 | www.powershares.com |
| — | PowerShares Networking | ST | 06-23-2005 | PXQ | Powershares | 800-843-2639 | www.powershares.com |
| — | PowerShares Pharma | SH | 06-23-2005 | PJP | Powershares | 800-843-2639 | www.powershares.com |
| — | PowerShares Semiconductor | ST | 06-23-2005 | PSI | Powershares | 800-843-2639 | www.powershares.com |
| — | PowerShares Software | ST | 06-23-2005 | PSJ | Powershares | 800-843-2639 | www.powershares.com |
| — | PowerShares Tel&Wireless | SC | 12-06-2005 | PTE | Powershares | 888-983-0903 | www.powershares.com |
| — | PowerShares Val Line Time | LG | 12-06-2005 | PIV | Powershares | 888-983-0903 | www.powershares.com |
| — | PowerShares Water Res | SU | 12-06-2005 | PHO | Powershares | 888-983-0903 | www.powershares.com |
| — | PowerShares WilderHill | SN | 03-04-2005 | PBW | Powershares | 800-843-2639 | www.powershares.com |
| 131 | PowerShares Zacks MicroCp | SB | 08-18-2005 | PZI | Powershares | 800-843-2639 | www.powershares.com |
| — | Rydex Russell Top 50 | LB | 05-10-2005 | XLG | Rydex | 800-820-0888 | www.rydex.com |
| — | SPDR Dividend ETF | LV | 11-08-2005 | SDY | State Street Global Advisors | 866-787-2257 | www.advisors.ssga.com |
| — | streetTRACKS DJ Large Cap | LB | 11-08-2005 | ELR | State Street Global Advisors | 866-787-2257 | www.advisors.ssga.com |
| — | streetTRACKS DJ Mid Cap | MB | 11-08-2005 | EMM | State Street Global Advisors | 866-787-2257 | www.advisors.ssga.com |
| — | streetTRACKS DJ Mid Value | MV | 11-08-2005 | EMV | State Street Global Advisors | 866-787-2257 | www.advisors.ssga.com |
| — | streetTRACKS DJ MidGrowth | MG | 11-08-2005 | EMG | State Street Global Advisors | 866-787-2257 | www.advisors.ssga.com |
| — | streetTRACKS DJ Small Cap | SB | 11-08-2005 | DSC | State Street Global Advisors | 866-787-2257 | www.advisors.ssga.com |
| — | streetTRACKS KBW Bank ETF | SF | 11-08-2005 | KBE | State Street Global Advisors | 866-787-2257 | www.advisors.ssga.com |
| — | streetTRACKS KBW Cap Mkt | SF | 11-08-2005 | KCE | State Street Global Advisors | 866-787-2257 | www.advisors.ssga.com |
| — | streetTRACKS KBWInsurance | SF | 11-08-2005 | KIE | State Street Global Advisors | 866-787-2257 | www.advisors.ssga.com |
| 146 | Vanguard EmergMkts VIPERs | EM | 03-10-2005 | VWO | Vanguard | 866-499-8473 | www.vanguard.com |
| 148 | Vanguard Euro Stk VIPERs | ES | 03-10-2005 | VGK | Vanguard | 866-499-8473 | www.vanguard.com |
| 156 | Vanguard Pacif Stk VIPERs | JS | 03-10-2005 | VPL | Vanguard | 866-499-8473 | www.vanguard.com |

# ETFs by Family

Morningstar's ETF Universe

| ETF Family | Page | Name | Ticker | Category | Inception Date | Expense Ratio % |
|---|---|---|---|---|---|---|
| BLDRS | — | BLDRS Asia 50 ADR Index | ADRA | DP | 11-08-2002 | 0.30 |
| | — | BLDRS Dev Mkts 100 ADR | ADRD | FB | 11-08-2002 | 0.30 |
| | — | BLDRS Emerg Mkts 50 ADR | ADRE | EM | 11-08-2002 | 0.30 |
| | — | BLDRS Europe 100 ADR | ADRU | ES | 11-08-2002 | 0.30 |
| Barclays | — | iShares Australia | EWA | PJ | 03-12-1996 | 0.57 |
| | — | iShares Austria Index | EWO | ES | 03-12-1996 | 0.57 |
| | — | iShares Belgium Indx | EWK | ES | 03-12-1996 | 0.57 |
| | — | iShares Brazil Index | EWZ | LS | 07-10-2000 | 0.74 |
| | 72 | iShares C&S Realty | ICF | SR | 01-29-2001 | 0.35 |
| | — | iShares Canada Index | EWC | FV | 03-12-1996 | 0.57 |
| | — | iShares COMEX Gold Trust | IAU | SP | 01-21-2005 | — |
| | — | iShares DJ BMaterial | IYM | LV | 06-12-2000 | 0.60 |
| | — | iShares DJ Cons Services | IYC | LB | 06-12-2000 | 0.60 |
| | — | iShares DJ Consumer Goods | IYK | LB | 06-12-2000 | 0.60 |
| | — | iShares DJ Fin Sectr | IYF | SF | 05-22-2000 | 0.60 |
| | — | iShares DJ Fin Svcs | IYG | SF | 06-12-2000 | 0.60 |
| | 73 | iShares DJ Health | IYH | SH | 06-12-2000 | 0.60 |
| | — | iShares DJ Industry | IYJ | LB | 06-12-2000 | 0.60 |
| | 74 | iShares DJ RE Index | IYR | SR | 06-12-2000 | 0.60 |
| | 75 | iShares DJ Sel Dividend | DVY | MV | 11-03-2003 | 0.40 |
| | 76 | iShares DJ Tech | IYW | ST | 05-15-2000 | 0.60 |
| | 77 | iShares DJ Telecom | IYZ | SC | 05-22-2000 | 0.60 |
| | 78 | iShares DJ Total Mkt | IYY | LB | 06-12-2000 | 0.20 |
| | 79 | iShares DJ US Energy | IYE | SN | 06-12-2000 | 0.60 |
| | 80 | iShares DJ Utilities | IDU | SU | 06-12-2000 | 0.60 |
| | — | iShares Dow Jones TransAv | IYT | MB | 10-06-2003 | 0.60 |
| | 81 | iShares EMU Index | EZU | ES | 07-25-2000 | 0.58 |
| | — | iShares France Index | EWQ | ES | 03-12-1996 | 0.57 |
| | 82 | iShares FTSE/Xinhua China | FXI | PJ | 10-05-2004 | 0.74 |
| | — | iShares Germany Indx | EWG | ES | 03-12-1996 | 0.57 |
| | — | iShares GS Nat Res | IGE | SN | 10-22-2001 | 0.50 |
| | — | iShares GS Network | IGN | ST | 07-10-2001 | 0.50 |
| | — | iShares GS Software | IGV | ST | 07-10-2001 | 0.50 |
| | 84 | iShares GS Tech | IGM | ST | 03-13-2001 | 0.50 |
| | 83 | iShares GS$ InvesTop | LQD | CL | 07-22-2002 | 0.15 |
| | — | iShares Hong Kong | EWH | PJ | 03-12-1996 | 0.57 |
| | — | iShares Italy Index | EWI | ES | 03-12-1996 | 0.57 |
| | 85 | iShares Japan Index | EWJ | JS | 03-12-1996 | 0.57 |
| | 86 | iShares KLD Sel Soc Idx | KLD | LB | 01-24-2005 | 0.50 |
| | 87 | iShares Lehman 1-3 T | SHY | GS | 07-22-2002 | 0.15 |
| | — | iShares Lehman 20+ | TLT | GL | 07-22-2002 | 0.15 |
| | — | iShares Lehman 7-10 | IEF | GI | 07-22-2002 | 0.15 |
| | 88 | iShares Lehman Aggregate | AGG | CI | 09-22-2003 | 0.20 |
| | 89 | iShares Lehman TIPS Bond | TIP | GL | 12-04-2003 | 0.20 |
| | — | iShares Malaysia | EWM | PJ | 03-12-1996 | 0.57 |
| | — | iShares Mexico Index | EWW | LS | 03-12-1996 | 0.57 |
| | 90 | iShares MSCI EAFE | EFA | FB | 08-14-2001 | 0.36 |
| | 91 | iShares MSCI EAFE Growth | EFG | FG | 08-01-2005 | — |
| | 92 | iShares MSCI EAFE Value I | EFV | FV | 08-01-2005 | — |
| | 93 | iShares MSCI Emerg Mkts | EEM | EM | 04-07-2003 | 0.77 |
| | 94 | iShares MSCI ex-Japn | EPP | PJ | 10-25-2001 | 0.50 |
| | — | iShares MSCI South Africa | EZA | EM | 02-03-2003 | 0.74 |
| | — | iShares MstarLargeCore | JKD | LB | 07-02-2004 | — |
| | — | iShares MstarLargeGrowth | JKE | LG | 07-02-2004 | — |
| | — | iShares MstarLargeValue | JKF | LV | 07-02-2004 | — |
| | — | iShares MstarMidCore | JKG | MB | 07-02-2004 | — |
| | — | iShares MstarMidGrowth | JKH | MG | 07-02-2004 | — |
| | — | iShares MstarMidValue | JKI | MV | 07-02-2004 | — |
| | — | iShares MstarSmallCore | JKJ | SB | 07-02-2004 | — |
| | — | iShares MstarSmallGrowth | JKK | SG | 07-02-2004 | — |
| | — | iShares MstarSmallValue | JKL | SV | 07-02-2004 | — |
| | 95 | iShares NASD Biotech | IBB | SH | 02-05-2001 | 0.50 |
| | — | iShares Netherlands | EWN | ES | 03-12-1996 | 0.57 |

Disclosure: Barclays Global Investors (BGI), which is owned by Barclays, currently licenses Morningstar's 16 style-based indexes for use in BGI's iShares exchange-traded funds. iShares are not sponsored, issued, or sold by Morningstar. Morningstar does not make any representation regarding the advisability of investing in iShares that are based on Morningstar indexes.

# ETFs by Family
Morningstar's ETF Universe

| ETF Family | Page | Name | Ticker | Category | Inception Date | Expense Ratio % |
|---|---|---|---|---|---|---|
| | — | iShares NYSE 100 Index | NY | LV | 03-29-2004 | 0.20 |
| | 96 | iShares NYSE Composite | NYC | LB | 03-30-2004 | 0.25 |
| | 97 | iShares R. Midcap | IWR | MB | 07-17-2001 | 0.20 |
| | 98 | iShares R. Midcap Gr | IWP | MG | 07-17-2001 | 0.25 |
| | 99 | iShares R. Midcap Vl | IWS | MV | 07-17-2001 | 0.25 |
| | 100 | iShares R1000 Growth | IWF | LG | 05-22-2000 | 0.20 |
| | 101 | iShares R1000 Index | IWB | LB | 05-15-2000 | 0.15 |
| | 102 | iShares R1000 Value | IWD | LV | 05-22-2000 | 0.20 |
| | 103 | iShares R2000 Growth | IWO | SG | 07-24-2000 | 0.25 |
| | 104 | iShares R2000 Index | IWM | SB | 05-22-2000 | 0.20 |
| | 105 | iShares R2000 Value | IWN | SV | 07-24-2000 | 0.25 |
| | 106 | iShares R3000 Growth | IWZ | LG | 07-24-2000 | 0.25 |
| | 107 | iShares R3000 Index | IWV | LB | 05-22-2000 | 0.20 |
| | 108 | iShares R3000 Value | IWW | LV | 07-24-2000 | 0.25 |
| | 109 | iShares Russell Microcap | IWC | SB | 08-12-2005 | — |
| | 110 | iShares S&P 100 Ind. | OEF | LB | 10-23-2000 | 0.20 |
| | — | iShares S&P 1500 Index | ISI | LB | 01-20-2004 | 0.20 |
| | 111 | iShares S&P 500 | IVV | LB | 05-15-2000 | 0.09 |
| | 112 | iShares S&P Euro-350 | IEV | ES | 07-25-2000 | 0.60 |
| | 113 | iShares S&P Glob 100 | IOO | WS | 12-05-2000 | 0.40 |
| | — | iShares S.Korea Indx | EWY | PJ | 05-09-2000 | 0.74 |
| | — | iShares Semiconductor | IGW | ST | 07-10-2001 | 0.50 |
| | — | iShares Singapore | EWS | PJ | 03-12-1996 | 0.57 |
| | 115 | iShares SP 400 Growth | IJK | MG | 07-24-2000 | 0.25 |
| | 116 | iShares SP 400 Value | IJJ | MV | 07-24-2000 | 0.25 |
| | 117 | iShares SP 500 Growth | IVW | LG | 05-22-2000 | 0.18 |
| | 118 | iShares SP 500 Value | IVE | LV | 05-22-2000 | 0.18 |
| | 119 | iShares SP 600 Growth | IJT | SG | 07-24-2000 | 0.25 |
| | 120 | iShares SP 600 Value | IJS | SV | 07-24-2000 | 0.25 |
| | — | iShares SP Glb Enrgy | IXC | SN | 11-12-2001 | 0.65 |
| | — | iShares SP Glb Fincl | IXG | SF | 11-12-2001 | 0.65 |
| | 121 | iShares SP Glb Hlth | IXJ | SH | 11-13-2001 | 0.65 |
| | — | iShares SP Glb Tech | IXN | ST | 11-12-2001 | 0.66 |
| | — | iShares SP Glb Tele | IXP | SC | 11-12-2001 | 0.65 |
| | 114 | iShares SP Latin 40 | ILF | LS | 10-25-2001 | 0.50 |
| | 122 | iShares SP MidCap400 | IJH | MB | 05-22-2000 | 0.20 |
| | 123 | iShares SP Small 600 | IJR | SB | 05-22-2000 | 0.20 |
| | 124 | iShares SP TOPIX 150 | ITF | JS | 10-23-2001 | 0.50 |
| | — | iShares Spain Index | EWP | ES | 03-12-1996 | 0.57 |
| | — | iShares Sweden Index | EWD | ES | 03-12-1996 | 0.58 |
| | — | iShares Switzerland | EWL | ES | 03-12-1996 | 0.57 |
| | — | iShares Taiwan Index | EWT | PJ | 06-20-2000 | 1.03 |
| | — | iShares U.K. Index | EWU | ES | 03-12-1996 | 0.57 |
| Fidelity Group | 68 | Fidelity Nasdaq Comp Trac | ONEQ | LG | 09-25-2003 | 0.30 |
| First Trust | — | First Trust DJ S MicroCap | FDM | SB | 09-30-2005 | — |
| Nasdaq-Amex Investment Prod Svcs | 126 | Nasdaq 100 Trust | QQQQ | LG | 03-10-1999 | 0.20 |
| PDR SERVICES LLC | 66 | DIAMONDS Trust | DIA | LV | 01-20-1998 | 0.18 |
| | 125 | MidCap SPDR Trust | MDY | MB | 05-04-1995 | 0.25 |
| | 133 | SPDR Trust Series 1 | SPY | LB | 01-29-1993 | 0.11 |
| Powershares | — | PowerShares Aero&Defense | PPA | ST | 10-26-2005 | — |
| | — | PowerShares Biotech & Gen | PBE | SH | 06-23-2005 | — |
| | — | PowerShares Div Achievers | PFM | LV | 09-15-2005 | — |
| | — | PowerShares Dyn Building | PKB | LB | 10-26-2005 | — |
| | — | PowerShares Dyn Energy | PXE | SN | 10-26-2005 | — |
| | — | PowerShares Dyn Insurance | PIC | SF | 10-26-2005 | — |
| | — | PowerShares Dyn Lg Growth | PWB | LG | 03-04-2005 | 0.63 |
| | — | PowerShares Dyn Lg Value | PWV | LV | 03-04-2005 | 0.63 |
| | — | PowerShares Dyn Mid Value | PWP | MV | 03-04-2005 | 0.63 |
| | — | PowerShares Dyn MidGrowth | PWJ | MG | 03-04-2005 | 0.63 |

# ETFs by Family
## Morningstar's ETF Universe

| ETF Family | Page | Name | Ticker | Category | Inception Date | Expense Ratio % |
|---|---|---|---|---|---|---|
| | — | PowerShares Dyn Oil & Gas | PXJ | SN | 10-26-2005 | — |
| | — | PowerShares Dyn Retail | PMR | LB | 10-26-2005 | — |
| | — | PowerShares Dyn Sm Growth | PWT | SG | 03-04-2005 | 0.63 |
| | — | PowerShares Dyn Sm Value | PWY | SV | 03-04-2005 | 0.63 |
| | — | PowerShares Dyn Utilities | PUI | SU | 10-26-2005 | — |
| | 128 | PowerShares Dynam Mkt | PWC | LB | 05-01-2003 | 0.60 |
| | 127 | PowerShares Dynam OTC | PWO | MG | 05-01-2003 | 0.60 |
| | — | PowerShares Food & Bevera | PBJ | LB | 06-23-2005 | — |
| | 129 | PowerShares Halter USX | PGJ | PJ | 12-09-2004 | 0.70 |
| | — | PowerShares High Gr Div | PHJ | LV | 09-15-2005 | — |
| | 130 | PowerShares HY Div Achiev | PEY | MV | 12-09-2004 | 0.60 |
| | — | PowerShares Intl Div Ach | PID | FV | 09-15-2005 | — |
| | — | PowerShares Leisure & Ent | PEJ | LB | 06-23-2005 | — |
| | — | PowerShares Lux Nanotech | PXN | ST | 10-26-2005 | — |
| | — | PowerShares Media | PBS | SC | 06-23-2005 | — |
| | — | PowerShares Networking | PXQ | ST | 06-23-2005 | — |
| | — | PowerShares Pharma | PJP | SH | 06-23-2005 | — |
| | — | PowerShares Semiconductor | PSI | ST | 06-23-2005 | — |
| | — | PowerShares Software | PSJ | ST | 06-23-2005 | — |
| | — | PowerShares WilderHill | PBW | SN | 03-04-2005 | 0.70 |
| | 131 | PowerShares Zacks MicroCp | PZI | SB | 08-18-2005 | — |
| Rydex | — | Rydex Russell Top 50 | XLG | LB | 05-10-2005 | — |
| | 132 | Rydex S&P Equal Weight | RSP | LB | 04-24-2003 | 0.40 |
| State Street Global Advisors | — | Consumer Discr SPDR | XLY | LB | 12-22-1998 | 0.26 |
| | 65 | Consumer Staple SPDR | XLP | LB | 12-22-1998 | 0.26 |
| | 67 | Energy SPDR | XLE | SN | 12-22-1998 | 0.26 |
| | 69 | Financial SPDR | XLF | SF | 12-22-1998 | 0.26 |
| | 70 | Health Care Sel SPDR | XLV | SH | 12-22-1998 | 0.26 |
| | 71 | Industrial SPDR | XLI | LB | 12-22-1998 | 0.25 |
| | — | Materials Sel SPDR | XLB | LV | 12-22-1998 | 0.26 |
| | — | SPDR Dividend ETF | SDY | LV | 11-08-2005 | — |
| | — | SPDR O-Strip | OOO | LB | 09-09-2004 | — |
| | 138 | streetTRACK DJ Small Gr | DSG | SG | 09-25-2000 | 0.26 |
| | 135 | streetTRACK Global T | DGT | WS | 09-25-2000 | 0.51 |
| | — | streetTRACKS DJ Euro 50 | FEZ | ES | 10-21-2002 | 0.32 |
| | — | streetTRACKS DJ Large Cap | ELR | LB | 11-08-2005 | — |
| | 136 | streetTRACKS DJ Lg Growth | ELG | LG | 09-25-2000 | 0.21 |
| | 137 | streetTracks DJ Lg Value | ELV | LV | 09-25-2000 | 0.21 |
| | — | streetTRACKS DJ Mid Cap | EMM | MB | 11-08-2005 | — |
| | — | streetTRACKS DJ Mid Value | EMV | MV | 11-08-2005 | — |
| | — | streetTRACKS DJ MidGrowth | EMG | MG | 11-08-2005 | — |
| | 139 | streetTRACKS DJ Small Val | DSV | SV | 09-25-2000 | 0.26 |
| | 134 | streetTRACKS DJ STOXX 50 | FEU | ES | 10-21-2002 | 0.32 |
| | — | streetTRACKS MS Tech | MTK | ST | 09-25-2000 | 0.51 |
| | 140 | streetTRACKS Total Market | TMW | LB | 10-04-2000 | 0.21 |
| | 141 | streetTRACKS WR REIT | RWR | SR | 04-23-2001 | 0.26 |
| | 142 | Technology SPDR | XLK | ST | 12-22-1998 | 0.26 |
| | 143 | Utilities SPDR | XLU | SU | 12-22-1998 | 0.26 |
| Vanguard | 144 | Vanguard Cons Disc VIPERs | VCR | LG | 01-26-2004 | 0.26 |
| | 145 | Vanguard Cons Stap VIPERs | VDC | LB | 01-26-2004 | 0.26 |
| | 146 | Vanguard EmergMkts VIPERs | VWO | EM | 03-10-2005 | 0.30 |
| | 147 | Vanguard Energy VIPERs | VDE | SN | 09-29-2004 | 0.26 |
| | 148 | Vanguard Euro Stk VIPERs | VGK | ES | 03-10-2005 | 0.18 |
| | 149 | Vanguard ExMkt VIPERs | VXF | MB | 12-27-2001 | 0.20 |
| | 150 | Vanguard Financial VIPERs | VFH | SF | 01-26-2004 | 0.26 |
| | 151 | Vanguard Growth VIPERs | VUG | LG | 01-26-2004 | 0.15 |
| | 152 | Vanguard HealthCar VIPERs | VHT | SH | 01-26-2004 | 0.26 |
| | — | Vanguard Indstrls VIPERs | VIS | LB | 09-29-2004 | 0.26 |
| | 153 | Vanguard InfoTech VIPERs | VGT | ST | 01-26-2004 | 0.26 |
| | 154 | Vanguard Large Cap VIPERs | VV | LB | 01-27-2004 | 0.12 |
| | — | Vanguard Materials VIPERs | VAW | SN | 01-26-2004 | 0.26 |

| ETF Family | Page | Name | Ticker | Category | Inception Date | Expense Ratio % |
|---|---|---|---|---|---|---|
| | 155 | Vanguard Mid Cap VIPERs | VO | MB | 01-26-2004 | 0.18 |
| | 156 | Vanguard Pacif Stk VIPERs | VPL | JS | 03-10-2005 | 0.18 |
| | 157 | Vanguard REIT Index VIPER | VNQ | SR | 09-23-2004 | — |
| | 160 | Vanguard Sm Cap Gr VIPERs | VBK | SG | 01-26-2004 | 0.22 |
| | 159 | Vanguard Sm Cp Val VIPER | VBR | SV | 01-26-2004 | 0.22 |
| | 158 | Vanguard Small Cap VIPERs | VB | SB | 01-26-2004 | 0.18 |
| | 161 | Vanguard TelcomSrv VIPERs | VOX | SC | 09-29-2004 | 0.26 |
| | 162 | Vanguard TSM VIPERs | VTI | LB | 05-31-2001 | 0.13 |
| | 163 | Vanguard Utilities VIPERs | VPU | SU | 01-26-2004 | 0.26 |
| | 164 | Vanguard Value VIPERs | VTV | LV | 01-26-2004 | 0.15 |
| World Gold Trust Services, LLC | — | streetTRACKS Gold Shares | GLD | SP | 11-18-2004 | — |

# ETFs by Index Family

| ETF Index Family | Page | Name | Ticker | Category | Inception Date | Expense Ratio % |
|---|---|---|---|---|---|---|
| Amex Intellidex | — | PowerShares Biotech & Gen | PBE | SH | 06-23-2005 | — |
| | — | PowerShares Dyn Building | PKB | LB | 10-26-2005 | — |
| | — | PowerShares Dyn Energy | PXE | SN | 10-26-2005 | — |
| | — | PowerShares Dyn Insurance | PIC | SF | 10-26-2005 | — |
| | — | PowerShares Dyn Lg Growth | PWB | LG | 03-04-2005 | 0.63 |
| | — | PowerShares Dyn Lg Value | PWV | LV | 03-04-2005 | 0.63 |
| | — | PowerShares Dyn Mid Value | PWP | MV | 03-04-2005 | 0.63 |
| | — | PowerShares Dyn MidGrowth | PWJ | MG | 03-04-2005 | 0.63 |
| | — | PowerShares Dyn Oil & Gas | PXJ | SN | 10-26-2005 | — |
| | — | PowerShares Dyn Retail | PMR | LB | 10-26-2005 | — |
| | — | PowerShares Dyn Sm Growth | PWT | SG | 03-04-2005 | 0.63 |
| | — | PowerShares Dyn Sm Value | PWY | SV | 03-04-2005 | 0.63 |
| | — | PowerShares Dyn Utilities | PUI | SU | 10-26-2005 | — |
| | 128 | PowerShares Dynam Mkt | PWC | LB | 05-01-2003 | 0.60 |
| | 127 | PowerShares Dynam OTC | PWO | MG | 05-01-2003 | 0.60 |
| | — | PowerShares Food & Bevera | PBJ | LB | 06-23-2005 | — |
| | — | PowerShares Leisure & Ent | PEJ | LB | 06-23-2005 | — |
| | — | PowerShares Media | PBS | SC | 06-23-2005 | — |
| | — | PowerShares Networking | PXQ | ST | 06-23-2005 | — |
| | — | PowerShares Pharma | PJP | SH | 06-23-2005 | — |
| | — | PowerShares Semiconductor | PSI | ST | 06-23-2005 | — |
| | — | PowerShares Software | PSJ | ST | 06-23-2005 | — |
| Bank of New York ADR | — | BLDRS Asia 50 ADR Index | ADRA | DP | 11-08-2002 | 0.30 |
| | — | BLDRS Dev Mkts 100 ADR | ADRD | FB | 11-08-2002 | 0.30 |
| | — | BLDRS Emerg Mkts 50 ADR | ADRE | EM | 11-08-2002 | 0.30 |
| | — | BLDRS Europe 100 ADR | ADRU | ES | 11-08-2002 | 0.30 |
| Cohen & Steers | 72 | iShares C&S Realty | ICF | SR | 01-29-2001 | 0.35 |
| Dow Jones | 66 | DIAMONDS Trust | DIA | LV | 01-20-1998 | 0.18 |
| | — | First Trust DJ S MicroCap | FDM | SB | 09-30-2005 | — |
| | — | iShares DJ BMaterial | IYM | LV | 06-12-2000 | 0.60 |
| | — | iShares DJ Cons Services | IYC | LB | 06-12-2000 | 0.60 |
| | — | iShares DJ Consumer Goods | IYK | LB | 06-12-2000 | 0.60 |
| | — | iShares DJ Fin Sectr | IYF | SF | 05-22-2000 | 0.60 |
| | — | iShares DJ Fin Svcs | IYG | SF | 06-12-2000 | 0.60 |
| | 73 | iShares DJ Health | IYH | SH | 06-12-2000 | 0.60 |
| | — | iShares DJ Industry | IYJ | LB | 06-12-2000 | 0.60 |
| | 74 | iShares DJ RE Index | IYR | SR | 06-12-2000 | 0.60 |
| | 75 | iShares DJ Sel Dividend | DVY | MV | 11-03-2003 | 0.40 |
| | 76 | iShares DJ Tech | IYW | ST | 05-15-2000 | 0.60 |
| | 77 | iShares DJ Telecom | IYZ | SC | 05-22-2000 | 0.60 |
| | 78 | iShares DJ Total Mkt | IYY | LB | 06-12-2000 | 0.20 |
| | 79 | iShares DJ US Energy | IYE | SN | 06-12-2000 | 0.60 |
| | 80 | iShares DJ Utilities | IDU | SU | 06-12-2000 | 0.60 |
| | — | iShares Dow Jones TransAv | IYT | MB | 10-06-2003 | 0.60 |
| | — | streetTRACKS DJ Euro 50 | FEZ | ES | 10-21-2002 | 0.32 |
| | 134 | streetTRACKS DJ STOXX 50 | FEU | ES | 10-21-2002 | 0.32 |
| Dow Jones Wilshire | 138 | streetTRACK DJ Small Gr | DSG | SG | 09-25-2000 | 0.26 |
| | 135 | streetTRACK Global T | DGT | WS | 09-25-2000 | 0.51 |
| | — | streetTRACKS DJ Large Cap | ELR | LB | 11-08-2005 | — |
| | 136 | streetTRACKS DJ Lg Growth | ELG | LG | 09-25-2000 | 0.21 |
| | 137 | streetTracks DJ Lg Value | ELV | LV | 09-25-2000 | 0.21 |
| | — | streetTRACKS DJ Mid Cap | EMM | MB | 11-08-2005 | — |
| | — | streetTRACKS DJ Mid Value | EMV | MV | 11-08-2005 | — |
| | — | streetTRACKS DJ MidGrowth | EMG | MG | 11-08-2005 | — |
| | — | streetTRACKS DJ Small Cap | DSC | SB | 11-08-2005 | 0.00 |
| | 139 | streetTRACKS DJ Small Val | DSV | SV | 09-25-2000 | 0.26 |
| | 140 | streetTRACKS Total Market | TMW | LB | 10-04-2000 | 0.21 |
| | 141 | streetTRACKS WR REIT | RWR | SR | 04-23-2001 | 0.26 |
| FTSE/Xinhua China | 82 | iShares FTSE/Xinhua China | FXI | PJ | 10-05-2004 | 0.74 |

# ETFs by Index Family
## Morningstar's ETF Universe

| ETF Index Family | Page | Name | Ticker | Category | Inception Date | Expense Ratio % |
|---|---|---|---|---|---|---|
| Goldman Sachs | — | iShares GS Nat Res | IGE | SN | 10-22-2001 | 0.50 |
| | — | iShares GS Network | IGN | ST | 07-10-2001 | 0.50 |
| | — | iShares GS Software | IGV | ST | 07-10-2001 | 0.50 |
| | 84 | iShares GS Tech | IGM | ST | 03-13-2001 | 0.50 |
| | 83 | iShares GS$ InvesTop | LQD | CL | 07-22-2002 | 0.15 |
| | — | iShares Semiconductor | IGW | ST | 07-10-2001 | 0.50 |
| Halter USX | 129 | PowerShares Halter USX | PGJ | PJ | 12-09-2004 | 0.70 |
| KLD Research & Analytics | 86 | iShares KLD Sel Soc Idx | KLD | LB | 01-24-2005 | 0.50 |
| Keefe, Bruyette & Woods | — | streetTRACKS KBW Bank ETF | KBE | SF | 11-08-2005 | 0.00 |
| | — | streetTRACKS KBW Cap Mkt | KCE | SF | 11-08-2005 | 0.00 |
| | — | streetTRACKS KBWInsurance | KIE | SF | 11-08-2005 | 0.00 |
| Lehman Brothers | 87 | iShares Lehman 1-3 T | SHY | GS | 07-22-2002 | 0.15 |
| | — | iShares Lehman 20+ | TLT | GL | 07-22-2002 | 0.15 |
| | — | iShares Lehman 7-10 | IEF | GI | 07-22-2002 | 0.15 |
| | 88 | iShares Lehman Aggregate | AGG | CI | 09-22-2003 | 0.20 |
| | 89 | iShares Lehman TIPS Bond | TIP | GL | 12-04-2003 | 0.20 |
| Lux Research | — | PowerShares Lux Nanotech | PXN | ST | 10-26-2005 | — |
| MSCI | — | iShares Australia | EWA | PJ | 03-12-1996 | 0.57 |
| | — | iShares Austria Index | EWO | ES | 03-12-1996 | 0.57 |
| | — | iShares Belgium Indx | EWK | ES | 03-12-1996 | 0.57 |
| | — | iShares Brazil Index | EWZ | LS | 07-10-2000 | 0.74 |
| | — | iShares Canada Index | EWC | FV | 03-12-1996 | 0.57 |
| | 81 | iShares EMU Index | EZU | ES | 07-25-2000 | 0.58 |
| | — | iShares France Index | EWQ | ES | 03-12-1996 | 0.57 |
| | — | iShares Germany Indx | EWG | ES | 03-12-1996 | 0.57 |
| | — | iShares Hong Kong | EWH | PJ | 03-12-1996 | 0.57 |
| | — | iShares Italy Index | EWI | ES | 03-12-1996 | 0.57 |
| | 85 | iShares Japan Index | EWJ | JS | 03-12-1996 | 0.57 |
| | — | iShares Malaysia | EWM | PJ | 03-12-1996 | 0.57 |
| | — | iShares Mexico Index | EWW | LS | 03-12-1996 | 0.57 |
| | 90 | iShares MSCI EAFE | EFA | FB | 08-14-2001 | 0.36 |
| | 91 | iShares MSCI EAFE Growth | EFG | FG | 08-01-2005 | — |
| | 92 | iShares MSCI EAFE Value I | EFV | FV | 08-01-2005 | — |
| | 93 | iShares MSCI Emerg Mkts | EEM | EM | 04-07-2003 | 0.77 |
| | 94 | iShares MSCI ex-Japn | EPP | PJ | 10-25-2001 | 0.50 |
| | — | iShares MSCI South Africa | EZA | EM | 02-03-2003 | 0.74 |
| | — | iShares Netherlands | EWN | ES | 03-12-1996 | 0.57 |
| | — | iShares S.Korea Indx | EWY | PJ | 05-09-2000 | 0.74 |
| | — | iShares Singapore | EWS | PJ | 03-12-1996 | 0.57 |
| | — | iShares Spain Index | EWP | ES | 03-12-1996 | 0.57 |
| | — | iShares Sweden Index | EWD | ES | 03-12-1996 | 0.58 |
| | — | iShares Switzerland | EWL | ES | 03-12-1996 | 0.57 |
| | — | iShares Taiwan Index | EWT | PJ | 06-20-2000 | 1.03 |
| | — | iShares U.K. Index | EWU | ES | 03-12-1996 | 0.57 |
| | 144 | Vanguard Cons Disc VIPERs | VCR | LG | 01-26-2004 | 0.26 |
| | 145 | Vanguard Cons Stap VIPERs | VDC | LB | 01-26-2004 | 0.26 |
| | 146 | Vanguard EmergMkts VIPERs | VWO | EM | 03-10-2005 | 0.30 |
| | 147 | Vanguard Energy VIPERs | VDE | SN | 09-29-2004 | 0.26 |
| | 148 | Vanguard Euro Stk VIPERs | VGK | ES | 03-10-2005 | 0.18 |
| | 150 | Vanguard Financial VIPERs | VFH | SF | 01-26-2004 | 0.26 |
| | 151 | Vanguard Growth VIPERs | VUG | LG | 01-26-2004 | 0.15 |
| | 152 | Vanguard HealthCar VIPERs | VHT | SH | 01-26-2004 | 0.26 |
| | — | Vanguard Indstrls VIPERs | VIS | LB | 09-29-2004 | 0.26 |
| | 153 | Vanguard InfoTech VIPERs | VGT | ST | 01-26-2004 | 0.26 |
| | 154 | Vanguard Large Cap VIPERs | VV | LB | 01-27-2004 | 0.12 |
| | — | Vanguard Materials VIPERs | VAW | SN | 01-26-2004 | 0.26 |
| | 155 | Vanguard Mid Cap VIPERs | VO | MB | 01-26-2004 | 0.18 |

# ETFs by Index Family

**Morningstar's ETF Universe**

| ETF Index Family | Page | Name | Ticker | Category | Inception Date | Expense Ratio % |
|---|---|---|---|---|---|---|
| | 156 | Vanguard Pacif Stk VIPERs | VPL | JS | 03-10-2005 | 0.18 |
| | 157 | Vanguard REIT Index VIPER | VNQ | SR | 09-23-2004 | — |
| | 160 | Vanguard Sm Cap Gr VIPERs | VBK | SG | 01-26-2004 | 0.22 |
| | 159 | Vanguard Sm Cp Val VIPER | VBR | SV | 01-26-2004 | 0.22 |
| | 158 | Vanguard Small Cap VIPERs | VB | SB | 01-26-2004 | 0.18 |
| | 161 | Vanguard TelcomSrv VIPERs | VOX | SC | 09-29-2004 | 0.26 |
| | 162 | Vanguard TSM VIPERs | VTI | LB | 05-31-2001 | 0.13 |
| | 163 | Vanguard Utilities VIPERs | VPU | SU | 01-26-2004 | 0.26 |
| | 164 | Vanguard Value VIPERs | VTV | LV | 01-26-2004 | 0.15 |
| Mergent | — | PowerShares Div Achievers | PFM | LV | 09-15-2005 | — |
| | — | PowerShares High Gr Div | PHJ | LV | 09-15-2005 | — |
| | 130 | PowerShares HY Div Achiev | PEY | MV | 12-09-2004 | 0.60 |
| | — | PowerShares Intl Div Ach | PID | FV | 09-15-2005 | — |
| Merrill Lynch Pierce Fenner & Smith | — | Consumer Discr SPDR | XLY | LB | 12-22-1998 | 0.26 |
| | 65 | Consumer Staple SPDR | XLP | LB | 12-22-1998 | 0.26 |
| | 67 | Energy SPDR | XLE | SN | 12-22-1998 | 0.26 |
| | 69 | Financial SPDR | XLF | SF | 12-22-1998 | 0.26 |
| | 70 | Health Care Sel SPDR | XLV | SH | 12-22-1998 | 0.26 |
| | 71 | Industrial SPDR | XLI | LB | 12-22-1998 | 0.25 |
| | — | Materials Sel SPDR | XLB | LV | 12-22-1998 | 0.26 |
| | 142 | Technology SPDR | XLK | ST | 12-22-1998 | 0.26 |
| | 143 | Utilities SPDR | XLU | SU | 12-22-1998 | 0.26 |
| Morgan Stanley | — | streetTRACKS MS Tech | MTK | ST | 09-25-2000 | 0.51 |
| Morningstar | — | iShares MstarLargeCore | JKD | LB | 07-02-2004 | — |
| | — | iShares MstarLargeGrowth | JKE | LG | 07-02-2004 | — |
| | — | iShares MstarLargeValue | JKF | LV | 07-02-2004 | — |
| | — | iShares MstarMidCore | JKG | MB | 07-02-2004 | — |
| | — | iShares MstarMidGrowth | JKH | MG | 07-02-2004 | — |
| | — | iShares MstarMidValue | JKI | MV | 07-02-2004 | — |
| | — | iShares MstarSmallCore | JKJ | SB | 07-02-2004 | — |
| | — | iShares MstarSmallGrowth | JKK | SG | 07-02-2004 | — |
| | — | iShares MstarSmallValue | JKL | SV | 07-02-2004 | — |
| NYSE | — | iShares NYSE 100 Index | NY | LV | 03-29-2004 | 0.20 |
| | 96 | iShares NYSE Composite | NYC | LB | 03-30-2004 | 0.25 |
| Nasdaq | 68 | Fidelity Nasdaq Comp Trac | ONEQ | LG | 09-25-2003 | 0.30 |
| | 95 | iShares NASD Biotech | IBB | SH | 02-05-2001 | 0.50 |
| | 126 | Nasdaq 100 Trust | QQQQ | LG | 03-10-1999 | 0.20 |
| Russell | 97 | iShares R. Midcap | IWR | MB | 07-17-2001 | 0.20 |
| | 98 | iShares R. Midcap Gr | IWP | MG | 07-17-2001 | 0.25 |
| | 99 | iShares R. Midcap Vl | IWS | MV | 07-17-2001 | 0.25 |
| | 100 | iShares R1000 Growth | IWF | LG | 05-22-2000 | 0.20 |
| | 101 | iShares R1000 Index | IWB | LB | 05-15-2000 | 0.15 |
| | 102 | iShares R1000 Value | IWD | LV | 05-22-2000 | 0.20 |
| | 103 | iShares R2000 Growth | IWO | SG | 07-24-2000 | 0.25 |
| | 104 | iShares R2000 Index | IWM | SB | 05-22-2000 | 0.20 |
| | 105 | iShares R2000 Value | IWN | SV | 07-24-2000 | 0.25 |
| | 106 | iShares R3000 Growth | IWZ | LG | 07-24-2000 | 0.25 |
| | 107 | iShares R3000 Index | IWV | LB | 05-22-2000 | 0.20 |
| | 108 | iShares R3000 Value | IWW | LV | 07-24-2000 | 0.25 |
| | 109 | iShares Russell Microcap | IWC | SB | 08-12-2005 | — |
| | — | Rydex Russell Top 50 | XLG | LB | 05-10-2005 | — |
| SPADE Defense Index | — | PowerShares Aero&Defense | PPA | ST | 10-26-2005 | — |
| Standard & Poors | 110 | iShares S&P 100 Ind. | OEF | LB | 10-23-2000 | 0.20 |
| | — | iShares S&P 1500 Index | ISI | LB | 01-20-2004 | 0.20 |

# ETFs by Index Family

**Morningstar's ETF Universe**

| ETF Index Family | Page | Name | Ticker | Category | Inception Date | Expense Ratio % |
|---|---|---|---|---|---|---|
| | 111 | iShares S&P 500 | IVV | LB | 05-15-2000 | 0.09 |
| | 112 | iShares S&P Euro-350 | IEV | ES | 07-25-2000 | 0.60 |
| | 113 | iShares S&P Glob 100 | IOO | WS | 12-05-2000 | 0.40 |
| | 115 | iShares SP 400 Growth | IJK | MG | 07-24-2000 | 0.25 |
| | 116 | iShares SP 400 Value | IJJ | MV | 07-24-2000 | 0.25 |
| | 117 | iShares SP 500 Growth | IVW | LG | 05-22-2000 | 0.18 |
| | 118 | iShares SP 500 Value | IVE | LV | 05-22-2000 | 0.18 |
| | 119 | iShares SP 600 Growth | IJT | SG | 07-24-2000 | 0.25 |
| | 120 | iShares SP 600 Value | IJS | SV | 07-24-2000 | 0.25 |
| | — | iShares SP Glb Enrgy | IXC | SN | 11-12-2001 | 0.65 |
| | — | iShares SP Glb Fincl | IXG | SF | 11-12-2001 | 0.65 |
| | 121 | iShares SP Glb Hlth | IXJ | SH | 11-13-2001 | 0.65 |
| | — | iShares SP Glb Tech | IXN | ST | 11-12-2001 | 0.66 |
| | — | iShares SP Glb Tele | IXP | SC | 11-12-2001 | 0.65 |
| | 114 | iShares SP Latin 40 | ILF | LS | 10-25-2001 | 0.50 |
| | 122 | iShares SP MidCap400 | IJH | MB | 05-22-2000 | 0.20 |
| | 123 | iShares SP Small 600 | IJR | SB | 05-22-2000 | 0.20 |
| | 124 | iShares SP TOPIX 150 | ITF | JS | 10-23-2001 | 0.50 |
| | 125 | MidCap SPDR Trust | MDY | MB | 05-04-1995 | 0.25 |
| | 132 | Rydex S&P Equal Weight | RSP | LB | 04-24-2003 | 0.40 |
| | — | SPDR Dividend ETF | SDY | LV | 11-08-2005 | — |
| | — | SPDR O-Strip | OOO | LB | 09-09-2004 | — |
| | 133 | SPDR Trust Series 1 | SPY | LB | 01-29-1993 | 0.11 |
| | 149 | Vanguard ExMkt VIPERs | VXF | MB | 12-27-2001 | 0.20 |
| WilderShares | — | PowerShares WilderHill | PBW | SN | 03-04-2005 | 0.70 |
| Zacks Investment Research | 131 | PowerShares Zacks MicroCp | PZI | SB | 08-18-2005 | — |

# Glossary

This section contains a glossary of investment terms. It explains how to use the data found in this publication to make better investment decisions.

# Glossary

The following is a complete alphabetical listing of the terms and features found in the pages of *Morningstar ETFs 100*.

## A

**% Annual Change**

A company's year-on-year growth in a given measure, such as sales per quarter or earnings/share per quarter. This number is expressed as a percentage.

**90-Day Treasury Bill**

*See U.S. 90-Day Treasury Bill*

**Actual Fees**

Taken from the ETF's prospectus, this area qualifies the management and 12B-1 distribution and service fees. Actual Fees most commonly represent the costs shareholders paid for management and distribution services over the fund's prior fiscal year. If fee levels have changed since the end of the most recent fiscal year, the actual fees will most commonly be presented as a recalculation based on the prior year's average monthly net assets using the new, current expenses. Although contract-type management and distribution costs are listed in a fund's prospectus, these are maximum amounts, and funds may waive a portion, or possibly all, of those fees. Actual Fees thus represent a close approximation of the true costs to shareholders.

**Address**

Usually the location of the fund's distributor, this address is where to write to receive a prospectus.

**Advisor**

This is the company that takes primary responsibility for managing the fund.

**Alpha**

*See Modern Portfolio Theory Statistics*

**Analysis**

*See Morningstar's Take*

**Arbitrage Mechanism**

This is the market mechanism that allows an ETF's market price to trade roughly in line with the net asset values of their underlying portfolios. ETFs create and redeem shares in-kind. That means they exchange ETF shares for baskets of their underlying stocks and vice versa. When ETF shares trade at a discount to their net asset values, institutional investors can assemble 50,000-share blocks in the open market at the discounted price, redeem them for the underlying stocks, and sell those stocks at a profit. The actual transaction isn't quite that simple, but the idea is the same: The arbitrage opportunity generates sufficient demand for the discounted ETF shares to close the gap between their market price and the net asset value of the underlying portfolio.

**Authorized Participant**

*See Also Creation Unit*

Typically large institutional investors or intermediaries (specialists, market makers, or broker dealers, for example), authorized participants directly enter participation agreements with ETF sponsors to purchase or redeem creation units of ETF shares. Authorized participants transfer a portfolio of stocks to a fund manager or trustee, who then places these stocks into a trust and issues creation units back to the authorized participant in exchange for the underlying securities. The authorized participant can then sell these creation units on a secondary market and redeem the units for its underlying securities.

**Average Credit Quality**

*See Also Credit Analysis*

Average credit quality gives a snapshot of the portfolio's overall credit quality. It is an average of each bond's credit rating, adjusted for its relative weighting in the portfolio. For the purposes of Morningstar's calculations, U.S. government securities are considered AAA bonds, nonrated municipal bonds generally are classified as BB, and other nonrated bonds generally are considered B.

**Average Daily Volume**

The average number of shares of an ETF traded per day, usually measured over the previous 12 months. This number, in addition to total net assets, can be a rough gauge of an ETF's popularity in the market.

**Average Effective Duration**

Average effective duration provides a measure of a fund's interest-rate sensitivity. The longer a fund's duration, the more sensitive the fund is to shifts in interest rates. The relationship among funds with different durations is straightforward: A fund with a duration of 10 years is expected to be twice as volatile as a fund with a five-year duration. Duration also gives an indication of how a fund's net asset value (NAV) will change as interest rates change. A fund with a five-year duration would be expected to lose 5% of its NAV if interest rates rose by 1 percentage point, or gain 5% if interest rates fell by 1 percentage point. Morningstar surveys fund companies for this information.

**Average Effective Maturity**
*See Also Average Nominal Maturity*
Average effective maturity is a weighted average of all the maturities of the bonds in a portfolio, computed by weighting each bond's effective maturity by the market value of the security. Average effective maturity takes into consideration all mortgage prepayments, puts, and adjustable coupons. (Because Morningstar uses fund company calculations for this figure and because different companies use varying interest-rate assumptions in determining call likelihood and timing, we ask that companies not adjust for call provisions.) Funds with longer maturity are generally considered more interest-rate sensitive than their shorter counterparts.

**Average Nominal Maturity**
*See Also Average Effective Maturity*
Listed only for municipal-bond funds, this figure is computed by weighting the nominal maturity of each security in the portfolio by the market value of the security, and then averaging these weighted figures. Unlike a fund's effective maturity figure, it does not take into account prepayments, puts, or adjustable coupons.

**Average Return**
*See Also Total Return and Market Return*
The annualized return of the ETF over a multiyear period, such as three or five years. This represents the annual return that an investor would have received if the fund's returns were evenly spread across the time period.

**Average Stock Percentage**
*See also Composition*
For stock-oriented funds, we provide a yearly average stock position calculated by averaging all reported composition numbers for the year. These averages provide a valuable complement to the current composition numbers; investors can compare a fund's current level of market participation with its historical averages.

**Average Weighted Coupon**
*See Also Coupon Range*
Average weighted coupon is computed by averaging each bond's coupon rate adjusted for its relative weighting in the portfolio. This figure indicates whether the fund is opting for a high- or low-coupon strategy, and it may serve as an indicator of interest-rate sensitivity, particularly for mortgage-backed funds or other funds with callable bonds. A high coupon frequently indicates less sensitivity to interest rates; a low coupon, the opposite.

**Average Weighted Price**
Average weighted price is computed for most bond funds by weighting the price of each bond by its relative size in the portfolio. This number reveals whether the fund favors bonds selling at prices above or below face value (premium or discount securities, respectively) and can also serve as an indicator of interest-rate sensitivity. This statistic is expressed as a percentage of par (face) value. This statistic is not calculated for international-bond funds, because their holdings are often expressed in terms of foreign currencies.

---

# B

**Bear Market**
*See Also Bull Market*
A period when stock prices fall and investors are pessimistic about market returns. Bear markets usually are not labeled as such until stock prices have slipped by at least 15%. The opposite of a bear market is a bull market.

**Benchmark Index**
A benchmark index gives the investor a point of reference for evaluating a fund's performance. In all cases in which such comparisons are made, Morningstar uses the S&P 500 Index as the basic benchmark for stock-oriented funds, including moderate- and conservative-allocation funds and convertible-bond funds. The Lehman Brothers Aggregate Bond Index is used as the benchmark index for all bond funds. We also provide a comparison with a secondary, specialized benchmark. Because the S&P 500 Index is composed of almost entirely large-cap domestic stocks, it is a good performance measure for large-cap domestic stocks funds and the overall market, but other comparisons are less useful. Comparing a foreign large-value fund with the S&P 500 Index, for example, does not show how the fund has done relative to foreign stock markets, so a fund's total return in the History and Performance sections is compared with a more specialized index. Benchmark also can refer to the index that an ETF tracks.

**Best Fit Index**
*See Also Modern Portfolio Theory Statistics*
The Best Fit Index is the market index whose monthly returns have correlated the most closely with a given fund's in the most recent 36 consecutive months. Morningstar regresses the fund's monthly excess returns against monthly excess returns of several well-

known market indexes. Best Fit signifies the index that provides the highest R-squared, or correlation with a given fund.

### Beta
*See Modern Portfolio Theory Statistics*

### Bid/Ask Spread
The difference in the price at which an investor can buy and sell ETF shares. A wide bid/ask spread allows market makers to buy at a lower price and sell at a higher price.

### Bull Market
*See Also Bear Market*
A period when stock prices rise and investors are optimistic about market returns. Bull markets usually are not labeled as such until stock prices have risen by at least 15%. The opposite of a bear market is a bull market.

---

# C

### Capital Gains
Capital gains are the profits received and distributed from the sale of securities within a portfolio. This line shows a summary of the ETF's annual capital gains distributions expressed in per-share dollar amounts. Both short- and long-term gains are included, as are options premiums and distributions from paid-in capital. Most ETFs realize and distribute fewer capital gains than conventional mutual funds because ETFs do not have to sell securities to satisfy redemptions. As a result, ETFs are often considered to be more tax efficient than mutual funds.

### Capital Return %
*See Also Income Return % and Total Return*
Morningstar provides the portion of a fund's total returns that was generated by realized and unrealized increases in the value of securities in the portfolio. Frequently, a stock fund's returns will be derived entirely from capital return. By looking at capital return and income return, an investor can see whether the fund's returns come from capital, from income, or from a combination of both. Adding capital and income return will produce the fund's total return.

### Category
*See Morningstar Category*

### Closed-End Fund
A type of fund that offers a limited number of shares and trades throughout the day on an exchange. Unlike ETFs, the shares of closed-end funds cannot be continuously created and redeemed. Closed-end funds sell shares to investors only once, in an initial public offering (IPO). When shareholders want to sell their closed-end fund shares, they must sell to other investors through brokers, as with a common stock, paying a commission when they do so. If you buy a closed-end fund on its IPO you also have to pay a built-in underwriting charge, similar to a mutual fund load, that can be as large as 7%. Most closed-end funds are listed on the New York Stock Exchange. Like open-end funds, closed-end funds gather money from large and small investors alike. Portfolio managers from investment firms, some of which are the same fund companies familiar to mutual fund investors, manage the combined assets. The value of one share of this pool of money is called the closed-end fund's net asset value (NAV) just like with open-end funds.

Because they trade on exchanges, closed-end funds have a second price besides their NAV. The price at which investors actually buy and sell shares is called the market price. Investors can learn the market price of a closed-end fund at any minute of the day, as with a stock price.

The two prices of a closed-end fund mean that it usually is bought and sold at a price higher or lower than its NAV. (The two prices could be identical, but they rarely are.) Most closed-end funds sell at discounts to their NAV. For years, academics and other researchers have come up with a variety of theories why that's so, but none of the theories has proven itself consistently enough to be considered a definitive explanation.

### Commission
The fee paid to a broker to buy or sell a security on behalf of an investor. Like stock trades, commissions for ETFs are typically assessed on a per-trade basis. As a result, it can be more cost-effective for frequent traders to purchase no-load indexed mutual funds in lieu of an ETF with a similar portfolio. Brokerage commissions vary greatly according to account size, individual trading frequency, and the brokerage company used.

## Composition

*See Also Average Stock Percentage*

The composition percentages provide a simple breakdown of the fund's portfolio holdings, as of the date listed, into general investment classes at the bottom of the Portfolio Analysis section. Cash encompasses both the actual cash and the cash equivalents (fixed-income securities with maturities of one year or less) held by the portfolio. A negative percentage of cash indicates that the portfolio is leveraged, meaning it has borrowed against its own assets to buy more securities or that it has used other techniques to gain additional exposure to the market. The percentage listed as Stocks incorporates only the portfolio's straight common stocks. Bonds include every fixed-income security with a maturity of more than one year, from government notes to high-yield corporate bonds. Other includes preferred stocks (equity securities that pay dividends at a specified rate), as well as convertible bonds and convertible preferreds, which are corporate securities that are exchangeable for a set amount of another form of security (usually shares of common stock) at a prestated price. Other also includes all those not-so-neatly categorized securities, such as warrants and options.

## Country Exposure

For each international portfolio the country exposure information displays the top five countries in which the fund is invested. This information is gathered directly from the portfolios given by the fund companies.

## Coupon Range

*See Also Average Weighted Coupon*

Taxable-bond funds feature a table listing the breakdown of each portfolio's bond coupons, or rates of interest payments. The coupon range is designed to help an investor complete the picture suggested by the average weighted coupon statistic. These ranges differ according to Morningstar category and, due to changing interest rates, are subject to alteration over time. Whatever the breakdown may be, the first number is always exclusive and the second number is always inclusive. A range of 8% to 10% for example, would exclude bonds that have a weighted coupon rate of exactly 8% but would include bonds with a weighted coupon rate of 10%. High-yield bond funds include PIKs in their coupon breakdown, which are payment-in-kind issues that make interest payments in the form of additional securities rather than cash.

The overall percentage of bond assets that fall within each coupon range is noted in the % of Bonds

column. The Rel Cat column compares a fund with others in its Morningstar Category. The category average is set at 1.0.

## Creation Unit

*See Also Authorized Participant*

The smallest block of ETF shares that can be bought or sold from the ETF at net asset value, usually 50,000. These are only bought and sold "in-kind." For example, when you sell one, you receive a portfolio of securities that approximates the ETF's holdings, not cash. Creation units' size means that only market makers and institutions can afford to buy or sell them. Such investors are referred to as authorized participants. All other investors can buy or sell ETF shares in any size lot at the market price, rather than at NAV, over an exchange.

## Credit Analysis

*See Also Average Credit Quality*

This section depicts the quality of bonds in a bond fund's portfolio. The credit analysis shows the percentage of fixed-income securities that fall within each credit-quality rating as assigned by Standard & Poor's or Moody's.

At the top of the ratings are U.S. government bonds. Bonds issued and backed by the government, as well as those backed by government-linked organizations such as Fannie Mae and Freddie Mac, are of extremely high quality and thus are considered equivalent to bonds rated AAA, which is the highest possible rating a corporate issue can receive. Morningstar gives U.S. government bonds a credit rating separate from AAA securities to allow for a more accurate credit analysis of a portfolio's holdings. Bonds with a BBB rating are the lowest grade that are still considered to be investment-grade. Bonds that are rated BB or lower (often called junk bonds or high-yield bonds) are considered to be speculative. Any bonds that appear in the NR/NA category are either not rated by Standard & Poor's or Moody's, or did not have a rating available at the time of publication.

## Current Investment Style

*See Also Investment Style Box*

For equity funds, this section lists a fund portfolio's current averages for various portfolio statistics, including price/earnings, price/cash flow, and historical earnings growth. To provide perspective, we compare these measures with the funds' category average.

For bond funds, this section lists a portfolio's current duration, as well as averages for effective maturity, credit quality, weighted coupon, and price. These numbers are helpful in determining how much interest-rate and credit risk the portfolio currently has. For example, funds with high durations typically are very sensitive to changes in interest rates, whereas those with durations of just a year or two tend to be relatively insensitive to interest-rate changes. Funds with AAA or AA average credit-quality rankings take on less credit risk than those with, for example, B ratings, which indicate the portfolio holds a lot of high-yield (or junk) debt.

Morningstar currently uses price/cash flow, price/book, and median market capitalization to categorize foreign funds. This section also compares international-stock funds' current valuations with those of the MSCI EAFE Index, which is the most widely used benchmark for international offerings. Funds with low valuations typically hold stocks that aren't expected to grow rapidly, and therefore land in one of the value style boxes. By contrast, portfolios with high valuations typically hold fast-growing issues.

---

# D

### Diamonds
*See Also Unit Investment Trust*
Shares in the Diamonds Trust Series I DIA, an ETF that tracks the Dow Jones Industrial Average. The fund is structured as a unit investment trust.

### Discount to NAV
Unlike regular open-end mutual funds, which are bought and sold directly from the fund company at the net asset value (NAV) of their portfolio securities, ETFs and closed-end funds trade at prices determined by the market forces of supply and demand. A fund that trades at a price less than its NAV is said to trade at a discount to its NAV. Any discount or premium should be small and short-lived due to the arbitrage mechanisms inherent in ETF structures.

### Dividend
The portion of a company's profit paid directly to shareholders, generally expressed in a per-share amount. Most ETFs pay dividends at least semiannually or annually. Some ETFs such as the iShares Dow Jones Select Dividend Index, actively mimic indexes that identify high dividend-paying stocks. The way in which an ETF pays out its dividends depends on the legal structure of the ETF. The open-end index ETFs automatically reinvest dividends and pay shareholders

through a quarterly cash distribution; unit investment trust ETFs do not reinvest dividends, instead putting them in a non-interest-bearing account until quarterly payout; and grantor trust ETFs allow investors to receive dividends directly from the companies of the underlying securities, instead of from the authorized participant. For an ETF's specific distribution policy, you must read the ETF's prospectus or consult with your financial advisor.

### Dollar-Cost Averaging
The practice of making investments in fixed amounts at regular intervals, such as monthly, quarterly, semiannually or annually. The process allows investors to lower their average costs by forcing them to buy more shares at low prices and fewer at high prices. Also referred to as systematic investing or constant-dollar plan. Conventional fund companies often will waive normal minimum investments for investors to commit to make direct deposits from their savings or checking accounts into such regular investment plans. However, because investors must pay brokerage commissions each time they purchase or redeem ETF shares, investing small sums of money at regular intervals for ETFs may not be very cost-efficient.

### Dow Jones Industrial Average
The Dow Jones Industrial Average, or Dow, is the most widely known stock-market index. The index is composed of 30 companies selected by the editors of the Wall Street Journal. The prices of the companies are added together and divided by a divisor that changes when a new company replaces an old one in the index, or when any company in the index splits its stock. While the Dow is not an accurate measure of the market, it is still popular because it is so well known and the companies in it are generally well-established blue-chips. Other indexes, such as Standard & Poor's 500 (S&P 500) or the Wilshire 5000, are considered to be more accurate representations of the market.

### Duration
*See Average Effective Duration*

# E

### ETF
*See Also Open-Index ETF, Unit Investment Trust, and Grantor Trust*

An abbreviation for exchange-traded funds. ETFs are baskets of securities that are traded on an exchange and, unlike open-end mutual funds, can be bought and sold throughout the trading day. They can also be sold short and bought on margin. In brief, anything you might do with a stock, you can do with an ETF. Currently most ETFs are index funds and are composed of holdings that mimic a given index or specialize in certain commodities and offer diversification, low costs, and trading flexibility to investors. Unlike mutual funds, there are options available on many ETFs. There are three different legal structures for ETFs: open-end funds, unit investment trusts, and grantor trusts. The first two structures are registered with the SEC under the Investment Company Act of 1940, while the third is not. The primary differences among these three structures regard their dividend distribution schedules and purchase/redemption policies.

### Equity Style
*See Investment Style Box*

### Exchange
Where ETFs are traded, including the American Stock Exchange (AMEX), New York Stock Exchange (NYSE), and Nasdaq Stock Market. Exchanges are formal organizations approved and regulated by the Securities and Exchange Commission and whose members use the facilities to trade securities. Because ETFs' shares are traded on an exchange, their prices will fluctuate according to supply and demand and offer investors the kind of real-time flexibility not available with traditional mutual funds.

### Expense Projections (Three-, Five-, and 10-Year)
The SEC mandates that each fund administered by a registered investment company list its expense projections. Found in the fund's prospectus, these figures show how much an investor would expect to pay in expenses, sales charges (loads), and fees over the next three, five, and 10 years, assuming a $10,000 investment that grows by 5% per year with redemption at the end of each time period. Expense projections are commonly based on the past year's incurred fees or an estimate of the current fiscal year's fees, should a portion of the overall fee structure change as of the printing of the fund's most current prospectus. Newer funds are required to print expense projections for only one- and three-year time periods, as longer-term projections may not be possible to estimate.

### Expense Ratio
The annual fee that all ETFs charge their shareholders. It is taken from the ETF's annual report and expressed as a percentage of the ETF's average daily net assets deducted each fiscal year for fund expenses. It may include such items as the management fee, trustee's fee, and license fee, among others. The expense ratio is deducted from the ETF's average net assets and accrued on a daily basis. It does not include the commissions paid to trade ETF shares, or the costs incurred by the fund in trading its underlying securities. If the ETF's assets are small, its expense ratio can be quite high because the ETF must meet its expenses from a restricted asset base. Conversely, as the net assets of the fund grow, the expense percentage should ideally diminish because expenses are spread across the wider base. To note, HOLDRs do not express their fees as expense ratios, but instead charge a flat quarterly fee per 100 shares.

# F

### Fixed-Income Style
*see Investment Style Box*

### Fair Value
*See Also Morningstar Price/Fair Value Measure*

Morningstar stock analysts estimate a stock's fair value using a discounted cash flow model that takes into account their estimates of the company's growth, profitability, risk, and many other factors over the next five years. This fair value is then compared with the stock's market price to figure its Morningstar Rating.

Morningstar uses the fair values its analysts set for stocks to help determine if an ETF is over- or undervalued.

# G

### Grantor Trust
An ETF structure not registered under the Investment Company Act of 1940. Grantor trusts create shares in lots of 100 and can only be purchased or redeemed in multiples of these units. They are unique in structure because investors retain the voting rights to

the underlying securities of the shares and can receive dividends immediately. Merrill Lynch's HOLDRs are examples of ETFs structured as grantor trusts.

## Growth

*See Also Investment Style Box*

Often contrasted with a value approach to investing, the term growth is used to describe an investment style in which a manager looks for equity securities with high rates of revenue or earnings growth. A company's valuations are generally not emphasized as much as they are in value-style investing.

## Growth of $10,000

The Growth of $10,000 graph shows an ETF's performance based on how $10,000 invested in the fund would have grown over time. The returns used in the graph are not load-adjusted. The growth of $10,000 begins at the date of the fund's inception, or the first year listed on the graph, whichever is appropriate. Located alongside the ETF's graph line is a line that represents the growth of $10,000 in either the S&P 500 Index (for stock funds and hybrid funds) or the LB Aggregate Index (for bond funds). The third line represents the fund's Morningstar category average (see definition below). These lines allow investors to compare the performance of the fund with the performance of a benchmark index and the ETF's Morningstar category. Both lines are plotted on a logarithmic scale, so that identical percentage changes in the value of an investment have the same vertical distance on the graph.  For example, the vertical distance between $10,000 and $20,000 is the same as the distance between $20,000 and $40,000 because both represent a 100% increase in investment value. This provides a more accurate representation of performance than would a simple arithmetic graph. The graphs are scaled so that the full length of the vertical axis represents a tenfold increase in investment value. For securities with returns that have exhibited greater than a tenfold increase over the period shown in the graph, the vertical axis has been compressed accordingly.

## Growth Measures

*Long-Term Earnings Growth*

Earnings are what are left of a firm's revenues after it pays all of its expenses, costs, and taxes. Companies whose earnings grow faster than those of their industry peers usually see better price performance for their stocks. Projected earnings growth is an estimate of a company's expected long-term growth in earnings, derived from all polled analysts' estimates. When reported for an ETF, it shows the weighted average of

the projected growth in earnings for each stock in the ETF's portfolio. This measure helps determine Morningstar's growth score for each stock and the overall growth orientation of the ETF.

*Historical Earnings Growth*

Historical earnings growth shows the rate of increase in a company's earnings per share, based on up to four time periods. When reported for an ETF, it shows the weighted average of the growth in earnings for each stock in the ETF's portfolio. This measure helps determine Morningstar's growth score for each stock and the overall growth orientation of the ETF.

*Sales Growth*

Sales growth shows the rate of increase in a company's sales per share, based on up to four time periods, and it is considered the best gauge of how rapidly a company's core business is growing. When reported for an ETF, it shows the weighted average of the sales-growth rates for each stock in the ETF's portfolio. This measure helps determine Morningstar's growth score for each stock and the overall growth orientation of the ETF.

*Cash Flow Growth*

Cash flow tells you how much cash a business is actually generating—in other words, its earnings before depreciation, amortization, and noncash charges. Sometimes called cash earnings, it's considered a gauge of liquidity and solvency. Cash flow growth shows the rate of increase in a company's cash flow per share, based on up to four time periods. When reported for an ETF, it shows the weighted average of the growth in cash flow for each stock in the ETF's portfolio. This measure helps determine Morningstar's growth score for each stock and the overall growthorientation of the ETF.

*Book Value Growth*

Book value is, in theory, what would be left over for shareholders if a company shut down its operations, paid off all its creditors, collected from all its debtors, and liquidated itself. In practice, however, the value of assets and liabilities can change substantially from when they are first recorded. Book value growth shows the rate of increase in a company's book value per share, based on up to four time periods. When reported for an ETF it shows the weighted average of the growth rates in book value for each stock in the ETF's portfolio. This measure helps determine Morningstar's growth score for each stock and the overall growth orientation of the ETF.

# H

### Hedge

Broadly, hedging is an investment strategy that aims to offset risk through a variety of techniques such as crosshedge, dynamic hedge, static hedge, and direct hedge. The aim of all of these techniques is to offset any gains or losses in an uncertain market environment.

### HOLDR

An abbreviation for Holding Company Depository Receipts. Unlike other ETFs, HOLDRs can be bought and sold only in 100-share increments and are structured as grantor trust ETFs. As such, they have unique characteristics regarding voting rights and distributions (as compared with open-end index ETFs and unit investment trusts). HOLDRs are currently offered by Merrill Lynch and the ones that currently exist focus on narrow industry groups.

---

# I

### Inception

The date on which the ETF commenced operations by offering its shares for sale to investors.

### Income $

Income reflects the dividends and interest generated by an ETF's holdings. This area shows a fund's yearly income distribution expressed in per-share dollar amounts.

### Income Distribution

The number of times per year that an ETF intends to make income payments (from either dividends or interest). This will differ according to the legal structure of the ETF and is specified in the ETF's prospectus or marketing document

### Income Ratio %

The fund's income ratio reveals the percentage of current income earned per share. It is calculated by dividing the ETF's net investment income by its average net assets. (Net investment income is the total income of the ETF, less expenses.) An income ratio can be negative if an ETF's expenses exceed its income, which can occur with funds that have high costs or that tend to emphasize capital gains rather than income. Because the income ratio is based on an ETF's fiscal year and is taken directly from the fund's annual shareholder report, it may not exactly correspond with other calendar-year information on the page.

### Income Return %
*See Also Capital Return % and Total Return*
Income return is that portion of an ETF's total returns that was derived from income distributions. Income return will often be higher than capital return for bond-tracking ETFs, and typically lower for equity-tracking ETFs. Adding the income return and the capital return together will produce the fund's total return.

### Index Fund

A fund type that attempts to passively track the composition and returns of a given index, rather than actively trying to select securities to beat the bogy. The portfolios of index funds provide a complete or near complete representation of their benchmark indexes. Their performance should be similar the performance of the benchmark. All ETFs are currently index funds, though there are plans for actively managed ETFs.

### Industry Weightings
*see also Relative Comparisons and Sector Weightings*
For specialty ETFs (also called sector ETFs), we replace the standard sector weightings, which include broad industry classifications such as hardware, with a breakdown of the ETFs weightings in the sector's subindustries, or subsectors. Each sector has its own breakdown of subsectors, which can help investors decide which specific areas of an industry the ETF invests in, and how pure its focus is. The industry weightings show at a glance whether a ETF is conservatively diversified across a sector, betting on just a couple of risky subsectors to charge up returns, or crouching defensively in the mildest corner of the specialty. The ETF's weightings relative to its category average are also shown.

Each specialty's breakdown also includes an Other classification, but a large weighting there shouldn't be interpreted as meaning the ETF is investing outside of its specialty. This is merely a catchall designation to classify the stocks that don't meet the exact criteria for any specific subsector. It's impossible to capture every nook and cranny of the sprawling technology category, for example, in the eight subsectors included on the page. Thus, a fair number of tech stocks fall into Other.

### In-Kind Redemption

When redeeming investors receive the underlying securities of an ETF instead of cash.

## Institutional Investor

An entity, company, or firm that manages assets on behalf of other investors (individual or otherwise). Some examples of institutional investors include mutual fund companies, insurance companies, and brokerage firms. Because of the large volume of assets traded by institutional investors, they can act as market makers and also often qualify for lower expense charges. Institutional investors often can enter into authorized participation agreements with ETF sponsors.

## Investment Company (Open-End Fund)

A company regulated under the Investment Company Act of 1940 whose primary business is to invest, reinvest, or trade in securities. The investment company offers its own securities to the public and must comply with the specified regulations.

## Investment Style Box

*See Also Current Investment Style, Growth, Market Capitalization, Morningstar Category, and Value*

To help investors cut through the confusion and profusion of mutual funds and ETFs, Morningstar designed the style box, a visual tool for better understanding a fund's true investment strategy. Based on an analysis of a fund's portfolio, the Morningstar style box is a snapshot of the types of securities held by the fund. The style box is calculated with methodology similar to that used to assign the Morningstar Categories. By providing an easy-to-understand visual representation of stock and fund characteristics, the Morningstar style box allows for informed comparisons and portfolio construction based on actual holdings, as opposed to assumptions based on a fund's name or how it is marketed. The style box also forms the basis for Morningstar's style-based fund categories and market indexes.

### Domestic-Stock Style Box

The Morningstar domestic-stock style box is a nine-square grid that provides a graphical representation of the "investment style" of stocks, mutual funds, and ETFs. It classifies securities according to market capitalization (the vertical axis) and growth and value factors (the horizontal axis). Note: Fixed-income funds are classified according to credit quality (the vertical axis) and sensitivity to changes in interest rates (the horizontal axis).

### How It Works

Style box assignments begin at the individual stock level. Morningstar determines the investment style of each individual stock in its database. The style attributes of individual stocks are then used to determine the style classification of stock ETFs.

### The Horizontal Axis

The scores for a stock's value and growth characteristics determine its placement on the horizontal axis of the stock style box:

## Value Score Components and Weights

**Forward-looking measures**

| | |
|---|---|
| Price-to-projected earnings | 50.0% |

**Historical-based measures**

| | |
|---|---|
| Price-to-book | 12.5% |
| Price-to-sales | 12.5% |
| Price-to-cash flow | 12.5% |
| Dividend yield | 12.5% |

## Growth Score Components and Weights

**Forward-looking measures**

| | |
|---|---|
| Long-term projected earnings growth | 50.0% |

**Historical-based measures**

| | |
|---|---|
| Historical earnings growth | 12.5% |
| Sales growth | 12.5% |
| Cash flow growth | 12.5% |
| Book value growth | 12.5% |

Growth and value characteristics for each individual stock are compared with those of other stocks within the same capitalization band and are scored from zero to 100 for both value and growth.

## Stock Style Box

| Risk | Investment Style | | | Average Weighted Market Capitalization |
|---|---|---|---|---|
| | Value | Blend | Growth | |
| Low ○ | Large-cap Value | Large-cap Blend | Large-cap Growth | Large |
| Moderate ○ | Mid-cap Value | Mid-cap Blend | Mid-cap Growth | Mid |
| High ◉ | Small-cap Value | Small-cap Blend | Small-cap Growth | Small |

Within the stock style box grid, nine possible combinations exist, ranging from large-cap value for the safest funds to small-cap growth for the riskiest.

To determine the overall style score, the value score is subtracted from the growth score.

The resulting number can range from 100 (for low-yield, extremely growth-oriented stocks) to -100 (for high-yield, low-growth stocks). A stock is classified as growth if the net score equals or exceeds the "growth threshold" (normally about 25 large-cap stocks). It is deemed value if its score equals or falls below the "value threshold" (normally about -15 for large-cap stocks).

And if the score lies between the two thresholds, the stock is classified as "core."

The thresholds between value, core, and growth stocks vary to some degree over time, as the distribution of stock styles changes in the market. However, on average, the three stock styles each account for approximately one third of the total free float in each size category.

*The Vertical Axis*
Rather than a fixed number of large-cap or small-cap stocks, Morningstar uses a flexible system that isn't adversely affected by overall movements in the market to classify stocks as small, medium, or large. Large-cap stocks are defined as the group that accounts for the top 70% capitalization of the Morningstar domestic-stock universe; mid-cap stocks represent the next 20%; and small-cap stocks represent the balance. The Morningstar stock universe represents approximately 99% of the U.S. market for actively traded stocks.

*Moving from Individual Stocks to Funds*
A stock-tracking ETF is an aggregation of individual stocks and its style is determined by the style assignments of the stocks it owns. By plotting all of an ETF's stocks on the stock style grid, the range of stock styles included in the fund immediately becomes apparent. An asset-weighted average of the stocks' net value/growth scores determines a fund's horizontal placement-value, growth, or blend.

A fund's vertical placement is determined by its "market cap," which is defined as the geometric mean of the market capitalization (or average weighted market cap) for the stocks it owns.

Cap1 = the capitalization of stock 1 and W1 = the % weight in the portfolio and the geometric mean of market capitalization
$$=(Cap1^{W1})(Cap2^{W2})(Cap3^{W3})(Cap4^{W4})\ldots(CapN^{WN})$$

For a simple example, consider a fund that owns just three stocks:

25% stake in Stock A, market cap = $1.85 Billion
35% stake in Stock B, market cap = $3.56 Billion
40% stake in Stock C, market cap = $8.58 Billion

Its geometric mean of market capitalization would equal:

$($1.85 bil$^{.25})($3.56 bil$^{.35})($8.58 bil$^{.40}) = $4.30$ Billion

Note that this number is larger than the fund's median market cap-the capitalization of the median stock in its portfolio. That's because stock C, with a relatively higher market cap, occupies the biggest slice of the portfolio. The geometric mean better identifies the portfolio's "center of gravity." In other words, it provides more accurate insight into how market trends (as defined by capitalization) might affect the portfolio.

Style box assignments for stocks are updated each month. Assignments for ETFs are recalculated whenever Morningstar receives updated portfolio holdings for the ETF.

*Using the Style Box*
In general, a growth-oriented ETF will hold the stocks of companies that the portfolio manager believes will increase earnings faster than the rest of the market. A value-oriented ETF contains mostly stocks the manager thinks are currently undervalued in price and will eventually see their worth recognized by the market. A blend fund might be a mix of growth stocks and value stocks, or it may contain stocks that exhibit both characteristics.

Understanding how different types of stocks behave is crucial for building a diversified, style-controlled portfolio of stocks, mutual funds, or ETFs. The Morningstar style box helps investors construct portfolios based on the characteristics, or style factors, of all the stocks and funds that portfolio includes.

*International-Stock Style Box*
These style boxes are similar to the domestic-stock style boxes described above, although the methodology is different.

On the vertical axis, international-stock ETFs are grouped as small, medium, or large. ETFs with median market capitalizations of less than $1 billion are grouped in the small-cap box. ETFs with median market caps equal to or greater than $1 billion but less than or equal to $5 billion are labeled as mid-cap offerings. ETFs with median market caps exceeding $5 billion are large cap. On the horizontal axis, international-stock ETFs, like their domestic counterparts, are separated into value, blend, or growth ETFs. We take the stock portfolio's average price/cash-flow ratio relative to the MSCI EAFE Index and add it to the portfolio's average price/book figure relative to the MSCI EAFE Index. (The MSCI EAFE average in each case is set equal to 1.00.) If the sum of the relative price/cash flow and the relative price/book is less than 1.75, the ETF is defined as a value offering if the sum lands from 1.75 to 2.25 the ETF is classified as a blend vehicle; if the sum is greater than 2.25 the ETF falls into the growth column.

## Bond Style Box

Domestic- and international-bond ETFs feature their own Morningstar style box, which focuses on two pillars of bond performance: interest-rate sensitivity and credit quality. Morningstar splits bond ETFs into three groups of rate sensitivity as determined by duration (short, intermediate, and long) and three credit-quality groups (high, medium, and low). These groupings graphically display a portfolio's average effective duration and credit quality. As with stock funds, nine possible combinations exist, ranging from short duration/high quality for the safest funds to long duration/low quality for the most volatile.

Along the horizontal axis of the style box lies the interest-rate sensitivity of an ETF's bond portfolio based on average effective duration. This figure, which is calculated by the ETF sponsors, weights each bond's duration by its relative size within the portfolio. Duration provides a more accurate description of a bond's true interest-rate sensitivity than does maturity because it takes into consideration all mortgage prepayments, puts and call options, and adjustable coupons. ETFs with an average effective duration of less than 3.5 years qualify as short term. ETFs with an average effective duration of greater than or equal to 3.5 years and less than or equal to six years are classified as intermediate. ETFs with an average effective duration of greater than six years are considered long term.

Along the vertical axis of a bond style box lies the average credit-quality rating of a bond portfolio. ETFs that have an average credit rating of AAA or AA are categorized as high quality. Bond portfolios with average ratings of A or BBB are medium quality, and

### Bond Style Box

| Risk | Duration | | | Quality |
|---|---|---|---|---|
| | Value | Blend | Growth | |
| Low ◯ | Short-term High Quality | Interm-term High Quality | Long-term High Quality | High |
| Moderate ◯ | Short-term Medium Quality | Interm-term Medium Quality | Long-term Medium Quality | Medium |
| High ◉ | Short-term Low Quality | Interm-term Low Quality | Long-Term Low Quality | Low |

Within the bond style box grid, nine possible combinations exist, ranging from short duration or maturity/high quality for the safest funds to long duration or maturity/low quality for the riskiest.

those rated BB and below are categorized as low quality. For the purposes of Morningstar's calculations, U.S. government securities are considered AAA bonds, nonrated municipal bonds generally are classified as BB, and all other nonrated bonds generally are considered B.

# L

## Lehman Brothers Aggregate Index

An index that measures the value of a wide variety of investment-grade government and corporate bonds, as well as asset-backed and mortgage-backed securities. This is one of the most popular benchmarks for bonds, bond funds, and bond-tracking ETFs.

## Lehman Brothers Corporate Index

An index that measures the value of a wide variety of U.S. corporate bonds and is commonly used as a benchmark for corporate bonds and corporate bond funds.

## Leverage

An investment technique that involves investing borrowed money to increase returns. Certain financial instruments, such as options, also are said to have leverage relative to the underlying stock or ETF because price changes in the stock can cause larger increases or decreases in the value of the option.

## Limit Order

A price order that stipulates the maximum price at which a buyer is willing to purchase shares or the minimum price at which he or she is willing to sell shares.

---

# M

## Management Fee

The management fee is the maximum percentage deducted from a ETF's average net assets to pay an advisor or subadvisor. Often, as the ETF's net assets grow, the percentage deducted for management fees decreases. Alternatively, the ETF may compute the fee as a flat percentage of average net assets. Management fees for ETFs should be relatively low compared with mutual funds, with most being well under 1.00%.

## Manager

*see Portfolio Manager*

## Market Cap

*See Also Market Capitalization*

Shown for domestic-stock ETFs, this section gives investors a view of the different sizes of companies in a fund's portfolio. Every month, we break down a stock portfolio into five different sizes of companies by their market capitalization and show what percentage of a fund's stock assets is devoted to each. Instead of using stationary market-cap cut-offs, we base our boundaries on percentiles: We call the largest 1% of U.S. companies Giant, the next 4% Large, the next 15% Medium, the next 30% Small, and the bottom 50% Micro. The Market Cap section is designed to help investors complete the picture suggested by the median market cap statistic. While average weighted market cap pinpoints the size of the average holding, this section allows investors to see the whole range of companies held by the fund.

## Market Capitalization (Average Weighted)

*See Also Market Cap, Relative Comparisons, and Investment Style Box*

For domestic-stock offerings, this measures the portfolio's "center of gravity," in terms of its market-cap exposure. A market capitalization is calculated for each stock. Its weight in the average weighted market cap calculation is then determined by the percentage of stocks it consumes in the overall portfolio. For example, a stock that is a 10% position in a fund will have twice as much influence on the calculation than a stock that is a 5% stake.

## Market Maker

A dealer, such as a brokerage or bank, who fulfills buy and sell orders from investors for particular stocks. Market makers display a publicly offered price for securities in their inventory and the number of securities offered for sale. They have an important role in providing liquidity and efficiency for the securities in which they traffic.

## Market Order

A price order executed with no specified price maximum or minimum. Instead, brokers buy or sell securities at the best price available on the market at the time.

## Market Price

An ETF's share price as determined by market supply and demand. The market price can be expressed as the bid or offer price, the midpoint between the bid/offer spread, or the last sale price. Its expression depends on the policy of the quoting entity.

## Market Return

*See Also Total Return and NAV Return*

The total return of an ETF based on its market price at the beginning and end of the holding period. This may differ from the ETF's NAVreturn. The market return is the return earned by ETF investors, except for those who hold creation units (authorized participants).

## Maturity

*See Average Effective Maturity and Average Nominal Maturity*

## Mean

*See Standard Deviation*

## Modern Portfolio Theory (MPT) Statistics

*See Also Benchmark Index*

Developed in the 1950s by Harry Markowitz, Modern Portfolio Theory statistics (or MPT statistics) are standard financial and academic statistical tools for assessing the risk and return of a portfolio relative to its benchmark. The main theory behind MPT is that a certain risk level will produce a certain corresponding return. Its statistical tools are best-fit beta, alpha, and R-squared. Morningstar bases alpha, beta, and R-squared on a least-squares regression of the portfolio's excess return over Treasury bills compared with the excess returns of the fund's benchmark index. These calculations are computed for the trailing 36-month period. For ETFs, the benchmark index should have a high R-squared, because index-tracking

ETF's underlying portfolio should replicate the composition of its target index.

### Alpha

Alpha represents the amount by which a portfolio has outperformed or underperformed what was expected based on its risk (beta). If alpha is positive, it means the portfolio's returns were higher than its regression line predicted. With mutual funds, investors often view alpha as a measurement of the value added or subtracted by active fund managers. With index-tracking ETFs, the alpha should correlate with the accepted beta of the benchmark. There are limitations to alpha's ability to accurately depict a fund's added or subtracted value. In some cases, a negative alpha can result from the expenses that are present in the fund figures but are not present in the figures of the comparison index. Alpha is completely dependent on the accuracy of beta: If the investor accepts beta as a conclusive definition of risk, a positive alpha would be a conclusive indicator of good fund performance.

### Beta

Beta is a measure of a fund's sensitivity to market movements. It measures the relationship between a fund's excess return over T-bills and the excess return of the benchmark index. Morningstar calculates beta using the same regression equation as the one used for alpha, which regresses excess return for the fund against excess return for the index. This approach differs slightly from other methodologies that rely on a regression of raw returns. By definition, the beta of the benchmark (in this case, an index) is 1.00. Accordingly, a fund with beta 1.10 has performed 10% better than its benchmark index after deducting the T-bill rate in up markets and 10% worse in down markets, assuming all other factors remain constant. Conversely, a beta of 0.85 indicates that the fund has performed 15% worse than the index in up markets and 15% better in down markets. A low beta does not imply that the fund has a low level of volatility, though; rather, a low beta means only that the fund's market-related risk is low. A specialty fund that invests primarily in gold, for example, will usually have a low beta (and a low R-squared), as its performance is tied more closely to the price of gold and gold-mining stocks than to the overall stock market. Thus, although the specialty fund might fluctuate wildly because of rapid changes in gold prices, its beta will remain low. With index-tracking ETFs, the beta coefficient should not deviate greatly from 1.00 because the portfolio aims to replicate the composition of the underlying benchmark. Hence, its volatility should also approximate that of the benchmark.

### R-Squared

R-squared ranges from zero to 100 and reflects the percentage of an ETF's movements that are explained by movements in its benchmark index. An R-squared of 100 means that all movements of an ETF are completely correlated with movements in the index. Thus, index ETFs that invest only in S&P 500 stocks will have an R-squared very close to 100. Conversely, a low R-squared indicates that very few of the ETF's movements are explained by movements in its benchmark index. An R-squared measure of 25, for example, means that only 25% of the ETF's movements can be explained by movements in its benchmark index. Therefore, R-squared can be used to ascertain the significance of a particular beta or alpha. Generally, a high R-squared will indicate a more reliable beta figure. If the R-squared is low, then the beta explains less of the ETF's performance.

**Morningstar Category**

*See Also Investment Style Box*

While the investment objective stated in a fund's prospectus may or may not reflect how the ETF actually invests, the Morningstar Category is assigned based on the underlying securities in each portfolio. Morningstar assigns categories based on three years of composition and style boxes. For ETFs that are not yet three years old an average of the portfolios since the ETF's inception is used.

The Morningstar Category helps investors make meaningful comparisons between mutual funds and ETFs. The categories make it easier to build well-diversified portfolios, assess potential risk, and identify the top-performing mutual funds and ETFs.

The following is a list and explanation of the categories. We place funds in a given category based on their portfolio statistics and compositions over the past three years. If the fund is new and has no portfolio history, we estimate where it will fall before giving it a more permanent category assignment. When necessary, we may change a category assignment based on recent changes to the portfolio.

## Stock ETFs
### Domestic-Stock ETFs
ETFs with at least 70% of assets in domestic stocks are categorized based on the style and size of the stocks they typically own. The style and size divisions reflect those used in the investment style box: value, blend, or growth style and small, medium, or large. Based on their investment style over the past three years, diversified domestic-stock funds are placed in one of the nine categories shown below:

| | | |
|---|---|---|
| Large Growth | Mid-cap Growth | Small Growth |
| Large Blend | Mid-cap Blend | Small Blend |
| Large Value | Mid-cap Value | Small Value |

Morningstar also includes several other domestic-stock categories:

Communications, Financial, Health Care, Natural Resources, Precious Metals, Real Estate, Technology, Utilities, Convertible Bond (convertible-bond funds have at least 50% of their assets invested in convertible securities), Conservative Allocation (conservative-allocation funds invest in both stocks and bonds, with just 20% to 50% of assets in stocks), and Moderate Allocation (moderate-allocation funds invest in both stocks and bonds, with more than 50% in stocks).

## International-Stock ETFs
Stock funds and ETFs that have invested 40% or more of their equity holdings in foreign stocks (on average over the past three years) are placed in an international-stock category, based on the following parameters:

Europe: at least 75% of stocks invested in Europe.

Latin America: at least 75% of stocks invested in Latin America.

Diversified Emerging Markets: at least 50% of stocks invested in emerging markets.

Diversified Asia/Pacific: at least 65% of stocks invested in Pacific countries, with at least an additional 10% of stocks invested in Japan.

Asia/Pacific ex-Japan: at least 75% of stocks in Pacific countries, with less than 10% of stocks invested in Japan.

Japan: at least 75% of stocks invested in Japan.

Foreign Large Value: a majority of assets invested in large-cap foreign stocks that are value-oriented (based on low price/book and price/cash flow ratios, relative to the MSCI EAFE Index).

Foreign Large Blend: a majority of assets invested in large-cap foreign stocks, where neither growth nor value characteristics predominate.

Foreign Large Growth: a majority of assets invested in large-cap foreign stocks that are growth-oriented (based on high price/book and price/cash flow ratios, relative to the MSCI EAFE Index).

Foreign Small/Mid-Cap Value: a majority of assets invested in small- and mid-cap foreign stocks that are value-oriented (based on low price/book and price/cash flow ratios, relative to the MSCI EAFE Index).

Foreign Small/Mid-Cap Growth: a majority of assets invested in small- and mid-cap foreign stocks that are growth-oriented (based on high price/book and price/cash flow ratios, relative to the MSCI EAFE Index).

World: at least 40% of stock holdings invested in foreign stocks, with at least 10% of stocks invested in the United States.

World Allocation: a fund with stock holdings of greater than 20% but less than 70% of the portfolio where 40% of the stocks and bonds are foreign. Also, must have at least 10% of assets invested in bonds.

## Bond ETFs
ETFs with 80% or more of their assets invested in bonds are classified as bond ETFs. Note: For all bond funds, maturity figures are used only when duration figures are unavailable.

### Taxable-Bond ETFs
Long-Term Government: at least 90% of bond portfolio invested in government issues with a duration of greater than six years, or an average effective maturity of greater than 10 years.

Intermediate-Term Government: at least 90% of bond portfolio invested in government issues with a duration of greater than or equal to 3.5 years and less than or equal to six years, or an average effective maturity of greater than or equal to four years and less than or equal to 10 years.

Short-Term Government: at least 90% of bond portfolio invested in government issues with a duration of greater than or equal to one year and less than 3.5 years, or an average effective maturity of greater than or equal to one year and less than four years.

Long-Term Bond: focuses on corporate and other investment-grade issues with an average duration of more than six years, or an average effective maturity of more than 10 years.

Intermediate-Term Bond: focuses on corporate and other investment-grade issues with an average duration of greater than or equal to 3.5 years but less than or equal to six years, or an average effective maturity of greater than or equal to four but less than or equal to 10 years.

Short-Term Bond: focuses on corporate and other investment-grade issues with an average duration of greater than or equal to one but less than 3.5 years, or an average effective maturity of greater than or equal to one but less than four years.

Ultrashort Bond: used for etfs with an average duration or an average effective maturity of less than one year. This category includes general corporate and government bond funds, and excludes any international, convertible, multisector, and high-yield bond funds.

High-Yield Bond: at least 65% of assets in bonds rated below BBB.

Multisector Bond: seeks income by diversifying assets among several fixed-income sectors, usually U.S. government obligations, foreign bonds, and high-yield domestic debt securities.

## Morningstar Price/Fair Value Measure

A ratio that offers a bottom-up assessment of whether an ETF portfolio is cheap or expensive by gauging if its holdings, on average, are trading above or below their Morningstar fair value estimates. The process draws on the research of Morningstar's stable of 75 in-house equity analysts who research and estimate fair values for more than 1,700 stocks. Morningstar calculates the market value of all the holdings in a given ETF for which it has fair value estimates. Then it uses the fair value estimates of those stocks to calculate a fair value of the same portfolio. Lastly, Morningstar compares the two numbers and calculates the percentage premium or discount of the market value compared to the fair value. The result is expressed as a ratio. A measure higher than 1.0 means the ETF is overvalued, according to Morningstar estimates. A reading lower than 1.0 means the offering is undervalued. Because Morningstar does not estimate a fair value for every stock an ETF might own, the relevance of the results of the price/fair value depends on how many stocks in a given portfolio have received a fair value estimate and the percentage of that portfolio's assets these stocks represent. As it turns out, Morningstar's stock coverage is pretty comprehensive for the vast majority of the domestic large-cap ETFs: Morningstar analysts have assigned fair value estimates to stocks representing 75% or more of the asset values of all but a handful of the ETFs in that space.

## Fair Value Estimate ($)

This is the per share fair value of the ETF's stock holdings that Morningstar equity analysts cover. Morningstar compares this fair value estimate to the price of those same holdings to determine if the ETF is overvalued, fairly valued or undervalued. Since Morningstar equity analysts do not always cover every stock in a given portfolio, an ETF's price per share and fair value per share may differ significantly from the portfolio's actual net asset value shown at the top of the page.

## Hit Rate (%)

This is the percent of an ETF portfolio's asset value that Morningstar stock analysts cover. It helps investors determine the relevance an ETF's Price/Fair Value measure. For example, an 80% hit rate means that Morningstar analysts have estimated fair values for stocks representing 80% of the portfolio's assets. A hit rate can be good, fair or poor, depending on the percent of assets under coverage. A hit rate of more than 83% is good, between 66.6% and 83% is fair, and between 50% and 66.6% is poor. Morningstar does not calculate Price/Fair Value ratios for ETFs with hit rates below 50%.

## Morningstar Style Box

*See Investment Style Box*

## Morningstar's Take

Morningstar's analysis of a fund that interprets and enhances the numerical data in an effort to provide an assessment of an ETF's worth. To accomplish this, a Morningstar analyst scrutinizes past shareholder reports, puts historical performance into the perspective of market trends, and whenever possible, interviews an ETF manager or other fund official. Although many people are involved in for producing this Morningstar page, the analyst is ultimately responsible for its content.

## MSCI EAFE (Morgan Stanley Capital International Europe, Australasia, Far East)

An index that measures the combined market value of a selected group of stocks from Europe, Australasia, and the Far East. This is one of the most widely used benchmarks for international stocks, funds, and ETFs.

### MSCI Emerging Markets

An index maintained by Morgan Stanley Capital International that measures the combined market value of a selected group of stocks from 26 emerging markets including Latin America, Eastern Europe, and most of Asia except for Japan and Australia. It is commonly used as a benchmark for emerging-markets stocks, funds, and ETFs.

# N

### Nasdaq Composite

An index that measures the cumulative market cap of all of the stocks traded on the Nasdaq stock market exchange. Because the Nasdaq exchange is heavily weighted with technology stocks, the Nasdaq Composite is often used as a proxy for the performance of the technology sector.

### NAV

*See Net Asset Value*

### Nav Return

*See Also Total Return, Market Return*

The total return of an ETF, based on its NAV at the beginning and end of the holding period and assuming reinvested dividends. This may be different from the ETF's market return. The market return, not the NAV return, is the return actually earned by ETF investors, except for those who hold creation units (authorized participants).

### Net Assets

*See Total Net Assets*

### Net Asset Value

An ETF's net asset value (NAV) represents its per-share price. An ETF's NAV is derived by dividing the total net assets of the ETF by the number of shares outstanding. Note that the Net Asset Value of ETFs may differ from the market price, which is the price at which the ETF shares are traded on an intraday market.

# O

### Open-End Index ETF

The most common type of ETF structure and registered under the Investment Act of 1940, open-end ETFs automatically reinvest dividends and pay them out to shareholders through a quarterly cash distribution. Open-end ETFs are authorized to use derivatives and generate income by loaning securities of its underlying portfolio.

### Options

The right, but not the obligation, to buy or sell a specific number of securities at a set price until a specified date. Like stocks and unlike traditional mutual funds, many ETFs offer options trading. Because options offer the right and not the obligation to buy shares, they can buffer price fluctuations for investors and are often profitably traded on the rise and fall of their premium prices. Call options allow the buyer to buy 100 shares of the underlying security by a certain date in the future for a certain price; put options allow the buyer to sell a certain number of shares within a certain time period for a certain price.

# P

### Percentile Rank (% Rank)

*See also Performance*

Located in the Performance and History sections these rankings allow investors to compare a fund's total returns with those of other funds.

In the Performance section we compare the fund's total return for various time periods against the same Morningstar Category (% Rank Cat). In the History section, we compare a fund's calendar-year total returns with its category's (Total Rtn % Rank Cat). In both sections, a fund's total returns are ranked on a scale from 1 to 100 where 1 represents the highest-returning 1% of funds and 100 represents the lowest-returning 1% of funds. Thus, in the performance section, a Percentile rank of 15 under the % Rank Cat column for the trailing three-month period indicates that the fund's three-month return placed in the top 15% of all funds in its category for that time period.

### Performance

*See Also Percentile Rank, Tax Analysis, and Total Return*

A fund's total return figures for various time periods.

*Investment Value Graph*

The Investment Value graph line shows a fund's performance trend, derived from the fund's historical growth of $10,000. It provides a visual depiction of how a fund has amassed its returns, including the performance swings its shareholders have endured along the way. The growth of $10,000 begins at the date of the fund's inception; if the fund has been in existence for more than 12 years, the growth of $10,000 begins at the first year listed on the graph. Also, featured in the graph is the performance of an index (S&P 500 or MSCI EAFE) that allows investors to compare the performance of the fund with the performance of the benchmark index.

### Quarterly Returns

The first section provides the fund's quarterly and year-end total returns for the past five years. The quarterly returns are compounded to obtain the year-end total return shown on the right. (Calculating the sum of the four quarterly returns will not produce the year-end total return because simple addition does not take into account the effects of compounding.)

### Total Return %

*See Also Total Return for more information about the calculation*

This figure is calculated by taking the change in net asset value, reinvesting all income and capital-gains distributions during the period, and dividing by the starting net asset value.

### +/- S&P 500

This statistic measures the difference between a stock ETF's total return and the total return of the S&P 500 Index. A negative number indicates that the ETF underperformed the index by the given amount, while a positive number indicates that the ETF outperformed the index by the given amount. For example, a listing of -2.0 indicates that the fund underperformed the index by 2 percentage points. The difference between each stock ETF's performance and the S&P 500 Index is listed. Bond ETFs are compared with the Lehman Brothers Aggregate Bond Index. The next column shows the same performance figure relative to another more specialized benchmark index.

### % Rank Cat

*See also Percentile Rank*

Morningstar lists each ETF's total return for various time periods against the funds in the same Morningstar Category (% Rank Cat). One is the highest or best percentile ranking and 100 is the lowest, or worst.

### Portfolio Analysis

Occupying much of the right side of the Morningstar page is the Portfolio Analysis section. Prominent in this section are an ETF's most recently reported top securities (excluding cash and cash equivalents for all but short-term bond funds), ranked in descending order by the percentage of the portfolio's net assets they occupy. With this information, investors can more clearly identify what drives the fund's performance.

Morningstar makes every effort to gather the most up-to-date portfolio information from a fund. By law, however, funds need only report this information four times during a calendar year, and they have two months after the report date to actually release the shareholder report and portfolio. Therefore, it is possible that a fund's portfolio could be up five months old or more at the time of publication. We print the date the portfolio was reported. Older portfolios should not be disregarded, however; although the list may not represent the exact current holdings of the fund, it may still provide a good picture of the overall nature of the fund's management style.

### Total Stocks/Total Fixed-Income

Total Stock indicates the total number of stock securities in a fund's portfolio, and Total Fixed-Income denotes the number of bond securities a fund holds. Theses do not simply refer to the stocks or bonds listed on the page; rather, they represent all stocks and bonds in the portfolio. These listings can be quite useful for gaining greater insight into the portfolio's diversification.

### Share Change

Applied only to common Stocks, the share change entry indicates the change in the number of shares of each stock from the previously reported portfolio. If the change column shows a minus sign for one of the portfolio's stocks, that means the ETF's manager sold shares of that stock since the previous portfolio was reported. Similarly, a plus sign next to the holding means that management added shares of that stock to the portfolio. The sunshine symbol indicates that the stock is a new addition to the portfolio. We list the date of the previously reported portfolio in the column heading, so that you know how much time has passed between the current portfolio and the previously reported portfolio.

### Security

This column lists the names of the stock or bond securities held as of the portfolio date. For stock holdings, this line typically displays just the name of the issuing company. Other stock labels are included where appropriate, such as ADR, which distinguishes an American Depository Receipt. Bond holdings, however, will usually include more information to differentiate among the many types of bonds available. For most bonds, the coupon rate is listed as a percentage figure after the name of the bond. Adjustable-rate mortgages and floating-rate notes will have ARM or FRN (or IFRN for inverse-floating rate notes) listed after the name of the bond to indicate that the coupon rate is variable.

Some adjustable-rate bond listings will include the formula by which the coupon rate is calculated, which is usually a fixed percentage plus some benchmark value. Securities followed by the abbreviation IO are interest-only securities, or those that consist only of the interest portion of a security, not the principal portion. PO indicates a principal-only security that sells at a discount to par and carries a coupon rate of zero.

### Sector
*See also Sector Weighting and Industry Weightings*
The industry sector of each stock holding is reported in this column this gives investors greater insight into where an ETF's top holdings are concentrated and where its vulnerabilities lie.

### P/E
*See also Price/Earnings Ratio and Value Measures*
To add depth to the average P/E number for the entire portfolio (listed under Current Investment Style), the P/E ratio for each stock is reported here. NMF means the stock's P/E is 100 or more. A minus sign means the company has no earnings or the figure is not available.

### YTD Return %
The year-to-date stock returns show whether one or two big winners (or losers) are driving fund performance, or a lot of little successes. In some cases, losses in top holdings can suggest a bargain-hunting strategy if a position in a losing stock is new or expanded.

### % Assets
The % Assets column indicates what percentage of the portfolio's net assets a given security constitutes. Morningstar calculates the percentage of net assets figure by dividing the market value of the security by the ETF's total net assets. If a given security makes up a large percentage of the fund's net assets, the fund uses a concentrated portfolio strategy, at least with respect to the security in question. If, however, the percentage figures are low, then the manager is simply not willing to bet heavily on a particular security.

### Date of Maturity
Maturity, located in the portfolio section for bond ETFs only, indicates the date on which a bond or note comes due. This information can be used in determin-ing the portfolio's basic fixed-income strategy. For example, if most of these dates are a year or two away, the fund is taking a conservative, short-term approach. The maturity dates listed here, however, are not adjusted for calls (rights an issuer may have to redeem outstanding bonds before their scheduled maturity) or for the likelihood of mortgage prepayments. Thus, they might not accurately state the actual time to repayment of a bond, and might overstate a portfolio's sensitivity to interest-rate changes.

### Amount
Found on bond ETF pages, the amount column refers to the size of the fund's investment in a given security as to the portfolio dates listed above. This figure reflects the principal value of the security in thousands of dollars.

### Value
Value simply gives the market value of a particular security in thousands of dollars as of the portfolio date. The value column allows investors to gauge whether a fixed-income security is selling at a premium or a discount to its face value, as reflected in the amount column.

## Portfolio Manager (s)
The portfolio manager is the individual or individuals responsible for the overall ETF strategy, as well as the buying and selling decisions for the securities in an ETF's portfolio. To help investors know who is running an ETF, we detail management with a brief biography. We note the manager's background, experience, analytical support, other funds managed, and whether the manager invests in his or her own fund. Because ETFs are often passively managed, the portfolio manager may take a less forthright role than would a mutual fund manager.

## Premium
*See Also NAV and Discount to NAV*
The amount by which an ETF's market price is greater than its net asset value (NAV). Any discount or premium is usually small and short-lived because ETFs' in-kind redemption process allows market makers to arbitrage away the difference.

## Price/Book Ratio
*See Also Relative Comparisons and Value Measures*
The price/book ratio of an ETF is the weighted average of the price/book ratios of all the stocks in an ETF's portfolio. Book value is the total assets of a company, less total liabilities. A company's price/book ratio is calculated by dividing the market price of its out-

standing stock by the company's book value and then adjusting for the number of shares outstanding. (Stocks with negative book values are excluded from this calculation.) In computing a fund's average price/book ratio, Morningstar weights each portfolio holding by the percentage of equity assets it represents; larger positions thus have proportionately greater influence on the final price/book. A low price/book may indicate that the stocks are bargains, priced below what the companies' assets could be worth if liquidated.

### Price/Cash Flow

*See Also Relative Comparisons and Value Measures*
Price/cash flow is a weighted average of the price/cash flow ratios of the stocks in an ETF's portfolio. Price/cash flow represents the amount of money an investor is willing to pay for a dollar of cash generated from a particular company's operations. Price/cash flow shows the ability of a business to generate cash and can be an effective gauge of liquidity and solvency. Because accounting conventions differ among nations, reported earnings (and thus P/C ratios) may not be comparable across national boundaries. Price/cash flow attempts to provide an internationally standardized measure of a firm's stock price relative to its financial performance. In computing the average, Morningstar weights each portfolio holding by the percentage of stock assets it represents; larger positions thus have proportionately greater influence on the ETF's final price/cash flow ratio.

### Price/Earnings Ratio

*See Also Relative Comparisons and Value Measures*
The price/earnings ratio of an ETF is the weighted average of the price/earnings ratios of the stocks in a fund's portfolio. The P/E ratio of a company, which is a comparison of the price of the company's stock and its estimated earnings per share, is calculated by dividing these two figures. In computing the average, Morningstar weights each portfolio holding by the percentage of stock assets it represents; larger positions thus have proportionately greater influence on the ETF's final P/E. A high P/E usually indicates that the market will pay more to obtain the company's earnings because it believes in the firm's ability to increase its earnings. (P/E can also be artificially inflated if a company has very weak earnings, which may be temporary. For example, during recessions, cyclical firms' earnings fall and their P/E s rise.) A low P/E indicates the market has less confidence that the company's earnings will increase.

### Profitability Measures

*Return on Assets (ROA)*
This measures how effectively companies use their assets to generate profits. The formula for an individual firm is net income divided by assets. Companies with high returns on assets include software firms and beverage companies. Both types of companies frequently generate high profits but have relatively small investments in plant, equipment, and other assets. Firms with low returns on assets are typically in manufacturing or other capital-intensive industries. Companies with low returns on assets tend to have low valuations and are mostly held by value ETFs; by contrast, growth managers favor firms with high returns on assets. An ETF's ROA is equal to the weighted average ROA of its individual holdings.

*Return on Equity (ROE)*
This calculation reveals how effectively management has invested shareholders' equity, which is the amount of money initially invested in the business plus retained earnings. ROE is simply net income divided by average shareholder equity. A high ROE is often a sign that a company's management uses its resources wisely, and the company is often located in a growing industry with high barriers to entry. For example, thanks to its dominance of the software operating-systems market, Microsoft usually has high ROEs. By contrast, companies with low ROEs frequently operate in stagnant industries in which there is overcapacity. For example, automakers frequently earn low returns on equity. Companies with high ROEs generally have better business models, but as a reflection of that, their share prices arc often expensive. Growth managers typically prefer companies with high and rising ROEs, while valuation concerns may lead value managers to buy firms with low ROEs. A fund's ROE is the weighted average of its individual holdings' ROEs.

*Net Margin*
We arrive at net margin by dividing a firm's net income (after all expenses, including taxes) by its sales. This measures how effective a company is at wringing profits out of each dollar of revenues. Companies with high net margins tend to have strong competitive positions, while those with low net margins often operate in highly price-competitive industries such as retailing. Companies that consistently earn high net margins include pharmaceuticals and successful software companies. Low-margin businesses include supermarkets and other retailers. High-margin firms earn superior returns but also

garner premium valuations, so the stocks are often too expensive for value managers. At the ETF level, net margin represents the weighted average of the individual stocks' net margins.

# Q

## Qube

Shares in the ETF that tracks the Nasdaq 100 Index. The name Qube is derived from its old ticker symbol, QQQ. The fund is the most heavily invested ETF by volume. Qubes have a unit investment trust structure. In 2005 the fund switched from the American Stock Exchange to the Nasdaq Stock Market and changed its ticker symbol to QQQQ.

# R

## Rank
*See Percentile Rank*

## Regional Exposure
All international stock funds feature a regional exposure listing. This table displays the percentage of the fund's total net assets invested in the U.K./Western Europe, Japan, Asia ex-Japan, North America, and Latin America. Below the regional information on each page we list the five largest country exposures. The information in this section is gathered from portfolios and is the most recent available.

## Relative Comparisons
*See also Market Capitalization, Price/Book Ratio, Price/Cash Flow, Price/Earnings Ratio, and Industry Weightings*
At various places in the Portfolio Analysis section, Morningstar shows how an individual ETF compares with the average of all ETFs within its category (Rel Cat) or a benchmark index (Rel S&P 500). The category average (or index) is always set equal to 1.00. For example, a domestic stock ETF with a utilities weighting of 1.50 relative to its category has 50% more in utilities issues than its average peer. Stock statistics are displayed in comparison with the S&P Index. In this case, 1.00 represents the index. A relative P/B ratio of 0.43, for example, indicates that the fund's P/B is 57% lower than that of the index.

## Restricted/Illiquid Securities
*See Special Securities*
## Return
*See Total Return*

## Risk
*See Modern Portfolio Theory Statistics and Standard Deviation*

## Russell 2000
An index, updated annually by the Frank Russell Company, that is composed of the 1,001st through 3,000th largest companies in the United States in terms of market capitalization. This is one of the most commonly used benchmarks for measuring the performance of small-cap stocks, and numerous funds and ETFs mimic all or portions of this index.

# S

## S&P 500 Index (Standard & Poor's 500 Index)
Also known simply as the "S&P," this is one of the most common indexes used to represent the U.S. stock market. Contrary to popular belief, it does not consist of the 500 largest U.S. companies, but is composed of a range of small capitalization to large capitalization companies selected by the Standard & Poor's Index Committee. The S&P 500 is a market-cap-weighted index, however, and the largest companies have more influence on its performance than the smaller-cap companies. Many stocks, funds, and ETFs are measured against this benchmark.

## Sector Breakdown for Fixed-Income Funds
The fixed-income sector illustrates the type of bonds a fund owns. These sectors help investors compare and understand the sector exposure of each mutual fund. These data are especially useful for comparing two funds that may be in the same Morningstar Category. The fixed-income sectors are calculated for all domestic taxable-bond portfolios. It is based on the securities in the most recent portfolio. This information shows the percentage of bond and cash assets invested in each of the 14 fixed-income sectors.

Morningstar groups all fixed-income assets into the following sectors:

*U.S. Government*
U.S. Treasuries
This sector includes all conventional fixed-rate debt issued by the Treasury department of the United

States government (i.e. this sector excludes TIPS). Some examples of this type of debt are Treasury bonds and Treasury notes. Treasury bills are included under % Cash, because they mature in less than 12 months.

### TIPS

TIPS are inflation-indexed debt issued by the U.S. Treasury. (The term TIPS derives from their former name, Treasury Inflation-Protected Securities.) These bonds have principal and coupon payments that are linked to movements in the Consumer Price Index. They are a defensive measure against expectations of inflation, which typically erodes the real yield of conventional bonds. Even if inflation fears are in check, these bonds can benefit when the yields fall on traditional Treasuries. These unique securities act very differently than any other fixed-rate bond, and their volatility can change over time, depending on the level of interest rates.

### U.S. Agency

This sector includes debt securities issued by government agencies-such as the Federal National Mortgage Association (FNMA), also known as Fannie Mae, or the Federal Home Loan Mortgage Corporation (FHLMC), also known as Freddie Mac-to raise capital and finance their operations. These "debentures" are not secured by physical assets, so they differ from most of the mortgage bonds that are issued by these agencies.

## Mortgage

### Mortgage Pass-Throughs

These are fixed-income securities that represent a claim to the cash flows associated with a pool of mortgages. The bondholders are entitled to a share of the principal and interest payments paid by the homeowners. The majority of these bonds are issued by a government agency such as FNMA, GNMA, or FHLMC. A few private corporations and banks also securitize and package mortgages in this way, and those are also included in this sector.

### Mortgage CMO

Collateralized mortgage obligations (CMO) are similar to pass-through mortgage securities, but investors have more control over whether they will be paid sooner or later. CMOs are structured by time, so that some investors can line up for the first series of cash flow payments, while others may choose to put themselves at the end of the line. A fund manager would buy a late-paying CMO if he or she believed that there would be a lot of mortgage refinancing in the near term. This would protect the fund from

getting its money back too early, which would require it to be reinvested at a lower interest rate. Most CMOs are based on mortgages from government agencies, such as FNMA or GNMA.

### Mortgage ARM

Adjustable-rate mortgage (ARM) securities are backed by residential home mortgages where the interest rate is reset periodically in relation to a benchmark. Most ARMs are from government agencies, such as FNMA and GNMA.

## Credit

### U.S. Corporate

This sector includes all fixed-income securities that are issued by corporations domiciled in the United States. Corporate bonds are issued with a wide range of coupon rates and maturity dates.

### Asset-Backed

Asset-backed securities are based on the expected cash flow from such things as auto loans, credit-card receivables, and computer leases. The cash flows for asset-backed securities can be fixed (e.g. auto loans have a defined payment schedule and a fixed maturity) or variable (credit-card debt is paid at random intervals). These securities typically range in maturity from two to seven years.

### Convertible

Convertible bonds give the owner an opportunity to convert the bond to a certain number of shares of common stock at a certain price. As the stock approaches that price, the option to convert becomes more valuable and the price of the convertible bond also rises. These securities usually provide lower interest payments, because the option to convert to stock could potentially be quite valuable at some point in the future.

### Municipal

Local and state governments issue municipal bonds in order to raise money for operations and development. This financing is sometimes used to build or upgrade hospitals, sewer systems, schools, housing, stadiums, or industrial complexes. Some municipal bonds are backed by the issuing entity while others are linked to a revenue stream, such as from a tollway or a utility. Municipal bonds are exempt from federal tax and often from state and local taxes, too. The tax break allows municipal governments to sell the bonds at a lower interest rate, because the investor gets an additional tax benefit. Currently there are no municipal bond ETFs.

### Corporate Inflation-Protected

Inflation-protected securities are similar to TIPS, but they are issued by a private entity rather than by the U.S. government. These bonds are linked to an index of inflation, and the principal and coupon payments increase when inflation increases. As with TIPS, these securities behave quite differently from conventional bonds.

### Foreign

#### Foreign Corporate

These fixed-income securities are issued by corporations that are based outside of the United States.

#### Foreign Government

These fixed-income securities are issued by governments outside the United States.

### Cash

Cash can be cash in the bank, certificates of deposit, currency, or money market holdings. Cash can also be any fixed-income securities that mature in less than 12 months. Cash also includes commercial paper and any repurchase agreements held by the ETF. Because this data point is based on only the cash and bond assets in the ETF, it can be different than the % Cash in the composition breakdown, which is expressed as a percent of total assets.

### Sector Weightings/Economic Spheres
*See Also Subsector Weightings*

Morningstar divides the stock market into three broad "economic spheres," each of which contains four specific industry sectors. Sectors are based on what companies actually do. That is, unlike some other sector classification systems, sectors aren't based on expected behavior of the stocks of these companies.

The economic spheres with their major inclusive sectors are as follows:

#### Information Sphere
Made up of the Software, Hardware, Media, and Telecommunications sectors.

#### Service Sphere
Made up of the Health Care, Consumer Services, Business Services, and Financial Services sectors.

#### Manufacturing Sphere
Made up of the Consumer Goods, Industrial Materials, Energy, and Utilities sectors.

The sectors with their major inclusive industries are as follows:

#### Software
Companies engaged in the design and marketing of computer operating systems and applications. Examples include Microsoft, Oracle, and Siebel Systems.

#### Hardware
Manufacturers of computer equipment, communication equipment, semiconductors, and components. Examples include IBM, Cisco Systems, and Intel.

#### Media
Companies that own and operate broadcast networks and those that create content or provide it for other media companies. Examples include Time Warner, Walt Disney, and Washington Post.

#### Telecommunications
Companies that provide communication services using fixed-line networks or those that provide wireless access and services. Examples include, AT&T, and Alltel.

#### Health Care
Includes biotechnology, pharmaceuticals, research services, HMOs, home health, hospitals, assisted living, and medical equipment and supplies. Examples include Abbott Laboratories, Merck, and Cardinal Health.

#### Consumer Services
Includes retail stores, personal services, home builders, home supply, travel and entertainment companies, and educational providers. Examples include Wal-Mart, Home Depot, and Expedia.

#### Business Services
Includes advertising, printing, publishing, business support, consultants, employment, engineering and construction, security services, waste management, distributors, and transportation. Examples include Manpower, R.R. Donnelley, and Southwest Airlines.

#### Financial Services
Includes banks, finance companies, money-management firms, savings and loans, securities brokers, and insurance companies. Examples include Citigroup, Washington Mutual, and Fannie Mae.

### Consumer Goods

Companies that manufacture or provide food, beverages, household and personal products, apparel, shoes, textiles, autos and auto parts, consumer electronics, luxury goods, packaging, and tobacco. Examples include PepsiCo, Ford Motor, and Kraft Foods.

### Industrial Materials

Includes aerospace and defense firms, companies that provide or manufacture chemicals, machinery, building materials, and commodities. Examples include Boeing, DuPont, and Alcoa.

### Energy

Companies that produce or refine oil and gas, oilfield services and equipment companies, and pipeline operators. Examples include ExxonMobil, Schlumberger, and BP.

### Utilities

Electric, gas, and water utilities. Examples include Duke Energy, Exelon, and El Paso.

### SEC Yield

*See Also Yield*

SEC yield is a standardized figure that the Securities and Exchange Commission requires funds to use to calculate rates of income return on a fund's capital investment. SEC yield is an annualized calculation that is based on a trailing 30-day period. This figure will often differ significantly from Morningstar's other yield figure, which reflects trailing 12-month distributed yield, because of differing time periods as well as differing accounting policies. For example, SEC yield is based on a bond's yield to maturity, which takes into account amortization of premiums and discounts, while Morningstar's distributed yield is based on what funds actually pay out.

### Share Change

*see Portfolio Analysis*

### Sharpe Ratio

The Sharpe ratio is a risk-adjusted measure developed by Nobel Laureate William Sharpe. It is calculated using standard deviation and excess return to determine reward per unit of risk. First, the average monthly return of the 90-day Treasury bill (over a 36-month period) is subtracted from the fund's average monthly return. The difference in total return represents the fund's excess return beyond that of the 90-day Treasury bill, a risk-free investment. An arithmetic annualized excess return is then calculated by multiplying this monthly return by 12. To show a relationship between excess return and risk, this number is then divided by the standard deviation of the ETF's annualized excess returns. The higher the Sharpe ratio, the better the ETF's historical risk-adjusted performance.

### Short Sale

Selling a borrowed security with the intention of buying it back at a lower price in the future and pocketing the difference. In essence, short sales are bets that a ETF will fall. To sell short, an investor borrows ETF shares from one party and then sells them to another on the open market. The investor hopes the ETF drops, because he or she would be able to buy the shares back at a lower price and then return them to the lender. The difference between the original price and the price the investor pays to buy the shares back is the profit or loss. Short sales can slow returns in a rising market, but reduce losses or even produce gains in a falling market. One of the risks of short sales is that the maximum gain is 100%, but potential losses are unlimited.

### SPDR

An abbreviation for Standard & Poor's Depository Receipts. SPDRs are ETFs that track a variety of S&P indexes. For example, the popular SPDR Trust Series 1, tracks the S&P 500 Index. Select Sector SPDRs track various sector indices that carve up the S&P 500 index into separate industry groups. SPDR Trust, Series 1 is structured as a unit investment trust, but Select Sector SPDRs are open-end funds.

### Specialist

A member of a given stock exchange (an individual or a firm) who maintains an inventory of specific securities and is responsible for executing limit orders and buying or selling to maintain the specialist's own account. (See Also market maker).

### Special Securities

This section shows an ETF's exposure to a variety of complex or illiquid securities, including derivatives. The percentage of total net assets represented by each type of security is listed to the right of each group. Some securities may fall under more than one type.

### Restricted/Illiquid Securities

Restricted and illiquid securities are issues that may be hard to accurately price and difficult to sell because an investor may be unable to find a buyer quickly. Private placement issues and 144(a) securities are both included here. Both types have varying degrees of liquidity and are exempt from some of the cumbersome registration and disclosure requirements that public offerings usually face.

### Exotic Mortgage-Backed Securities

This section indicates how much of an ETF's net assets are held in unusual mortgage-backed derivatives. Specifically, we delineate those securities that see their price changes magnified when interest rates or mortgage-prepayment speeds change. Because not all mortgage-backed derivatives have these traits, we include the following: interest-only (IOs) and principal-only paper (POs), inverse floating-rate securities (IFRNs), and Z-tranche collateralized mortgage obligation issues, all of which are fairly clearly labeled in a fund's shareholder reports. Kitchen-sink bonds, a complex mix of interest-only, principal-only bonds, and cast-off CMO tranches, are also tallied here. For stock funds, which rarely hold mortgage-backed issues of any kind, we combine exotic mortgage-backed securities with structured notes.

### Emerging-Markets Securities

Debt or equity securities from emerging markets are listed here. These figures are calculated from the most recently available portfolio. Morningstar classifies as an emerging market anything aside from the following developed markets: Australia, Austria, Belgium, Canada, Denmark, Finland, France, Germany, Greece, Hong Kong, Ireland, Italy, Japan, the Netherlands, New Zealand, Norway, Portugal, Singapore, South Korea, Spain, Sweden, Switzerland, Taiwan, the United Kingdom, and the United States. This list is subject to change as markets become more developed or vice versa.

### Options/Futures/Warrants

Options and futures may be used speculatively, to leverage a portfolio, or cautiously, as a hedge against risk. We don't show the percentage of assets devoted to options or futures because it is difficult to determine from shareholder reports how much of a portfolio is affected by an options or futures contract. We also include forward contracts and warrants in this area.

### Standard Deviation

A statistical measure of the range of an ETF's performance. When an ETF has a high standard deviation, its range of performance has been very wide, indicating greater volatility. Investors use the standard deviation of historical performance to try to predict the range of returns that are most likely for a given portfolio. Standard deviation is based on a bell-curve distribution, so approximately 68% of the time, returns will fall within one standard deviation of the

mean return for the portfolio, and 95% within two standard deviations. The most important thing to note is that the greater the standard deviation, the greater the fund's volatility has been.

For example, an investor can compare two ETFs with the same average monthly return of 5%, but with different standard deviations. The first ETF has a standard deviation of 2, which means that its range of returns for the past 36 months has typically remained between 1% and 9%. On the other hand, assume that the second ETF has a standard deviation of 4 for the same period. This higher deviation indicates that this ETF has experienced returns fluctuating between -3% and 13%. With the second ETF, an investor can expect greater volatility.

### Mean

The mean represents the annualized average monthly return from which the standard deviation is calculated. The mean will be the same as the annualized trailing, three-year return figure for the same time period.

### Stop Loss Order

A trading technique designed to limit losses by designating a specified threshold at which shares must be sold.

### Strategy

While the Morningstar Category gives investors an idea of what sorts of investments a ETF makes, it does not fully capture the nuances of the construction methodology of the ETFs underlying index. In this section, Morningstar analysts explain the criteria ETF bogies use in selecting securities and how risky a given methodology may be. On the equity side, the strategy description often focuses on what size and type of company an index keys on, or a discussion regarding how a style-based benchmark, for instance defines growth and value stocks. With bond ETFs, the strategy section explains how the ETF manager goes about tracking the often wide ranging fixed income indexes. Strategy section also often notes whether an ETF manager uses representative sampling to track the underlying index and the benchmarks rebalancing schedule.

### Strategic Asset Allocation
*See Also tactical asset allocation*

A passive investment strategy or portfolio construction model by which investments are selected according to a fixed asset allocation model. This asset allocation model is defined by broad asset class (stocks, bonds, cash, or alternative instruments). Strategic asset allocators often rebalance portfolios under management on a monthly or quarterly basis and strictly adhere to the pre-ordained asset allocation model. This investment model can be used in conjunction with tactical asset allocation model, but is sometimes viewed as its opposite.

### StreetTracks

A group of ETFs managed by State Street Global Advisors. These ETFs track various indexes, including Dow Jones Wilshire style-specific and global indexes, technology indexes from Morgan Stanley, and the Dow Jones Wilshire REIT index. StreetTracks are structured as open-end funds (as opposed to unit investment trusts and grantor trusts) and are traded on the American Stock Exchange. (See Also index fund, unit investment trust, grantor trust).

### Style Box

*See Investment Style Box*

---

# T

### Tactical Asset Allocation

*See Also strategic asset allocation*

An active investment strategy or portfolio construction model by which investments are selected with deference to a particular asset allocation model but is regularly rebalanced to benefit from favorable investment climates, sectors, or subgroups. Tactical asset allocators will also shift their strategies in accordance with fundamental investment principles such as returns, various measures of volatility, and risk while keeping in mind the original asset allocation strategy. Tactical asset allocation models are sometimes used in conjunction with strategic asset allocation models, though the two strategies are also considered to be opposites.

### Tax-Adjusted Return %

*See Tax Analysis*

### Tax Analysis

The information provided in the Tax Analysis section can be used to evaluate an ETF's aftertax returns and its efficiency in achieving them. Additionally, the potential capital-gain exposure figure can provide a glimpse at a shareholder's vulnerability to taxation. All these figures can help an investor judge which ETFs have been tax-friendly.

### Tax-Adjusted Return

The Tax-Adj Rtn % column shows an estimate of an ETF's annualized aftertax total return for the three-, five-, and 10-year periods, excluding any capital-gains effects that would result from selling the ETF at the end of the period. Consistent with SEC guidance regarding tax-adjusted returns, these figures reflect the maximum load paid by fund shareholders. To determine this figure, all income and short-term (less than one year) capital-gain distributions are taxed at the maximum federal rate at the time of distribution. Long-term (more than one year) capital gains are taxed at a 20% rate. The aftertax portion is then reinvested in the fund. The category percentile rank (% Rank Cat) for each fund's tax-adjusted return is also listed. This ranking helps investors compare a fund's estimated aftertax performance with that of other funds in the category.

### Tax-Cost Ratio

This represents the estimated percentage-point reduction in an annualized return that has resulted from income taxes over the past three-, five-, and 10-year periods. The calculation assumes investors pay the maximum federal rate on capital gains and ordinary income.

### Telephone Numbers

These are the local and toll-free (if available) numbers that an investor may use to contact the fund, call for a prospectus, or get marketing information.

### Ticker

A ticker is the symbol assigned to the ETF based on the exchange on which it's sold. ETF tickers range from three to four characters and are commonly used to locate a fund on electronic price-quoting systems.

### Total Net Assets (TNA)

This figure gives the ETF's asset base, net of fees and any expenses, at year-end of past calendar years and at month-end for the current year. Both total net assets and average trading volume can indicate the popularity of an ETF with investors (See Also average trading volume).

### Total Return
*See Also Capital Return %, Income Return %, and Market Return*
All references to total return represent an ETF's gains over a specified period of time. Total return includes both income (in the form of dividends or interest payments) and capital gains or losses (the increase or decrease in the value of a security). Morningstar calculates total return by taking the change in an ETF's NAV, assuming the reinvestment of all income and capital-gains distributions (on the actual reinvestment date used by the ETF) during the time period, and then dividing the initial NAV. The quarterly returns, listed in the Performance section, express the ETF's return for each individual quarter; the total shown on the right is the compounded return for the four quarters of that year. An asterisk next to the total return number indicates that the return is calculated for a partial quarter or partial year because the ETF began operations during that time period.

Note that market return calculates total return by using market prices in place of the ETF's net asset value (NAV). Thus, the market total return and NAV total return may differ slightly.

### Total Stocks/Total Fixed-Income
*See Portfolio Analysis*

### Tracking Error
As applied to index exchange-traded funds, this refers to the amount by which the ETF portfolio's returns differ from that of the benchmark it tries to follow. In general, an index ETF's tracking error should be no greater than its expense ratio. That shows the fund is doing a good job tracking its underlying index before expenses are deducted. Tracking error greater than an ETF's expense ratio could indicate the fund's manager isn't doing a good job running the fund, or that the fund has selected an inefficient index to follow.

### Transaction Costs
The costs of buying or selling securities, including brokerage costs and commissions.

### Turnover Rate
The rate that represents, roughly, the percentage of the portfolio's holdings that have changed over the past year, this number provides a rough measure of the ETF's level of trading activity. This publicly reported figure is calculated by funds in accordance with SEC regulations, and Morningstar gathers the information from fund shareholder reports. An ETF divides the lesser of purchases or sales (expressed in dollars and

excluding all securities with maturities of less than one year) by the ETF's average monthly assets. The resulting percentage can be loosely interpreted to represent the percentage of the portfolio's holdings that have changed over the past year. The turnover ratio is most accurate, however, when an ETF's asset base remains stable. A low turnover figure (typically less than 30%) might indicate that the manager is following a buy-and-hold strategy. High turnover (more than 100%) could be an indication of an investment strategy involving considerable buying and selling of securities. For index-tracking ETFs, the turnover ratio should be low (ie. generally in single digits) because they are not actively managed; however, the turnover rate can be greater based on the methodology of the particular index tracked.

# U

### Unit Investment Trust
An ETF structure registered under the Investment Company Act of 1940. Unit Investment Trusts replicate their benchmark but cannot invest greater than 25% of its assets in any single issuer. Unlike open end funds, unit investment trusts do not reinvest dividends immediately. Instead, dividends are placed in a non-interest bearing account until they are paid out on a quarterly basis. This can create a slight drag on the performance of these ETFs.

### U.S. 90-day Treasury Bill
Also known as the 90-day "T-bill", these debt securities, issued by the U.S. government, are used as a common measure of short-term interest rates.

# V

### Value
*See Also Growth and Investment Style Box*
The investment style commonly referred to as a value approach focuses on stocks that an investor or fund manager thinks are currently undervalued in price and will eventually have their worth recognized by the market. It is often contrasted with a growth style approach to investing.

### Value Measures
*Price/Projected Earnings*
Projected earnings are the consensus analyst opinion of how much a company will earn during its next

fiscal year. Price/projected earnings represents the amount investors are paying for each dollar of expected earnings per share. When reported for an ETF, it shows the weighted average of the price/projected earnings ratio for each stock in the ETF's portfolio. This measure helps determine Morningstar's value score for each stock and the overall value orientation of the ETF.

### Price/Book Value

Book value is, in theory, what would be left over for shareholders if a company shut down its operations, paid off all of its creditors, collected from all of its debtors, and liquidated itself. In practice, however, the value of assets and liabilities can change substantially from when they are first recorded. Many investors use the price/book ratio-the ratio of a company share price to its total book value per share-as a way to value a stock. If the share price is less than total equity per share, the company is selling for less than its break-up value. When reported for an ETF, it shows the weighted average of the price/book ratio for each stock in the ETF's portfolio. This measure helps determine Morningstar's value score for each stock and the overall value orientation of the ETF.

### Price/Sales

Price/sales represents the amount investors are paying for each dollar of sales generated by the company. Price/sales is usually a less volatile measure than either price/earnings or price/book and can be especially useful when evaluating companies with volatile earnings. When reported for an ETF, it shows the weighted average of the price/sales ratio for each stock in the ETF's portfolio. This measure helps determine Morningstar's value score for each stock and the overall value orientation of the ETF.

### Price/Cash Flow

Cash flow tells you how much cash a business is actually generating-its earnings before depreciation, amortization, and noncash charges. Sometimes called cash earnings, it's considered a gauge of liquidity and solvency. Price/cash flow represents the amount investors are paying for each dollar generated from a company's operations. When reported for an ETF, it shows the weighted average of the price/cash flow ratio for each stock in the ETF's portfolio. This measure helps determine Morningstar's value score for each stock and the overall value orientation of the ETF.

### Dividend Yield

Dividends are the per-share amount taken from a company's profits and paid to shareholders. Dividend yield is equal to a company's annual dividend divided by its share price. It works as a kind of valuation measure-the lower the yield, the more investors have to pay for each dollar of dividends. Investors often consider stocks with high dividend yields potentially undervalued investments. When reported for an ETF, it shows the weighted average of the dividend yield for each stock in the ETF's portfolio.

This measure helps determine Morningstar's value score for each stock and the overall value orientation of the ETF.

# W

### Wilshire 5000

An index commonly known for measuring the performance of the entire U.S. stock market, including companies of all sizes. Although it originally contained 5,000 stocks, the index now measures the combined market value of more than 6,500 stocks. Wilshire REIT (Real Estate Investment Trusts) An index that measures the combined market value of equity real estate investment trusts (as opposed to mortgage REIT s) with market capitalizations above 1 billion USD. It is widely used as a benchmark for equity REIT performance and its composition is mimicked by numerous funds and ETFs.

### Wilshire REIT (Real Estate Investment Trusts)

An index that measures the combined market value of equity real estate investment trusts (as opposed to mortgage REITs) with market capitalizations above 1 billion USD. It is widely used as a benchmark for equity REIT performance and its composition is mimicked by numerous funds and ETFs.

# Y

### YTD

An abbreviation for year-to-date, or since the beginning of the current calendar or fiscal year. When evaluating YTD total returns, for example, the beginning price is the first day of the current calendar or last day of the current calendar (usually December 31 or January 1) to the present date.

## Yield

*See Also SEC Yield*

Yield, expressed as a percentage, represents a fund's income return on capital investment for the past 12 months. This figure refers only to interest distributions from fixed-income securities and dividends from stocks. Money generated from the sale of securities, from options and futures transactions, and from currency transactions are considered capital gains, not income. Return of capital is also not considered income. NMF (No Meaningful Figure) appears in this space for those ETFs that do not properly label their distributions. We list N/A if an ETF is less than one year old, in which case we cannot calculate yield. Morningstar computes yield by dividing the sum of the fund's income distributions for the past 12 months by the previous month's NAV(adjusted upward for any capital gains distributed over the same period).